BUILDING TRADES
PRINTREADING - Part 2
RESIDENTIAL AND LIGHT COMMERCIAL CONSTRUCTION

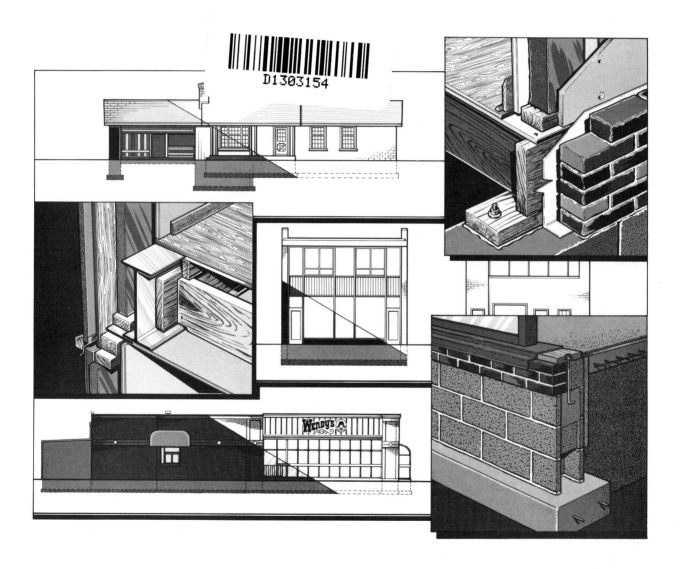

AMERICAN TECHNICAL PUBLISHERS, INC.
HOMEWOOD, ILLINOIS 60430

Elmer W. Sundberg
Thomas E. Proctor

Acknowledgments

The authors and publisher are grateful to the following companies and organizations.

For providing plans:

Barclay and Associates
Design Concept Associates
Ekroth, Martorano, and Ekroth, Architects
Erickson, Kristman, and Stillwaugh, Inc.

Emory L. Jackson, Architect
Metropolis Architecture and Interior Design
Wendy's International, Inc.

For providing technical information and assistance:

Alcoa Building Products
Ansul Fire Protection
American Institute of Steel
  Construction, Inc.
American National Standards
  Institute
American Plywood Association
Ametek, Houston Instrument
  Division
Autodesk, Inc.
Barclay and Associates
William Brazley and Associates
Brick Institute of America
Rodger A. Brooks, Architect

Concrete Reinforcing Steel Institute
Construction Specifications
  Institute
Dur-O-Wal Products, Inc.
The Garlinghouse Company
Hearlihy and Company
Inland Ryerson
Intergraph Corporation
The Institute of Electrical and
  Electronics Engineers, Inc.
JonesMayer Architecture, Inc.
Harold L. LePere and Assoc. Inc.,
  Architects, Planners, and Interior
  Designers

National Forest Products
  Association
National Gypsum Co.
Owens Corning Fiberglas
Plywood Fabricator Service, Inc.
Rock Island Millwork
Simpson Strong-Tie Co., Inc.
J.H. Svenson
Trus Joist Corporation
United States Gypsum Company
United Steel Products Company
Wheeling-Pittsburgh Steel Corp.
Wire Reinforcement Institute

1 2 3 4 5 6 7 8 9 - 87 - 9 8 7 6 5 4 3

Printed in the United States of America

Library of Congress Cataloging-in-Publication Data

Sundberg, Elmer W.
  Building trades printreading.

  Includes index.
  Contents: p. 2. Residential and light commercial
construction.
  1. Building—Details—Drawings. 2. Blueprints.
I. Proctor, Thomas E., 1939–   . II. Title.
TH431.S83 1987   692´.1   87-18840
ISBN 0-8269-0449-1 (soft)

CONTENTS

INTRODUCTION

BUILDING TRADES PRINTREADING - PART 2 provides printreading experience in residential and light commercial construction. The text/workbook is designed to reinforce concepts regarding elements commonly found on prints. Chapters 1 and 2 cover information such as symbols, abbreviations, and conventions. Sketching principles and practices in orthographic and pictorial form are also included. Computer-aided drafting (CAD) is introduced in Chapter 1. The plans for Wendy's Restaurant (Chapter 9) are CAD-generated.

Five sets of plans are included in BUILDING TRADES PRINTREADING - PART 2. These plans show different types of construction and regional applications. These plans are North Carolina Residence, Commercial Building, Fisher Residence, Branch Bank, and Wendy's Restaurant. Four *Trade Plans* are included for study as assigned by your instructor. These plans provide an opportunity to develop additional printreading skills in your trade area. These plans include

Trade Plan 1: Residence—Framed Wall
Trade Plan 2: Residence—Masonry Wall
Trade Plan 3: Bathhouse for Swimming Pool
Trade Plan 4: Office Renovation

Review Questions and Trade Competency Tests follow each chapter. For the five chapters related to specific plans, Review Questions are based on the chapter text and the Trade Competency Test is based on the plans. Types of questions included are True-False, Multiple Choice, Completion, Identification, Matching, Definition, Math, and Printreading. Always record your answer in the space provided. Answers for all questions are in the Instructor's Guide for BUILDING TRADES PRINTREADING - PART 2.

True-False

Circle T if the answer is true. Circle F if the answer is false.

T (F)   **8.** Aluminum should not be used for framing dwellings and small commercial buildings.

Multiple Choice

Select the response that correctly completes the statement. Write the appropriate letter in the space provided.

__C__   **6.** A _____ is an electromechanical device used to input information into a CAD system.
   A. plotter
   B. light pen
   C. stylus
   D. CPU

Completion

Determine the response that correctly completes the statement. Write the appropriate response in the space provided.

__plot__   **1.** A(n) _____ plan contains lot and building dimensions.

Identification

Select the response that correctly matches the given word(s). Write the appropriate letter in the space provided.

__D__   **1.** Rough member (section)

__A__   **2.** Concrete (elevation)

__B__   **3.** Earth (section)

__C__   **4.** Brick (elevation)

Matching

Select the response that correctly matches the given word(s). Write the appropriate letter in the space provided.

__*C*__	**1.**	Drawing	A. EXT
__*A*__	**2.**	Exterior	B. DW
__*D*__	**3.**	Bathroom	C. DWG
__*B*__	**4.**	Dishwasher	D. B

Definitions

Write a short statement to define the term. Use the space provided.

3. Subcontractor— *Any person, firm, or corporation working for the contractor.*

Math

Solve the problem by performing the mathematical function(s) required. Write the answer in the space provided.

__*$4\frac{1}{4}''$*__ **1.** A partition is framed with $2'' \times 4''$ studs and finished with $^3/_8''$ drywall on both sides. What is the actual thickness of the partition?

Printreading

Study the referenced plan. Questions may be True-False, Multiple Choice, Completion, Matching, and so forth. Write the answer in the space provided.

(T) F **1.** The width of the bench is $1'\text{-}11^1/_2''$.

T (F) **2.** The scale of the Bench Detail is $^1/_2'' = 1'\text{-}0''$.

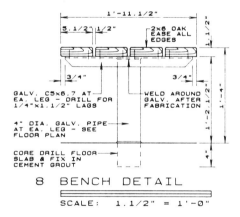

```
                        1'-11.1/2"
        5.1/2" 1/2"        2x6 OAK
                          EASE ALL
                          EDGES

        3/4"              3/4"

GALV. C5x6.7 AT           WELD AROUND
EA. LEG - DRILL FOR       GALV. AFTER
1/4"x1.1/2" LAGS          FABRICATION

4" DIA. GALV. PIPE
AT EA. LEG - SEE
FLOOR PLAN

CORE DRILL FLOOR
SLAB & FIX IN
CEMENT GROUT

   8   BENCH DETAIL
```

SCALE: 1.1/2" = 1'-0"

Plans

Five sets of plans are separately packaged for convenience. Note that the size of each print has been modified and should not be scaled. Information along the border of each sheet identifies the print on each side of the sheet. For example,

- Wendy's—Sheet 1 (Sheet 2)   •   Wendy's—Sheet 1 (Sheet 2)   •

  PRINT ON   PRINT ON
  THIS SIDE   OPPOSITE SIDE

An Index to Plans is located inside the cover of the box containing the prints. A brief listing of the contents of each print is also included.

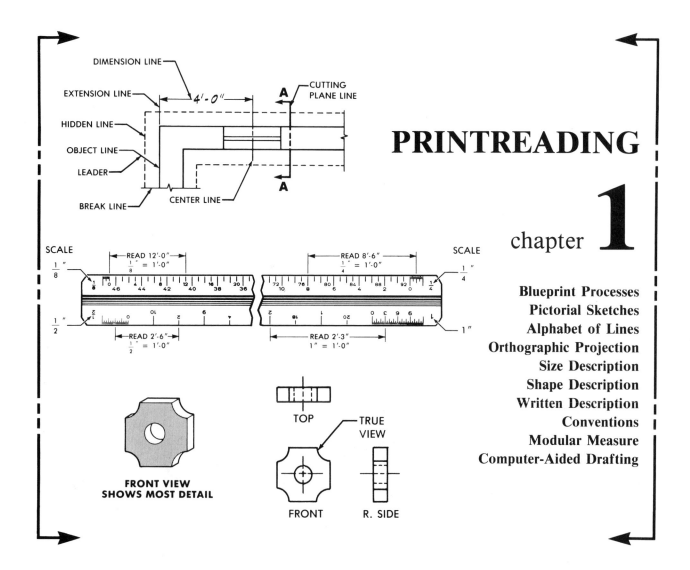

PRINTREADING

chapter 1

Blueprint Processes
Pictorial Sketches
Alphabet of Lines
Orthographic Projection
Size Description
Shape Description
Written Description
Conventions
Modular Measure
Computer-Aided Drafting

BLUEPRINT PROCESSES

Before the blueprint process was invented, architects drew the working drawings for a building in ink on heavy, durable paper. Each original drawing was the only one available during construction of the building unless additional copies were made by tracing them on transparent (clear) paper or by making an exact duplicate on the same kind of paper.

When the blueprint process was perfected, the original working drawings were made on transparent paper. Each sheet was then placed over a sheet of paper that was treated with light-sensitive chemicals. The two sheets were firmly held in position and exposed to sunlight or some other light source. Wherever a line, dimension, or notation appeared on the tracing, an area of the same image was shielded from

the light. When the sensitized paper was washed with water, these areas remained white. The whole background turned a deep blue because the light had changed the chemicals in the paper. The great advantage of the blueprint process was that numerous blueprints could be made from the same tracings. The blueprints were distributed to estimators, builders, and owners. The tracings were stored carefully in the architect's office to be used to make additional blueprints as needed.

Many refinements have been made in the blueprint process. With the new types of light-sensitive paper, new developing methods, and new high speed printing, better prints are available for use by estimators, owners, builders (both contractors and subcontractors), architects, and others. One of the new processes uses an aniline dye in the paper which,

1

when exposed to light, provides prints with a blue line on a white background. See Figure 1-1. The diazo process provides a black line on a white background.

All reproductions of original tracings, regardless of color, line, or background, are commonly referred to as blueprints although they are not technically blueprints. These are thought of as direct copies of the original working drawings. Technically, a distinction is made between blueprints, blue line prints, and black line prints.

PICTORIAL SKETCHES

Pictorial sketches look like a "picture" because they convey a sense of perspective and realism of the object being viewed. Height, length, and depth of the object are easily shown by utilizing various types of pictorial drawings. While pictorial drawings or sketches are only occasionally used when prepar-

ing prints, an understanding of their basic concepts aids in the interpretation of prints. Additionally, the ability to quickly sketch a pictorial drawing of an object or detail aids in conveying technical information to others. Three basic types of pictorial drawings are *axonometric, oblique,* and *perspective.* See Figure 1-2.

Axonometric

Axonometric drawings are drawn using three principle axes. The three basic methods utilized in making axonometric drawings are *isometric, dimetric,* and *trimetric.* Of these, the isometric method is the most commonly used. Dimetric and trimetric drawing methods are rarely utilized. In isometric drawings, the axes are 120° apart. Dimetric drawings have two axes drawn on equal angles and one axis containing either fewer or more degrees. In trimetric drawings, all axes are drawn at different angles. See Figure 1-3.

Figure 1-1. Prints with a blue line on a white background are commonly used in the building trades.

TYPES OF PICTORIALS

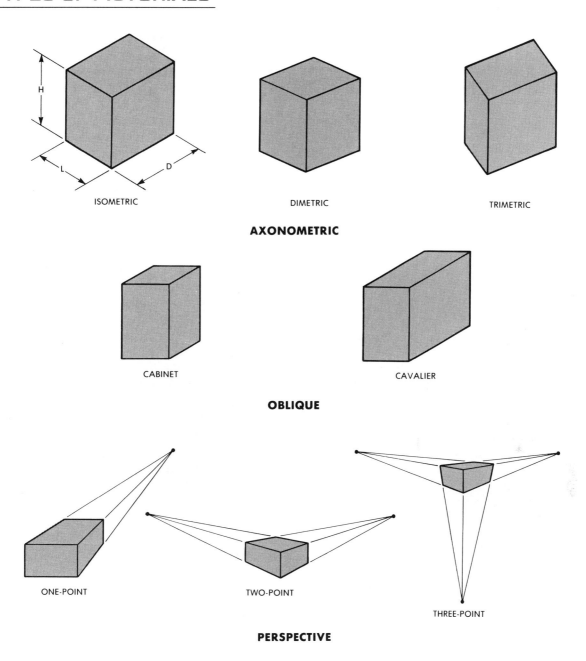

Figure 1-2. Pictorial drawings show height, length, and depth. They convey a "picture" of an object or detail.

Isometric. Isometric drawings are created using drafting instruments such as a T-square and 30°-60° triangle. An isometric sketch can be developed quickly by following the same basic principles used when making isometric drawings with instruments. Isometric drawings contain three equal axes that are drawn 120° apart. Because of this 120° angle, no surface appears as a *normal view* (line of sight is perpendicular to the surface); however, the object has a natural appearance since it is shown as a solid. Because of the skewed sides, circles (drilled holes, counterbores, etc.) appear as ellipses on isometric surfaces. Additionally, arcs appear as portions of ellipses. All surfaces not in one of the three princi-

TYPES OF AXONOMETRICS

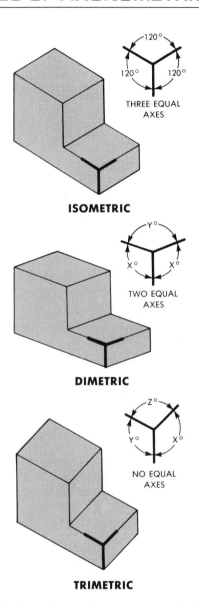

ISOMETRIC

DIMETRIC

TRIMETRIC

Figure 1-3. Isometrics are the most commonly drawn type of axonometric drawings.

ple isometric surfaces must be drawn by locating end points of the skewed surface. The end points are connected to complete the skewed surface. See Figure 1-4.

Sketching Isometrics. To make isometric sketches of objects, follow the procedure shown in Figure 1-5.
1. Locate the isometric axes and "block in" the front view using length and height measurements from the multiview. There are two front

surfaces on this particular object. These two surfaces are parallel to one another. The depth dimension used to establish the location of the second front surface is taken from either the top or right side view of the multiview.
2. Sketch the outline shape of the front surfaces. Measurements are determined from the multiview. Notice that the arc on the second front surface is drawn as a portion of an ellipse.
3. Locate the centerpoint of the drilled hole on the second front surface. Construct an ellipse using measurements from the front view of the multiview.
4. Draw all receding lines. These lines must be drawn long enough to mark the depth of the object. Receding lines are parallel to the isometric axis.
5. Refer to the multiview for depth dimensions and mark depth.
6. Draw lines to establish the back surface. These lines are parallel to the isometric axis. The skewed line on the back surface representing the V portion is drawn to its corresponding line in the front surface. Find the depth through the drilled portion to determine if the back portion of the drilled hole will show through on the front view. Draw portion of ellipse as required.
7. Darken all object lines to complete the isometric sketch.

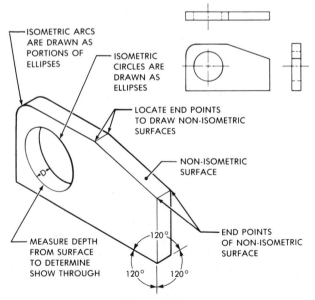

Figure 1-4. Circles on isometric drawings appear as ellipses. Non-isometric surfaces are drawn by locating their end points.

SKETCHING ISOMETRICS

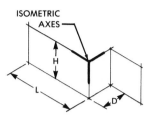

1. "Block in" front view. Use measurements from the multiview.

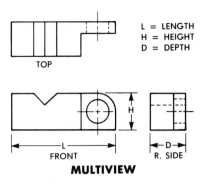

L = LENGTH
H = HEIGHT
D = DEPTH

TOP

FRONT

R. SIDE

MULTIVIEW

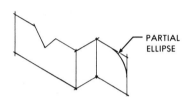

PARTIAL ELLIPSE

2. Sketch outline shape of front view.

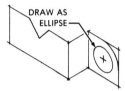

DRAW AS ELLIPSE

3. Locate centerpoint shown in front view. Sketch ellipse for drilled hole.

RECEDING LINE ORIGINATING FROM THIS POINT

4. Draw receding lines.

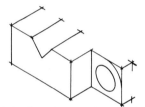

5. Establish depth.

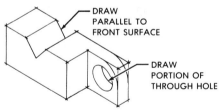

DRAW PARALLEL TO FRONT SURFACE

DRAW PORTION OF THROUGH HOLE

6. Draw lines to establish back surface.

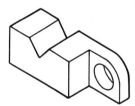

7. Darken all object lines.

Figure 1-5. Isometric sketches can be quickly sketched to convey a "picture" of an object.

Non-isometric Surfaces. Non-isometric (skewed) surfaces on isometric sketches do not lie in one of the three principle isometric planes. To draw a skewed surface, all end points must first be located on surfaces in isometric planes. These points are connected to complete the skewed surface. See Figure 1-6. Note in the figure shown that surface A, B, C is the skewed surface. It does not lie in an isometric surface.

Circles on Isometrics. Circles on isometric surfaces are drawn as ellipses. An ellipse is a plane curve with two focal points (*foci*). The sum of the distances from these two focal points to any point on the ellipse determines the shape of the ellipse. As the distance between the focal points decreases, the ellipse becomes more circular in shape.

Several methods of constructing ellipses with drafting instruments are available to drafters. Ellipse

SKETCHING SKEWED SURFACES ON ISOMETRICS

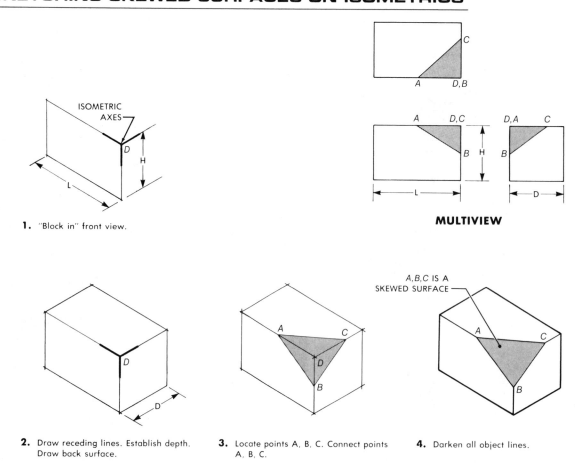

MULTIVIEW

1. "Block in" front view.

2. Draw receding lines. Establish depth. Draw back surface.

3. Locate points A, B, C. Connect points A, B, C.

4. Darken all object lines.

Figure 1-6. Skewed surfaces on isometric sketches are drawn by locating their end points.

templates also are commercially available. For sketching, the *parallelogram* method may be used. In this method, dimensions from the multiview are used to determine the size of the parallelogram. Arcs are then drawn or sketched using the intersecting points as centerpoints. See Figure 1-7.

Oblique

Oblique drawings show one face (surface) of an object as a *true view* (line of sight is 90° to the face). All other faces of the object are distorted by the angle of the receding, oblique lines. All features shown on the face containing a true view are drawn as they appear. Additionally, right angles are shown at 90° on surfaces having a true view. For example, a drilled hole shown on the true view face of an oblique drawing is shown as a circle. Drilled holes on any other surface of the oblique drawing appear

as ellipses. The angle at which an ellipse is drawn on these surfaces is determined by the angle of the receding line. Normally, these lines are drawn on a 30° or 45° angle. See Figure 1-8. The two types of oblique drawings are oblique *cabinet* and oblique *cavalier*.

Cabinet. Oblique cabinet drawings show a true view of one surface with all receding lines drawn to one-half the length of corresponding lines in the true view. This is the most commonly used type of oblique drawing. Cabinet drawings, as the name implies, are often used to show kitchen and bathroom cabinets. This method of drawing allows a true view of the major surfaces (usually the front of the cabinets) and conveys a sense of perspective with receding lines showing other surfaces. See Figure 1-9. Circles, arcs, and all lines 90° to line-of-sight that

SKETCHING ISOMETRIC CIRCLES

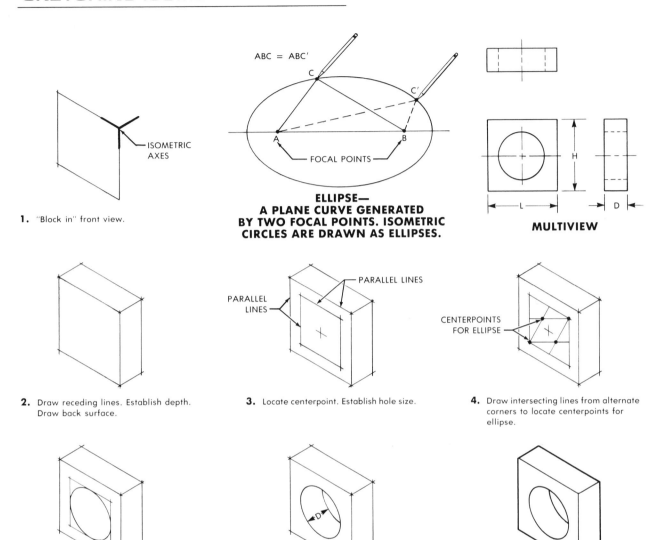

1. "Block in" front view.

ABC = ABC'

**ELLIPSE—
A PLANE CURVE GENERATED
BY TWO FOCAL POINTS. ISOMETRIC
CIRCLES ARE DRAWN AS ELLIPSES.**

FOCAL POINTS

MULTIVIEW

2. Draw receding lines. Establish depth. Draw back surface.

3. Locate centerpoint. Establish hole size.

4. Draw intersecting lines from alternate corners to locate centerpoints for ellipse.

5. Draw arcs to complete ellipse.

6. Establish depth of drilled hole. Draw arc on back surface.

7. Darken all object lines.

Figure 1-7. Circles on isometrics appear as ellipses.

are shown in the true (usually front) view appear as seen and are not distorted. All surfaces drawn with receding lines do not provide a true view. Circles on these surfaces appear as ellipses.

Cavalier. Oblique cavalier drawings show a true view of one surface with all receding lines drawn to the same scale used to draw lines in the true view.

The use of the same scale to draw all oblique lines of an oblique cavalier drawing produces a distorted pictorial drawing. Consequently, this type of drawing is seldom utilized. Circles, arcs, and oblique lines are drawn in the same manner as for oblique cabinet drawings with the view showing the most features commonly selected to be drawn as the front view. See Figure 1-10.

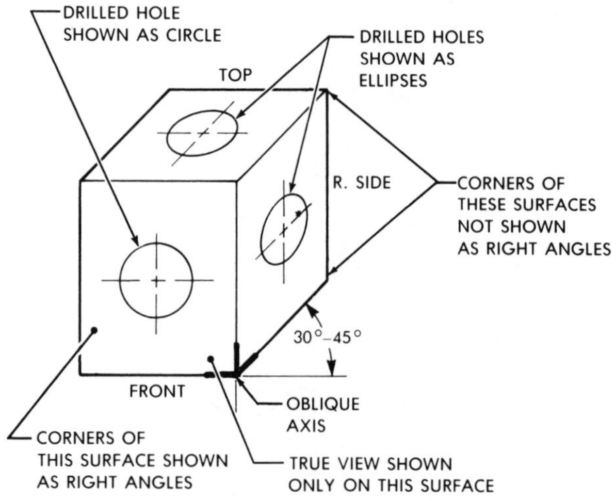

DRILLED HOLE
SHOWN AS CIRCLE

DRILLED HOLES
SHOWN AS
ELLIPSES

TOP

R. SIDE

CORNERS OF
THESE SURFACES
NOT SHOWN
AS RIGHT ANGLES

FRONT

30°–45°

OBLIQUE
AXIS

CORNERS OF
THIS SURFACE SHOWN
AS RIGHT ANGLES

TRUE VIEW SHOWN
ONLY ON THIS SURFACE

Figure 1-8. Features shown on true view surface of an oblique drawing are drawn as they appear.

Sketching Obliques. To make oblique sketches of objects, follow the procedure shown in Figure 1-11.

1. Determine if the object will be shown as as oblique cabinet or oblique cavalier sketch. (An oblique cabinet is shown in this exercise.)
2. "Block in" the front view (usually the view with the most detail). The length and height sizes shown in the multiview are used for this step.
3. Add lines to complete the outline shape as shown in the front view of the multiview.
4. Locate all centerpoints of circles and/or arcs shown in the front view. Sketch circles and arcs.
5. Draw receding lines. (The receding lines shown in this step are drawn at approximately a 30° angle. They could also be drawn at a 45° angle.)

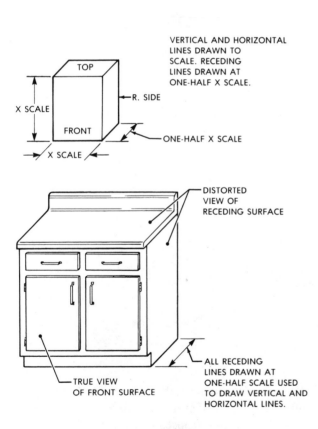

VERTICAL AND HORIZONTAL
LINES DRAWN TO
SCALE. RECEDING
LINES DRAWN AT
ONE-HALF X SCALE.

TOP

R. SIDE

X SCALE

FRONT

ONE-HALF X SCALE

X SCALE

DISTORTED
VIEW OF
RECEDING SURFACE

TRUE VIEW
OF FRONT SURFACE

ALL RECEDING
LINES DRAWN AT
ONE-HALF SCALE USED
TO DRAW VERTICAL AND
HORIZONTAL LINES.

OBLIQUE CABINET

Figure 1-9. All receding lines of oblique cabinet drawings are drawn at one-half the scale used to draw vertical and horizontal lines.

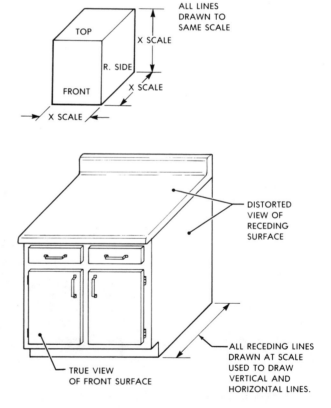

ALL LINES
DRAWN TO
SAME SCALE

TOP

X SCALE

R. SIDE

FRONT

X SCALE

X SCALE

DISTORTED
VIEW OF
RECEDING
SURFACE

TRUE VIEW
OF FRONT SURFACE

ALL RECEDING LINES
DRAWN AT SCALE
USED TO DRAW
VERTICAL AND
HORIZONTAL LINES.

OBLIQUE CAVALIER

Figure 1-10. All lines of oblique cavalier drawings are drawn at the same scale.

SKETCHING OBLIQUES

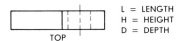

L = LENGTH
H = HEIGHT
D = DEPTH

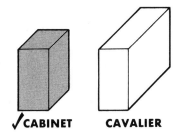

√CABINET **CAVALIER**

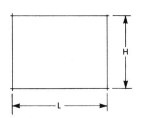

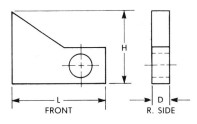

MULTIVIEW

1. Determine which oblique to sketch. (Cabinet is shown in following steps.)

2. "Block in" front view. Use L and H measurements from the multiview.

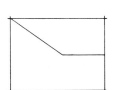

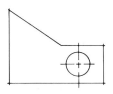

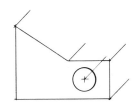

3. Sketch outline shape of front view.

4. Locate centerpoint shown in front view and sketch circle.

5. Draw receding lines.

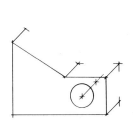

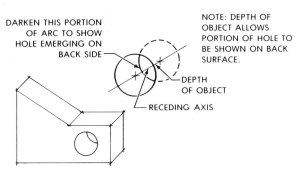

DARKEN THIS PORTION OF ARC TO SHOW HOLE EMERGING ON BACK SIDE

NOTE: DEPTH OF OBJECT ALLOWS PORTION OF HOLE TO BE SHOWN ON BACK SURFACE.

DEPTH OF OBJECT

RECEDING AXIS

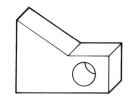

6. Establish depth.

7. Draw lines to establish back surface.

8. Darken all object lines.

Figure 1-11. Oblique drawings can be quickly sketched to convey a "picture" of an object.

6. Establish depth. This dimension is taken from the right side or the top view of the multiview. Note that only one-half the dimension shown is drawn for depth of the oblique cabinet.

7. Draw lines to represent the object's back surface. When holes are drilled completely through the object being drawn, determine if the back side of the hole will show by measuring the depth along a receding line drawn from the centerpoint of the hole on the front surface.

8. Darken all object lines. Construction lines may be erased, if desired.

When sketching oblique drawings, notice that the true view represents a plane surface. If an object has two or more plane surfaces to be shown in the true view, the drawing is blocked out and receding lines are used to connect the plane surfaces. The view showing the most shape of the object, the view containing the larger number of circles and arcs, or the view commonly thought of as the front is selected

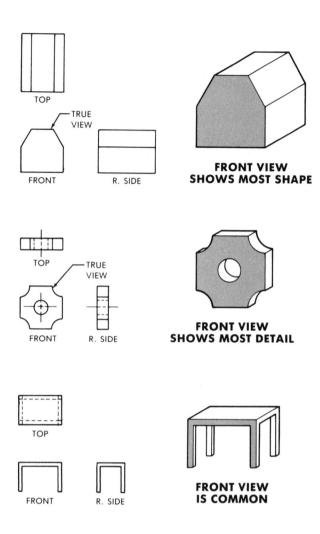

TOP

TRUE VIEW

FRONT R. SIDE

FRONT VIEW SHOWS MOST SHAPE

TOP

TRUE VIEW

FRONT R. SIDE

FRONT VIEW SHOWS MOST DETAIL

TOP

FRONT R. SIDE

FRONT VIEW IS COMMON

Figure 1-12. The front view of an oblique object is selected by determining which view shows the most shape, has the most detail, or is commonly thought of as the front view.

for the front view when making oblique drawings. See Figure 1-12.

Perspective

Perspective drawings are the most realistic of all pictorial drawings. In order to produce a technically accurate perspective drawing, many measurements involving the position of the observer, location of the picture plane, and distances to various vanishing points are required. For perspective sketching, however, this process is simplified and fairly accurate perspective sketches can be drawn quickly and easily. The perspective sketching method is often utilized when preparing an artist's rendering of a proposed building. Such a rendering is useful to allow the owner to see how the completed building will look and for presentation to the various boards when applying for zoning. See Figure 1-13.

Three basic types of perspective drawings are *one-point, two-point,* and *three-point* perspectives. Of these, the two-point perspective is most commonly used. Each of these three types of perspective drawings may be completed with the observer perceived to be in a *bird's-eye, eye-level,* or *worm's-eye* position. See Figure 1-14.

The location of the vanishing points alters the angle of receding perspective lines. When the vanishing points of two-point and three-point perspectives are spaced close together, the receding lines converge much more sharply than when the vanishing points are spaced farther apart. Vanishing points spaced too closely together produce a distorted view

Figure 1-13. Artists' renderings utilize perspective sketching.

of the drawn object. Refer to Figure 1-14 and note the position of the vanishing points for the two-point and three-point perspective sketches. The third sketch of each shows the vanishing points spaced apart, producing a more realistic sketch.

When labeling vanishing points for referencing during sketching, abbreviations are used. For example, the vanishing point in a one-point perspective sketch is abbreviated *VP*. The vanishing points for a two-point perspective are labeled *VPL* for vanishing point left and *VPR* for vanishing point right. For three-point perspectives, *VPB* or *VPT* indicates either a bottom or a top vanishing point.

Sketching Perspectives. To make perspective sketches of objects, follow the procedure shown in Figure 1-15.

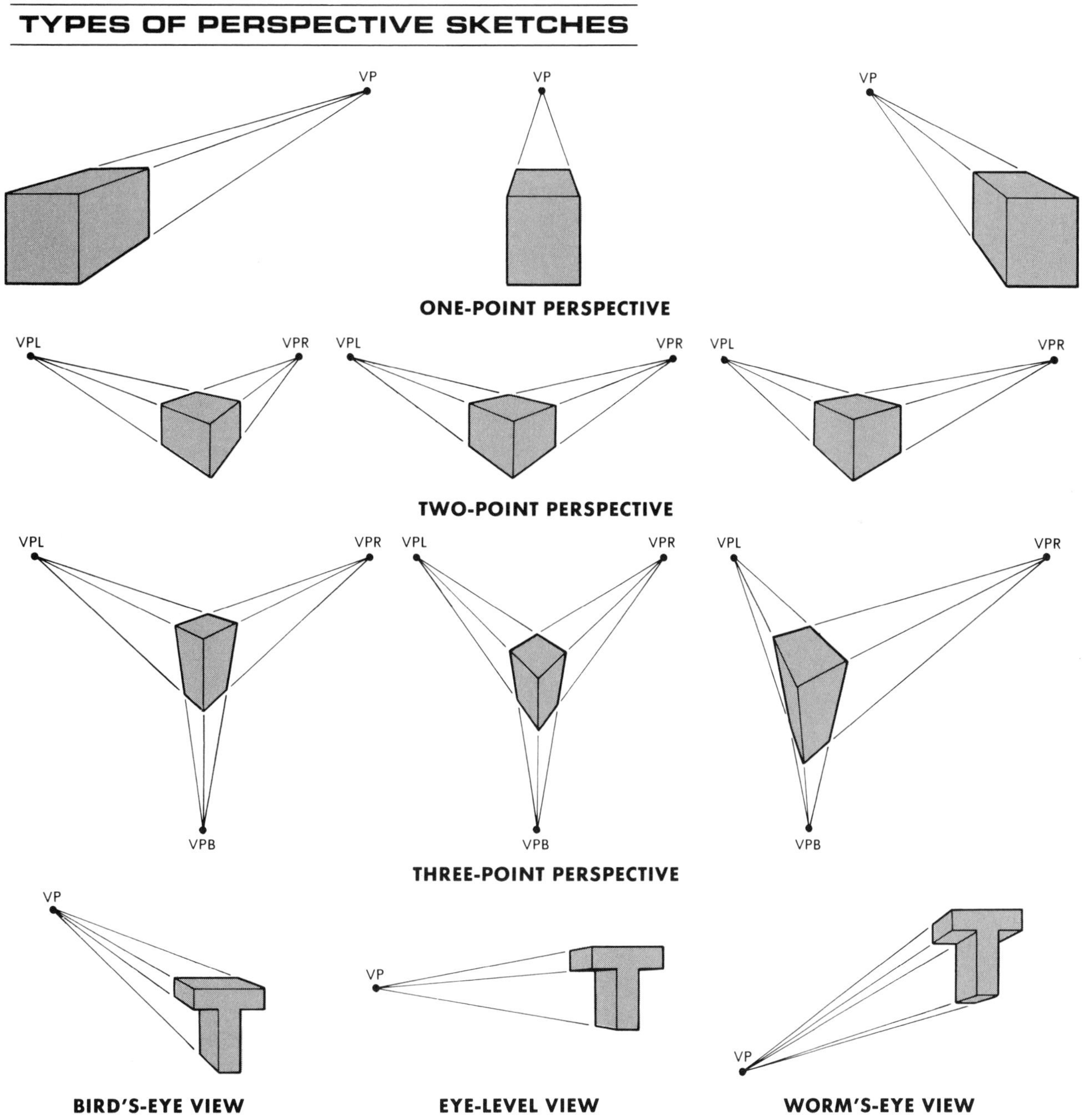

TYPES OF PERSPECTIVE SKETCHES

Figure 1-14. Perspective sketches may be one-, two-, or three-point. They are drawn as bird's-eye, eye-level, or worm's-eye views.

SKETCHING PERSPECTIVES

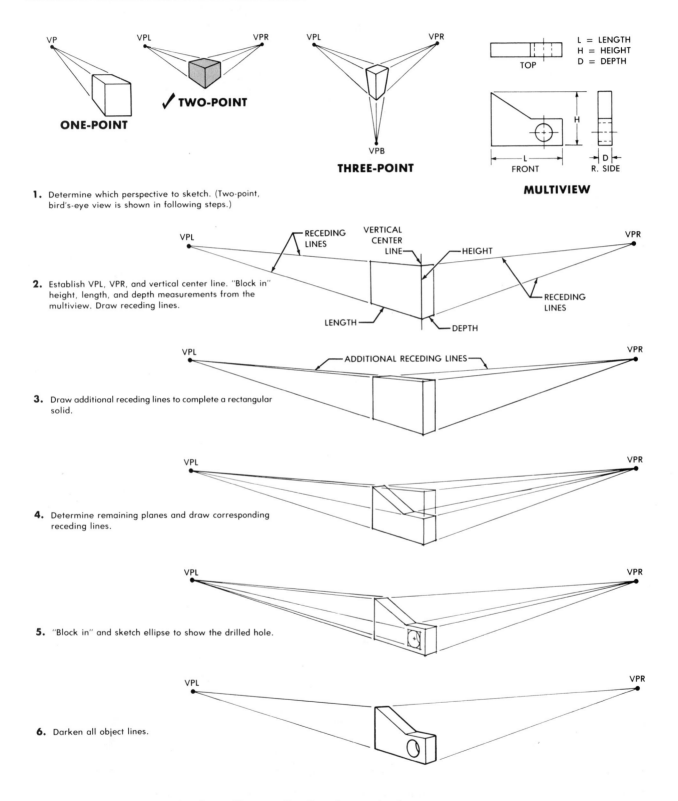

1. Determine which perspective to sketch. (Two-point, bird's-eye view is shown in following steps.)

2. Establish VPL, VPR, and vertical center line. "Block in" height, length, and depth measurements from the multiview. Draw receding lines.

3. Draw additional receding lines to complete a rectangular solid.

4. Determine remaining planes and draw corresponding receding lines.

5. "Block in" and sketch ellipse to show the drilled hole.

6. Darken all object lines.

Figure 1-15. Perspective sketches utilize receding lines for a natural appearance.

1. Determine if the object will be shown as a one-point, two-point, or three-point perspective and whether it will be sketched as a bird's-eye, eye-level, or worm's-eye view.
2. Establish vanishing points and "block in" the height, length, and depth dimensions (shown in the multiview sketch). Draw appropriate receding lines. Note: Selection of the vertical line nearest the viewer will determine orientation of the completed sketch.
3. Draw additional receding lines to complete a rectangular solid with proper height, length, and depth dimensions.
4. Determine any remaining lines and draw corresponding receding lines to appropriate vanishing points. Note: Oblique planes (those not in one of the planes defined by the rectangular solid) may be determined by locating their end points on appropriate lines. They are then completed by drawing receding lines from the located points to the appropriate vanishing points.
5. "Block in" any squares, arcs, or other shapes and sketch as full or partial ellipses. Note: Construction of a "square" with appropriate receding lines will determine orientation and aid in sketching of circular parts.
6. Darken all object lines to complete the perspective sketch.

ALPHABET OF LINES

The conventional representation of lines is fundamental to drafting practice and printreading. Conventional representation of lines refers to prescribed line types as specified in ANSI Y14.2M. The American National Standards Institute (ANSI) sets standards for use in many areas (for example, plumbing and hardware).

By drawing lines to ANSI standards, an "alphabet of lines" is established and easily read. For example, a line that is always drawn with a series of dashes of equal length is immediately identified as a hidden line.

Lines used on drawings include object lines, hidden lines, center lines, dimension lines, extension lines, leaders, break lines, and cutting plane lines. See Figure 1-16. Other types of lines are also used on drawings. Refer to ANSI Y14.2M. All drawing lines are sharp and dark so that good quality reproduction can be made.

All lines on prints that are visible are shown with object lines. For example, object lines are used extensively on elevation views. A floor plan and a section view are made by passing cutting plane lines through the building. Lines that become visible on or behind the cutting plane are shown with object lines. Lines that are hidden below a surface or behind an object are drawn as hidden lines. Note: Lines above the cutting plane are drawn as hidden lines in plan views.

As a general practice, architects rarely use hidden lines on working drawings unless they are necessary to provide information to the builder. Center lines are particularly useful in locating the centers of columns, windows, doors, and openings. Occasionally section views are taken through walls or parts of buildings, such as windows or cabinets, to show greater detail. The location of such sections, as well as the direction in which they are viewed, is indicated by cutting plane lines, arrows, and identifying letters or numbers.

Dimension lines are terminated by extension lines projecting from the feature to be dimensioned. Dimensions are lettered above a continuous dimension line or centered along the dimension line. Break lines are useful when the architect wishes to terminate a detail or show that it continues but is not drawn. See Figure 1-17.

ORTHOGRAPHIC PROJECTION

Drawings utilizing orthographic projection (drawn at right angles) techniques are referred to as *multiview* drawings. In this method of drawing, each view is shown two-dimensionally. The six basic views of a multiview drawing are front, top, right side, back, left side, and bottom. The front, top, and right side views are most commonly shown. See Figure 1-18. Notice the relationship of one view to another. The right side view is always drawn on the right side of the front view and the top view is always drawn directly above the front view. These views are *projected* from one another.

Prints are drawn orthographically. The front, back, right and left side views are drawn as *elevations*. Top views (looking from above) are drawn as *plans*. *Sections* may be drawn from any of the six basic orthographic views, although for building trades prints they are commonly drawn from front, back, right or left side views.

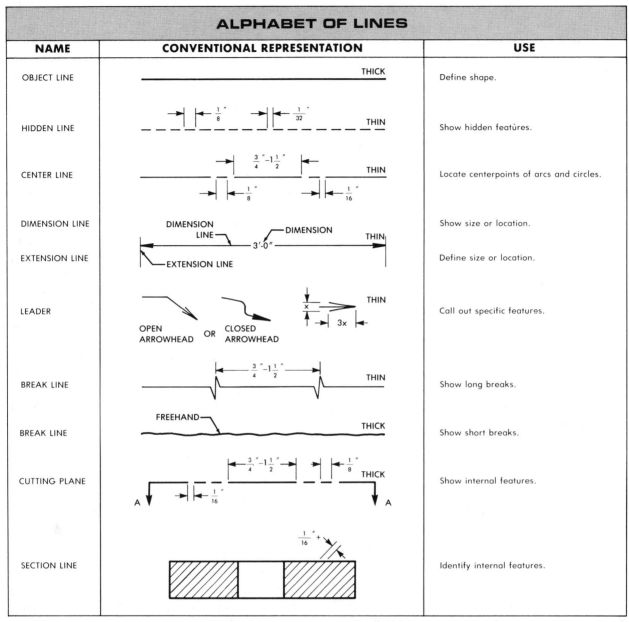

Figure 1-16. The alphabet of lines is specified in ANSI Y14.2M.

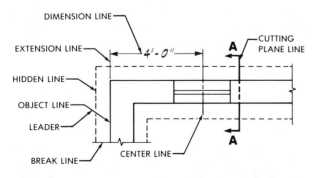

Figure 1-17. Each line on a drawing has a specific function.

Multiview Principles

Multiview drawings are based on the principle of showing one view of an object in detail. All objects have three basic dimensions; *length, height,* and *depth.* Any one view of a multiview drawing can only show two of these dimensions. For example, the front view shows length and height; the top view shows length and depth; and the right side view shows height and depth. See Figure 1-19.

All visible lines of a multiview are drawn as object lines. Lines that are not visible are drawn as

ORTHOGRAPHIC PROJECTION [MULTIVIEWS]

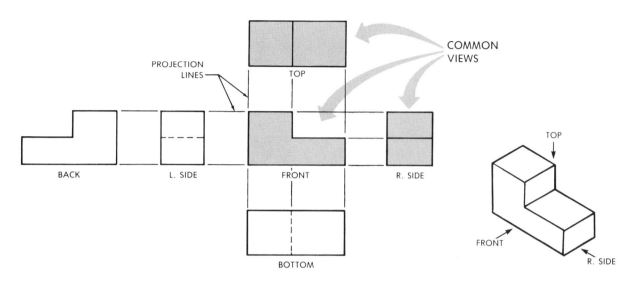

Figure 1-18. The front, top, and right side of a multiview drawing are the most common views.

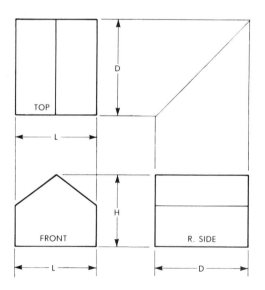

VIEW	SHOWS
Front	Length and height
Top	Length and depth
Right side	Height and depth

Figure 1-19. Any one view of a multiview drawing shows two dimensions.

hidden lines. The front view of a multiview drawing is generally the view showing the most shape. Front views are also selected to show a minimal number of hidden lines. Additionally, the view normally considered the front is often selected.

Sketching Multiviews. To make multiview sketches of objects, follow the procedure shown in Figure 1-20. Note that the object shown in this procedure is similar to the object shown in Figure 1-18. The front, top, and right side views are to be drawn.

1. "Block in" the length and height dimensions of the front view. Note: Pay particular attention to the location of the front view to allow even spacing of views.
2. Project the length and height dimensions of the front view to the top and right side views.
3. Establish depth dimensions of the top and right side views. The depth dimension is shown through a 45° miter line on the right side of the top view to establish the same depth dimension in the right side view.
4. Sketch the drilled hole in the top view. Project hole dimensions to the front and right side views and draw hidden lines.
5. Darken all object lines. Show center lines to complete the sketch of the multiview drawing.

SKETCHING MULTIVIEWS

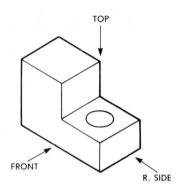

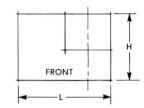

1. "Block in" length and height dimensions of front view.

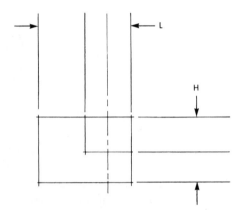

2. Project length and height dimensions of front view to top and right side views.

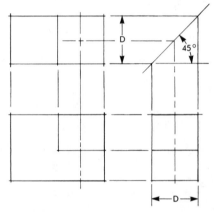

3. Establish depth dimensions of top and right side views. Note use of 45° turn.

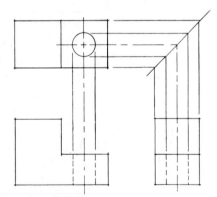

4. Sketch drilled hole in top view. Project size of hole to front and right side views and sketch hidden lines.

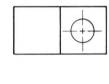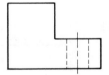

5. Darken all object lines. Show center lines for drilled hole.

Figure 1-20. Dimensions of views in a multiview drawing are projected from adjacent views.

SIZE DESCRIPTION

Prints are drawn to scale and dimensioned to give a complete and accurate size description of the building. While different print drawings may be drawn to different scales in order to show small details and fit the drawing on the sheet, all parts of a single drawing are drawn to the same scale to clearly show size relationships. Additionally, dimensions applied to the drawings establish particular size and location of the features shown.

In Figure 1-21, the Shelf Detail is drawn to the scale of $1\frac{1}{2}'' = 1'-0''$. This large-size scale allows the architect to show small parts clearly. The $\frac{3}{4}''$ oak varnished shelf is $5'-8''$ above the finished floor. Oak braces, at 32" OC, support the 30° inclined shelf which projects $1'-4''$ from the $\frac{5}{8}''$ gypsum board wall. The note (N.I.C. BY OWNER) indicates that the shelf is not included in the contract. It is to be supplied by the owner.

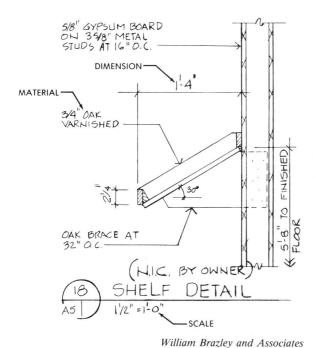

William Brazley and Associates

Figure 1-21. Prints are drawn to scale and clearly dimensioned to give a complete size description.

Scale

Scale is the relative size to which an object is drawn. It is impractical to draw plans of a building, or even major parts of a building, at actual or even half-size scale. The architect has two objectives, clarity and size, which can work against each other. Plans must be drawn large enough to clearly show all necessary information, yet must fit the drawing sheet and not be too large to handle. The difficulty of showing parts clearly is solved by applying appropriate scales to the drawings.

The most common scale for working drawings is $\frac{1}{4}'' = 1'-0''$ (read "one-quarter of an inch equals one foot"). Ordinarily this scale provides the architect with enough space to draw plans on a reasonably large sheet and also permits the various parts of the building, dimensions, and notes to be clearly shown. A quick, comprehensive idea of most buildings' layout, size, and unique features can be formed with a set of plans drawn to a scale of $\frac{1}{4}'' = 1'-0''$.

Other scales are used when necessary. Scales of $\frac{1}{2}'' = 1'-0''$ or $\frac{3}{4}'' = 1'-0''$ are often used to show elevations of rooms and section views through walls. Detail drawings are an example of showing particular features at a larger scale. The scales of $1'' = 1'-0''$, $1\frac{1}{2}'' = 1'-0''$, and $3'' = 1'-0''$ are used when complex parts require extensive dimensioning or detail.

Extremely complex features may be drawn to a scale of $6'' = 1'-0''$ (half size) or $12'' = 1'-0''$ (full size). These scales are often required when molding or other trim pieces have special profiles which must be shown.

Architect's Scale

An architect's scale is used by architects and drafters to draw objects to a particular scale. The architect's scale is triangular in shape with six faces. Five faces have two scales each and one face is divided into inches and fractional parts of an inch. See Figure 1-22.

To use the architect's scale, place the 0 of the appropriate scale on one end of the line and read the largest increment falling on the other end of the line. Inches are read between the 0 designation and the scale size shown near the end of the architect's scale. Notice that scales read right *or* left—not both. Scales that are multiples of one another are shown on the same edge to conserve space. For example, the $\frac{1}{8}''$ scale and the $\frac{1}{4}''$ scale are located on the same edge with the $\frac{1}{8}''$ scale read from left to right and the $\frac{1}{4}''$ scale read from right to left. Refer to Figure 1-22. Notice on the $\frac{1}{8}''$ scale that extension lines have been drawn to show $12'-0''$ when $\frac{1}{8}'' = 1'-0''$. Also, on the $\frac{1}{2}''$ scale, extension lines show $2'-6''$ on a scale of $\frac{1}{2}'' = 1'-0''$.

Dimensions

It is the architect's responsibility to supply all dimensions where possible. Individual dimensions must be correct so that they add up to equal overall dimensions. Cross checks should be made to ensure that all partitions are correct. It is the responsibility of the worker on the job to correctly read dimen-

ARCHITECT'S SCALE

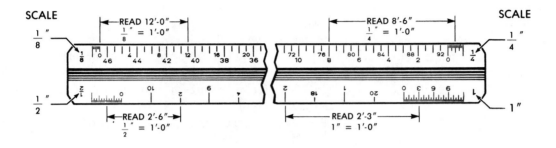

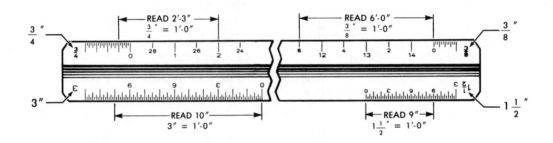

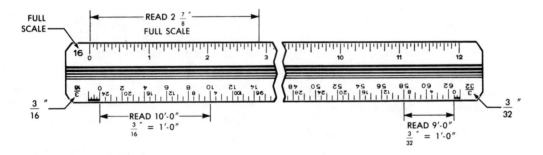

SCALE		SIZE	
3″	= 1′-0″	¹/₄	actual size
1¹/₂″	= 1′-0″	¹/₈	actual size
1″	= 1′-0″	¹/₁₂	actual size
¹/₂″	= 1′-0″	¹/₂₄	actual size
³/₄″	= 1′-0″	¹/₁₆	actual size
³/₈″	= 1′-0″	¹/₃₂	actual size
¹/₄″	= 1′-0″	¹/₄₈	actual size
¹/₈″	= 1′-0″	¹/₉₆	actual size
³/₁₆″	= 1′-0″	¹/₆₄	actual size
³/₃₂″	= 1′-0″	¹/₁₂₈	actual size

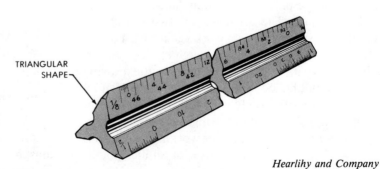

TRIANGULAR SHAPE

Hearlihy and Company

Figure 1-22. The architect's scale is used to draw plans to scale.

sions from the plans and frequently check that they are being followed as the work progresses.

Dimensions are shown to locate points from other points on the prints. The extension lines or leaders are drawn so that the point of reference is clear. Dimension lines on architectural drawings are generally drawn as a continuous line with dimensions appearing above the line. This technique saves drafting time and is easy to read. Dimensions may also be centered in a break in the dimension line. Arrows, dots, or slashes on the end of dimension lines limit each dimension. See Figure 1-23.

Dimensions on plan and elevation drawings are shown in feet and inches (such as 3'-0", 4'-8", and 28'-3"). Note that a dash mark is used between the feet and inch designations to avoid confusion.

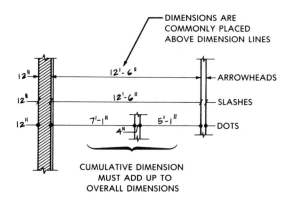

Figure 1-23. Dimension lines are terminated by arrowheads, slashes, or dots.

When laying out buildings, care must be exercised to use full feet and inch measurements as shown on the plans while making slight adjustments for material variations. Laying out partitions is somewhat difficult because of varying partition sizes. Drywall partitions are usually indicated on plans as 4" thick. When $3/8$" drywall is used on both sides of the studs, the actual partition thickness is $4\frac{1}{4}$" ($3/8$" + $3\frac{1}{2}$" + $3/8$" = $4\frac{1}{4}$"). For $1/2$" drywall on each side of the studs, the actual partition thickness is $4\frac{1}{2}$" ($1/2$" + $3\frac{1}{2}$" + $1/2$" = $4\frac{1}{2}$"). A partition with $3/4$" lath and plaster on each side might be shown on the prints as 6" thick. However, the actual thickness is 5". The discrepancy will show up in each room, which will be slightly larger or smaller than the dimensions shown on the plans.

When such dimensions are shown over a series of rooms across a building, a significant cumulative

error could occur in the last room. The tradesworker responsible for the partitions avoids error by laying out all of the partitions on the floor according to the dimensions of the floor plan and then centering each partition within these marks. Note: When using this method, pay particular attention to window or door openings near room corners. Precise dimensioning is also difficult in concrete work. It is almost impossible to erect rough formwork so precisely that dimensions will not vary slightly from the plans.

In the manufacture of modular homes and components such as trusses and wall sections, factory standards can be maintained by using jigs (holding devices) to maintain position of members during assembly. Accuracy is critical for such parts as there is little opportunity on the job for adjustments.

Dimensions should be placed on drawings to avoid confusion. The same dimension should not be shown twice, unless marked REF (reference). This procedure avoids cluttering the drawing with unnecessary dimensions and prevents the possibility of two dimensions referring to the same measurement not being the same.

SHAPE DESCRIPTION

Each print of a set of working drawings represents a part of a building drawn as a flat plane. This method of drawing allows the individual parts of the building to be shown in their true shape and not distorted as they would be on pictorial drawings.

A substantial number of individual prints may be required to clearly show the shape and size of all components. Generally, the architect draws only those plans required to completely show and describe the building. The most essential plans required include plot plans, floor plans, elevations, section views, and detail views.

Plot Plans

The plot plan shows the location and orientation of the structure on the lot and the size of the lot. Additionally, other pertinent information as required by local ordinances is given. When designing a building for an urban community, the architect must comply with local building and zoning ordinances. The first requirement is a legal survey of the property made by a licensed surveyor who establishes the corners of the lot in relation to official points of measurement in the vicinity. The compass direction and the angles at the corners of the lot are included. The survey locates existing buildings, shows the contour of the land, large trees, and other physical features. Location of water, sewer, and electrical power may be included.

Zoning ordinances restrict the use of land in each community of the town or city to single-family dwellings, multi-family dwellings, commercial buildings, and so forth. The distance from the front sidewalk to the building, the width of side yards, and the area covered by the building in relation to the area of the lot are some of the provisions. For example, community building ordinances may stipulate that a commercial building can occupy no more than 40% of the lot size and that the minimum front setback is 65'-0" from the center line of the street. Building codes specify materials and methods of construction. For example, all-masonry buildings may be required in a commercial development to ensure continuity of exterior appearances.

The architect must observe all zoning restrictions when drawing the plot plan. Information given in the survey is shown and the new structure is located on the plot of ground. The *point of beginning* is a mark on a sidewalk or some other fixed point at the lot from which all measurements, both vertical and horizontal, are made. The point of beginning, in turn, is related to a bench mark or city datum point. These datum points may be concrete markers within sighting distance of the lot, a mark on a fire hydrant, the top of a sewer in the street, or other points established by the city as a local point of reference.

The datum points are not only points from which the point of beginning is located by horizontal measurement, but are also the basic points for vertical dimensions. For example, a bench mark and the point of beginning for a particular building are both at a height of 220' above sea level. The finished first floor is at +224' elevation and the basement floor at +215' elevation. (*Elevation* here refers to height above sea level and not an elevation view. The "+" designation in this case indicates the number of feet above sea level.) The finished first floor is 4'-0" above the point of beginning and the basement is 5'-0" below. The point of beginning may be set at zero (+0'-0") elevation. The finished first floor is then +4'-0" elevation and the basement floor is −5'-0" elevation.

The point of beginning is important to the excavator who must dig an excavation at the correct location and to the correct depth. It is equally important to the concrete formworker who must build or erect forms so that the walls are the correct distance from the lot lines and the basement and first floor elevations are correct.

When buildings are to be erected on sloped ground, information about the slope is shown by contour lines which pass through points of the same elevation. The lines are spaced at graduated intervals, such as 2'-0" or 4'-0" elevations, depending on the amount of slope. Additional contour lines are added if significant changes in the finished grading are desired. The new lines are designated *finished grade* (FG).

Two types of contour lines are used to show grade on plot plans. Dashed contour lines show existing grade. Solid lines show finished grade. Contour lines spaced close together indicate steeper slopes. Contour lines spaced farther apart indicate less slope.

Figure 1-24 shows a typical plot plan. The point of beginning, shown at the intersection of the sidewalks, is +0'-0". Other information about grading, location of water, sewer, utilities, large trees, walks, and drives important to various workers is shown on this plot plan. The lot shown on this plot plan is 90'-2" × 126'-4" and contains approximately 11,391 sq. ft. Note that opposite sides of the property shown on this plot plan are not the same lengths. Consequently, the square footage obtained is only an approximate figure.

The existing sidewalks are located on the South and East sides of the lot. These sidewalks are 4'-0" wide and are bordered by an 8'-0" parkway. The sidewalks extend to the curbs of Green and Oak Streets. These streets are concrete paved. The utility pole is located on the North side of the lot. The pole indicates that electrical service will be *overhead*. (Underground electrical service is referred to as *lateral service*.) Water and sewer lines are run under the concrete paved street (Green Street) in front of the house.

The front and side setbacks are 30'-0" from the existing sidewalks. The first floor elevation is +2'-0" above the point of beginning. Floor size of finished space is 38'-0" × 50'-0" less 8'-0" × 14'-0" on the Northeast corner. There are 1788 sq. ft. of finished floor space (38'-0" × 50'-0" = 1900 sq. ft. − 112 sq. ft. = 1788 sq. ft.) and the garage, which is 1'-0" above the point of beginning, contains an additional 576 sq. ft. Front porch length

PLOT PLAN

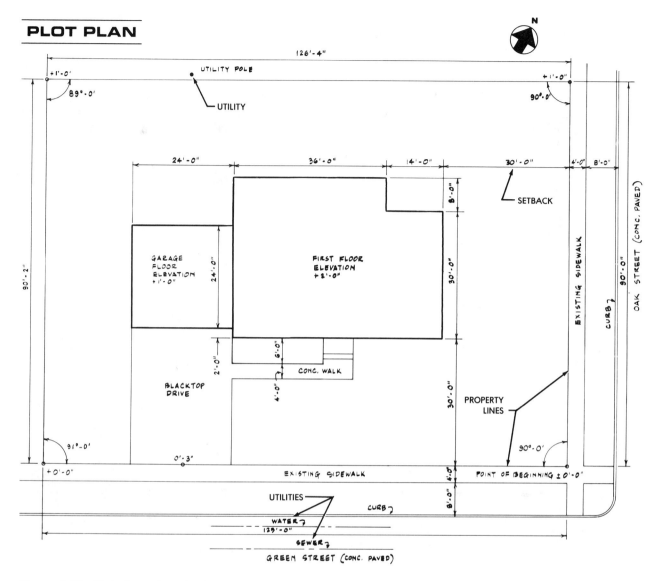

Figure 1-24. Plot plans show the location of the building on the lot.

is not given on this plot plan and no indication is made to show that the front porch is either open or enclosed. The front entrance of the house is reached by a 4'-0" concrete walk from the blacktop drive which exits into Green Street.

Floor Plans

Floor plans are views of a building as though cutting planes were made through it horizontally. The cutting plane is generally taken 5'-0" above the floor being shown. A one-story house requires one floor plan. Buildings with more than one story generally require a floor plan for each level.

The location of all exterior walls and interior partitions are shown and dimensioned on the floor plans. Overall size dimensions and specific location dimensions are given. Door and window openings are shown. Reference letters or numbers refer to door and window schedules showing the type and size of door or window required at each opening.

Plumbing fixtures such as water closets, sinks, shower stalls, and bathtubs are shown on residential floor plans. On smaller sets of plans, electrical information is shown on the floor plans. The general location of receptacles, lights, and switches are shown. On larger sets of residential plans and on commercial plans, electrical information is usually shown on electrical plans. Information pertaining to heating, ventilating, and air conditioning (HVAC) systems may also be shown on floor plans. Registers connecting to the system are located on the floor plan. On larger sets of plans, HVAC information is usually shown on mechanical plans.

When designing floor plans, the architect must keep in mind the overall room relationships and their functions. For multistory buildings, load bearing walls and openings for stairs must be provided.

Room volume in relation to floor space must be considered as the architect makes calculations for ventilation and glass area in accordance with building codes.

Floor plans are generally considered to be one of, if not the most, used plans in the complete set of prints for a building and should be carefully studied to gain an overall mental picture of the building to be constructed.

Figure 1-25 shows a portion of a floor plan for

FLOOR PLAN

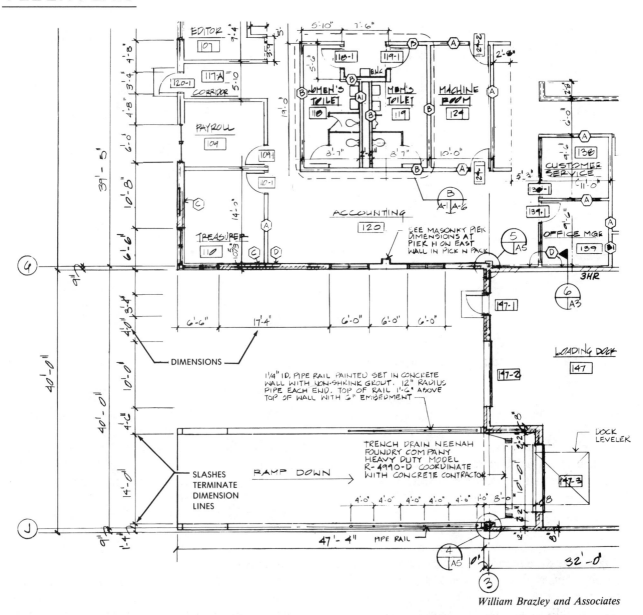

William Brazley and Associates

Figure 1-25. Floor plans show locations of walls, partitions, doors, windows, and other components. The cutting plane is taken 5'-0" above the floor.

a commercial building. Overall dimensions are shown on dimension lines terminated by extension lines leading from the building. Slash marks are used on the ends of dimension lines. The loading dock area is 40'-0" wide. This area is designated as Room 147. Doors leading from this area are designated 147-1, 147-2, and 147-3. The door schedule for this set of plans gives additional door information.

Door 147-1 swings out from the loading dock area onto a floor-level stoop as required by building codes. The purpose of this requirement is to assure continuous footing during an emergency exit, thus avoiding potential falls. Doors 147-2 and 147-3 are overhead doors allowing for delivery or shipping of goods. Door 147-2 is at floor level.

The ramp leading to the overhead door (147-3) at the dock leveler has a 1¼" inside diameter (ID) pipe rail on either side. The pipe rails are set 1'-6" above poured concrete walls. Notice that the masonry wall between the dock area and the office portion of the building has a 3-hour fire rating.

Room 109 is the payroll office. This small office has two windows. Room 110, belonging to the treasurer of the company, is a larger office and has four windows arranged in a corner unit. The letters in the hexagons indicate wall treatment. This information is found elsewhere on the plans.

The accounting room (120) has four windows and serves as a common area to payroll, treasurer's office, office manager's office, customer service office and the machine room. The 5/A5 reference refers to a steel column detail found on sheet A5. The B/A-1—A-6 reference refers to a separate toilet detail found on sheet A-6. Partitions around the water closets are sized to accommodate individuals with special needs.

Elevations

Elevations are orthographic drawings showing vertical planes of a building. Depending on building size, shape, and complexity, four or more elevations may be required to clearly show all exterior walls. Generally, however, four exterior views are sufficient. These are the front, rear, right side, and left side or North, South, East, and West. The North Elevation of a building is a view of the North side seen from a point opposite the North side looking South. Elevations are identified and the scale is given on elevation drawings. Interior elevations are used

to clarify locations of such items as cabinets, mantels, and bookcases.

The interior elevations in Figure 1-26 show a master bath. The floor to ceiling height in this bathroom is 7'-0". The walls are of gypsum board. A water closet (W.C.) is located between the shower and vanity. The shower has a glass door. The vanity has two lavatories separated by an all-drawer unit. The countertop and backsplash are Formica (a brand of plastic laminate). Medicine cabinets, on each side of the mirror, are hinged on the outside.

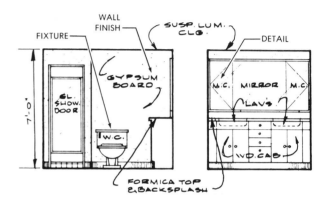

Figure 1-26. Interior elevations are orthographic drawings of interior walls and partitions.

The exterior elevation in Figure 1-27 is a portion of the Revised West Elevation of a commercial building. Masonry control joints (MCJ) are shown on either side of the window units. Three of these joints extend the full height of the wall and two extend from the windows to the top of the wall.

Casement clad windows are 7'-4" above the finished floor. The two corner windows are 30" × 48". They are designated 3048 CC-2. The remaining windows shown are 30" × 30". They are designated 3030 CC-2. Dashed lines show hinged and opening sides of the windows. The apex of the triangle indicates the hinged side. Skylights shown on the lower roof are not called out in this elevation.

Sections

Sections are views created by passing a cutting plane (either horizontal or vertical) through a portion of a building. Section views are shown wherever

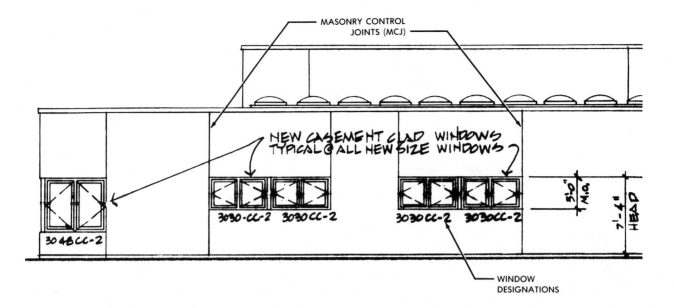

MASONRY CONTROL
JOINTS (MCJ)

NEW CASEMENT CLAD WINDOWS
TYPICAL @ ALL NEW SIZE WINDOWS

5'-0"
M.O.

7'-4"
HEAD

3048CC-2

3030-CC-2   3030CC-2

3030CC-2   3030CC-2

WINDOW
DESIGNATIONS

REVISED WEST ELEVATION

William Brazley and Associates

Figure 1-27. Exterior elevations are orthographic drawings of exterior walls.

an important part of a building is not apparent on the plan views or elevation views. Cutting planes are passed through the building at the most advantageous point to provide clear information.

The most common section view is taken through an outside wall. It shows information such as details of the foundation wall and footing, details of wall and floor framing, height of windows above the floor, eave construction, and roof construction.

Cutting planes for section views are shown on the floor plan. Refer to Figure 1-25. Direction arrows indicate line of sight and a code reference shows the sheet number (6-A3) on which the identified section is found.

Several section views may be required if the construction varies from one part of the building to another part of the building. In some instances, cutting planes are taken lengthwise or crosswise in a building. Sections taken lengthwise are *longitudinal* sections. Sections taken crosswise are *transverse* sections.

In Figure 1-28, a vertical cutting plane has been passed through an exterior wall to show construction details. This pictorial section shows an inverted-T foundation for a two-story house constructed by the platform framing method. The wall section in Figure 1-29 shows a 4″ (jumbo) brick and 4″ concrete block wall. Elevation at the concrete slab is

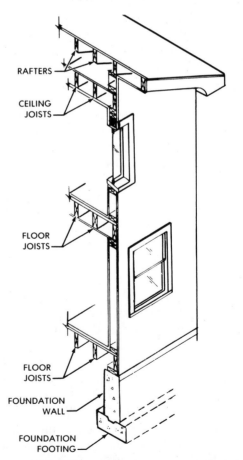

RAFTERS

CEILING
JOISTS

FLOOR
JOISTS

FLOOR
JOISTS

FOUNDATION
WALL

FOUNDATION
FOOTING

Figure 1-28. Pictorial sections are not commonly found on prints because of the drawing time required.

SECTIONS

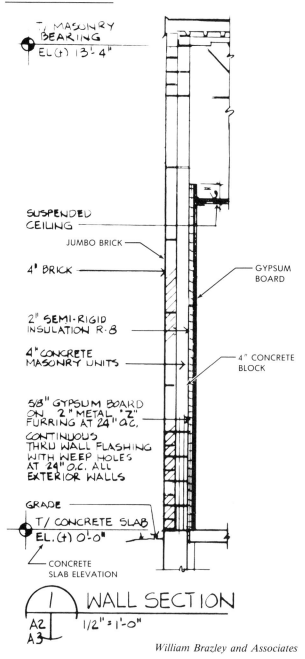

T/ MASONRY BEARING
EL(+) 13'-4"

SUSPENDED CEILING

JUMBO BRICK

4" BRICK

2" SEMI-RIGID INSULATION R-8

4" CONCRETE MASONRY UNITS

5/8" GYPSUM BOARD ON 2" METAL "Z" FURRING AT 24" O.C.

CONTINUOUS THRU WALL FLASHING WITH WEEP HOLES AT 24" O.C. ALL EXTERIOR WALLS

GRADE
T/ CONCRETE SLAB
EL.(+) 0'-0"

CONCRETE SLAB ELEVATION

GYPSUM BOARD

4" CONCRETE BLOCK

1 WALL SECTION
A2 A3   1/2" = 1'-0"

William Brazley and Associates

Figure 1-29. Sections show the inside details of walls.

+ 0'-0". Semi-rigid insulation is 2" thick with an insulation value of R-8. Gypsum board is 5/8" thick and attached to 2" metal "Z" furring at 24" OC (on center). Continuous-through wall flashing with weep holes at 24" OC is located on all exterior walls. A suspended ceiling is shown. Insulation and drywall extend 6" above the ceiling. Roof steel is supported at a height of 13'-4" on the masonry bearing wall.

Details

Details may be either a part of a plan, elevation, or section view drawn at a larger scale. Often the plan, elevation, and section views do not show all the information the builder must have to construct the building. The basic set of prints is generally drawn at a very small scale and does not always show small details clearly. When this occurs, the architect takes a small part of the building and draws it at a larger scale or full size, if possible. Details may be drawn of any part of the building that cannot be shown clearly and conveniently on the working drawings. Thus, a detail drawing is an elevation, plan, or section view drawn at a larger scale. See Figure 1-30.

WRITTEN DESCRIPTION

Working drawings show all walls, partitions, and other features of a building by means of lines, symbols, and conventional representations. With few exceptions, each part is located by precise dimensions. However, in order to develop accurate cost estimates and to quickly solve problems that may arise during construction, information is shown on the prints in the form of notations. Also, additional information is included in the specifications which may consist of a few typed sheets or a book of several hundred pages, depending on the complexity of the project.

Written information is shown on prints in four ways.

1. Some information is found in the title block.
2. Descriptive titles are placed near a specific item and connected with a leader line terminated by an arrowhead or a dot.
3. Specific information that refers to only one situation may be placed near the situation.
4. General information applying to several sheets in the prints may be placed in any convenient space.

Title Block

The title block is the logical place to begin reading a set of prints. Information in the title block includes the name of the project, project location, architect's name and office location, date on which plans were completed, initials of the drafter, number of the sheet, number of sheets in the set of prints, name

DETAILS

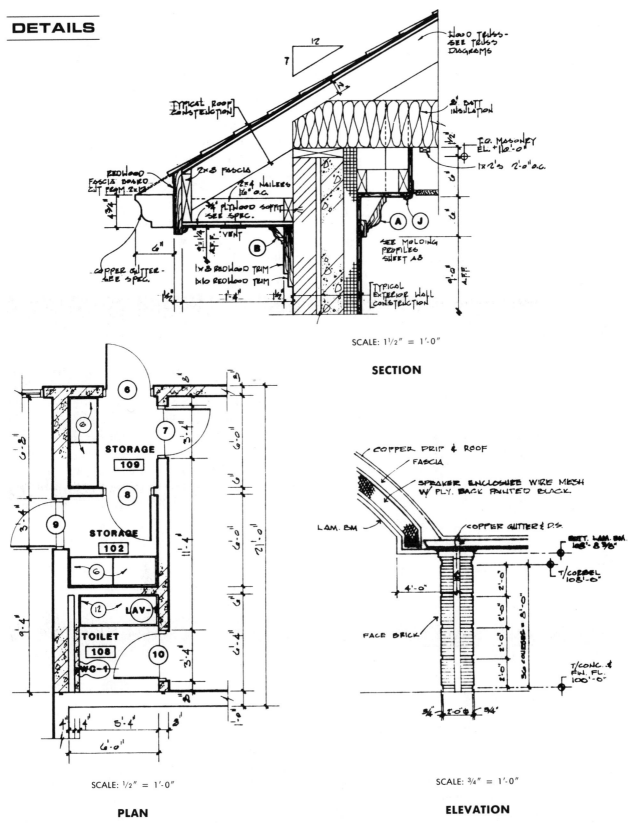

SCALE: $1\frac{1}{2}'' = 1'\text{-}0''$

SECTION

SCALE: $\frac{1}{2}'' = 1'\text{-}0''$

PLAN

SCALE: $\frac{3}{4}'' = 1'\text{-}0''$

ELEVATION

Barclay and Associates

Figure 1-30. Details are section, plan, or elevation views drawn to a larger scale.

TITLE BLOCK

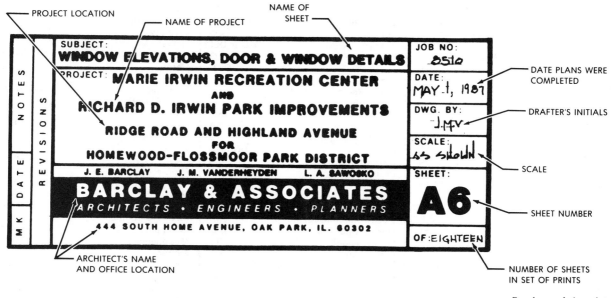

— PROJECT LOCATION

— NAME OF PROJECT

NAME OF SHEET —

SUBJECT:
WINDOW ELEVATIONS, DOOR & WINDOW DETAILS

PROJECT: **MARIE IRWIN RECREATION CENTER**
AND
RICHARD D. IRWIN PARK IMPROVEMENTS

RIDGE ROAD AND HIGHLAND AVENUE
FOR
HOMEWOOD-FLOSSMOOR PARK DISTRICT

J. E. BARCLAY   J. M. VANDERHEYDEN   L. A. SAWOSKO

BARCLAY & ASSOCIATES
ARCHITECTS • ENGINEERS • PLANNERS
444 SOUTH HOME AVENUE, OAK PARK, IL. 60302

N O T E S

R E V I S I O N S

M K   D A T E

JOB NO: 0516

DATE: MAY 1, 1987

DWG. BY: J.MV

SCALE: AS SHOWN

SHEET: **A6**

OF: EIGHTEEN

— DATE PLANS WERE COMPLETED

— DRAFTER'S INITIALS

— SCALE

— SHEET NUMBER

— ARCHITECT'S NAME AND OFFICE LOCATION

— NUMBER OF SHEETS IN SET OF PRINTS

Barclay and Associates

Figure 1-31. Title blocks give basic information for the complete set of prints.

of the sheet, and other information as determined by the architect. See Figure 1-31.

Abbreviations

Abbreviations are used throughout a set of plans to describe materials and processes while conserving space on the drawing sheets. They save drafting time while presenting information in a standard manner.

Only uppercase letters are used for abbreviations. All abbreviations that make an actual word end in a period in order to distinguish the abbreviation from the actual word. For example, IN. is the abbreviation for inch.

While many abbreviations are accepted by virtue of their common usage, only standardized abbreviations should be used on drawings. Standardized abbreviations eliminate confusion and misinterpretation. Although some words use the same standardized abbreviations, an interpretation based upon the context in which they are used will help clarify the specific use. Examples of the same abbreviations for different words are WF and R. WF is the abbreviation for wide flange and wood frame. R is the abbreviation for riser and room. See Figure 1-32.

CONVENTIONS

Relatively complex building parts are simplified so that they may be drawn at a scale to fit the sheets on which plans are drawn. Examples of building plans drawn as conventions include windows, doors, masonry, plumbing, and electrical parts. These parts are shown on plans as symbols.

A constant effort is made on the part of manufacturer's associations and government agencies to establish and use uniform symbols and conventions. The American National Standards Institute (ANSI), American Welding Society (AWS), and American Society of Mechanical Engineers (ASME) are some of the organizations that develop and establish standard methods of material representation on drawings.

Symbols

Symbols used for residential and commercial prints facilitate the architect's work and provide a uniform representation of building materials, fixtures, and structural parts that are easily recognizable. Symbols are shown on plan views (plot, floor, framing, etc.), elevation views, sections, and details.

ABBREVIATIONS COMMONLY USED ON PLAN VIEWS

Term	Abbrev.	Term	Abbrev.	Term	Abbrev.
Access Panel	AP	Copper	CPR or COP	Lath	LTH
Acoustic	AC or ACST	Counter	CTR	Laundry	LAU
Acoustical Tile	ACT or AT	Cubic Feet	CFT or CU FT	Laundry Tray	LT
Adjustable	ADJT or ADJ	Cut Out	CO	Lavatory	LAV
Aggregate	AGG or AGGR	Detail	DTL or DET	Leader	L
Air Conditioning	A/C or AIR COND	Diagram	DIAG	Length	L, LG or LGTH
Aluminum	AL	Dimension	DIM.	Library	LIB
Anchor Bolt	AB	Dimmer	DIM.	Light	LT
Apartment	APT.	Dining Room	DR	Limestone	LMS or LS
Approximate	APX or APPROX	Dishwasher	DW	Linen Closet	L CL
Architectural	ARCH	Ditto	DO.	Lining	LN
Area	A	Double-Acting	DA	Linoleum	LINO
Area Drain	AD	Double Strength Glass	DSG	Living Room	LR
Asbestos	ASB	Down	DN or D	Louver	LVR or LV
Asbestos Board	AB	Downspout	DS	Main	MN
Asphalt	ASPH	Drain	D or DR	Marble	MRB or Mr
Asphalt Tile	AT.	Drawing	DWG	Masonry Opening	MO
Basement	BSMT	Dressed and Matched	D & M	Material	MTL or MATL
Bathroom	B	Dryer	D	Maximum	MAX
Bathtub	BT	Electric Metallic Tubing	EMT	Medicine Cabinet	MC
Beam	BM	Electric Operator	ELECT. OPR.	Minimum	MIN
Bearing Plate	BPL or BRG PL	Electric Panel	EP	Miscellaneous	MISC
Bedroom	BR	End to End	E to E	Mixture	MIX.
Blocking	BLKG	Excavate	EXCA or EXC	Modular	MOD
Blueprint	BP	Expansion Joint	EXP JT	Mortar	MOR
Boiler	BLR	Exterior	EXT	Molding	MLD or MLDG
Book Shelves	BK SH	Exterior Grade	EXT GR	Nosing	NOS
Brass	BRS	Finish	FIN.	Obscure Glass	OBSC GL
Brick	BRK	Finished Floor	FIN. FLR or FIN. FL	On Center	OC
Bronze	BRZ	Firebrick	FBRK	Open Web Joist	OJ or OW JOIST
Broom Closet	BC	Fireplace	FPL or FP	Opening	OPG or OPNG
Building	BLDG	Fireproof	FP or FPRF	Outlet	OUT.
Building Line	BL	Fixed Window	FX WDW	Overall	OA
Cabinet	CAB.	Fixture	FIX.	Overhead	OH. or OVHD
Caulking	CK or CLKG	Flashing	FLG or FL	Pantry	PAN.
Casing	CSG	Floor	FLR or FL	Partition	PTN
Cast Iron	CI	Floor Drain	FD	Per Square Inch	PSI
Cast Stone	CST or CS	Flooring	FLR or FLG	Plaster	PLAS or PL
Catch Basin	CB	Fluorescent	FLUR or FLUOR	Plastered Opening	PO
Ceiling	CLG	Flush	FL	Plate	PL
Cellar	CEL	Footing	FTG	Plate Glass	PG or PL GL
Cement	CEM	Foundation	FND	Platform	PLAT.
Cement Asbestos Board	CEM AB	Frame	FR	Plumbing	PLBG
Cement Floor	CEM FL	Full Size	FS	Porch	P
Cement Mortar	CEM MORT	Furring	FUR	Precast	PRCST
Center	CTR	Galvanized Iron	GI	Prefabricated	PFB or PREFAB
Center to Center	C to C	Galvanized Steel	GS	Pull Switch	PS
Center Line	CL	Garage	GAR	Quarry Tile	QT
Center Matched	CM	Gas	G	Radiator	RAD
Ceramic	CER	Glass	GL	Random	RDM
Channel	CHAN	Glass Block	GLB or GL BL	Range	R
Cinder Block	CIN BL	Grill	G	Recessed	REC
Circuit Breaker	CIR BKR	Gypsum	GYP	Refrigerator	REF
Cleanout	CO	Gypsum Board	GYP BD	Register	REG
Clean Out Door	CODR	Hardware	HDW	Reinforce or Reinforcing	RE or REINF
Clear Glass	CL GL	Hollow Metal Door	HMD	Reinforcing Steel Bar	RE BAR
Closet	C, CL, or CLOS	Hose Bibb	HB	Revision	REV
Cold Air	CA	Hot Air	HA	Riser	R
Cold Water	CW	Hot Water	HW	Roof	RF
Collar Beam	COL B	Hot Water Heater	HWH	Roof Drain	RD
Concrete	CONC	Inside Diameter	ID	Room	RM or R
Concrete Block	CONC BLK	Insulation	INS	Rough	RGH
Concrete Floor	CONC FLR or CONC FL	Interior	INT	Rough Opening	RO or RGH OPNG
Concrete Masonry Unit	CMU	Iron	I	Rubber Tile	RBT or R TILE
Conduit	CND	Jamb	JB	S-Beam	S
Construction	CONST	Kitchen	KIT. or K	Scale	S
Contract	CONTR or CONT	Landing	LDG	Schedule	SCH

Figure 1-32. Abbreviations conserve space on drawing sheets.

ABBREVIATIONS COMMONLY USED ON PLAN VIEWS

Screen	SCN or SC	Standard	STD	Vent Stack	VS
Scuttle	S	Steel	ST or STL	Vestibule	VEST
Section	SEC or SECT	Steel Sash	SS	Vinyl Tile	VT or V TILE
Select	SEL	Storage	STO or STG	Vitreous Tile	VIT TILE
Service	SERV	Structural Clay	SCR	Wainscot	WSCT or WAIN.
Sewer	SEW.	Products Research Foundation		Warm Air	WA
Sheathing	SHTH or SHTHG	Switch	SW or S	Washing Machine	WM
Sheet	SHT or SH	Telephone	TEL	Water	W
Shelf and Rod	SH & RD	Tempered Plate Glass	TEM PL GL	Water Closet	WC
Shelving	SH or SHELV	Terra Cotta	TC	Water Heater	WH
Shower	SH	Terrazzo	TZ or TER	Water-resistant	WR
Sill Cock	SC	Thermostat	THERMO	Waterproof	WP
Single Strength Glass	SSG	Threshold	TH	Weather Stripping	WS
Sink	SK or S	Toilet	T	Weephole	WH
Sliding Door	SL DR	Tongue-and-groove	T & G	Welded Wire Fabric	WWF
Soil Pipe	SP	Tread	TR or T	White Pine	WP
Specification	SPEC	Typical	TYP	Wide Flange	W or WF
Square Feet	SQ FT	Unfinished	UNF	Wood	WD
Stained	STN	Unexcavated	UNEXC	Wood Frame	WF
Stairs	ST	Utility Room	U RM	Yellow Pine	YP
Stairway	STWY	Vent	V		

ABBREVIATIONS COMMONLY USED ON ELEVATIONS

Aluminum	AL	Flashing	FLG or FL	Overhead	OH or OVHD
Asbestos	ASB	Floor	FLR or FL	Panel	PNL
Asphalt	ASPH	Foot or Feet	FT	Perpendicular	PERP
Basement	BSMT	Footing	FTG	Plate Glass	PG or PL GL
Beveled	BLV or BEV	Foundation	FND	Plate Height	PL HT
Brick	BRK	Full Size	FS	Radius	RAD or R
Building	BLDG	Galvanized	GV or GALV	Revision	REV
Cast Iron	CI	Galvanized Iron	GI	Riser	R
Ceiling	CLG	Galvanized Steel	GS	Roof	RF
Cement	CEM	Gauge	GA	Roof Drain	RD
Center	CTR	Glass	GL	Roofing	RFG
Center Line	or CL	Glass Block	GLB or GL BL	Rough	RGH
Clear	CLR	Grade	GD or GR	Saddle	SDL or S
Column	COL	Grade Line	GL	Scale	SC
Concrete	CONC	Height	HT	Schedule	SCH
Concrete Block	CONC BLK	High Point	H PT	Section	SEC or SECT
Concrete Masonry Unit	CMU	Horizontal	HOR	Sheathing	SHTH or SHTHG
Copper	CPR or COP	Hose Bibb	HB	Sheet	SHT or SH
Corner	COR	Inch or Inches	IN.	Shiplap	SHLP
Detail	DTL or DET	Insulating (Insulated)	INS	Siding	SDG
Diameter	DIAM or DIA	Length	L	South	S
Dimension	DIM	Length Over All	LOA	Specifications	SPEC
Ditto	DO	Level	LEV	Square	SQ
Divided	DIV	Light	LT	Square Inch	SQ IN.
Door	DR	Line	L	Stainless Steel	SST
Double-Hung Window	DHW	Lining	LN	Steel	ST or STL
Down	DN or D	Long	LG	Stone	STN
Downspout	DS	Louver	LVR or LV	Terra Cotta	TC
Drawing	DWG	Low Point	L PT or LP	Thick or Thickness	THK or T
Drip Cap	DC	Masonry Opening	MO	Typical	TYP
Each	EA	Metal	MET. or M	Vertical	VERT
East	E	Moulding	MLD or MLDG	Waterproofing	WP
Elevation	EL	Mullion	MULL	West	W
Entrance	ENT	North	N	Width	W or WTH
Excavate	EXCA or EXC	Number	NO.	Window	WIN or WDW
Exterior	EXT	Opening	OPG or OPNG	Wire Glass	WG or W GL
Finish	FIN.	Outlet	OUT	Wood	WD
Fixed Window	FX WDW	Outside Diameter	OD	Wrought Iron	WI

Figure 1-32 (continued)

Figure 1-33 shows a detail at the entrance to a commercial building. Symbols are used to depict building materials. The 2 × 6s at the top of the wall are shown by intersecting lines drawn from corner to corner of each piece. Gravel is placed on top of the roofing. Insulation is shown behind the continuous aluminum closure angle and 2″ semi-rigid insulation is shown behind the spandrel glass. The steel beam is shown in profile with two diagonal lines closely spaced.

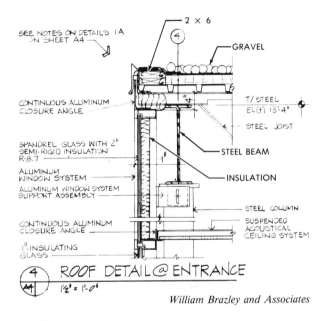

ROOF DETAIL @ ENTRANCE

William Brazley and Associates

Figure 1-33. Symbols are used on detail drawings to clearly show different parts and materials.

Windows

Windows are shown on prints of plan views and elevations with symbols. Windows are often complex when drawn in detail and little is gained by showing more than the basic information on plans since the windows are factory-built and installed on the job site. The three classes of windows are *fixed sash, sliding sash,* and *swinging sash.* See Figure 1-34.

Fixed sash windows are usually large and often fitted with insulating glass. Sliding sash windows include double-hung windows with two sashes that slide vertically past each other, and horizontal sliding windows with sashes that slide horizontally past each other. Swinging sash windows include *casement, awning,* and *hopper* types. Casement windows may be single, in pairs, or multiples. They swing outward

with hinges on the vertical sides of the sash. Converging dashed lines in plan view show the hinged side of the window. Awning windows have hinges on the top horizontal rail of the sash and swing outward. Hopper windows have hinges on the bottom rail of the sash and swing inward. Out-swing windows have screens toward the room side and are closed by crank or lever mechanisms.

As dimensions are not generally repeated on plans, it is often necessary to refer to a plan view, an elevation, and a section view to obtain all the information about a window. The plan view gives the location of the windows from the corner of the building, from other openings, or either. See Figure 1-35. Dimensions for windows in brick or stone walls are usually given to the masonry opening. Dimensions locating windows in framed walls or masonry veneer walls are usually given to the centers of the windows.

Elevation views give information about the type of window and its light (glass) size. See Figure 1-36. The size of the light is described by means of two numbers, such as 30/48, 30–48, 30 × 48, or 3048, unless there is a window schedule included in the working drawings. The first numbers represent the width of the light and the second numbers represent the height. Additional letters and numbers are often used to provide more information. For example, the glass shown on the corner on the Revised West Elevation in Figure 1-37 is 30″ wide by 48″ high. Two casement clad windows are specified.

The use of windows in combination in the same frame is common. The elevation view shows the arrangement of mullions (vertical members of the frame between the sash). Two hidden lines which form two sides of a triangle are shown on the swinging sash. The point of intersection of the two lines indicates the side of the window where the hinges are located. When no lines are shown on one sash of a multiple casement window, one sash is fixed and the others open. The vertical location of the window in the wall can be shown in several places. The best place to show the height above the floor is on the vertical section view taken through the outside wall. It may also be shown on the elevation views. This height may be given from the finished floor level to the top of the window stool (the inside window sill), or to the bottom of the top window jamb. See Figure 1-37. The latter is preferred if there are windows of different sizes because the top members will usually line up.

TYPES OF WINDOWS

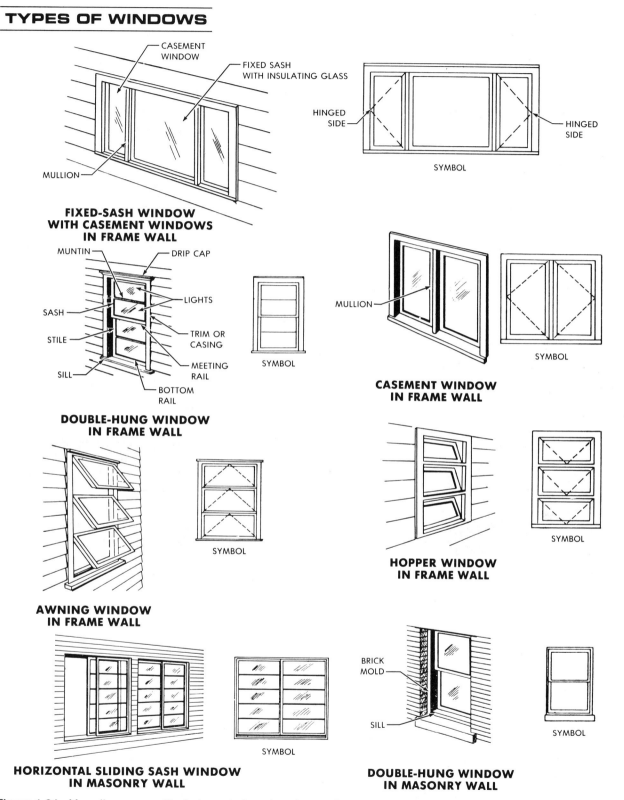

Figure 1-34. Many lines are omitted when window elevation symbols are drawn. Wood windows have wider sash parts than metal windows. Windows in frame walls have wood trim. Windows in masonry walls have a narrow brick mold. The side that has the hinges on swinging windows is indicated by the apex (or point) of a dashed triangle. (Note the swing symbol for a casement window, an awning window, and a hopper window.)

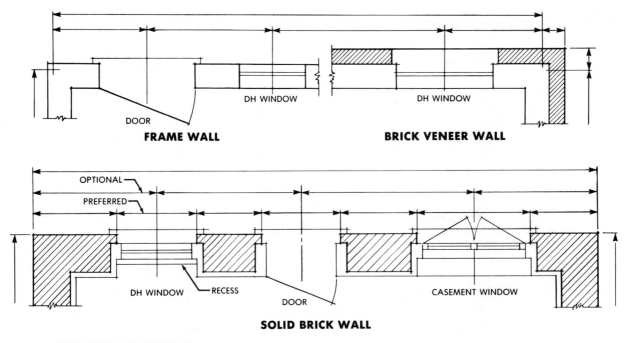

FRAME WALL   **BRICK VENEER WALL**

DH WINDOW   DH WINDOW

DOOR

SOLID BRICK WALL

DH WINDOW   RECESS   DOOR   CASEMENT WINDOW

OPTIONAL

PREFERRED

WINDOWS MAY BE LOCATED BY:
DIMENSIONS TO OPENINGS (PREFERRED)
DIMENSIONS TO CENTERS (OPTIONAL)

Figure 1-35. Plan views show window locations.

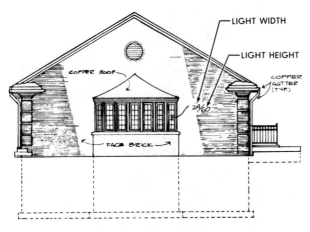

LIGHT WIDTH

LIGHT HEIGHT

COPPER ROOF

COPPER GUTTER (TYP.)

FACE BRICK

Barclay and Associates

Figure 1-36. Light size is shown on elevation drawings. The first two digits show width. The last two digits show height.

The majority of windows and frames used in residential construction are made in factories and are ready to install. The carpenter prepares the wall by building the structural members on each side and above and below the opening. Prints are read to find the dimensions locating the window frame from the

building corner or previous opening. After determining the height above the finished floor, the carpenter makes allowances in the rough opening to permit the window to be adjusted into a perfectly level position.

When windows differ from stock windows in trim or installation, a large scale detail view is shown elsewhere on the prints. Figure 1-38 shows a detailed section view through a double-hung window taken from a manufacturer's catalog. In order to read this figure, place a narrow piece of paper over the part marked *Jamb*. Notice how the top and bottom sash slide up and down in grooves made by the window frame members. The section through the jamb is a slice through the side jamb of the window looking down. It is revolved into place as shown in the figure for convenience. Rough structural members are shown as rectangles with diagonal cross lines.

Windows in masonry walls are set with the cooperation of the carpenter and bricklayer. When the brickwork has been laid to the required height and the window sill is in place, the carpenter will place and brace the frame with members extending back to the subfloor to hold it firmly in place. The brick-

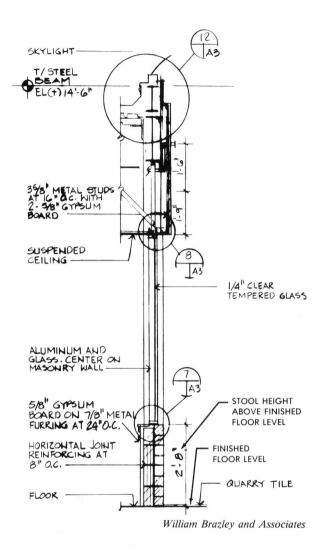

SKYLIGHT

T/ STEEL
BEAM
EL(+)14'-6"

3⅝" METAL STUDS
AT 16" O.C. WITH
2-⅝" GYPSUM
BOARD

SUSPENDED
CEILING

¼" CLEAR
TEMPERED GLASS

ALUMINUM AND
GLASS. CENTER ON
MASONRY WALL

⅝" GYPSUM
BOARD ON ⅞" METAL
FURRING AT 24" O.C.

HORIZONTAL JOINT
REINFORCING AT
8" O.C.

FLOOR

STOOL HEIGHT
ABOVE FINISHED
FLOOR LEVEL

FINISHED
FLOOR LEVEL

QUARRY TILE

William Brazley and Associates

Figure 1-37. Window height above a finished floor is usually given to the bottom of the top window jamb.

layer then proceeds to lay brick courses on each side. See Figure 1-39.

When several windows are of the same type and size, the architect does not show dimensions and light sizes for each. This information is given for one window with a note indicating that the type and size are typical.

Window schedules are normally included on a set of plans. See Figure 1-40. Often, window schedules are combined with door information as a door and window schedule. The window schedule describes each window by type, size, and special features, such as insulated or tinted glass, and factory number. A letter or number code on the floor plan and on the schedule identifies each window.

Building Code—Windows. The Uniform Building Code requires that light and ventilation be provided for all great rooms, dormitories, and habitable rooms in dwellings. Glazed openings, whose total area is not less than $1/10$ (10%) of the floor area of these rooms, are utilized to provide natural light. For example, glazed openings located in the exterior wall of a 12'-0" × 20'-0" dormitory room (240 sq. ft.) must total 24 sq. ft. The minimum area for ex-

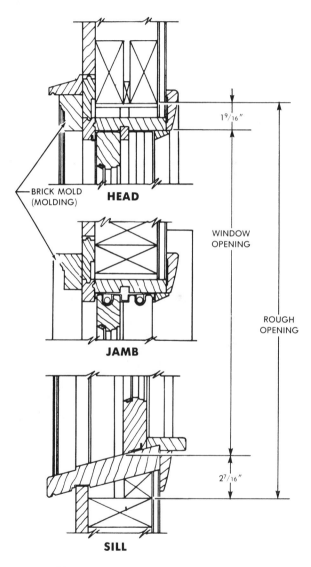

BRICK MOLD
(MOLDING)   **HEAD**

19/16"

WINDOW
OPENING

JAMB

ROUGH
OPENING

2⁷/16"

SILL

**4³/4″ FRAME WALL CONSTRUCTION
³/4″ SHEATHING—¹/2″ DRYWALL**

Rock Island Millwork

Figure 1-38. A vertical cutting plane passing through the window head and sill and a horizontal cutting plane passing through the jamb provides a detailed section view of a window.

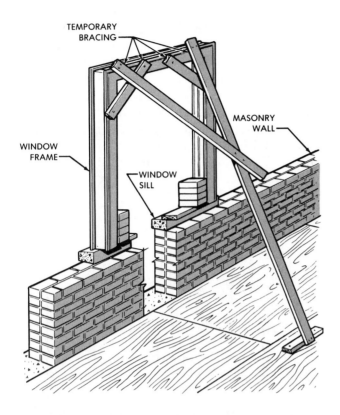

Figure 1-39. Carpenters and bricklayers must coordinate their work when setting window frames in masonry walls.

terior glazed openings serving guest rooms, dormitories, and habitable rooms in dwellings is 10 sq. ft. This applies whenever such a room contains less than 100 sq. ft.

These rooms must be ventilated with openable exterior openings (sliding glass doors may be utilized) whose total area is not less than 1/20 (5%) of the floor area. Additionally, the minimum total area that provides natural ventilation cannot be less than 5 sq. ft. For example, a 9'-0" × 10'-0" room contains 90 sq. ft. Multiplying 90 × 1/20 produces 4.5 sq. ft. For this room, the minimum size openable exterior opening is 5 sq. ft.

When mechanical ventilating systems are used to provide natural ventilation, requirements of openable exterior openings do not apply. Mechanical systems must take at least 20% of their air supply directly from the outside. Two complete air changes per hour are required.

Doors

The symbol for swinging doors on plan views is a single line with an arc to show the direction of swing. See Figure 1-41. Special doors, including bi-fold doors, sliding doors, accordion doors, and pocket doors, have their own symbols. *Door hand* is the direction in which a door swings. When determining door swing, the viewer is always standing on the outside of the door. The outside may be a hallway or the street side of an entrance door. For doors that open between rooms, the keyed side of the lock is considered the outside.

Doors are usually described in a door schedule that is keyed to letters shown at their location on the floor plan. The schedule gives the size, type, special description, and the factory number. Doors may also be described by notations at each door and descriptions in the specifications. The designation 2'-8" × 6'-8" × 1¾" gives the width, height, and thickness in that order.

Two general types of doors are *flush* and *panel* doors. See Figure 1-42. Flush doors are distinguished by flat surfaces on each side. Flush wooden doors are covered with plies of veneer with adjacent plies placed at right angles to minimize movement and warpage. Two types of flush doors are *solid-core* and *hollow-core*.

Solid-core wood doors are manufactured of solid blocks of wood or particleboard glued together and covered with veneer plies. These doors are heavier than hollow-core doors, prevent sound transmission better, and have less tendency to warp. Solid-core doors are also manufactured with a fire-resistant, mineral core and are commercially available with various fire ratings. Solid-core doors are weather-resistant and commonly used for exterior openings. Three hinges are required for hanging.

Hollow-core doors are composed of wooden strips glued together on edge in the form of a large egg crate and covered with veneer plies. Also, some hollow-core doors contain a cardboard core which is edge glued and covered with veneer. Wooden strips are used to frame and strengthen these doors. Many hollow-core doors are covered with plastic laminate and require no staining or finishing. Hollow-core doors are not permitted for use in exterior openings as they do not have the strength of solid-core doors. Building codes require that interior doors be at least 1⅜" thick. Due to their light weight, only two hinges are required.

Panel doors are made of solid strips or planks arranged in several different ways and rabbeted (grooved) to hold thin panels. They are used for both outside and inside doors in buildings with traditional

WINDOW SCHEDULE						
CODE	QUANTITY	NUMBER OF LIGHTS	GLASS SIZE	SASH SIZE	ROUGH OPENINGS	REMARKS
E	3	2	39″ × 51″ 19″ × 51″	3'-6″ × 6'-6″	3'-4¾″ × 4'-0¾″	NO. 4456 Fix Over 4424 Pella Multi-purpose Windows
F	2	1	35″ × 43″	3'-2″ × 3'-10″	3'-4¾ × 4'-0¾″	NO. 4048 Fix Pella Multi-purpose Windows
G	1	1	15″ × 35″	1'-6″ × 3'-2″	1'-8¾″ × 3'-4¾″	NO. 4020 Pella Multi-purpose Window
H	2	1	15″ × 27″	1'-6″ × 2'-6″	1'-8¾″ × 2'-8¾″	NO. 3220 Pella Multi-purpose Windows

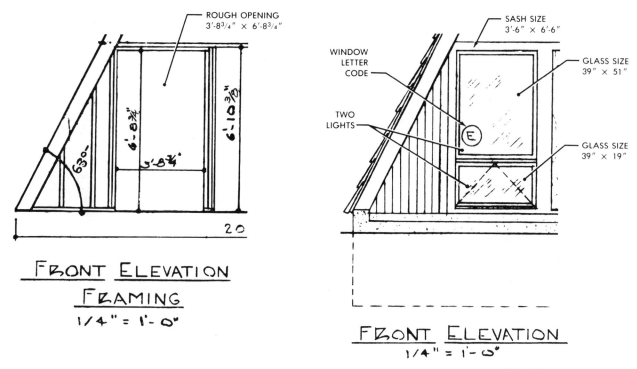

The Garlinghouse Company

Figure 1-40. Window schedules describe each window by type, size, and special features. The window manufacturer's part number is often given.

architecture. *Package* (flush or panel) doors have come into common use. They are either wood or metal and consist of the frame with the door already hung and the hardware installed. They are delivered to the job ready for insertion in the rough opening.

Openings in exterior walls are dimensioned in the same way as the windows. Doors inside of the building are not usually located by dimensions. In many cases the door is centered on a hallway. When a door is located near a corner of a room, the carpenter constructing the rough opening must allow sufficient room for the trim. Interior doors stand open much of the time and should be placed so that they are close to the wall when opened.

Building Codes—Doors. Building codes related to doors, and passageways leading to doors, are very specific as the passageways and doors may be used to exit from a building during emergencies. Building

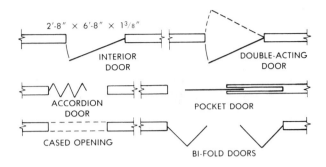

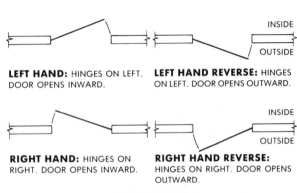

FACE OUTSIDE OF DOOR WHEN
DETERMINING "DOOR HAND."

Figure 1-41. Door symbols are shown on plan views. Door hand is the direction in which a door swings.

codes generally require 1¾″ thick by 3′-0″ wide doors for exterior use. See Figure 1-43. The architect has the responsibility of designing exits and passageways in accordance with all applicable codes to provide safe ingress and egress to a building. Generally speaking, specific code requirements for doors and passageways are determined by the type of occupancy (such as residential or commercial) and the occupancy load.

All buildings are required to have at least one exit. Additional exits (other than elevators) are required where occupancy loads exceed a minimum number of people. For example, hotels and apartments with an occupancy load exceeding ten people must have at least two doors. Commercial kitchens with an occupancy load exceeding 30 people must have a minimum of two doors. Other use areas requiring a minimum of two exits other than elevators and their given minimum occupancy loads include:

manufacturing areas 30
classrooms 50
offices 30
school shops and vocational rooms 50
retail stores
  basement level 11
  ground floor 50
  upper floors 10
warehouses 30

Location and distance to exits are determined by the size and layout of the room or building. For example, a classroom with an occupancy load of over 50 people must have two doors placed a distance apart that is not less than one-half the maximum overall diagonal length of the classroom.

For all doors serving hazardous areas with occupancy levels of 50 people or more, exit doors must swing in the direction of exit travel. Force required to open such doors shall not exceed 30 pounds ap-

TYPES OF DOORS

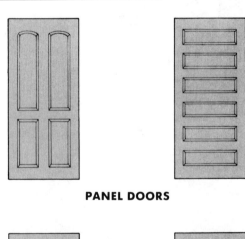

PANEL DOORS

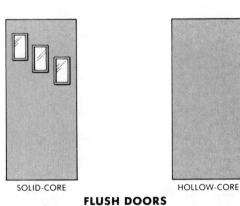

FLUSH DOORS

Figure 1-42. Two general types of doors are panel doors and flush doors.

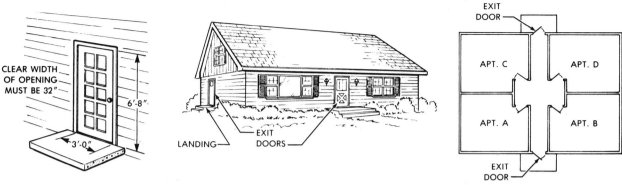

MINIMUM SIZE OF EXIT DOOR	**ALL BUILDINGS MUST HAVE AT LEAST ONE EXIT DOOR. LANDINGS ARE REQUIRED ON ALL EXIT DOORS.**	**APARTMENTS WITH OVER 10 OCCUPANTS MUST HAVE AT LEAST TWO EXIT DOORS.**

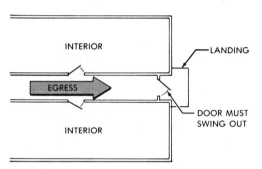

FOR BUILDINGS WITH OVER 50 OCCUPANTS OR FOR ANY HAZARDOUS AREA, EXIT DOORS MUST SWING IN DIRECTION OF EXIT TRAVEL.

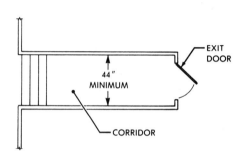

CORRIDORS SERVING 10 OR MORE OCCUPANTS MUST BE AT LEAST 44″ WIDE.

Figure 1-43. The type of building and occupancy load determines minimum specifications for doors.

plied to the latch side. Note: Exit doors must be openable from the inside without using a key, special effort, or applying special knowledge.

All exit doors must be at least 3′-0″ wide and 6′-8″ high. The clear width of the opening must be at least 32″ when the door is in the open position. No leaf of an exit door can exceed 4′-0″ in width. Special doors, such as revolving doors, sliding doors, and overhead doors, may not be used as required exits.

A floor or landing is required on each side of a door regardless of the occupancy load. This prevents the possibility of a fall during exit due to an unexpected floor level change. Additionally, any corridor serving an occupancy load of 10 or more must be at least 44″ wide to prevent any unnecessary crowding. For private dwellings, minimum hallway width is 36″.

Stairs

The conventional representations for stairs on plan views is a series of parallel lines representing risers. Designations such as *14 R Up* (14 Risers Up) and *13 R Down* (13 Risers Down) indicate the number of risers to the floor immediately above or below. An arrow with the designation points up or down, depending upon the direction of travel. See Figure 1-44.

Stairs provide a means of going from one level in a building to another. In many buildings they are constructed with broken flights, right angle turns, or windings. Stairs may be straight-run, straight-run with landing, L-shaped with landing, U-shaped with winders, circular, or spiral. See Figure 1-45. Other shapes may be developed through combinations of these basic shapes.

The total rise of a stairway is its total height. The total run of a stairway is its total length. Unit rise is the height of each riser and unit run is the width of each tread, not including the nosing. A rule-of-thumb formula for determining riser and tread dimensions is "the width of the tread plus the height

of the riser shall be 17″ to 18″″". Applying this rule of thumb, some common riser and tread dimensions are

RISER	TREAD	TOTAL
6″	11″	17″
6½″	11½″	18″
6¾″	11¼″	18″

Many other riser and tread dimensions are possible. Architects must design stair riser and treads to fit within accepted dimensions and code standards. See Figure 1-46.

Preferred angles for stairs are between 30° and 35°. Lesser angles will produce larger total runs. Higher angles will produce stairways that are too steep for easy climbing.

Building Codes—Stairs. Any stairway that has two or more risers must comply to minimum code standards. See Figure 1-47. All stairways serving an occupancy load of 49 people or less must be at least 36″ wide. All stairways serving an occupancy load of 50 people or more must be at least 44″ wide. The minimum rise of a step is 4″. The maximum rise of a step is 7″. Riser height variance in a flight of stairs shall not exceed 3/8″. With the exception of winding stairways or spiral stairways, the run of a step must be at least 11″.

Landings for stairways must extend in the direction of travel a distance equal to the stairway width. For straight runs, this distance need not exceed 44″. Distances between landings shall not exceed 12′-0″ vertically.

Stairways for dwellings and stairways less than 44″ wide must have at least one handrail. Stairways 44″ or more in width must have at least two handrails. An intermediate handrail is required for stairways more than 88″ wide. Handrails are located 30″–34″ above the nosing of the stairway treads and must run continuously for the full length of the stairway. Additionally, one handrail must extend 6″ beyond the top and bottom riser of all stairways other than private stairways. Ends of handrails must return or be terminated in newel posts or safety terminals. The cross-sectional area of a handrail must be not less than 1¼″ nor more than 2″ and must have a smooth surface with no sharp corners. Handrails must be provided with an opening space of not less than 1½″ between wall and handrail. See Figure 1-48.

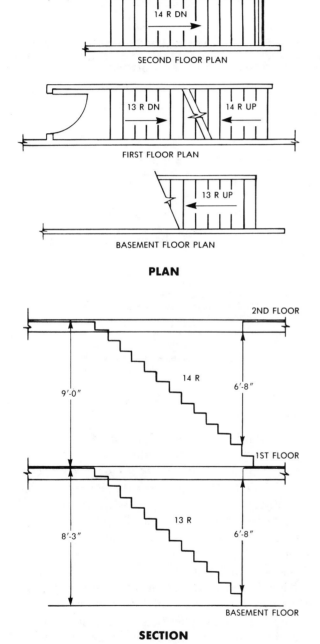

Figure 1-44. Stairs may be shown on plan and section views of prints.

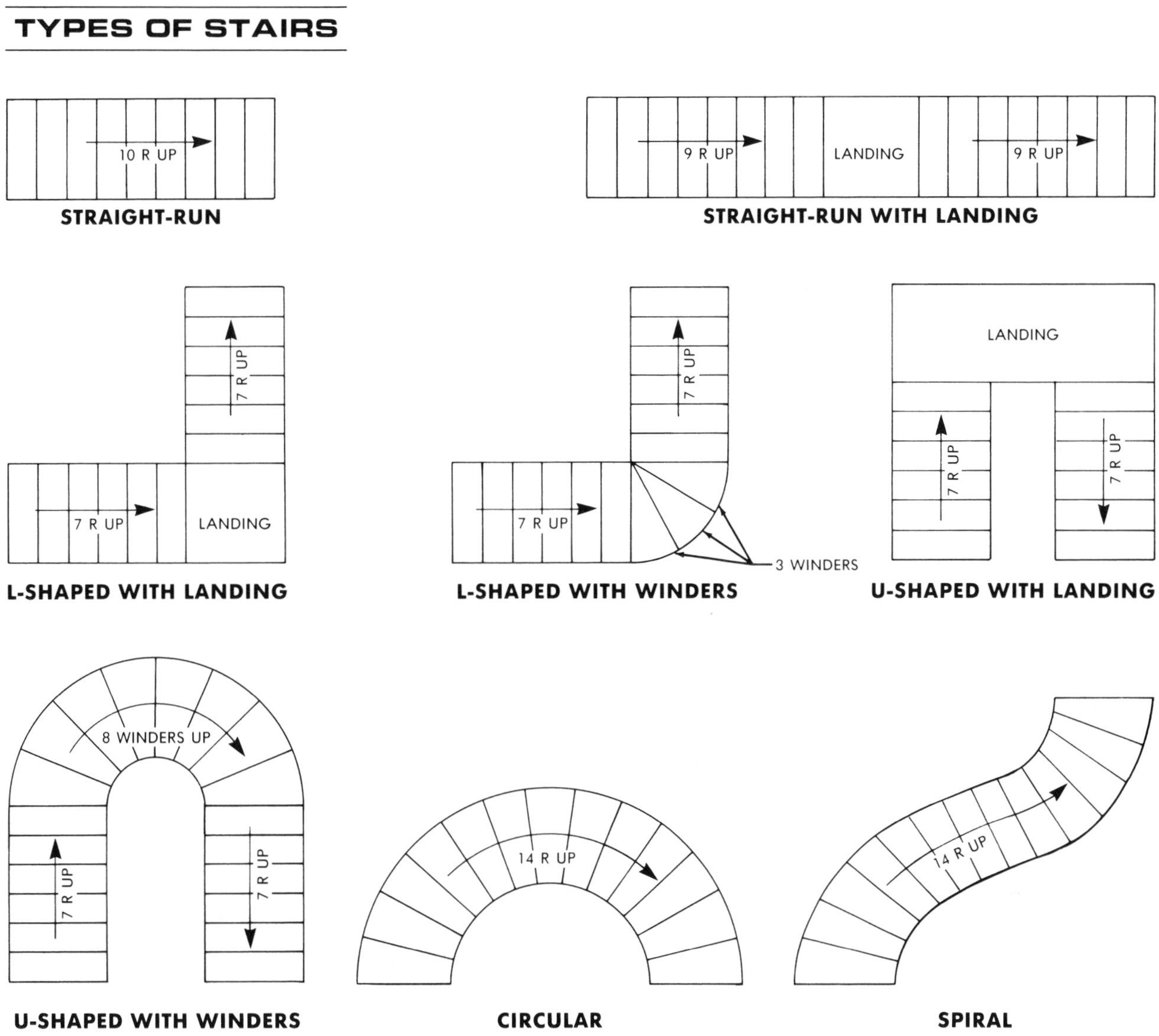

TYPES OF STAIRS

STRAIGHT-RUN

10 R UP

STRAIGHT-RUN WITH LANDING

9 R UP   LANDING   9 R UP

L-SHAPED WITH LANDING

7 R UP

7 R UP   LANDING

L-SHAPED WITH WINDERS

7 R UP

7 R UP   3 WINDERS

U-SHAPED WITH LANDING

LANDING

7 R UP   7 R UP

U-SHAPED WITH WINDERS

8 WINDERS UP

7 R UP   7 R UP

CIRCULAR

14 R UP

SPIRAL

14 R UP

Figure 1-45. Stairway layouts are shown on plan views.

All stairways must have a minimum headroom of 6′-6″. Greater headroom is desirable for moving larger objects in or out of areas connected by stairways.

MODULAR MEASURE

A trend has developed toward the use of modular measurement. A grid with a unit of 4″ is used in the drawing of the plans. Material used for construction is manufactured to fit the grid spaces. In the past, materials have been manufactured in a number of sizes and shapes that have been accepted by the industry. The purpose of introducing modular measure is to cut down on waste and to fulfill the need of builders to stock many sizes of material. It also provides a means for the building units to fit together with greater precision. A whole new era in the construction industry has opened up in the building of components such as wall, partition, roof, and floor sections, and the manufacture of roof trusses. Modular measure has played a large part in coordinating these units so that they fit when they are delivered to the job.

In making a preliminary layout for a building, the architect uses graph paper with 1/4″ squares. Each square is divided into three parts to make a grid representing 4″ modules. Sketches made on this

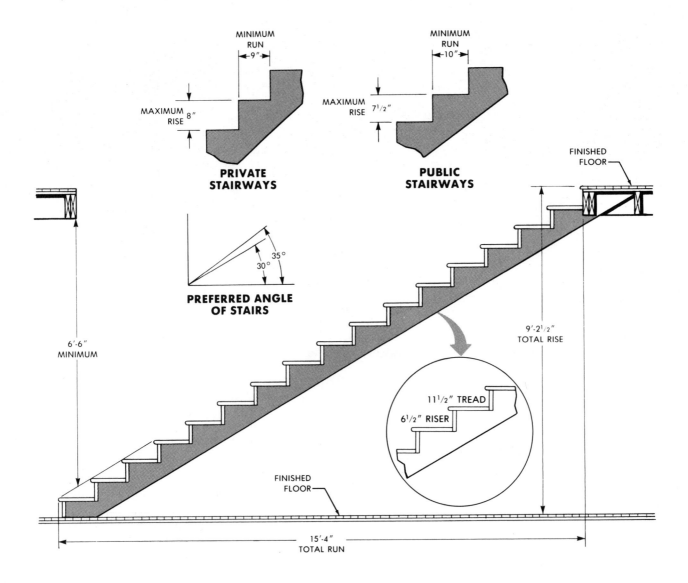

Figure 1-46. Minimum headroom for stair openings is 6'-6". Preferred angle for stairs is 30°–35°.

paper give the designer some idea of scale while retaining the modular concept. Many sketches will have to be made of the rooms, closets, stairways, windows, and other parts of the building before the working drawings are attempted. See Figure 1-49.

One part of the building trades industry has concentrated on the manufacture of modules, which may be complete bathrooms, kitchens, or houses made in two parts then delivered to the job and lifted into place. (The two concepts of *module* can be easily confused. A module is both a small unit of measure and a large cubical part of a building.) Under the *stick* (piece-by-piece) method of building, some adjustments are possible because there are oppor-

tunities to cut and fit the building parts. Everything must fit exactly when prebuilt members and units are used.

COMPUTER-AIDED DRAFTING

Computer-aided drafting (CAD) utilizes computer systems to produce drawings. These systems are rapidly becoming more common in architectural and engineering offices because of their efficiency and the quality of drawings produced.

Construction tradesworkers reading CAD-generated plans benefit from the excellent quality and consistency of line work, symbol representation, and lettering. Architects benefit from increased drafting productivity achieved in the planning, design, drafting, and reproduction of prints. See Figure 1-50. Six primary factors contributing to increased productivity are

1. Consistency—constant sameness in line width, symbol depiction, and representation of drawing components.
2. Changeability—revisions, additions, and deletions are easily made.
3. Layering—a method, similar to using overlays on manually generated drawings, in which base work is used to generate additional drawings.
4. Modeling—viewing of the complete building in pictorial form and subjection to stress tests.
5. Storage—drawings, stored on magnetic tapes

or small magnetic disks, require minimal space.
6. Repeatability—an unlimited number of sheets may be reproduced, each with original quality.

CAD systems utilize *hardware* and *software* to generate drawings. Hardware is the physical components of the system, including the input devices, central processing unit (CPU), and output devices. A large variety of commercially available components are used to control, manage, and process information in CAD systems. See Figure 1-51. Software is the operating system, on magnetic tape or disks, that provides operational instructions for capturing and formatting keystrokes and generated lines. See Figure 1-52. Software allows system hardware components to interact in the production of drawings.

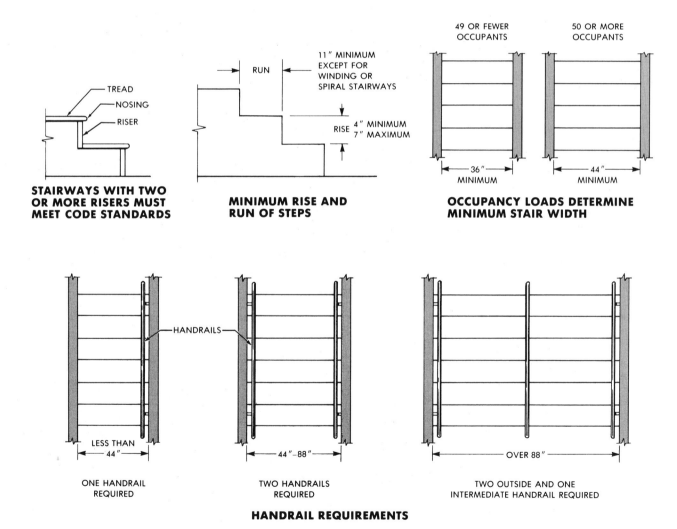

Figure 1-47. Any stairway with two or more risers must comply with minimum code standards.

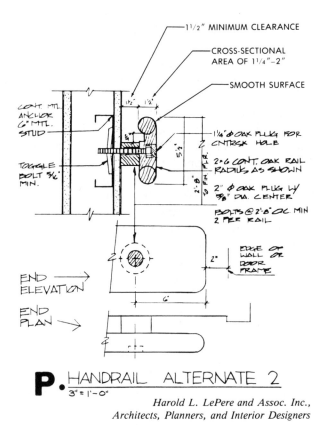

Harold L. LePere and Assoc. Inc., Architects, Planners, and Interior Designers

Figure 1-48. Detail drawings are used to show critical dimensions of handrails.

Input Devices

Input devices are pieces of equipment used to enter information into a CAD system. The input devices are interfaced (connected) with the central processing unit, which controls the CAD system. Information may be input by the use of *electronic* or *electromechanical* devices. Electronic devices use electronic signals to relay information to the CPU. Electromechanical devices use mechanical actuation to input electronic information. Common input devices include the *graphics tablet, digitizing tablet, keyboard,* and *light pen.* Tablet accessories include the stylus, mouse, joystick, thumbwheel, and trackball.

Graphics Tablet. A graphics tablet is a common input device used with a CAD system. It consists of a drawing area and a menu. See Figure 1-53. The menu is a group of commands. Menu selections may consist of simple commands such as inserting circles and erasing lines, or more complex operations such as drawing tangent lines and dimensioning objects.

An electronic or electromechanical device is used with the graphics tablet to choose a function from the menu and "draw" the object in the space provided. For example, a CAD operator may choose "INSERT CIRCLE" from the menu with a stylus (pen-like device). The stylus is placed in the drawing area and a *cursor* on the display screen shows its present location. A cursor is the solid or flashing pointer indicating position of work. As the stylus

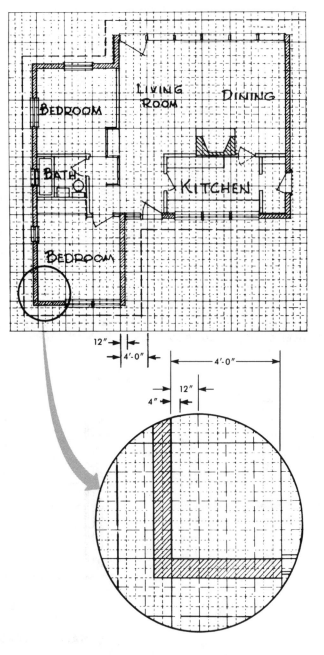

Figure 1-49. All dimensions are multiples of 4″ in the modular concept.

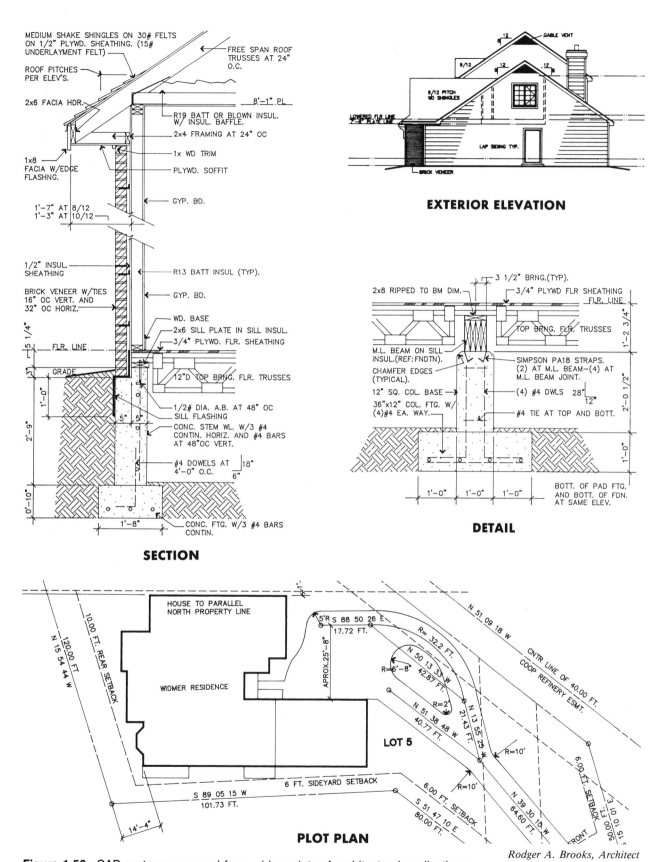

MEDIUM SHAKE SHINGLES ON 30# FELTS ON 1/2" PLYWD. SHEATHING. (15# UNDERLAYMENT FELT)

FREE SPAN ROOF TRUSSES AT 24" O.C.

ROOF PITCHES PER ELEV'S.

2x6 FACIA HDR.

8'-1" .PL

R19 BATT OR BLOWN INSUL. W/ INSUL. BAFFLE.

2x4 FRAMING AT 24" OC

1x WD TRIM

1x8 FACIA W/EDGE FLASHNG.

PLYWD. SOFFIT

GYP. BD.

1'-7" AT 8/12
1'-3" AT 10/12

1/2" INSUL. SHEATHING

R13 BATT INSUL (TYP).

BRICK VENEER W/TIES 16" OC VERT. AND 32" OC HORIZ.

GYP. BD.

WD. BASE

2x6 SILL PLATE IN SILL INSUL.

3/4" PLYWD. FLR. SHEATHING

5 1/4"

FLR. LINE

12"D TOP BRNG. FLR. TRUSSES

3"

GRADE

1'-0"

1/2# DIA. A.B. AT 48" OC
SILL FLASHING

CONC. STEM WL. W/3 #4 CONTIN. HORIZ. AND #4 BARS AT 48"OC VERT.

2'-9"

#4 DOWELS AT 4'-0" O.C.

18"

6"

0'-10"

1'-8"

CONC. FTG. W/3 #4 BARS CONTIN.

SECTION

EXTERIOR ELEVATION

GABLE VENT

12

9/12

12

12

9/12 PITCH WD SHINGLES

LOWERED FLR LINE
7'-8" PLAT LINE

LAP SIDING TYP.

BRICK VENEER

DETAIL

3 1/2" BRNG.(TYP).

2x8 RIPPED TO BM DIM.

3/4" PLYWD FLR SHEATHING
FLR. LINE

TOP BRNG. FLR. TRUSSES

1'-2 3/4"

M.L. BEAM ON SILL INSUL.(REF: FNDTN).

CHAMFER EDGES (TYPICAL).

12" SQ. COL. BASE

36"x12" COL. FTG. W/ (4)#4 EA. WAY.

SIMPSON PA18 STRAPS. (2) AT M.L. BEAM—(4) AT M.L. BEAM JOINT.

(4) #4 DWLS   28"
                       12"

#4 TIE AT TOP AND BOTT.

2'-0 1/2"

1'-0"

1'-0"   1'-0"   1'-0"

BOTT. OF PAD FTG. AND BOTT. OF FDN. AT SAME ELEV.

PLOT PLAN

HOUSE TO PARALLEL NORTH PROPERTY LINE

10.00 FT. REAR SETBACK

120.00 FT
N 15 54 44 W

WIDMER RESIDENCE

5'R S 88 50 26 E
17.72 FT.

APROX.25'-8"

R= 32.2 FT.

R=6'-8"

N 50 13 33 W
42.87 FT.

R=2'

N 51 38 48 W
40.77 FT.

N 13 55 25

21.43 FT.

LOT 5

R=10'

N 51 09 18 W

CNTR LINE OF 40.00 FT.
COOP REFINERY ESMT.

6 FT. SIDEYARD SETBACK

S 89 05 15 W
101.73 FT.

14'-4"

6.00 FT. SETBACK

S 51 47 10 E
80.00 FT.

R=10'

N 39 30 10 W
64.60 FT.

FRONT

6.00 FT. SETBACK

5.00 FT.
N 15 10 00 W

Rodger A. Brooks, Architect

Figure 1-50. CAD systems are used for a wide variety of architectural applications.

Autodesk, Inc.

Figure 1-51. Hardware components of a CAD system are the input devices, central processing unit, and output devices.

Autodesk, Inc.

Figure 1-52. Software is the operating system that provides instructions to the hardware components.

is moved to its desired location, the cursor moves accordingly. Once in position, the size of the circle may be input by using the keyboard or stylus. In addition to standard commands, the graphics tablet may display a library of symbols. Common symbols include doors, windows, plumbing fixtures, and electrical fixtures. A symbol that is frequently used, but not part of the original symbols library, can be created and stored. When needed again, the symbol can be recalled from the library and used in its desired location.

Digitizing Tablet. A larger version of the graphics tablet, known as a digitizing tablet, can be used to convert existing drawings to CAD without reinputting all drawing components. An existing print is placed on the digitizing tablet and digitized (traced) with a stylus or mouse. The digitized drawing is then treated as other CAD drawings and may be revised to required specifications. See Figure 1-54.

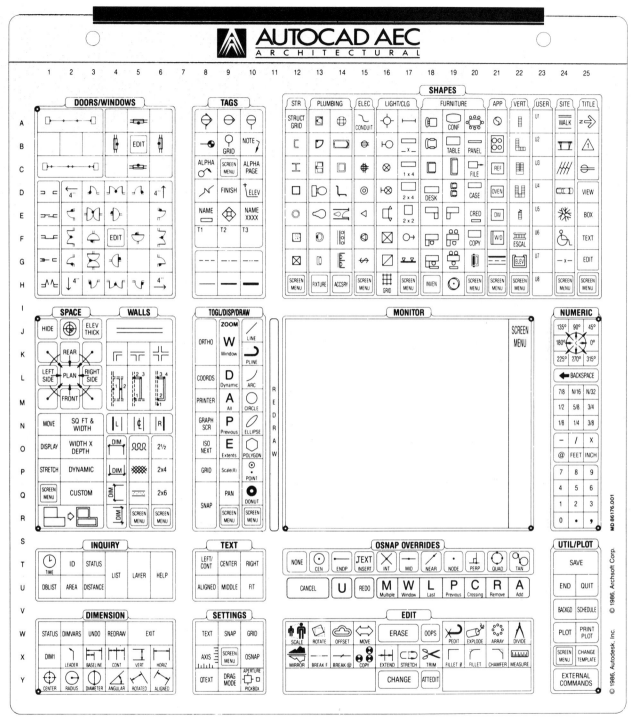

Figure 1-53. A graphics tablet consists of a group of commands and a drawing area.

Autodesk, Inc.

Keyboard. The keyboard is the most common input device. The number and letter arrangement is similar to a typewriter. For example, the standard QWERTY letter arrangement is utilized. Keyboards are electronic devices that send signals to the CPU.

The keyboard has the capability of inputting notes and dimensions as well as positioning the cursor on the display monitor. A keyboard may be the sole input device or it may be used in conjunction with other input devices.

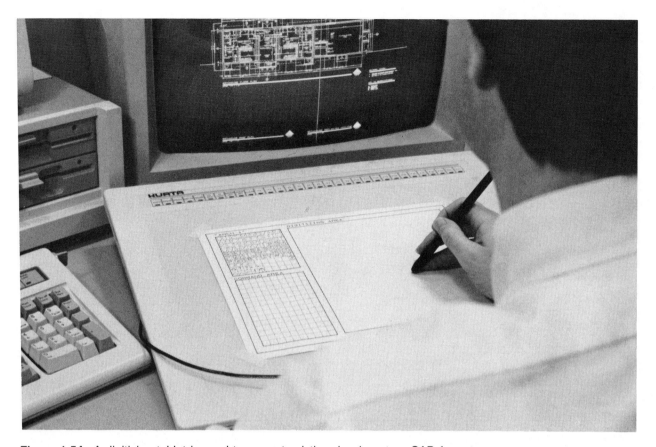

Figure 1-54. A digitizing tablet is used to convert existing drawings to a CAD format.

Light Pen. A light pen is a photosensitive electronic device used to enter data into the CAD system. Data (information) is input when the tip of the light pen is pressed directly on the screen. The operator may choose various commands listed along the edge of the screen in the same manner as when using a graphics tablet. An advantage of using the light pen is that the operator is working directly on the drawing rather than indirectly as with the graphics tablet.

Tablet Accessories. A stylus, mouse, joystick, thumbwheels, and trackballs are common accessories used in conjunction with tablets to input information. These accessories are either electronically or electromechanically operated.

A *stylus* is an electromechanical device used to input information into the CAD system. The stylus is used to select commands from the menu and position the cursor in the required area. When the desired command or position is located, the tip of the stylus is depressed against the surface of the tablet. As the tip is depressed, the stylus relays an electronic signal to the CPU.

A *mouse* is an electronic device used to input information into the CAD system. A mouse may be interfaced with a tablet or used separately. When used separately, the mouse controls the cursor on the display screen through movement on a hard surface. Menu selections are made by moving the cursor to the edge of the display screen and selecting the desired command.

A *joystick* is an electromechanical device used to control the cursor on the display screen and enter information into the CAD system. It may be used to choose a command from the display screen and locate its position on the drawing area.

A *thumbwheel* is an electromechanical device used to control the position of the cursor in vertical and horizontal planes. Two thumbwheels are required. One thumbwheel controls the vertical movement and the other controls the horizontal movement of the cursor.

A *trackball* is an electromechanical device similar to a thumbwheel in that it is only used to control cursor movement. A single trackball controls both the horizontal and vertical movement of the cursor and also has the capability of moving it diagonally. The cursor is moved by rolling the trackball in the desired direction.

Central Processing Unit

The central processing unit (CPU) is the control center of the CAD system. The CPU receives information through the input devices and manages and manipulates it to produce an output image. A CPU is classified by its memory capacity and the speed at which it carries out commands. A larger memory capacity generally has a greater capability of producing quality drawings. The central processing unit stores information through the use of magnetic tapes, disks, and internal memory.

CPUs may be dedicated for CAD systems only or may also run other software, such as word or data processing programs. The CAD system used to develop the plan for Wendy's restaurant (see chapter 9) is Interact™, which is a dedicated system manufactured by Intergraph™. This complete workstation includes a dual-screen display system and worksurface with alphanumeric (letters and numbers) keyboard and cursor. One screen is monochromatic (single color) and the other screen can simultaneously display up to 256 colors selected from a palette of 16 million colors. This wide range of colors provides virtually unlimited modeling capabilities. The Interact™ worksurface incorporates a digitizing tablet large enough for a standard D-size (22″ × 34″) drawing. See Figure 1-55.

Intergraph™

Figure 1-55. A central processing unit may be dedicated to CAD applications.

Output Devices

Output devices are hardware that either display or generate drawings. The basic types of output devices are *monitors* (screens), *printers*, and *plotters*.

Display Monitor. A display monitor is a necessity for all CAD stations. The monitor displays the drawing that the operator is developing. Monitors are available in many sizes and are chosen based upon the application. A large display monitor may be required when using a light pen because the large working surface enables an operator to work more accurately with the drawing. On some types of CAD systems two monitors are used. One monitor displays the drawing and the other displays the menu.

Printer. Printers produce drawings on paper. They provide a fast and convenient method of checking the placement of drawing features. The drawing generated by a printer consists of small dots that form shapes to produce the various parts of the drawing. The copy produced by a printer is generally of less-than-desirable quality. Consequently, final drawings are seldom produced by a printer.

Plotter. Plotters generate finished drawings with pens. They are available with single-color or multiple-color pens. The quality of a plotted drawing is much better than a printed drawing. Plotters vary in size and are chosen based upon the application. Larger plotters have the capability of plotting E-size (36″ × 48″) sheets of paper or film. Plotters are available in two major styles: the *rotary-drum* and the *flatbed* plotter.

On a rotary-drum plotter, the paper is mounted on a drum and moves with the drum's rotation. The pen moves parallel with the length of the drum. Vertical lines are drawn with the drum remaining in a fixed position while the pen moves along the sheet of paper. Horizontal lines are drawn with the pen remaining stationary and the drum rotating. A flatbed plotter allows the piece of paper to lie flat on its bed. The pen moves along the width and height of the paper while the paper remains stationary. See Figure 1-56.

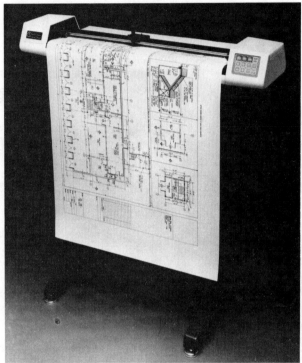

Ametek, Houston Instrument Division

Figure 1-56. A plotter produces high-quality drawings.

Name _____   Date _____

Multiple Choice

_____ 1. Isometric drawings utilize axes that are drawn _____° apart.
A. 60
B. 90
C. 120
D. 180

_____ 2. Cutting planes for section views are generally shown on _____.
A. elevations
B. floor plans
C. details
D. none of the above

_____ 3. Common input devices for a CAD system include a _____.
A. keyboard
B. light pen
C. digitizing tablet
D. all of the above

_____ 4. Drawings utilizing orthographic projection techniques are referred to as _____.
A. multiviews
B. pictorials
C. isometrics
D. obliques

_____ 5. For a hazardous area with an occupancy load exceeding 50 people, _____.
A. exit doors must swing in the direction of travel
B. force required to open exit doors shall not exceed 40 pounds
C. both A and B
D. neither A nor B

_____ 6. A _____ is an electromechanical device used to input information into a CAD system.
A. plotter
B. light pen
C. stylus
D. CPU

_____ 7. Dimensions on a print show _____.
A. size
B. location
C. size relationship of parts
D. all of the above

_____ 8. Two types of oblique drawings are _____.
A. orthographic and pictorial
B. perspective and front view
C. cabinet and cavalier
D. none of the above

_____ 9. The most commonly used scale for working drawings is _____.
A. $1/8'' = 1'-0''$
B. $1/4'' = 1'-0''$
C. $1'-0'' = 1/8''$
D. $1'-0'' = 1/4''$

_____ 10. A _____ produces the highest quality print.
A. display monitor
B. plotter
C. printer
D. keyboard

_____ 11. Finished grade is shown on a plot plan with _____ contour lines.
A. solid
B. dashed
C. dotted
D. broken

_____ 12. _____ is a method of viewing an object in its final form.
A. Layering
B. Modeling
C. Wire-framing
D. none of the above

_____ 13. The conventional representation for stairs on plan views is a series of _____.
A. horizontal lines representing treads
B. vertical lines representing risers
C. parallel lines representing risers
D. parallel lines representing runs and risers

_____ 14. An architect's scale may be read from _____.
A. left to right
B. right to left
C. both A and B
D. neither A nor B

_____ 15. Stairways between _____ " and 88" in public buildings shall have two handrails.
A. 30
B. 36
C. 40
D. 44

True-False

T F   **1.** Blueprints have white lines on a blue background.

T F   **2.** Written information is often found in title blocks of plans.

T F   **3.** Dimensions should be shown in each room on a floor plan giving its exact size.

T F   **4.** The front view of an isometric drawing shows a true view of the object.

T F   **5.** As the space between contour lines increases, the lot becomes steeper.

T F   **6.** The most common section views are taken through exterior walls.

T F   **7.** All information on windows is shown on floor plans or section views.

T F   **8.** Dimensions should not be repeated on prints unless marked REF.

T F   **9.** Floor plans are generally the most used plans in a set of prints.

T F **10.** Corridors in buildings with occupancy loads of 10 or more must be at least 44″ wide.

T F **11.** Interior doors generally require only two hinges.

T F **12.** Modular measurement is based upon grids with 4″ units.

T F **13.** Hollow-core doors have a core of wood blocks.

T F **14.** Four elevations are generally sufficient to clearly show exterior walls of a building.

T F **15.** Door hand is the direction in which a door swings.

Identification

_____ **1.** Multiview (top)

_____ **2.** Oblique (cabinet)

_____ **3.** Isometric

_____ **4.** Perspective

_____ **5.** Multiview (front)

_____ **6.** Oblique (cavalier)

_____ **7.** Multiview (right side)

Completion

_____   1. Circles on isometric drawings appear as _____.

_____   2. Three basic types of _____ drawings are one-point, two-point, and three-point.

_____   3. All visible print lines are shown with _____ lines.

_____   4. Dimension lines are terminated by _____ lines.

_____   5. The architect's scale is _____ in shape.

_____   6. Drywall partitions on floor plans are usually indicated as _____" thick.

_____   7. A legal _____ is required to establish the corners of a building lot in relation to official points of measurement in the vicinity.

_____   8. Building _____ specify types of materials that must be used for particular aspects of construction.

_____   9. The location of all exterior walls and interior _____ are shown on floor plans.

_____   10. The _____ elevation is a view of the South side of a building seen from a point opposite the South side, looking North.

_____   11. The _____ block is the logical place to begin reading a set of prints.

_____   12. The three classes of _____ are fixed, sliding, and swinging sash.

_____   13. Complex building parts such as doors and windows are simplified and drawn as _____.

_____   14. Mechanical ventilating systems must take at least _____% of their air supply directly from the outside.

_____   15. When determining door swing, the viewer is considered to be standing on the _____ of the door.

_____   16. Flush doors may be either solid-core or _____-core.

_____   17. Interior doors for single and multi-family dwellings must be at least _____" thick.

_____   18. The vertical distance between stair landings should not exceed _____'.

_____   19. Hidden lines are drawn with _____" dashes and $1/32$" spaces.

_____   20. A right-hand door hinges on the right and opens _____.

_____   21. When using the architect's scale, the _____ should always be placed on the beginning of the line being scaled.

_____   22. Underground electrical service is known as _____ service.

_____   23. A skewed surface on an isometric drawing is not in an isometric _____.

_____   24. Extension lines define size or _____.

_____   25. The abbreviation for foundation is _____.

Math

_____ 1. A partition is framed with 2″ × 4″ studs and finished with ³/₈″ drywall on both sides. What is the actual thickness of the partition?

Refer to the plot plan for Highland Office Supply to answer questions 2 through 7.

Local ordinances require the following for commercial office buildings:
Setbacks—40′-0″ from front street curb; 25′-0″ on each side; 20′-0″ on back
Parking—two 200 sq. ft. parking spaces per 1,000 sq. ft. of office building
Green space—10% minimum of total lot size
Maximum building size—40% of total lot size

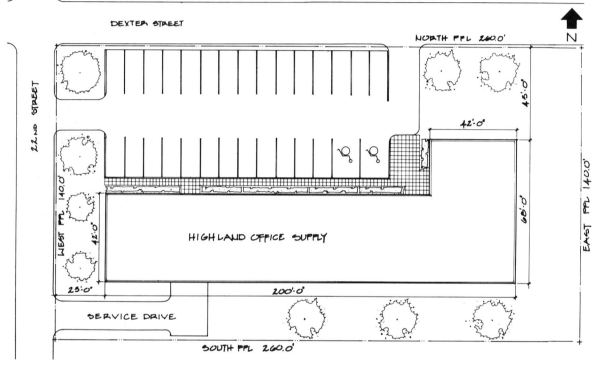

_____ 2. Are front and back setbacks sufficient?

_____ 3. What is the East setback?

_____ 4. How many square feet does the building contain?

_____ 5. Is the number of parking spaces sufficient?

_____ 6. What is the South setback?

_____ 7. How many square feet does the lot contain?

_____ 8. The point of beginning for a single-family dwelling is shown on the plot plans as 312′-0″. A one-story house with full basement is to be built on the lot. The first floor elevation is 316′-6″. The basement floor is 9′-0″ below the first floor. What is the elevation of the basement?

_____ 9. A single pane window is designated 30/36. What is the area in square inches?

_____ 10. A set of straight-run stairs is designated 16 R UP. Each riser is 6″ high. What is the total rise of the stairs?

Sketching

Sketch isometrics of problems 1–6.

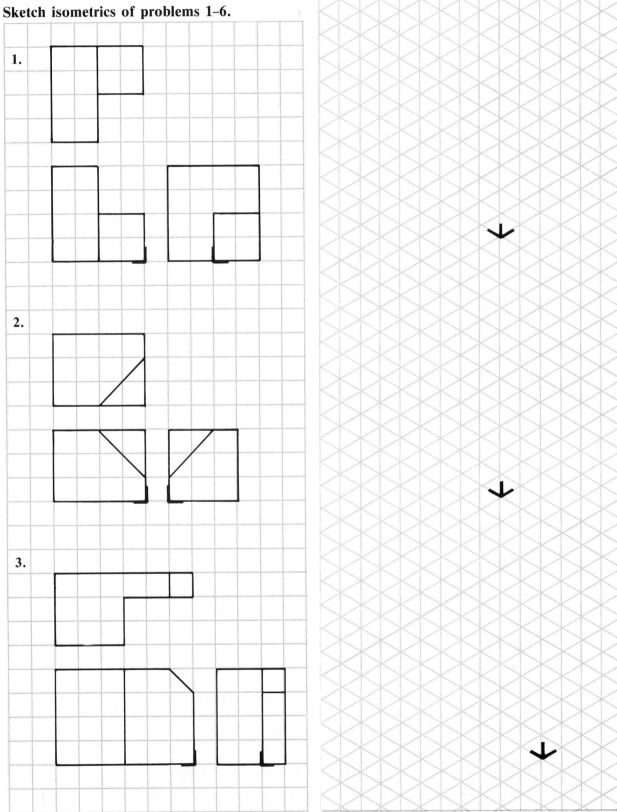

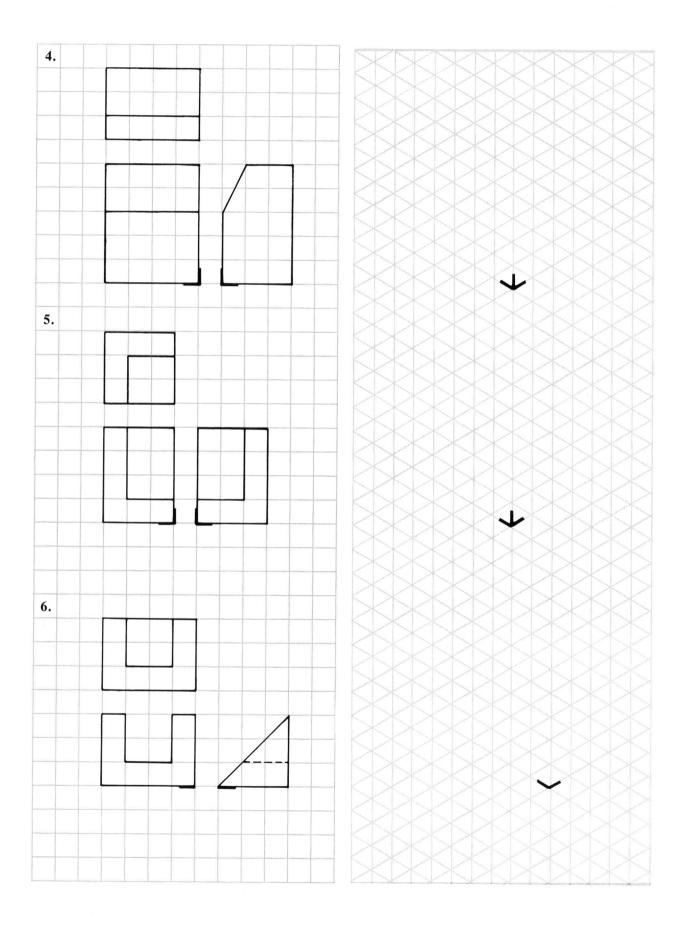

Sketch multiviews (front, top, and right side) of problems 7–9.

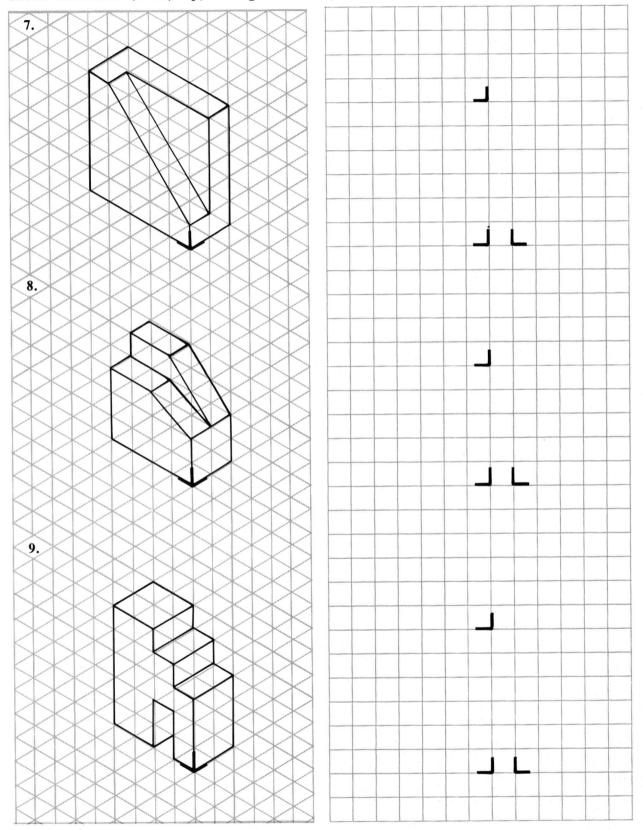

7.

8.

9.

Sketch one-point perspective for problem 10 and two-point perspective for problem 11.

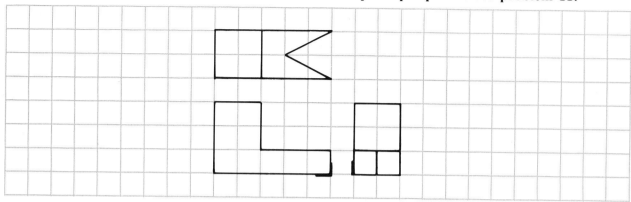

10.

•

⌐

11.

•   •

⌐

Matching

_____	1. Drawing	A. DW
_____	2. Exterior	B. FLG or FL
_____	3. Bathroom	C. EXCA or EXC
_____	4. Dishwasher	D. DWG
_____	5. Footing	E. B
_____	6. Flashing	F. CTR
_____	7. Excavate	G. CER
_____	8. Center	H. EXT
_____	9. Ceramic	I. FTG
_____	10. Bedroom	J. BR

Identification

_____	1. Front view—length
_____	2. Top view—depth
_____	3. Top view—length
_____	4. Right side view—depth
_____	5. Front view—height
_____	6. Right side view—height

Matching

_____	1. Printer	A. Common input device similar to a typewriter
_____	2. Keyboard	B. Central Processing Unit
_____	3. Digitizing tablet	C. Used to convert existing prints to CAD
_____	4. Mouse	D. Electronic input device
_____	5. CPU	E. Output device that produces rough copy

Trade Competency Test

Name   Date

Multiple Choice

_____   1.   The three basic types of axonometric drawings are _____, _____, and
                   _____.
                   A. oblique, perspective, trimetric
                   B. cavalier, cabinet, isometric
                   C. perspective, dimetric, cabinet
                   D. isometric, dimetric, trimetric

_____   2.   The _____ has the responsibility of providing all required dimensions for
                   the plans.
                   A. owner
                   B. builder
                   C. architect
                   D. contractor

_____   3.   A door designated 2'-8″ × 6'-8″ × 1¾″ _____.
                   A. may be used as an exterior door
                   B. is a left-hand door
                   C. is a flush door
                   D. none of the above

_____   4.   The input devices, central processing unit, and output devices are _____
                   components.
                   A. software
                   B. hardware
                   C. digitizing
                   D. none of the above

_____   5.   Cross-sectional areas of handrails must not be less than 1¼″ nor more than
                   _____″.
                   A. 1¾
                   B. 2
                   C. 2¼
                   D. 2½

_____   6.   _____ on the ends of dimension lines limit each dimension on a print.
                   A. Arrows
                   B. Dots
                   C. Slashes
                   D. all of the above

7. The minimum area for exterior glazed openings serving habitable rooms in dwellings, per the Uniform Building Code, is _____ sq. ft.
   A. 6
   B. 8
   C. 10
   D. 12

8. A _____ is a solid or flashing pointer indicating the position of work on a CAD system.
   A. stylus
   B. mouse
   C. cursor
   D. light pen

9. The minimum number of complete air changes required per hour for mechanical ventilating systems is _____ per the Uniform Building Code.
   A. no minimum is required
   B. 1
   C. 2
   D. 4

10. Preferred angles for stairs are between 30° and _____°.
    A. 35
    B. 40
    C. 45
    D. none of the above

11. A _____ is a photosensitive input device used to enter information into a CAD system by pressing the tip directly on the screen.
    A. mouse
    B. trackball
    C. stylus
    D. light pen

12. Dimensions on plan and elevation drawings are shown in _____.
    A. feet
    B. inches
    C. both A and B
    D. neither A nor B

13. The numbers 30/48 near windows shown on a set of plans indicate that _____.
    A. 30 window lights are 48″ high
    B. from 30 to 48 windows are installed
    C. window lights are 30″ wide and 48″ high
    D. window lights are 30″ high and 48″ wide

14. Electrical information on plans is shown on _____.
    A. floor plans for most residential construction
    B. floor plans for small commercial jobs
    C. electrical plans for large residential and most commercial construction
    D. all of the above

_____ 15. The minimum clear width of an exit door is _____.
    A. 2'-6"
    B. 2'-8"
    C. 3'-0"
    D. no such requirement

_____ 16. The cutting plane for a floor plan is generally taken _____ the floor being shown.
    A. on
    B. 5'-0" above
    C. at any convenient height above
    D. below

_____ 17. All buildings are required to have at least _____ exit(s).
    A. one
    B. two
    C. three
    D. no such requirement

_____ 18. Minimum headroom required for stairs is _____.
    A. 6'-0"
    B. 6'-6"
    C. 6'-8"
    D. 7'-0"

True-False

T F **1.** A section through the jamb on a detail drawing of a window is a slice through the side jamb looking down.

T F **2.** Package doors include the door frames and hardware.

T F **3.** The working drawings include all of the information needed to build a house.

T F **4.** A printer produces a better finished drawing than a plotter.

T F **5.** Concrete walks and drives are shown on plot plans.

T F **6.** Drawings on a single print sheet must be drawn to the same scale.

T F **7.** Location of water, sewer, and electrical power is generally indicated on plot plans.

T F **8.** A flatbed plotter allows a piece of paper to remain stationary while the pen plots lines horizontally and vertically.

T F **9.** Commercial kitchens with occupancy loads exceeding 30 people must have at least four exit doors.

T F **10.** Isometrics are the most commonly drawn type of axonometric drawings.

T F **11.** The central processing unit is the control center of a CAD system.

T F **12.** Stair unit rise is the height of each riser.

T F **13.** Casement windows swing outward.

T F **14.** Door openings on plan views are dimensioned in the same general manner as window openings.

T   F   **15.** A graphics tablet is a larger version of a digitizing tablet.

T   F   **16.** Isometric drawings have one surface that is a true view.

T   F   **17.** L-shaped stairs must have one landing.

T   F   **18.** Dimensions for windows in masonry walls are generally given to the opening.

T   F   **19.** Software is the operating system of a CAD system that allows hardware components to interact.

T   F   **20.** The use of hidden lines on working drawings is minimized to avoid confusion.

T   F   **21.** Elevations are always drawn to the same scale as floor plans.

T   F   **22.** The minimum hallway width for private dwellings is 44″.

T   F   **23.** Symbols may be used on floor plans and elevations but should not be used on details or sections.

T   F   **24.** The two general types of doors are flush and panel.

T   F   **25.** When windows are of the same size and type, the dimensions and light size of each are given for clarity.

T   F   **26.** General information pertaining to drawings on several sheets in a set of plans must be recorded in the title block.

T   F   **27.** Window parts are shown in detail on floor plans.

T   F   **28.** An extension line is always terminated by an arrowhead.

T   F   **29.** The hinged side of a window is shown by the apex of a dashed triangle drawn on the window in an elevation view.

T   F   **30.** The abbreviation for center is CNT.

Completion

_____   **1.** Axonometric drawings are drawn with _____ principal axes.

_____   **2.** _____ pictorial drawings show one surface of the object as a true view.

_____   **3.** The location of _____ points alters the angles of receding lines in perspective drawings.

_____   **4.** Conventional representation of lines used for drawings are prescribed in ANSI _____.

_____   **5.** Lines below a surface or behind an object are drawn as _____ lines.

_____   **6.** _____ is the relative size to which an object is drawn.

_____   **7.** _____ are shown to locate points from other points on the prints.

_____   **8.** _____ are holding devices used to maintain accuracy of members during assembly.

_____   **9.** Each print of a set of working drawings represents a part of a building drawn as a(n) _____ plane.

_____   **10.** _____ plans show the location and orientation of a building on the lot.

_____ 11. _____ ordinances restrict the use of land to particular types of businesses or dwellings.

_____ 12. _____ contour lines show existing grade.

_____ 13. HVAC information for commercial buildings is generally shown on _____ plans.

_____ 14. Elevations are _____ drawings showing vertical planes of a building.

_____ 15. A(n) _____ is created by passing a cutting plane through a portion of a building.

_____ 16. Working drawings show all features of a building with lines, _____, and conventional representations.

_____ 17. Only _____ case letters are used for abbreviations on plans.

_____ 18. _____ may be drawn of any part of a building that is not clearly shown on the plans.

_____ 19. Out-swing windows are closed by crank or _____ mechanisms.

_____ 20. _____ hinges are required for hanging solid-core doors.

_____ 21. The minimum size of an exit door is _____ wide and 6'-8" high.

_____ 22. The total _____ of a stairway is its total height.

_____ 23. Leaders may be terminated with open or closed _____.

_____ 24. The front view of a multiview drawing shows the dimensions of _____ and height.

_____ 25. Window height above a finished floor is usually given to the bottom of the top window _____.

_____ 26. A(n) _____ line is utilized to show that a detail continues but is not drawn.

_____ 27. Drawings completed with _____ projection techniques are commonly referred to as multiview drawings.

_____ 28. _____ plans show the location of existing buildings on the property.

_____ 29. An oblique _____ has receding lines drawn to the same scale as the front view.

_____ 30. A(n) _____ axonometric has no equal axes.

True-False

T F 1. Each axis of a trimetric drawing is drawn at a different angle.

T F 2. Plumbing fixtures are generally shown on residential floor plans.

T F 3. Details may be part of a plan, elevation, or section view drawn at a larger scale.

T F 4. A casement window is a type of sliding sash window.

T F 5. The keyed side of a lock is considered the inside for doors that open between rooms.

T F 6. Hollow-core doors may be used for any room or any entrance of a single-family dwelling.

T   F   **7.** Elevators do not count toward the minimum number of exits that are required for a building.

T   F   **8.** A floor or landing is required on each side of a door.

T   F   **9.** The minimum rise of a step meeting minimum code standards is 6″.

T   F   **10.** Pictorial drawings show height, length, and depth of an object.

T   F   **11.** A bathroom may be constructed as a module.

T   F   **12.** Awning windows swing outward.

T   F   **13.** Hollow-core doors have a core of wood blocks.

T   F   **14.** Exterior elevations are used to show cabinet details.

T   F   **15.** In an oblique cabinet drawing, receding lines are drawn at one-half scale.

T   F   **16.** Two handrails are required for stairs over 44″ and less than 88″ wide.

T   F   **17.** A code reference near a cutting plane indicates the sheet number on which the identified section is found.

T   F   **18.** Symbols are not used on sections in order to avoid confusion on the drawings.

T   F   **19.** Bird's-eye, eye-level, and worm's-eye in relation to perspective sketches refer to the position of the observer.

T   F   **20.** The diazo print process produces a black line on a white background.

T   F   **21.** A perspective bird's-eye view may be drawn with one, two, or three vanishing points.

T   F   **22.** A dimension, without other notation, should only be shown once on a plan.

T   F   **23.** Steep stairs have wide treads and low risers.

T   F   **24.** A center line and a cutting plane line are drawn with the same symbol.

T   F   **25.** A standardized abbreviation on a plan can only have one meaning.

Matching

_____   **1.** Water closet   A. W

_____   **2.** Wood   B. WP

_____   **3.** Riser   C. WS

_____   **4.** Waterproof   D. WC

_____   **5.** Roof   E. R

_____   **6.** Elevation   F. EL

_____   **7.** Entrance   G. WD

_____   **8.** Water   H. E

_____   **9.** Weather stripping   I. ENT

_____   **10.** East   J. RF

Identification

_____ **1.** Straight-run

_____ **2.** Total rise

_____ **3.** Circular

_____ **4.** Straight-run with landing

_____ **5.** Finished floor

_____ **6.** Riser

_____ **7.** Tread

_____ **8.** Total run

_____ **9.** Headroom

_____ **10.** Stair angle

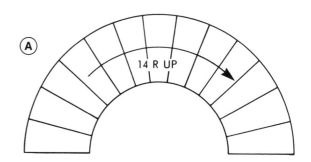

Ⓐ 14 R UP

Ⓑ 10 R UP

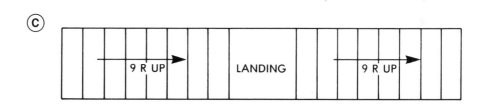

Ⓒ 9 R UP LANDING 9 R UP

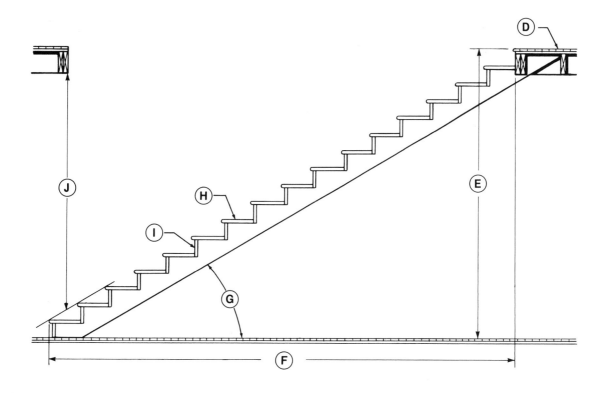

Identification

_____ 1. Leader (open arrowhead)

_____ 2. Section line

_____ 3. Break line (long)

_____ 4. Hidden line

_____ 5. Object line

_____ 6. Break line (short)

_____ 7. Cutting plane

_____ 8. Leader (closed arrowhead)

_____ 9. Centerpoint

_____ 10. Center line

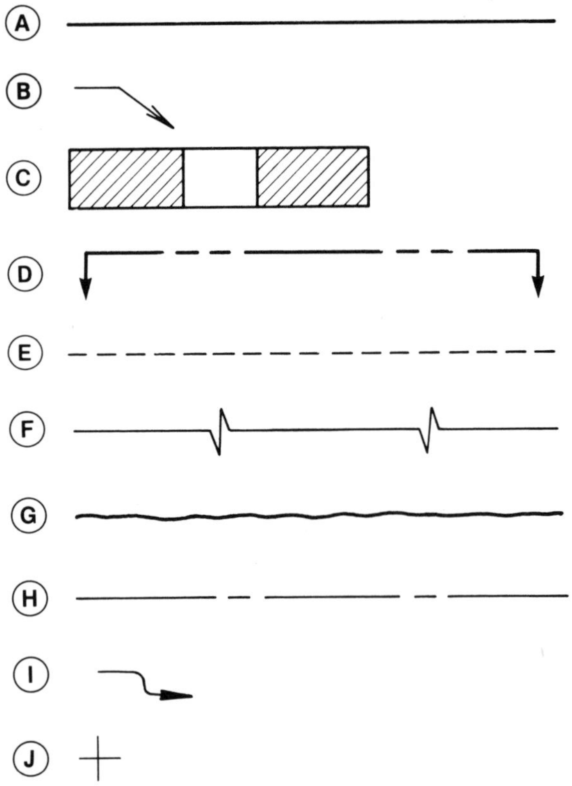

Ⓐ ————————————————

Ⓑ ⟍

Ⓒ ▨☐▨

Ⓓ ↓ – – – – ↓

Ⓔ – – – – – – – –

Ⓕ ———⋀———⋀———

Ⓖ 〜〜〜〜〜〜

Ⓗ —— – —— – ——

Ⓘ ⌐→

Ⓙ ＋

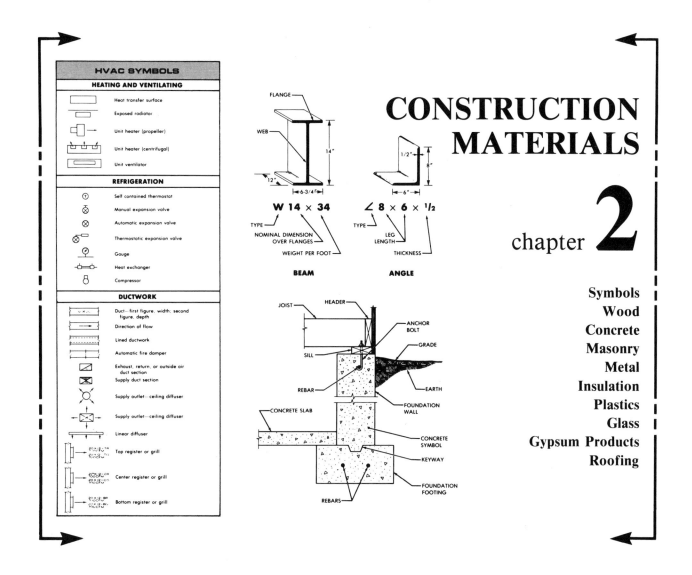

CONSTRUCTION MATERIALS

chapter 2

Symbols
Wood
Concrete
Masonry
Metal
Insulation
Plastics
Glass
Gypsum Products
Roofing

SYMBOLS

Building a structure of any type involves using a great number of raw or processed materials that come in a variety of sizes, shapes, and finishes. Materials range from concrete, which goes into footings, foundation walls, and slabs to the roofing. A number of materials are used in the structure itself, which is covered with many kinds of interior and exterior finish. All of the equipment needed for heating, cooling, plumbing, and electricity must be included. Printreading involves how to understand, with full comprehension, the symbols and conventional representations of the plans.

Persons who read prints are concerned with factors such as choosing the best material for the application in terms of both serviceability and attractiveness. In addition, builders and tradesworkers

must know the available sizes and forms, the response of materials to tools, and the modification of materials for specific use. Those responsible for ordering material and preparing cost estimates are more concerned with sizes, shapes, and costs.

The symbols used on prints indicate the materials to be used at each location, thus frequently eliminating the need for descriptive notations. See Figure 2-1. Some symbols are standardized; others are optional. One of several symbols may be used, depending on the architect's preference or training. Electrical symbols are used to show objects such as general outlets, convenience outlets, switch outlets, special outlets, panels, and circuits. Plumbing symbols are used to show fixtures, drains, piping, pipe fittings, valves, and other plumbing items. Architectural symbols show earth, brick, block, stone, tile,

ELECTRICAL SYMBOLS

GENERAL OUTLETS

CEILING	WALL	
○	─○	Outlet
Ⓑ	─Ⓑ	Blanked outlet
Ⓔ	─Ⓔ	Electrical outlet—for use when circle alone may be confused with other symbols
Ⓙ	─Ⓙ	Junction box
Ⓛ	─Ⓛ	Outlet controlled by low-voltage switching when relay is installed in outlet box
Ⓢ	─Ⓢ	Pull switch
Ⓧ	─Ⓧ	Surface or pendant exit light
ⓍⓇ	─ⓍⓇ	Recessed exit light
▭○▭	▭─▭○▭	Surface or pendant individual fluorescent fixture
▭○R▭	▭─▭○R▭	Recessed individual fluorescent fixture

CONVENIENCE OUTLETS

⊖	Duplex receptacle outlet
⊕	Triplex receptacle outlet
⊖WP	Weatherproof duplex outlet
⊖R	Range outlet
⊖S	Switch and convenience outlet
▲	Special purpose outlet—use subscript letters to indicate function
⊟	Floor duplex receptacle outlet
⊖GFCI	Outlet equipped with ground-fault circuit interrupter

SWITCH OUTLETS

S	Single-pole switch
S_2	Double-pole switch
S_3	Three-way switch
S_4	Four-way switch
S_D	Automatic door switch
S_P	Switch and pilot lamp
S_{CB}	Circuit breaker
S_{WCB}	Weatherproof circuit breaker
S_{MC}	Momentary contact switch
S_{RC}	Remote control switch
S_{WP}	Weatherproof switch
S_F	Fused switch
S_{WF}	Weatherproof fused switch

SPECIAL OUTLETS

$O_{a,b}$	Any standard symbol with the addition of a lowercase subscript.
⊖$_{a,b}$	Letter may be used to designate a variation in standard equipment.
$S_{a,b}$	When used on a drawing, they must be listed in the Key of Symbols on each drawing and, if necessary, further described in the specifications.

PANELS, CIRCUITS, AND MISCELLANEOUS SYMBOLS

▬	Lighting panel
▨	Power panel
───	Wiring concealed in ceiling or wall
─ ─ ─	Wiring concealed in floor
─ ─ ─ ─	Wiring exposed
⟶ 2 1	Home run to panelboard. Number of arrows indicates number of circuits.
	Note: Any circuit without further identification indicates a two-wire circuit. For greater number of wires indicate with inclined lines: (three wires) ─///─ (four wires) ─////─
▬	Feeders. Note: Use heavy line and designate by number corresponding to Feeder Schedule.
⊟	Underfloor duct and junction box. Triple duct system. For single or double duct systems, use either a single or double line.
MC	Motor or other power controller
⟋	Constant current transformer
⬎	Externally operated disconnection switch
⊠⊐	Combination controller and disconnecting means

AUXILIARY SYSTEMS

▫•	Pushbutton
◻⟍	Buzzer
◻○	Bell
◇	Annunciator
◀	Outside telephone
◁	Interconnecting telephone
BT	Bell-ringing transformer
D	Electric door opener
TV	Television outlet
CH	Chime
─▫	Smoke alarm device
F○	Fire alarm bell
F	Fire alarm station
⊠	City fire alarm station
FA	Fire alarm central station
FS	Automatic fire alarm device
SC	Signal central station
▭	Interconnection box
╫	Battery
Ⓣ	Thermostat
◁	Sound system
◁2	Microphone

The Institute of Electrical and Electronics Engineers, Inc.

Figure 2-1. Symbols are conventional representations used to show building materials, piping fixtures, circuits, and other building objects.

PLUMBING AND PIPING SYMBOLS

PLUMBING

Corner Bath	
Recessed Bath	
Roll Rim Bath	
Sitz Bath	SB
Foot Bath	FB
Bidet	B
Shower Stall	
Shower Head	(Plan) (Elev.)
Overhead Gang Shower	(Plan) / (Elev.)
Pedestal Lavatory	PL
Wall Lavatory	WL
Corner Lavatory	LAV
Manicure Lavatory Medical Lavatory	ML
Dental Lavatory	DENTAL LAV
Plain Kitchen Sink	S
Kitchen Sink, R & L Drain Board	
Kitchen Sink, L H Drain Board	
Combination Sink & Dishwasher	
Combination Sink & Laundry Tray	S & T
Service Sink	SS
Wash Sink (Wall Type)	
Wash Sink	
Laundry Tray	L │ T
Water Closet (Low Tank)	
Water Closet (No Tank)	
Urinal (Pedestal Type)	
Urinal (Wall Type)	
Urinal (Corner Type)	
Urinal (Stall Type)	
Urinal (Trough Type)	TU
Drinking Fountain (Pedestal Type)	DF
Drinking Fountain (Wall Type)	DF

PLUMBING

Drinking Fountain (Trough Type)	DF
Hot Water Tank	HWT
Water Heater	WH
Meter	M
Hose Rack	HR
Hose Bibb	HB
Gas Outlet	G
Vacuum Outlet	
Drain	D
Grease Separator	G
Oil Separator	
Cleanout	
Garage Drain	
Floor Drain With Backwater Valve	
Roof Sump	

PIPING

Soil and Waste	———————
Soil and Waste, Underground	— — — —
Vent	- - - - - - -
Cold Water	- - - · - - - ·
Hot Water	- - - - - - -
Hot Water Return	- - - - - - -
Fire Line	—F— —F—
Gas	—G— —G—
Acid Waste	———ACID———
Drinking Water Supply	——————
Drinking Water Return	——————
Vacuum Cleaning	—V— —V—
Compressed Air	———A———

PIPE FITTINGS

	Screwed	Bell and Spigot
Joint		
Elbow - 90°		
Elbow - 45°		
Elbow - Turned up		
Elbow - Turned Down		

PIPE FITTINGS

	Screwed	Bell and Spigot
Elbow - Long Radius		
Side Outlet Elbow - Outlet Down		
Side Outlet Elbow - Outlet Up		
Base Elbow		
Double Branch Elbow		
Single Sweep Tee		
Double Sweep Tee		
Reducing Elbow		
Tee		
Tee - Outlet Up		
Tee - Outlet Down		
Side Outlet Tee Outlet Up		
Side Outlet Tee Outlet Down		
Cross		
Reducer		
Eccentric Reducer		
Lateral		
Expansion Joint Flanged		

VALVES

	Screwed	Bell and Spigot
Gate Valve		
Globe Valve		
Angle Globe Valve		
Angle Gate Valve		
Check Valve		
Angle Check Valve		
Stop Cock		
Safety Valve		
Quick Opening Valve		
Float Opening Valve		
Motor Operated Gate Valve		

American National Standards Institute

Figure 2-1 (continued)

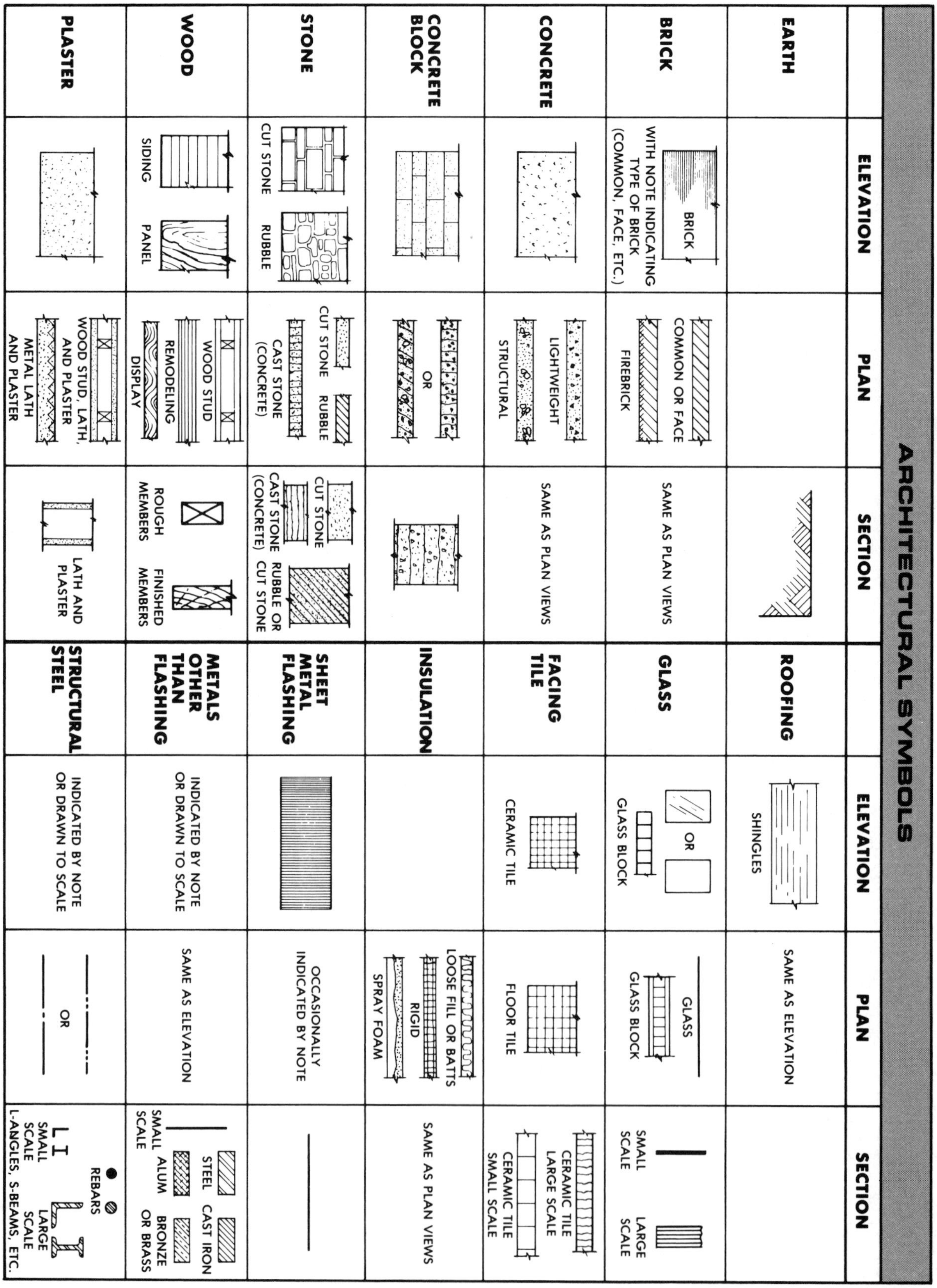

ARCHITECTURAL SYMBOLS

	ELEVATION	PLAN	SECTION		ELEVATION	PLAN	SECTION
EARTH				ROOFING	SHINGLES	SAME AS ELEVATION	
BRICK	BRICK / WITH NOTE INDICATING TYPE OF BRICK (COMMON, FACE, ETC.)	COMMON OR FACE / FIREBRICK	SAME AS PLAN VIEWS	GLASS	GLASS BLOCK / OR	GLASS / GLASS BLOCK	SMALL SCALE / LARGE SCALE
CONCRETE		LIGHTWEIGHT / STRUCTURAL	SAME AS PLAN VIEWS	FACING TILE	CERAMIC TILE	FLOOR TILE	CERAMIC TILE SMALL SCALE / CERAMIC TILE LARGE SCALE
CONCRETE BLOCK		OR		INSULATION		LOOSE FILL OR BATTS / RIGID / SPRAY FOAM	SAME AS PLAN VIEWS
STONE	CUT STONE / RUBBLE	CAST STONE (CONCRETE) / CUT STONE (CONCRETE) RUBBLE	CUT STONE / CAST STONE (CONCRETE) RUBBLE OR CUT STONE	SHEET METAL FLASHING		OCCASIONALLY INDICATED BY NOTE	
WOOD	SIDING / PANEL	WOOD STUD / REMODELING DISPLAY / WOOD STUD	ROUGH MEMBERS / FINISHED MEMBERS	METALS OTHER THAN FLASHING	INDICATED BY NOTE OR DRAWN TO SCALE	SAME AS ELEVATION	SMALL SCALE ALUM / STEEL CAST IRON / BRONZE OR BRASS
PLASTER		WOOD STUD, LATH, AND PLASTER / METAL LATH AND PLASTER	LATH AND PLASTER	STRUCTURAL STEEL	INDICATED BY NOTE OR DRAWN TO SCALE	OR	REBARS / L-ANGLES, S-BEAMS, ETC. / SMALL LARGE SCALE SCALE

Figure 2-1 (continued)

American National Standards Institute

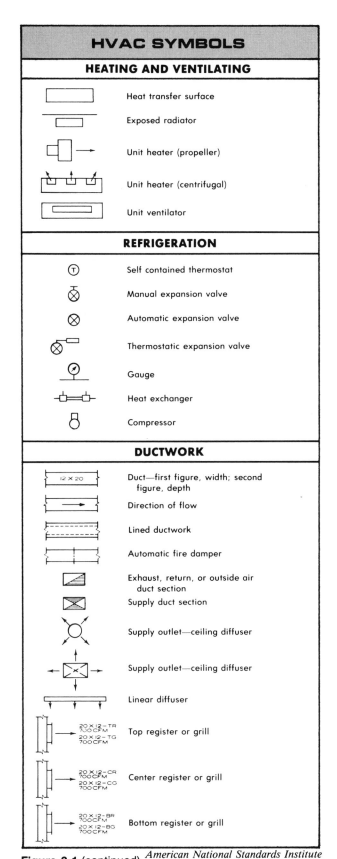

HVAC SYMBOLS

HEATING AND VENTILATING

	Heat transfer surface
	Exposed radiator
	Unit heater (propeller)
	Unit heater (centrifugal)
	Unit ventilator

REFRIGERATION

	Self contained thermostat
	Manual expansion valve
	Automatic expansion valve
	Thermostatic expansion valve
	Gauge
	Heat exchanger
	Compressor

DUCTWORK

12 × 20	Duct—first figure, width; second figure, depth
	Direction of flow
	Lined ductwork
	Automatic fire damper
	Exhaust, return, or outside air duct section
	Supply duct section
	Supply outlet—ceiling diffuser
	Supply outlet—ceiling diffuser
	Linear diffuser
20×12–TR 700CFM / 20×12–TG 700CFM	Top register or grill
20×12–CR 700CFM / 20×12–CG 700CFM	Center register or grill
20×12–BR 700CFM / 20×12–BG 700CFM	Bottom register or grill

Figure 2-1 (continued) *American National Standards Institute*

glass, wood, plaster, and other building materials. Heating, ventilating, and air conditioning (HVAC) symbols are used to show valves, gauges, heaters, ductwork, diffusers, and other HVAC items.

WOOD

Wood is relatively inexpensive, has good structural strength, and has a beauty of its own when used as finish. However, it is flammable and is subject to the flaws developed during growth and processing. Each species has its own qualities. Some types of pine, hemlock, and fir have excellent structural qualities and are used for the rough members of the building. Maple and oak are hard, wear resistant, and fine grained. They are used for finished flooring. Mahogany is used as a veneer to cover doors and panels. Birch and some species of pine are among woods used for trim. Walnut and fruitwoods are generally used for furniture because of their beauty but only rarely for trim in houses or commercial buildings because of their cost.

Rough lumber lengths are available in 2′ increments and are described by their nominal sizes, such as 2 × 4, 2 × 6, and 1 × 6. These are not actual sizes but are used for descriptive purposes among lumber dealers, tradesworkers, and architects. A 2 × 4 piece of wood is actually $1^{1}/_{2}'' \times 3^{1}/_{2}''$. The $^{1}/_{2}''$ difference is accounted for in the drying and cutting necessary to bring the rough sawed pieces down to finished size.

The symbol for wood-framed walls and partitions on small-scale plan views is to leave the space blank between the two lines representing the two faces of the wall or partition. Walls are generally considered to be load-bearing while partitions are considered non-bearing. This symbol for walls and partitions is the most commonly used symbol as it does not unnecessarily clutter the plans. See Figure 2-2. An alternate symbol is often used to show walls and partitions when plans are drawn for magazines or display work. This symbol, for display drawings, allows the walls and partitions to stand out clearly on the plans. Another option for showing walls and symbols is particularly useful when a building is to be remodeled, or an addition is to be made. The architect uses closely drawn parallel lines to show parts which are new or which require changes. The contractor thus has detailed information regarding the nature and extent of the changes and can prepare a realistic cost estimate. See Figure 2-3.

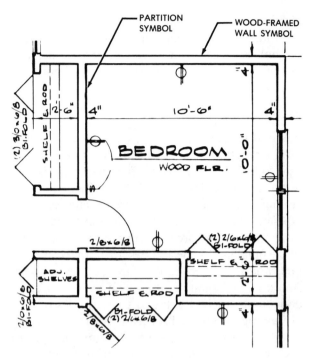

Figure 2-2. The symbol for wood-framed walls and partitions is two parallel lines with blank space in between.

Different symbols are used when wood members are shown in cross section, such as in a cutting plane view through an exterior wall or in a special section detail showing construction or assembly. See Figure 2-4. The end views of rough wood structural (framing) members are indicated by diagonal lines, forming an ''X,'' within each piece. Face views of framing members are shown by two parallel lines. Finished wood members, such as moldings and trim, are shown with lines drawn freehand to represent woodgrain. Plywood drawn at a small scale is shown by the same symbol as wood trim members. When the print scale is large, horizontal lines are added to indicate the plies. No attempt is made to show the exact number of plies in the particular piece.

Structural Qualities of Wood

The proper use of wood in building is the joint responsibility of the architect and the tradesworker. The architect must decide on a species of wood that is available and has the best structural qualities for the job. Figure 2-5 shows a typical stress table taken from the building code of a large city. It gives maximum allowable unit stresses in pounds per square inch for the eight most common varieties of wood, plywood, and laminated timber used in that area.

Extreme fiber stress is the resistance to the shortening and lengthening of the fibers when a member is placed in a position where it tends to bend under a load.

Horizontal shear is the resistance to the tendency of the fibers to slide past one another lengthwise in a member placed in a position where it tends to bend under a load.

Compression across grain is the resistance to compression at right angles to the axis of the member.

Compression parallel to grain is the resistance to compression parallel to the axis of the member.

Modulus of elasticity is the relation of the unit stress to unit elongation. When a member is placed under stress it will elongate at a uniform rate until it reaches its limits of elasticity after which it will no longer return to its original length.

The architect must also calculate whether a 2 × 8 or 2 × 10 floor joist is needed to span a certain distance on 16″ centers and make similar decisions regarding other structural members. The tradesworker, who must follow the prints and specifications regarding materials and their installation, is responsible for framing openings and fastening all members.

Plywood

Plywood has become increasingly important in the building industry because it is relatively inexpensive and has many fine characteristics. Plywood derives its name from the crossbands (or plies) which are glued together to form the piece. Plywood always contains an uneven number of plies, generally 3, 5, or 7 depending upon the thickness of the sheet. The odd number of plies assures that the grain on each face runs in the same direction. The common facegrain direction for plywood is along the long side of the sheet, although crossgrain plywood is available for specific applications.

Structural plywood has stiffness and strength, which gives it stress-resistant qualities. It is water-resistant because of the type glues now used. Builders use plywood for concrete forms, exterior walls, roof sheathing, and rough flooring. Most plywood is supplied in 4′ × 8′ sheets ranging in thickness from 1/4″ to 7/8″. Plywood is also supplied with surface veneers from many types of beautiful wood, such as birch, maple, and oak. These are used for

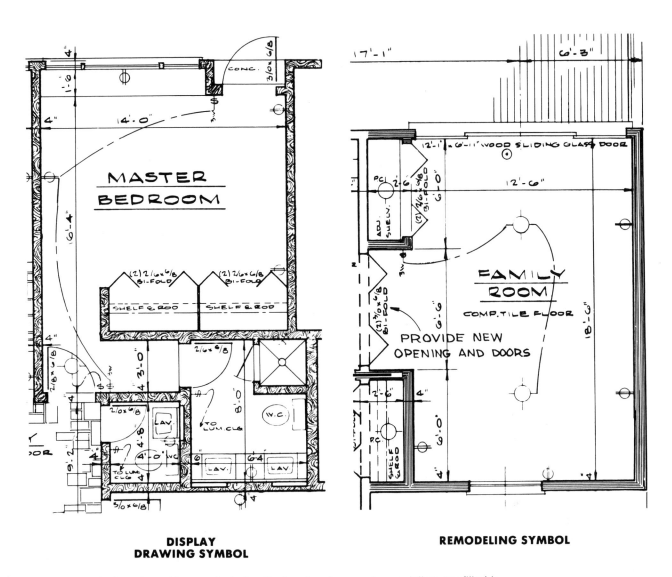

DISPLAY DRAWING SYMBOL

REMODELING SYMBOL

Figure 2-3. Wall and partition symbols for display drawings and remodeling are filled in.

paneling walls to provide interesting interiors and for building cabinets, vanities, and shelving.

CONCRETE

One uniform concrete symbol is used for *monolithic* (one piece) concrete in sectional views, regardless of the makeup of the concrete itself. The cross-sectional area is covered with small dots with a random sprinkling of small triangular shapes. See Figure 2-6.

Concrete is an extremely useful basic material because of its strength and because it can be cast in place in a plastic state to take the shape of formwork. Concrete is a mixture of cement, sand, and aggregate with water to make it plastic and to bring

about a chemical action. The aggregate is usually crushed stone or gravel of near uniform size but may be cinders, slag, or a mineral product such as expanded mica (*vermiculite*). Concrete made with some of these aggregates is lighter in weight than stone, when used. Chemical additives provide still different qualities in the concrete, such as air entrainment, which gives the concrete higher resistance to freezing and high early strength.

The concrete mixture is important because, when the proportions are changed, load-bearing and other qualities are modified. The mixture is determined by the ratio of materials in the concrete. A ratio of 1:2:4 indicates 1 part of cement, 2 parts of sand, and 4 parts of gravel (or other aggregate). The concrete sets during the first 12 to 24 hours after place-

WOOD SYMBOLS

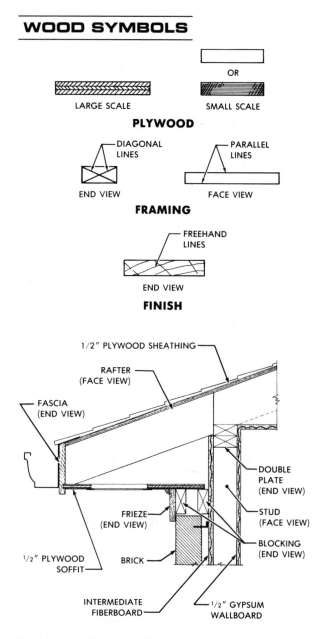

OR

PLYWOOD

LARGE SCALE   SMALL SCALE

DIAGONAL LINES   PARALLEL LINES

END VIEW   FACE VIEW

FRAMING

FREEHAND LINES

END VIEW

FINISH

1/2" PLYWOOD SHEATHING

RAFTER (FACE VIEW)

FASCIA (END VIEW)

DOUBLE PLATE (END VIEW)

FRIEZE (END VIEW)

STUD (FACE VIEW)

BLOCKING (END VIEW)

1/2" PLYWOOD SOFFIT   BRICK

INTERMEDIATE FIBERBOARD

1/2" GYPSUM WALLBOARD

Figure 2-4. The symbol for end views of wooden members in section views is diagonal lines drawn through the member.

ment, depending on the atmospheric temperature, the size of the mass, and other factors. The forms may generally be removed after three or four days. The chemical process of curing, during which the concrete develops its load-bearing qualities and design strength, takes place within the first 28 days.

Architects design concrete footings to bear the load of the foundation walls and the building, including its contents, based on the type of soil they must rest on. Steel reinforcing bars (rebars) are used in the footing and foundation wall if there is any possibility of settling or movement of the earth, or if the weight of the building is a factor. Rebars are also used to tie together adjacent parts of foundations, walks, and steps. Concrete is able to withstand great compressive stress but is relatively poor in counteracting bending or tension. Rebars provide the necessary structural qualities to concrete parts of buildings.

Tradesworkers have the responsibility of reading the specifications and prints so that they can build the forms that provide the desired shapes in the finished concrete. The formwork must be constructed so that it will be able to hold the plastic, almost liquid, material during placement and until it sets. Reinforcing bars, when specified, must be placed and supported in the exact position shown on the prints to provide the strength for which the structure is designed.

In many buildings, particularly in warm climates, concrete floors are placed over a bed of sand or gravel fill at or near grade level. *Slab-on-grade* construction utilizes plastic sheeting to prevent moisture entry into the slab from the ground. Slab thicknesses are specified on the plans. Wood flooring or carpeting is laid over the concrete slab. Another type of finished floor surface for concrete is *terrazzo*. A separate layer of concrete is placed over the concrete floor with marble chips pressed into the top surface before it sets. After the concrete sets, the surface is ground and polished to a smooth finish.

MASONRY

Masonry construction is the process of building with brick, concrete block, terra cotta, stone, or other material laid as units with a mortar binding them together. The early struggle to provide shelter included using stone that could be carried or pieces of sod that could be arranged to form a wall. Tradesworkers eventually learned to mix clay and water and dry the mixture in the sun to make rough bricks somewhat uniform in size and shape. These adobe bricks made it possible for the tradesworkers to make a better wall with less work and frustration. Eventually, they learned how to make bricks by burning clay and cut stone, marble, and granite to precision size.

In modern times, new units have been added to masonry, including concrete block and facing tile.

MAXIMUM ALLOWABLE UNIT STRESSES (POUNDS PER SQUARE INCH)					
SPECIES AND COMMERCIAL GRADE	EXTREME FIBER STRESS AND TENSION PARALLEL TO GRAIN	HORIZONTAL SHEAR	COMPRESSION ACROSS GRAIN	COMPRESSION PARALLEL TO GRAIN	MODULUS OF ELASTICITY
Cypress	1300	120	300	900	1,200,000
Douglas Fir	1300	100	325	1200	1,600,000
Plywood (Fir) Built-up Section	1500	100	400	1500	1,600,000
Laminated Timber	1100	75	400	1500	1,600,000
Hemlock	1000	90	350	1100	1,400,000
Oak	1300	120	600	1000	1,500,000
Redwood	1100	75	300	1000	1,200,000
Southern Pine Longleaf	1300	120	450	1000	1,600,000
Shortleaf	1100	120	400	900	1,600,000
Spruce Sitka or Eastern	1000	75	300	800	1,200,000

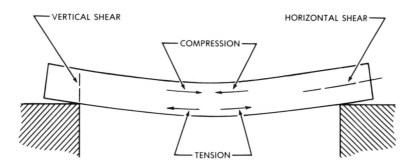

Figure 2-5. Wood for construction jobs is selected based upon special characteristics.

The cost of laying individual units to make a wall is expensive because of the time factor. Manufacturers have developed other sizes of masonry material to produce varying wall textures and appearances and respond to the demand for more cost-effective materials. For example, jumbo brick (4″ × 4″ × 12″) is becoming increasingly popular because of the area that can be covered as compared to an equivalent number of standard brick, which would require the same time to lay. Other factors such as low maintenance cost, weather resistance, and good appearance keep masonry among the most popular methods of construction today.

Brick

Architects only rarely show individual bricks on drawings. This occurs when the architect is drawing a large-scale plan or sectional detail view where brick is involved or when the brick mason is to lay the brick in a particular decorative pattern. Brick is indicated on small-scale plan views, such as floor plans, by 45° hatched lines which show the type of brick in the symbol itself. For example, common brick is shown on plan views with a series of 45° parallel, diagonal lines spaced apart. Face brick is shown with the 45° lines spaced closer together and

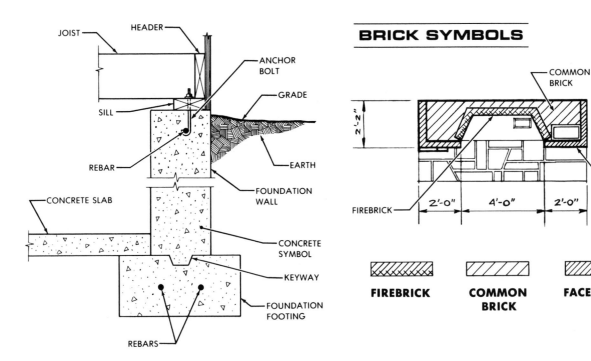

Figure 2-6. The symbol for concrete is a series of small dots and random triangles.

BRICK SYMBOLS

Figure 2-7. The symbol for brick in plan views is a series of inclined, parallel lines, or cross-hatched lines.

firebrick is shown with 45° cross-hatched lines. See Figure 2-7.

On exterior elevation views, horizontal lines are used to indicate brick. A notation of the type of brick used, such as *face brick* or *building brick* (common brick) is lettered in open space between the horizontal lines. See Figure 2-8.

The raw materials for bricks are clay and shale found in many parts of the country. The clay or shale is ground and mixed with water to the proper consistency then placed in molds and formed into bricks. Brick can also be made by the extrusion process. The material is forced through a die and cut off to make individual bricks. The brick made by

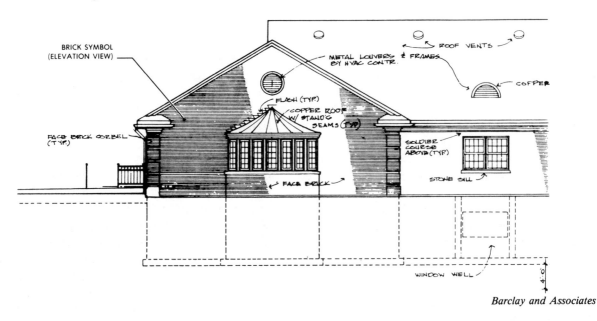

Barclay and Associates

Figure 2-8. The symbol for brick in elevation views is a series of horizontal lines. The type of brick is specified in the specs.

either process is dried to the proper moisture content before it is placed in the kiln. It is then burned at a high temperature from 40 to 150 hours. Building brick is made of local clay or shale and may have several colors. Face brick is made of select clay so that distinctive uniform colors will result. It is also treated to give it a special surface. Firebrick is made of clay found in only a few areas. Firebrick has the property of withstanding high temperatures without disintegrating.

The size of the brick and the width or thickness of the mortar joints must be considered when laying bricks because the units must work out to specified dimensions, both horizontally and vertically. Face brick is nominally 2″ × 4″ × 8″ but its actual size is approximately 2¼″ × 3¾″ × 8″. Dimensions of face brick and other types of brick are shown in Figure 2-9. These dimensions were established before the new measuring system, called *modular measure*, was adopted and will continue to be used until it is phased out and modular size brick is specified for all jobs.

Modular measure is a system in which buildings are designed and materials manufactured to fit a grid based on a 4″ square (or cube). The 4″ unit is a *module*. Figure 2-10 shows the new regulation brick sizes that are used with each particular thickness of

MODULAR BRICK

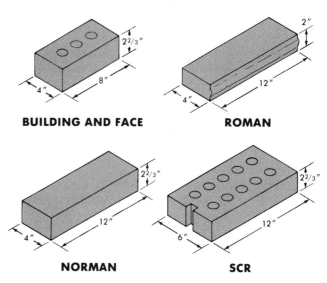

**ACTUAL SIZES FOR
MODULAR BUILDING AND FACE BRICK**

FOR ¼″ JOINT 2⅜″ × 3¾″ × 7¾″
FOR ⅜″ JOINT 2¼″ × 3⅝″ × 7⅝″
FOR ½″ JOINT 2³/₁₆″ × 3½″ × 7½″

Brick Institute of America

Figure 2-10. Modular brick varies in size depending upon the width of the mortar joint.

mortar joint to achieve the modular concept. The *SCR brick* is designed so that a 6″ load-bearing wall can be constructed with a single wythe. Core holes reduce the weight and a notch in one end provides a means to anchor window or door frames. The amount of time spent in laying SCR units is less than conventional brick. *Modular brick* is laid so that every third horizontal joint falls on a multiple of 4″. See Figure 2-11. Modular and SCR brick will become more common as the design of buildings calls for modular measure.

The architect is careful to locate the windows so that the window sills and members over the head of the windows (*lintels*) fall in place, using full brick courses, if at all possible. On tall buildings, the arrangement of brick in courses is very important because the floor-to-floor height is fixed and the brickwork must fit the spaces exactly. The architect also tries to keep in mind that it is expensive for the bricklayer to do too much cutting of brick. If horizontal measurements can be kept to widths that divide approximately into full or half brick, money is saved.

STANDARD BRICK

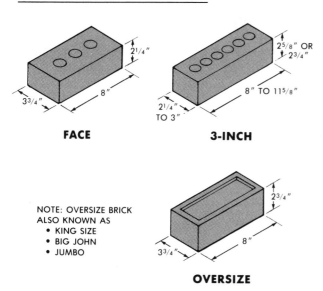

NOTE: OVERSIZE BRICK
ALSO KNOWN AS
• KING SIZE
• BIG JOHN
• JUMBO

Brick Institute of America

Figure 2-9. Standard brick sizes may vary in different localities.

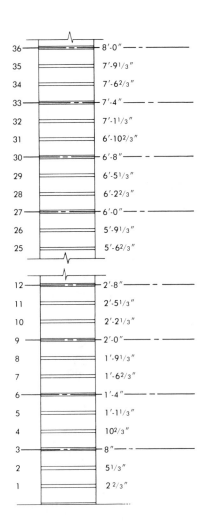

Figure 2-11. Modular brick is laid so that every third joint falls on a multiple of 4″.

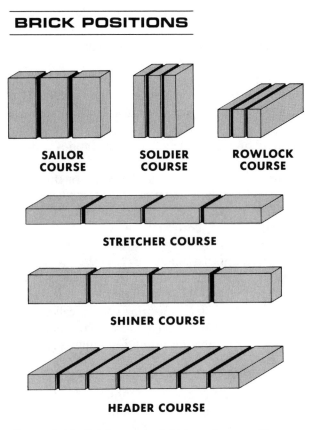

Figure 2-12. Brick may be laid in various positions.

The mason must make frequent reference to the prints to make sure the measurements work out accurately. Corners and openings must be perfectly vertical (plumb) and each course perfectly level. The mortar joints must be uniform in order that heights will be accurate as the wall is built up. The brick joints should coincide with the bottom of window sills, the tops of windows, and floor levels. The brickwork should be laid out carefully for the openings and corners in order to use as many complete units as possible.

The various positions for brickwork as it appears on the face of the wall are shown in Figure 2-12. When the architect wishes to use brick in a special way, the information is usually included with a note in the specifications by showing an example of the brickwork on the elevation views, or by a large-scale detail view. For example, a window sill laid in row-

lock fashion or the brick over a window laid as a soldier course might be shown on the elevation views or as a detail drawing.

Brick can be laid in various *bonds* (patterns) that make the wall more interesting. The common bond is the most frequently used. It has a header course every sixth course to tie the front and back *wythes* (rows) of brick together. See Figure 2-13. The English and Flemish bonds are used in buildings or garden walls when special or architectural effects consistent with the building itself are desired. The English bond is made with alternate header and stretcher courses. The Flemish bond is made with alternate headers and stretchers in each course. The headers tie the wall together. Stack bond is used mainly for decorative rather than structural purposes. It is used as brick veneer or as a garden wall. When brick is used with other backing units, such as concrete block or structural tile, metal ties are laid in the mortar joints to fasten the two parts together. Concrete block made to receive the headers serves this function also.

Brick Veneer. Brick veneer has become common in light construction. A brick veneer building is essentially a frame building with a skin of one wythe brick. The brick wall and the frame wall are separated by 1″ air space for ventilation and moisture control. Refer to Figure 2-4. The brick part of the wall and the frame part are held together by galvanized ties that are laid in the brick joints and extended across the air space to be nailed into the face of the wood wall sheathing.

Stone

Stone is indicated on plan views by a sprinkling of dots. Lines indicate cast stone or rubble. Refer to Figure 2-1. It is shown on elevation views with lines to resemble the stones. Natural stone is used as a structural material and is generally backed up by brick, structural clay tile, concrete block, or concrete. It is used in thin pieces as wall facing over walls of other masonry. Natural stone is desirable because of its color, compressive strength, and its beauty, whether used as rough stones or with a smooth, cut- and-polished surface. Some of the more common types of stone used are granite, limestone, sandstone, marble, and slate. Cast stone, made of concrete, shares many of the fine qualities of natural stone and is manufactured with relative ease.

The size of pieces of stone varies greatly and is directly related to the effect desired. Rough stones are fashioned by the mason with greater regard for their usefulness than their dimensions or shape. Cut stone may be uniform in size but can be made in a number of sizes and shapes for use in the same wall. In working out details of a stone wall, the architect keeps in mind the type of backing to be used, either brick or concrete block. The horizontal joints must fall so that ties can be used at intervals between the stone and the back-up material.

Stone Classifications. The most common classifications of stone available for building are *rubble, squared stone,* and *ashlar.* Rubble is any rough stone found locally as field stone or blasted in a quarry. Squared stone is rough stone made approximately square either at the quarry or on the job. Ashlar is stone cut to precise measurements according to plan. When a building is to use rubble or squared stone, the architect shows the general character of the stonework on the elevation drawings. No detailed plans are drawn up. The stone mason's skill and artistry are used in bringing about the general effect. When ashlar stonework is to be used, the architect draws the elevations and detail views showing each stone in place. The stone company's drafters make shop drawings closely related to the architect's prints, giving the size, finish, and anchors to

BRICK BONDS

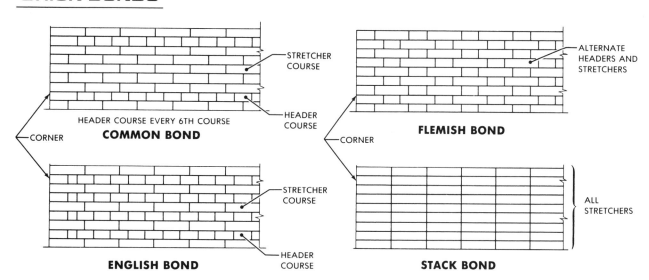

Figure 2-13. Brick may be laid in various bonds.

be used. They assign a number to each piece. The shop drawings are submitted to the architect before the stones are cut. See Figure 2-14.

Another method of classifying stonework is in the way it is laid. The simplest divisions are *coursed, broken range,* and *random.* Refer to Figure 2-14. Course stonework is laid so that pieces of stone are arranged in continuous horizontal rows with vertical joints in line on alternate rows. Each course can be made of a different thickness of stone as long as the mortar joints are unbroken horizontal lines. The range is a horizontal row of stones extending across the width of the wall. No attempt is made to line up the joints vertically when the courses are broken. When the range is broken, the horizontal mortar joints break against larger stones. Random stonework is laid with stones of different sizes with-

out maintaining courses or ranges. When working with ashlar stone, even in a random arrangement, the mason is required to follow the prints carefully to achieve precise mortar joints. The anchoring devices specified are designed to provide support and safety.

A mason who works with rubble or roughly squared stones must have special skills. In some types of walls, the mason takes rubble and makes a beautiful arrangement that has no coursed or range effect. If the plans call for roughly squared stones, the mason selects each stone from a pile. With a minimum amount of cutting, the stones are laid in the wall in a coursed, broken range, or random arrangement.

Concrete Block

Concrete block construction is shown in elevation views with the courses laid out with a sprinkling of dots and small circles or triangles to indicate concrete and with a series of lines to distinguish it from monolithic concrete. Refer to Figure 2-1.

Standard modular block is made $7\frac{5}{8}'' \times 7\frac{5}{8}'' \times 15\frac{5}{8}''$ so that when laid in a wall with allowances for mortar joints, it will measure $8'' \times 8'' \times 16''$. Concrete block is laid to fit the $4''$ module of modular measure and can be used to back up brick or other materials. The mortar joints in the facing material come out to the same level so that metal ties can be put in place in the joints to bridge the two materials.

Blocks are made with hollow cores to reduce weight to a minimum yet provide the desired strength and fire-resistance. Core size, shape, and number vary. Two-core blocks are most commonly used because they are lightweight and easy to produce. They are available in widths of $2''$, $3''$, $4''$, $6''$, $8''$, $10''$, and $12''$ and in heights of $4''$ and $8''$. Because of the many sizes available, all thickness can be easily adjusted to the desired dimension. One wythe of modular blocks (stretchers) is used to form foundations or exterior walls. The narrower blocks, including $8''$ block, back up brick or stone. Blocks of two different thicknesses can be used to make a wall of the desired dimensions.

Concrete Block Types. Concrete blocks are available in various shapes to serve various functions. See Figure 2-15. The most commonly used building

STONE BONDS

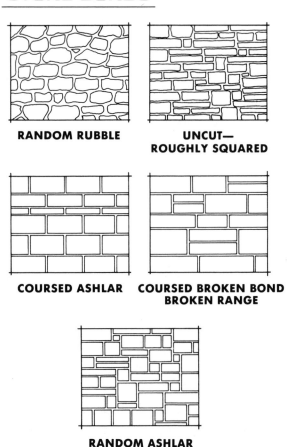

RANDOM RUBBLE

UNCUT— ROUGHLY SQUARED

COURSED ASHLAR

COURSED BROKEN BOND BROKEN RANGE

RANDOM ASHLAR

Figure 2-14. Elevation views of stone show whether it is rubble, roughly squared, or ashlar. The type of bond is also shown.

CONCRETE BLOCK

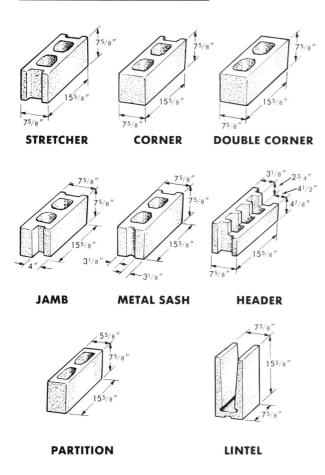

STRETCHER **CORNER** **DOUBLE CORNER**

JAMB **METAL SASH** **HEADER**

PARTITION **LINTEL**

Figure 2-15. Concrete blocks fit modular measure. Core size, shape, and number vary. Two-core block is most commonly used.

blocks are the *stretcher* (used for running walls), the *corner* block (used for square corners), and the *bull-nose* block (used for rounded corners). *Solid top* blocks finish off the top of the wall and provide a flat bearing surface for wood framing members or brick or stone masonry. The *double corner* blocks are used to make columns, piers, and pilasters. *Jamb* and *metal sash* blocks are placed at the sides of windows and doors. *Header* blocks back up brick or stone. The header course of brick or stone fits into the shelf on the concrete block to hold the wall together. *Partition* blocks either back up other masonry or form partitions. *Lintel* blocks are used over openings to make bond beams. The lintel blocks are laid in a row, rebars are suspended in the hollow

of the blocks, and then the hollow is filled with concrete. Lightweight blocks, made of concrete with one of several lightweight aggregates, are also available.

Miscellaneous Masonry Products

Decorative concrete blocks form interesting designs when laid in a wall. They are used to provide privacy for patios or a screen between rooms. They are not intended for load-bearing structural purposes.

Clay facing tile (not to be confused with ceramic facing tile) are masonry units made of clay baked in a kiln. They are used for interior facing material. Some types are given a high glaze achieved by coating the faces with salt, chemicals, ceramic glazes, or enamel before firing. Their major use is in situations where sanitation or moisture is a problem. Food manufacturing plants, locker rooms, and swimming pools are some examples calling for the use of clay facing tile.

Structural facing tile is also made of baked clay. It is made in large units and may be used for load-bearing walls. One surface is faced with glaze and color. The color and glaze are achieved by coating the tile with salt, chemicals, ceramic glazes, or enamel before firing it in the kiln. Structural tile is nominally 6" × 12" and 2", 6", or 8" deep. A number of thinner shapes are available for fitting around windows, door openings, and base and corner trim.

Terra cotta is a masonry building material made by burining molded units of clay on a kiln. The symbol used on plan views for terra cotta is similar to the symbol for cast stone. Terra cotta is primarily used for wall coping, although it also provides colorful exterior wall facings. It is finished with color and glaze in the same manner as facing tile. Wall coping is made in pieces to fit the tops of walls that have different thicknesses and are made up to 36" long. See Figure 2-16. The pieces of terra cotta are fastened to the face of the building by means of mortar placed between the pieces and the backup material. Some are anchored with wire or metal ties. Terra cotta facing material is generally available in several large sizes, as specified by the architect.

Terra cotta is among the most colorful and beautiful building materials available, but it must be manufactured so that the surface can withstand the weather in the area. It must be applied to the building carefully to prevent moisture and frost from getting between or behind the facing.

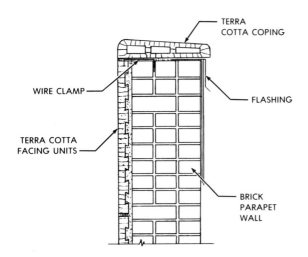

Figure 2-16. Terra cotta may be used for wall coping and facing.

Ceramic tile is made of baked clay with a glazed surface. It is available in many colors and degrees of glaze. Ceramic tile is shown on elevation views as squares or rectangles. These may be drawn to scale, showing their exact arrangement, or a small section of the wall may be drawn to indicate tile. When large scale sectional views are shown, tile is indicated by wavy cross lines. Refer to Figure 2-1.

One type of ceramic tile, called *ceramic wall tile*, is supplied in units that are $4^1/4''$ square, $6''$ square, and $4^1/4'' \times 6''$. The nominal thickness is $5/16''$. These large wall units are laid individually in plaster or adhesive. Plaster or grout is spread over the surface to fill the joints and is wiped off. Tile is also available in large assembled units with flexible joints so they can be applied more quickly.

Mosaic tile is used to cover walls or floors. It is available in sizes of $1''$ square, $2''$ square, and $1'' \times 2''$. The tile is glued to a mesh in $1'$ squares with even spaces between each tile. The units of tile are embedded in mortar or adhesive and made perfectly level. A grout is then spread over the surface to fill the joints. The excess is wiped off the surface.

Quarry tile is made from natural clay and shale and is used for floors and base trim. It is supplied in red or dark tones and smooth or rough surfaces. The most common sizes are $6'' \times 6''$ and $4'' \times 8''$, with a thickness of either $1/2''$ or $3/4''$.

METAL

There is no special symbol for metal when it is shown on elevation drawings. Information about metal is usually covered with a note or described in the specifications. In plan views or sectional views, the metal parts are often so thin it would be difficult to draw them with any type of symbol. They are drawn as solid lines. However, in large-scale section views the various metal symbols shown in Figure 2-1 are used. Structural members such as beams and girders are shown with a dot-dash line on plan views.

Metal plays an increasingly important part in the construction industry. It is primarily used for the framework of tall buildings, but it is becoming increasingly common in residential framing as joists and studs. Metal is used in windows, doors, exterior trim, the facing of buildings, and the covering of roofs. Metal gutters and metal flashing protect all types of buildings from water damage. Concrete is used extensively in modern building construction because of the use of rebars. Metal is widely used in many phases of building construction, from conduit, pipe, and ducts, to electrical appliances and fixtures.

Structural Steel

Structural steel is available in basic shapes to serve as load-bearing units in building construction. See Figure 2-17. The manufacturers of structural steel must roll the members with close tolerance and check the chemical properties constantly so that the finished product will have the required strength. Architects and engineers can readily solve design problems because most types of steel members are available in several sizes and weights.

W beams are described by their nominal dimensions over the flanges and the weight per foot. Dimensions vary with each weight and size of beams. An example of a description for a W beam is W 14 $\times$ 34. The size over the flanges is $14''$. The weight per running foot is 34 pounds. W 14 $\times$ 30 is another W beam with the same basic dimensions. The difference in weight (and therefore, strength) is accounted for by the flange and web thickness. The height over the flanges is $13^7/8''$ instead of $14''$. The nominal size is $14''$; however, $14''$ W beams actually vary from $13^3/4''$ to $14^3/4''$. Dimensions for other beams can be found in steel construction manuals.

Steel angles are made with either equal or unequal legs. They are described by the width of the legs measured along the back of the angle and the thickness of the legs instead of the weight per foot.

STEEL SHAPES

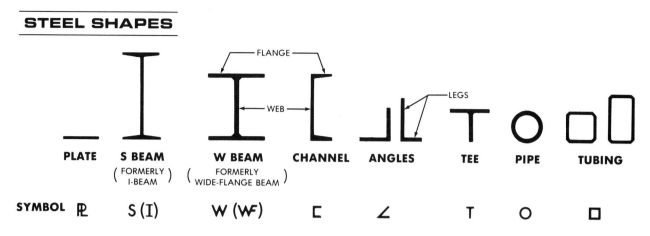

Figure 2-17. Symbols designate typical steel shapes used in light construction.

For example, a ∠ 6 × 6 × ⁷/₈ steel angle measures 6″ along the back of each leg, which is ⁷/₈″ thick. See Figure 2-18.

Aluminum is manufactured in a number of sizes and structural shapes similar to steel shapes. Both steel and aluminum are used for framing residences and other small buildings. The metal members are used for floor joists and wall studs.

Rebars are shown on plan views with solid lines and on sectional views with filled-in circles. Rebars are used in concrete construction to help counteract the tension and bending stresses in beams and floors and compressive stresses in columns. The identifying marks on the bars indicate the manufacturer, the type of steel, the grade (or tensile yield point) and the diameter. See Figure 2-19. The size of rebars is given in ⅛ths of an inch. A number 4 bar is ⁴/₈″, or ½″, in diameter. Projections on the bars are called *deformations* (ridges). These ridges keep the bars from pulling through the concrete. Rebars are bent in the fabricating shop to the shape specified. Both bent and straight bars serve specific functions in the structure.

Concrete floors are reinforced with *welded wire fabric* (WWF), which is a mesh of heavy wire laid before the concrete pour, designed to strengthen the concrete. Welded wire fabric is arranged in a square or rectangular pattern and welded at each intersection. It is commercially available in sheets and rolls.

Two types of welded wire fabric are *smooth* and *deformed*. Anchoring qualities in concrete are achieved by welded intersections of smooth wire. Anchoring of deformed wire is achieved by either 2, 4, or 6 lines of deformations and the welded intersections of the fabric. The American Society for Testing and Materials (ASTM) uses the letter "W" to designate smooth wire. The letter "D" is used to designate deformed wire. Smooth wire has a lower tensile strength and yield strength and a higher shear strength than deformed wire.

Welded wire fabric is designated by two numbers and two letter-number combinations. For example, in the designation 6 × 6—W1.4 × W1.4, the first two numbers, 6 × 6, indicate spacing of wire in inches. The first number gives the longitudinal (length)

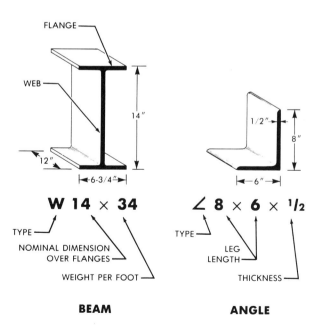

Figure 2-18. Steel beams and angles are designated by abbreviated descriptions.

REBARS

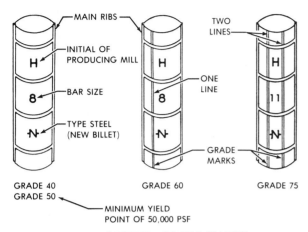

LINE SYSTEM—GRADE MARKS

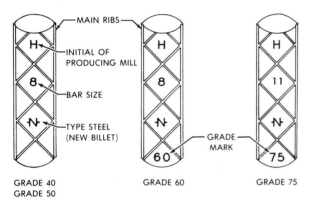

NUMBER SYSTEM—GRADE MARKS

Concrete Reinforcing Steel Institute

Figure 2-19. Rebars show manufacturer's identification, size, type of steel, and tensile yield point. The grade is the tensile yield point.

spacing and the second number gives the transversal (width) spacing. The letter-number combinations, W1.4 × W1.4, give the type and size of wire. Both of these wires (W) are smooth. The first 1.4 designation gives longitudinal wire size and the second 1.4 gives transversal wire size. Both of these 1.4 wires are .042 sq. in. in cross-sectional area. See Figure 2-20.

An older method used to designate welded wire fabric indicates wire size by its gauge. For example, the designation WWF 6 × 8 × #6 represents welded wire fabric with wires spaced 6″ apart longi-

tudinally, 8″ apart transversally, and made of #6 gauge wire. Another older method gives the wire gauge in two numbers. For example, the designation WWF 6 × 8 × 6 × 6 represents the same size wire as in the preceding example.

Open web steel joists are made of steel angles with bars bent back and forth between the upper and lower sets of angles. The lower chord of open web steel joists may be made of two round bars. These joists are used extensively in light construction to support floors and roofs. See Figure 2-21. Open web steel joists is discussed in greater detail in chapter 6, Types of Light Frame Construction.

Thin gauge metal is frequently used in buildings for weather protection, ductwork, structural purposes, facing, and ornamental work. The thinner metal sheets can be cut and bent with ease and shaped into gutters and downspouts. Flashing made of thin metal is used to protect wood and masonry parts from water damage. Ducts used in the heating and cooling plant are also shaped from thin metal. Metal siding has become popular because it is easy to apply and its finish virtually eliminates the need for painting.

Heavier gauge metal is cold rolled into shapes used for structural purposes, such as wall studs, floor joists, and window and door frames. Much of the sheet metal is steel galvanized with a coating of zinc to prevent corrosion. Light structural members are furnished unfinished, with a coating (black) to prevent rusting. Aluminum, bronze, and steel alloys are used extensively as curtain walls on tall buildings. The metal is in sheet form and treated with finishes and coatings that are colorful, decorative, and weather-resistant. The same base metals are particularly useful in the manufacture of parts for windows, window and door frames, and ornamental metal work. The shapes are made in long lengths by a process called *extrusion*. The metal is forced through an aperture (die opening) that is shaped like the cross section of the desired product.

A major use of steel, cast iron, and copper is in the manufacture of pipe and pipe fittings. Piping for plumbing and heating is not generally shown on prints for light construction. However, a plumbing diagram is often included showing the drainage system. Single lines represent each pipe. Pipe is described by inch sizes, corresponding roughly to the inside diameter. See Figure 2-22. The water diagram is drawn as an isometric drawing. Pipe diameters are given along the various runs of pipe.

WELDED WIRE FABRIC

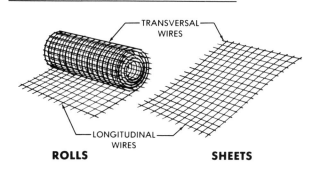

ROLLS **SHEETS**

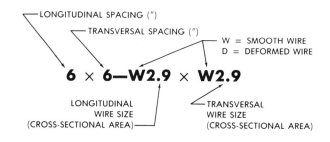

LONGITUDINAL SPACING (") TRANSVERSAL SPACING (") W = SMOOTH WIRE D = DEFORMED WIRE

6 × 6—W2.9 × W2.9

LONGITUDINAL WIRE SIZE (CROSS-SECTIONAL AREA) TRANSVERSAL WIRE SIZE (CROSS-SECTIONAL AREA)

WIRE SIZE COMPARISON

W & D SIZE NUMBER		AREA (SQ. IN.)	NOMINAL DIAMETER (IN.)	AMERICAN STEEL & WIRE GAUGE NUMBER
SMOOTH	DEFORMED			
W8.5		.085	.329	
W8	D8	.080	.319	
W7.5		.075	.309	
		.074	.3065	1/0
W7	D7	.070	.298	
W6.5		.065	.288	
		.063	.283	1
W6	D6	.060	.276	
W5.5		.055	.264	
		.054	.2625	2

COMMON STOCK SIZES OF WELDED WIRE FABRIC

STYLE DESIGNATION		STEEL AREA SQ. IN. PER FT.		WEIGHT APPROX. LBS. PER 100 S.F.
NEW DESIGNATION (BY W-NUMBER)	OLD DESIGNATION (BY STEEL WIRE GAUGE)	LONGIT.	TRANS.	
ROLLS				
6 × 6—W1.4 × W1.4	6 × 6—10 × 10	.028	.028	21
6 × 6—W2.0 × W2.0	6 × 6—8 × 8*	.040	.040	29
6 × 6—W2.9 × W2.9	6 × 6—6 × 6	.058	.058	42
SHEETS				
6 × 6—W2.9 × W2.9	6 × 6—6 × 6	.058	.058	42
6 × 6—W4.0 × W4.0	6 × 6—4 × 4	.080	.080	58
6 × 6—W5.5 × W5.5	6 × 6—2 × 2**	.110	.110	80

*Exact W-number size for 8 gauge is W2.1.
**Exact W-number size for 2 gauge is W5.4.

Wire Reinforcement Institute

Figure 2-20. Welded wire fabric (WWF) is designated by a numbering system related to the cross-sectional area of the wire.

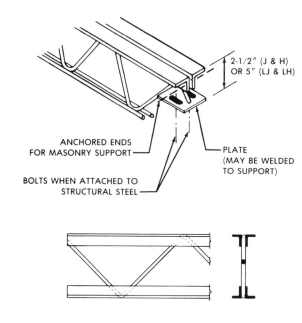

Figure 2-21. Open web steel joists support wide spans in light steel construction.

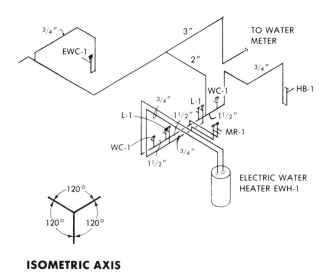

ISOMETRIC AXIS

Figure 2-22. Piping is shown with one-line isometric drawings.

INSULATION

The symbols for the different types of insulation are shown in Figure 2-1. The most common types of insulation used in light construction are the loose-fill or the batt types. They are used in the hollow parts of frame walls and over the ceiling in the attic space. See Figure 2-23. Batt-type insulation consists of mineral fiber, vegetable fiber, or glass wool covered by waterproof paper made to fit exactly between studs and joists. It is supplied in short lengths called *batts* or in continuous rolls.

Loose-fill is granular mineral wool or pellets made from glass, slag, rock, or expanded mica. It is poured in place between joists over the ceiling in new buildings. Loose-fill insulation is poured or blown into the stud spaces of old buildings that have no insulation. It is used because it is very difficult to apply batts in an already enclosed wall space.

Rigid insulation board sheathing is made of wood fibers pressed to a thickness of $1/2''$ or $25/32''$ and usually impregnated with bituminous waterproofing. It covers the outside wall as sheathing. It also provides some insulation. The insulating value, however, is not great. Polyurethane is used as sheets to replace conventional wall sheathing or is forced into stud spaces by pressure.

Insulation is rated by *R value*, which is the resistance to heat flow. As R numbers of insulation increase, the resistance value of the insulation also increases. For example, recommended R values for dwellings in the North Central portion of the United States call for the following:

Walls 19R
Floors 22R
Ceilings 33R

PLASTICS

Plastics are usually manufactured as thin material and are shown on prints by a solid line or by two lines spaced close together to indicate the two faces. When the material has any amount of thickness, the architect may use a symbol of choice. A designation or note is included, with an arrow pointing to the material in place.

Plastics serve many purposes in the construction industry. A number of products are available, each having different physical and chemical properties. Plastics are most commonly used for countertops and wall and floor coverings. These products are extremely durable and waterproof. They are available in many colors and decorator designs such as woodgrains and patterns. Countertops and cabinet facings are manufactured using plastic laminate veneers. These veneers are available in stock sizes up to $5' \times 12'$ and may be ordered in many smaller sizes as specified.

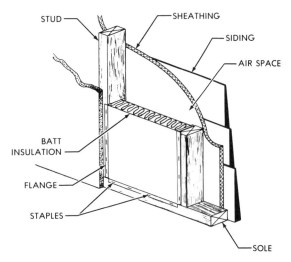

BATT INSULATION IS STAPLED TO STUDS

Owens Corning Fiberglas

**LOOSE-FILL INSULATION IS
BLOWN BETWEEN CEILING JOISTS**

Figure 2-23. Batt or loose-fill insulation is placed between framing members.

Plastic coatings in several forms are bonded to sheets of hardboard (fiberboard) and make attractive interior wall coverings. Resilient flooring made from vinyl tile and sheet goods is used in kitchens, dining areas, hallways, and entries.

Translucent plastic is used for ceiling light panels, light fixtures, and skylights. Large plastic sheets of polyethylene film are fitted over sand or gravel fill before a concrete slab is placed. This serves as a waterproofing agent. Other plastic materials are used instead of flashing and caulking where two different materials that make up part of the building meet, or where water might seep into a wall. Plastic gutters, downspouts, and fittings are becoming increasingly popular because they do not rust and their color is even throughout. Exterior siding, rain gutters, and downspouts are available in solid vinyl. These can be cut and assembled using simple hand tools and adhesives. They are almost indestructible and never need painting. Siding and the exterior parts of windows, doors, and window and door frames are available with a vinyl covering bonded to the wood. This provides permanent weather resistance and a colorfast surface.

Plastic pipe and fittings have been assembled by cementing and used as drainage for many years. Now plastics are accepted in many parts of the country for general plumbing. Plastic and fiberglass have been combined to make lightweight tub and shower units as integral parts of the walls, eliminating the need for further wall finish.

GLASS

Figure 2-1 shows how glass appears on elevation, plan, and sectional views. Usually the architect shows glass in elevations as blank rectangles. Because glass is thin, it is shown on plan views and sectional views as a thin line. When the details are drawn at large scale or full size, glass is shown with a series of closely drawn parallel lines.

Sheet window glass is supplied in three thickness classifications: single strength ($3/32''$ thick), double strength ($1/8''$ thick), and heavy sheet (from $3/16''$ to $7/16''$ thick). *Plate glass* is ground and polished to have a very smooth surface. It is generally manufactured in $1/8''$ and $1/4''$ thicknesses but can be obtained up to $1/2''$ thick. Plate glass is available in bronze, gray, or blue-green tints. The difference between sheet glass and plate glass is in the manufac-

turing process. Sheet glass is made in a continuous sheet and cut to size without further processing. Plate glass is rolled out and polished.

Insulating glass is made of two pieces of glass (usually sheet or plate glass) separated by a sealed air space. The edges are sealed on all four sides by a closure of either glass or metal. A typical piece of insulating glass is made of two sheets of double strength glass ($1/8''$) with a $3/16''$ air space and a glass closure. It measures $7/16''$ thick.

Patterned glass has one side finished with a fine grid or an unpolished surface so that it is translucent. It is used in office partitions and for doors and windows when privacy is desired. *Cathedral glass* (art glass) is available in a wide range of colors and with several surface treatments. It is cut into small pieces then reassembled with the use of lead channels to make artistic color effects. The windows made from cathedral glass are often used in churches and public buildings. Because the assembly process is a highly skilled art involving considerable time, the windows are very expensive. *Laminated glass* is used in schools and other public buildings where safety is a prime factor. It is the same glass that is used for automobiles. Several layers of glass are bonded together with plastic sheets between each layer. *Wire glass* is glass embedded with wire mesh to provide some measure of safety and security. It will not shatter like other glass because the wire mesh holds it together. Mirrors are included among the glass products used in light construction.

Glass block is occasionally used to provide light in rooms when ventilation is not a factor. Glass block must be laid carefully so that it is waterproof in the wall. It is not a weight-bearing material. Lintels of steel are provided so that the weight of the masonry above will not rest on the glass block. Glass block is available in $6''$, $8''$, and $12''$ (nominal) squares in assorted thicknesses. These sizes allow for a $1/4''$ mortar joint.

GYPSUM PRODUCTS

Figure 2-1 shows that the symbol for plaster in elevation views is a sprinkling of small dots. This is optional. In plan views there is no special symbol for frame walls to be finished with lath and plaster or drywall. When a brick wall is to be plastered, a line is added to represent the thickness of the lath and plaster. A solid plaster wall is repre-

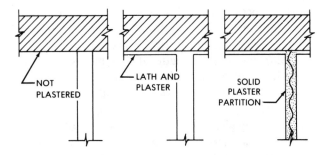

Figure 2-24. A line indicates lath and plaster on a masonry wall. A solid plaster partition is shown with wavy lines and dots.

sented by a wavy line and a sprinkling of dots. See Figure 2-24. When lath and plaster are shown in large sectional views, the symbol used is an overall pattern of dots.

The major uses of gypsum are in the manufacture of gypsum lath, wallboard, and plaster. Gypsum lath is a base for plaster coating. Gypsum wallboard is used in the drywall system.

Gypsum lath consists of an air-entrained core of gypsum between two layers of fibrous absorbent paper. It comes in thicknesses of $3/8''$ and $1/2''$. The overall size of the pieces is $18'' \times 48''$. The lath is fastened to the studs with clips or nailed.

The traditional method of plastering (now required only when expanded wire lath is used for lathing) is the three-coat method. After the lath is fastened to the studs and joists, a *scratch coat* is applied. This is either a lime putty or gypsum-type plaster with fiber in its composition. The surface is scratched to provide good bond for the next coat. The second coat, which is the *brown coat*, contains hair or other fiber. The *finish coat* presents a smooth, level, white finish. Depending on local ordinances, one or two coats of finished plaster are used over the gypsum lath. Exterior *stucco*, a combination of gypsum plaster and portland cement, is put on over metal-mesh lath in three coats of different compositions.

The *drywall* system requires the use of gypsum wallboard. Drywall is a wall treatment that includes (1) the application of gypsum board panels to wood or metal studs, (2) the application of gypsum joint compound and paper tape to the joints, and (3) sanding and applying additional coats until a smooth

finish is achieved. The wallboard is a core of gypsum between two layers of special paper. Gypsum wallboard is the same as gypsum lath except in size and thickness. The thickness of gypsum wallboard ranges from $1/4''$ to $5/8''$. It is available in standard sheets of $4' \times 8'$, but longer lengths of $12'$ and $14'$ are more common because less installation time is required. The wallboard is applied to wood studs with nails and adhesive, or drywall screws (self-tapping screws). It is applied to steel studs with self-tapping screws. The screws are driven by a power screwdriver, which indents the surface of the wallboard without breaking the paper covering. When more than one layer of wallboard is applied to a wall, the first layer is nailed to the studs and the second layer is laminated at right angles to the first layer, using gypsum compound for adhesive. See Figure 2-25.

ROOFING

Roofing is usually shown on elevation drawings with a few parallel lines to indicate the rows of roofing material. A note describes the material. Additional information about the roofing and how it is to be applied is given in the specifications. Asphalt-saturated felt shingles covered with mineral granules is the most common type used in residential construction. It is generally supplied in strips of 3-tab shingles ($3'$ long and $12''$ wide). Roll roofing of the same material is available for special applications, such as on the roofs of barns and secondary buildings. Roofing is sold by the square, which covers 100 sq. ft. when it is laid. It is described by the weight per square. A typical order would be 10 squares of 235# felt roofing.

Other types of roofing are wood shingles and shakes, mineral asbestos, cement tile, and clay tile. Each of these is available as individual shingles. Flat and near-flat roofs require the use of a built-up roof which is made of several layers of asphalt- or tar-saturated felt. Each layer is mopped with hot asphalt or coal-tar pitch before placing the next layer. Gravel is spread over the top surface. Other flat roofs are constructed of steel panels welded to the ceiling joists and covered with sheets of rigid insulation, followed by rolls of rubber that are glued together at the seams and covered with gravel.

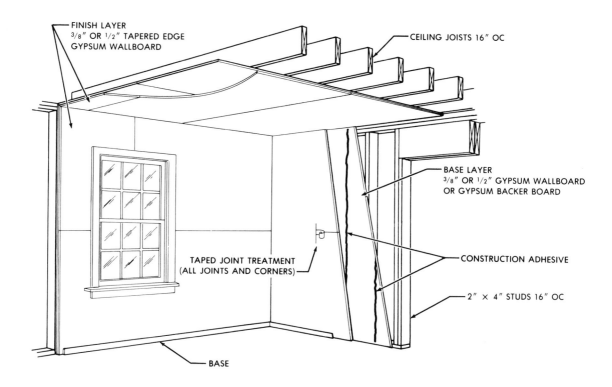

FINISH LAYER
³/₈″ OR ¹/₂″ TAPERED EDGE
GYPSUM WALLBOARD

CEILING JOISTS 16″ OC

BASE LAYER
³/₈″ OR ¹/₂″ GYPSUM WALLBOARD
OR GYPSUM BACKER BOARD

TAPED JOINT TREATMENT
(ALL JOINTS AND CORNERS)

CONSTRUCTION ADHESIVE

2″ × 4″ STUDS 16″ OC

BASE

Figure 2-25. Drywall is taped to cover the joints. In double-thick applications, drywall is placed at 90° over the base sheets.

Name _____ Date _____

True-False

T F   **1.** The cross-sectional size of today's 2 × 4 studs is $1^5/_8'' \times 3^5/_8''$.

T F   **2.** Maple and oak are often used for rough flooring.

T F   **3.** Concrete may be cast in place because of its plastic state.

T F   **4.** Concrete normally sets within 12 to 24 hours after pouring.

T F   **5.** SCR bricks require less laying time than conventional bricks.

T F   **6.** Concrete block has four cores.

T F   **7.** Terra cotta is made by cutting masonry sheets into squares or rectangles.

T F   **8.** Aluminum should not be used for framing dwellings and small commercial buildings.

T F   **9.** Rebars are shown in section views as filled-in circles.

T F   **10.** Drywall may be hung on metal stud walls with nails or screws.

Completion

_____   **1.** Electrical _____ are used to show outlets and receptacles on plans.

_____   **2.** Plywood always has a(n) _____ number of plies.

_____   **3.** _____ brick can withstand high heat without crumbling.

_____   **4.** _____ bricks of modular size are $2'' \times 4'' \times 12''$.

_____   **5.** _____ are used to attach brick veneer walls to the frame of a building.

_____   **6.** _____ are projections on rebars that keep them from pulling through concrete.

_____   **7.** Light structural sheet metal is generally galvanized with a coating of _____ to prevent corrosion.

_____   **8.** Countertops may be manufactured with plastic _____ veneers.

_____   **9.** The _____ coat is the first coat applied when plastering a wall.

_____   **10.** Ceramic tile has a(n) _____ surface developed during the firing process.

Multiple Choice

_____ 1. A plan view is a view looking _____ of a building.
A. at either end view
B. down on the inside
C. at the front or back view
D. from the inside to the outside

_____ 2. Adjacent layers of plywood _____.
A. are parallel to one another
B. are turned 90° to one another
C. either A or B
D. neither A nor B

_____ 3. The aggregate for concrete is usually _____.
A. slag and sand
B. cinders, slag, or vermiculite
C. crushed stone or gravel
D. none of the above

_____ 4. A Flemish bond has _____.
A. headers in each course
B. headers in no courses
C. headers and stretchers in each course
D. headers and stretchers in no courses

_____ 5. Three methods of laying stone are _____.
A. even, uneven, and interspersed
B. horizontal, vertical, and perpendicular
C. coursed, broken range, and random
D. none of the above

_____ 6. Reinforcing mesh is described by a note such as _____.
A. RM $6 \times 6 \times$ #8
B. RWM $6 \times 6 \times$ #6
C. WWF 6×6—1.4×1.4
D. WWF $6 \times 1.4 \times$ #6

_____ 7. Roofing is sold by the square, which covers _____ square feet when laid.
A. 72
B. 100
C. 144
D. 200

_____ 8. Regarding thin gauge metal, _____.
A. all thin gauge metal is galvanized
B. window parts are made of sheet metal
C. the symbol for flashing, when shown on elevation views, is closely drawn vertical lines
D. sheet metal is made by the extrusion process

_____ 9. Regarding glass, _____.
- A. insulating glass consists of two sheets of glass with an air space between, sealed all around by a glass or metal closure
- B. the symbol for glass in small or large section views is a heavy black line
- C. sheet glass and plate glass look the same and are made by the same process
- D. laminated glass is another name for insulating glass

_____ 10. Regarding symbols for wood, _____.
- A. the use of wavy lines or closely spaced parallel lines are accepted ways to show a wood frame wall on a floor plan
- B. the standardized symbol for a wood frame wall on a floor plan is a blank space between two lines
- C. a piece of structural wood shown in cross section is indicated by lines representing wood grain
- D. the number of plies in plywood shown in a section view is indicated by closely drawn parallel lines

Identification

_____ 1. Earth (section)

_____ 2. Brick (elevation)

_____ 3. Sheet metal flashing (elevation)

_____ 4. Finished wood member (section)

_____ 5. Concrete (section)

_____ 6. Lath and plaster (section)

_____ 7. Rebar (section)

_____ 8. Rough wood member (section)

_____ 9. Wood stud (plan)

_____ 10. Steel (section)

Multiple Choice

_____ 1. Regarding insulation, _____.
- A. loose-fill is the best material for use in walls of new buildings
- B. batts are made by enclosing insulating material in a waterproof paper covering provided with nailing flanges
- C. rigid wood fiber insulation board has enough insulating value to serve in place of batt insulation
- D. polyurethane sheets are installed over plywood sheathing

_____ 2. Regarding plastics, _____.
- A. plastic pipe and fittings are assembled in the same way as steel pipe
- B. polyethylene film is laid over gravel fill under s slab on the ground to provide a means to retain the concrete
- C. symbols for plastics have been standardized to one symbol
- D. solid vinyl exterior trim never needs painting

_____ 3. Regarding gypsum products, _____.
- A. gypsum lath and gypsum wallboard are the same
- B. three coats of plaster are required to finish a wall
- C. gypsum wallboard is applied in two parallel layers
- D. drywall is a term used for the application of gypsum wallboard with taped joints

_____ 4. Regarding concrete block, _____.
- A. the main use for concrete block is to back up brick or stone facing units
- B. concrete block is not intended to be used with modular measure
- C. the same symbol is used for concrete and for concrete block
- D. screen blocks are used for decorative purposes but not to carry weight

_____ 5. Regarding wood, _____.
- A. all types of wood have the same structural value to carry loads
- B. wood is not a satisfactory material for use as floor supporting members because of the flaws that occur during growth
- C. important considerations in choosing the wood for specific applications are cost and whether or not it will best serve the purpose
- D. wood of the same species is used for finish flooring, trim, furniture, and structural members

Trade Competency Test

Name   Date

Multiple Choice

_____   **1.** Diagonal lines intersecting on a wood member indicate _____.
A. a finished wood member on a plan view
B. a rough wood member on a section view
C. that wood members should not be used for the application shown
D. none of the above

_____   **2.** A concrete ratio of 1:2:4 indicates _____.
A. 1 part sand, 2 parts cement, and 4 parts aggregate
B. 1 part cement, 2 parts sand, and 4 parts aggregate
C. 1 part aggregate, 2 parts cement, and 4 parts sand
D. none of the above

_____   **3.** Modular brick fit a square based on a _____ ″ unit.
A. 3
B. 4
C. 6
D. 8

_____   **4.** Wythe refers to the _____ of brick walls.
A. height
B. depth
C. length
D. none of the above

_____   **5.** The actual size of standard modular concrete block is _____.
A. $7^1/2''\times 7^1/2''\times 15^1/2''$
B. $7^5/8''\times 7^5/8''\times 15^5/8''$
C. $7^3/4''\times 7^3/4''\times 15^3/4''$
D. $8''\times 8''\times 16''$

_____   **6.** A beam designated W 12 × 30 has _____.
A. one flange 12″ wide and 30″ long
B. two flanges 12″ wide and 30″ long
C. one flange 12″ wide and weighs 30 lbs/ft
D. two flanges 12″ wide and weighs 30 lbs/ft

7. Open web steel joists are used in light construction to support _____.
   A. floors
   B. roofs
   C. both A and B
   D. neither A nor B

8. The diameters of rebars are given in _____.
   A. eighths of an inch
   B. tenths of an inch
   C. decimal sizes
   D. none of the above

9. In the extrusion process of making metal shapes, metal is _____.
   A. pulled through a die
   B. forced through a die
   C. pounded into shape
   D. poured into a mold

10. Roofing is generally shown on elevation drawings with _____ lines.
    A. hidden
    B. dashed
    C. parallel
    D. none of the above

11. Batt insulation is commercially available in _____.
    A. short lengths
    B. continuous rolls
    C. either A or B
    D. neither A nor B

12. Quarry tile used for floors and base trim is _____.
    A. supplied in $4\frac{1}{4}''$ square units
    B. made of baked clay with a glazed surface
    C. both A and B
    D. neither A nor B

13. _____ is/are available in solid vinyl.
    A. Exterior siding
    B. Rain gutter
    C. Down spouts
    D. all of the above

14. Regarding the reinforcing of concrete, _____.
    A. rebars help concrete beams resist bending and tension
    B. a #8 bar is $\frac{1}{2}''$ in diameter
    C. the deformations on rebars are made to provide a grip for handling them
    D. WWF 8 × 8 × #8 means a mesh made of #8 rebars welded to form $8''$ squares

15. Regarding roofing, _____.
    A. shingles can be used on any roof, regardless of slope
    B. most asphalt shingles are single-tab shingles
    C. roll roofing is used exclusively for built-up roofs
    D. a square of roofing covers 100 sq. ft. when it is laid

Completion

_____ 1. Rough lumber is described by its _____ size.

_____ 2. Concrete usually requires _____ days to cure.

_____ 3. Bricks are laid in arrangements referred to as _____.

_____ 4. A horizontal row of bricks is known as a(n) _____.

_____ 5. _____ is any rough stone found locally as field stone or blasted in a quarry.

_____ 6. Rebars are shown on plan views as _____ lines.

_____ 7. Open web steel _____ are used to support floors and roofs.

_____ 8. Plumbing systems are generally drawn on plans as one-line _____ drawings.

_____ 9. _____ glass is ground and polished to a smooth finish.

_____ 10. Standard drywall sheets are _____' wide and 8' long, or longer.

Identification

_____ 1. Power panel

_____ 2. Outside telephone

_____ 3. Single-pole switch

_____ 4. Floor outlet

_____ 5. Junction box

_____ 6. Circuit breaker

_____ 7. Duplex convenience outlet

_____ 8. Lighting panel

_____ 9. Pushbutton

_____ 10. Ceiling pull switch

(A) ⊖   (B) ▨

(C) Ⓙ   (D) Ⓢ

(E) ◄   (F) ▬

(G) S   (H) S$_{CB}$

(I) ⊜   (J) ▫

Identification

_____ **1.** Elbow—90° (screwed)

_____ **2.** Tee

_____ **3.** Water heater

_____ **4.** Gate valve (screwed)

_____ **5.** Soil and waste

_____ **6.** Soil and waste—underground

_____ **7.** Compressed air

_____ **8.** Cross (screwed)

_____ **9.** Vent

_____ **10.** Drinking water supply

True-False

T	F	**1.**	Rough lumber lengths are available in 2′ increments.
T	F	**2.**	Walnut is rarely used for interior trim because of its cost.
T	F	**3.**	Plywood should not be used for concrete formwork because it is not water-resistant.
T	F	**4.**	The type of symbol used to show concrete plans is dependent upon the mixture used.
T	F	**5.**	Concrete forms should be removed immediately after pouring the concrete.
T	F	**6.**	A common brick and a face brick are the same size.
T	F	**7.**	The English bond is the most commonly used arrangement for laying bricks.
T	F	**8.**	Bricks in a header course are laid on their side.
T	F	**9.**	Bullnose concrete blocks are used in the center run of solid walls.
T	F	**10.**	Concrete blocks of two different thicknesses should not be used in the same wall.
T	F	**11.**	W beams were formerly known as wide flange beams.
T	F	**12.**	Steel angles always have equal leg lengths.
T	F	**13.**	Rebars are shown on plan views with solid lines.
T	F	**14.**	Single strength glass is $1/8''$ thick.
T	F	**15.**	Glass block may be used as a load-bearing material.

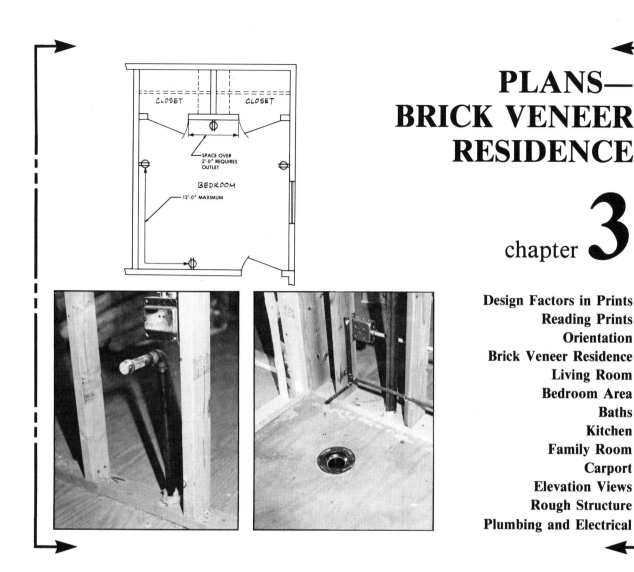

PLANS—BRICK VENEER RESIDENCE

chapter 3

DESIGN FACTORS IN PRINTS

One prime factor in designing a residence is that it provides for the needs and lifestyle of the occupants. There should be space for all the residents and their activities. The design should be flexible enough so the residence continues to be useful over a long period of time. Formal areas, work areas, and recreational and rest areas, each with their own special features must be provided. See Figure 3-1.

Another factor that is given high priority is the outward appearance of the structure. All parts of the building should fit together into a harmonious whole. The building will be attractive when attention is paid to all details and the overall effect. It will have added charm if it is designed to fit its surroundings and is placed on the plot of ground to the greatest advantage.

Another extremely important factor affecting design is cost. It is rare that "cost is no object." Cost is determined by the choice of the building lot, overall size of the building, size of individual rooms, and the equipment and materials used in construction. Cost is also affected by planning, whether good or poor, and the efficient use of labor to construct the building. A factor closely related to cost is the choice of mechanical and electrical parts for the building. Plumbing and electrical work should be within the budget set up for total cost of the structure. However, this does not imply unnecessary cost cutting. Heating and cooling plants must be sized to carry the loads imposed by climatic conditions. Safety must also be considered. A strict adherence to building codes and ordinances that are written to restrict unsafe practices is basic.

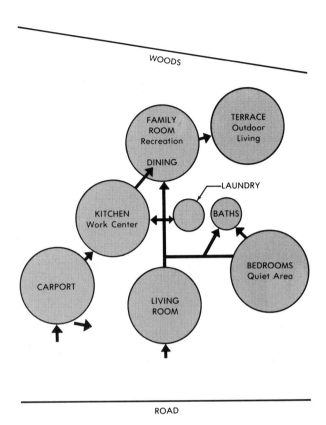

Figure 3-1. The areas of a dwelling are designed to provide for the needs of the occupants.

READING PRINTS

The tradesworkers in the various trades must strive to be efficient and skillful in their work. To be efficient means that the tradesworker avoid wasting effort or time. The material should always be applied as intended, with a minimum of waste. The skill of many trades is evident in the finished building. Well-laid brick and stone work, interior wood finish, custom-designed and constructed cabinet work, and properly laid resilient floor coverings are examples of how the finished product speaks for the tradesworker. Other tradesworkers whose work is hidden in walls, floors, or the ceiling, and often taken for granted, are equally important because their skill and know-how provide the owner with many years of trouble-free service.

Reading prints is part of the intelligent approach to pride in a job well-done. In order to be efficient and develop skills to the fullest, tradesworkers must not only understand the parts of working drawings and specifications that directly concern them but also have an overall knowledge of the structure as

well. They are responsible for following the plans exactly as drawn. If they find errors or discrepancies or have other suggestions, they should consult the contractor. The architect, after discussing the matter with the contractor and owner, will make the necessary changes.

Tradesworkers make many decisions during the construction of buildings. Many specific details are left to them because they are experts in their field and do the work every day. Plans often call for measurements to be made on the job. Notes are included that building details are to be modified to meet job conditions.

Certain phases of building construction have always been the responsibility of the tradesworker. Only rarely is the rough structure detailed for the carpenters. They have the job of framing walls and floors for openings, arranging joists, laying out roof rafters, and working out other structural members. The electricians run conduit or nonmetallic sheathed cable to outlets wherever power or light is needed and efficiently arrange circuits for convenience so that overloading is prevented. The plumbers have similar tasks in providing water, waste, and vent piping. See Figure 3-2. Heating and cooling require careful planning by the architect and attention to installation details by the tradesworker because of the size of the ducts that must pass through floors and walls. Frequent adjustments are made on the job while the building is in progress. The accurate reading of plans, coupled with extensive trade know-how, is the key to doing a good job.

Orientation

Orientation is a method for getting acquainted with the prints. When the sheets for the dwelling to be studied in this chapter are spread out and examined one by one, it is immediately evident that there is a great deal of information to be studied and digested. Prints are designed to be read by tradesworkers who are familiar with all the information displayed and are able to quickly locate the information that applies to them.

The plans for study are a North Carolina Residence. See Figure 3-3. This set of plans contains five sheets. Each sheet is identified in the lower right-hand corner. The sheets and their contents are

    SHEET 1: Basement Plan
               Floor Plan
    SHEET 2: Exterior Elevations
               Exterior Sections

Figure 3-2. Electricians run conduit to outlets wherever power or light is required. Plumbers provide supply, waste, and vent piping.

Figure 3-3. The North Carolina Residence is a three-bedroom, brick veneer house with a carport.

SHEET 3: Sections
               Interior Elevations
               Exterior Sections
               Details

SHEET 4: Plot Plan
               Interior Sections
               Piping
               Door Schedule

SHEET 5: Floor Framing Plan
               Roof Framing Plan

BRICK VENEER RESIDENCE

The brick veneer residence entitled North Carolina Residence is situated on the outskirts of a small city in North Carolina among the rolling foothills of the Blue Ridge Mountains. The plot of ground comprises an acre of land facing a road that serves a half dozen similar plots and ends in a cul-de-sac. The residence is a single-family dwelling designed to be architecturally harmonious with other houses in the area.

The Plot Plan shows the location of the house on the lot. See Sheet 4. The house faces Northeast and is located on an irregular-shaped lot, which extends 213' deep on the carport end on the house and 164' on the bedroom end. The lot is 227'-0" wide at the rear. The driveway is not part of the contract.

Elevation points are not shown on this plan. Groundwork called for is minimal. Approximately 1'-0" of dirt is to be scraped off at the back of the house and fill is to be placed along the front and near the front corner of the house. A septic tank with tile field is located between the bedroom wing and the Northwest property line.

The plan of the first floor shows the relationship of rooms. See Sheet 1. The exterior entrance to the living room is from a sheltered porch directly accessible to the carport. The living room has a fireplace at the carport end. This fireplace is also shown on the Basement Plan, Sheet 1, and the Exterior Elevations, Sheet 2.

Sufficient lighting is available from the large windows. The kitchen, which is the work center of the house, is designed to be efficient in every way. Natural light is provided by the large windows above the kitchen sink. A breakfast area is included in the kitchen. Direct entrance to the kitchen from the carport allows groceries to be carried in easily and trash to be taken from the kitchen without passing through other rooms of the dwelling.

There is convenient access from the kitchen to the family room, which doubles as a dining room. These rooms are adjacent, but also equipped with a wide counter opening between the two areas. The laundry area is only a few steps away so that it is easy to observe when in use. Bi-fold doors conceal laundry appliances when not in use.

The family room contains a large amount of glass and brings it in close touch with the outdoors throughout the year. The adjacent open terrace, which is a 4" concrete slab, provides outdoor living.

The bedroom wing provides quiet, privacy, adequate light, cross ventilation, and ample closets. Three bedrooms are entered from a common hall. One bathroom is accessible from the hallway and the other from Bedroom 1, which is the master bedroom. Each bathroom has a lavatory, water closet, and tub. These fixtures are backed up to a common wall.

The basement extends under part of the kitchen and living room and is reached by stairs from the carport. It contains the furnace, water heater, sump pump, and room for storage. The balance of space below the living area is crawl space.

The Elevation Views, Sheet 2, and Figure 3-4, complete the survey of the house. Front, Rear, Right Side, and Left Side Elevations are shown. The exterior walls are constructed of light brown brick veneer. Wood trim at cornices, wood siding on the exterior wall outside of the living room, and the carport are stained gray. The colors chosen for the building harmonize with its rustic setting at the edge of the woods. The change in material along the front elevation, the gable roof with raised ridge over the central portion, and the double-hung windows toward the road divided by muntins give the dwelling a traditional character, which is appropriate for its place in the community.

The rear of the dwelling cannot be seen from the road and faces the woods. This increases privacy. Wide expanses of insulated glass windows give unobstructed views of the natural setting toward the Southwest. The terrace at the rear of the house promotes use of the rear yard.

Living Room

The plan of the living room, Figure 3-5, is taken directly from Sheet 1. The dimensions of the living

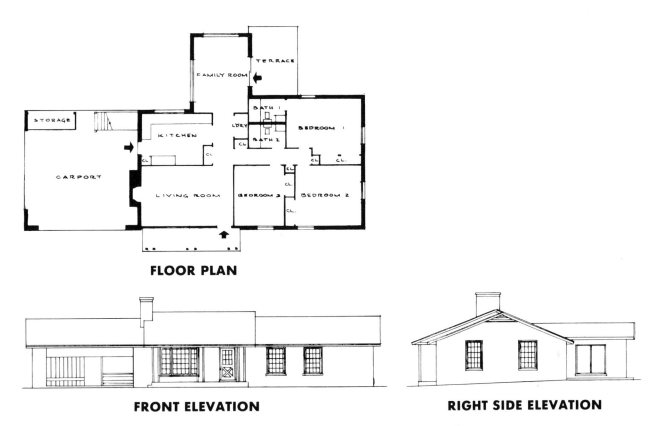

FLOOR PLAN

FRONT ELEVATION   **RIGHT SIDE ELEVATION**

Figure 3-4. Floor plans and elevation views help form an overall view of the dwelling.

room are 12′-10″ × 20′-2″. These dimensions are not to finished walls, but to the rough framing members (studs). The 4″ dimension on partitions and the exterior wall represents the nominal measurement. A 2″ × 4″ member is actually 1½″ × 3½″. In laying out the rough framing, it is difficult to work to fractions of an inch. The wall finish is ½″ gypsum board for drywall application. The exterior wall is 5¼″ thick. For example, ½″ (drywall) + 3½″ (stud) + ½″ (fiberboard sheathing) + ¾″ (siding) = 5¼″. See Figure 3-6.

The living room floor has ½″ rough flooring plywood laid over 2″ × 10″ floor joists. Nailed to the subfloor are 1″ × 2″ strips which provide air space between the subfloor and the finished floor. The finished floor is ⅝″ plywood.

Sometimes it is necessary to look at several sheets in order to gather all of the required data. Dimensions on the Plan View, Sheet 1, locate the set of windows horizontally. The symbol tells the type of window. The Front Elevation View, Sheet 2, shows how the windows are arranged with larger, lower sash and dividing bars (muntins). The dimensions shown (36/24) on the sash are light sizes (glass sizes) measured as though there were no muntins. The first

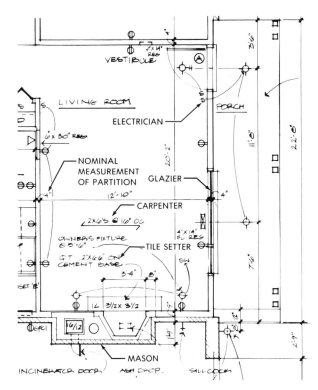

Figure 3-5. The plan of the living room includes information for carpenters, masons, electricians, and other tradesworkers.

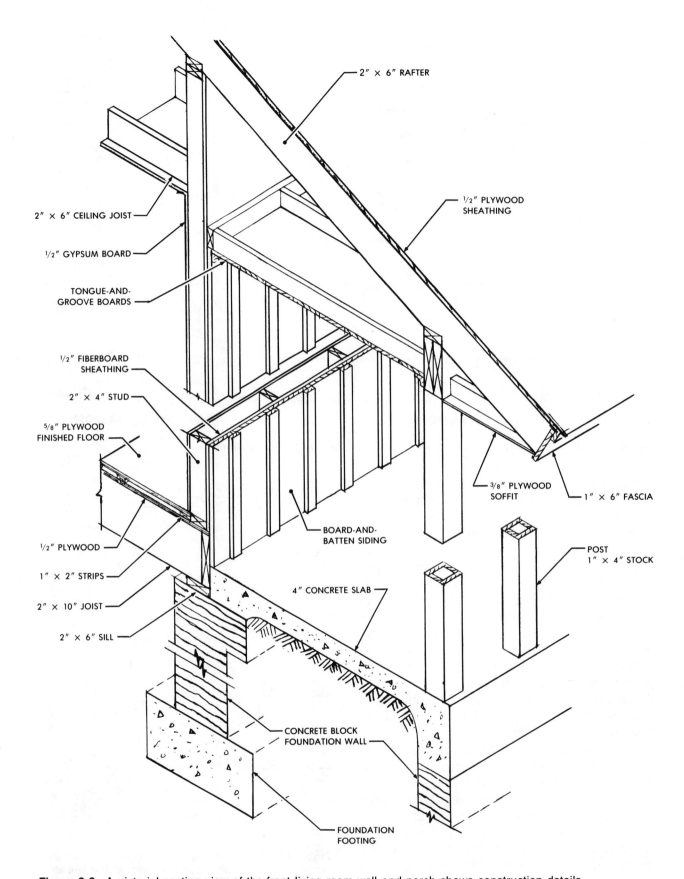

Figure 3-6. A pictorial section view of the front living room wall and porch shows construction details.

number (36) is the width and the second number (24) is the height.

The muntins in these particular windows are grills that snap into place on the outside of the glass to give the illusion of real dividing bars. The ends of the bars fit into grooves in the sash. The one remaining required dimension for the windows is the height above the floor. The Typical Wall Section, Detail 1, Sheet 3, and Figure 3-7 gives this information for all of the double-hung windows in the building. This is a section cut through the brick veneer. This section view shows a dimension of 6'-8½" from the finished floor to the underside of the head jamb of the double-hung window. Information about the double-hung windows in the living room is shown on the First Floor Plan, Sheet 1, the Front Elevation, Sheet 2, and Section A-A, Sheet 3.

The only door in the living room is the front entrance door. It is shown as a line in a full open position indicating the side of the door with butts (hinges). The designation "A" refers to the Door Schedule, Sheet 4, which describes the size, type, and material of the door itself and tells about the frame and casing. The Front Elevation shows that the door is a panel door with nine lights surrounded with trim. Details 3 and 4, Sheet 3, give important instructions about the door frame. They show the jambs, trim, and rough framing.

The fireplace and chimney are shown to some extent on the living room floor plan. For additional information, refer to Sections A-A and B-B, Sheet 3, and the Basement Plan, Sheet 1. The section through the living room, Section A-A, shows the face of the wall and wall below extending to the basement floor where cleanouts are located. The mason will provide and install the cleanout doors. The section through the carport, Section B-B, is viewed looking toward the chimney. It shows all of the flues with hidden lines. An incinerator (if permitted by local and state building codes) is accessible to the carport.

The section view through the living room, Section A-A, indicates how the fireplace will actually look. It is to have a brick face with a finishing mold on the sides and top. The finishing mold is 1⅛" × 2¾" oak. See Sheet 3, Section A-A and Detail 5. The Plan View, Sheet 1, shows the chimney masonry, which extends almost to the corner of the room, concealed by wall finish as indicated by the line that passes in front of it. This plan shows all of the dimensions needed by the mason except the height

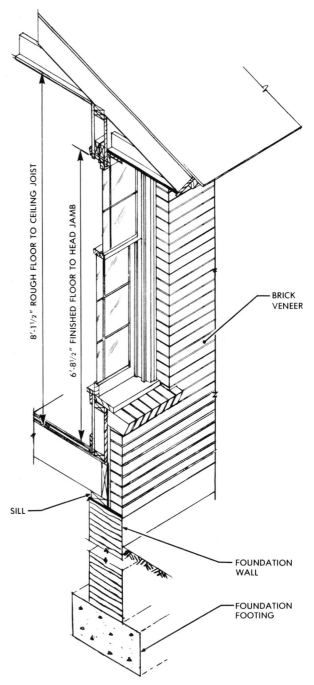

Figure 3-7. A pictorial section view through the bedroom window shows brick veneer construction.

of the opening, which is shown on Section A-A, Sheet 3. The 16" × 12" flue shown on the plan view is not for the fireplace but for the incinerator. Two hidden lines from this flue indicate the opening toward the carport.

The round flue, made of 8" tile, is for the furnace. This is shown on the Basement Plan, Sheet

1. The flue for the fireplace begins above the *throat* and does not show on the first floor plan. The throat is the opening at the top of the fire chamber into the smoke chamber where the damper is located. If there were an attic plan or a section taken through the chimney, the fireplace flue would appear in place. Section B-B, Sheet 3, shows how the three flues, the back wall of the fireplace, and the throat are arranged. An ash drop is placed in the hearth of the fireplace with a cleanout opening in the basement. A steel angle iron is used to support the masonry above the fireplace opening. This angle iron has $3^1/_2''$ legs.

Electrical features in the living room include convenience outlets and switched lighting outlets. The lighting outlets on the porch and at the entrance door are controlled by switches near the door. Note that the symbol shown indicates that these are ceiling lights. The letter designations refer to the Light Fixture Schedule, Sheet 4. For example, the light in the vestibule is indicated by the letter H. The Light Fixture Schedule shows a #1716, surface-mounted fixture with one 60 W bulb.

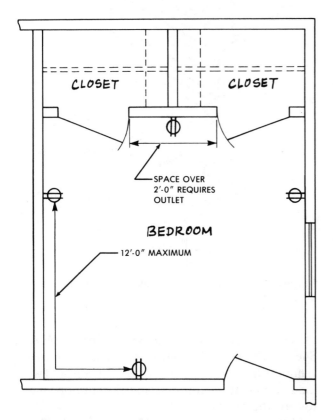

Figure 3-8. Installation of wall outlets must comply with applicable sections of the NEC®.

Several duplex convenience outlets are shown around the living room walls. The exact location of these outlets is determined by the electrician, who will follow applicable sections of the National Electrical Code®. For example, Article 210-52(a) of the NEC® states that all wall space over 2'-0" in length must be provided with an outlet. Additionally, wall outlets must be no more than 12'-0" apart measured along the wall. See Figure 3-8. Wall outlets are placed 16" above the finished floor. The grounding plug of the receptacle normally is located on the lower side of the receptacle.

Two warm air supply registers and one return air register for the living room are shown on the Floor Plan, Sheet 1. One 4" × 14" register is placed in the floor in front of the windows. The other supply register is in the wall near the entrance door. This wall register is 6" × 14". The 6" × 30" return register is on the long wall across from the door. The actual location of registers is determined by the HVAC subcontractor based upon placement of wall studs, floor joists, and ceiling joists. Additionally, the HVAC subcontractor locates the registers to provide good air flow.

The designation 2 × 6s @ 16" OC under the 12'-10" dimension refers to the size and spacing of the joists in the ceiling above. The arrows below the designation show the direction of run for the ceiling joists. The Roof Framing Plan and Floor Framing Plan are shown on Sheet 5. The Roof Framing Plan calls for 2" × 6" × 14' rafters spaced 16" OC above the living room. The Floor Framing Plan calls for 2" × 10" × 14' floor joists spaced 16" OC below the living room area.

Bedroom Area

The bedroom wing is enclosed in walls of brick veneer. This is shown in Figures 3-7 and 3-9 and on Sheet 3, Detail 1. A brick veneer building is essentially a frame building with a skin of brick. Frame construction is used with 2" × 4" studs and with wood floor joists, ceiling joists, and rafters supported in the conventional way. Sheathing of $^1/_2''$ fiberboard is placed on the outside of the frame wall and a 1" space is provided between the frame wall and the brick wall for ventilation. The 4" brick wall is laid resting on the foundation. It is tied to the frame wall with anchors that bridge the air space. One anchor is provided for each 2 sq. ft. of area. The brick wall is laid around window and door openings to give the appearance that the wall is solid brick masonry. The wall is built up tight to the cornice without serving as the support of the structure above. On the gable end, the brick veneer wall is built past the soffit. See Sheet 2, Detail 1. The window is shown in place on Sheet 3, Detail 1, to show the rough framing and trim. The 9″ dimension for wall thickness, shown on the plan and Figure 3-9, is comprised of the following parts: 3½″ stud, ½″ sheathing, 1″ air space, and 4″ brick. This does not include the interior wall finish which is ½″ gypsum board.

The windows in all the bedrooms are identical and are shown on the Front, Right, Side, and Rear Elevation Views, Sheet 2. Two sizes of sash are used

in each window. Each sash has a one-piece insulating glass. The muntins are in the form of snap-in grills.

A careful study of the doors, using the Door Schedule, Sheet 4, should be made to determine their size, description, and special provisions. Sliding doors are used for Bedrooms 1 and 3 because swinging doors would interfere with furniture or another door. Closets A and C are equipped with bi-fold doors, shelves, and hanger rods. The doors for Closet A in Bedroom 1 are O and P doors. These doors are 8′-0″ high. They have one solid panel and open louvers. They are made of pine with ranch-type stock, oak trim, and oak jambs. The O doors are 4′-0″ wide and the P doors are 5′-0″ wide. The doors for Closet C in Bedroom 2 are designated as

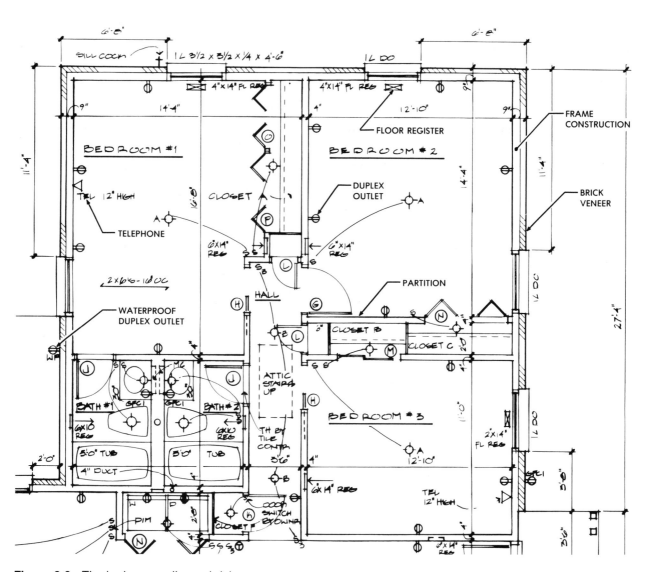

Figure 3-9. The bedroom walls are brick veneer.

N doors on the plan and the door schedule. N doors are 5'-0" × 6'-8" × 1³/₈". Their style and finish are the same as the style and finish of O and P doors. Closet B has sliding doors. These are designated as M doors. These doors are paired doors. The bypass track for M doors is installed by the carpenter.

Switches control ceiling and closet lights. Telephone outlets are provided in Bedrooms 1 and 3. A pair of three-way switches controls the light in the hall. A disappearing stairway, providing access to the attic, is located in the hall.

Warm air registers are placed in the floor beneath the windows in each bedroom. Air returns are situated in walls across the rooms. The size of the registers is shown on the floor plan.

Ceiling joists in the bedroom area are 2" × 6" spaced 16" OC. Their direction of run is shown by the arrows. The note showing ceiling joist information is shown on the floor plan for Bedroom 1.

Baths

Baths 1 and 2 are similar, but reversed. They are shown on the Floor Plan, Sheet 1, and with detailed, large-scale elevations on Sheet 4. A plumbing wall that is 6" thick accommodates all of the supply, waste, and vent piping. Warm air is provided through registers on the long walls across from the fixtures. Exhaust fans are provided in the ceiling with ducts extending into the attic space. These exhaust fans are controlled from the wall switch.

A notation, 4" DUCT, over the tub in Bath 1 refers to a vent duct for the clothes dryer. The notation, TH BY TILE CONTR., indicates that the tile contractor is responsible for supplying and installing the threshold between the bath and hall needed because of a change in flooring material. The elevation drawings of the bathroom walls on Sheet 4 are necessary to show how much of the wall is to be covered with ceramic tile. The tile extends 6'-4" from the floor around the tub. On all other bath walls, it extends 4'-2" from the floor. Base and door casing and the location of accessories are also shown on the elevation drawings. A tile cove base is applied to the ceramic tile walls. Wood casings are used for the doors. Refer to the Door Schedule, Sheet 4, for information on J doors. A towel bar, tumbler and toothbrush holder, and soap dish are shown above the water closet and vanity. The medicine cabinets in the bathrooms are not fully recessed

because they are placed back-to-back on the common wall.

Kitchen

Many factors are involved in the planning of an efficient and adequate kitchen. The placement of the sink, refrigerator, range, oven, and counter space is of primary importance in saving steps and providing convenience. The three major areas in a kitchen are storage, preparation, and cooking areas. Storage areas include base and wall cabinets, pantries, refrigerators, and freezers. Preparation areas include sink and adequate countertop space. Cooking areas include stoves, grills, countertop units, and ovens. Microwave ovens, whether free-standing or built-in, must also be considered when planning contemporary kitchens. In addition to the three major areas of a kitchen, adequate provision for clean-up must be considered. Portable or built-in dishwashers are utilized in clean-up. Built-in dishwashers are placed under the countertop adjacent to the sink for convenience and short plumbing runs.

An efficient kitchen is designed so that work is minimized and steps are saved. The three sides of a triangle drawn on the floor plan of an efficiently designed kitchen should total 12'-0" to 21'-0". See Figure 3-10. Distances less than 12'-0" result in

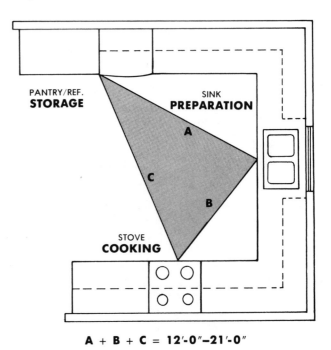

Figure 3-10. Well-designed kitchens have 12'-0" to 21'-0" between storage, preparation, and cooking areas.

crowding of the kitchen appliances. Distances over 21'-0" require too much walking between areas.

Cabinets should be adequate for the needs of the family. Base cabinets are 24" deep and 36" high. The countertop (generally plastic laminate) overhangs the base cabinet by 1". A minimum of 5 running feet of drawers is required for a kitchen. As the number of base cabinets increases, the number of drawers must also increase. All-drawer base cabinets provide additional drawer space. Special base cabinets, such as corner units, may also be utilized. Base cabinets are shown on floor plans with solid lines.

Wall cabinets are 12" deep and 30" high. Three shelves provide storage space. Wall cabinets extending to an 8'-1" ceiling are 42" high and generally have a smaller door at the top. Other wall cabinets vary in height based upon their particular use. For

example, wall cabinets above a stove are generally 18" shorter than other wall cabinets in the kitchen. Wall cabinets are shown on floor plans with hidden lines. The recommended vertical clearance between base and wall cabinets is 18". See Figure 3-11.

Kitchen windows provide adequate light and ventilation. Generally, kitchen windows are placed above the sink. A valance (decorative molding strip) is often placed between wall cabinets and above the kitchen sink for continuity and to provide mounting space for light fixtures above the sink.

Special provisions are made for electrical equipment such as ranges, dishwashers, ventilating fans, and small appliances. Space for a table and chairs is often provided. Access to the more formal dining area should be convenient. Kitchens are frequently planned with access to the carport or garage so that supplies can be brought in with a maximum of convenience. All of these elements have been considered and provided for in the kitchen of the North Carolina Residence.

In order to gather all of the information about the kitchen, see Figure 3-12 and the Kitchen Cabinets

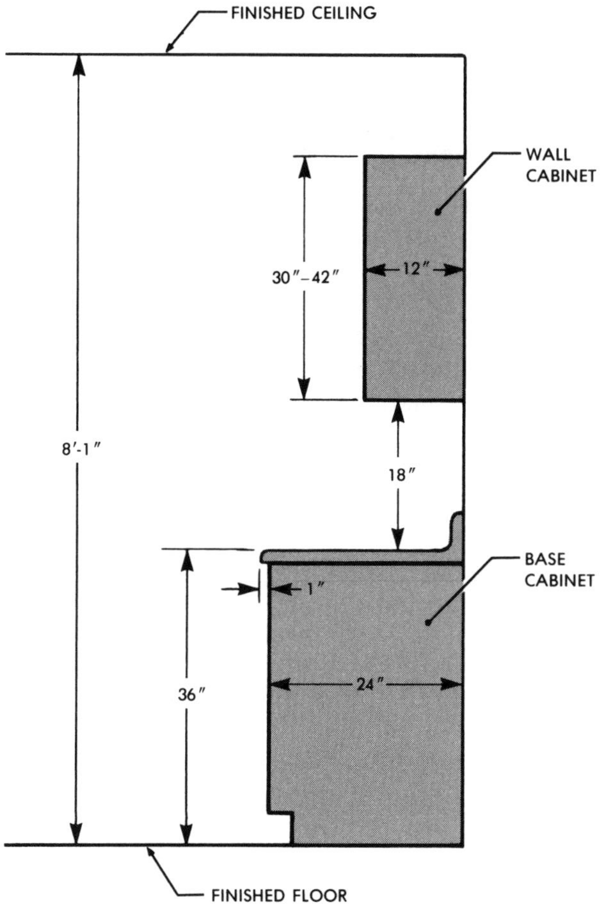

Figure 3-11. Kitchen cabinets should conform to standard dimensions.

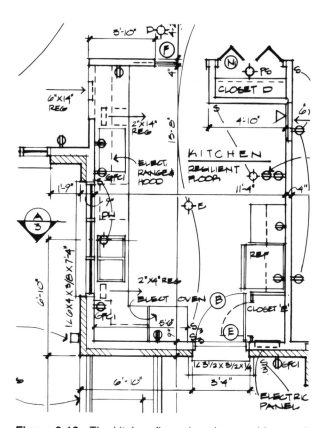

Figure 3-12. The kitchen floor plan shows cabinet and appliance layout.

drawings on Sheet 3. Section A-A, Sheet 3, is drawn through the kitchen and gives additional information. The Rear Elevation View, Sheet 2, gives the details of the windows.

The windows are shown on the plan view and elevation view as triple casement sash with the center window fixed. Optional sizes are available from different manufacturers. The glass is insulating glass. The height of the windows above the floor or the top of the counter is not given directly, but the interior view of the kitchen cabinets shows the top of the window trim touching the soffit at a height of 7'-1". The Door Schedule, Sheet 4, indicates the exterior door is made of steel. The exterior door is shown on Section B-B, Sheet 3.

The Floor Plan, Sheet 1, shows an L-shaped arrangement on the window side. The utility closet (Closet E), space for refrigerator, a refrigerator cabinet, base and wall cabinet, and a space for a kitchen table are shown on the other side. The Kitchen Cabinet Elevations, Sheet 3, give detailed views of three sides of the kitchen. At the far left side of Elevation A, a base cabinet is shown which is alongside the kitchen-dining area. This base cabinet has a maple countertop and a Formica® backsplash. Above the base cabinet is a wall cabinet with one fixed and two adjustable shelves. Note that only the two adjustable shelves are called out in the note as one fixed shelf is required in the construction of a wall cabinet.

The soffit begins above this cabinet and continues around the room to the corner nearest the family room. Next to this cabinet is a space for the refrigerator, with cabinets above. The minimum recommended width of a refrigerator space is 32". The cabinetmaker should verify the refrigerator size before making working drawings to construct the kitchen cabinets. Closet E is located between the refrigerator space and the carport end wall of the kitchen. The Door Schedule, Sheet 4, gives E door dimensions as 1'-8" × 6'-8" × 1³/₈". Closet E has a flush door.

Elevation B shows Door B (refer to Door Schedule, Sheet 4) and the oven space with a cabinet above and below the oven space. A wall cabinet with two adjustable shelves and a lazy susan (revolving) base cabinet finished with Formica® top and backsplash is shown. Elevation B meets the cabinet on the adjacent wall at the corner.

Elevation C shows the wall with the window, the location of the sink, dishwasher, range top with hood above, the cabinets with drawers or doors and shelves. A special drop-in cutting board is located over the dishwasher. It is useful for kitchen operations. A portion of the wall at the far right is open, providing a pass-through to the family room. The wall cabinet with doors on either side is accessible from the kitchen and the family room.

Basic measurements are given on the Floor Plan, Sheet 1, and on the Kitchen Cabinet Elevations, Sheet 3. The window, pass-through opening, utility closet, soffit, and wall finish are built or installed before accurate measurements for cabinets can be taken.

Types of outlets not previously shown are power outlets for the range and oven and a clock outlet. See Floor Plan, Sheet 1. A three-way switch controls the ceiling light from two locations. The electrical panel is in the utility closet.

Warm air is supplied to the kitchen through registers in the toekick under the base cabinets as shown on Sheet 1 and the Kitchen Cabinet Elevations, Sheet 3. An exhaust fan is part of the range hood. A vent extends from the hood through the wall cabinet and exits through the roof.

Family Room

The family room, Sheet 1, is enhanced by large windows and the full-length glass doors to the terrace. See Figure 3-13. They are shown on the Rear, Right, and Left Side Elevations, Sheet 2.

Item C in the Door Schedule, Sheet 4, describes the sliding glass doors, one of which is stationary. Tempered insulating glass is used. The door height is 6'-8" with a threshold of ³/₄", placing the head jamb 6'-8³/₄" above the floor. The window head jambs are set at the same height.

Warm air registers are placed in the floor under a window and in front of the fixed door. The size of these registers is 4" × 14". The air return is located on the wall under the pass-through. This register is 6" × 14".

Light fixtures in the family room are recessed. The recessed fixture in the dining area is 2'-4" from the wall. Another recessed light fixture is located 3'-6" from the end windows and 2'-4" from the finished wall adjacent to the terrace. The main recessed light fixture is located in the center of the room. Light fixtures are controlled from a bank of switches near the passage.

Three closets are located next to the passage.

Closet F, Sheet 1, faces the hall and is equipped with a light that is controlled by a door switch. Closet D, Sheet 1, is a guest closet in the passage near the living room. It is equipped with a light that is controlled by a pull switch. The closet across from the kitchen has a receptacle for the dryer and a 4″ duct that serves as a vent to the outside.

Carport

The carport, Sheet 1, is built on a 4″ concrete slab with solid brick masonry at three corners. A W 12 × 27 beam supports the roof structure over the wide opening. The roof is supported at the rear by 6″ × 6″ posts. Siding on a wood framework with fiberglass panels closes in the left side of the carport. The storage area wall is covered with siding. See Detail 2, Sheet 2. A fiberglass screen windbreak protects the stairs to the basement. The lights in front of the carport are controlled by a single switch alongside the kitchen door. The ceiling light and the light at the head of the stairs are controlled by a three-

way switch inside the kitchen door and another three-way switch on the brick wall outside the door.

Elevation Views

Many of the items that appear on the Elevation Views, Sheet 2, have been discussed as they relate to the rooms of the dwelling. The roof is covered with asphalt shingles. The roof pitch symbol shows a 4½″ rise per foot. All roofs on this dwelling have the same pitch. Metal diverters are indicated on the Rear, Right Side, and Left Side Elevations. These are used to divert water into the valleys of the intersecting gable roofs. There are no gutters or downspouts on the dwelling. Wood louvers are installed in both gable ends of the main roof to ventilate the attic space. These are shown on the Right and Left Side Elevations.

Wherever brick veneer appears above the heads of windows, steel angle lintels are necessary to support the brick. This occurs on the right side gable end, at the glass doors in the family room, the end

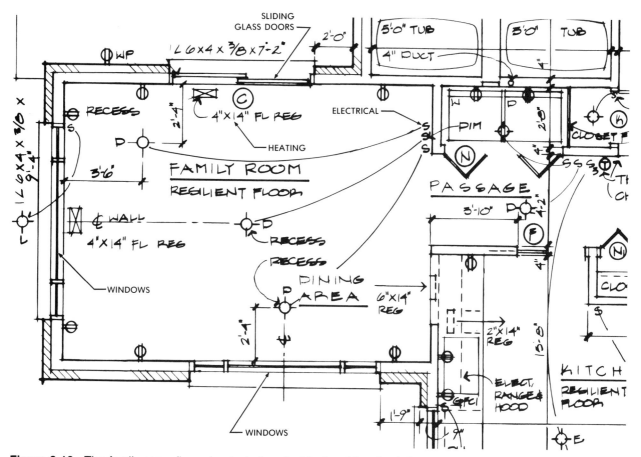

Figure 3-13. The family room floor plan includes electrical and heating information.

windows in the family room, and the kitchen windows. The lintels are shown on the Floor Plan, Sheet 1. For example, the lintel over the end windows in the family room is 6″ × 4″ × ³/8″. It is 9′-4″ long. Information the bricklayer needs concerning the chimney is shown on the Front and Left Side Elevations, Sheet 2. The chimney is 3′-0″ above the main roof ridge. Its nominal dimensions are 2′-5″ × 5′-6″. Metal flashing is shown at the intersection of the chimney and roofs.

The exterior finish of the wall outside the living room shown on the Front Elevation, Sheet 2, is wood siding using boards and battens. This area is located between the front entrance door and the living room windows. Three doubled pairs of wood posts are shown across the front porch.

The views of the carport, Sheet 2, give additional information on the variety of materials used for exterior finish. The siding, posts, and railings shown on the Front Elevation, Sheet 2, are for the storage room and the stairs at the rear. The fiberglass screen and wood siding, shown on the Rear Elevation, Sheet 2, form the back wall with an open space between. The Left Side Elevation, Sheet 2, shows wood siding with fiberglass panels above.

Rough Structure

The elements that comprise the rough structure are the footings and foundation, the wood frame-

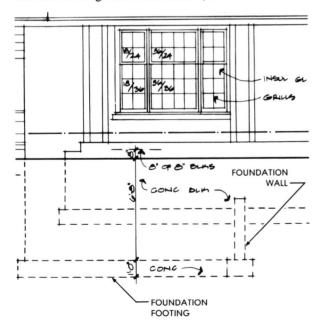

Figure 3-14. Hidden lines show deep footings at basement and stairs.

work of floor joists, walls, partitions, ceiling joists, and roof, and brick and brick veneer. Several sheets must be studied for a review of the rough structure.

The footings are shown with hidden lines on the Basement Plan, Sheet 1, and on the four Elevation Views on Sheet 2. They are shown again on Sections A-A and B-B and the Typical Wall Section, Detail 1, Sheet 3. The foundation wall is shown on the Basement Plan, Sheet 1, with two thicknesses. The footings vary in width accordingly. Footing dimensions vary when there is an added load, such as at the garage corners. The footing under the chimney takes the shape of a large pad. Square footings are provided under each column in the crawl space. The wall footings are 1′-0″ thick and reinforced with two continuous #4 rebars. Additional reinforcing is placed across the chimney footing. The bottoms of the footings are set at three different elevations. See the Right Side Elevation, Sheet 2.

One elevation example is the deep footing around the basement portion, which extends under the living room and porch. See Figure 3-14. Other footing elevations provide for the change in grade. The ground slopes down toward the front of the building. Provisions for the change are achieved by a stepped footing on each side.

The foundation walls consist of concrete masonry units (concrete blocks) laid on the footings according to the Basement Plan, Sheet 1, and the Elevation Views, Sheet 2. The mason must study the elevation views because the foundation wall is not to be laid to the same elevation (height) all around. The Right Side Elevation, Sheet 2, shows how the top of the foundation wall is stepped so the brickwork follows the slope in grade more closely. The Basement Plan, Sheet 1, shows that the wall toward the crawl space is 4′-0″ high. The foundation wall around the carport is modified to compensate for the slope in grade, to give direct support to the corner piers which are built before the floor is placed, and to provide for concrete grade beams at the front opening and the side. Steel reinforcing is usually required between alternate block courses. See note beside Basement Plan, Sheet 1, and Figure 3-15.

The steel members supporting the floor joists are W 8 × 17 beams resting on pipe columns and masonry walls. See Detail 1, Sheet 1. The top concrete masonry units are filled with concrete in which anchor bolts are placed at 6′-0″ intervals. Sills are laid in grout so they can be adjusted to be level around the building. They are then fastened in place with

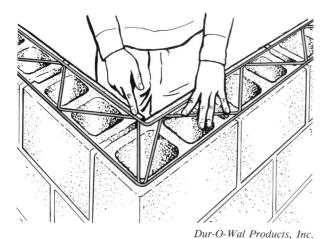

Dur-O-Wal Products, Inc.

Figure 3-15. Steel reinforcing provides added lateral strength for a concrete block foundation wall.

the anchor bolts. Care must be taken to ensure building dimensions, as shown on the First Floor Plan, Sheet 1, are followed accurately and that corners are square. The joists are then put in place and fastened. The Floor Framing Plan, Sheet 5, gives the dimensions. Notice that the joists under the bathrooms, where there is additional weight because of the fixtures, are placed on 12″ centers. Cross bridging is required at the center of each span. See Figure 3-16.

The Typical Wall Section, Detail 1, Sheet 3, shows

BRIDGING

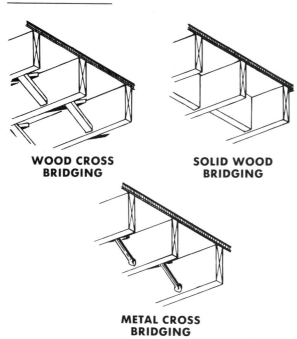

WOOD CROSS BRIDGING

SOLID WOOD BRIDGING

METAL CROSS BRIDGING

Figure 3-16. Bridging strengthens floors and distributes loads.

the next operation, which is the laying of the rough floor. The rough floor is made of ¹/₂″ plywood extending to the outside of the headers at the ends of the joists. The framing of the walls and partitions can then proceed. The sections are made on the floor with the bottom sole and double top plates nailed to the studs. They are made in lengths so they can be conveniently handled for tilting up in place. The double top plate permits them to be tied together at intersections and corners. See Figure 3-17.

Detail 1, Sheet 3, shows two members (2″ × 4″) on edge to form a header over the window. They are headers for the double-hung windows in the bedrooms. The ceiling joists rest on the wall plates and the bearing partition which extends the length of the house near the center. One row of solid bridging is required in each span to make the joists rigid.

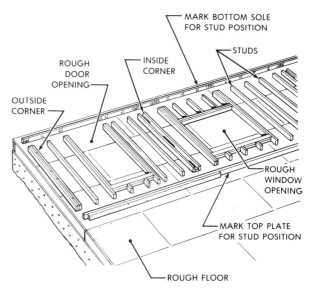

Figure 3-17. Wall and partition sections are laid out and nailed together on the rough floor, then tilted into place.

The roof rafters, shown on Detail 1, Sheet 3, are notched to fit over the wall plate and extend down to form support for the overhang. Sheet 5 shows the arrangement of the rafters, and Figure 3-18 shows how roof rafters are placed. The Roof Framing Plan, Sheet 5, and the Elevation Views, Sheet 2, show how the roof is erected. Some of the items to be noted are the different ridge heights and the valleys that develop over the family room wing. The elevation views show that the eaves are not at the same height all around the house. This makes it necessary to extend some of the rafters. Part of the roof over the family room is supported from partitions below.

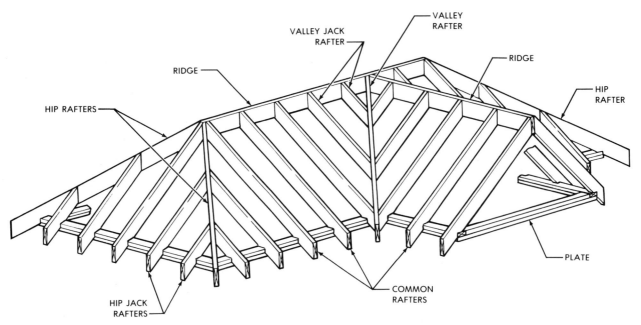

Figure 3-18. A hip roof with a gable has several types of rafters.

Laying the brick veneer can be done as soon as the frame walls are finished, the rough window frames installed, and the sheathing applied. The brick corners of the carport and the chimney are built at the same time. Placing the slabs for the carport, the terrace, and front porch are among the last outside jobs to be done. The Basement Plan, Sheet 1, and Section B-B, Sheet 3, show a grade beam for the front of the carport slab strengthened with two rebars. The other two sides of the carport slab, the terrace, and porch slabs are made with edges thicker than the slabs themselves. The Section Views, Sheet 3, provide this information.

Print Details

Detail 1, Sheet 1, shows the typical basement column and also shows the first floor construction and the framing of the bearing partition. The Right Side Gable Overhang, Detail 1, Sheet 2, shows the continuation of the brick veneer wall. It also shows how lookouts are used to support the last rafter, soffit, and trim at the right end wall over the bedrooms. The section through the carport gable wall is for the gable at the opposite side of the building. See Detail 2, Sheet 2. For framing above the openings in the screen, 2″ × 6″ members are used. The construction of the carport screen is also shown. Detail 2, Sheet 3, shows the cornice at the carport entrance and gives information on how the rafters and cornice are supported by the W beams and how the face

of the wall is finished. The porch detail shows important features of trim. See Detail 3, Sheet 3.

Plumbing and Electrical

An examination of the Floor Plan, Sheet 1, and the Water Piping Diagram, Sheet 4, reveals how the plumbing has been carefully arranged for efficiency and economy. The floor plan shows how the kitchen fixtures have been placed in a line, beginning with the kitchen sink. The sink, dishwasher, washing machine, bathroom fixtures for Bathrooms 1 and 2 (all arranged on the same plumbing partition), and the sill cock on the side of the house outside Bedroom 1 are all approximately in line. The Water Piping Diagram, Sheet 4, also includes the water heater and the supply line for the sill cock in the carport. The soil pipe is shown on the Basement Plan, Sheet 1, going to the septic tank. The septic tank is indicated with the tile field on the Plot Plan, Sheet 4. The basement is protected by drain tile along the footings. See Basement Plan, Sheet 1, and Section A-A, Sheet 3. The tile extends back to the family room and to the floor drain at the foot of the stairs. The water is diverted into a tile settling basin to reduce the silt and then expelled by a sump pump to drain tile under the lawn.

The electrical system has been discussed as each outlet appeared for the first time in relation to its use. The Light Fixture Schedule, Sheet 4, refers to catalog descriptions of the fixtures chosen for each location.

Name _____ Date _____

True-False

(T)   F   **1.**   Wall cabinets may have adjustable shelves.

T   F   **2.**   The rough structure of a building is generally very detailed so that carpenters can locate each measurement.

T   F   **3.**   A set of plans always contains an even number of sheets.

T   F   **4.**   Exterior elevations show complete kitchen details.

T   F   **5.**   A gable roof slopes in two directions.

T   F   **6.**   The imaginary cutting plane to produce a floor plan is taken 5'-0" above the floor.

T   F   **7.**   Panel doors are not suitable for exterior use.

T   F   **8.**   All ceiling lights are required to be controlled by a switch.

T   F   **9.**   The abbreviation OC indicates off-center.

T   F   **10.**   Warm air registers may be located in floors or walls.

T   F   **11.**   Kitchen wall cabinets are generally 30" or 42" high.

T   F   **12.**   The recommended vertical clearance between base and wall cabinets is 18".

T   F   **13.**   Elevation views may be either interior or exterior.

T   F   **14.**   Window head jambs in a building are normally set at the same height.

T   F   **15.**   A #4 rebar is 5/8" in diameter.

T   F   **16.**   Floor registers are often placed below windows.

T   F   **17.**   The arrows on a cutting plane line indicate the direction of sight.

T   F   **18.**   Details and floor plans are drawn to the same scale for uniformity.

T   F   **19.**   The setback for a single-family dwelling may vary depending upon local ordinances.

T   F   **20.**   Plastic laminate is the standard countertop material.

Completion

_____   **1.**   A(n) _____ plan shows the location of the house on a lot.

_____   **2.**   The light size of a window refers to the size of _____.

_____   **3.**   A section view is made by passing a cutting _____ through the object.

_____ 4. A brick _____ building is essentially a frame building with a skin of brick.

_____ 5. The standard depth for wall cabinets is _____ ".

_____ 6. The furred-down area above kitchen cabinets is the _____ .

_____ 7. A(n) _____ switch controls lights from two locations.

_____ 8. The standard height of a door is _____ .

_____ 9. The _____ is the highest point of a gable roof.

_____ 10. Roof _____ are notched to fit over the top plate.

_____ 11. The standard depth for base cabinets is _____ ".

_____ 12. The actual size of a 2" × 4" stud is _____ .

_____ 13. The first number in a window notation gives the _____ of the glass.

_____ 14. Wall cabinets are shown on floor plans with _____ lines.

_____ 15. Electrical wall outlets must be located no more than _____ from the nearest wall outlet measured along the wall.

_____ 16. The minimum triangular distance between the three major work areas of a kitchen is _____ .

_____ 17. A door _____ is often included on prints to give such information as door size, number, and trim.

_____ 18. The roof pitch symbol ⟍¹² ₅ indicates a(n) _____ " rise per foot.

_____ 19. Foundation footings on basement plans are shown with _____ lines.

_____ 20. A(n) _____ pump is placed in a basement to remove excess groundwater.

Identification

_____ 1. Sill cock

_____ 2. Center line

_____ 3. Concrete

_____ 4. Pull switch

_____ 5. Hidden line

_____ 6. Earth (section)

_____ 7. Telephone

_____ 8. Steel (section)

_____ 9. Lighting panel

_____ 10. Duplex convenience outlet

Ⓐ — — — — —

Ⓑ ⊥

Ⓒ ◀

Ⓓ ⊖

Ⓔ — — · — —

Ⓕ Ⓢ

Ⓖ

Ⓗ

Ⓘ

Ⓙ

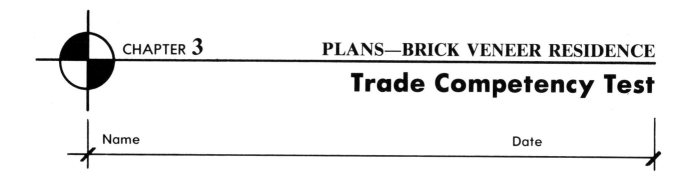
Refer to Plans for a North Carolina Residence

Multiple Choice

_B_   1. The roof for the North Carolina Residence is a _____ roof.
A. hip
B. gable
C. mansard
D. gambrel

_B_   2. The plan views show _____.
A. a direct access to the living room from the carport
B. basement under part of the living room and kitchen
C. that each bedroom has a bath
D. a laundry in the basement

_D_   3. The living room _____.
A. measures 13'-2" × 20'-2" to the finished walls
B. has all of the convenience outlets controlled by switches
C. has casement windows
D. has a designation regarding joist size referring to joists overhead

_A_   4. The kitchen has _____.
A. a pass-through opening to the family room
B. a soffit all around the room at the ceiling
C. double-hung windows
D. stock cabinets to be fitted by the carpenter on the job

_C_   5. The family room has _____.
A. a pair of sliding glass doors, both of which open
B. two warm air registers and no return air register
C. two sets of casement windows that are alike in size
D. a doorway leading to the kitchen

_B_   6. Regarding the bedroom wing, _____.
A. each bedroom has a closet with bi-fold doors
B. the bathrooms are identical but reversed, except for the placement of the doors and switches
C. the bedroom doors are sliding doors
D. warm air is supplied to the bathroom by a ceiling fan

_A_ 7. The carport _____.
A. includes a storage space with doors opening toward the rear of the building
B. is enclosed on two sides with wood screens
C. has an inner wall of solid brick masonry
D. is equipped with a sill cock and a floor drain

_C_ 8. Regarding windows, _____.
A. all windows are located horizontally on the plan view with dimensions to the sides of the brick openings
B. the window size 36/24 means that the outside dimensions of wood sash are 36″ high and 24″ wide
C. double-hung windows in the bedrooms are placed 6′-8½″ above the finished floor to the bottom of the top jamb
D. all sashes in the kitchen windows open

_C_ 9. Regarding doors, _____.
A. the front entrance door is a wood panel door with nine lights
B. doors are all 6′-8″ high and either 1⅜″ or 1¾″ thick
C. the basement door is a wood panel door with six lights
D. closet doors in bedrooms and hall are either sliding or bi-fold doors

_A_ 10. Regarding concrete footings, _____ .
A. wall footings are to be reinforced with two continuous #4 rebars
B. the stepped footings on both right and left sides of the house have the same amount of drop
C. only one basement column is supported on a footing
D. all wall footings are 2′-6″ × 1′-0″

_D_ 11. Regarding foundation walls, _____.
A. the foundation walls around the basement are 12″ thick
B. the top of the foundation wall is level around the building where the brick veneer is to be laid
C. the chimney foundation up to the first floor elevation is made of concrete instead of concrete block
D. alternate courses of concrete block are to be reinforced with horizontal steel reinforcing

_B_ 12. Regarding concrete slabs, _____.
A. the carport slab is 4″ thick out to the rear and side edges
B. the grade beam for the carport entrance is described on the Basement Plan and shown in Section B-B
C. the steps to the basement are wood and rest on the 4″ thick basement floor
D. the terrace is laid on compact fill without a foundation wall or footing

_A_ 13. Regarding steel support members, _____.
A. a W 12 × 27 beam is used to support the roof rafters and cornice over the front of the carport
B. two steel angles are used at each bedroom window on the right elevation to support the brick veneer
C. the W 8 × 17 beam down the center of the building is supported by steel pipe columns 7′-4″ long
D. steel angle lintels hold up the masonry over the living room windows

_B_ 14. Regarding brick veneer walls, _____.
- A. the brick veneer part of the wall is erected before the frame part
- B. a 1″ air space is provided for ventilation
- C. the brick veneer is set back 1″ from the face of the foundation
- D. anchors are placed on 2′-0″ centers in the course of brick

_C_ 15. Regarding the fireplace and chimney, _____.
- A. flue linings are not permitted to extend above the top of the chimney masonry
- B. a fireplace ash drop opens into the carport
- C. the round flue shown on the first floor plan is for the furnace
- D. details to build the chimney top are given in Section B-B

_D_ 16. Regarding wood framing, _____.
- A. headers over all windows and doors are 2″ × 6″ members
- B. there are no ceiling joists in the carport
- C. cross bridging is required for both floor and ceiling joists
- D. the joists under the bathrooms are placed on 12″ centers

_D_ 17. Regarding the roof, _____.
- A. the eaves are at the same elevation around the roof
- B. a hip roof extends over the bedroom wing
- C. the ridge over the living room-kitchen area is at the same elevation as the ridge over the bedroom area
- D. ventilation is provided by louvers in the right and left side gable ends

_A_ 18. Regarding plumbing, _____.
- A. a settling basin and sump pump are connected to drain tile and serve to help keep the basement dry
- B. the piping diagram on Sheet 4 shows water supply and drainage from fixtures
- C. the water heater is located directly below the washing machine
- D. the soil pipe from the bathrooms is connected directly to the tile field

_C_ 19. The electrical installation includes _____.
- A. an electrical panel in the basement
- B. power outlets for the clothes dryer, dishwasher, and sump pump
- C. three-way switches to control ceiling lights in the kitchen and carport
- D. thermostat and chimes located in the hall to the bedrooms

_B_ 20. The heating installation includes _____.
- A. a gas-fired, warm air furnace
- B. warm air supply registers in the baseboard under kitchen cabinets
- C. air returns placed under windows in the bedrooms
- D. an air conditioning system with the condenser located behind the house

True-False

T F 1. The family room and kitchen have a cabinet that opens to both rooms.

T F 2. The front elevation of the carport shows an opening in the back wall.

T F 3. The windows in the bedroom have the same size top and bottom sash.

T F 4. The same type of windows are used on the front and rear of the house.

T F 5. Bedroom windows use insulating glass.

T	F	**6.**	Bedroom doors are solid-core doors 1³/₄″ thick.
T	F	**7.**	Information about footings is shown on the Basement Plan and Elevation Views.
T	F	**8.**	The footing for the basement wall toward the crawl space is 20″ wide.
T	F	**9.**	The concrete block foundation wall is reinforced with vertical rebars.
T	F	**10.**	Section B-B shows how the flues are arranged in the chimney.
T	F	**11.**	The concrete grade beam at the front of the carport rests on a footing and foundation wall.
T	F	**12.**	A steel angle supports brick veneer over the family room glass doors.
T	F	**13.**	The brick veneer part of the wall supports the roof structure and the overhang at the bedroom gable end.
T	F	**14.**	The solid brick masonry at the front carport corner has different thicknesses on each side of the corner.
T	F	**15.**	Anchor bolts hold down the wood sill at 6′-0″ intervals.
T	F	**16.**	The rough floor is ³/₄″ plywood.
T	F	**17.**	The roof slopes 4¹/₂″ per foot.
T	F	**18.**	Diverters are used on the roof near the family room to direct water to the gutters and downspouts.
T	F	**19.**	There is no access provided to the attic space.
T	F	**20.**	The detail views of the bathroom walls show towel bars and other accessories.
T	F	**21.**	The plumbing fixtures are placed in a line to promote economy of piping and to make plumbing work easier.
T	F	**22.**	Lights in the front of the carport are controlled from the kitchen.
T	F	**23.**	A ceiling light in the family room can be dimmed by a dimmer switch.
T	F	**24.**	Windows may be one of three types.
T	F	**25.**	Cleanout doors for the fireplace are provided and installed by the mason.
T	F	**26.**	Sill plates in exterior walls are 2 × 8s.
T	F	**27.**	The basement floor is a 6″ slab.
T	F	**28.**	All siding on the dwelling is applied vertically.
T	F	**29.**	A double top plate is shown on top and rear walls.
T	F	**30.**	Closet B is larger than Closet A.

Completion

_____ 1. The telephone jack in Bedroom 3 is _____ " high.

_____ 2. The terrace has _____ electrical convenience outlets.

_____ 3. Exhaust fans in bathrooms are controlled by _____ switches.

_____ 4. A(n) _____, forced-air furnace is located in the basement.

_____ 5. The foundation wall at the bedroom end of the dwelling is _____ in length.

_____ 6. Basement columns are _____ " diameter standard pipe.

_____ 7. Registers in toekicks of kitchen base cabinets are 2 " × _____ ".

_____ 8. _____ flashing is placed around the chimney.

_____ 9. Brick veneer is anchored to the house frame every _____ sq. ft.

_____ 10. _____ " exterior grade plywood is used for the soffit at the porch.

_____ 11. Kitchen cabinets have _____ " plywood backs.

_____ 12. The fireplace opening is _____ high.

_____ 13. Plumbing supply lines inside a house are _____.

_____ 14. Door _____ is a sliding door with tempered, insulated glass.

_____ 15. Ceramic tile is placed to a height of _____ around tubs.

_____ 16. The plot plan is drawn to a scale of 1 " = _____ '.

_____ 17. A(n) _____ step is shown at Door B leading to the carport.

_____ 18. Kitchen cabinet elevations are drawn at a scale of _____ " = 1'-0 ".

_____ 19. The concrete slab is thickened to _____ " at the front entrance of the carport.

_____ 20. Section B-B is drawn to a scale of _____ " = 1'-0 ".

_____ 21. The septic tank is located _____ ' from the bedroom end of the dwelling.

_____ 22. Hot and cold water pipes to the washer are _____ " in diameter.

_____ 23. Ridge boards in roof framing are 2 " × _____ ".

_____ 24. Floor joists over the basement area are spaced _____ " OC.

_____ 25. Foundation footings under the main structure are _____ wide.

_____ 26. The front porch is supported by _____ 6 " × 6 " posts.

_____ 27. A(n) _____ " hood is placed above the drop-in cooktop.

_____ 28. The family room has a(n) _____ floor.

_____ 29. Bedroom _____ measures 14'-4 " × 16'-8 ".

_____ 30. Crawl space is excavated to the top of the _____.

_____ 31. Concrete steps leading to the basement have _____ risers.

_____ 32. Access to the attic is located in the ceiling of the _____.

_____ 33. The electrical panel is located in Closet _____.

_____ 34. Soil beneath the terrace is _____.

_____ 35. The front entrance door is Door _____.

_____ 36. Bedroom 3 is 11'-0" × _____.

_____ 37. The storage area in the carport has a(n) _____ light fixture.

_____ 38. The tile _____ provides the thresholds for bathroom doors.

_____ 39. The electric water heater is located in the _____.

_____ 40. The electric meter is located on the exterior wall of the _____.

Identification

_____ 1. Soffit

_____ 2. Foundation wall

_____ 3. Sole plate

_____ 4. Sill

_____ 5. Ceiling joist

_____ 6. Roof pitch symbol

_____ 7. Floor joist

_____ 8. Foundation footing

_____ 9. Window apron

_____ 10. Brick veneer

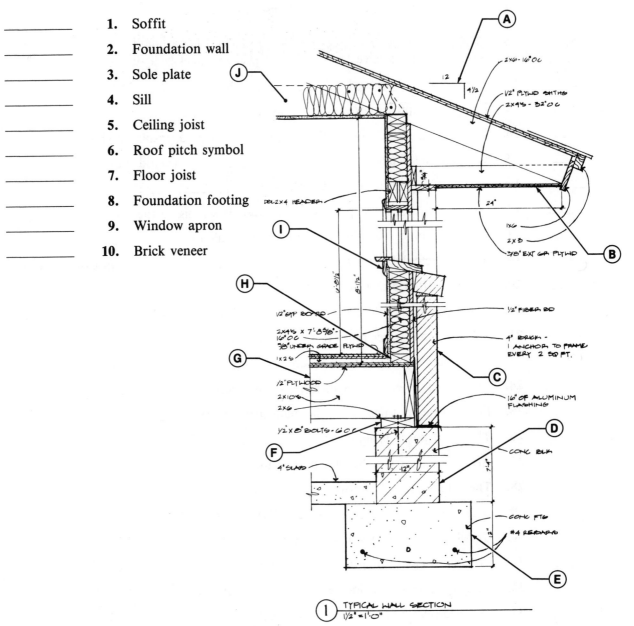

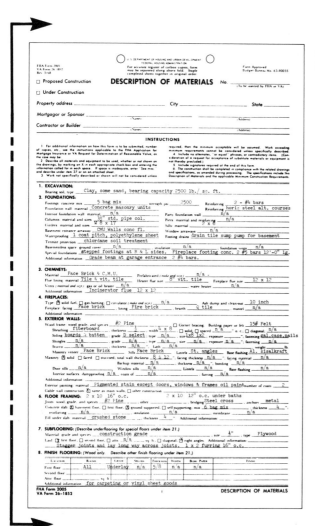

SPECIFICATIONS— BRICK VENEER RESIDENCE

chapter 4

General Requirements
Site Work
Concrete
Masonry
Metals
Wood
Thermal and Moisture Protection
Doors and Windows
Finishes
Equipment
Mechanical
Electrical

SPECIFICATIONS

Specifications are typed sheets gathered together into a pamphlet (or into several volumes for a large building) covering a number of subjects in detail. These subjects include information, in paragraph form, that describes the building to be constructed, the materials to be used, and the responsibilities of those involved.

Even the simplest type of construction job should have specifications. These specifications consist of short statements about the work to be done and the materials to be used. Such specifications are included with a sketch or a working drawing and a written contract to become the basis for agreement between the owner and the contractor.

Complete specifications are written to give detailed information about the job. This information cannot conveniently be shown on a set of prints because it is too lengthy.

The general purpose of specifications includes the following:

1. They provide the general conditions giving the broad provisions of the contract and outline the responsibilities of the owner, architect, contractor, and subcontractors. Guarantees of performance are included.

2. They supplement the working drawings with detailed technical information about the work to be done, specifying the material, equipment, and fixtures to be used.

3. They serve, with the contract agreement and the working drawings, as the legal basis for the transaction of erecting the building from start to finish.

The specifications are intended to supplement the set of prints with data that will spell out the job in a general sense. The specifications also include the details of the job to be done by each individual trade. The set of prints and the specifications are intended to be in agreement. In the event of any discrepancy or conflict between the two, the specifications take precedence.

The architect, who is responsible for the specifications, carefully accounts for all the details in writing. Specifications spell out the architect's role in the project and the personal responsibility that must be assumed for inspection.

The owner uses the specifications to verify that materials specifically desired in the building are provided and to obtain a specific and detailed overview of the finished building. The owner reviews the various guarantees of performance for future reference in the event that the structure or its equipment does not prove satisfactory.

The specifications provide the contractor and subcontractors with detailed information for precise and competitive bidding when estimating the costs of labor and material. Suppliers of building materials such as roofing, lumber, insulation, etc. are able to determine the quality and type of material to be used. Equipment and fixture suppliers find detailed descriptions, with catalog numbers or names, for plumbing fixtures, furnace and air conditioning equipment, and similar items. Subcontractors bid their work based upon codes referenced in the specifications. For example, electricians comply with the requirements of the National Electrical Code® when estimating cost for specific materials.

The building department of the town or city in which the building is to be constructed uses the specifications and the prints to determine their compliance with all applicable building codes and zoning ordinances to meet structural, fire, and health standards. Banks and loan agencies use the same information to help appraise the building to determine its value. When governmental agencies such as the Veterans Administration (VA) or the Federal Housing Administration (FHA) provide part of the financing, they require a copy of the specifications for their approval. Certain sections of the specifications must be written on forms supplied by the individual agency when either VA or FHA financing is to be used.

The importance of complete and concise specifications cannot be overemphasized. They are part of the legal contract and may be used in court in the event of a lawsuit. If the working drawings are correct, and the specifications written with care, the possibility of problems arising are largely averted.

Writing Specifications

The architect is responsible for writing the specifications so that they are consistent with the prints. New developments in materials and methods of construction must be studied so that the architect can recommend specific products to be used and building techniques to be followed. When preparing the specifications, the architect includes the exact materials to be used and lists the equipment by catalog numbers or suggests an alternative. This requires experience acquired from specifying and observing the performance of materials and equipment and watching for new developments in the field.

The architect has an extensive library of catalogs supplied by manufacturers as well as literature from other sources. One of the architect's most useful tools is the *Sweet's Architectural Catalog File*, which is a series of volumes consisting of manufacturers' catalogs organized as ready reference. *Sweet's Architectural Catalog File* (commonly referred to as *Sweet's Catalogs*) is arranged alphabetically by product (for example, doors, windows, etc.) with product manufacturers' specific catalog material giving technical information such as size, color, and application. This file is updated yearly.

Another example of reference material that the architect consults is the *Building Materials Directory* published by Underwriters' Laboratories Inc. Product classifications are given alphabetically, followed by manufacturers of those particular products. Underwriters' Laboratories Inc. also publishes a number of other directories in specific areas. Examples of these directories are *Electrical Construction Materials Directory* and *Electrical Appliance and Utilization Directory*. These directories are updated on an annual basis.

The American Institute of Architects provides standard forms and overall directions for specification writing. These are particularly useful in stating the general conditions. The general conditions are stated at the beginning of the set of specifications, but they govern all of the separate areas of construction. The general conditions also provide uniform legal language, which protects all of the participants (owner, architect, contractor, and subcontractors).

The Construction Specifications Institute (CSI) has developed standard procedures that are helpful in writing the specifications, particularly in writing in the CSI format. See Figure 4-1. Specification writing is divided into 16 technical divisions, each with several broadscope (smaller subheads) section headings. These technical divisions are

1. Division 1—General Requirements
2. Division 2—Site Work
3. Division 3—Concrete
4. Division 4—Masonry
5. Division 5—Metals
6. Division 6—Wood and Plastics
7. Division 7—Thermal and Moisture Protection
8. Division 8—Doors and Windows
9. Division 9—Finishes
10. Division 10—Specialties
11. Division 11—Equipment
12. Division 12—Furnishings
13. Division 13—Special Construction
14. Division 14—Conveying Systems
15. Division 15—Mechanical
16. Division 16—Electrical

Sweet's Architectural Catalog File and catalogs of manufacturers generally follow the CSI format numbering system so that reference to products is made with relative ease. All specifications written according to the CSI format are similar in the arrangement of content. This format helps avoid overlapping between trade areas. Specifications for small buildings with light construction, however, do not always follow the CSI format. A number of divisions may not apply. For example, Division 14—Conveying Systems may not apply and, consequently, is not included. The architect can write the specifications using a condensed form and arrange the divisions to fit the particular building being planned.

The specifications usually begin with general conditional statements, such as the responsibility for examining the site, the liability due to delay in the work, periodic cleaning of the construction area, etc. The remainder of the specifications is devoted to technical information about the divisions of work to be done by each trade. Each technical division covering an area of work should contain four parts:

1. Scope—information that is included in this section of the work.
2. Materials—what specific materials are to be used in each instance.

3. Application—special instructions on how the material is to be applied or used.
4. Guarantee—a statement binding the contractor to a certain quality of work over a specified time. The guarantee can be general, applying to all the trade groups, and inserted in the general conditions.

Specifications are prepared in several ways to serve different purposes. Minimum specifications (for a minor repair job or remodeling) might consist of a sketch showing the work to be done, and a simple statement about the materials to be used. Some specifications are prepared to give general information about the construction and the features of a building without going into detail about procedure. True specifications cover every conceivable area of the building and the building site that is not shown in detail on the working drawings.

Outline Specifications. Outline specifications consist of short statements about the work to be done and the materials to be used. One type of outline specification is that which accompanies *stock plans*. Stock plans are well-designed working drawings prepared by an architectural service to meet the needs of a large cross section of prospective owners located in various parts of the country. These plans are sold for a reasonably moderate fee. In order for the plans and specifications to meet local building code requirements, they should be reviewed and revised as required by a local architect.

Another form of outline specification is prepared by a subdivision builder for prospective buyers. These specifications feature the details in the houses available in the subdivision. The outline specification shown on page 128 is for the North Carolina Residence, which is covered in chapter 3.

Description of Material Specification Forms. Governmental agencies, such as the Federal Housing Administration and the Veterans Administration, require the use of a standard form, entitled *Description of Materials*, as part of the procedure for obtaining a mortgage. This form, shown on pages 129 to 132, is such a document prepared for the building in chapter 3. The form requires the architect to make decisions in the choice of materials and gives the governmental agency a uniform and quick check on the contents. The Description of Materials form cannot be considered a complete set of specifications

CSI FORMAT

DIVISION 1—GENERAL REQUIREMENTS
Reference
Numbers *

01010	SUMMARY OF THE WORK
01100	ALTERNATIVES
01200	PROGRESS AND PAYMENT
01300	SUBMITTALS
01400	TESTING LABORATORY SERVICES
01500	TEMPORARY FACILITIES AND CONTROLS
01600	MATERIAL AND EQUIPMENT
01700	PROJECT CLOSEOUT

DIVISION 2—SITE WORK
Reference
Numbers *

02010	SUBSURFACE EXPLORATION
02100	CLEARING
02110	DEMOLITION
02200	EARTHWORK
02250	SOIL POISONING
02300	PILE FOUNDATIONS
02350	CAISSONS
02400	SHEETING, SHORING AND BRACING
02500	SITE DRAINAGE
02550	SITE UTILITIES
02600	PAVEMENTS AND WALKS
02700	SITE IMPROVEMENTS
02800	LANDSCAPING
02850	RAILROAD WORK
02900	MARINE WORK
02950	TUNNELING

DIVISION 3—CONCRETE
Reference
Numbers *

03100	CONCRETE FORMWORK
03150	EXPANSION AND CONTRACTION JOINTS
03200	CONCRETE REINFORCEMENT
03300	CAST-IN-PLACE CONCRETE
03350	SPECIALLY FINISHED CONCRETE
03360	SPECIALLY PLACED CONCRETE
03400	PRECAST CONCRETE
03500	CEMENTITIOUS DECKS

DIVISION 4—MASONRY
Reference
Numbers *

04100	MORTAR
04150	ACCESSORIES
04200	UNIT MASONRY
04400	STONE
04500	MASONRY RESTORATION AND CLEANING
04550	REFRACTORIES

DIVISION 5—METALS
Reference
Numbers *

05100	STRUCTURAL METAL
05200	STEEL JOISTS
05300	METAL DECKING
05400	LIGHTGAGE FRAMING
05500	MISCELLANEOUS METAL
05700	ORNAMENTAL METAL

DIVISION 6—WOOD AND PLASTICS
Reference
Numbers *

06100	ROUGH CARPENTRY
06130	HEAVY TIMBER CONSTRUCTION
06150	TRESTLES
06170	PREFABRICATED STRUCTURAL WOOD
06200	FINISH CARPENTRY
06300	WOOD TREATMENT
06400	ARCHITECTURAL WOODWORK
06500	PREFABRICATED STRUCTURAL PLASTICS
06600	PLASTIC FABRICATIONS

* Note:
The reference numbers shown relate, insofar as
possible, to the *Uniform System* cost accounting
numbers and the current document identifying
system of the Institute.

DIVISION 7—THERMAL AND MOISTURE PROTECTION
Reference
Numbers *

07100	WATERPROOFING
07150	DAMPPROOFING
07200	INSULATION
07300	SHINGLES AND ROOFING TILES
07400	PREFORMED ROOFING AND SIDING
07500	MEMBRANE ROOFING
07600	FLASHING AND SHEET METAL
07800	ROOF ACCESSORIES
07900	CAULKING AND SEALANTS

DIVISION 8—DOORS AND WINDOWS
Reference
Numbers *

08100	METAL DOORS AND FRAMES
08200	WOOD AND PLASTIC DOORS
08300	SPECIAL DOORS
08500	METAL WINDOWS
08600	WOOD AND PLASTIC WINDOWS
08700	HARDWARE AND SPECIALTIES
08800	GLAZING
08900	CURTAINWALL SYSTEM
08950	STOREFRONT SYSTEM

DIVISION 9—FINISHES
Reference
Numbers *

09100	LATH AND PLASTER
09250	GYPSUM DRYWALL
09300	TILE
09400	TERRAZZO
09450	VENEER STONE
09500	ACOUSTICAL TREATMENT
09550	WOOD FLOORING
09650	RESILIENT FLOORING
09680	CARPETING
09700	SPECIAL FLOORING
09800	SPECIAL COATINGS
09900	PAINTING
09950	WALL COVERING

DIVISION 10—SPECIALTIES
Reference
Numbers *

10100	CHALKBOARDS AND TACKBOARDS
10130	CHUTES
10150	COMPARTMENTS AND CUBICLES
10230	DISAPPEARING STAIRS
10240	DOCK FACILITIES
10250	FIREFIGHTING DEVICES
10300	FIREPLACES
10350	FLAGPOLES
10400	IDENTIFYING DEVICES
10500	LOCKERS
10530	PLASTIC SPECIALTIES
10550	POSTAL SPECIALTIES
10600	PARTITIONS
10650	SCALES
10670	STORAGE SHELVING
10700	SUN CONTROL DEVICES (EXTERIOR)
10750	TELEPHONE ENCLOSURES
10800	TOILET AND BATH ACCESSORIES
10900	WARDROBE SPECIALTIES
10950	WASTE DISPOSAL UNITS

DIVISION 11—EQUIPMENT
Reference
Numbers *

11100	BANK EQUIPMENT
11150	COMMERCIAL EQUIPMENT
11170	CHECKROOM EQUIPMENT
11180	DARKROOM EQUIPMENT
11200	ECCLESIASTICAL EQUIPMENT
11300	EDUCATIONAL EQUIPMENT
11400	FOOD SERVICE EQUIPMENT
11500	ATHLETIC EQUIPMENT
11550	INDUSTRIAL EQUIPMENT
11600	LABORATORY EQUIPMENT
11630	LAUNDRY EQUIPMENT
11650	LIBRARY EQUIPMENT
11700	MEDICAL EQUIPMENT

11800	MORTUARY EQUIPMENT
11830	MUSICAL EQUIPMENT
11850	PARKING EQUIPMENT
11880	PRISON EQUIPMENT
11900	RESIDENTIAL EQUIPMENT
11960	SHIPYARD EQUIPMENT
11970	THEATER EQUIPMENT

DIVISION 12—FURNISHINGS
Reference
Numbers *

12100	ARTWORK
12200	BLINDS AND SHADES
12300	CABINETS AND FIXTURES
12500	DRAPERY AND CURTAINS
12600	FURNITURE
12670	RUGS AND MATS
12700	SEATING

DIVISION 13—SPECIAL CONSTRUCTION
Reference
Numbers *

13010	AIR SUPPORTED STRUCTURES
13050	ACCESS FLOORING
13100	AUDIOMETRIC ROOM
13250	CLEAN ROOM
13300	GREENHOUSE
13350	HYPERBARIC ROOM
13400	INCINERATORS
13440	INSTRUMENTATION
13450	INSULATED ROOM
13500	INTEGRATED CEILING
13540	NUCLEAR REACTORS
13550	OBSERVATORY
13650	PREFABRICATED STRUCTURES
13700	RADIATION PROTECTION
13750	CHIMNEYS
13770	SOUND ISOLATION
13800	STORAGE VAULTS
13850	SWIMMING POOL

DIVISION 14—CONVEYING SYSTEMS
Reference
Numbers *

14100	DUMBWAITERS
14200	ELEVATORS
14300	HOISTS AND CRANES
14400	LIFTS
14500	MATERIAL HANDLING SYSTEMS
14600	MOVING STAIRS AND WALKS
14700	PNEUMATIC TUBE SYSTEMS

DIVISION 15—MECHANICAL
Reference
Numbers *

15010	GENERAL PROVISIONS
15100	BASIC MATERIALS AND METHODS
15180	INSULATION
15200	WATER SUPPLY AND TREATMENT
15300	WASTE WATER DISPOSAL AND TREATMENT
15400	PLUMBING
15550	FIRE PROTECTION
15600	POWER OR HEAT GENERATION
15650	REFRIGERATION
15700	LIQUID HEAT TRANSFER
15800	AIR DISTRIBUTION
15900	CONTROLS AND INSTRUMENTATION

DIVISION 16—ELECTRICAL
Reference
Numbers *

16010	GENERAL PROVISIONS
16100	BASIC MATERIALS AND METHODS
16200	POWER GENERATION
16300	OUTSIDE POWER TRANSMISSION AND DISTRIBUTION
16400	SERVICE AND DISTRIBUTION
16500	LIGHTING
16600	SPECIAL SYSTEMS
16700	COMMUNICATIONS
16850	HEATING AND COOLING
16900	CONTROLS AND INSTRUMENTATION

Figure 4-1. The CSI format technical grouping is divided into 16 divisions.

Construction Specifications Institute

because it does not contain the general conditions nor outline the work to be done.

Complete Specifications. The complete specifications for the building studied in chapter 3 are given on pages 133 to 150. It follows the CSI divisions architects might use when writing such specifications. The specifications, however, can be arranged in some other sequence, depending on the architect's preference. The two primary objectives are to make the specifications complete and concise. Complete specifications are generally broken down into divisions of trade areas and written in detail so that the contractor is assured that everything has been covered in estimating labor and material costs.

References are generally made to specific products. Specifying material may take several forms and often includes optional choices. In some cases, a product that has recognized high quality may be in-dicated. For example, "Formica® or equal" indicates that Formica® brand plastic laminate or its equal must be used. In other cases, several choices may be given in this manner: "Windows by Andersen, Pella, or ROW." In still another instance, a product may be specified by name and catalog number because it will function best in the particular situation.

The specifications for the North Carolina Residence are arranged with the divisions used in the CSI format to parallel the numbering system in *Sweet's Architectural Catalog File* and literature from manufacturers. Refer to Figure 4-1. Four divisions, 10, 12, 13, and 14 are omitted because they do not apply. A set of specifications such as this is not too complex. The numbering system can be simplified to serve the purpose of positively identifying paragraphs. When a set of specifications is lengthy and covers a great number of items, the CSI broadscope sections are carefully followed.

OUTLINE SPECIFICATIONS

North Carolina Residence

This specification is a brief outline of building features. Cost estimates and construction are to be based on the detailed specifications and the working drawings.

1. Foundation:		Cast in place footings formed to size and shape as shown on the working drawings. Basement walls of concrete masonry units with horizontal metal reinforcing. Outside of basement walls to be water proofed with pitch and membrane. Chemical termite protection shall be applied as directed. Slabs to be a minimum of 4″ concrete with a reinforced grade beam at the carport entrance.
2. Walls:		<u>Building</u>. Face brick veneer as shown on elevations. Wall at living room to have board and batten siding.
		<u>Carport</u>. Solid brick piers at corners. Storage room with board and batten siding. Stair windbreak screen of fiberglass.
		<u>Chimney</u>. Concrete block with brick veneer and solid brick masonry as shown on the plans.
3. Rough Framing:		Steel beams on steel posts support 2 × 10 floor joists. Studs 2 × 4. Ceiling joists and roof rafters 2 × 6. Spacing 16″ o.c. for all framing members except under baths 12″ o.c.
4. Roof:		Asphalt shingles over plywood sheathing.
5. Floors:		Plywood rough floors. 1 × 2 inch furring strips. Finish floor underlayment grade plywood. Ceramic (mosaic) tile in baths.
6. Resilient Floors:		Vinyl sheet goods and cove base in passage, kitchen, and family room.
7. Interior Finish:		Gypsum board drywall walls and ceilings. Ceramic tile bathroom walls as shown on the working drawings.
8. Windows:		Wood windows with insulating glass.
9. Doors:		Front and rear entrance doors of insulated steel. Exterior basement door is wood panel with lights. Interior doors to be flush hollow core except one louvered closet door.
10. Kitchen:		Wood custom built kitchen cabinets. Equipment includes oven and range top. Vented hood above range. Dishwasher by owner.
11. Baths:		Built-in vanities with laminated plastic countertops. Vent fans in ceilings.
12. Heating:		Oil-fired, forced warm air system, with 55 gal. capacity electric water heater.
13. Electricity:		200 ampere service
14. Painting:		2 coats oil base paint on exterior except where stain is specified. Interior painting not included in contract.

FHA Form 2005
VA Form 26 1852
Rev. 3/68

U. S. DEPARTMENT OF HOUSING AND URBAN DEVELOPMENT
FEDERAL HOUSING ADMINISTRATION

For accurate register of carbon copies, form
may be separated along above fold. Staple
completed sheets together in original order.

Form Approved
Budget Bureau No. 63-R0055

☐ Proposed Construction

DESCRIPTION OF MATERIALS

No. _____
(To be inserted by FHA or VA)

☐ Under Construction

Property address _____ City _____ State _____

Mortgagor or Sponsor _____
(Name)   (Address)

Contractor or Builder _____
(Name)   (Address)

INSTRUCTIONS

1. For additional information on how this form is to be submitted, number of copies, etc., see the instructions applicable to the FHA Application for Mortgage Insurance or VA Request for Determination of Reasonable Value, as the case may be.
2. Describe all materials and equipment to be used, whether or not shown on the drawings, by marking an X in each appropriate check-box and entering the information called for in each space. If space is inadequate, enter "See misc." and describe under item 27 or on an attached sheet.
3. Work not specifically described or shown will not be considered unless

required, then the minimum acceptable will be assumed. Work exceeding minimum requirements cannot be considered unless specifically described.
4. Include no alternates, "or equal" phrases, or contradictory items. (Consideration of a request for acceptance of substitute materials or equipment is not thereby precluded.)
5. Include signatures required at the end of this form.
6. The construction shall be completed in compliance with the related drawings and specifications, as amended during processing. The specifications include this Description of Materials and the applicable Minimum Construction Requirements.

1. EXCAVATION:
Bearing soil, type __Clay, some sand, bearing capacity 2500 lb./ sq. ft.__

2. FOUNDATIONS:
Footings: concrete mix __5 bag mix__ ; strength psi __2500__   Reinforcing __2 - #4 bars__
Foundation wall: material __Concrete masonry units__   Reinforcing __horiz steel alt. courses__
Interior foundation wall: material __n/a__   Party foundation wall __n/a__
Columns: material and sizes __3½" std. pipe col.__   Piers: material and reinforcing __n/a__
Girders: material and sizes __W 8 x 17__   Sills: material __2 x 6__
Basement entrance areaway __CMU Walls conc fl.__   Window areaways __n/a__
Waterproofing __1 coat pitch, polyethylene sheet__   Footing drains __drain tile sump pump for basement__
Termite protection __chlordane soil treatment__
Basementless space: ground cover __n/a__ ; insulation __n/a__ ; foundation vents __n/a__
Special foundations __stepped footings at R & L sides. Fireplace footing conc. 2 #5 bars 12'-0" lg.__
Additional information: __Grade beam at garage entrance 2 #4 bars.__

3. CHIMNEYS:
Material __Face Brick & C.M.U.__   Prefabricated (make and size) __n/a__ .
Flue lining: material __Tile & vit. tile__   Heater flue size __8" vit. tile__   Fireplace flue size __12 x 12__
Vents (material and size): gas or oil heater __n/a__ ; water heater __n/a__
Additional information: __Incinerator flue 12 x 12__

4. FIREPLACES:
Type: ☒ solid fuel; ☐ gas-burning; ☐ circulator (make and size) __n/a__   Ash dump and clean-out __10 inch__
Fireplace: facing __Face brick__ ; lining __Fire brick__ ; hearth __Q tile__ ; mantel __n/a__
Additional information:

5. EXTERIOR WALLS:
Wood frame: wood grade, and species __#2 Pine__   ☐ Corner bracing. Building paper or felt __15# Felt__
Sheathing __fiberboard__ ; thickness __½__ ; width __4 x 8__ ; ☐ solid; ☐ spaced __n/a__ " o. c.; ☐ diagonal; __n/a__
Siding __boards & batten__ ; grade __D select__ ; type __n/a__ ; size __1x8 1x2__ ; exposure ____"; fastening __gal.case.nails__
Shingles __n/a__ ; grade __n/a__ ; type __n/a__ ; size __n/a__ ; exposure __n/a__ "; fastening __n/a__
Stucco __n/a__ ; thickness __n/a__ "; Lath __n/a__ ; weight ____ lb.
Masonry veneer __Face Brick__   Sills __Face Brick__   Lintels __St. angles__   Base flashing __Al. sisalkraft__
Masonry: ☒ solid ☐ faced ☐ stuccoed; total wall thickness __8 & 12__ "; facing thickness __n/a__ "; facing material __n/a__
Backup material __n/a__ ; thickness __n/a__ "; bonding __n/a__
Door sills __n/a__   Window sills __n/a__   Lintels __n/a__   Base flashing __n/a__
Interior surfaces: dampproofing, __n/a__ coats of __n/a__ ; furring __n/a__
Additional information:
Exterior painting: material __Pigmented stain except doors, windows & frames oil paint__ number of coats __2__
Gable wall construction: ☒ same as main walls; ☐ other construction ____

6. FLOOR FRAMING: 2 x 10 16" o.c.   2 x 10 12" o.c. under baths
Joists: wood, grade, and species __#2 Pine__ ; other ____ ; bridging __Steel cross__ ; anchors __metal__
Concrete slab: ☒ basement floor; ☐ first floor; ☒ ground supported; ☐ self-supporting; mix __6 bag mix__ ; thickness __4__ ";
reinforcing __n/a__ ; insulation __n/a__ ; membrane __n/a__
Fill under slab: material __crushed stone__ ; thickness __4__ ". Additional information:

7. SUBFLOORING: (Describe underflooring for special floors under item 21.)
Material: grade and species __construction grade__ ; size __½__ ; type __Plywood__
Laid: ☒ first floor; ☐ second floor; ☐ attic __n/a__ sq. ft.; ☐ diagonal; ☒ right angles. Additional information: ____
__Stagger joints and lay long way across joists. 1 x 2 furring 16" o.c.__

8. FINISH FLOORING: (Wood only.   Describe other finish flooring under item 21.)

Location	Rooms	Grade	Species	Thickness	Width	Bldg. Paper	Finish
First floor	All	Underlay	n/a	5/8	n/a	n/a	
Second floor							
Attic floor	___ sq. ft.						

Additional information: __for carpeting or vinyl sheet goods__

FHA Form 2005
VA Form 26-1852

1

DESCRIPTION OF MATERIALS

DESCRIPTION OF MATERIALS

9. PARTITION FRAMING:
Studs: wood, grade, and species __#2 Pine__ size and spacing __2 x 4 16" o.c.__ Other __n/a__
Additional information: __n/a__

10. CEILING FRAMING:
Joists: wood, grade, and species __#2 Pine 2 x 6__ Other _____ Bridging __Solid__
Additional information: _____

11. ROOF FRAMING:
Rafters: wood, grade, and species __#2 Pine 2 x 6__ Roof trusses (see detail): grade and species _____
Additional information: _____

12. ROOFING:
Sheathing: wood, grade, and species __Construction ½" Fir Plywood__ ; ☒ solid; ☐ spaced __n/a__ " o.c.
Roofing __Asph. Shingles__ ; grade __240#__ ; size __3 tab__ ; type __Class C__
Underlay __Roofing Felt__ ; weight or thickness __15#__ ; size _____ ; fastening __Zinc Ct.Nail__
Built-up roofing __n/a__ ; number of plies __n/a__ ; surfacing material __n/a__
Flashing: material __gal. st.__ ; gage or weight __26 gage__ ; ☐ gravel stops; ☐ snow guards
Additional information: _____

13. GUTTERS AND DOWNSPOUTS:
Gutters: material __n/a__ ; gage or weight __n/a__ ; size __n/a__ , shape __n/a__
Downspouts: material __n/a__ ; gage or weight __n/a__ ; size __n/a__ , shape __n/a__ ; number __n/a__
Downspouts connected to: ☐ Storm sewer; ☐ sanitary sewer; ☐ dry-well. ☐ Splash blocks: material and size _____
Additional information: __metal diverters at rear valley__

14. LATH AND PLASTER
Lath ☐ walls, ☐ ceilings: material __n/a__ ; weight or thickness __n/a__ Plaster: coats __n/a__ ; finish __n/a__
Dry-wall ☒ walls, ☒ ceilings: material __gypsum bd.__ ; thickness __½__ ; finish __smooth__
Joint treatment __Tape & spackle, sand smooth__

15. DECORATING: (Paint, wallpaper, etc.)

ROOMS	WALL FINISH MATERIAL AND APPLICATION	CEILING FINISH MATERIAL AND APPLICATION
Kitchen	Paint 3 coats	Paint 3 coats
Bath	Ceramic tile, Paint 3 coats above	Paint 3 coats
Other	Paint 3 coats	Paint 3 coats

Additional information: _____

16. INTERIOR DOORS AND TRIM:
Doors: type __H.C. Flush & louvered__ ; material __Flush Oak, Louvered Pine__ thickness __1 3/8 - 1 3/4__
Door trim: type __Solid__ ; material __oak__ Base: type __stock__ ; material __oak__ ; size __n/a__
Finish: doors __Stain & varnish__ ; trim __stain & varnish__
Other trim (item, type and location) __mantel trim oak stain & varnish__
Additional information: _____

17. WINDOWS:
Windows: type __D.H.& casement__ ; make __Andersen__ ; material __Pine__ ; sash thickness __1 3/8__
Glass: grade __Insulating__ ; ☐ sash weights; ☐ balances, type __Spring__ ; head flashing __n/a__
Trim: type __Wood casing__ ; material __Oak__ Paint __Stain & varnish__ ; number coats __2__
Weatherstripping: type __Friction__ ; material __st. st.__ Storm sash, number __n/a__
Screens: ☒ full; ☐ half: type __aluminum__ ; number __n/a__ ; screen cloth material __n/a__
Basement windows: type __n/a__ ; material __n/a__ ; screens, number __n/a__ ; Storm sash, number __n/a__
Special windows _____
Additional information: _____

18. ENTRANCES AND EXTERIOR DETAIL:
Main entrance door: material __Pease Steel Clad__ ; width __3'-0"__ ; thickness __3/4__ ". Frame: material __Pine__ , thickness __1 3/8__ "
Other entrance doors: material __Pease Steel Clad__ width __3'-0"__ ; thickness __3/4__ ". Frame: material __Pine__ ; thickness __1 3/8__ "
Head flashing __n/a__ Weatherstripping: type __Friction__ ; saddles __n/a__
Screen doors: thickness __n/a__ "; number __n/a__ ; screen cloth material __n/a__ Storm doors: thickness __n/a__ "; number __n/a__
Combination storm and screen doors: thickness __1 1/8__ ; number __2__ ; screen cloth material __Aluminum__
Shutters: ☐ hinged; ☐ fixed. Railings __Wood__ , Attic louvers __2 #2 Pine__
Exterior millwork: grade and species __D Select (West Coast)__ Paint __Pigmented stain__ ; number coats __2__
Additional information: __Oil paint windows, doors, and trim__

19. CABINETS AND INTERIOR DETAIL:
Kitchen cabinets, wall units: material __Oak__ ; lineal feet of shelves __28'__ ; shelf width __12"__
Base units: material __Oak__ ; counter top __Laminated plastic__ ; edging __Laminated plastic__
Back and end splash __Broderick 3309__ Finish of cabinets _____ ; number coats _____
Medicine cabinets: make _____ ; model _____
Other cabinets and built-in furniture _____
Additional information: __2 Bathroom vanities Laminated plastic top   Oak stain & varnish__

20. STAIRS:

STAIR	TREADS		RISERS		STRINGS		HANDRAIL		BALUSTERS	
	Material	Thickness	Material	Thickness	Material	Size	Material	Size	Material	Size
Basement	Conc.		Conc.		Conc.		Pipe	2"	n/a	
Main										
Attic										

Disappearing: make and model number __Super Simplex folding stair (wood)__
Additional information: _____

2

21. SPECIAL FLOORS AND WAINSCOT: ○　　　　　　○

	LOCATION	MATERIAL, COLOR, BORDER, SIZES, GAGE, ETC.	THRESHOLD MATERIAL	WALL BASE MATERIAL	UNDERFLOOR MATERIAL
FLOORS	Kitchen	3/16" Vinyl asbestos sheet goods	Aluminum	Vinyl	½" Plywood
	Bath	3/16" Vinyl asbestos sheet goods	Aluminum	Vinyl	½" Plywood

	LOCATION	MATERIAL, COLOR, BORDER, CAP. SIZES. GAGE, ETC.	HEIGHT	HEIGHT OVER TUB	HEIGHT IN SHOWERS (FROM FLOOR)
WAINSCOT	Bath	Ceramic tile, See Elevations	4'-2"	6'-4"	n/a

Bathroom accessories: ☐ Recessed; material _____ ; number _____ ; ☒ Attached; material __ceramic__ ; number _____
Additional information: __2 Soap dish, 2 tumbler holder, 4 towel bar, 2 toilet paper holder__

22. PLUMBING:

FIXTURE	NUMBER	LOCATION	MAKE	MFR'S FIXTURE IDENTIFICATION NO.	SIZE	COLOR
Sink	1	Kitchen	Crane	St.St. 2 comp 2 drbd.	5' - 6"	S.S.
Lavatory	2	Bath	Crane	with vanity		as selected
Water closet	2	Bath	Crane	siphon jet with tank		as selected
Bathtub	2	Bath	Crane		5' - 0"	as selected
Shower over tub △	2	Bath	Crane			
Stall shower △	n/a					
Laundry trays	n/a					
Dishwasher		Kitchen	By Owner			
Disposal		Kitchen	Insinkerator	77	½ h.p.	
Washer Dryer		Closet	By Owner			

△☒ Curtain rod　△☐ Door　☐ Shower pan: material _____
Water supply: ☒ public; ☐ community system; ☐ individual (private) system.★
Sewage disposal: ☐ public; ☐ community system; ☒ individual (private) system.★
★Show and describe individual system in complete detail in separate drawings and specifications according to requirements.
House drain (inside): ☐ cast iron; ☐ tile; ☒ other __PVC__ House sewer (outside): ☐ cast iron; ☒ tile; ☐ other _____
Water piping: ☐ galvanized steel; ☒ copper tubing; ☐ other _____ Sill cocks, number _____
Domestic water heater: type __Electric__ ; make and model __Rheem__ ; heating capacity _____
_____ gph. 100° rise. Storage tank: material __Glass__ ; capacity __55__ gallons.
Gas service: ☐ utility company; ☐ liq. pet. gas; ☐ other _____ Gas piping: ☐ cooking; ☐ house heating.
Footing drains connected to: ☐ storm sewer; ☐ sanitary sewer; ☐ dry well. Sump pump; make and model _____
_____ ; capacity _____ ; discharges into _____

23. HEATING:
☐ Hot water. ☐ Steam. ☐ Vapor. ☐ One-pipe system. ☐ Two-pipe system.
　☐ Radiators. ☐ Convectors. ☐ Baseboard radiation. Make and model _____
　Radiant panel: ☐ floor; ☐ wall; ☐ ceiling. Panel coil: material _____
　☐ Circulator. ☐ Return pump. Make and model _____ ; capacity _____ gpm.
　Boiler: make and model _____ Output _____ Btuh.; net rating _____ Btuh.
Additional information: _____
Warm air: ☐ Gravity. ☒ Forced. Type of system __Ducts in basement__
　Duct material: supply __Sheet metal__ ; return __sheet metal__ Insulation __n/a__ , thickness __n/a__ ☐ Outside air intake.
　Furnace: make and model __Lennox 09-105__ Input _____ Btuh.; output __84,000__ Btuh.
Additional information: _____
☐ Space heater; ☐ floor furnace; ☐ wall heater. Input _____ Btuh.; output _____ Btuh.; number units _____
　Make, model _____ Additional information: _____
Controls: make and types __Johnson   electric for above furnace__
Additional information: _____
Fuel: ☐ Coal; ☒ oil; ☐ gas; ☐ liq. pet. gas; ☐ electric; ☐ other _____ ; storage capacity __550 gal.__
Additional information: _____
Firing equipment furnished separately: ☐ Gas burner, conversion type. ☐ Stoker: hopper feed ☐; bin feed ☐
　Oil burner: ☒ pressure atomizing; ☐ vaporizing _____
　Make and model _____ Control _____
Additional information: _____
Electric heating system: type _____ Input _____ watts; @ _____ volts; output _____ Btuh.
Additional information: _____
Ventilating equipment: attic fan, make and model _____ ; capacity _____ cfm.
　kitchen exhaust fan, make and model __Thermador__
Other heating, ventilating. or cooling equipment __2 Bath fans   Tradewind Model 1201__

24. ELECTRIC WIRING:
Service: ☒ overhead; ☐ underground. Panel: ☐ fuse box; ☒ circuit-breaker; make __Bryant__ AMP's __200__ No. circuits _____
Wiring: ☒ conduit; ☐ armored cable; ☐ nonmetallic cable; ☐ knob and tube; ☐ other _____
Special outlets: ☒ range; ☒ water heater; ☒ other __oven, clothes dryer__
☐ Doorbell. ☒ Chimes. Push-button locations __Front & Back Doors__ Additional information: _____

25. LIGHTING FIXTURES:
Total number of fixtures __12__ Total allowance for fixtures, typical installation, $_____
Nontypical installation _____
Additional information: _____

3

DESCRIPTION OF MATERIALS

DESCRIPTION OF MATERIALS

26. INSULATION:

LOCATION	THICKNESS	MATERIAL, TYPE, AND METHOD OF INSTALLATION	VAPOR BARRIER
Roof	n/a		
Ceiling	6	foil faced fiberglass	
Wall	2"	foil faced fiberglass	
Floor	n/a		

HARDWARE: (make, material, and finish.) ___ Schlage, bronze

SPECIAL EQUIPMENT: (State material or make, model and quantity.   Include only equipment and appliances which are acceptable by local law, custom and applicable FHA standards.   Do not include items which, by established custom, are supplied by occupant and removed when he vacates premises or chattels prohibited by law from becoming realty.)_____
Counter top range
Built-in oven
Garbage disposal

27. MISCELLANEOUS: (Describe any main dwelling materials, equipment, or construction items not shown elsewhere; or use to provide additional information where the space provided was inadequate.   Always reference by item number to correspond to numbering used on this form.) _____

PORCHES: 4" concrete slab and covered porch at front door

TERRACES: 4" poured concrete slab with troweled finish

GARAGES:

WALKS AND DRIVEWAYS:
Driveway: width __n/a__ ; base material _____ ; thickness _____"; surfacing material _____ ; thickness _____"
Front walk: width __n/a__ ; material _____ ; thickness _____". Service walk: width _____ ; material _____ ; thickness _____"
Steps: material __n/a__ _____; treads _____"; risers _____". Cheek walls _____

OTHER ONSITE IMPROVEMENTS:
(Specify all exterior onsite improvements not described elsewhere, including items such as unusual grading, drainage structures, retaining walls, fence, railings, and accessory structures.)
Entire site to be fine graded.

LANDSCAPING, PLANTING, AND FINISH GRADING:
Topsoil __4__ " thick; ☒ front yard; ☒ side yards; ☒ rear yard to ____15____ feet behind main building.
Lawns (seeded, sodded, or sprigged): ☐ front yard __n/a__ ; ☐ side yards _____ ; ☐ rear yard_____
Planting: ☐ as specified and shown on drawings; ☐ as follows:
| | |
__n/a__ Shade trees, deciduous, _____" caliper.   __n/a__ Evergreen trees. _____' to _____', B & B.
__n/a__ Low flowering trees, deciduous, _____' to_____'   __n/a__ Evergreen shrubs. _____' to _____', B & B.
__n/a__ High-growing shrubs, deciduous, _____' to_____'   _____ Vines, 2-year _____
__n/a__ Medium-growing shrubs, deciduous, _____' to_____'
__n/a__ Low-growing shrubs, deciduous, _____' to_____'

IDENTIFICATION.—This exhibit shall be identified by the signature of the builder, or sponsor, and/or the proposed mortgagor if the latter is known at the time of application.

Date_____   Signature _____

Signature _____

FHA Form 2005
VA Form 26–1852

4

COMPLETE SPECIFICATIONS FOR
A NORTH CAROLINA RESIDENCE

(Prints studied in Chapter 3)

INDEX

DIVISIONS 10, 12, 13, and 14 do not apply.

GENERAL CONDITIONS

The latest edition of the standard form of "General Conditions of the Contract" published by the American Institute of Architects shall be understood to be a part of this specification and shall be adhered to by the Contractor (the General Contractor).

SPECIAL CONDITIONS

Sec. 1.   EXAMINATION OF SITE. It is understood that the Contractor has examined the site and is familiar with all conditions which might affect the execution of this contract and has made provisions therefor in his bid.

Sec. 2.   TIME FOR COMPLETION. The work shall be completed within 150 calendar days after written Notice to Proceed is issued to the Contractor.

Sec. 3.   EXISTING TREES. Existing trees within 15 feet of the foundation line for the new structure shall be carefully protected by the Contractor from injury which might result from any operation connected with the execution of this contract.

Sec. 4.   GUARANTEE. The acceptance of this contract carries with it a guarantee on the part of the Contractor to make good any defects in the work of the building arising or discovered within one year after completion and acceptance of same by the Architect, whether from shrinkage, settlement, or faults of labor or materials.

Sec. 5.   RESPONSIBILITIES OF CONTRACTOR. Except as otherwise specifically stated in the Contract, the Contractor shall provide and pay for all materials, labor, tools, equipment, water, light, heat, power, transportation, temporary construction of every nature, taxes legally collected because of the work, and all other services and facilities of every nature whatsoever necessary to execute the work to be done under this contract and to bring the building to completion in every respect within the specified time, all in accordance with the drawings and specifications. The Contractor shall carry public liability, workmen's compensation, and vehicular insurance. The Contractor shall coordinate all trades.

DIVISION 1—GENERAL REQUIREMENTS

1.01   SUMMARY OF THE WORK

1.01.1   Work under the Contract shall include all work shown on the drawings and indicated in these specifications. All work shall conform to local rules and ordinances. The General Contractor shall complete all work within the allotted time as indicated in the Method of Bidding.

1.01.2   The carpenter shall do cutting of wood necessary for other trades and shall erect ladders inside of building. Scaffolding shall be erected, maintained, and removed by Contractor for whose work it is necessary. Ditches for mechanical trades shall be dug and refilled by Contractor for whose work they are necessary.

1.01.3   Items provided by Owner are shown on the drawings and will be installed by Owner unless noted to be installed by the General Contractor.

1.01.4   Owner occupancy shall occur at the completion of the work. The General Contractor must complete the work within 30 days after the substantial completion. (Substantial completion date is the date when owner, architect, and contractor go over a check list of things in the contract.)

1.1 PROGRESS AND PAYMENT (Project meetings)

1.1.1 Progress of the work for payment purposes shall be determined by the Architect. The Contractor shall submit his claim for payment to the Architect for approval. The Architect shall determine that the work in place meets the quality specified and the claim for payment is for the work in place and material stored at the building site.

1.1.2 Payment to the Contractor shall be made by the Owner within ten (10) days of the Architect's approval of the claim for payment.

1.2 SUBMITTALS

1.2.1 Shop Drawings and Samples of finish materials shall be submitted to the Architect for his approval before shop fabrication.

1.2.2 Cost Breakdown for purposes of payment shall be submitted within 30 days of the signing of the contract.

1.3 TEMPORARY FACILITIES AND CONTROLS

1.3.1 Utilities for temporary use shall be provided by the Contractor.

1.4 PROJECT CLOSEOUT

1.4.1 Cleaning up shall be the responsibility of the General Contractor. All rubbish shall be removed from the building and hauled to the city land fill site each week. Floors, walls, windows, and all other surfaces shall be cleaned ready for occupancy. Turn over building broom clean. The owner will wash windows and the plumbing fixtures.

1.4.2 Final Inspection shall be held with the Owner, Contractor, and Architect, or a representative of each, present. Within one week (7 days) the Contractor shall correct all items found to be defective.

DIVISION 2—SITE WORK

2.1 SUBSURFACE EXPLORATION

2.1.1 Subsurface Soil Data from previous projects in the area indiciate an allowable bearing load of 2500 lbs./sq. ft. The Contractor shall notify the Architect, who shall inspect the excavation prior to placing of footings.

2.2 CLEARING

2.2.1 Topsoil Stripping and Storage. Strip all topsoil up to a depth of 6 inches and stockpile within the site. Keep topsoil free from all trash. See plot plan.

2.3   EARTHWORK

2.3.1   Site Grading. Do all cutting, filling, backfilling, and grading required to bring the entire project area, outside of buildings to subgrade. Subgrade for lawn and planting areas is 4 inches below finished grade.

2.3.2   Trench for footings and carport foundations allowing sufficient room for form work. Place footings and foundations upon undisturbed and firm bottoms.

2.3.3   Excavate for basement and crawl space to 18 inches outside of foundation line.

2.3.4   Backfill and compaction against foundation wall shall be trashfree material in 8 inch lifts. Rough grade around building to be 4 inches below top of foundation. Care must be taken not to damage the foundation walls or the dampproofing and waterproofing.

2.3.5   Waste Material Disposal. Remove from the site, and dispose of, all debris and all excavated materials not suitable or needed for fill.

2.3.6   Finish grading shall be to elevations shown on the drawings. Use topsoil from stockpile on the site. Slope all work away from the building with no abrupt changes.

2.4   SOIL POISONING
(Author's note: The soil is poisoned around the foundation and under slabs to prevent termites from invading the building.)

2.4.1   Chemical—Chlordane applied in oil solution or water emulsion, 1.0% concentration.

2.4.2   Apply at rate of 1 gallon per $2^1/_2$ lineal feet of depth along both sides of basement and crawl space foundation walls.

2.4.3   Under floors of basement, carport, basement stairs, and porches and around column footings in crawl space, apply overall treatment at rate of one gallon per 10 square feet.

2.4.4   In voids of unit masonry foundation walls apply at rate of 1 gallon per 5 lineal feet.

2.4.5   Treatment shall not be made when the soil or fill is excessively wet or immediately after heavy rains. Unless treated areas are to be immediately covered, take precautions to prevent disturbance of treatment.

2.5   PAVEMENTS AND WALKS

        not in contract

2.6   LANDSCAPING

        not in contract

DIVISION 3—CONCRETE

3.1   CONCRETE FORMWORK

3.1.1   Forms for footings and edges of slabs shall conform to the shapes, lines, and dimensions called for on plans and be substantial and tight to prevent leakage of concrete. Prior to placing concrete, concrete forms shall be thoroughly wetted or oiled.

3.1.2   Remove forms without damage to concrete.

3.2   CONCRETE REINFORCEMENT

3.2.1   Provide and install reinforcing bars as indicated on drawings.

3.3   CAST-IN-PLACE CONCRETE

3.3.1   Portland cement shall conform to ASTM Specifications for Portland Cement, C150.

3.3.2   Aggregates for concrete shall conform to ASTM Specifications for Concrete Aggregates, C33. Grade course aggregate from 1 inch to $1^1/_2$ inches.

3.3.3   Water shall be clean and free from injurious amounts of deleterious substances.

3.3.4   Place concrete only on undisturbed earth. Concrete shall be ready-mixed and shall comply with ASTM Specifications for Ready-mixed Concrete, C94.

3.3.5   All debris and ice shall be removed from the space to be occupied by the concrete. Reinforcement shall be free of ice and other coatings and shall be thoroughly cleaned.

3.3.6   Compacted fill under basement and carport slabs shall be approved by the Architect. A 95% compaction is required.

3.3.7   The 4 inch porous fill under the slab shall be composed of gravel or crushed stone of uniform-size particles, $^3/_4$ inch in size, compact and level. Cover this fill with a vapor barrier polyethylene sheet 6 mils nominal thickness.

3.3.8   Concrete for slabs and steps shall not be less than 4 inches thick. Concrete floor finish shall be true and level as called for by the drawings with maximum tolerance of $^1/_8$ inch in 6 feet. Pitch basement floor to drain. Pitch porch floors away from building. Trowel finish slabs.

3.3.9   Concrete shall be maintained in a moist condition for at least 7 days by water curing or membrane curing.

DIVISION 4—MASONRY

4.1   MORTAR

4.1.1   Mortar: Proportioning. By volume, one part portland cement, one part lime putty, six parts sand.

4.1.2   Mortar consistency shall be as wet as can be conveniently handled. Do not use stiffened mortar.

4.2   ANCHORS AND TIES

4.2.1.   Brick veneer shall be secured to backing with corrosion resisting ties. Install one metal tie for each 2 square feet of area.

4.3   CONCRETE BLOCK

4.3.1   Build foundations of concrete block accurately as shown on drawings. Key mesh or Durowall reinforcing in alternate block courses. Bond walls together at intersections.

4.3.2   Fill voids in top units with concrete. Install anchor bolts 6 feet-0 inches o.c.

4.4   BRICK VENEER AND BRICK WALLS

4.4.1   Build brick veneer walls and solid brick walls as shown on drawings. Figure $00.00 per thousand for brick delivered to the job as selected by the Owner.

4.4.2   Build walls straight and plumb, courses level. Fill all joints with mortar as units are laid. Full head joints. Tool exposed brick joints with concave tool. Lay solid brick walls with common bond.

4.4.3   Install lintels furnished by other contractor under Division 5.

4.5   CHIMNEY AND FIREPLACE

4.5.1   Build chimney as shown on drawings.

4.5.2   Install vitrified tile flue for furnace, and tile flues for incinerator and fireplace.

4.5.3   Build fireplace as shown on drawings. Line with firebrick, face with same brick as on exterior. Install ratchet type cast iron damper, ash drop. Mason contractor is responsible to make fireplace operate properly.

4.5.4   Furnish and install three iron cleanout doors, incinerator grating. Install lintels furnished by others.

6

4.6   CLEANING MASONRY

4.6.1   Clean brick from top down with a solution of non-staining soap and clean water or solution of one part muriatic acid to ten parts water. Scrub surface with stiff bristle brushes and rinse well with clean water.

DIVISION 5—METALS

5.1   STRUCTURAL STEEL

5.1.1   Basement beams, steel pipe columns, carport entrance beam, and lintels as shown on drawings.

5.1.2   All steel shall be painted one shop coat of rust inhibiting paint.

DIVISION 6—WOOD

6.1   CARPENTRY

6.1.1   Workmanship shall conform to FHA standards. Interior finish shall be installed by trim carpenters. Trim shall be set level and plumb, well joined. Set nails.

6.2   ROUGH CARPENTRY

6.2.1   Material. Mudsills, floor joists, ceiling joists, studs, and rafters shall be construction grade Douglas fir or No. 2 or better yellow pine. Sub-floor shall be utility grade west coast wood or yellow pine sheathing or $1/2$ inch CD plywood. Roof boards same. Wall sheathing $1/2$ inch water resistant fiber board. At both sides of four corners of house, install $1/2$ inch plywood sheathing.

6.2.2   <u>Methods of Framing</u>

6.2.2.1   Lay out carpenter work as called for by the drawings. Cut and fit for conditions encountered. All work shall be plumbed, leveled, and braced with nails, spikes, bolts, etc., to ensure rigidity. Steel cross bridging for floor joists. Solid bridging for ceiling joists.

6.2.2.2   Clearance around chimneys and flues shall conform to NBFU (National Bureau of Fire Underwriters) Building Code and local code.

6.2.2.3   Sole framing members shall be single, 2 inch nominal thickness members for all walls and partitions.

6.2.2.4   Studs shall be 2 × 4 inch wood at 16 inch o.c., doubled at openings and tripled at corners, placed to provide end nailing for sheathing and wall board. Toenail to sole with two 8d nails on each side face of each stud. One stud per four feet of exterior wall shall be fastened by means of 19 gauge zinc coated metal anchor, as per manufacturer's instructions.

6.2.2.5   Top plates shall be double, 2 inch nominal thickness members for all partitions.

6.2.2.6   Plates shall be same width as studs and form continuous horizontal ties. Ends of soles shall be provided with splice plates, nailed to studs and corner posts. Top plates shall be nailed together with 10d nails at 24 inch o.c. Two 10d nails shall be used at ends of upper members. No joint in upper member shall occur over a joint in a lower member. Lintels shall occur over openings in walls and bearing partitions. Plate splices shall not occur where plate forms part of a lintel.

6.2.2.7   All wood members shall be anchored and fastened together to ensure sound, sturdy construction.

6.2.3   <u>Wood Blocking</u>

6.2.3.1.   Wood blocking, nailers, and grounds shall be provided for woodwork, cabinets, and other finished items.

6.3   FINISH CARPENTRY

6.3.1   Material: Fascia boards and siding shall be D select west coast lumber. Plywood soffit AB exterior grade plywood. 6 × 6 posts shall be standard grade fir or No. 2 yellow pine. Top flooring shall be underlayment grade $5/8$ inch plywood on 1 × 2 inch strips 16 inches o.c. Face nail with 8d ring or coated nails 12 inches o.c. and 6 inches o.c. at edges. Stock oak jambs and stops. Stock $2^{1}/_4$ inch ranch type oak casings.

6.3.2   Vanities by Owner to be installed by this Contractor. Oak mantel trim. Install window trim, base, closet plywood partitions, shelves, hanging rods as shown on drawings.

6.3.3   Custom built oak kitchen cabinets to be built and installed by kitchen cabinet sub-contractor.

6.4   <u>Methods of Framing</u>

6.4.1   Exterior millwork and trim shall be installed with tight joints, securely nailed with galvanized case nails. Interior trim and finish lumber shall be fastened in place with finishing nails, the heads set for putty, and finish sanded.

6.4.2   Millwork shall be in long lengths with jointing where solid fastenings can be made and bedded in white lead paste. Corners shall be mitered or coped as is standard practice.

6.5   WOOD TREATMENT

6.5.1   All sills in contact with concrete shall be treated with preservative meeting Federal Specifications TTW571.

DIVISION 7— THERMAL AND MOISTURE PROTECTION

7.1   FOUNDATION WATERPROOFING

7.1.1 Outside of foundation walls around basement and crawl space and basement stair. Crawl space side of wall between crawl space and basement.

7.1.2 Apply one heavy coat of pitch. Over this apply 6 mil polyethylene sheets in as wide widths as practical, well lapped.

7.2 DAMPPROOFING

7.2.1 Vapor barrier applied over plywood sheathing shall be 15 lb. felt, asphalt saturated.

7.2.2 One-ply felt on walls.

7.3 INSULATION

7.3.1 Between studs in outside walls install 2 inch foil faced fiberglass batts. Between ceiling joists install 6 inch foil face fiberglass batts or blow in rock wool to joist depth. If blown-in insulation is used, install foil back gypsum board on ceilings.

7.4 ROOFING

7.4.1 Cover roofs with 15 lb. roofing felt. Over this install 12 × 36 inch 240 lb. asphalt shingles, class C label, standard color as selected by Owner. Five inch exposure, six nails per shingle, zinc coated nails.

7.5 FLASHING AND SHEET METAL

7.5.1 Install flashing around chimney and where carport roof meets gable wall. Diverters where shown on drawings. 26 gauge galvanized iron. Install 20 × .019 inch aluminum valley flashing in valleys.

7.6 CAULKING AND SEALANTS

7.6.1 Caulking shall conform to F. S. TT-C-598 Grade 1, color to be selected by architect.

7.6.2 Sealant to be poly-sulfide.

7.6.3 Set all thresholds in sealant. Caulk and seal all windows, doors, and joints.

7.6.4 Apply materials with pressure gun.

DIVISION 8—DOORS AND WINDOWS

8.1 METAL DOORS

8.1.1 Outside entrance doors. Insulated steel doors. (Pease Co.) Keyed alike. Owner to choose style.

8.2   WOOD DOORS

8.2.1   Basement door wood panel door per schedule. Key alike with entrance doors.

8.2.2   Interior doors, premium grade hollow core flush oak doors or stock pine louver doors with panels, as scheduled.

8.2.3   Interior and exterior door frames pine, stock design.

8.2.4   Install all doors to fit snugly without binding. All faces, edges, tops, and bottoms to be finished. $^1/_{16}$ inch clearance at top and sides and $^1/_2$ inch at the bottom.

8.3   SPECIAL DOORS

8.3.1   Wood sliding glass doors, 6 feet wide minimum sash opening, stock type by Andersen, Pella, or ROW, with $^5/_8$ inch tempered insulating glass and manufacturer's screen.

8.3.2   Provide and install attic access door, stock type.

8.4   WOOD WINDOWS

8.4.1   Double hung by same manufacturers of similar stock types, with insulating glass, grills, and manufacturer's full screens. Casement window same, no grills, rototype operators.

8.4.2   Provide screen louvers for right and left gable ends, stock type.

8.5   HARDWARE

        All material and work in this section by carpentry contractor.

8.5.1   Rough hardware, nails, screws, hangers, anchor bolts, and fastening as required.

8.5.2   Tracks and associated hardware for bi-fold and sliding doors. Pocket door frames. Hinges, lock and latch sets, cabinet hardware, medicine cabinets. Bedroom and bathroom doors shall have push button knob locks. Allow $000.00 Contractor's cost for same as selected by Owner. Install same.

8.5.3   Aluminum thresholds with vinyl inserts at two outside doors. Weatherstrip jambs. Caulk around all outside masonry openings with best grade caulking paste.

DIVISION 9—FINISHES

9.1   GYPSUM DRYWALL

9.1.1   Gypsum board. Basement ceiling, $1/2$ inch fireshield board. Bathroom walls, $1/2$ inch water resisting type. On ceilings and other walls and partitions, $1/2$ inch gypsum board for taping. Install metal beads at outside corners. Apply with ring shank nails as per manufacturer's instructions. Tape joints, putty nail heads, and corner beads to smooth finish job. No taping in basement.

9.2   CERAMIC TILE

9.2.1   Conform to specifications of Tile Council of America. Standard colors and patterns as selected by Owner. Same in both baths.

9.2.2   On bathroom floors install mosaic tile floors by thin set method over plywood installed by others. On bathroom walls install $4^1/4 \times 4^1/4$ inch tile on water resistant gypsum board installed by others. See drawings. Allow $00.00 for accessories as selected by Owner.

9.2.3   Tile hearth. Quarry tile, $12'' \times 6''$ on $1^1/4$ inch cement base by this Contractor.

9.3   RESILIENT FLOORS

9.3.1   Apply materials as per manufacturer's directions. Lay out for minimum number of seams, which shall be tight. Fit tight to base, door jambs, and casings, etc. Check condition of floors before starting work. If not satisfactory, report to general contractor for correction.

9.3.2   In kitchen, passage, and family room, install Armstrong Castilian sheet goods in twelve foot widths. All same pattern, as selected by Owner.

9.4   PAINTING

9.4.1   General

9.4.1.1   Furnish labor and materials to complete painting of all surfaces; drywall, wood, and metal as hereinafter specified and shown on the drawings. Prime window and door frames.

9.4.1.2   Materials: Paint shall be best grade oil base house and interior paint as made by Moore, O'Brien, Pittsburgh, Sherwin-Williams, or as approved by Owner. Cabot's oil stain and Galvinoleum as specified in Painting Schedule.

9.4.1.3   Architect shall furnish a color schedule showing where various colors are used. Owner will give final approval of colors.

9.4.1.4   Each coat of paint shall be slightly darker than preceding coat unless otherwise directed. Undercoats shall be tinted similar to finish coats.

9.4.1.5   Commencing of work indicates acceptance of surfaces by painter.

9.4.1.6   Cover materials and surfaces, including floors, adjoining or below work in progress, with clean drop cloths or canvas. Remove hardware, accessories, plates, lighting fixtures, and similar items or provide protection by masking. Upon completion, replace above items or remove protection and clean.

9.4.1.7   Before applying paint or finish, surfaces, including floors, shall be clean, dry, smooth, and free of loose dirt and dust.

9.4.2   Workmanship

9.4.2.1   Brush, spray, or roll on materials smoothly in solid, even colors without drips, runs, lumps, defective brushing, discoloration, or any other faulty workmanship.

9.4.2.2   Coats shall be thoroughly dry before applying succeeding coats. Allow 48 hours drying time between coats for exterior work and 24 hours for interior work.

9.4.3   Painting Schedule

9.4.3.1   Exterior Finish

9.4.3.1.1   Window sash and frames, paint two coats. Two wood doors and frames, same.

9.4.3.1.2   Two outside entrance doors, wood frames, paint two coats. These doors are metal. Paint one coat red lead or Rustoleum, one coat house paint.

9.4.3.1.3   Fascias, soffits, siding, porch woodwork, two coats Cabot's oil stain. Chimney flashing, one coat Galvinoleum, one coat house paint.

9.4.3.1.4   Check colors with Owner before applying paint or stain.

9.4.3.2   Interior Finish

9.4.3.2.1   Kitchen and bath walls: one coat primer, one coat Semi-Gloss.

9.4.3.2.2   Other walls and ceilings: one coat primer, one coat Alkyd flat.

9.4.3.2.3   Interior wood: one coat stain; two coats dull varnish.

9.4.3.2.4   Check colors with Owner before applying paint or stain.

DIVISION 11—EQUIPMENT (RESIDENTIAL)

11.1   KITCHEN EQUIPMENT

11.1.1   Electric cook top surface unit shall be Sears 43420 or equal.

11.1.2   Built-in oven shall be Sears double oven 42720 or equal.

12

11.1.3   Dishwasher shall be furnished by the Owner.

11.1.4   Refrigerator shall be furnished by the Owner.

11.1.5   Garbage disposal shall be stainless steel.

11.1.6   Kitchen cabinets, backsplashes, and counter tops shall be by Brammer or equal. Oak wood finish and hardware by manufacturer.

11.2   LAUNDRY EQUIPMENT

11.2.1   Laundry equipment shall be one washer and one dryer by Sears or equal. Washer shall be 10-cycle washer No. 22801. Dryer shall be Gas Electronic Sensor dryer No. 72801.

DIVISION 15—MECHANICAL

15.1   GENERAL PROVISIONS

15.1.1   Scope of Work

15.1.1.1   All plumbing, heating, and air conditioning for a complete job as specified and on the drawings.

15.1.1.2   It is not the intention of the specification to mention specifically each and every item shown on the plans and, therefore, does not excuse the Contractor from the responsibility of furnishing or having the proper subcontractor furnish and install such items without extra cost to the Owner.

15.1.2   Codes and Standards

15.1.2.1   All codes of the local and state jurisdiction shall be applied and shall take precedence over any item mentioned in this specification. Conform to National Plumbing Code.

15.1.2.2   Standards of the trades and materials shall be the highest quality.

15.1.2.3   The General Conditions and General Requirements shall apply to this Division.

15.2   PLUMBING

15.2.1   Provide complete systems as called for and/or shown or specified including but not limited to the following items.

15.2.2   Electrical work by others. Waterproof patch where plumbing pipes are cut through foundation walls.

15.2.3   Sewerage. Four inch PVC pipe inside of building and to four feet outside, then closed four inch tile to 1,000 gallon concrete septic tank. Tile field as required by seepage tests. Install 200 feet of agricultural tile in gravel, or more if required.

15.2.4   Drain tile. Install four inch perforated plastic pipe or agricultural tile set in crushed stone at footings as indicated on plan. Connect to 21 inch tile settling basin and sump. Iron covers and concrete bottoms for same.

15.2.5   Sump pump, Weil SS 605 automatic submersible, $1/3$ hp with automatic reset overload protection, waterproof power cord with heavy duty plug and grounded lead. $1^{1}/_{4}$ inch galvanized steel pipe to 20 feet from building, discharge into 20 feet of 4 inch perforated plastic pipe. Set in gravel or crushed stone, about 2 feet deep.

15.2.6   Wastes and vents shall be plastic like Carlon ABS-DWV with corresponding fittings or galvanized steel with cast iron soil stack.

15.2.7   Two inch water main is at front of lot. Tap into same with $3/_4$ inch tap. Water pipe in earth or concrete shall be lead or copper, elsewhere copper with copper fittings or galvanized steel schedule 40 with galvanized malleable fittings. Shutoff valve where service pipe enters building. See piping diagram.

15.2.8   Hot water to sink, dishwasher, clothes washer, lavatories, bath tubs. Cold water to same except dishwasher, and to water closets, water heater, and to sill cocks, with shut off valves. Valve dishwasher riser. (Dishwasher by Owner) Provide recessed metal panel at clothes washer with hot and cold water faucets, drain, and electric receptacles for washer and dryer. Insulate pipes in danger of freezing.

15.2.9   Water heater, as made by Rheem, Ruud, or A. O. Smith, 55 gallon electric, glass liner, with temperature and pressure relief valve. Send manufacturer's guarantee to Owner before final payment for this contract.

15.2.10   Fixtures. Stops at all fixtures. Crane, Eljer, American Standard, or Kohler, with manufacturer's chrome or stainless steel trim. Check selection with Owner before ordering.

15.2.11   Bath tubs. Color as selected by Owner. Five foot, 14 inches high, built-in, cast iron; built-in shower with diverter spout, pop up waste, curtain rod.

15.2.12   Lavatories. Color as selected by Owner. About 17×14 inches oval, vitreous china, for building into counter top. Include stainless steel sink rim. Combination faucet, pop up waste.

15.2.13   Water closets. Color as selected by Owner. Close coupled, round front, floor mounted, siphon jet with tank, plastic seat and cover to match.

15.2.14   Five foot, 6 inch sink. Stainless steel two compartment, drainboard, with mixing faucet like Moen, hose spray. Disposal, Insinkerator model 77, $1/_2$ hp.

15.2.15   Connect Owner's dishwasher

15.2.16   Floor drain at basement stair shall be cast iron, Blake, Wade, Crane, or equal, black body and cover.

15.2.17   Install all appliances as called for in Division 11.

14

15.2.18   Testing and cleaning of all plumbing, soil, waste, drain, vent piping, and sewers shall be as required by the City Plumbing Inspector.

15.2.19   Verify locations of the city and utility company services. Secure and pay for all permits, fees, inspections, etc., required by the city or utility company.

15.2.20   Materials shall be new and of the grade and quality specified. Work shall be performed by trained, experienced workers, skilled in their various crafts.

15.2.21   All openings in roof shall be flashed with 3 lb. sheet lead in one piece, extending under and over the shingle roof at least 12 inches, measured with the vertical, turned down into the extension of the increaser pipe through the roof.

15.2.22   All excavation and backfilling required shall be done for the proper installation of the work.

15.2.23   All work shall be in accordance with the plumbing ordinances of the city.

15.2.24   The entire installation shall be guaranteed against defects in workmanship and material for the period of one year from the date of final acceptance. The installation shall be guaranteed against water hammer, rattling of pipes, gurgling of traps, and to be a complete and noise-free installation.

15.3   HEATING

15.3.1   Provide complete blower system warm air heating system for the residence including, but not limited to, the following:

15.3.2   Oil burning furnace.

15.3.3   All piping and electrical connections and disconnect switch.

15.3.4   Thermostat.

15.3.5   Supply and return duct system.

15.3.6   Grilles and registers.

15.3.7   Guarantee to heat all rooms to 70 degrees in zero weather. Design and installation shall conform to standards of the National Warm Air and Air Conditioning Association. Design system for addition of future air cooling. A complete layout showing sizes of pipe, thermostat location, register location, ducts, distribution system, size, and type of furnace shall be submitted before award of contract. The owner shall accept or reject the heating bids on the basis of quality as well as price.

15.3.8   Include electrical work for heating. Fused disconnect near furnace furnished by others. Include one plain room thermostat.

15.3.9   Oil fired forced air furnace, Lennox 09-105, 84,000 btu/hour output. Include filters, fan controls, limit control, safety controls on primary oil burner relay.

15.3.10   Bury 550 gallon oil tank under carport slab, with necessary piping projecting above slab near house wall.

15.3.11   Ducts all full lined aluminum and/or galvanized iron, adequate size, tightly joined. Dampers as required to balance system. Floor and wall registers, where indicated on plan, with dampers and adjustable vanes. Include register in ductwork to provide warm air to basement.

15.3.12   Thermostat shall be Johnson Control or equal electric system.

15.3.13   Workmanship shall be such to require a minimum of cutting and patching.

15.3.14   Secure and pay all required heating permits and inspections required by the city and the utility company and all other fees, etc.

15.3.15   Put system into operation, lubricated and adjusted, balance room temperatures.

15.3.16   The Contractor shall guarantee the system in writing to be and remain in good working condition for one year from the date of the first heating season, beginning October 1. The guarantee shall state that all rooms shall be heated to 70° in zero weather.

15.3.17   Include ducts between three fans and roof jacks installed by others. Include 4 inch round duct and roof jack for dryer vent.

DIVISION 16—ELECTRICAL

16.1   GENERAL PROVISIONS

16.1.1   <u>Scope of Work</u>

16.1.1.1   Items provided by the Owner or other trades shall be checked carefully so as to avoid duplicating material or labor provided by others. Electrical installation shall include, but not be limited to, the following:

16.1.1.2   New 120/240 volt, 1 phase, 3-wire overhead service and main switch.

16.1.2   <u>Codes and Standards</u>

16.1.2.1   Equipment, devices, apparatus, and installation shall be in full compliance with applicable standards, requirements, rules, regulations, codes, statutes, ordinances, etc., of the city, county, state, and the utility company.

16.1.2.2   Electrical equipment, wiring, etc., shall comply with National Bureau of Fire Underwriter's requirements and National Electrical Code requirements for the particular type of installation, and labeled UL approved.

16.1.3   Guarantee and Testing

16.1.3.1   The entire installation shall be guaranteed for workmanship and material for a period of one year from acceptance.

16.1.3.2   The entire conduit system and the solid neutral wires shall be tested for shorts and grounding in the presence of the Architect.

16.1.3.3   The Contractor must guarantee that all joints are soldered or tightly screwed and that all wire joints are thoroughly insulated as specified.

16.2   BASIC MATERIALS AND METHODS

16.2.1   All materials shall be new and of the grade and quality specified. Work must be performed by trained, experienced workers, skilled in their various crafts.

16.2.2   The location of all outlets, switches, convenience outlets, and devices shall be as shown on the plans and as directed by the Architect.

16.2.3   Do all excavation and backfilling required to install the work properly.

16.2.4   Wiring shall be electrical metallic tubing (EMT). Wiring in concrete slabs or in fill shall be galvanized rigid conduit and moisture proof. Wiring shall be concealed in construction except in attic, basement, and carport. Cut in straps or receptacle boxes to make a flush surface for drywall.

16.2.5   Install branch circuits for lighting, complete with wire, receptacles, wiring devices, silent switches. Dimmer switch as noted on plan, like Moe 6502, 600 watt. Install circuits for convenience outlets, complete with wire, wiring devices, receptacles, cover plates. All plugs three point for grounding. Cover plates at switches and convenience outlets, chrome in kitchen and baths, prime coat elsewhere. Outlet boxes shall be stamped steel octagonal or square, of suitable and ample sizes, mounted with hangers, of same finish as conduit. Junction and pull boxes shall be of adequate size and of correct gauge steel to meet requirements of the N.E.C. (National Electrical Code). Wiring devices, switches, convenience outlets, etc., shall be of Sierra, Hubble, Bryant, Hart, and Hageman, or approved equal, 125V.

16.2.6   Furnish and install bathroom ceiling fans. Provide roof jacks. Ducts by others. Kitchen range hood and fan, same.

16.2.7   Provide and install chimes with transformer and push buttons.

16.2.8   Set lamp post in concrete near front of lot. Install waterproof cable underground to same. Install photo electric control to operate lamp post lamp.

16.2.9   Kitchen exhaust range hood shall be special "Thermador," as shown on the drawings, complete with duct through ceiling and roof. Bathrooms shall be exhausted with "Trade-Wind," Model 1201, complete with electrical connection to light switch and 4 inch round duct to attic space.

17

16.2.10   Install fused disconnect for furnace. Heating wiring by others. Make electric connections to water heater and Disposal, furnished by others, and range top and oven.

16.3   SERVICE AND DISTRIBUTION

16.3.1   Three wire 200 ampere single phase. Install galvanized iron pipe conduit for same.

16.3.2   Install circuit breaker panel with 200 ampere main breaker and 20 breakers as follows: One 30 amp each to range top, water heater, clothes dryer; 50 amp to oven. One 20 amp each to dishwasher, garbage disposal, refrigerator, furnace, and 2 circuits for kitchen convenience outlets. Four 20 amp for convenience outlets, and four for lighting outlets, two spares. Label circuits on circuit breaker panel.

16.4   LIGHTING

16.4.1   Provide and install light fixtures with lamps as scheduled.

16.5   DOOR BELL SYSTEMS

16.5.1   Provide transformers and low voltage lines for door chimes. Provide lighted push buttons at front and rear doors. Owner will provide chimes to be installed by Contractor. Divide system to indicate different signal from each door.

16.6   COMMUNICATIONS

16.6.1   Telephone outlets as indicated on plan, with $1/2$ inch thin wall conduit from outlet to below floor.

Name   Date

Matching

_____   **1.** Division 1   A. Concrete

_____   **2.** Division 2   B. Electrical

_____   **3.** Division 3   C. General Requirements

_____   **4.** Division 4   D. Wood and Plastics

_____   **5.** Division 5   E. Doors and Windows

_____   **6.** Division 6   F. Metals

_____   **7.** Division 7   G. Thermal and Moisture Protection

_____   **8.** Division 8   H. Site Work

_____   **9.** Division 15   I. Mechanical

_____   **10.** Division 16   J. Masonry

True-False

T   F   **1.** When there is a conflict between the information shown on the prints and the specifications, the specifications are to be followed.

T   F   **2.** The working drawings, specifications, and contract are considered the legal documents to be used in case of a lawsuit.

T   F   **3.** The owner decides on all of the materials to be used in the building and tells the architect, who then writes the specifications.

T   F   **4.** The divisions in the CSI format can be rearranged in order to suit the purpose of the architect.

T   F   **5.** Small remodeling jobs should have specifications.

T   F   **6.** Outline specifications do not tell how material is to be applied.

T   F   **7.** The Description of Material form is used mainly to provide information on which to base a mortgage loan.

T   F   **8.** Complete specifications cover the ordering of specific materials, suitable options, and ''or equal'' products.

T   F   **9.** Information in *Sweet's Architectural Catalog File* is arranged alphabetically by product.

T   F   **10.** Subcontractors are not required to comply with the specifications of a building as the contractor verifies that all items in the specifications are met.

Refer to Outline Specifications for the North Carolina Residence.

True-False

T   F   **1.**   No information is given about the mix of concrete or about formwork.

T   F   **2.**   Exterior finish above the first floor level shall be brick veneer or wood siding.

T   F   **3.**   Vanities may be either plastic laminate countertop or marble, depending on cost.

T   F   **4.**   Floors in the baths and family room are to be mosaic tile.

T   F   **5.**   Doors are made of wood or steel.

T   F   **6.**   The roof is constructed of asphalt shingles over plywood sheathing.

T   F   **7.**   The electrical service for this house is 200 amps.

T   F   **8.**   The kitchen cabinets are factory-built.

T   F   **9.**   The electric water heater has a 65-gallon capacity.

T   F   **10.**   Interior painting is not included in this contract.

Refer to Description of Materials for the North Carolina Residence.

True-False

T   F   **1.**   The mixes of concrete are a 5-bag mix for the footings and a 6-bag mix for the slab.

T   F   **2.**   The fireplace and chimney are built of face brick and firebrick.

T   F   **3.**   The exterior is finished with select siding using $1'' \times 8''$ boards with $1'' \times 2''$ battens.

T   F   **4.**   Floor joists are placed on $12''$ or $16''$ centers.

T   F   **5.**   Underlayment grade plywood is used for the finished wood floor.

T   F   **6.**   Cross bridging is used between floor and ceiling joists.

T   F   **7.**   Stock roof trusses are used to support the roof.

T   F   **8.**   The roofing is 240 lb. asphalt shingles over 15 lb. roofing felt.

T   F   **9.**   Interior and exterior finish coating consists of three coats of paint.

T   F   **10.**   Exterior doors are $1^3/4''$ thick.

T   F   **11.**   Disappearing stairs are provided to reach the attic space.

T   F   **12.**   The heating section includes information on the make and model of hood and vent fans.

T   F   **13.**   Gutters and downspouts are vinyl-clad metal.

T   F   **14.**   Kitchen cabinets are made of oak.

T   F   **15.**   Lath and plaster walls are painted light blue.

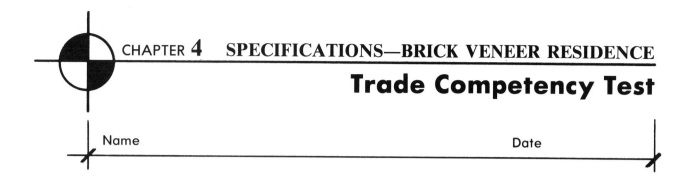

CHAPTER **4**   **SPECIFICATIONS—BRICK VENEER RESIDENCE**

Trade Competency Test

Name _____   Date _____

Refer to Complete Specifications for the North Carolina Residence.

SPECIAL CONDITIONS AND DIVISION 1

T   F   **1.** The work must be completed within 150 days after the written Notice to Proceed is issued to the contractor.

_____   **2.** Existing trees within _____ ' of the foundation line must be protected by the contractor.

_____   **3.** The guarantee requires that the contractor make good any defects in the work arising or discovered within _____ year(s) after completion and acceptance.

T   F   **4.** The owner shall provide and pay for all material, labor, and other costs necessary to complete the building within the specified time.

_____   **5.** Progress of the work for payment purposes is determined by the _____.

T   F   **6.** The contractor is responsible for providing utilities for use during construction.

_____   **7.** All rubbish must be removed from the building and hauled to the city land fill on a _____ basis.

_____   **8.** The _____ is responsible for cleaning windows and plumbing fixtures prior to occupancy.

_____   **9.** The owner, contractor, and architect, or a representative of each, are required to be present for the final _____.

_____   **10.** The _____ shall be responsible for coordinating the work of all trades.

DIVISION 2

_____   **1.** The allowable bearing load of the soil is _____ lbs./sq. ft.

_____   **2.** All topsoil shall be stripped to a depth of _____ ".

T   F   **3.** The subgrade for lawn and planting areas is _____ " below the finished grade.

_____   **4.** Trenches for footings and carport foundations must be made wide enough to provide room for _____.

_____   **5.** The basement and crawl space are to be excavated to _____ " outside of the foundation line.

153

_____   6. Trash-free material for backfill and compaction against the foundation walls is placed in _____ " lifts.

_____   7. Finish grading must be to _____ shown on the plans.

T   F   8. All finished grading is to slope away from the building.

_____   9. The chemical used for soil poisoning is _____.

_____   10. Pavements, walks, and _____ are not part of the site work under this contract.

DIVISION 3

_____   1. Concrete forms must be wetted or _____ before placing concrete.

_____   2. _____ are used to reinforce concrete as shown on the plans.

T   F   3. Portland cement must conform to ASTM standards.

T   F   4. Concrete may be placed only on undisturbed earth.

_____   5. A _____% compaction of fill is required under the slabs.

_____   6. The porous fill under the slab is _____ ".

_____   7. Concrete for all slabs must be at least _____ " thick.

_____   8. All slabs are _____-finished.

T   F   9. The basement floor is pitched to drain.

T   F   10. Concrete must be kept moist for at least seven days.

DIVISION 4

_____   1. Mortar shall have 1 part portland cement, 1 part lime putty, and _____ part(s) sand.

T   F   2. Stiffened mortar may be used as required.

_____   3. The brick veneer shall be tied to the wall sheathing with one tie for each _____ sq. ft. of area.

_____   4. Anchor bolts to tie down the wood sill are to be placed at _____ ' intervals in the concrete block foundation wall.

_____   5. _____ bond is used for solid brick walls.

T   F   6. The fireplace is faced with the same brick used on the exterior.

_____   7. The furnace flue is to be _____ tile.

T   F   8. The architect is to select the bricks to be used.

_____   9. The _____ is responsible for the proper operation of the fireplace.

_____   10. Non-staining soap and water or _____ acid and water (1:10) may be used to clean the brick.

DIVISION 5 AND DIVISION 6

T   F   **1.** All steel must be painted with one shop coat of rust-inhibiting paint.

_____   **2.** All carpentry work must conform to _____ standards.

_____   **3.** The interior finish work is to be completed by _____ carpenters.

T   F   **4.** All nails must be set on all trim work.

T   F   **5.** Floor and ceiling joists may be construction grade Douglas fir or #2, or better, yellow pine.

T   F   **6.** Wall sheathing is to be 1/2″ water-resistant fiberboard except at the corners.

_____   **7.** _____ sheathing is placed at the corners of the house.

_____   **8.** _____ bridging is to be used for ceiling joists.

_____   **9.** Studs are to be 2 × 4s placed _____″ OC.

T   F   **10.** Studs are doubled at openings and corners.

_____ **11.** Metal anchors shall be used on one stud every _____′.

T   F   **12.** All top plates are to be doubled.

_____ **13.** Nails used for top plates shall be _____d.

T   F   **14.** The soffit is finished with AB exterior grade plywood.

_____ **15.** Vanities are provided by the _____.

T   F   **16.** The fireplace mantel is trimmed with #1 select pine.

T   F   **17.** The cabinets are 3/4″ birch plywood.

T   F   **18.** Kitchen cabinets are custom-made and installed by the cabinetmaker.

_____ **19.** _____ case nails are used for nailing exterior trim.

T   F   **20.** All sills in contact with concrete must be treated with a preservative.

DIVISION 7

T   F   **1.** The inside of all foundation walls are to be waterproofed.

_____   **2.** The initial step in waterproofing foundation walls is the application of a heavy coat of _____.

_____   **3.** A membrane of _____ mil polyethylene sheets is applied over the base coat on foundation walls.

_____   **4.** The vapor barrier applied over plywood sheathing is _____-lb. felt.

_____   **5.** Insulation placed between studs in outside walls is 2″ foil faced _____ batts.

T   F   **6.** Insulation between ceiling joists is 6″ batts or rock wool to joist depth.

_____   **7.** Roofing shingles are 12″ × 36″, 240 lb., _____.

_____   **8.** Roofing shingles have a(n) _____″ exposure.

_____   **9.** Flashing around the chimney is 26-gauge _____ iron.

T   F   **10.** Caulking color is selected by the architect.

DIVISION 8

T   F   **1.** Outside entrance doors are metal.

T   F   **2.** All outside entrance doors are keyed alike.

_____   **3.** Interior flush doors are _____-core.

_____   **4.** The clearance for tops and sides of all interior doors is _____".

_____   **5.** Sliding glass doors have ⁵/₈" tempered _____ glass.

T   F   **6.** Grills are to be placed over all casement windows.

T   F   **7.** Double-hung windows are to be of insulating glass.

_____   **8.** Door and window hardware is to be installed by _____.

_____   **9.** Bathroom and _____ doors have pushbutton knob locks.

_____   **10.** _____ thresholds are placed at exterior doors.

DIVISION 9

_____   **1.** _____ beads are to be used at all outside drywall corners.

_____   **2.** Drywall thickness for walls and ceilings is _____".

T   F   **3.** Drywall in the basement is to be taped horizontally.

_____   **4.** Bathroom walls are covered with $4\frac{1}{4}" \times 4\frac{1}{4}"$ _____ tile.

_____   **5.** _____ tile is to be placed on the fireplace hearth.

_____   **6.** The _____ is to select the resilient flooring for the kitchen.

T   F   **7.** Exterior walls are to be painted with a primer and two coats of latex paint.

T   F   **8.** Paint may be brushed, sprayed, or rolled as determined by the painter.

_____   **9.** Interior paint shall be allowed to dry _____ hours before succeeding coats are applied.

_____   **10.** Interior wood trim is _____ and varnished.

DIVISION 15

_____   **1.** The sewer piping in the building is _____" PVC pipe.

_____   **2.** PVC sewer pipe extends _____' outside the building.

_____   **3.** The septic tank has a capacity of _____ gallons.

_____   **4.** The tile field shall consist of a minimum of _____' tile in gravel.

_____   **5.** Drain tile at the footings may be 4″ _____ plastic pipe.

T   F   **6.** The sump pump has a ½ HP motor.

T   F   **7.** The sump pump discharges into the main sewer line.

T   F   **8.** The soil stack is cast iron.

T   F   **9.** Plastic pipe is run from the 2″ water main into the house.

T   F   **10.** All water pipes inside the house are to be insulated if subject to freezing.

_____   **11.** The bathtub color is selected by the _____.

T   F   **12.** Round lavatories are built into the vanity countertop.

T   F   **13.** Water closets are wall-hung.

_____   **14.** Roof openings shall be flashed with 3 lb. sheet _____.

_____   **15.** The furnace shall have a capacity of _____ Btu/hr.

_____   **16.** The heating system must heat all rooms to _____ °F with an outside temperature of 0 °F.

_____   **17.** A(n) _____-gallon oil tank is to be buried under the carport slab.

T   F   **18.** The heating contractor must lubricate and adjust the heating system upon completion of installation.

T   F   **19.** A one-year warranty of the heating system shall be provided by the heating contractor.

T   F   **20.** The clothes dryer is vented to the outside with a 4″ round duct.

DIVISION 16

T   F   **1.** The electrical service is lateral.

_____   **2.** The size of the electrical service is _____ volts, single phase, three wire.

T   F   **3.** Electrical installations must comply with the requirements of the National Electrical Code®.

_____   **4.** The wiring inside the house shall be _____.

_____   **5.** The lamp post near the front of the lot has a(n) _____ electric control.

T   F   **6.** The duct for the range hood is vented through the kitchen wall to the outside.

_____   **7.** A fused _____ is to be installed for the furnace.

_____   **8.** The main panel has _____ circuit breakers.

_____   **9.** Door bell chimes are placed on a(n) _____ voltage system.

T   F   **10.** Outlets for TV hookups are installed by the electrical subcontractor.

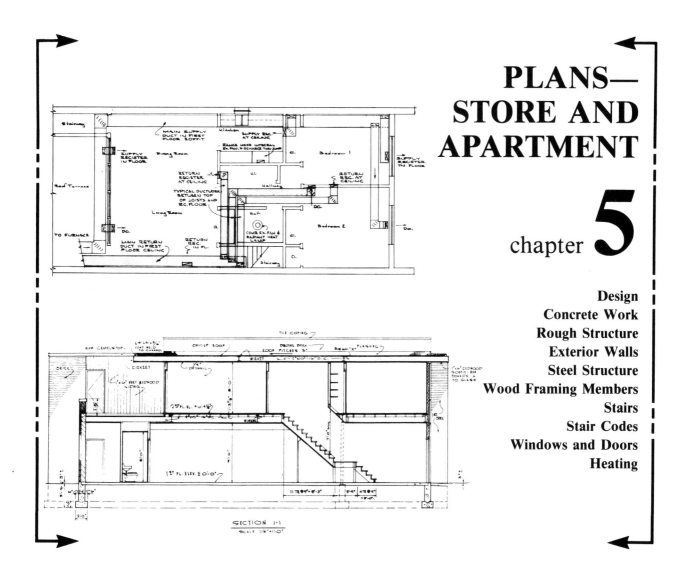

PLANS—
STORE AND
APARTMENT

chapter **5**

Design
Concrete Work
Rough Structure
Exterior Walls
Steel Structure
Wood Framing Members
Stairs
Stair Codes
Windows and Doors
Heating

DESIGN

The architect was commissioned to design a commercial building on a narrow lot with these general requirements:

1. The first floor is to be designed for commercial rental. It must be adaptable to suit the needs of different types of businesses. There will be no basement.
2. The second floor is to be an apartment with private front and rear entrances. It shall be the equivalent of a five-room apartment with the option of combining the living and dining areas. The living room shall be at the rear of the house opening onto a roof terrace.
3. Heating is to be forced warm air.

The prints, Sheets A-1, A-2, and A-3, represent the final solution that was accepted by the client.

The commercial space and apartment are well-planned within the severe limitations of the narrow lot and the fact that the two side walls are blank except for the kitchen window. The longitudinal section, designated Section 1-1, shows many construction features including the stair arrangement. Perhaps the most valuable part of the prints, from the standpoint of the builder, is the careful attention paid to detail drawings of the construction and building features.

The Front Elevation, Sheet A-2, is laid out as a symmetrical arrangement of doors and windows with redwood siding and cement plaster panels to fill open spaces. The brick walls and roof soffit extend beyond the face of the front wall in order to set the storefront back from the sidewalk.

The First Floor Plan, Sheet A-1, shows the large rectangular space for commercial use. The rear wall has an exterior door and an overhead door that provides a wide opening for merchandise or equipment. Although not open to the commercial area, the stairways for the apartment are drawn and dimensions given. The space under the stairs on the first floor is available for storage purposes. The toilet and heating room occupy the Southeast corner.

The Second Floor Plan, Sheet A-1, shows two bedrooms facing the street and the living-dining area at the rear. The kitchen, bath, and closets are placed across the center of the building. Both stairways ascend to the living-dining area. A hallway connects the living-dining area to the bedrooms and is flanked by a closet wall. The compact kitchen is placed adjacent to the dining area. Light and ventilation are provided for the living-dining area by a window wall to the South. A roof terrace provides for outdoor living and is partially protected by the projecting roof.

The Rear Elevation, Sheet A-2, gives information about openings for windows and doors for both levels and shows the exterior of the stair tower and chimney. Section 1-1, Sheet A-2, is a longitudinal section. Refer to the First Floor Plan, Sheet A-1, which shows that the cutting plane is parallel to and near the East wall, passing through the front stair hall, the commercial area, the toilet, and heater room. On the second floor the cutting plane passed through Bedroom 2, the linen closet over the stairs, the Living Room, and the Roof Terrace. The door shown on the terrace is for the storage room.

Rear Stair Section 2-2, Sheet A-2, is taken through the rear stairwell near the West wall. These two section drawings show how the foundation and footing are to be placed and give information about the steel, wood, and brick structure. The important part, which is difficult to include anywhere else on the plans, is the stair arrangement. The need to take advantage of every bit of space so that the upstairs rooms are adequate required a careful study of headroom and resulted in sloped soffits over the stairs. The manner in which the roof extends over the roof terrace is clearly shown in Section 1-1, Sheet A-2.

Sheet A-3 contains the plot plan which provides lot and building dimensions. This sheet also includes the details of construction. Detail 1, Sheet A-3, gives fundamental information about the special footings under the foundation walls where the building is placed on the property line. The rebars and welded wire fabric in the floor are shown.

Detail 2, Sheet A-3, is a section through the front wall from the first floor to the roof taken at a point passing through a front door. It shows steel members, rough wood members, wall and floor finish, trim members, and details about the roof. Detail 3, Sheet A-3, is a sectional view taken through the front windows of the commercial area and gives information the bricklayer, carpenter, and glazier need to prepare the opening, set the frame, and install the glass. Detail 4, Sheet A-3, shows the rough construction used to support the roof members. This occurs at two beam locations which may be seen on Section 1-1, Sheet A-2. Detail 5, Sheet A-3, shows how the ends of roof joists are supported over the front of the building by using a large steel channel. It also gives information about the fascia and soffit. Detail 6, Sheet A-3, is essentially for the purpose of showing how the steel channel is anchored in the brick walls. Detail 7, Sheet A-3, solves the problem of supporting the wall and compensating for the difference in floor heights at the door to the roof deck. The windows in the rear wall at the living-dining space are explained by Detail 8, Sheet A-3. Detail 9, Sheet A-3, indicates the ducts that run in the ceiling of the commercial space to supply heat to the second floor and provide for the return of cold air. The First Floor Plan, Sheet A-1, shows the supply air duct along the West wall and the return air duct along the East wall.

Three small-scale elevation views on Sheet A-2 are detailed studies of the cabinet arrangement, soffit and wall finish in the kitchen, and second floor bathroom.

CONCRETE WORK

No plan views of the foundation and footings were included in the set of working drawings because the building is a simple rectangle with the slab placed on the ground. The only unusual problem encountered is that the building is built on the East and West lot lines, which prevents the placing of the footing to center on the foundation wall. See Detail 1, Sheet A-3, and Front Elevation, Sheet A-2. The basic dimensions of the foundation wall and footing are found on Section 1-1, Sheet A-2. The foundation wall extends approximately 3″ above the grade. The hidden lines for the foundation in Section 1-1, Sheet A-2, and also on the front and rear elevations indicate footing and foundation wall. A concrete post and footing is placed under the column at the front stair hall and is shown on Section 1-1, Sheet A-2, and on the First Floor Plan, Sheet A-1.

Figure 5-1 shows how rebars are arranged to help the foundation wall and footing counteract strain. Rebars are described by a number that is equal to the number of $1/8''$ in diameter. The designation #4 @ 15″ indicates a $1/2''$ bar at 15″ spacings, and 2 #5 CONT. means two rebars $5/8''$ diameter continuous. The steel mesh in the floor is made of wire welded in a square or rectangular pattern. WWF 6 × 6 × #6 indicates welded wire fabric with a 6″ square pattern, using #6 gauge wire (6 gauge is .207″, or slightly more than $3/16''$ in diameter).

ROUGH STRUCTURE

The rough supporting structure includes brick and concrete block wall on the East, West, and South sides and a frame wall on the North side; steel members including wide flange beams and channels placed at right angles to the long side walls; and

wood joists running at right angles to the steel members.

Exterior Walls

Information about the masonry is indicated at several places on the prints. The First and Second Floor Plans, Sheet A-1, show that brick is used and indicates it is to be backed up by concrete block. The brick is returned into openings at the doors at the rear. Solid face brick is used at the front part of the side walls because they project beyond the storefront and under the storefront. Building (common) brick is used for the *parapet* wall. See Section 1-1, Sheet A-2. A parapet wall is a low, protective wall at the edge of a balcony or roof. The parapet wall shown extends 2′-8″ above the roof terrace deck. The chimney is made with concrete block units and brick to the second floor. Only brick is used from this elevation to the cap.

The bricklayer needs the elevation drawings because they show how the brick is to be laid and provide the vertical dimensions needed. See Sheet A-2.

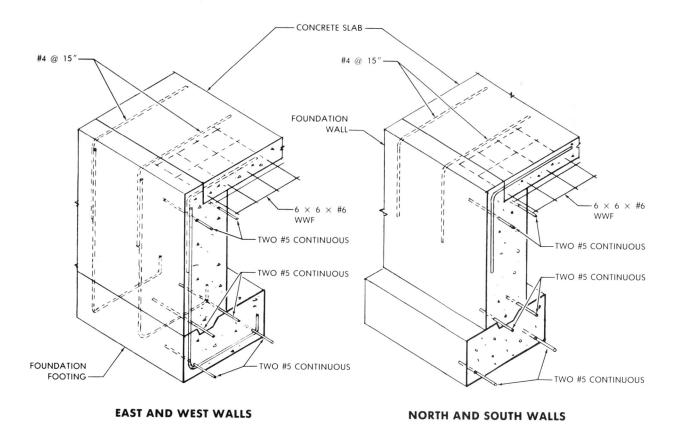

EAST AND WEST WALLS

NORTH AND SOUTH WALLS

Figure 5-1. Rebars allow foundation walls and footings to counteract strain.

By referring to the plan views, the bricklayer obtains horizontal dimensions and information about lintels. Further information is given in Details 3, 6, and 9, Sheet A-3. Detail 3, Sheet A-3, shows the brickwork under the storefront windows. It is face brick laid in a single tier (wythe). The bricklayer is also involved in the support and anchoring of some steel and wood members because their ends are embedded in the wall. Two notes on Sheet A-1 describe how to provide a firm base for beam ends.

The front wall of the building is a frame wall. The storefront part is supported by 2″ × 6″ vertical wood members. See Typical Vertical Mullion Section, Detail 3, Sheet A-3. The second floor part is a typical frame wall using 2″ × 4″ studs. It is supported by a steel plate welded to the wide flange beam, which is located above the storefront. See Detail 2, Sheet A-3. The first floor front wall carries little structural load because of the large wide flange beam, over the storefront. The roof load at the front of the building is supported by a wide flange beam (W 12 × 27) 17′-0″ from the front of the building and a channel in the fascia. See Details 4 and 5, Sheet A-3.

Steel Structure

The structural steel members used to support the second floor and the roof are shown on the First Floor Plan and Second Floor Plan, Sheet A-1. Details 2, 4, 6, and 7, Sheet A-3, give detailed information. See Figure 5-2.

The description and location of the beams for the second floor are shown on the First Floor Plan and those for the roof on the Second Floor Plan, Sheet A-1. The W beams (wide flange) are described by the nominal measurement outside of the flanges and the weight per running foot. A W 14 × 34 beam is 14″ high and weighs 34 pounds per running foot. For both beams used, the height is the actual dimension as well as the nominal dimension. Channels are designated by the actual measurement outside of the flanges and the weight per foot. See Figure 5-3. When other dimensions such as the width of flanges or thickness of web or flanges are required, it is necessary to refer to the *Manual of Steel Construction*.

The W members are set in the masonry walls on bearing plates, which in turn are supported by several courses of brick or solid concrete block. The beam at the storefront is modified by welding a ³/₈″ plate to its lower flange to project 3¹/₂″. This plate serves as a lintel. The next beam back of the storefront in the second floor is shorter so as not to project through the stairwell. It is supported by a *Lally column* (concrete filled steel post).

Details 5 and 6, Sheet A-3, point out the special construction used at the fascia at the North and South ends of the roof. Two steel members are required at each location, one of them a channel and the other an equal leg angle. They are tack welded together. The channel is needed to support the ends of the roof joists and must be anchored solidly in the masonry of the side walls. Detail 6, Sheet A-3,

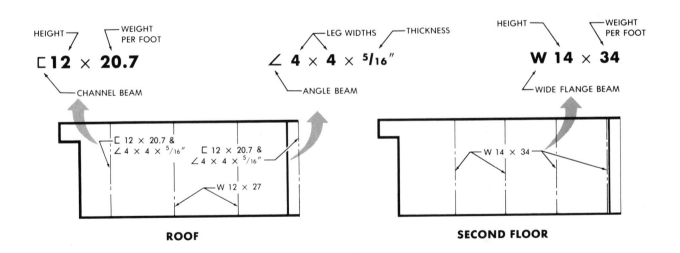

Figure 5-2. Structural steel members are used to support heavy loads.

STRUCTURAL STEEL

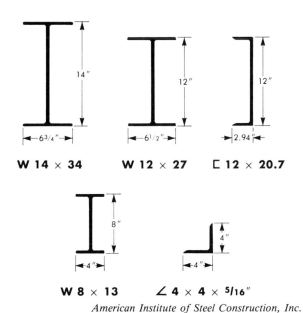

W 14 × 34   **W 12 × 27**   **⊏ 12 × 20.7**

W 8 × 13   **∠ 4 × 4 × 5/16"**

American Institute of Steel Construction, Inc.

Figure 5-3. Structural steel members are available in a variety of shapes and sizes.

and Figure 5-4 details this procedure. W beams, which are 4' long and 8" wide, are embedded in the wall and fastened to the fascia channels with bolts through clip angles.

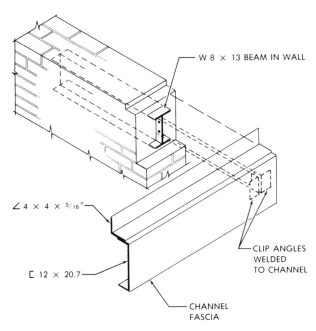

Figure 5-4. The channel fascia is hung from beams embedded in the brick wall.

METAL BRIDGING

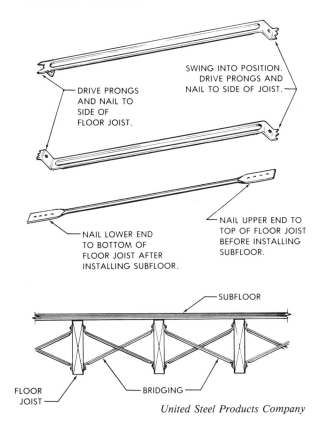

United Steel Products Company

Figure 5-5. Metal bridging is placed between joists to make them rigid and to keep them in line.

Other steel members are lintels consisting of angles over the opening in the rear wall. One angle supports the brick wythe and two angles support the concrete block.

Wood Framing Members

The rough framing support members in the second floor consists of 2" × 10" joists, 16" OC with two rows of metal cross bridging between each pair of steel supporting members and between the last beam and the South masonry wall. See Figure 5-5.

Detail 7, Sheet A-3, and Figure 5-6 show how the joists are cut to permit them to rest on the lower flange of the W beam so that gypsum board for the ceiling will be flush. The three joists nearest to the East and West walls are tied together at 6'-0" intervals with metal strips that are embedded in the masonry wall. See Detail 9, Sheet A-3.

Blocking is placed between each pair of joists at their ends to keep them in alignment. The 2" × 4"

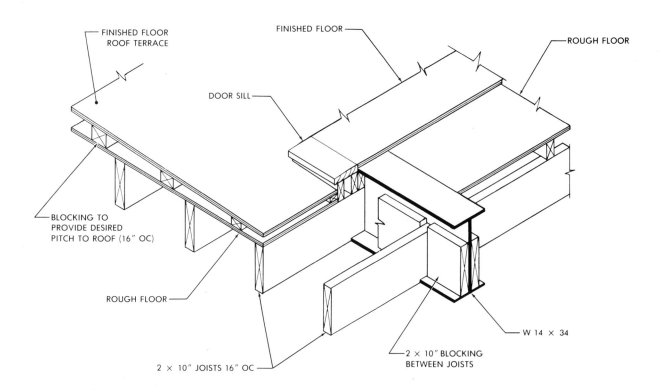

Figure 5-6. A pictorial detail at the roof terrace doorway shows floor construction.

members are placed 16″ OC at right angles to the joists to support the plywood rough floor and to provide a 3½″ space in which to run heating ducts. See Detail 9, Sheet A-3.

Detail 7, Sheet A-3, indicates how the roof terrace floor is to be constructed to provide for the change in elevation from the finished second floor and to give slope for drainage to the floor itself. The 2″ × 2″ blocking is to be ripped into increasingly narrower pieces until the plywood finished floor and sheathing touch each other.

In the construction of the roof supporting structure, the tops of the steel beams are to be kept at the same elevation, +19′-10⅜″. Detail 4, Sheet A-3, shows how the joists are cut to give maximum bearing on the blocking, which is bolted to the beams. See Figure 5-7. Blocking is placed between beams to keep the joists in line and rigid. The blocking under the joists is modified at each beam so that the roof is given a pitch of 3″ from front to rear. See Section 1-1, Sheet A-2.

The joists over the front of the building are hung from the steel channel. See Details 2 and 5, Sheet A-3. The gypsum wallboard ceiling panels for the drywall installation are hung from 2″ × 4″ ceiling joists, which are suspended from the roof joists. See

Detail 5, Sheet A-3. The wall above the storefront is a typical stud wall. See Detail 2, Sheet A-3.

STAIRS

A fundamental problem of the architect is to design stairs that comply with the local building code and fit the particular space problem of the building. The carpenter who installs the stairs has the responsibility of working out details of construction not covered specifically on the prints. This includes adequate support for the stairs and framework for the ceiling (soffit) above. Custom-built stairs are usually made in a shop by a carpenter who specializes in stair work. These stairs require accurate machine work to rout out the stringers to receive the treads and risers. See Figure 5-8. The staircase is often designed with winders or curved stair parts and railings.

Stair Codes

Local building codes vary, but all give minimum riser height and tread width. Headroom and stair landing restrictions are often specified. The following stair information is taken from several building

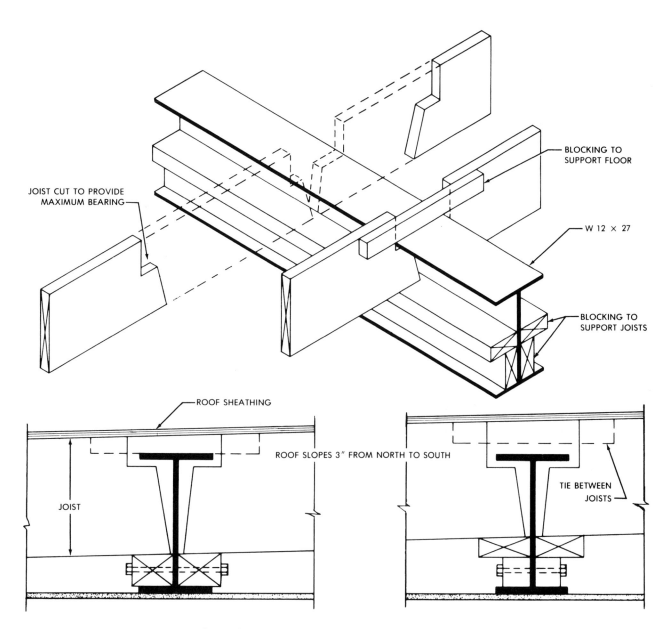

JOIST CUT TO PROVIDE MAXIMUM BEARING

BLOCKING TO SUPPORT FLOOR

W 12 × 27

BLOCKING TO SUPPORT JOISTS

ROOF SHEATHING

ROOF SLOPES 3″ FROM NORTH TO SOUTH

JOIST

TIE BETWEEN JOISTS

A CHANGE IN THE BLOCKING AT W BEAMS PROVIDES FOR A SLOPE IN THE JOISTS TO GIVE DRAINAGE TO THE ROOF

Figure 5-7. Roof joists are supported on blocking. A change in the height of the blocking gives pitch to the roof. (Blocking between joists has been omitted.)

codes and applies to the stairs in this chapter. The *CABO One and Two Family Dwelling Code* (Council of American Building Officials) standardizes requirements of building, plumbing, mechanical, and electrical codes. The *BOCA Basic Building Code* (Building Officials Conference of America) is a national code considered to be a source document for communities developing their own codes. The third code shows how a local community addresses stair construction. This code is for the city of Chicago,

but is typical of other cities. These three codes are similar, yet vary slightly in tread and riser dimension limitations, dimensions for landings, and other aspects.

From *CABO One and Two Family Dwelling Code:*

Run

Main stairs, closed or open riser minimum 9 inches plus 1 inch nosing.

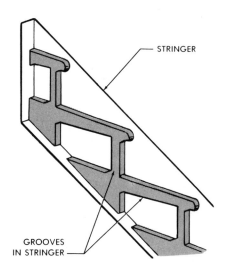

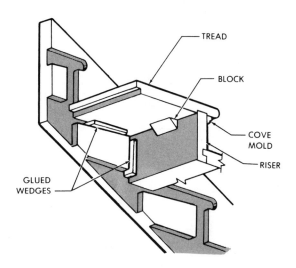

Figure 5-8. Stair stringers are housed to receive the treads, risers, and wedges. Glued wedges reinforce the center of the treads.

Rise

Main stairs, maximum 8¼ inches. All riser heights shall not vary by more than ⅜ inch in any one flight.

Landings

Provide a landing at each side of an exit door unless the door swings over interior stairs.

Minimum dimension of landing shall be not less than 3 feet. (Measured in direction of travel.)

Headroom

Continuous clear headroom measured vertically from the front edge of nosing to a line parallel with stair pitch:

Main stair, minimum 6 feet 8 inches.

Width clear of handrail

Main stair, minimum 2 feet 8½ inches.

From *BOCA Basic Building Code*
(Building Officials Conference of America):

Treads and Risers

One and two family dwellings. All stairs with closed risers, maximum riser 8¼ inches, minimum tread 9 inches plus 1¼ inch nosing.

Width

All interior required stairways shall be not less than forty-four (44) inches in width except that such width may be reduced to thirty-six (36) inches in one and two family dwellings.

Headroom

The minimum headroom in all parts of the stair enclosure shall be not less than six and two thirds (6⅔) feet.

Landings and Platforms

Width. The least dimension of landings and platforms shall be not less than the required width of the stairway. (The dimensions for a landing or a platform at the top or bottom of a stair shall be at least as great, measured in the direction of travel, as the stairs are wide.)

Vertical Rise. In assembly and institutional buildings (schools, churches, etc.) the height of a vertical rise shall not exceed eight (8) feet between landings and intermediate platforms. In all other buildings no stairway shall have a height of rise more than twelve (12) feet before landings, nor shall any single flight of stairs have less than three (3) risers.

From *a typical city code:*

Treads and Risers

In other occupancies (not Institutional or Assembly Units) the maximum height of a riser shall be eight inches, and the minimum width of a tread, exclusive of nosing, shall be nine inches. The width of a tread, including the nosing shall be not less than ten inches.

(Stair Ratio)

The height of two risers plus the width of one tread shall equal not less than twenty-four or more than twenty-seven inches.

Landings

The maximum vertical rise of a flight between floors, between landings or between a floor and a landing shall not exceed nine feet in Assembly Units nor twelve feet in all other occupancies.

The length of a landing in the direction of travel shall be not less than the width of the stair, but need not exceed four feet in a stair of any width.

Codes are specific on maximum riser height and minimum tread width. Local codes usually give a means of calculating stairs to vary *stair ratio* (riser height and tread width within safe limitations). Some typical ratios in use, expressed as formulas, are:

$$T + R = 17''\text{--}18''$$
$$T + R + R = 24''\text{--}27''$$

A riser height of $7\frac{1}{2}''$ and a tread width of $9\frac{1}{2}''$ satisfies both of these stair ratios. Generally speaking, the stair with the lowest riser height and widest tread width in keeping with the code requirements is preferred. A low riser height provides comfortable ascent. Section 2-2, Sheet A-2 shows that the floor-to-floor height is $10'\text{-}9\frac{5}{8}''$, or 129.62$''$. Any of the following riser heights could be used for the stairs:

$129.62''/18 = 7.20''$, or a riser height of $7\frac{3}{16}''$
$129.62''/17 = 7.62''$, or a riser height of $7\frac{5}{8}''$
$129.62''/16 = 8.10''$, or a riser height of $8\frac{1}{8}''$

The riser height chosen was 17 risers of $7\frac{5}{8}''$, each with a tread width of $9''$. The riser height and tread width produce a $16\frac{5}{8}''$ stair ratio. While slightly below the minimum recommended stair ratio, it is within safe limitations.

A platform is introduced at the top of the fifth riser on the front stairs because it provides a break in the stairs and there is ample room. See Section 1-1, Sheet A-2, and First Floor Plan, Sheet A-1. The landing is $3'\text{-}9'' \times 3'\text{-}0''$. Less room is available for the rear stairway. A platform space is provided at the top and bottom of the stair for safety.

Headroom is measured vertically from a line through the *nosing points* (pitch of the stairs) to the ceiling above. Usually the carpenter works out the framework for the soffit before the stairs are installed. The stairwell is framed with headers, against which the stair rests, as well as strong side members. The headroom dimensions shown on Section Views 1-1 and 2-2 comply with code requirements and should give the carpenter a sufficient allowance so that there is no need to cut into the ceiling or vertical wall above when the sloped soffit is formed.

WINDOWS AND DOORS

Windows and doors are often described in schedules, which give sizes and special characteristics. When there are not many varieties, the information is covered on the prints and in the specifications. Enough information is given for the storefront windows on the First Floor Plan, Sheet A-1, and in Detail 3, Sheet A-3 so that a schedule is not required. The bricklayer and carpenter are shown how to prepare the openings for the plate glass that is to be installed after the frame is ready. The front and rear windows on the second floor and the steel sash window in the heater room are stock windows ordered from a manufacturer's catalog.

Dimensions are given on the prints for the size and location of the overhead door. The name of the manufacturer and descriptive information is given in the specifications. Other doors throughout the building are described by a note on Sheet A-1. Width and height dimensions are shown at their location on the first and second floor plans.

HEATING

The heating of the building, with forced warm air, has been worked out using a long supply duct along the West wall at the ceiling of the commercial space and a return duct along the East wall. See First Floor Plan, Sheet A-1, Detail 9, Sheet A-3, and Figure 5-9. The greatest heat loss is at the windows and doors on the North and South walls. This is counteracted by supply registers in the floor in the living-dining area and in the bedrooms. Heat is supplied to the kitchen by a register in the soffit above the cabinets.

Return air is exhausted through registers in the bedroom partition and at two locations in the living-dining area. The ducts are run under the floor in the space between the joists in a North-South direction then turn toward the return trunk at the East wall. The ducts run in the space between the joists and the floor in an East-West direction. No return is required from the kitchen or the bathroom. The kitchen air is exhausted through the range hood. The bathroom has an exhaust fan in the ceiling. Both have ducts that pass through the roof.

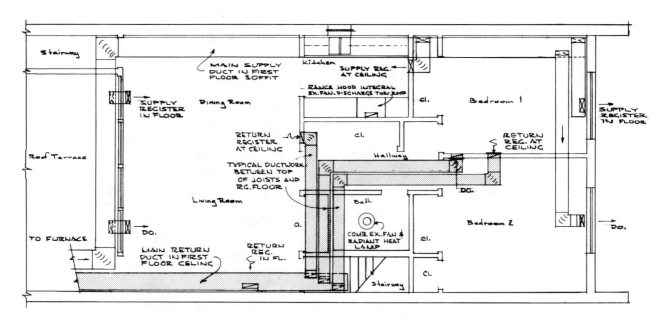

Figure 5-9. Supply and exhaust heating ducts pass in space under the floor or between joists. Kitchen exhaust is through range hood. Bath heat and exhaust are provided through ceiling unit.

Name	Date

Completion

_____	1. A(n) _____ plan contains lot and building dimensions.
_____	2. A #5 rebar is _____ " in diameter.
_____	3. A(n) _____ section runs from the front to the back of a building.
_____	4. WWF 6 × 8 × #6 indicates _____ wire fabric with a 6″ × 8″ pattern of 6 gauge wire.
_____	5. Building brick is also known as _____ brick.
_____	6. _____ drawings provide vertical dimensions needed by the bricklayer.
_____	7. A W 14 × 34 steel beam weighs _____ pounds per running foot.
_____	8. Steel channels are designated by the actual measurement _____ the flanges and the weight per foot.
_____	9. A concrete-filled steel post is commonly referred to as a(n) _____ column.
_____	10. _____ are steel angles placed above wall openings.
_____	11. _____ are the vertical parts of stairs.
_____	12. _____ are the horizontal parts of stairs.
_____	13. The minimum width for interior stairs in one-family and two-family dwellings is _____ ″.
_____	14. No stairway may have a rise of more than _____ between landings.
_____	15. _____ for stairs is measured vertically from the nosing to the ceiling directly above.
_____	16. The symbol for a supply register is a rectangle with _____ diagonal lines.
_____	17. The note, 4 @ 15″, indicates ½″ _____ spaced 15″ apart.
_____	18. In a(n) _____ layout, details on both sides of a common center line appear as mirror images of one another.
_____	19. The bricklayer obtains _____ dimensions from plan views.
_____	20. Drywall is also known as _____ board.

Identification

_____ 1. Object line

_____ 2. Concrete

_____ 3. Rough wood

_____ 4. Extension line

_____ 5. Break line

_____ 6. Stone

_____ 7. Dimension line

_____ 8. Finish wood

_____ 9. Dimension

_____ 10. Earth

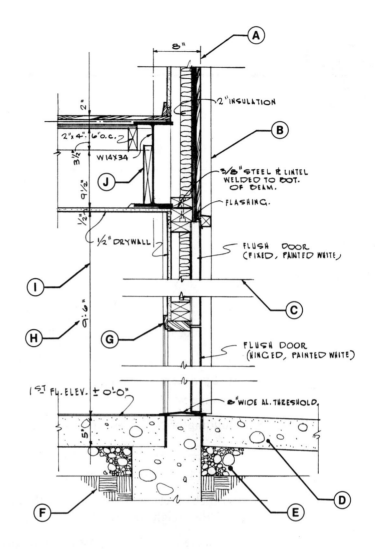

True-False

T   F   **1.** Metal bridging cannot be used with wood joists.

T   F   **2.** Steel angles are described by the size of each leg and the weight per running foot.

T   F   **3.** Rebars should not be completely concealed in foundations.

T   F   **4.** Local communities establish their own building codes which may be based on model codes.

T   F   **5.** The FHA requires a landing at the top of any stairs having a door that swings toward the stairs.

T   F   **6.** A tread and riser stair ratio of 17" to 18" produces stairs that are within safe limitations.

T   F   **7.** Window and door sizes are always specified in schedules on the prints.

T   F   **8.** A return air register is drawn as a rectangle with one diagonal line running from corner to corner.

T   F   **9.** The carpenter who installs stairs should work out any details of construction not specifically covered in the prints.

T   F   **10.** Ducts for heating and air conditioning may be concealed in soffits.

Trade Competency Test

Name _____ Date _____

Refer to Plans for a Commercial Building.

Completion

_____ 1. _____ bridging is installed between joists.

_____ 2. A(n) _____ switch controls the light in the stairs on the East side of the building.

_____ 3. The second floor elevation (plans) is + _____.

_____ 4. Four W 14 × 34 steel beams supporting the second floor are spaced _____ apart OC.

_____ 5. The first floor bathroom measures 4'-0" × _____.

_____ 6. Redwood soffit boards are placed _____ to the front glass.

_____ 7. The second floor ceiling is finished with _____ " drywall.

_____ 8. The concrete slab across the front of the building is sloped _____ " to provide runoff.

_____ 9. Ripped 2" × 2" _____ are placed on the rear deck and pitched from West to East.

_____ 10. A 15'-0" wide alley is located on the _____ side of the property.

_____ 11. One electrical outlet in each bedroom is _____-controlled.

_____ 12. The linen closet in the Northeast bedroom contains _____ shelves.

_____ 13. A combination radiant heat lamp and _____ is located in the bathroom ceiling.

_____ 14. A _____ " downspout is connected to the roof drain on the roof terrace.

_____ 15. The furnace is located on the _____ floor.

_____ 16. The rear stairs leading to the second floor contain _____ risers.

_____ 17. Four _____ windows are placed below fixed glass in the bedrooms.

_____ 18. Both front doors are wood with _____ " tempered plate glass.

_____ 19. The duct for the return air is enclosed in a(n) _____ on the ceiling of the first floor.

_____ 20. Horizontal trim members on the front of the building are painted _____.

171

_____ 21. The restroom in the commercial area measures 4'-0" × _____.

_____ 22. The front entrance door for the commercial area swings _____.

_____ 23. A(n) _____ is used to control the light in the storage room on the second floor.

_____ 24. The roof terrace is pitched toward the _____.

_____ 25. Lights in bedroom closets are controlled by _____.

_____ 26. Both stairways have _____ risers.

_____ 27. The bearing surface for roof beams must be _____" deep.

_____ 28. Soffit boards of 1" × 6" redwood are run _____ to the glass.

_____ 29. The Rear Stair Section 2-2 is drawn to the scale of _____" = 1'-0".

_____ 30. _____ tile is placed 4'-0" high on the East wall of the bathroom.

_____ 31. The minimum headroom clearance in the rear stairway is _____.

_____ 32. A(n) _____ and mirror are placed above the lavatory in the bathroom.

_____ 33. The plot plan is drawn to the scale of 1" = _____.

_____ 34. The door leading to the roof deck has an interlocking aluminum _____.

_____ 35. Horizontal trim members above the 1" × 6" vertical redwood are painted _____.

Multiple Choice

_____ 1. Regarding the general layout, _____.
  A. the second floor contains four rooms plus bath and closets
  B. the roof terrace is completely covered by a roof
  C. the building has a commercial space with approximately 1500 sq. ft.
  D. stairs lead from the commercial space to the second floor

_____ 2. The Elevation Views, Sheet A-2, show _____.
  A. two front doors that open on commercial space
  B. that face brick is used at the storefront and for the rear of the building
  C. elevation dimensions for floors, ceilings, and beams in relation to the First Floor elevation
  D. that blank wall spaces on the front wall are filled with redwood siding

_____ 3. Regarding Section Views 1-1 and 2-2, Sheet A-2, _____.
  A. Section 1-1 is taken through the center of the building on a North-South line
  B. the steel members supporting the second floor and the roof structure are shown
  C. dimensions are given locating both sets of stairs
  D. the door in elevation on the second floor opens into the dining area

_____ 4. The Plot Plan, Sheet A-3, shows _____.
  A. a point of beginning for horizontal measurements
  B. that the building is located from the concrete walk
  C. dimensions of the roofed area
  D. dimensions which outline the foundation

5. Regarding concrete work, _____.
   A. all of the dimensions needed for the footing and foundation are shown on the First Floor Plan, Section 1-1, and Detail 1
   B. the footing shown in Detail 1 is the same for all four walls
   C. the concrete floor is 5″ thick and reinforced with steel rebars
   D. the first floor concrete floor extends to the outside of the walls

6. Regarding masonry, _____.
   A. the East and West walls are made of solid brick
   B. the parapet wall extends the length of the building
   C. horizontal and vertical dimensions are given for the rear window and door openings on the Rear Elevation View
   D. three steel angles are specified for lintels over first floor window and door openings

7. Regarding the steel members, _____.
   A. all of the W beams are supported on steel plates resting on the brick and concrete block walls
   B. all of the W beams supporting the roof are set at the same elevation
   C. all W beams supporting the second floor are the same length
   D. channels over the front of the building serve only to provide a fascia

8. Joists _____.
   A. supporting the roof are all placed at the same elevation
   B. support the steel channel fascia at the front of the building
   C. under the roof terrace and under the rest of the second floor have the same cross section dimensions
   D. supporting the roof have square ends

9. Regarding the roof construction, _____.
   A. the slope of the roof is achieved by using different size W beams and wood joists
   B. changing the size of the blocking at each steel beam gives the roof a pitch from front to back
   C. the elevation of the top of the joists over beam "X" is + 19′-10³/₈″
   D. insulation is provided beneath the joists under the roof

10. Information and dimensions include _____.
    A. dimensions that total 22′-8³/₈″ from the top of the foundation to the top of the coping
    B. vertical measurements (elevations) measured from the sidewalk elevation
    C. exact dimensions locating stairwell soffits
    D. dimensions for the second floor hallway from the living room to the bedroom

11. Regarding the roof terrace, _____.
    A. the joists supporting the deck are sloped to support the sheathing
    B. the joists are supported on brick at their outer end
    C. the slope of the floor terrace and storage room deck is achieved by changing the thickness of the sleepers
    D. the partial roof over the roof terrace has no pitch

12. The Kitchen and Bathroom Plan and Elevation Views show _____.
    A. that the bathroom has a wainscot of ceramic tile 4'-0" high all around
    B. a soffit running around three sides of the kitchen
    C. a ceiling with fluorescent panels in the kitchen
    D. the cabinet door and drawer arrangement in the kitchen

13. Regarding stairs, _____.
    A. the first floor plan shows the complete flight of the front entrance stairs
    B. the front and rear stairs are located in the line of travel by dimensions from exterior walls
    C. the soffit over the rear stair can be at any angle as long as it is above the minimum headroom dimension
    D. all treads are 9" wide, not including the nosing

14. Regarding doors, _____.
    A. the two dashed lines on elevation drawings of doors point toward the side with the hinges
    B. all doors are flush solid-core, $1^3/_8$" or $1^3/_4$" thick
    C. only swinging and sliding doors are used
    D. all interior doors are 6'-8" high and either 2'-6" or 2'-8" wide

15. Regarding windows, _____.
    A. the kitchen window has two horizontal sliding sashes with light size 16" wide and 26" high
    B. only a vertical dimension is given for the heater room window
    C. the bedroom windows are a combination of a fixed sash with thermopane and a hopper sash below
    D. the living-dining area windows are shown with sash hinged at the bottom, above the large fixed sash

16. Interior finish includes _____.
    A. lath and plaster over $1/_2$" Sheetrock® on second floor walls and ceiling
    B. wood baseboard, drywall wall finish, and interior wood trim at the front of the building
    C. drywall over furring strips for sidewalls in the commercial space
    D. a ceramic tile bathroom floor

17. Wall Section View, Detail 2, and Fascia Section View, Detail 5, show _____.
    A. that panels over front doors are made using redwood siding
    B. the use of a $3^1/_2$" thick insulating blanket in the front wall
    C. how the second floor ceiling is hung by means of 2" × 4" ceiling joists
    D. that roof joists butt against blocking of 2" × 8" members

18. The heating requirements include _____.
    A. a fresh air intake in the heater room
    B. main supply and return ducts run between the joists along the sides of the ceiling in the commercial space
    C. warm air outlets for the commercial space shown on the First Floor Plan
    D. cold air returns in the kitchen and bathroom

_____ **19.** The electrical installation includes _____.
A. power outlets in furnace room
B. a ceiling fan and radiant heat lamp in the bathroom
C. a light outlet with three-way switches in the hall between the living-dining area and bedrooms
D. the location of the electrical panel

_____ **20.** The plumbing installation includes _____.
A. a plumbing stack located in the second floor partition behind the tub
B. a plumbing stack in the partition at the front stairs on the first floor
C. a downspout that passes through the heater room, carrying water from the roof
D. a floor drain in the heater room

True-False

T F **1.** The plot plan shows a point of beginning at the curb.

T F **2.** Section 1-1 is a longitudinal section through the building taken through the front stairs, first floor toilet, and heater room.

T F **3.** The Front Elevation shows that the building is symmetrical in appearance.

T F **4.** The East and West walls have no windows.

T F **5.** The rebars used in the foundation are all the same size.

T F **6.** A W 12 × 27 steel beam is 12″ high and weighs 27 pounds per foot.

T F **7.** The East and West walls are face brick with common brick backing.

T F **8.** The joists shown on the second floor plan support the second floor.

T F **9.** The two stairways terminate in the living-dining area.

T F **10.** The front and rear stairs have different riser heights.

T F **11.** Partitions are all shown 5″ thick except for the bathroom partition.

T F **12.** The heater room is lined with Sheetrock®.

T F **13.** Four return air registers are shown on the second floor.

T F **14.** The roof terrace is pitched toward the South.

T F **15.** The roof drain in the roof terrace floor connects to the drain from the roof.

T F **16.** Electrical outlets are shown for the commercial level.

T F **17.** Vinyl asbestos tile is used to cover the first floor.

T F **18.** Pull-chain light fixtures are placed in all closets on the second floor.

T F **19.** The area above the tub in the bathroom of the living quarters is furred-down.

T F **20.** Plans for the first and second floors are drawn to a scale of $1/8'' = 1'-0''$.

T F **21.** The width of the lot is 25′-0″.

T F **22.** Minimum headroom at the back stairway is 7′-0″.

T   F   **23.** Front window glass on the lower floor is ¼" polished plate.

T   F   **24.** The landing in the front stairs is 4'-9" long.

T   F   **25.** An existing 1½-story, frame building is located on the East side of the lot.

T   F   **26.** The heating room may be squared off if the alternate proposal for replacing the overhead door at the rear of the building is accepted.

T   F   **27.** The elevation at the top of the second floor steel is 9'-2¼".

T   F   **28.** Treads of the rear stairwell are 11" deep.

T   F   **29.** The total run of the front stairway is 15'-6".

T   F   **30.** A fresh air intake is located on the East wall of the building.

T   F   **31.** The refrigerator is located to the right of the sink.

T   F   **32.** The cutting plane for Section 2-2 is taken through the second floor plan.

T   F   **33.** A three-way switch controls lights in the rear stairwell.

T   F   **34.** One switched duplex receptacle is located in the living room.

T   F   **35.** The supply air riser is placed in the front stairwell near the landing.

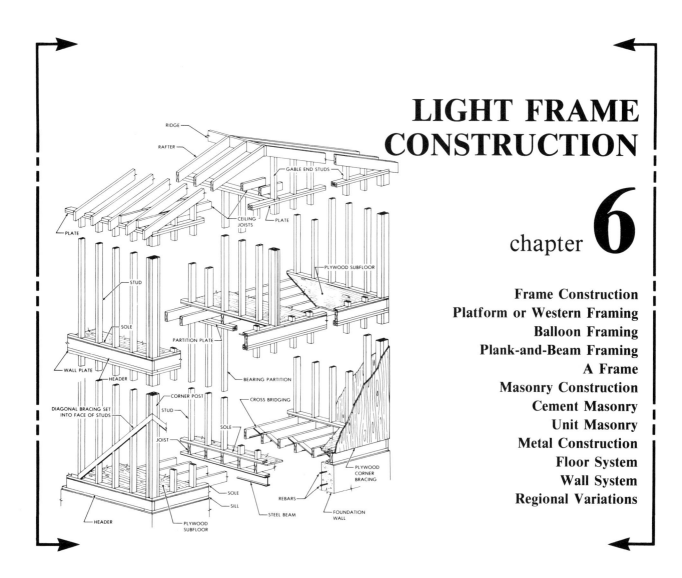

Labels in figure:
RIDGE
RAFTER
GABLE END STUDS
CEILING JOISTS
PLATE
PLATE
PLYWOOD SUBFLOOR
STUD
SOLE
PARTITION PLATE
WALL PLATE
HEADER
BEARING PARTITION
DIAGONAL BRACING SET INTO FACE OF STUDS
CORNER POST
STUD
CROSS BRIDGING
JOIST
SOLE
PLYWOOD CORNER BRACING
SOLE
SILL
REBARS
FOUNDATION WALL
HEADER
PLYWOOD SUBFLOOR
STEEL BEAM

LIGHT FRAME CONSTRUCTION

chapter 6

Frame Construction
Platform or Western Framing
Balloon Framing
Plank-and-Beam Framing
A Frame
Masonry Construction
Cement Masonry
Unit Masonry
Metal Construction
Floor System
Wall System
Regional Variations

FRAME CONSTRUCTION

The framework of a building forms a skeleton on which the exterior and interior finish is applied. The framework must be designed to withstand the stresses caused by the weight of people, equipment, and furniture and must be adequate to withstand external forces of wind, snow loads, and earthquake. Several methods of construction have been developed, each with its own advantage. These methods are designed to use available materials and labor in an efficient and economical manner.

Platform or Western Framing

The basic type of light construction using wood is *platform framing*. See Figure 6-1. The essential features of platform (western) framing are floor-ing laid over joists to the outside edges of the joists and headers, exterior walls and bearing partitions resting on the rough floor, and second floor joists resting on the exterior walls and bearing partitions. Most frame buildings use this type of construction. It is the most efficient method of assembly and erection of a building and the least costly for most applications. Light steel and aluminum framing systems are a direct application of platform framing with the use of different materials.

Some of the characteristics of platform framing are shown in the floor systems made of 2″ boards on edge over which a rough floor is placed. Walls and partitions made of 2″ × 4″ studs, complete with *sole* and *plates* (bottom and top members), are made in units and tilted up into place. Ceiling joists, which are also 2″ members on edge, rest on the wall and

PLATFORM FRAMING

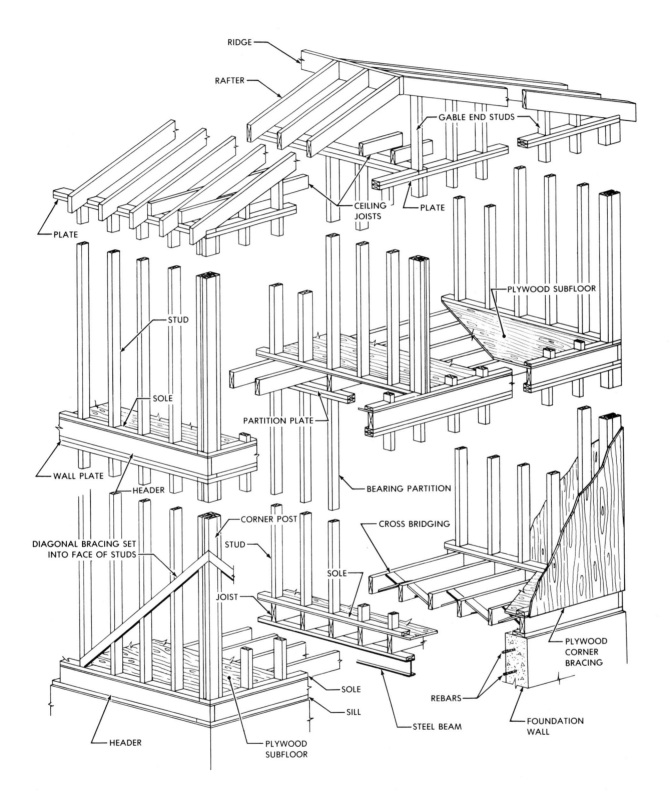

Figure 6-1. Platform framing is the most popular type of light construction framing.

on a *bearing partition* placed near the center of the building. A bearing partition is capable of carrying heavy loads. Joists and studs are usually placed on 16″ centers.

In typical platform framing, a sill rests on the foundation wall. It is bedded in mortar and is fastened down with anchor bolts firmly fixed in the foundation wall. Anchor bolts are commercially available in lengths from 6″ to 24″ and diameters from 3/8″ to 3/4″. Flat washers and hex nuts are used to secure the sill to the foundation wall. Anchor bolts are commonly placed on 4′-0″ or 6′-0″ centers. See Figure 6-2.

ANCHOR BOLTS

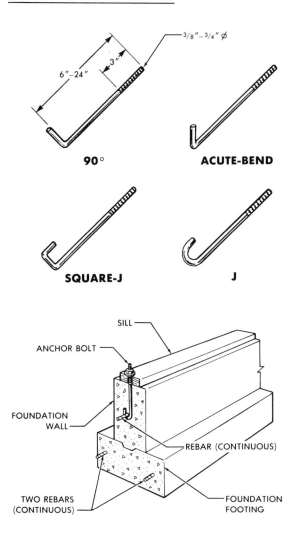

Figure 6-2. Anchor bolts secure the sill to the foundation wall.

The joists rest on the sill, lining up with the outside on two sides, and butts against a header on the two ends. Joists are supported by a beam at the center of the building. The rough flooring is placed on the joists. It is laid out to the outer edge of the joists and headers on all four sides to form a platform. Wide 1″ boards were used in the past for rough flooring, but builders today use plywood sheets fastened in a staggered pattern at right angle to the joists. Either glue or nails, or both, are used to secure the panels to the floor joist. These provide a very strong, quiet floor.

Exterior walls and partitions are assembled on the floor and tilted up into position to be nailed to the floor and through the floor into joists below. They are made with a single member at the bottom (sole) and a double member at the top (plate) arranged so that the members overlap at corners and intersections to provide good nailing. When there are enough carpenters in the crew, whole walls are often made in one piece and raised into position. Otherwise, they are made in lengths that can be conveniently handled.

When all of the rough walls and partitions are erected, the soles are nailed down securely, and plate corners and intersections are fastened together. This assembly is quite stable and plumb. However, it is not considered strong enough to withstand unusual wind or other external stresses encountered in some areas, without some form of bracing. When plywood sheathing is applied, there is generally no need for other bracing. See Figure 6-3. Diagonal bracing, which takes the form of members placed diagonally across the face of the studs, is cut into the studs to be flush. This method is still used in areas where there is great external wind stress placed on the building.

The basic structure is modified to provide stairwell openings in floors, window and door openings in walls, and additional strength under bearing partitions. Where bearing partitions are placed parallel to floor joists, double or triple joists are placed underneath the partition to carry the load transferred from the structure above. Openings in floors for stairwells or chimneys must be located according to the plan, regardless of the arrangement of joists. The joists are cut and reinforced by double joists at the side (double trimmers) and double headers at the ends. Openings in walls for doors and windows are located as shown on the working drawings, even though the studs are spaced on 16″ cen-

CORNER BRACING

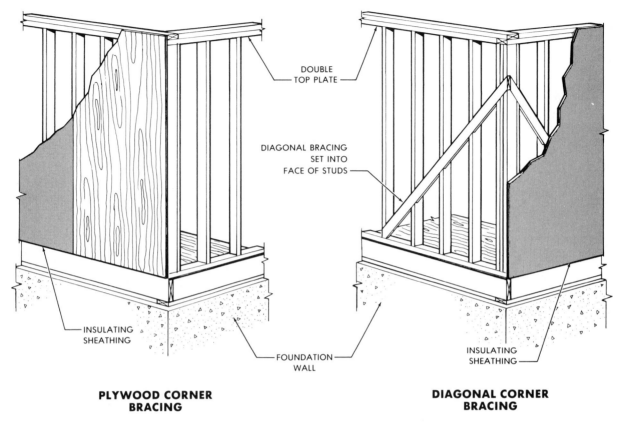

PLYWOOD CORNER BRACING

DIAGONAL CORNER BRACING

Figure 6-3. Plywood sheathing is used to brace corners in platform framing construction. An older method is the use of diagonal bracing let into the studs.

ters, regardless of the size openings. The studs, where openings appear, are cut out and replaced by trimmers (cripple studs) at the sides supporting headers over the opening. This can be accomplished in several ways, but the principle involved is to transfer the load imposed above the opening to the floor below and to provide the right size rough opening at the same time. See Figure 6-4.

Ceiling joists are positioned on 16″ centers with ends resting on the outside walls and the bearing partition. The floor plan may not always place the bearing partition near the center of the building. The joists may be much longer on one side than the other but will always be specified of sufficient size to support the load above and come within the allowed deflection limits. Joists are selected so that they do not bend more than a prescribed amount under the load of people, furniture, equipment, and the weight of the joist itself. Excessive deflection results in cracks in the interior finish. When there is a second

floor on the building, a rough floor is installed in the same manner as the first floor. Partitions are built and tilted up into place following the methods utilized for partition construction on the first floor.

When the floor plan of a building is a rectangle, the roof is often a simple gable roof (slopes in two directions). This permits the use of trusses, which are components built on the job or in an assembly plant to form the rough supporting structure for the roof sheathing and roofing. When the floor plan is irregular in shape or a special architectural effect is desired, the roof structure is made using rafters spaced on 16″ centers to support the complex surfaces of the roof itself.

Developments in industrial processes have taken platform framing and broken it up into components to be built away from the job. The components are made using costly machinery on a production basis with great precision. The National Forest Products Association took the initiative by developing the

Unicom (uniform component) system for making wall, floor, roof, and truss components. The components are based on strict adherence to the use of modular measure (4″ cube module). Assembly plants are common in all parts of the country to supply builders with the components they need. See Figure 6-5.

It was only a few steps from making two-dimensional components to developing *modules* (three-dimensional units) in the form of bathrooms, kitchens, plumbing cores, and other parts of houses. They are delivered to the job by truck and installed on the foundation or rough framework with a crane. See Figure 6-6. The use of modules decreases on-site construction time.

The plywood industry has made valuable contributions to perfecting platform framing. Plywood flooring provides a strong, flat surface for the direct application of carpet or other resilient flooring. Plywood wall and roof sheathing provide walls and roof surfaces that are strong and that permit the nailing of siding and shingles without searching for wood members below the sheathing, or installing

American Plywood Association

Figure 6-5. Components are built off site and quickly erected on site.

nailing strips. Experiments done have been successful using the platform frame for flooring and sheathing, with members on 2′-0″ centers. Proper gluing and nailing techniques must be observed.

Special components have been developed using plywood sheets over wood structural frames. One of these is the box beam or box header. See Figure 6-7. This system is used for floor and roof supports or to span wide distances over openings. Another pre-manufactured component that is used to span wide distances between supports because it has great structural value is the stressed skin panel. These panels are framed with 2 × 4s and covered on each side with plywood. The 2 × 4s are commonly placed 16″ OC. Ventilation holes are drilled in the 2 × 4s for air circulation. Plywood on the upper side of stressed skin panels is thicker than plywood on the lower side. Insulation may be placed inside the panels during assembly. See Figure 6-8.

Balloon Framing

Balloon framing is not as commonly used today as it once was. One problem with using wood as a

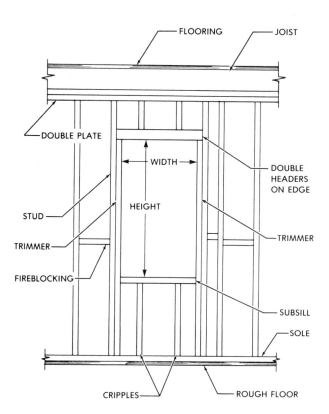

Figure 6-4. Trimmers at each side of the rough opening give support to the header and provide nailing for the trim. Full studs maintain 16″ OC.

American Plywood Association

Figure 6-6. Modules are placed on the foundation with a crane.

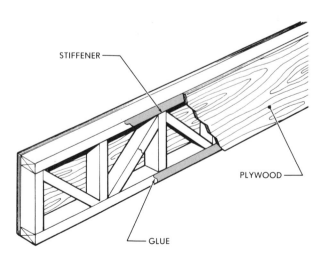

Figure 6-7. Box beams made of plywood over a framework provide lightweight, strong support.

construction material is that it shrinks across the width of the grain. In balloon framing, this tendency of the wood to shrink is overcome with the use of studs which continue from the sill to the plate at the top of the wall with ribbons let (notched) into them at the second floor level. The joists are nailed to the sides of the studs as well. See Figure 6-9. This type of framing provides passageways to run ducts and raceway systems through the open stud spaces from floor to floor. However, the same stud spaces can act as flues, enabling fire to spread quickly, unless carefully blocked with pieces of wood fitted in place near the floor levels.

Balloon framing has some use in the central partition of split-level houses. It is generally awkward to assemble when compared to platform framing. Wall, partition, and floor components can be made to fit into the structure of a particular house. They are constructed on the job site, rather than transported from a distance. They must be built with care in order to fit together.

Plank-and-Beam Framing

Plank-and-beam framing is used in the light construction field. It is characterized by wide expanses of glass walls, high ceilings that are actually the underside of the roof planks, and heavy support members. The ceilings and roof are finished to show the beauty of the wood itself. See Figure 6-10.

The unique structural features of plank-and-beam framing are (1) the posts at the outside walls, (2) the beams below the floor and beams above supporting the roof planks, and (3) the posts supporting the ridge of the roof. All members are spaced at fixed wide intervals. The construction at the sill resembles platform framing, but little else is similar.

Floor beams are used in place of floor joists. The beams are spaced from 6'-0" to 8'-0" apart and support 2" (nominal dimension) floor planks. The floor planks are made with a tongue-and-groove joint and are thick, so that they have their own structural strength. Thicker decks spaced farther apart are used for heavy construction. Posts are erected with the same spacing as the floor beams to support plates and roof beams.

The roof beams support 2" planks for the roof. This type of framing requires heavy floor and roof beams. These beams may be solid timbers. However, modern gluing techniques provide laminated, large dimension members from a number of thin boards.

Plank-and-beam framing has several distinct advantages over platform or balloon framing. Since the outside walls are wide open, glass can be used without special framing for openings. Also, there are few structural members with only minor differences in size or shape. The only limitation for the architect is working within the various post locations. Rooms are usually planned so that the partitions run down the center of the building to enclose the posts, then out to exterior walls so that they meet posts located between window units.

Some of the problems posed by plank-and-beam framing are (1) difficulty in concealing wiring and heating ducts, (2) difficulty in providing additional floor reinforcement under heavy equipment and fixtures in kitchens and bathrooms, and (3) difficulty in adequately insulating the building. Wiring and ducts that go above floor level must be run in the central partition or concealed along posts between windows. Additional heavy beams are placed under heavy fixtures in kitchens and bathrooms. Insulating glass is used on outside walls. Thermal insulation, in the form of insulation board, is placed over the roof planks.

A Frame

An unusual type of building construction having a relationship to plank-and-beam framing is the *A frame*. The A frame is a popular type of construction for vacation homes. See Figure 6-11. The main structural members are large in dimension and are spaced 4'-0" to 6'-0" apart. They resemble the roof joists of plank-and-beam framing except that they are placed at a steep slope extending from the foundation, where they are firmly fastened, to the ridge. The roof boards are strong enough to carry the load of the roof over the span between the structural members. The exterior sides of the building are actually roof surfaces and the two gable ends. The gable ends have the windows and doors needed for light, ventilation, and access.

The living room is often left open to the roof above, creating a cathedral effect. The extensive use of glass in the gable end walls opens up the living space to the outdoors. A loft is often placed over the remainder of the house. It may contain bedrooms and an additional bathroom. The open space from the living area allows good lines of sight and

Plywood Fabricator Service, Inc.

Figure 6-8. Stressed skin panels span wide distances. They may be used for roof decks.

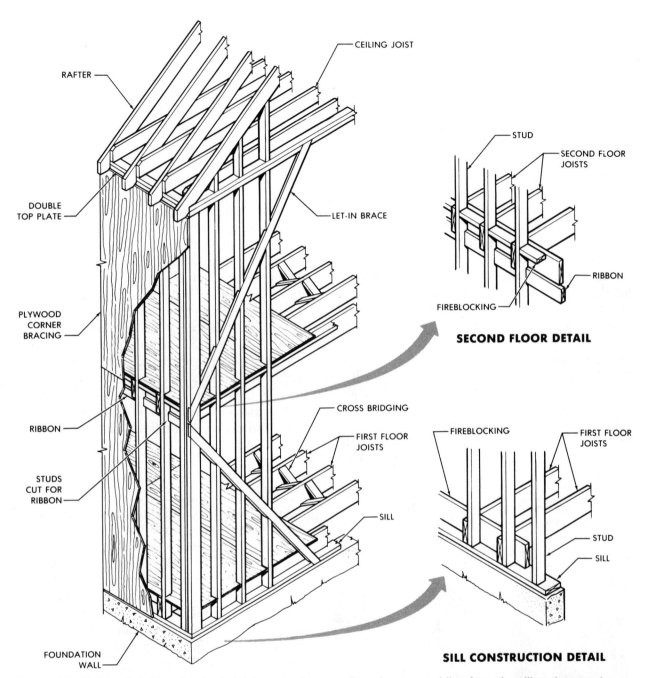

Figure 6-9. Balloon framing minimizes shrinkage by the use of continuous studding from the sill to the top plate.

an open feeling between the loft deck and the space below. Circular or steeply pitched stairs commonly lead to the loft.

MASONRY CONSTRUCTION

Masonry construction can be divided into two broad classes: *monolithic concrete construction* (cement masonry) and *unit masonry construction*. In monolithic concrete construction, concrete is formed into one mass (the prefix *mono* means one). Monolithic concrete construction is utilized for both residential and light commercial construction. It is most prevalent in heavy construction. Unit masonry construction uses brick, stone, concrete masonry unit (concrete block), or structural and facing tile. It is most prevalent in residential and light commercial construction.

Figure 6-10. Plank-and-beam framing uses heavy structural members and planks for floors and roofs. An open look is achieved.

Cement masonry and unit masonry construction are often used in combination. Cement masonry provides the most satisfactory means of making load-bearing footings and foundation walls. Concrete, when properly mixed and placed in the formwork, provides structurally sound continuous footings and walls that last indefinitely without deterioration. Cement masonry is also used for the walls of buildings and parts of walls above ground.

Brick masonry provides one of the most durable and easily maintained walls available. When properly constructed of sound material, the brick unit gives almost unlimited service. The units must be laid carefully to form a strong wall. Precautions are taken to provide waterproofing in the form of flashing or parging where necessary. Masonry units are often laid in combination, with one type on the outside face of the wall and another type backing it up.

For example, a brick wall may be backed up with a concrete block wall.

Cement Masonry

Building with cement masonry is primarily a matter of preparing formwork designed to take the desired shape of the footings and walls, making the forms to the correct dimensions, and locating them as specified on the working drawings. The concrete is mixed according to specifications in a mixing plant and delivered to the job as *ready mix* (ready to pour) concrete. The placing of concrete is a routine job; however, care must be taken that all voids are filled. This is done with the help of a mechanical vibrator. After three or four days, the forms are carefully removed so as not to damage the *green* (not cured) concrete. Bricklaying or wood construction can then begin, but it must be remembered that the concrete does not develop its full strength until about 28 days after placement.

Footings. Much work takes place before the actual placing of a footing can be done. A carpenter or a cement mason lays out the building lines with a level and a steel tape from a *point of beginning* (reference point) on the lot. The location of the building lines are marked on batterboards set back from the foundation location so that they will not

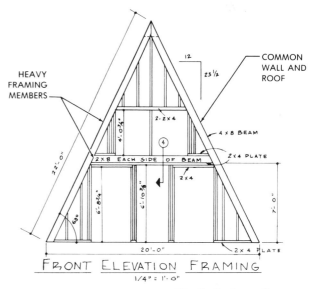

Figure 6-11. In A frame construction, heavy framing members form a common wall and roof.

be disturbed when the excavation is made. See Figure 6-12. The excavation is dug to the specified depth with a backhoe or other piece of earth-removal equipment. Sufficient room is left on the sides for the tradesworkers to work as they erect the forms. Often, the walls must be shored to prevent cave-ins. Specific instructions must be followed when shoring walls for excavated areas. The foundation footings must be placed on undisturbed earth.

Lines are strung horizontally between the batterboards, representing the faces of the foundation wall. Plumb (vertical) lines are dropped, which serve to locate points from which the foundation footing forms can be located. Simple forms, consisting of boards that are spaced to give the footing the specified width and adjusted for the specified height, are erected and braced. Rebars are often required in the

footing. They must be located as shown on the section view through the foundation wall on the working drawing. Wiring and special wire devices hold the rebars in position during the concrete pour.

Foundation Walls. The foundation wall may be made of concrete masonry units, as in the North Carolina Residence in chapter 3, or monolithic concrete. When a foundation wall is made of concrete, several forming methods may be used, depending on the preference of the builder and the thickness and height of the foundation wall.

Most foundation formwork is made with panel forms that can be reused many times. These forms are often made by carpenters. See Figure 6-13. Patented panel forms, complete with hardware (holding devices), are commercially available. These forms

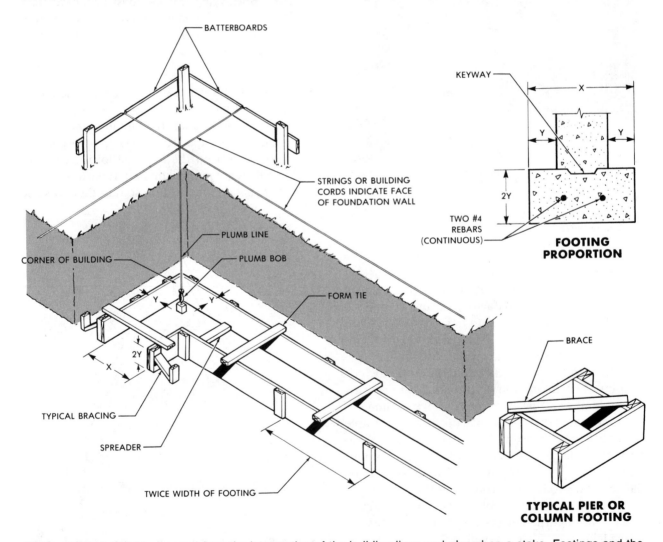

Figure 6-12. A point is dropped from the intersection of the building lines and placed on a stake. Footings and the face of the foundation are located from this point.

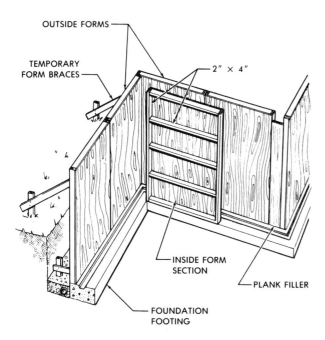

Figure 6-13. Panels with fillers of various sizes can be adapted to most forming problems. They may be reused many times. Forms of this type are generally made by the carpenter.

are easily assembled and may be adapted to solve specific construction problems. The forms are placed on the footing and tied together with *snap ties*. See Figure 6-14. Snap ties are commercially available in a variety of types. They serve to keep the two inside form faces the proper distance apart and to take the full thrust of the pressure of the concrete when

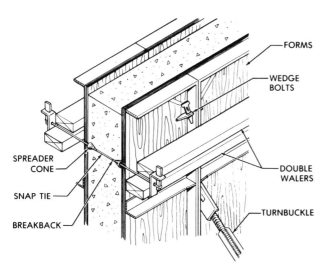

Figure 6-14. Patented panel systems use a variety of holding devices to maintain wall spacing. Snap ties are common.

it is placed in the forms. Snap ties are broken off (snapped) when the forms are stripped.

If windows and doors are to appear in the foundation wall, boxes are fastened inside of the forms, or the jambs are set. When the concrete is placed, the boxes or jambs remain until the forms are stripped.

Concrete stairs are formed in several ways, depending on their design. A simple method is to erect side stringers and braces to hold the riser form boards in position. See Figure 6-15. The cement mason will trowel the treads to a smooth finish.

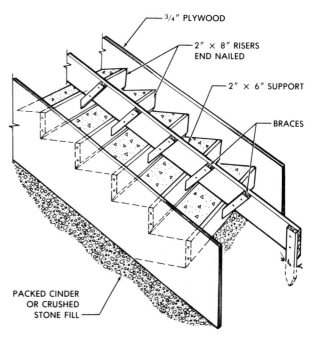

Figure 6-15. Concrete stairs are formed by risers that are held in place by braces.

Waterproofing Foundations. Foundations and footings are waterproofed in various ways, depending on the condition of the soil, depth of footing below grade, and the general climatic conditions of the area. Usually the outside of the foundation wall and footing is mopped with tar or asphaltum before the earth is back filled. If this is not considered to be sufficient, a membrane of wide sheets of polyethylene is placed over the tar to form an overlapping waterproof cover. When the conditions are extreme, several layers of felt are applied over coats of tar or asphaltum.

Drain tile is laid around the perimeter of the building. It is either plastic pipe with holes, or clay tile laid with open joints so that the water can enter and be carried away from the foundation walls. The tile terminates in a sump pump, which expels the water to a storm sewer or to a dispersion field away from the building. Note: Many local ordinances will not allow such water to be pumped into the storm sewer. In this case, the water should be pumped far enough from the foundation wall of the dwelling so that it is not likely to re-enter the sump pump.

Unit Masonry

Unit masonry consists of brick, stone, concrete block, and tile. These units are laid as (1) solid brick walls with no backup, (2) brick walls with backup, (3) cavity walls, or (4) brick veneer over a wood frame.

Solid Brick Walls with No Backup. Bearing-wall construction, or ordinary construction, is construction using solid brick walls that serve to carry the load of floor and roof joists. See Figure 6-16. The

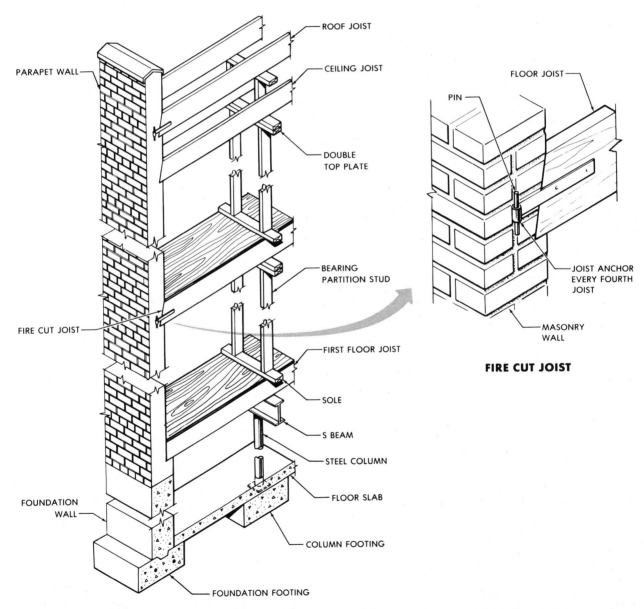

Figure 6-16. Construction for a masonry building consists of wood joists and wood-bearing partitions. Joists are fire cut.

walls are laid with two wythes of brick bonded together every sixth course by a header course. In some cities, building codes require a 12″ wall of three wythes for buildings more than one-story tall. Joists are *fire cut* (cut on an angle) to rest in the brick wall. In the event of a severe fire, the burned-out joist would drop without disturbing the wall. A joist with a square cut on the end would exert a prying action, forcing the wall to fall outward. The joists are tied to the wall by metal anchors spaced at every fourth joist. The anchors pull out of the wall in case of fire. The rest of the structure is constructed in the same manner as platform framing.

SCR brick, developed by the Structural Clay Products Research Foundation, is designed to provide a 6″ (nominal) load-bearing wall with only a single wythe of brick. It is primarily used for one-story structures, although it has been used for high, load-bearing walls with good results. SCR brick saves time since it is larger than building brick and is laid without backup material. In order to provide sufficient bearing for the joists, the wall is *corbeled*. A corbel is a ledge built into the wall to provide bearing space. Furring strips are usually placed on the inside of all masonry walls in order to provide a flat surface for lath or drywall. In Figure 6-17, 2″ × 2″ members are fastened, using clips, to the brick. The space serves to ventilate the wall. Moisture due to condensation runs down to the flashing, then to weep holes in the mortar joints directly above the flashing.

Another typical framing method for building with masonry walls is to use steel columns and beams to support floor joists or open web steel joists in the place of a bearing partition.

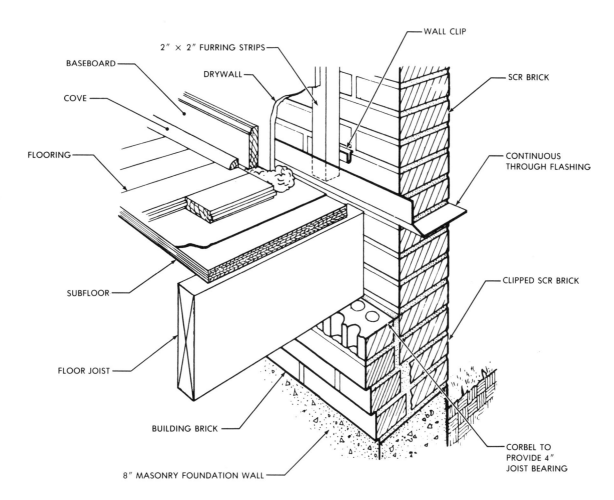

Figure 6-17. SCR brick may be used to make a strong, durable wall with only one thickness of brick. Note the corbel used to provide joist bearing, the through wall flashing, and the furring strips fastened with clips to the wall.

Brick Walls with Backup. Brick is often used in conjunction with a backup material of a different size, such as concrete block or tile. See Figure 6-18. The courses of brick and the backup material must be arranged so that the wall is tied together at intervals. When brick and concrete block are laid to make up a 12″ wall, a *full cut header* (special concrete block) is used. The full cut header is notched out to receive a header course. The backing tier (wythe) is *parged* with mortar. Parging is the application of mortar to provide additional waterproofing. See Figure 6-19.

Stone may be laid so that the units extend through the wall, but generally they are laid with brick or concrete block to back them up. The manner of tying the wythes together is similar to that for masonry walls using brick and other materials for backup.

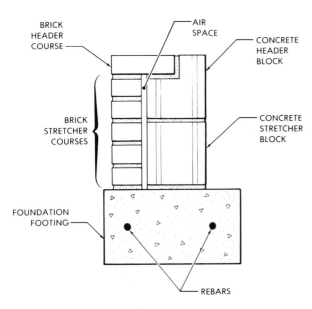

Figure 6-18. Brick backed up by concrete block is tied together with a header course.

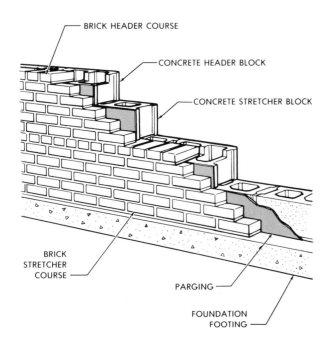

Figure 6-19. The backing tier is often parged to provide additional waterproofing.

Cavity Walls. Cavity walls are a type of construction using two wythes of brick separated by a 2″ air space. Individual ties are usually embedded in the mortar joints of every sixth course on 24″ centers. See Figure 6-20. Continuous flashing is provided in the same manner as for the SCR brick. The core of the cavity wall may be filled with insulation. The interior walls can be prepared for plaster or drywall by the application of furring strips and gypsum lath or wallboard. Cavity wall construction is commonly used in buildings designed to have the inside face of exterior walls finished with exposed brick.

Brick Veneer Walls. One wythe of brick is used as a skin over wood-framed walls in brick veneer construction. Stone may be used for the same purpose. The foundation is made wide enough to support the sill for the joists and the brick. See Figure 6-21. The frame of the building is erected first and provides the supporting structure for floor joists, ceiling joists, and rafters. The brick is laid and tied to the frame wall with clips. One clip is required for each 2 sq. ft. of area. An air space is provided between the wall sheathing and the back of the brick because a slight movement between the brick and the frame wall will result due to shrinkage of the wood members. The air space also provides ventilation for the wall. Flashing is used to divert any moisture toward the outside. Weep holes are placed in brick joints.

METAL CONSTRUCTION

Wood and masonry have always been considered the basic materials for light construction. The steel industry supplies structural shapes for supporting beams, lintels to support masonry over openings, and miscellaneous straps, anchors, and rebars. Developments in the steel and aluminum industries,

CAVITY WALLS

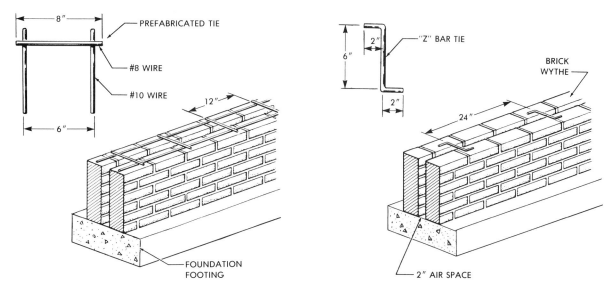

Figure 6-20. A cavity wall contains two wythes of brick separated by a 2″ air space and tied together every sixth course.

however, have produced framing systems that are competitive in price and offer several advantages for some applications. Steel and aluminum members will not warp, shrink or rot, and are impervious to termites. They are available in stock sizes and are assembled with relative ease. The members are designed to be light in weight and can be adapted to meet the needs of any plan layout.

Non-load-bearing walls using steel studs and tracks have been adopted for general use for partitions in commercial and apartment buildings. Metal tracks are fastened to the floor and ceiling with nails, screws, or powder-actuated fasteners, depending on the material of the surface. The studs are snapped into place on 24″ centers and fastened with screws or crimped to stay in position. Gypsum board for

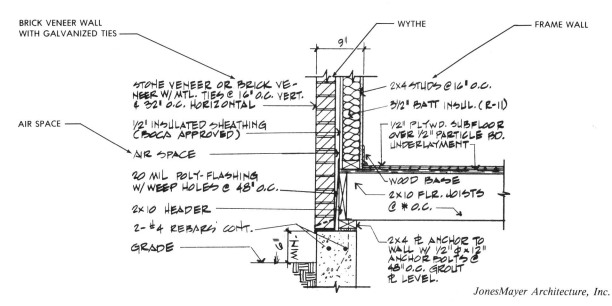

JonesMayer Architecture, Inc.

Figure 6-21. A brick veneer wall contains one wythe of brick secured to the frame wall with galvanized ties. An air space separates the brick from the frame wall.

the drywall is fastened to the studs and channels with screws driven by a power screwdriver. Frames for doors are included in the framework wherever needed. See Figure 6-22.

Comprehensive structural arrangements for the framing of the whole building with either steel or aluminum members have been developed to provide floor systems with metal joists, exterior wall systems with bearing properties, and internal partition systems. The wall and partition assemblies are particularly valuable for use as components assembled in a shop, although they can be assembled on the job.

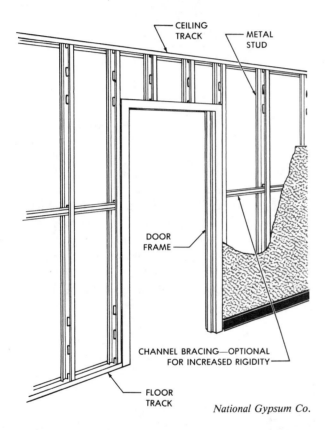

National Gypsum Co.

Figure 6-22. Steel non-load-bearing partitions consist of floor and ceiling tracks and studs. Doubled drywall adds rigidity.

Floor System

A conventional W beam is used to support the center of the steel joists. The joists are either C-shaped sections or nailable joists. They are made in several depths (6″ to 12″) and with several gauges of metal. See Figure 6-23. They rest in pockets provided in the foundation wall or on top of the wall

STEEL FRAMING MEMBERS

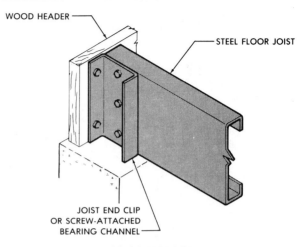

WOOD HEADER ON FOUNDATION WALL

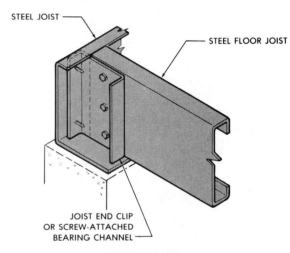

STEEL JOIST ON FOUNDATION WALL

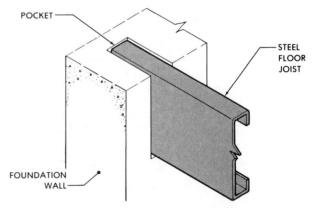

POCKET IN FOUNDATION WALL

Inland Ryerson

Figure 6-23. Steel framing members are used to build light construction framework.

with a wood header member or a steel joist closure placed to serve this purpose. The joists are tied together by bridging resting on top and screwed to three adjacent joists. Plywood flooring is applied over the joists with screws driven by a power screwdriver or with nails, if nailable joists are used. Figure 6-24 shows the floor structure assembled with an opening for a stairway.

Lightweight aluminum W beams and joists serve the same purpose. A perimeter plate (rim joist) is used on the ends of joists and is fastened to the joists with screws. The floor assembly is fastened to the foundation with powder-actuated fasteners through the flanges of the perimeter joists.

Wall System

The wall system consists of load-bearing studs with top and bottom channel plates. Steel studs are supplied in the shape of a channel or a letter C. They are available either solid or punched with holes which permit the passage of pipe or conduit. Aluminum studs are made in the shape of the letter I. Wood liners are provided for window and door openings in buildings with steel or aluminum superstructure. Metal frames, integral with the walls, are also used. The studs are placed on 24″ centers to fit plywood or other sheets of sheathing. See Figure 6-25. Racking loads (distortions diagonally across the wall) are counteracted by using plywood sheathing at corners or by means of diagonal straps or wires.

Internal partitions that are generally non-load-bearing are made of lighter gauge metal. See Figure 6-26. When load-bearing partitions are required, the same studs as those used in the outside wall are used. The metal members can be arranged so that room layouts and the locations of windows and doorways are completely flexible. Gypsum wallboard is then applied as drywall finish with power-driven screws.

Metal framing systems are often used in conjunction with *open web steel joists* in the construction industry. These joists are made in several styles by different manufacturers. All of the joists have a top and bottom chord with bars bent back and forth between them to give a truss effect. See Figure 6-27. Standards have been set by the Steel Joist Institute regarding length, depth, carrying capacity, and details of support at the ends. Two series, designated J and H and differing in load-bearing capacity, are supplied from 8″ to 24″ in depth, in 2″ increments,

Alcoa Building Products

Figure 6-24. Framing members are assembled to provide solid floor support. The plywood subfloor is fastened with an air-driven nail gun.

to span up to 48′-0″. Other series can span up to 144′-0″ without center support.

The joists are spaced on 24″ centers for floors and up to 30″ centers for roofs. If stronger decks are required, roof spacing can be 5′-0″ to 6′-0″. Bridging is installed at intervals to provide firmness. Extensions are installed so that ceiling materials can be applied. Floors and roof decks are made of 2″ tongue-and-groove wood decking, reinforced concrete over steel decking, or *paper-backed wire mesh.* This is specially prepared heavy paper, strong enough to support the thin lightweight concrete deck until it sets. The mesh provides reinforcement for the concrete. Ceilings can be made by fastening wire lath or gypsum lath to the bottom of the joists and applying plaster.

Steel joists have several advantages. Their light weight permits them to be installed easily and cuts down the *dead load* of the building. The dead load is the weight of the structure itself. They are designed to serve exceptionally wide spans between supports. The joists rest on the walls with such precision that floor decks and ceilings can be installed with little or no adjustment to make them level. Pipe and conduit can pass through the open webs with ease.

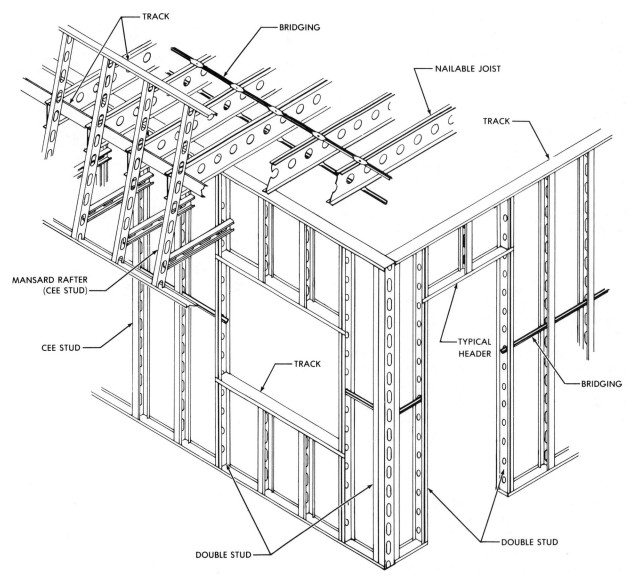

Figure 6-25. Metal framing members provide flexibility in layout.

Wheeling-Pittsburgh Steel Corp.

REGIONAL VARIATIONS

The manner of building footing and foundation walls has more contrast in various parts of the country than any other building feature. The factors of climate, moisture, and soil conditions have to be considered. Some of the primary choices are the full basement, crawl space, slab-on-grade, or the use of grade beams.

Basements are desired in cold climates and in cities because the most economical use of space is to build the house as near the shape of a cube as possible. The basement is used for the heating plant, laundry, and family or recreation room. Foundation walls are made of solid concrete placed in one piece or concrete block, if the moisture and soil conditions will permit. Footings and foundations extend below the frost line in cold climates. In warmer climates, the buildings have crawl spaces with low foundations because there is no frost problem. The slab-on-grade foundation is used extensively also. In warmer climates, the foundation walls are omitted and a thickened perimeter support is substituted. See Figure 6-28.

The plan of the house is directly related to the choice of the type of foundation. In warm climates, the family room is generally located on the first floor

Figure 6-26. Interior partitions are framed with lighter gauge metal studs.

level and is often designed as a porch with jalousie windows. The heating plant is in a closet space and the laundry appliances are in the utility room. Certain types of buildings are not limited, however, to one locality. Houses with crawl spaces and slabs-on-grade are also found in the North. Special precautions are taken to insulate the foundations. Foundations for houses with crawl spaces can be made to extend below the frost line. Radiant heating may be embedded in the floor in buildings with slabs-on-grade.

A grade beam is used where soil is unstable in warmer climates. It provides a continuous support to the buildings with piers spaced at intervals. See Figure 6-29.

In many parts of the country, precautions must be taken against termites by providing metal shields on top of the foundation, on pipes, and by poisoning the soil. The need for waterproofing the foundation and footing varies with the amount of moisture in the soil and the nature of the soil.

The basic structure, whether made of masonry or platform framing, does not vary greatly in different

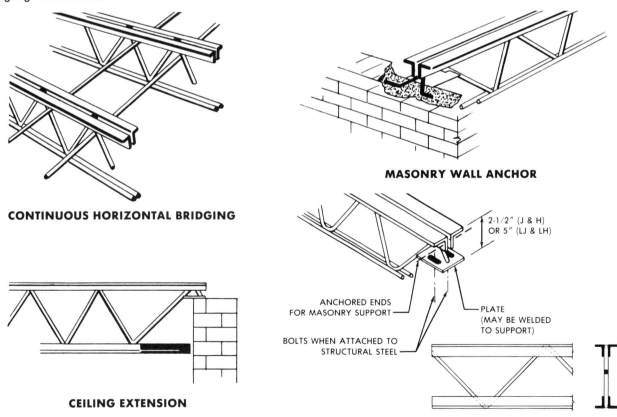

CONTINUOUS HORIZONTAL BRIDGING

MASONRY WALL ANCHOR

2-1/2″ (J & H)
OR 5″ (LJ & LH)

ANCHORED ENDS
FOR MASONRY SUPPORT

PLATE
(MAY BE WELDED
TO SUPPORT)

BOLTS WHEN ATTACHED TO
STRUCTURAL STEEL

CEILING EXTENSION

Figure 6-27. Open web steel joists support wide spans for floors and roof decks.

SLAB-ON-GRADE FLOOR

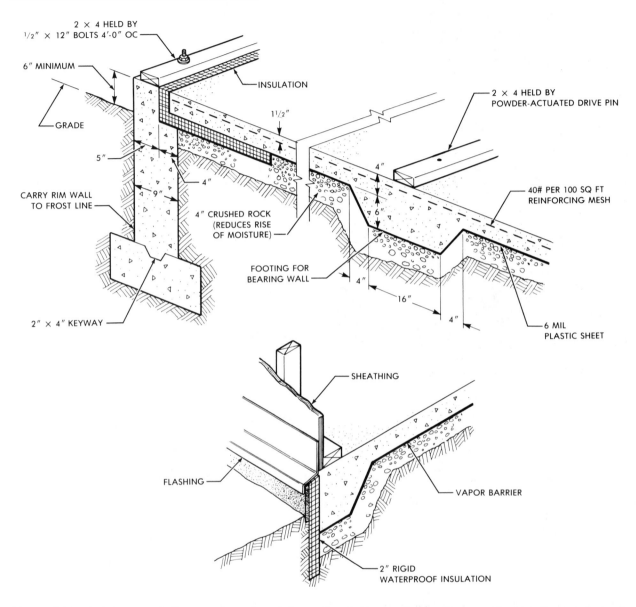

2 × 4 HELD BY
½″ × 12″ BOLTS 4′-0″ OC

6″ MINIMUM

INSULATION

GRADE

2 × 4 HELD BY
POWDER-ACTUATED DRIVE PIN

1½″

5″

4″

9″

CARRY RIM WALL
TO FROST LINE

4″ CRUSHED ROCK
(REDUCES RISE
OF MOISTURE)

40# PER 100 SQ FT
REINFORCING MESH

4″

6″

FOOTING FOR
BEARING WALL

4″

2″ × 4″ KEYWAY

16″

4″

6 MIL
PLASTIC SHEET

SHEATHING

FLASHING

VAPOR BARRIER

2″ RIGID
WATERPROOF INSULATION

Figure 6-28. A slab-on-grade floor requires a foundation wall and edge insulation when used in cold climates. A simple perimeter support suffices in warm climates.

parts of the country. Building with components occurs more frequently near urban centers where they are readily available. In areas where there are hurricane or tornado hazards, special precautions are made to tie down the framing to the foundation with sufficient anchor bolts and to tie the framing members together with steel straps. The rigidity of the walls is increased by using strong diagonal braces and thicker plywood sheathing. The choice of lum-

ber, flashing, and waterproofing is important in areas where there is high moisture.

In warm parts of the country, such as the Southeast, concrete blocks are used for exterior walls. Where there is a possibility of damage from high winds, reinforced concrete piers are used. A horizontal reinforced concrete beam is placed around the top of the wall. See Figure 6-30.

In areas where high earthquake frequency is encountered, buildings are designed to counteract horizontal shear forces in the framework. Ductility is achieved by providing a frame that is not rigid at the connecting points. Great care must be used in the design of tall buildings. Stress is not as significant a factor in residential or light construction because of the relative size of the building. Most buildings of this type are confined to one floor.

Experiments have been conducted building small houses with monolithic concrete walls on a production basis. In *tilt-slab construction*, the walls are formed on the ground with frames for openings in place. After the concrete is set, the walls are lifted up into place.

The simple gable roof, using trussed rafters or trusses for support, is the most common roof type used in residential construction. These supporting members are made as components in a shop. Flat roofs, using built-up roofing, and roofs of other shapes are not necessarily regional. Their use depends on the desired architectural effect. Asphalt shingles are accepted as the most economical type of roofing. In areas where high wind may dislodge ordinary shingles, cement roof tile cemented or nailed in place is used. Snow and ice on roofs in cold climates pose special problems. These can be solved by increasing the protection at the eaves and insulating the attic space to prevent loss of heat through the roof.

GRADE BEAMS

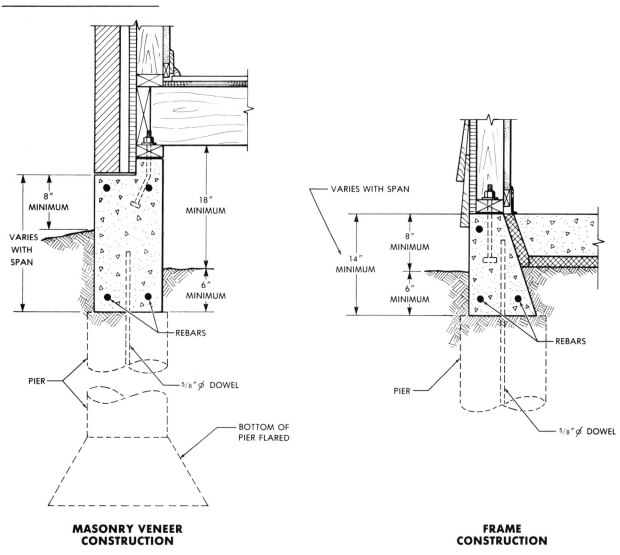

MASONRY VENEER CONSTRUCTION

FRAME CONSTRUCTION

Figure 6-29. Grade beams are used for houses with slabs-on-grade or crawl spaces where conditions warrant.

A PIER REBARS EMBEDDED IN FOUNDATION.

B SPACE FOR PIERS PROVIDED IN WALL.

C CONCRETE FORMWORK CONSTRUCTED.

D HORIZONTAL REINFORCED CONCRETE BOND BEAM PLACED AROUND TOP OF WALL.

E FINISHED WALL READY FOR SURFACE TREATMENT.

F REINFORCEMENT PLACED AT CORNERS AND IN WALL. CEMENT ROOF TILE READY FOR LAYING.

J. H. Svenson

Figure 6-30. In areas where there is a possibility of high-wind damage, walls are reinforced with concrete piers.

Name   Date

Identification

_____   1. Header

_____   2. Sole

_____   3. Diagonal bracing

_____   4. Gable end studs

_____   5. Rafter

_____   6. Sill

_____   7. Ridge

_____   8. Cross bridging

_____   9. Ceiling joists

_____   10. Foundation wall

_____   11. Steel beam

_____   12. Symbol—
                  rough wood

_____   13. Bearing partition

_____   14. Symbol—
                  concrete

_____   15. Doubled top
                  plate

_____   16. Symbol—
                  break line

_____   17. Partition plate

_____   18. Corner post

_____   19. Joist

_____   20. Subfloor

Completion

_____ 1. Frame wall partitions are made with a(n) _____ as the top member.

_____ 2. _____ (or trimmers) are placed at each side of the rough window opening to support the header.

_____ 3. Shrinkage is minimized in _____ framing through the use of continuous studs from the sill to the top plate.

_____ 4. Stairs in A frame houses generally have a(n) _____ pitch.

_____ 5. _____ ties are used to maintain spacing in foundation walls before the concrete is poured.

_____ 6. A(n) _____ is a brick ledge designed to support a load.

_____ 7. Brick veneer is _____ wythe(s) thick.

_____ 8. The _____ load of a building is the weight of the structure.

_____ 9. Walls and partitions in platform framing are _____ at the corners for nailing.

_____ 10. _____ framing provides an open architectural effect.

True-False

T F 1. SCR brick is used for cavity walls.

T F 2. Brick walls backed up by concrete block are tied together with header courses of the brick.

T F 3. Cavity walls are brick walls made of two wythes with an air space between.

T F 4. Brick veneer is combined with wood platform framing.

T F 5. The brick part of a brick veneer wall supports the rafters or trusses.

T F 6. Windows and doors are difficult to fit into buildings using steel or aluminum framework.

T F 7. Walls of metal framework buildings are strengthened by diagonal straps or the use of plywood sheathing at the corners.

T F 8. An advantage of open web joists is the ease of installing raceway systems.

T F 9. Crawl space houses are limited to the South.

T F 10. The ranch house is built with the same foundation construction in all parts of the U.S.

T F 11. Earthquake damage can be minimized by making the framework as rigid as possible.

T F 12. Snow and ice damage to roofs can be eliminated by increasing the strength of roof supports.

Trade Competency Test

Name _____   Date _____

Completion

_____   1. The type of frame construction most commonly used is _____ construction.

_____   2. A partition located near the center of a building supporting ceiling joists is a(n) _____ partition.

_____   3. Anchor bolts hold the _____ to the foundation.

_____   4. Frame walls and partitions are made with a(n) _____ as the bottom member.

_____   5. The roof shape most commonly used is the _____ roof.

_____   6. Parts of buildings, such as wall sections and trusses, are _____.

_____   7. A unit of a house, such as a kitchen or bathroom, made off the job site is a(n) _____.

_____   8. Components made of wood frames with plywood facing which are used for decking are _____.

_____   9. The beams in plank-and-beam framing are placed 6'-0" to _____ OC.

_____   10. The roof beams in residential plank-and-beam framing support boards that are _____ " thick.

_____   11. Buildings that are made with heavy structural members extending from the ridge to the foundation diagonally are _____ buildings.

_____   12. Concrete reaches its design strength in about _____ days.

_____   13. Foundation footings must be placed on _____ earth.

_____   14. Foundation walls are waterproofed with tar or asphaltum and a membrane of _____ sheets.

_____   15. The ends of joists supporting floors in a solid brick building are given _____ cuts.

_____   16. SCR brick are laid in a single _____.

_____   17. Brick walls are usually lined with _____ strips before lath or gypsum board is applied.

_____   18. The base of a brick wall is often protected by metal _____ for moisture control.

_____   19. Stone is backed up by brick or _____ masonry units.

_____   20. Cavity walls usually have a(n) _____ " air space.

_____ 21. An air space of _____ " is provided in a brick veneer wall.

_____ 22. Clips hold the brick veneer to the sheathing with a clip for each _____ sq. ft. of area.

_____ 23. Steel non-load-bearing studs support gypsum board for _____ finish.

_____ 24. Studs in metal-framed houses are placed on _____ " centers.

_____ 25. Steel open web joists are made with top and bottom _____ and bent bars.

_____ 26. J and H series open web joists span up to _____.

_____ 27. Foundations and footings in the North extend below the _____ line.

_____ 28. Metal shields are placed on foundation walls to overcome the _____ problem.

_____ 29. In order to counteract high winds, framing members are tied together with steel _____.

_____ 30. Gable roofs are generally supported by trusses, trussed rafters, or _____.

True-False

T   F   1. Boards of 2" nominal thickness with headers across the ends are used in platform framing to support floors.

T   F   2. Plywood sheets used for flooring are fastened with the long dimension parallel to the joists.

T   F   3. Glue may be used to help fasten plywood to framing members.

T   F   4. Windows are moved by the builder to fall in line with stud spacing.

T   F   5. Clearance is allowed between the rough frame opening and the window frame to permit adjustment.

T   F   6. Rafters are used instead of trusses on most roofs that are rectangular in shape.

T   F   7. The module used for modular measure is the same as a building module.

T   F   8. Siding can be nailed directly to plywood sheathing.

T   F   9. Members of platform framing are always placed on 16" centers.

T   F   10. Posts and beams line up in plank-and-beam framing.

T   F   11. The framing members in plank-and-beam framing are laminated.

T   F   12. The A frame can only be used for plans with a single floor.

T   F   13. The mix of concrete is varied for different applications.

T   F   14. Parging is placing a metal shield at the bottom of a brick wall for moisture control.

T   F   15. Rebars are often used in concrete footings.

T   F   16. Voids in concrete are filled with the aid of a vibrator.

T   F   17. Drain tile is laid tight to keep the water from leaking out.

T   F   18. Corbeling a brick wall means increasing its thickness.

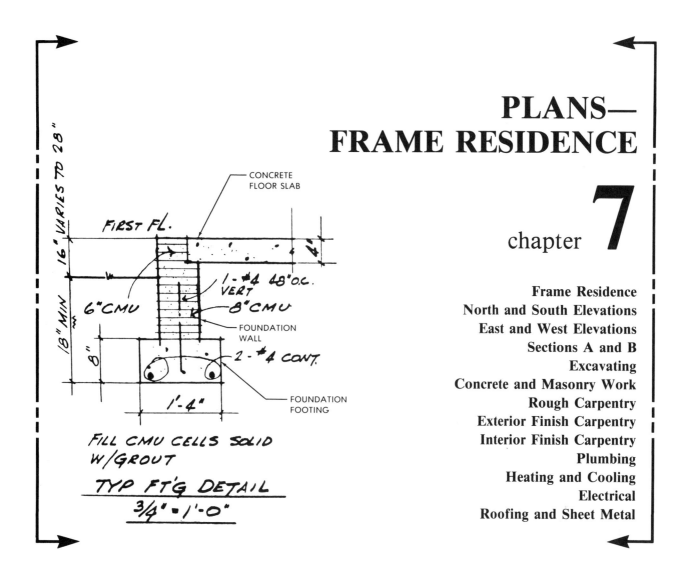

CONCRETE
FLOOR SLAB

FIRST FL.

16" VARIES TO 28"

18" MIN

6"CMU

8"

1 - #4 48" O.C.
VERT
8" CMU

FOUNDATION
WALL

2 - #4 CONT.

FOUNDATION
FOOTING

1'-4"

FILL CMU CELLS SOLID
W/GROUT

TYP FT'G DETAIL
3/4" = 1'-0"

PLANS—
FRAME RESIDENCE

chapter **7**

Frame Residence
North and South Elevations
East and West Elevations
Sections A and B
Excavating
Concrete and Masonry Work
Rough Carpentry
Exterior Finish Carpentry
Interior Finish Carpentry
Plumbing
Heating and Cooling
Electrical
Roofing and Sheet Metal

FRAME RESIDENCE

The one-family dwelling is situated high on a mountainside in North Central Arizona with a view over the valley to the South. The lot is irregular in shape and has a drop of nearly 70′ from one end to the other, a distance of about 260′. To cut out a level place for the building that would take full advantage of the view was an important consideration for the architect.

The South Elevation, Sheet 5, shows large glass areas that open up the front of the building. The rooms included are the living room, dining room, den, and one bedroom. Toward the valley, flanking the living room, are two porches with extended solar screens, providing opportunity for outdoor living.

The entrance to the house is from the North. It

is approached over a terrace, paved with local sandstone. The terrace leads to steps and a platform made of brick pavers. A sturdy door is flanked by wide fixed-glass sash, which provides a glimpse of the entry hallway.

Provision for an adequate heating and cooling system required careful study. Temperatures vary greatly during the year in this part of the country. The dual heating and air conditioning plant is located in a small room off the garage. Heated or cooled air is supplied and returned through ducts enclosed in concrete below the floor. Insulation maintains comfortable indoor temperatures in both summer and winter. Meticulous attention is given to interior planning for function and charm.

Several procedures might be used to study this set of plans which includes many sheets. One way is to study them in numerical order, examining each plan, elevation, section, detail, and schedule as it appears with the objective that everything will fall into place. A more logical approach is to study the larger elements and ideas first, starting with plan views, then going to elevation and section views and winding up with details. A third approach is to study the set of prints from the viewpoint of each tradesworker involved in the work in the order of work on the job.

ORIENTATION, FIRST METHOD

It is important that the tradesworker be familiar with what the prints contain before making a formal study of their content. This is much like studying the table of contents of a book before approaching the text material in the individual chapters. The following list gives an overview of the contents of the prints:

Reference numbers are shown on various views in circles. The upper number is the detail number and the lower number is the number of the sheet on which it appears. See Figure 7-1. The two numbers are separated by a horizontal line passing through the circle.

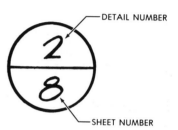

Figure 7-1. Reference numbers on prints refer to the sheet on which the particular detail is located.

ORIENTATION, SECOND METHOD

The second approach to studying a set of prints, and perhaps the most satisfactory, is to analyze the more important features of the building first and then study all the details. This procedure entails studying the first floor plan for the general layout, followed with closer attention to its minor features. Afterwards, the elevation and section views are analyzed to see how they relate to the first floor plan.

First Floor Plan, Sheet 3

Figure 7-2 is a simplification of Sheet 3. It provides a layout of the rooms so that their relationship can be easily studied. Study each room, beginning with the entry hallway to observe its general shape, the location of doorways, the sources of light and ventilation, and the placement of closets. The circulation (passage of persons) from room to room should be considered. Returning to Sheet 3, study each room in further detail and also note the porches, the terrace, and the entrance platform. Observe the swing of doors, the windows, kitchen and bathroom fixtures, and the cabinets. All of the notations should be read carefully.

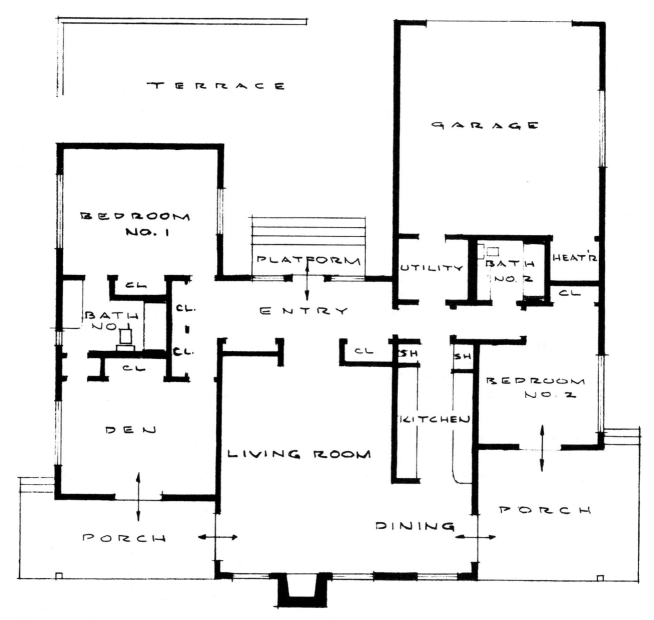

Figure 7-2. Simplified floor plan sketches provide room relationships.

References to information contained on other sheets, such as Sections A and B (see Sheet 7), the door schedule (which corresponds to the letter designation at each door), and notations indicating details on other sheets, will be discussed later. One additional point to note is the manner of showing the change in floor level in the garage and at the apron. There are two 7″ steps down from the utility room floor to the garage floor shown by turning the profile of the floor at right angles. A 1″ drop is shown at the overhead door from the garage to the apron.

North and South Elevations, Sheet 5

The North and South Elevation views of the building display its character. It is set low against the mountainside with strong horizontal lines at the base and the *fascia*. The fascia is the top wide horizontal trim member on the face of the wall. The indentation between the base member and siding and those above and below the fascia are painted black to accent the horizontal lines. The treatment at the chimney cap, the brick paver steps, and the porch handrail continue this horizontal accent. A vertical contrast is provided by the glazed openings, the vertical siding, and the balustrade.

The footing and foundation walls are shown with hidden lines. The footings are shown with two different elevations (levels) because they must be erected to accommodate the slope of the ground. The actual conditions at the job site determine the dimension to the finish grade. Notice all of the notations explaining the materials and how they are to be applied. The window and door details will be examined later.

Trade names, such as those on sliding glass doors and the front door, appear throughout the prints and in the specifications on Sheet 1 and Sheet 9. Specific reference to products represents the suggestions of the architect and/or the choice of the owner. In many cases other products serve the same purpose with equal success.

Study the North and South Elevations, Sheet 5, along with the First Floor Plan, Sheet 3, to determine how the windows and doors are related to rooms.

East and West Elevations, Sheet 6

The strong horizontal lines on the North and South Elevation views are continued around the building. Of special interest, on the East and West Elevations, are the two side views of the front of the building which show that the chimney and balustrades for the porches are important design features. The balustrades continue past the corners of the building to provide a railing for stairs shown on the First Floor Plan, Sheet 3. A fascia member continues to the corner post to provide a support for the solar screen.

Hidden lines indicate stepped footings near walls at the face of the den (West Elevation) and Bedroom No. 2 (East Elevation). They are necessary to accommodate the drop in grade at the South end of the building.

Refer to the First Floor Plan, Sheet 3, to see how the sliding glass doors and awning windows shown on the Elevation views relate to the rooms.

Sections A and B, Sheet 7

Longitudinal and transverse section views taken through buildings serve several purposes such as (1) to show interior elevations of walls, doors, and cabinets, (2) to show sectional views of parts of the building that require further explanation, and (3) to show details of the foundation and rough structure. Section A is taken through the building on an East-West line. Section B is taken on a North-South line. In order to understand the two section views on Sheet 7, it is necessary to study the First Floor Plan, Sheet 3, at the same time.

The cutting plane line for Section A passes through the den and living room and then is offset so that when it passes through the kitchen, it cuts through the skylight. It is offset again in Bedroom No. 2 so that it passes through the wall instead of the window.

Doors, cabinets, and wall finish are illustrated in some detail. Special attention is given to the skylight, kitchen lighting, and the soffit over the cabinets. Among the structural features shown are the footings, foundation walls, concrete floor slab, the exterior frame walls, bearing partitions, and the roof joists.

Section B is taken through the entry and living room and also shows the exterior elevation of the wall of Bedroom No. 1. It allows the architect an opportunity to give details and dimensions for the fireplace and chimney. The glass sliding doors near the fireplace open to the porch. The portion of the drawing at the entrance doorway and through the entry affords an opportunity that is not available elsewhere to show the concrete work that supports the brick paver floor and steps, as well as details of the canopy above.

ORIENTATION, THIRD METHOD

A third approach to studying a set of prints is to use the viewpoint of particular trades. After an orientation to the building as a whole, study is directed toward breaking the construction into the various trade areas. All of the parts of the working drawings not discussed up to this point are covered as the work of each trade is considered. A breakdown into trade divisions common in the building of a residence follows. There may be other divisions and subdivisions.

Excavating, Filling, and Grading
Concrete Work
Masonry
Steel Work
Carpentry and Millwork
Roofing and Sheet Metal

Glass and Glazing
Finishes
    Ceramic tile
    Resilient floor covering
    Painting
Mechanical Trades
    Plumbing
    Heating and Cooling
Electrical Trades

In the following material, the arrangement of topics roughly follows the construction of a building. For example, the work of the excavator is covered first and that of the painter last.

Whole divisions may be omitted if they do not apply. In this instance the only steel items are rebars used in the footings, some steel accessories used in the masonry wall and for fastening wood in place. They are covered under concrete work, masonry, and carpentry. Much of the information is covered in written form in specifications such as those shown on Sheets 1 and 9.

Excavating

Preparing the land for the building site and excavating for footings requires a study of the Plot Plan, Sheet 1, the Foundation Plan, Sheet 2, Elevations, Sheets 5 and 6, and miscellaneous details. The plot plan shows the information obtained from the official survey regarding dimensions and contour lines so that a relatively flat place is provided for the location of the building. The excavator, in following the new lines, is required to move earth so that the elevation at the building site will range between $+4476'$ and $+4478'$. The first floor level is to be brought to $+4479.33'$, including the fill and the slab itself. See Figure 7-3. The point of beginning for measurements is the Northeast corner with building lines to be made at right angles and parallel to the East lot line.

Excavating for the footings requires close attention to the Foundation Plan, Sheet 2. All of the linear dimensions are shown on this plan along with cross section detail views through the foundation wall and footing. A stepped footing is necessary at each side to lower the footing at the front of the building because of the slope of the ground. See Figure 7-4. These footings are indicated near the

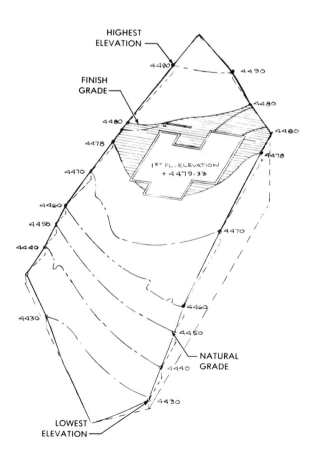

Figure 7-3. Contour lines spaced at 10'-0" intervals show the slope of the lot.

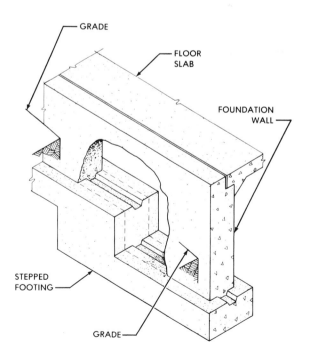

Figure 7-4. A stepped footing provides a transition in the footing and foundation wall to allow for a change in grade.

Southwest and Southeast corners of the side walls of the Foundation Plan, Sheet 2, and on the East and West Elevations, Sheet 6.

Concrete and Masonry Work

Concrete and masonry work, grouped together because of their interdependence, are shown on the Foundation Plan, Sheet 2, and details of other sheets. Included are the following operations:

1. To build the forms for the footings and place the concrete.
2. To lay the concrete masonry units to the prescribed heights to form the foundation walls and the retaining walls.
3. To build the forms for the stair platform, the stairs, and depressed tub areas and to place the concrete.
4. To strip the forms.
5. To build the forms to block out the depressed floor areas in the entry, hall, and kitchen.
6. To place floor slabs.
7. To lay brick for the fireplace and chimney.

The Foundation Plan, Sheet 2, is the main source of information for the footings. *Building lines* (lines strung between the batterboards) outline the faces of the 8″ foundation wall. The detail on Sheet 2 shows that the foundation footing is 1′-4″ wide and 8″ thick. It is reinforced with two #4 rebars run continuously. The foundation wall consists of 8″ concrete masonry units on which the 4″ concrete floor slab rests. The foundation wall is completed with 6″ concrete masonry units. See Figure 7-5. The foundation footing forms are built so that the outer faces are 4″ outside of the building lines. The stepped footings are to be formed at the same time as the rest of the footings.

The retaining wall is supported by a larger footing. See Detail 4, Sheet 8. Steel rebars are suspended horizontally inside the footing forms before the concrete is placed. The porch corner piers have concrete foundation footings, which are shown in Sheet 2.

Masonry work follows after the formwork is stripped from the foundation footings. The 8″ × 8″ × 16″ (nominal size) units, and narrower units as needed, build up the wall to the floor level as prescribed on the Plot Plan and shown in the Details on Sheet 2.

The Mechanical and Electrical Plan, Sheet 9, shows where the ducts are located at the perimeter of the building. Additional information from the mechanical contractor is needed to locate the ducts which follow the exterior walls and the path of both supply and return ducts as they connect to the heating-cooling plant away from the walls. The Foundation Details on Sheet 2, the section through the retaining wall, Detail 4, Sheet 8, and a note in the General Notes on Sheet 1 further outlines the procedure for laying and reinforcing concrete masonry wall units.

Support for the porch floor consists of 2″ × 12″ (nominal size) wood framing members fastened flat against the masonry with 3/8″ anchor bolts at 4′-0″ intervals. Information is shown on the Typical Wall Section, Detail 1, Sheet 8, and also on Sheet 2. Anchor bolts are also provided to hold down the sill of exterior frame walls at intervals of 4′-0″ around the perimeter of the building. See Typical Wall Section, Detail 1, Sheet 8.

Once the foundation walls are laid up to the first floor elevation, preparations can be made to place the slab. Fill must be leveled to the correct height and compacted. The entry, hallway, kitchen, and utility room are to be paved with brick. The brick

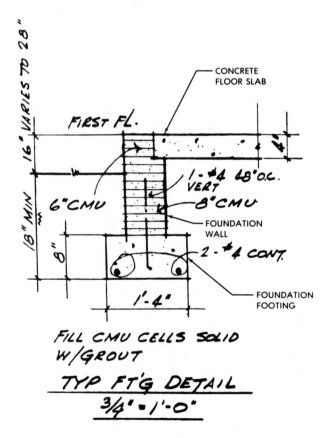

Figure 7-5. Concrete masonry units may be utilized for foundation walls.

is to be depressed so that the top surface will be at the same elevation as the flooring elsewhere. Some concrete forming is necessary at the front entrance and stairs. See Section B, Sheet 7.

The tubs in the bathrooms are sunk to near floor level and surrounded by a concrete wall. A detail on Sheet 2 shows a section view through this concrete wall. The outside of the wall is formed against the earth. The inside of the wall requires the building of a form of the size suggested by the manufacturer and to provide a 6″ thickness. When the forming for the depressed slab, the entry platform and base for the steps, and the tub enclosures are completed, the concrete is poured and finished. The cement mason may decide to complete the job in two or three operations, with the pouring and finishing of the floor slab as the final step.

The remaining masonry jobs include the erection of the retaining walls, porch piers, fireplace, and chimney. Completion of these jobs is coordinated with the contractor in order to assure continuity of work among the various trades.

Carpentry

Because wood is used almost extensively in most light construction, carpentry usually accounts for the greatest number of working hours and a substantial portion of the total cost for materials of all the building trades involved in the building. Carpentry is generally considered in two distinct categories—*rough carpentry* and *finish carpentry*. Rough carpentry is the building of the structure, including building and stripping of forms, framing of walls, roofs, and floors. Finish carpentry includes applying exterior and interior wall coverings and trim, hanging windows and doors, and installing cabinet work.

Rough Carpentry. The rough carpenters who work on the building must review the complete set of plans. However, the rough carpenter's primary concerns are in the Foundation Plan (Sheet 2), First Floor Plan (Sheet 3), Framing Plan (Sheet 4), and the Typical Wall Section (Detail 1, Sheet 8).

The first job is to erect the exterior walls and the bearing partitions. The bearing partitions are the main North-South partitions on which the roof joists rest. See Sheet 4. The Typical Wall Section (Detail 1, Sheet 8) shows the outside stud walls made with a 2″ × 4″ sill. The sill is fastened to the concrete

block foundation with anchor bolts. Two 2″ × 4″ plates are nailed to the top of the studs to support the roof joists.

Two exceptions to the Typical Wall Section are the walls at the entry and the South wall of the living room and dining room. The sills, studs, and plates for these walls are 2″ × 6″ material. See Fixed Window Details, Sheet 5. The studs are cut to length so that the ceiling height is 8′-0″. The outside face of the wall lines up with the face of the masonry wall. With this information and the layout of walls and partitions shown on Sheets 3 and 4, the work can proceed. Rough openings for exterior windows and doors are framed with clearance to permit the frames to be inserted and adjusted. Members at each side of the openings are doubled. The members over windows and exterior doors are two 2″ × 6″ or two 2″ × 12″ boards as shown or noted on Sheet 7. The larger members are necessary in several locations because they support the roof joists. Vertical location dimensions of windows, which do not extend to the floor, are shown on the elevation drawings.

Interior partitions are laid out carefully so that all room dimensions are correct. Doors are placed with allowances for trim. Certain partitions are to be built up in thickness. The plumbing partition containing the vent is 8″ thick, and partitions are increased in thickness at the ends of the bathroom tubs. Pocket doors require special framing.

The Mechanical and Electrical Plan, Sheet 9, shows the location of several air returns to the heating-cooling unit. Provisions are made in the partitions to match their locations.

When the partitions are in place, the carpenter can prepare for the erection of the roof joists. Sheet 4, shows the size of the roof joists and the direction in which they are placed. The roof joists rest on the wall plates and lap over each other at the bearing partitions. They are hung from the 2″ × 12″ members placed over window and door openings with the use of joist hangers because they are at the same level. See Figure 7-6. One end of the joists over the entrance platform is hung from a fascia beam. The other end rests on the members over the door and windows. Double headers are required at skylight openings as shown in Section A, Sheet 7.

The porch structure is studied last. Dimensions are shown on the First Floor Plan, Sheet 3; structural information on the Foundation Plan, Sheet 2; the Framing Plan, Sheet 4; and details on Sheet 8.

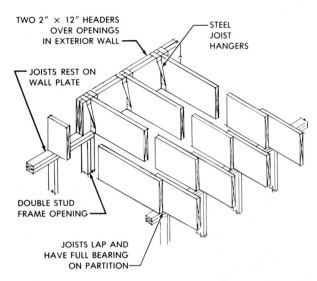

Figure 7-6. Joists are given firm support at walls and partitions.

The 6″ × 6″ wood columns are erected and fastened to the concrete masonry unit piers as shown in Details 3 and 6 on Sheet 8. Framing members that are fastened to the masonry wall and between the wall and the columns to support the floor joists are 2″ × 12″. The floor joists are installed and bridging put in place to make the joists more rigid.

Information about the solar screen over the porches is found on the Framing Plan, Sheet 4; Details 1, 2, and 5 on Sheet 8; and the East and West Elevation, Sheet 6. See Figure 7-7. Horizontal 2″

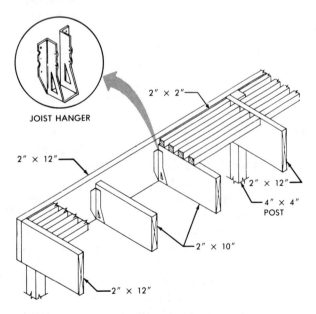

Figure 7-7. Solar screen for the Fisher Residence is built of 2″ × 2″ lattice members.

× 12″ headers are extended from the East and West corners of the building to rest on posts. The solar screen joists hang from the headers and from the 2″ × 12″ members over the sliding glass doors.

The sheathing for both the exterior walls and the roof is ³/₄″ plywood. This material is rigid enough to make it unnecessary to place bridging in the walls. A 2″ × 6″ block serves as both a roof edge and a gravel stop. It is cut to provide for the galvanized iron flashing and drip. See Detail 1, Sheet 8. An opening is left in the roof on each side of the entry platform, as shown on Sheets 3 and 4, to provide light for the entry windows.

The roofing, made up of four plies of felt covered with tar and then gravel, is installed by the roofer before insulation is placed or interior finish is begun. The note "4 PLY T&G ROOFING" denotes the type of roofing.

Exterior Finish Carpentry. Exterior finish carpentry includes the siding, base and fascia members, windows and doors and their trim, and the handrail and balustrade. The Typical Wall Section, Detail 1, Sheet 8, and the elevation drawings give details of the exterior finish. A 1″ × 12″ fascia and a 2″ × 12″ base member extend around the building with 1″ × 4″ cedar shiplap boards used as siding. See Figure 7-8. The windows and doors are explained on the elevation views, Sheets 5 and 6. No exterior trim is provided at windows or doors. The jambs extend beyond the face of the siding which is cut back to show ¹/₂″ of the sheathing. The sheathing is prepainted black. This is illustrated in part C of the Fixed Window Details, Sheet 5.

Details of the handrails and balusters for the porch, and the top members and siding for the retaining wall are shown on Sheet 8.

Interior Finish Carpentry. Interior finish carpentry includes the wall and ceiling finish, the floors, interior doors, trim, and cabinet work. Two important schedules are a part of the working drawings. The schedule for room finish is on Sheet 1. The schedule covering doors is on Sheet 5.

Other items of information on interior finish are shown in Sections A and B, Sheet 7, and Details spread over Sheets 5, 6, 7, and 8. The logical place to start is with the Typical Wall Section, Detail 1, Sheet 8, and the Room Finish Schedule. A 1″ × 6″ base is nailed to the studs at the floor on outside

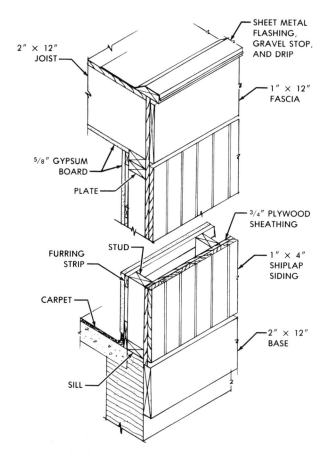

2″ × 12″ JOIST

SHEET METAL FLASHING, GRAVEL STOP, AND DRIP

1″ × 12″ FASCIA

5/8″ GYPSUM BOARD

PLATE

3/4″ PLYWOOD SHEATHING

FURRING STRIP

STUD

1″ × 4″ SHIPLAP SIDING

CARPET

2″ × 12″ BASE

SILL

Figure 7-8. Exterior walls are covered with 1″ × 4″ ship-lap siding applied vertically.

walls, and 1″ furring strips are nailed horizontally at intervals above it. Gypsum wallboard is then fastened to the furring strips, beginning 2¼″ above the floor to permit the carpeting to turn up to form a cove. Usually a wood baseboard is used at the bottom of the interior walls. In this building, however, the carpeting is turned up along the walls to a height of 2⅛″, as shown on Section View 1, Sheet 8.

Columns under *Walls* in the Room Finish Schedule, Sheet 1, show 5/8″ one-hour gypsum board on 1″ × 2″ furring. The one-hour gypsum board designation indicates that it has a one-hour fire rating.

The column in the schedule with a reference to furring pertains to outside walls of rooms. The column omitting reference to furring strips pertains to the interior partitions of rooms. Ceilings are covered with 5/8″ gypsum board fastened to the roof joists. The Room Finish Schedule calls for wood paneling to be placed over the gypsum board in the living

room, dining room, and the entry. A wood base trim is placed in the entry where there is no carpeting to form a cove.

The Door Schedule on Sheet 5 keys each door to a letter on the First Floor Plan, Sheet 3. For example, the C door is shown on the Floor Plan, Sheet 3, as an entrance door from the garage into the house. The swing of the door and its location are shown on the Floor Plan and the Door Schedule gives width, height, and thickness of the door. The sizes are given as well as descriptive information for all doors. The details alongside the schedule show how the interior doors are to be trimmed. The jambs are made wide enough to extend beyond the face of the wall finish. The gypsum board is held back ½″. The studs are prepainted black to accent the door frame (or jamb).

The doors are unusually high, at 7′-10″, extending to within 2″ of the ceiling. The Door Detail, Head Section, Sheet 5, shows the simple arrangement of concealed rough blocks used to fasten the head jamb.

Details of cabinet work in the Kitchen, bathrooms, Bedroom No. 1. and Living Room are shown in elevation and section views. The arrangement of doors and indication as to how they swing and the placement of drawers and shelves are shown. Notations cover materials, rollers, pulls, wall finish, soffit, lighting, and other information. The cabinetmaker measures the spaces for the cabinets after the wall finish is in place. Cabinets are built in the cabinet shop and brought to the job for installation and final trim. The only other items of concern to the carpenter in the Room Finish Schedule are the wood decking floor on the porch and the solar screen, which extends over the porches on the South side of the building.

Mechanical Trades

The work of the mechanical trades includes water supply, waste water disposal, heating, and cooling. Electrical work is a separate division. See Mechanical and Electrical Plan, Sheet 9.

Some architects include the plumbing, heating and cooling, and the electrical information on the floor plan, while other architects include a separate sheet containing this information. Note that although Sheet 9 resembles a floor plan, no dimensions are given. Dimensions have already been included on the floor plan.

Plumbing. The plumbing work presents little difficulty except that the drainage and waste pipes are buried under the concrete slab and the tub is sunk to floor level. Hot and cold water is supplied to fixtures through overhead pipes that pass in the joist spaces to drop down in plumbing partitions in back of the fixtures. The plumber makes a sketch showing how the lines are to run. The fixtures are designated by manufacturer's name and factory numbers in specifications on Sheet 9.

Heating and Cooling. One of the important functions of the Mechanical and Electrical Plan, Sheet 9, is to show details of the heating and cooling plant. The furnace is located in a closet adjacent to the garage. It is described in the Equipment Specifications on Sheet 9. The furnace is gas-fired with an input of 125,000 Btu/hr to deliver an output of 96,000 Btu/hr and 1500 CFM. It is equipped with a *humidifier* for use in the heating cycle. Humidifiers add moisture to the air. Cooled air is provided by the same unit, with a condenser located outside of the building.

The supply air (hot or cooled) is delivered to diffusers (registers) generally located in the floor below windows and doors. The supply ducts follow the perimeter of the house and are placed before the slab is cast in place. See Detail on Sheet 2.

The size of the grills and ducts for the return air ducts is shown by a symbol and notations. These ducts return to the furnace by the shortest route possible under the slab. This layout is not provided in the working drawings but is the responsibility of the sheet metal workers who work closely with the cement masons.

Electrical. Electrical outlets and the electrical panel are shown on Sheet 9 instead of on the First Floor Plan. The conductors all run above the ceiling to the locations where they drop down to the outlets. Special outlets for the furnace, range, and telephones are indicated by symbols. Vent fan information is shown either at the location or in a note. The electrician makes a sketch showing the distribution of outlets into circuits, which is presented to the owner for reference.

Miscellaneous Trades

Other trades involved in the construction and the finishing of the building should refer to the working drawings and specifications. Information needed by these trades to complete their work is found on various prints.

Roofing and Sheet Metal. Roofing and sheet metal work might be done by the same contractor employing two types of tradesworkers. The roof is made up of four plies of felt. Each ply is saturated with tar. A final layer of tar and a sprinkled layer of gravel provide the top coating. The sheet metal worker provides a metal flashing gravel stop and drip around the roof made to fit over a $2'' \times 6''$ wood member at the edge of the roof. *Scuppers* (openings) are placed near each corner of the building to permit excess water to run off. See East and West Elevations, Sheet 6. The sheet metal worker may contract for miscellaneous items, such as the furnace chimney and the exhaust fan ducts that pass through the roof.

Glass and Glazing. Most of the windows and the door with glass come to the job preglazed. The glazier is responsible, however, for the fixed plate-glass windows flanking the entrance doorway and the three large plate-glass windows facing the South. Details in the lower left corner of Sheet 5 show how the glass is to be held in place. The glazier is also responsible for the large plate-glass bathroom mirrors shown on the bathroom elevations, Sheet 6.

Ceramic Tile and Resilient Floors. Mosaic tile is laid in several places. The tub enclosures in bathrooms and the face of the fireplace are laid by tile setters. Details are given on Sheets 6 and 7. Resilient floor coverers lay both carpeting and resilient tile or sheet goods. The Room Finish Schedule, Sheet 1, indicates where each material is used. For example, in Bathroom No. 2, the floor is finished with vinyl asbestos (VA) tile.

Painting. Painting is covered in the specifications on Sheet 1. The material to be used and the number of coats are itemized. The painter is available at several early stages of the construction sequence to paint the black accent on the exterior siding at the fascia, the base member, and the openings for the door and windows. When the interior work has progressed to the point where the gypsum board is to be applied, the painter first paints the rough framing member at each side of the doors and windows, as shown in the various details on Sheet 5.

Review Questions

Name   Date

Refer to Fisher Residence Plans.

True-False

T	F	**1.**	The plot plan shows all contour lines spaced at 10′-0″ increments.
T	F	**2.**	The plot plan shows the distance from the edge of the road to the property line.
T	F	**3.**	The specifications on Sheet 1 give the carpenter information on the rough framing members.
T	F	**4.**	Horizontal truss type steel reinforcing is used to strengthen the concrete masonry unit walls.
T	F	**5.**	Vinyl tile is used for the kitchen floor.
T	F	**6.**	Some of the rough wood framing members are indicated on the Foundation Plan.
T	F	**7.**	The retaining wall is located with dimensions on the Foundation Plan.
T	F	**8.**	Rebars in footings are ½″ in diameter.
T	F	**9.**	The dimension from the top of the footing to the top of the grade is given as 18″.
T	F	**10.**	All closets are equipped with bi-fold doors.
T	F	**11.**	The first floor plan shows the interior areas to be floored with brick.
T	F	**12.**	The canopy over the entrance platform has openings to provide light.
T	F	**13.**	The furnace is vented through a brick chimney.
T	F	**14.**	Vent fans in the bathrooms are indicated with symbols on Sheets 3 and 9.
T	F	**15.**	The Framing plan shows the joists in place inside the building.
T	F	**16.**	Wooden 6″ × 6″ posts support 2″ × 12″ solar screen frame members at the level of roof joists.
T	F	**17.**	The roof slopes to drain toward the East and West.
T	F	**18.**	The ceilings on the porches have drywall construction.
T	F	**19.**	Elevations of all four sides of the building are included in the working drawings.
T	F	**20.**	Porch balusters are spaced on 12″ centers.
T	F	**21.**	Doors are either 1⅜″ or 1¾″ thick.
T	F	**22.**	The footings under the house are lower on the South side of the building.
T	F	**23.**	A light is contained in the bathroom soffit in Bath No. 2.

T   F   **24.** Bathroom mirrors conceal medicine cabinets.

T   F   **25.** The inside of the North wall at Bedroom No. 1 is shown in Section A.

T   F   **26.** Double header framing members are used at skylights.

T   F   **27.** Ceramic tile is used on the face of the fireplace.

T   F   **28.** Anchor bolts are placed on 4'-0" centers to hold down the sill.

T   F   **29.** An electrical panel equipped with a 200-ampere service is shown.

T   F   **30.** Exterior lights along the retaining wall are controlled from the entry.

Completion

_____   **1.** The new grade on the Plot Plan is shown with _____ lines.

_____   **2.** _____, or equal, paint is to be used on the Fisher Residence.

_____   **3.** An allowance of $_____ is specified for the purchase of finish hardware.

_____   **4.** The kitchen floor is specified to be brick _____.

_____   **5.** The 4" concrete slab is reinforced with 6" × 6" No. _____ wire mesh.

_____   **6.** Ceiling height in the garage is _____.

_____   **7.** All exterior doors are to receive one coat of _____ filler, one coat of wood stain, and three coats of spar varnish.

_____   **8.** The blacktop driveway is _____" below the garage floor at the garage entrance.

_____   **9.** The 16'-0" × 7'-0" garage overhead door is _____" sectional wood.

_____   **10.** Backsplashes on bathroom vanities are _____" high.

_____   **11.** Wood used to finish kitchen cabinets is natural select _____.

_____   **12.** Section A-7 is drawn to a scale of _____" = 1'-0".

_____   **13.** Detail _____-8 shows wood railing and deck framing.

_____   **14.** All _____ water pipes are to be wrapped.

_____   **15.** The clothes dryer is to be located in the _____ room.

_____   **16.** The furnace has a(n) _____ horsepower blower motor.

_____   **17.** All concrete to be used on the the job shall be a minimum of _____ bag mix.

_____   **18.** Floor joists for porches are 2" × 12" members spaced _____" OC.

_____   **19.** Bedroom No. 1 measures 13'-0" × _____.

_____   **20.** The only elevation not showing the full chimney height is the _____ Elevation.

_____   **21.** Stair nosing detail is shown on Sheet _____.

_____   **22.** Face brick for the raised hearth of the chimney is laid as a(n) _____ course.

_____   **23.** The 1" × 12" fascia around the house is capped with _____ gauge flashing.

_____   **24.** Detail _____ of Sheet 8 shows the retaining wall detail.

_____   **25.** Moen model #_____ kitchen faucets are specified.

Trade Competency Test

Name

Date

Refer to Fisher Residence Plans.

SHEET 1
Completion

_____ 1. The plot plan is drawn to the scale of 1″ = _____′.

_____ 2. The blacktop drive has a 2″ topping over a(n) _____″ base.

_____ 3. The width of the driveway is _____′.

_____ 4. New grade elevations are shown with a(n) _____ line.

_____ 5. Lot depth along the Northwest property line is _____′.

_____ 6. The _____ shall render inspection of the project.

_____ 7. An allowance of $_____ is included for the purchase of finish hardware.

_____ 8. The garage has a ceiling height of _____.

_____ 9. The plot plan is Sheet _____ of 9.

_____ 10. The only room with wood base trim is the _____.

SHEET 2
True-False

T F 1. The foundation plan is drawn to the scale of $\frac{1}{4}$″ = 1′-0″.

T F 2. CMU cells in foundation walls are filled solid with grout.

T F 3. The floor slab is poured to a uniform height.

T F 4. Two #4 rebars are run continuously in foundation footings.

T F 5. Heating ducts adjacent to foundation walls are placed 2″ above the finished floor.

T F 6. Typical foundation footings are 8″ × 1′-4″.

T F 7. The longest straight run of foundation wall is 44′-0″.

T F 8. Pier size and location are shown on Sheet 6.

T F 9. The foundation walls are the same thickness throughout.

T F 10. Footing details are drawn to the same scale as the foundation plan.

215

SHEET 3
Multiple Choice

_____ 1. The overhang of the solar screen is _____.
  A. shown with a solid line
  B. shown with a dotted line
  C. supported by two metal posts
  D. not shown on Sheet 3

_____ 2. The fireplace _____.
  A. is located in the den
  B. has an ash drop on the left side
  C. serves as a divider between the kitchen and den
  D. is located in the living room

_____ 3. The garage _____.
  A. can be entered directly from the den
  B. has a floor pitch of 1″ from back to front
  C. has a 16′-0″ × 7′-0″ electrically operated door
  D. has two skylights

_____ 4. Bath No. 1 _____.
  A. can be entered directly from the entry
  B. has a double-bowl vanity
  C. contains more square feet than Bath No. 2
  D. is adjacent to the utility room

_____ 5. The living room _____.
  A. has one set of sliding glass doors leading to a porch
  B. contains built-in bookcases on both sides of the main entrance
  C. both A and B
  D. neither A nor B

_____ 6. Bedroom No. 3 _____.
  A. measures 13′-0″ × 13′-0″
  B. has one closet with folding doors
  C. has hardwood floors
  D. there is no bedroom No. 3

_____ 7. The den contains approximately _____ sq. ft. of floor space.
  A. 180
  B. 198
  C. 221
  D. 290

_____ 8. All closets _____.
  A. are located in the bedrooms
  B. have F doors
  C. are 2′-0″ deep
  D. have a pole and shelf

9. The largest porch may be entered from _____.
   A. the dining area
   B. Bedroom No. 2
   C. both A and B
   D. neither A nor B

10. The electrical panel is _____.
   A. located in the entry closet
   B. between the refrigerator and kitchen cabinet
   C. mounted in the end wall of the garage
   D. not shown on the floor plan

SHEET 4
Completion

1. The Framing Plan on Sheet 4 is drawn to a scale of _____ " = 1'-0".

2. Ceiling joists in the garage are 2" × 12" spaced _____ " OC.

3. The front entrance has a(n) _____ roof over 1" plywood sheathing.

4. The _____ over the garage door is spiked together.

5. Lattice strips forming the solar screen are spaced _____ " apart.

6. Typical roof insulation is 6" _____.

7. Unless otherwise shown, all headers over openings are doubled _____.

8. Detail A is drawn to a scale of _____ " = 1'-0".

9. A 2" × 12" _____ beam is shown over the front entrance roof.

10. Vents, stacks, and all other roof openings are to be _____.

SHEET 5
Completion

1. Type G doors are _____ wide.

2. The chimney is laid with _____ brick.

3. Vertical _____ siding is shown on North and South elevations.

4. All doors are _____ in height.

5. Finish floor to finish ceiling height is _____.

6. Door details are drawn to a scale of _____ " = 1'-0".

7. Exterior elevations are drawn to a scale of _____ " = 1'-0".

8. The minimum depth below grade for foundation footings is _____ ".

9. A(n) _____ " recess around exterior doors and windows is prepainted.

10. Door _____ is a custom-made door.

SHEET 6
True-False

T   F   **1.** Sheet 6 shows East and West exterior elevations, interior elevations, and an entrance step detail.

T   F   **2.** The cast concrete cap on the fireplace is reinforced $6'' \times 6''$ #10 WWF.

T   F   **3.** The West Elevation is drawn to a scale of $^3/_8'' = 1'-0''$.

T   F   **4.** The East Elevation shows the front entrance detail of the house.

T   F   **5.** Both baths have cultured marble vanity tops.

T   F   **6.** Bath No. 2 shows an all-drawer unit below the basin.

T   F   **7.** The exterior window head height is $7'-0''$.

T   F   **8.** Foundation footings are shown with solid lines.

T   F   **9.** The cabinetmaker is to furnish shop drawings of all cabinet work.

T   F   **10.** Exterior wood siding has a shiplap joint.

SHEET 7
Multiple Choice

_____   **1.** Paneling around the fireplace is selected by the _____.
     A. owner
     B. architect
     C. contractor
     D. cabinetmaker

_____   **2.** The chimney _____.
     A. is lined with firebrick from the hearth to the cap
     B. rests on a solid concrete footing and foundation wall
     C. has a $3'-8''$ vertical firebox opening
     D. flue is clay tile

_____   **3.** Section Y-Y shows a pantry cabinet with _____.
     A. one adjustable shelf
     B. three roll-out shelves
     C. narrow shelves built on the door
     D. all of the above

_____   **4.** The countertop in the kitchen has a _____.
     A. $6''$ backsplash
     B. built-in $24'' \times 24''$ cutting board
     C. both A and B
     D. neither A nor B

_____   **5.** The canopy over the main entrance door _____.
     A. extends $2'-0''$ beyond the front steps
     B. is supported on either side by a $6'' \times 6''$ column
     C. is shown as Detail 7 of Sheet 1
     D. none of the above

_____ 6. Kitchen walls cabinets _____.
    A. are hung by the carpenters
    B. are factory units
    C. have a 12″ furr down
    D. are 16″ above the countertop

_____ 7. The skylight in the kitchen _____.
    A. requires a 48″ square rough opening
    B. is 9′-0″ above the finished floor
    C. is detailed in Section X-X
    D. has an eggcrate grill with 1″ squares

_____ 8. The steps at the front entrance are _____.
    A. pitched 1″ toward the door
    B. shown in detail on Section A of Sheet 7
    C. reinforced with two #4 rebars
    D. finished with brick pavers

_____ 9. The fireplace is _____.
    A. shown in Section B of Sheet 7
    B. shown in elevation at a scale of ¼″ = 1′-0″
    C. trimmed out with 6″ × 6″ decorated ceramic tile
    D. all of the above

_____ 10. Sections X-X and Y-Y are taken from cutting planes in _____.
    A. Section A of Sheet 7
    B. Detail 1 of Sheet 7
    C. East and West Kitchen Elevations
    D. none of the above

SHEET 8
True-False

T   F   **1.** Detail 2 is drawn to the same scale as Detail 3.

T   F   **2.** Detail 4 shows three #4 rebars in the foundation footing.

T   F   **3.** The 1½″ × 4″ wood railing has a beveled handrail.

T   F   **4.** All measurements for building the cabinets are to be taken directly from the plans.

T   F   **5.** Wood columns are spiked to 2″ × 12″ members in Detail 5.

T   F   **6.** Finished grade elevation is specified in Detail 4.

T   F   **7.** Foil-backed insulation is used in all ceilings.

T   F   **8.** The all-drawer counter unit in the Master Bedroom has plastic laminate drawer faces.

T   F   **9.** The deck column detail at the roof is shown in Detail 3, Sheet 8.

T   F   **10.** Flashing at the roof edge is 26 gauge galvanized iron.

SHEET 9
Completion

_____   1. The overhead light and electric door opener in the garage are controlled by _____ switches.

_____   2. _____ duplex convenience outlets are shown in Bedroom No. 2.

_____   3. _____ weatherproof convenience outlets are shown on Sheet 9.

_____   4. Telephone outlets are shown in Bedroom No. 1 and the _____.

_____   5. Exterior light fixtures at the front entrance are _____.

_____   6. Three air supply registers in the living room and dining area provide _____ CFM and two air supply registers provide 120 CFM.

_____   7. _____ air returns with 18″ × 6″ grates are located throughout the house.

_____   8. The electric range in the kitchen is on a separate _____V circuit.

_____   9. A(n) _____ light fixture is located in the Heater Room.

_____   10. The furnace has an output of _____ Btu.

_____   11. All air supplies are sheet metal duct encased in _____.

_____   12. The AC condenser is located _____ the building.

_____   13. The _____ of all kitchen appliances and bath fixtures is to be selected by the owner.

_____   14. The _____ and hot water heater are vented together.

_____   15. All plumbing below the slab is to be _____.

_____   16. _____ duplex convenience outlets are located in the garage.

_____   17. The _____ fixture in the dining area is controlled by a wall-mounted switch.

_____   18. Bath No. 2 has a(n) _____-tube fluorescent fixture in the skylight.

_____   19. A shower head is shown over the tub in Bath No. _____.

_____   20. General lighting in the bedrooms is controlled by a wall-mounted _____.

Refer to Fisher Residence Plans.
Multiple Choice

_____ 1. The specifications, Sheet 1 and Sheet 9, _____.
A. contain information pertaining to the specific work of each trade involved in the building
B. give details regarding the laying of brick
C. include all of the items of equipment used in kitchen, baths, and utility room
D. direct the painter to use specific materials without exception

_____ 2. The Plot Plan, Sheet 1, shows _____.
A. a point of beginning that is also a local benchmark
B. a difference in elevation of 1.33′ between the grade at the Northwest corner of the building and the 1st floor elevation
C. the length of each side of the lot and angles at the corners
D. the location of the driveway and walks

_____ 3. The Foundation Plan and Details on Sheet 2 show _____.
A. information about rebars in the footing under the house and in the pad under the fireplace
B. dimensions for the size and location of the footings under the retaining wall
C. dimensions locating the stepped footings
D. location of the depressed slabs for brick floors and areas for tubs

_____ 4. The First Floor Plan, Sheet 3, shows _____.
A. thickness dimensions for partitions around bathrooms
B. exterior walls 6½″ and 8½″ thick
C. dimensions of the entrance platform
D. the furnace and location of the furnace chimney

_____ 5. The Framing Plan, Sheet 4, shows or notes that _____.
A. all joists including those over porches are spaced 16″ OC
B. all joists run in the same direction
C. all joists are the same size
D. headers over openings are made of either 2″ × 6″ or 2″ × 12″ boards spiked together

_____ 6. The North or South Elevations, Sheet 5, show _____.
A. the living room windows as sliding sash
B. the footing for the chimney with hidden lines
C. that both doors of the pair of glass doors slide open
D. dimensions of the fascia member

_____ 7. The Door Schedule and the Details on Sheet 5 show _____.
A. that the doors are typical 6′-8″ doors
B. that doors are either swinging or sliding
C. that window sills for plate-glass windows are at the floor level
D. interior wall finish held back ½″ from the door jambs

_____ 8. The East and West Elevations, Sheet 6, show _____.
A. stairs at the inner end of the porch railing
B. dimensions from finished floor to window sills
C. stepped footings with hidden lines
D. an unbroken gravel stop and drip above the fascia

_____ 9. Sections A and B and Detail 1, Sheet 7, show _____.
   A. the slab and concrete steel reinforcing under the stairs
   B. that Section A is taken on a straight East-West line through the entry
   C. that the fireplace foundation is completely made of concrete masonry units
   D. that 2″ × 12″ joists, 24″ OC, are used for the canopy over platform and stairs

_____ 10. The Typical Wall Section, Sheet 8, shows that _____.
   A. the section is taken through an exterior wall at a window
   B. the siding is nailed tight with no opening between it and the base member and the fascia
   C. the sill is held down by 3/8″ anchor bolts spaced 4′-0″ OC
   D. rigid insulation board sheathing is used for outside walls

_____ 11. The Mechanical and Electrical Plan, Sheet 9, shows _____.
   A. a 220-amp service
   B. light outlets on porches
   C. a gas outlet in the utility room
   D. three-way switches to control the electric garage door opener

_____ 12. Regarding concrete work and building lines, Sheets 1 and 2, show _____.
   A. footings for the retaining wall are the same size as those for the building
   B. the building lines are at right angles or parallel to the East property line
   C. the concrete floor slab extends to the outside of the foundation walls
   D. wood formwork is required for the inside and outside of the tub enclosure walls

_____ 13. Regarding masonry, _____.
   A. the foundation walls are built of standard 8″ × 8″ × 16″ concrete masonry units to the top of the walls
   B. the top of the foundation wall is at the same elevation on the East and West sides of the building
   C. the brick for the stairs and platform are laid flat
   D. the information on Sheet 7 is sufficient to build the fireplace and chimney

_____ 14. Regarding carpentry, _____.
   A. joists over the garage and those over the kitchen and Bedroom No. 2 are the same length
   B. the wall studs are 8′-0″ long
   C. fixed window frames fit into rough openings without any space for fitting
   D. cross bridging is unnecessary for the roof joists because of the 3/4″ plywood sheathing

_____ 15. Regarding exterior finish, _____.
   A. balusters for the porch handrails are nailed to the top of the porch decking
   B. 2″ × 12″ fascia and base members are nailed on top of the siding
   C. cedar shiplap siding is nailed over the sheathing
   D. support members and joists for the solar screen are 2″ × 12″ members

_____ 16. Regarding interior finish, Sheets 1, 5, and 8, _____.
   A. a vinyl tile floor is required in the utility room
   B. interior door jambs are flush with the wall surface
   C. wood trim base is specified for all rooms except bathrooms and kitchen
   D. gypsum board wall finish on exterior walls is applied over furring strips

17. Interior plan and elevation detail views, Sheets 6, 7, and 8, indicate _____.
    A. adjustable shelves, roll-out shelves, swing of doors, and drawer arrangement for kitchen cabinets
    B. soffit with concealed light in kitchen
    C. mosaic tile on all bathroom walls and lavatories with Formica® tops
    D. bedroom counter for Master Bedroom with doors and drawers to be made on the job

18. Plumbing and electrical information, Sheet 9, includes _____.
    A. the division of outlets into electrical circuits
    B. information on light fixtures in the entry
    C. a note that all plumbing pipes are under the slab
    D. detailed information for ordering plumbing fixtures

19. Heating and cooling features, Sheet 9, include _____.
    A. supply air ducts all placed in the floor in front of windows or doors
    B. a gas-fired furnace with a humidifier and a cooling coil coupled to a condenser for air conditioning
    C. return ducts to the furnace to pass overhead between joists
    D. supply and return air ducts with specified grill and duct sizes

20. Regarding other trades involved in the building, _____.
    A. the painter's work begins when the other workers have finished
    B. tile setters set ceramic tile of bathroom floors
    C. glaziers set plate-glass fixed windows
    D. sheet metal workers install gutter and downspout for the front entrance platform canopy

21. In Bedroom No. 1, _____.
    A. the finished floor is oak parquet
    B. carpeting is provided by the owner
    C. the general contractor installs the finished floor
    D. strip hardwood flooring runs parallel to the long dimensions of the room

22. Walls in the Entry are _____.
    A. drywall to be painted by the owner
    B. wallpaper over drywall
    C. wood paneling
    D. none of the above

23. Type B doors are _____.
    A. natural select birch
    B. 2'-8" wide
    C. 1¾" thick
    D. all of the above

24. Section X-X gives height and depth dimensions of the _____.
    A. bathroom vanities
    B. fireplace
    C. base and wall cabinets on the West wall
    D. china and storage cabinet on the East wall

_____ 25. A _____ is controlled by a switch near the door to the Den.
      A. ceiling light fixture
      B. wall-mounted receptacle
      C. both A and B
      D. neither A nor B

Identification

_____   **1.** Supply air

_____   **2.** Return air

_____   **3.** Weatherproof electrical receptacle

_____   **4.** Three-way switch

_____   **5.** Telephone

_____   **6.** Electrical circuit

_____   **7.** Incandescent ceiling fixture

_____   **8.** Fluorescent ceiling fixture

_____   **9.** Bi-fold door

_____   **10.** Pocket door

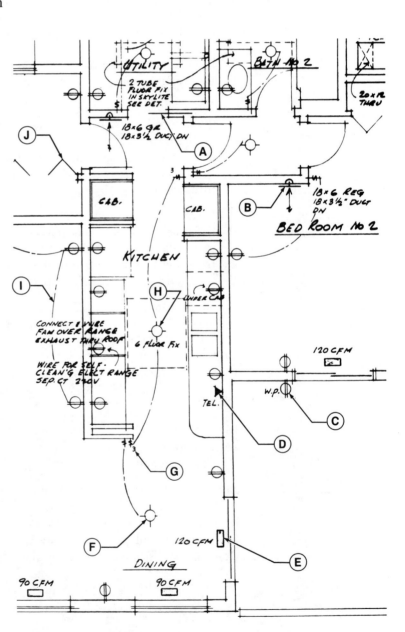

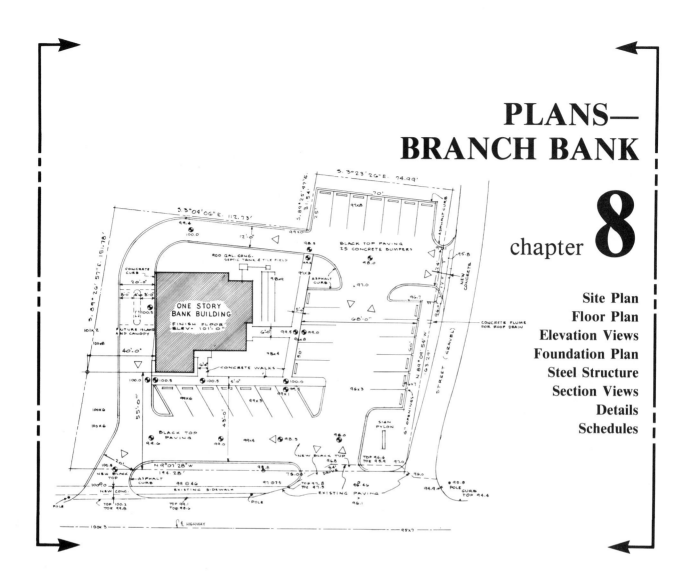

Site Plan
Floor Plan
Elevation Views
Foundation Plan
Steel Structure
Section Views
Details
Schedules

BRANCH BANK

The branch bank (a branch banking facility for a savings and loan association) is located at a corner of a major highway and a gravel street near the center of a small community. It is set on the highest portion of the lot, away from the highway and street, in order to create an open feeling and to provide ample parking for customers. The exterior of the branch bank is contemporary with wide expanses of tall glass windows and brick walls. Cantilevered open web steel joists support a wide facing of stone aggregate which projects beyond the building on three sides. The branch bank is designed to reflect the stability and progressive spirit of the institution and the community.

The building contains open web steel joists used in combination with a steel supporting structure, a

slab-on-grade foundation, metal windows and window walls, and masonry construction combining brick and concrete masonry units. A *heat pump* is used for heating and cooling. A heat pump is a unit that serves both heating and cooling purposes through a one-duct system. With modifications in the heating and cooling plant, and perhaps in the foundation, the building could be erected to serve as a branch bank facility anywhere in the country.

Five working drawings are included in the set, giving all of the basic information needed to complete the building, with the exception of heating, cooling, plumbing, and electrical work. The specifications, which contain 150 typed pages, are not included.

In studying a particular sheet, reference may be made to other sheets for further information. The working drawings for the branch bank will be studied in this order:

1. Site Plan, Sheet A-1.
   A study of the site, location of the building, elevations, grades, drives, and walks.
2. Floor Plan, Sheet A-2.
   A study of the layout, walls and partitions, windows, roof soffit, concrete work, and equipment.
3. Elevation Views, Sheet A-5.
   A study of the elevation views as they relate to the floor plan, windows, doors, roof projections, footings, foundation, and concrete curbs.
4. Foundation Plan, Sheet A-1.
   A study of the footings and foundation, the auto teller pit, and under-slab plumbing.
5. Steel Structure, Roof, and Lintels, Sheet A-3.
   A study of the steel members supporting the roof, roof slab, and lintels.
6. Section Views, Sheet A-4.
   Orientation of section views in relation to other working drawings.
7. Details, Sheets A-1, 2, 3, and 4.
   A review of the details to cover items not previously included.
8. Schedules, Sheet A-3.
   A study of the Interior Finish Schedule and the Door Schedule.

Site Plan, Sheet A-1

The site plan (plot plan) serves the following purposes: (1) to locate the lot lines and the lot corners, (2) to locate the building in relation to the lot lines, (3) to establish elevations, particularly the elevation of the finished floor, and (4) to indicate finished grade elevations at various points on the lot. Existing and new walks, curbs and drives, the location of the utility poles, gas lines, sewers, and large trees are often included on site plans. If there is a steep slope or any other unusual physical characteristics, the contour of the lot may be shown. This particular site plan shows new walks, drives, a complete layout of the parking facility, the septic tank location, and the drain field.

The basic information about the lot in its preconstruction state is provided by a licensed surveyor who is legally responsible for the accuracy of the survey. A survey drawing establishes the lot corners and the lot lines. The survey is also a means of determining elevations from *datum points* or *bench marks*. These are official location points established by local government. The surveyor shows information about present walks, curbs, and streets and usually gives some indication of the contour of the lot by using contour lines of grade elevations. The architect, using the survey as a base, draws the site plan which is included in the working drawings.

The site plan provides information for the excavator, carpenter, cement mason, and paving contractor. The excavator rough grades the lot so that not too much earth will have to be moved at the location where the floor slab is to be placed. Trenches for footings and foundations are dug to the correct depth and in the approximate location.

The carpenter lays out the building lines so that the building is located precisely where indicated on the site plan. The elevation for the top of the concrete foundation wall is established so that the finished floor elevation is at the correct height. Formwork is built as necessary. The excavator returns after the building is nearly completed to finish grade the entire lot.

Those responsible for walks, drives, and landscaping use the site plan to determine measurements and elevations. Building officials of the community study the site plan, along with the working drawings, to see that local ordinances have been followed.

Location. Figure 8-1 shows some of the basic information taken from the survey. Generally, a point of beginning from which measurements and elevations are taken is designated. The assumption is that point A is a mark on the pavement for horizontal measurements. A mark on the curb across the street is used for elevations (Curb Top 94.4'). The surveyor sets a transit over point A in a true North-South bearing, then moves it through an angle of 9°07'28" in a Northwesterly direction to sight a point 194.28' away. The angle is measured in *degrees* (9°), *minutes* (07'), and *seconds* (28"). A degree is 1/360 of a circle. A minute is 1/60 of a degree and a second is 1/60 of a minute.

Distances are measured in feet and hundredths of a foot instead of feet, inches, and fractions of an inch. The steel tape used for measuring is divided into tenths and hundredths of a foot to make measuring and calculating easy. The next step is to place a stake or marker at point B. The surveyor sets up the transit over point B, takes a bearing of 89°26'57"

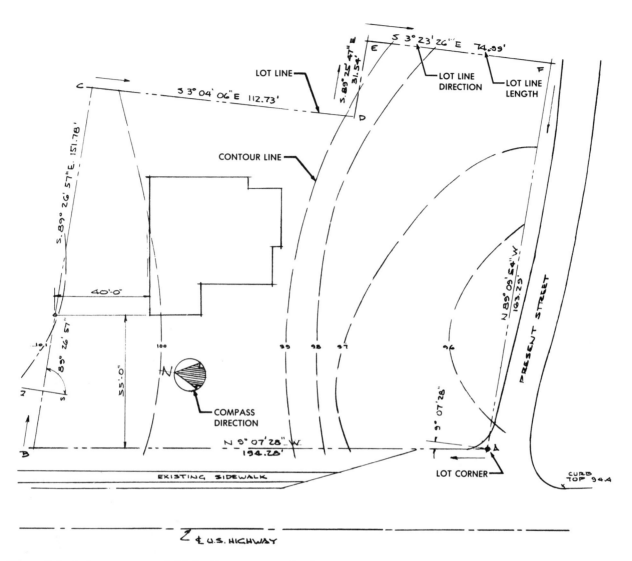

Figure 8-1. Lot corners are established by a surveyor. Lot lines are run by compass directions and measured in lengths. Contour lines show approximate slope.

from a North-South line, and locates point C 151.78′ away. Each stake is located in sequence until the final bearing returns to point A. None of the corners of the lot are right angles, nor are any two sides parallel.

When the architect draws the site plan, the building location must comply with local ordinances regarding setback from the street and dimensions to side and rear lot lines. The architect's primary interest is to place the building in the best location while providing convenient drives and parking within the legal limitations. The building is located on a line drawn parallel to and 55′-0″ away from the West lot line (A-B). The line is extended to cross the lot line (B-C). From the point of intersection,

a measurement of 40′-0″ locates the Northwest corner of the building. Other corners are established using a builder's level and a steel tape. Frequent reference is made to the Foundation Plan.

Elevations and Grades. Establishing elevations and grades are as important as establishing points on the lot. The bench mark officially designated by the building authorities is a mark on a curb across the street at an elevation of 94.4′ above local datum. The surveyor has supplied grade elevations at a number of points, which are recorded on the site plans. The rough contour of the lot slopes down from the North to the South.

The architect establishes elevations for the building, drives, and other pavements, taking advantage of the natural slope. This reduces the amount of moving and disposing of fill and provides drainage from around the building and the parking areas. A sudden change in grade to the North and East would present a problem for neighbors who would have to contend with the run off of the surface water.

Elevation symbols for the pavement resemble a target. See Figure 8-2. The South parking area is to be made level at 98.0'. The West parking lot is to rise from 98.0' to 99.6' to meet the drive that passes the North side of the building. The drive is required to be at an elevation of 100.5' at the location of the auto teller island. Elevation marks on the drive show that the drive and parking areas are sloped to allow water to run off to the South.

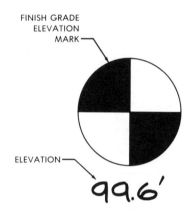

Figure 8-2. Elevation symbols are often shown with targets. Elevations are given in feet and tenths and hundredths of a foot.

The location of the septic tank and drain field is needed by the plumber and is required by the local building authorities. Additional information shown on the site plan include location, arrangement, and number of parking spaces. Seven parking spaces are located on the East side of the building. Eleven parking spaces are located on the South side of the building, and seven parking spaces are located on the West side of the building. The number of parking spaces for commercial buildings must comply with local ordinance requirements. Each parking space has a concrete bumper to prevent vehicles from driving too far into the spaces.

Triangles indicate direction of vehicular traffic flow. Two-way traffic is permitted in the main park-

ing area to the South. One-way traffic is indicated from the South parking area to the auto teller and continues out the Northwest exit to the highway. The West parking area is for one-way traffic. Vehicles may enter or exit from the Southeast and Southwest drives. The Northwest drive is for exiting only.

Sidewalks leading to the front and side entrances are 6'-0" wide. Sidewalks fronting the South and West parking areas are 5'-0" wide. An existing sidewalk is shown along the highway on the West side of the building. New blacktop and concrete is required at the junction of the Northwest drive and the highway while only new blacktop at the Southwest drive and new concrete at the Southeast drive are required.

Floor Plan, Sheet A-2

The plan of the building is essentially a 44'-8" × 56'-0" rectangle with an L-shaped area projecting toward the highway. All areas of the bank are clearly defined on the Floor Plan. These areas include a front entrance, lobby, closing office, teller area, secretary's area, manager's office, storage vault, workroom, lounge, janitor's closet, and men's and women's restrooms.

The lobby extends across the building. It comprises the largest, uninterrupted floor area in the branch bank. Glass walls face South and West and large windows face North. The lobby is entered through either the main doors on the West side of the building or doors on the South side of the building. These doors are "A" doors. The Door Schedule, Sheet A-3, gives detailed information about these and other doors.

Most of the business of the bank is conducted at the counter in the teller area. The counter is conveniently located on the East side of the lobby and is in view when entering from either set of entrance doors. Details 8 and 10 of Sheet A-4 contain dimensions and other information required to complete the counter.

The closing office provides privacy for business transactions. This large office area may be entered through two "C" doors located directly across the lobby from the teller area. Refer to the Door Schedule, Sheet A-3, for detailed information about these doors. The wall separating the closing office from the lobby is gypsum board over 2" × 6" wood studs placed 16" OC. Additional information concerning finish for the closing office is found on the Interior Finish Schedule, Sheet A-3.

Banking activities in the customer areas can be observed through the glass partitions in the manager's office. The Interior Finish Schedule, Sheet A-3, notes that these windows are ¼″ plate-glass in bronzed, anodized aluminum frames. The "B" door of the manager's office is detailed in the Door Schedule, Sheet A-3.

The secretary's area is open to the lobby and immediately adjacent to the manager's office and the teller area. The location of this office prevents unnecessary traffic in the lounge and restrooms and gives the secretary an excellent view of the banking activities. A railing separates the secretary's area from the teller area. This railing is shown on Detail 9, Sheet A-4. The 3′-4″ high railing is framed with 2 × 4s and capped with ¾″ oak. A 2′-0″ gate in the railing provides entrance into the teller area.

The wall separating the secretary's area from the lounge is a gypsum board wall over 2″ × 6″ wood studs placed 16″ OC. The "E" door located in this wall is detailed in the Door Schedule, Sheet A-3.

The storage vault is immediately behind the teller area, and is consequently isolated from inadvertent entry by unauthorized personnel. Note the wall material and thickness. Section 1, Sheet A-4, gives additional information concerning the vault floor, walls, and ceiling. The "J" door of the storage vault is stainless steel.

The workroom is located directly behind the teller area and between the storage vault and lounge. The Floor Plan shows 1″ × 2″ furring strips on the 1′-0″ core-filled concrete block wall separating the storage vault and the workroom. Gypsum board is applied to the furring strips. A 2′-0″ deep closet is located behind a "G" door. The closet contains a shelf and rod. The workroom is entered through a "D" door.

The lounge may be entered through an "E" door from the secretary's area or through an "F" door from the rear of the teller area near the workroom. A 39″ Dwyer unit is located in one corner of the lounge and a janitor's closet is behind the East wall. The janitor's closet contains a mop sink, 30-gallon electric water heater, and the electrical panels. A "G" door allows entry into the janitor's closet.

Restrooms are located off a very short hallway from the lounge. Each restroom contains a water closet and basin with vanity. The water closets are behind toilet partitions for privacy. A floor drain, indicated by the initials, FD, is located in each restroom. Note the use of insulation in partitions surrounding the restrooms. The restrooms are entered through "H" doors.

While some essential information is found on the Floor Plan, other information is found by studying one or more sheets in conjunction with the Floor Plan. For example, while the Floor Plan, Sheet A-2 shows all doors, their location, and their direction of swing, the Door Schedule, Sheet A-3, must be studied in order to determine size, type, material, frame, casings, and hardware for each door.

Exterior Walls. The exterior walls are face brick with concrete masonry unit backing. With the exception of the storage vault walls, all exterior walls are 1′-0″ thick. The exterior walls on the storage vault are 1′-4″ thick. They are made of 1′-0″ concrete blocks in which the cores are poured solid. The concrete block is then faced off with 4″ brick. Wood furring is placed on the inner surface of the exterior walls except for the storage vault. Gypsum board is applied to the furring strips for a drywall finish. Walls and partitions for the storage vault are specially constructed and reinforced for security. Cutting planes are made through the masonry exterior walls in two locations. These refer to Details 1 and 2, Sheet 4, where additional information concerning the exterior walls is found.

Glass Walls, Windows, and Exterior Doors. The glass walls and windows, shown on the West and South sides of the building, are *fixed*. Fixed glass walls and windows do not open. Dimensions are given on the Floor Plan, Sheet A-2, to locate glass walls and windows. Cutting planes denoting Details 3 and 4, Sheet A-4, are shown on the Floor Plan. These details give additional information about the glass walls, doors, and windows.

Exterior doors are "A" doors. These doors are referred to in the Door Schedule, Sheet A-3. Their size, type, material, frame, and hardware are noted. "A" doors are the only paired doors on this set of plans.

Partitions. Partitions are made with 2″ × 6″ wood studs with gypsum board facing for a drywall finish. The Finish Schedule, Sheet A-3, shows the finish that is to be applied on walls and partitions in all rooms. The partitions are made in accordance with Detail 1, Sheet A-2. Note in this detail the use of

2″ × 4″ staggered wood studs placed 16″ OC to form a thicker partition, allowing insulation to be placed around the offset studs. Vinyl-covered fiberglass blanket insulation placed in this manner provides sound-deadening qualities.

Two partitions for the manager's office are glass. The Finish Schedule, Sheet A-3, calls for ¼″ plate glass in bronzed, anodized aluminum frames. The glazing is flush. These glass partitions provide an open look to the main customer area of the bank while allowing the manager a certain amount of privacy.

Roof. The majority of the information concerning the supporting structure for the roof is shown on other drawings. The 3½″ pipe columns along the West wall and in the partition behind the secretary's area are shown on the Floor Plan, Sheet A-2. The footing for the 3½″ column is shown in Detail 2, Sheet A-1. The Roof Plan, Sheet A-3, shows column location and notes the size and location of connecting steel work.

The roof extends beyond the face of the building. A wide soffit begins at the exterior wall outside of the janitor's closet and surrounds three sides of the building to end at the Northwest corner. The soffit is shown with a hidden line on the floor plan because it is more than 5′-0″ above the finish floor elevation. The underside of the soffit is finished with cement plaster to withstand exposure to the weather. Expansion beads placed at intervals along the soffit prevent cracking due to temperature change. Detail 7, Sheet A-4, shows soffit details. The roof overhang is also shown on Detail 6 and Section Views 1–4 on Sheet A-4.

Concrete Work. The location of a future island and auto teller installation is shown on Sheet A-2. The window and counter for the auto teller are to be installed during the initial construction of the building. A note on the auto teller indicating "FUTURE" shows that the auto teller will be installed at a later date. The Foundation Plan, Sheet A-1, gives additional information concerning the auto teller. Note that the future work includes the installation of a canopy over the island and auto teller.

Concrete walks are shown on the Floor Plan, Sheet A-2. Both walks leading to the building are 6′-0″ wide. Additional information regarding the walks is obtained from the Site Plan, Sheet A-1.

A concrete curb is shown along the North wall of the building. This curb is 10″ wide at the Northeast corner and extends to 2′-0″ wide at the Northwest corner. The curb assures adequate clearance between the North wall of the building and vehicular traffic on the driveway. The night depository, located in the North exterior wall, is also protected by the concrete curb.

Equipment. Built-in counters for the teller area are shown on the Floor Plan, Sheet A-2. Notes on the Floor Plan refer to Details 8 and 10, Sheet A-4. These details show necessary dimensions for building the counter.

The hot water heater, mop sink, and electrical panels are located in the janitor's closet. The Dwyer unit shown in the lounge is a compact kitchen unit containing a stove, refrigerator, and sink. These compact units are often used in commercial locations where space is limited or larger equipment is not required based upon the number of employees in the building.

Detail 2, Sheet A-2, shows an elevation of the women's restroom wall. The men's restroom, in which the equipment is laid out on the opposite hand, is also finished as shown in this elevation. Tile on the restroom wall extends 4′-0″ above the finished floor. Information concerning the surface-mounted mirror and vanity is given. Note that the pipe supporting the front of the vanity is specified as chrome only in the women's restrooms.

Elevation Views, Sheet A-5

The Elevation Views, Sheet A-5, must be studied with the Floor Plans, Sheet A-2. These are drawn at the same scale for easy reference. Foundation walls and footings are shown with hidden lines on the four elevation views on this sheet. While some information concerning footings is given, reference should be made to Sections 1–4, Sheet A-4. Information concerning the stone aggregate panels, bronzed aluminum fascia, and divider channels is found on all elevations.

The West Elevation shows the front of the bank building. This elevation faces the highway. The doors and window wall shown in this elevation are part of the lobby. Letters are to be applied to this wall. The upper row of letters is 8″ high and the lower row of letters is 6″ high. The North Elevation shows a window in the closing office, the North lobby windows, and the window for the auto teller. The night depository is also located on this wall. The South Elevation shows the remaining lobby doors, part of the lobby window wall, and a window in the closing office. The East Elevation is a blank wall.

Windows and Doors. Windows in the closing office and in the North lobby are polished plate-glass with a horizontal bar located 2'-6" above the finished floor. These are fixed windows. The window for the auto teller counter is made of bullet-resistant glass and is to be supplied by the manufacturer of the auto teller.

Glass window walls with fixed sash are placed along the South and West sides of the lobby. The glass doors are integral parts of the metal frames for the window walls. Square metal members are 5" × 5". These are part of the frames concealing the pipe columns that support the roof.

Roof Projection. The roof projection is keyed to Details 6 and 7, Sheet A-4. These two section views show the open web steel joists and the rough framework of wood needed to support the facing and the soffit. The facing is made of panels of plywood covered with colored stone chips. The panels are cut to fit into 4'-0" spaces defined by vertical aluminum channels. See Joint Detail, Sheet A-4. The soffit is made of cement plaster on wire lath and is supported from 2" × 6" lookouts. The expansion beads are shown on the Floor Plan, Sheet A-2.

Footings and Foundations. Dimensions are shown relating the finished floor elevation, the finished grade, and the footing elevation. The finished floor elevation is 6" above the finished pavement on the North side of the building. The grade is at the same elevation on all of the views except the North elevation where the concrete curb is shown, and between the North and South elevations where the driveway is shown. The driveway on the North side of the building follows the curb and the wall under the closing office window. It is 6" below the finished floor.

The hidden lines below each elevation view show the footings and foundation. Vertical hidden lines occur at foundation corners and are identified by referring to the Foundation Plan, Sheet A-1. The deep foundation shown on the North Elevation is for the auto teller pit. The top of the foundation

is 8" below the finished floor elevation and 4" below grade. Two rowlock courses of brick, with one course showing above grade, are placed under the lobby windows and the windows in the closing office. Refer to Detail 2, Sheet A-1.

Foundation footings for the various locations are shown on the Foundation Plan, Sheet A-1. Three #4 rebars are run continuously in the foundation footings. Four #4 rebars are placed in column footings. Masonry reinforcing is placed in alternate horizontal joints in the concrete block foundation walls.

Steel Members. The locations of the ends of steel W members that support open web steel joists are shown on the North and South Elevations, Sheet A-5. Beam size called for varies from 8" to 14".

Foundation Plan, Sheet A-1

The Foundation Plan is drawn to the scale 1/4" = 1'-0". All of the information regarding the building of foundation footings, foundation walls, piers, and pouring of the concrete slab, with the exception of certain dimensions, is found on the West Elevation, Sheet A-5.

Foundation Footings. The function of the foundation footings is to transfer the load of the building and foundation to the earth. The size of the footing is increased as the load increases or as the load is concentrated in one area. A footing 1'-0" thick and 2'-4" wide is used under the 1'-0" foundation wall. Three #4 rebars are run continuously throughout. The footings vary in thickness under the specially constructed storage vault foundation, under the non-load-bearing walls of the lobby and around the auto teller pit.

Steel columns supporting the roof structure are located in the window wall. These and other columns toward the rear of the building are supported on 16" square pilasters.

Foundation Walls. The foundation walls are 2'-8" high. See South and West Elevations, Sheet A-5. The wall thicknesses are 8", 12", and 16". Pilasters with an 8" concrete cap are made at column locations in the lobby walls. See Detail 2, Sheet A-1. Concrete columns support the steel columns at the rear of the building. They are reinforced with four

#4 rebars that extend into the footing. See Section 2, Sheet A-4. Damp-proofing is applied to the outside of the foundation walls as detailed in the specifications. Styrofoam insulation, in 1″ thick by 24″ wide pieces, is cemented on the inside of the foundation walls. This is shown by the note on the West wall. See Detail 6, Sheet A-4.

Floor Slab. The concrete floor slab, which is 4″ thick, is placed over Sisalkraft Moistop® and at least 4″ of crushed stone. It is reinforced with 6 × 6 × #10 welded wire fabric. All under-slab piping, conduit, ducts, and other materials must be in place and verified before the slab is poured.

The manner of terminating the slab at the walls is shown in Detail 2, Sheet A-1, Detail 6, Sheet A-4, and in all of the section views on Sheet A-4. Note that the slab is thickened at the column bearing West wall.

The slab is depressed below the restrooms, providing space to lay a cement bed and a ceramic tile floor which will be flush with the slab elsewhere. A 4″ cast iron drain runs to the septic tank. It must be roughed-in prior to pouring the depressed slab.

Auto Teller. The auto teller is a convenience of modern banking that enables a person to make banking transactions without leaving the car. Electronic and electrical controls and pneumatic tubes are used to efficiently speed the cash, checks, pass book, and other currency and papers between customer and teller. The customer need not see the teller. In fact, the teller may be over 100′ away in the bank. The auto teller for this branch bank is to be completed at a later time, but as many provisions as possible are included at the time of initial construction. This will save costs when the island and canopy are built. See the Site Plan, Sheet A-1.

Section 1 on Sheet A-1 is related to the Foundation Plan, Sheet A-1. Note the cutting plane and the direction the section is taken in the Foundation Plan, then relate the two views. The section view shows the two walls of the pit itself and the masonry wall of the building supported on a reinforced concrete beam. A 4′-0″ galvanized steel culvert extends beyond the location of the future island to provide space for the equipment and a means to service it. An opening is provided in the floor of the bank for the passage of the pneumatic tubes and wiring. See the note, "OP'G IN FLOOR SLAB" on the Foun-

dation Plan. The sump pump and the manhole shown in the plan do not show in the section view because they are behind the cutting plane.

Under-slab Piping. A note calls attention to workers to "VERIFY THAT ALL UNDER SLAB PIPING, CONDUIT, DUCTS, ETC., ARE IN BEFORE PLACING SLAB." See Foundation Plan, Sheet A-1. This is important because it is impossible to rectify errors without tearing up the slab. Certain plumbing features are shown on the Foundation Plan. Downspouts carry water from the roof through pipes in the masonry walls. One pipe is shown in the North wall near the auto teller pit. It connects to a 4″ plastic pipe that passes under the floor slab, continuing out through a 6″ diameter pipe to a storm sewer in the street at the South end of the lot. The pipe is joined by a pipe carrying the discharge from the sump pump and a 3″ downspout pipe at the South wall. A third downspout connects to a pipe that passes outside of the building to join the line to the sewer on the South side of the building. The soil pipe to the septic tank is shown in its approximate location. Other supply lines to and waste lines from the restrooms, janitor's closet, and kitchen unit are not shown.

Steel Structure, Roof, and Lintels, Sheet A-3

The main feature of the steel structure is the use of open web steel joists. The joists are a combination of angles that serve as top and bottom chords with diagonal bars for reinforcement. Open web steel joists are particularly useful in light construction because they can span great distances, are lightweight, and the open webs allow a passageway for conduit, pipes, and ducts.

Sheets that best show the steel structure and that should be studied together are the Roof Plan, Sheet A-3; Section Views 1, 2, 3, and 4 on Sheet A-4; and Details 6 and 7 on Sheet A-4. The open web steel joists are supported by walls or structural steel members. See Figure 8-3. A variety of sizes of open web steel joists are used and are selected based upon their spans and loads to be supported.

The usual type of open web steel joist is *underslung*. In underslung joists, the joists are hung by a top member. Refer to the joists over the storage vault at the Northeast corner in Figure 8-3. The top ends of the joists rest on weld plates that are securely anchored in the masonry. The top of the masonry

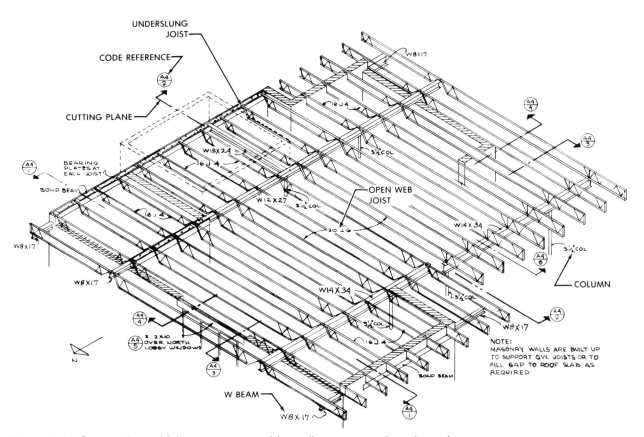

Figure 8-3. Open web steel joists are supported by walls or structural steel members.

wall is made into a reinforced concrete bond beam using U-shaped lintel blocks. See the exterior wall of the storage vault in Section 1, Sheet A-4. After the joists are placed in position, they are tack welded to hold them in alignment. Other underslung joists rest on the outside wall and on W beams. They are securely welded to the beams.

Whenever the joists project beyond the wall on the East or West side of the building, they are modified with square ends to support the facing panels and soffit. See Detail 6 and Section Views, Sheet A-4. Section 1 shows how they are supported when they pass through a masonry wall, and Detail 6 shows how they are supported by a W beam over the glass window wall of the lobby. The end joists at the North and South sides of the building are supported by short W beams embedded in the masonry and fastened with anchor bolts and by the ends of a large W 14 beam and W 8 beams.

An 8″ masonry *parapet* wall surrounding the roof where the heat pump is located is shown on the Roof Plan, Sheet A-3, and Section 2, Sheet A-4. A parapet wall is a short wall. The masonry wall rests on

a W 8 × 24 beam and a W 12 × 27 beam. On the other sides it rests on a continuation of the masonry of the storage vault wall and the exterior wall. Two 12″ × 8″ openings at roof level are provided for roof drainage.

Special steel members include the W 12 × 27 beam under the parapet wall where the heat pump is located. A 1/4″ × 7″ plate is welded to the W beam to provide a wider base for the masonry above. Steel angles are used to frame the curbs for the restroom's fans and heat pump at the roof. See Details 1 and 2, Sheet A-3.

Corrugated steel deck material is welded to the joists when they are in place. See Details 6 and 7, Sheet A-4. Welded wire fabric reinforcing (6 × 6 × #10) is then spread, and 2 1/2″ of lightweight concrete, using *perlite* as an aggregate, is placed. Perlite is a volcanic siliceous rock, crushed and heated at a high temperature, which expands it into lightweight glassy particles. A five-ply, built-up roof of tarred felt and pitch is then applied. The finish is a surface of fine gravel. Details 6 and 7, Sheet A-4, show how the roof edge is formed with a 4″ × 4″ wood member that stops the concrete, and how the metal fascia is put in position.

Lintels. The windows in the window wall do not need lintels because the wall is non-load-bearing. Details 6 and 7, Sheet A-4, show the blocking required to close the gap to open web steel joists above and to provide a means to fasten the ceiling and soffit material. A reference is made on the North Elevation View, Sheet A-5 to Detail 5, Sheet A-4, for the lintel over the North lobby windows. This detail shows two 2″ × 10″ members serving as a lintel over the windows. The masonry wall shown in the detail is beyond the opening. Lintels over the auto teller window and the two windows in the closing office are made of U-shaped concrete masonry units (lintel blocks) with rebars and filled with concrete. See Figure 8-4.

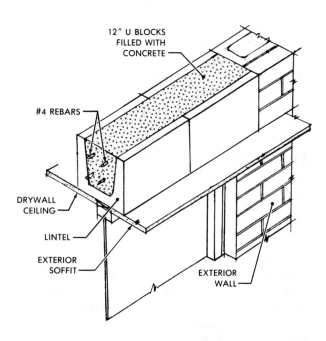

Figure 8-4. Lintels may be reinforced concrete in U blocks.

Details 1 and 2, Sheet A-3, shows how the roof slab breaks against the curbs for the heat pump and the fan openings in the roof to ease drainage. The slab is placed at an angle at the fan curb, while a 1″ × 6″ cant strip provides the corner angle at the heat pump curb. Three roof drains are shown on the Roof Plan. They are connected to 3″ pipes in

the space between the ceiling and roof to carry the water to downspouts in the walls. Four 4″ plastic overflow pipes are shown on the roof passing through the roof projection. The manner in which they are installed and flashed is shown in Detail 7, Sheet A-4. Note that they extend 1½″ above the roof.

Section Views, Sheet A-4

The purpose of section views in a set of working drawings is (1) to show interior elevations and details of finish, and (2) to show structural features of walls, partitions, foundation, and roof support. To help orientation, the cutting planes for section views are shown on the floor plan with direction arrows and a code reference. Note that the placement of sheet numbers and section or detail number may vary. Generally, the method of number placement for references may be determined by finding the sheet number first. The remaining number is either the section or detail number. See Figure 8-5. Sheet A-4 contains four sections taken through the building and additional sections through the counter.

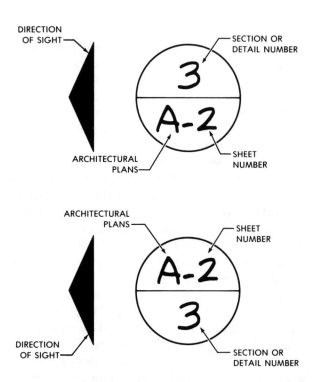

Figure 8-5. Code references key cutting planes to details and sections.

Section 1, Sheet A-4. Section 1 is a view taken parallel to the North wall looking toward the wall. The cutting plane passes through the closing office, lobby, teller area, and the storage vault. See Floor Plan, Sheet A-2. The manner in which brick is applied to the exterior of the masonry walls and the position of the reinforced U block bond beam are some of the structural features included here. The frame partition is shown extending above the ceiling and the lower chord of the open web steel joists to be anchored by bolts. The ceiling over the teller area is dropped to a clear height of 8′-0″ with the use of eggcrate luminous ceiling tile. A complete description of the reinforced concrete slab over the storage vault is given. Notice that the edges project into the masonry walls.

Section 2, Sheet A-4. Section 2 is taken through the workroom, the teller area, and the lobby looking South. The cutting plane passes through the roof portion where the heat pump is located. The door to the left is to a closet. The next door to the right is to the lounge. The doors and window wall to the right are in the South wall of the lobby. Details of the wood railing between the teller area and the secretary's area are shown. This railing, which is shown on the Floor Plan, Sheet A-2, might easily be mistaken for a partition if it was not for this section view.

Detail 9, Sheet A-4, gives additional information about the railing. The glass partition and door for the manager's office appear beyond the railing. The suspended acoustical ceiling is shown with a reference to Detail 7, Sheet A-4, for more information. The ceiling height in the workroom and restrooms is noted as 8′-0″. The ceiling in the janitor's closet extends to the joists. The manner of support and construction of the parapet wall on the roof is indicated. The parapet wall is 8″ solid brick.

Section 3, Sheet A-4. Section 3 is taken through the lobby looking West. It shows the wide expanse of the window wall, including the double entrance doors, in the lobby. The two doors to the right are for the closing office. The concrete curb outside of the North wall is shown with dimensions and reinforcing information.

Section 4, Sheet A-4. Section 4 is taken through the lobby looking East to show information about the arrangement of the teller counter and details of the glass partition in the manager's office. *Victrex* wall covering is to be applied by the painter. Victrex is a trade name for a vinyl material used for wall covering. *Element 1* is a designation for a particular type of finished plywood. Only a small portion (the right side of the teller area), including the gate, indicates how the entire counter will look when finished. The dropped ceiling over the teller area is shown with a plastered area above. The doors from left to right are the vault door, the door to the workroom, and the door to the lounge. The railing to the right of the counter separates the teller area from the secretary's area.

Section 8, Sheet A-4. Section 8 is taken through the counter in the teller area. The counter has two main working surfaces. The surface used by the tellers is 40″ high. The surface used by bank customers is 54″ high. *Formica*® is applied to these surfaces. Formica is a trade name for plastic laminate. Metal cabinets beneath the counter are not in the contract.

Section 10, Sheet A-4. Section 10 is also taken as if looking at the back (teller) side of the counter. The wood shelf unit is supplied by the general contractor. Letter and numerical designations refer to metal cabinets that are not part of this contract.

Details, Sheets A-1 to A-4

Details are generally section views that are enlarged to present detailed information that could not be clearly shown at a smaller scale. Details may be plan, elevation, or section views although section views are most common.

Detail 1, Sheet A-1. Detail 1 shows a section taken through the auto teller pit. This detail is drawn to the scale of $3/8″ = 1′-0″$. Foundation footings are 1′-8″ wide and 1′-0″ high. The concrete footings are reinforced with three #4 rebars.

A drain tile is shown and details of the 4′-0″ galvanized steel culvert are given. Compacted fill is placed on the steel culvert and covered with blacktop. Future work is indicated as the auto teller is not part of this contract.

Detail 2, Sheet A-1. Detail 2 is drawn in order to show how the pipe columns in the lobby window wall rest on a concrete base, which forms the top of the foundation wall. No scale is indicated for this detail. The detail also shows how the brick masonry and the floor slab are related. The 4″ slab is increased to 8″ to rest on the 8″ concrete base. The Styrofoam insulation is brought up to the top of the foundation wall and repeated behind the bricks.

Detail 3, Sheet A-2. Detail 3 is a section taken through the soffit over the teller counter. The detail is drawn to the scale of ¼″ = 1″, which is one-quarter size. It informs the carpenter how to frame the rough structure and how to hang it from the bar joists above. The wood finish on the face is shown.

The plastering work is indicated and is stopped on a *ground* inside the trough. A ground is a wood strip nailed in place and is used by the plasterer to end the work. It also serves as a guide for the thickness of the plaster. The soffit part of the plastering begins at a quarter round bead and continues to a corner bead where it follows the 2″ × 6″ vertical members. The beads provide a stop for the plaster, a protection for the corners, and also determine the level of the finished coat. The eggcrate ceiling is hung with exposed T's. One of the T's is shown at the plaster corner. See Figure 8-6.

Other Details. Details 1 and 2, Sheet A-3, were discussed in the section on the roof regarding miscellaneous steel members and again in the discussion on the placing of the roof slab. These details also show the wood framing members, the flashing, and dimensions for the openings.

A number of references have been made to Details 5, 6, and 7, on Sheet A-4. Details 8 and 9, Sheet A-4, show section views through the teller counter and railing to give all of the information needed to build them. The rough framework of wood members and plywood, the blocking, and finish are carefully detailed.

Detail 10, Sheet A-4, displays the arrangement of metal cabinets shown from the teller's side with manufacturer's numbers for each unit. This detail should be compared with the lobby elevation of the counter shown in Section 4 on the same sheet.

Schedules, Sheet A-3

The schedules make up an important part of a set of working drawings because they consolidate information. The number of schedules in a set of prints varies with the complexity of the project. The Branch Bank plans contain an Interior Finish Schedule and a Door Schedule. A window schedule is not required because there are no windows that open in the bank building.

Interior Finish Schedule. The Interior Finish Schedule gives information for finishing floors, walls, and ceilings. The type and size of baseboards for walls are also listed. Notice that carpet is not a part of this contract. Four different types of paint and stain finishes are detailed. These are noted as Finish 1, 2, 3, and 4.

Door Schedule. The Door Schedule describes each type and size of door completely, including the finish and frame. The Floor Plan, Sheet A-3, should be available to cross-check each door's location. Two pairs of entrance doors of aluminum are to be furnished with medium *stiles*. The stiles are the vertical side members of the door itself. Doors "B" and "F" are solid wood doors with cores of flakeboard and ventilating louvers. Door "G" to the janitor's closet and "H" to the restrooms are solid wood doors. The two doors marked "H" have push and pull plates.

The doors to the manager's office and the closing office have *locksets*. Locksets have locks with keys. They may have rectangular or beveled bolts, or both. Doors "E," "F," and "G" have *latchsets*. Latchsets have beveled bolts that hold the doors closed when they are shut. They are not meant for security and do not have keyed locks.

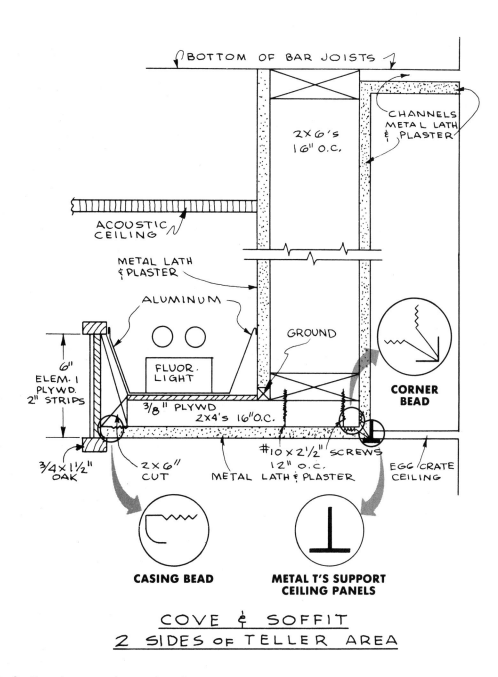

BOTTOM OF BAR JOISTS

2X6's
16" O.C.

CHANNELS
METAL LATH
& PLASTER

ACOUSTIC
CEILING

METAL LATH
& PLASTER

ALUMINUM

GROUND

**CORNER
BEAD**

6"
ELEM. 1
PLYWD.
2" STRIPS

FLUOR.
LIGHT

3/8" PLYWD
2X4's 16"O.C.

3/4 x 1½"
OAK

2 X 6"
CUT

#10 x 2½" SCREWS
12" O.C.
METAL LATH & PLASTER

EGG CRATE
CEILING

CASING BEAD

**METAL T'S SUPPORT
CEILING PANELS**

COVE & SOFFIT
2 SIDES OF TELLER AREA

Figure 8-6. Section views may be used to show carpentry construction and plaster finish.

Name _____   Date _____

Completion

_____ 1. A(n) _____ is a unit that provides heating or cooling for a building.

_____ 2. The survey provides a means of determining elevations from datum points or _____.

_____ 3. _____ view drawings show interior elevations.

_____ 4. _____ drawings are drawn to a larger scale to show the object more clearly.

_____ 5. A(n) _____ provides complete information on the type and size of doors specified.

_____ 6. Studs in walls and partitions may be _____ to allow insulation to be interweaved around the studs.

_____ 7. A(n) _____ line has arrows on each end to indicate the direction of sight.

_____ 8. _____ windows can not be opened.

_____ 9. Concrete foundation footings are usually reinforced with _____.

_____ 10. A surveyor's steel tape is divided into tenths and hundredths of a(n) _____.

True-False

T F 1. A section view is commonly shown with closely spaced, parallel lines drawn horizontally through the object.

T F 2. One of the primary functions of a site plan is to locate the lot lines and corners.

T F 3. Floor plans showing room size and layout are drawn with the line of sight parallel to the floor.

T F 4. Elevation symbols on prints often resemble a target.

T F 5. The size of a foundation footing is increased as loads are concentrated in one area.

T F 6. Concrete floor slabs must be poured at the same elevation throughout a building.

T F 7. Downspouts should always be run on the outside of exterior walls.

T F 8. A septic tank requires the pumping action of a sump pump.

T F 9. A W 12 × 27 beam weighs more per foot than a W 14 × 34 beam.

T F 10. Hidden lines on floor plans indicate features over 5'-0" above the floor.

T	F	**11.**	W beams can not be adequately supported by masonry walls.
T	F	**12.**	Parapet walls may be wood-framed or masonry construction.
T	F	**13.**	Acoustical ceilings must be suspended to prevent sound transmission.
T	F	**14.**	Latchsets do not have keyed locks.
T	F	**15.**	Door schedules describe each type and size of door, including the finish and frame.
T	F	**16.**	Stiles are horizontal members of a door.
T	F	**17.**	Locksets may have rectangular, beveled, or rectangular and beveled bolts.
T	F	**18.**	Prints drawn to the scale of ¼″ = 1′-0″ are one-quarter actual size.
T	F	**19.**	Site plans may be used to determine if property setbacks comply with local ordinances.
T	F	**20.**	Open web steel joists may be utilized in constructing cantilevered roofs.

Identification

_____ **1.** Architectural plans

_____ **2.** Scale

_____ **3.** Concrete

_____ **4.** Sheet number

_____ **5.** Break line

_____ **6.** Center line

_____ **7.** Framing member

_____ **8.** Detail or section number

_____ **9.** Door symbol

_____ **10.** Direction of sight

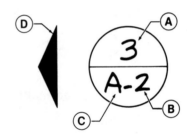

(E) 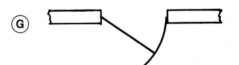 $\frac{1}{4}″ = 1′-0″$

(F)

(G)

(H)

(I)

(J)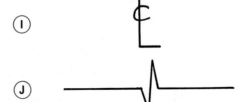

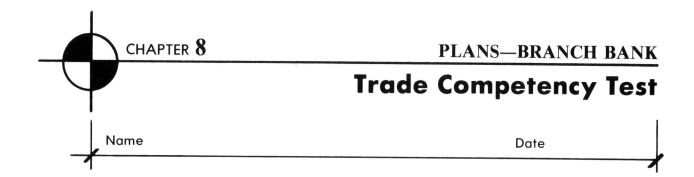
Refer to Branch Bank Plans.

SHEET A-1
Completion

_____ 1. The driveway is _____ wide on the East side of the building.

_____ 2. The sump pump drains into a 4″ _____ pipe that runs beneath the concrete slab.

_____ 3. _____ diagonal parking spaces are provided on the West side of the building.

_____ 4. The concrete slab is thickened to _____ ″ at the foundation walls.

_____ 5. The sump pump has a 6.6 A, _____ HP motor.

_____ 6. The Site Plan is drawn to the scale of 1″ = _____ ′.

_____ 7. A(n) _____ ″ diameter pipe is connected to the 3″ downspout on the West side of the building.

_____ 8. The street on the South side of the parking lot is _____.

_____ 9. The West property line extends _____ ′ along the highway.

_____ 10. The Northwest corner of the building is located _____ from the West property line.

SHEET A-2
Multiple Choice

_____ 1. The fan register in the women's restroom is located _____.
   A. on the wall across from the water closet
   B. in the floor near the East wall
   C. 3″ above the baseboard beneath the lavatory
   D. high on the wall above the lavatory

_____ 2. The hot water heater _____.
   A. has a 30-gallon capacity
   B. is located at the ceiling in the janitor's closet
   C. both A and B
   D. neither A nor B

_____ 3. The teller area _____.
   A. is immediately adjacent to the restrooms
   B. extends 8'-0" from the front wall of the storage vault
   C. is partitioned off from the lobby
   D. none of the above

_____ 4. The main entrance doors _____.
   A. open to the outside
   B. are paired
   C. are A doors
   D. all of the above

_____ 5. Sill cocks for outside use are located on the _____ walls.
   A. North and South
   B. South and West
   C. South and East
   D. East and West

_____ 6. The common partition between the restrooms _____.
   A. is 8'-0" high
   B. is 1'-0" thick
   C. contains sound-deadening insulation
   D. has two 3¼" × 8" ducts to a fan

_____ 7. Exterior masonry walls are _____.
   A. of uniform thickness
   B. 4" brick over 8" concrete block except for the storage vault
   C. painted concrete block below and brick above
   D. none of the above

_____ 8. The door for the storage vault _____.
   A. swings flush against the storage vault wall
   B. is furnished and installed by Diebold, Inc.
   C. is a J door
   D. all of the above

_____ 9. The partition between the secretary's area and the lounge _____.
   A. is framed with 2" × 4" wooden studs
   B. has stud placement 24" OC
   C. is 3'-6" high
   D. conceals a steel column

_____ 10. The North wall of the building _____.
   A. is 57'-4" in length
   B. contains six windows
   C. both A and B
   D. neither A nor B

SHEET A-3
Completion

_____   **1.** The roof _____ is thickened to meet the curb for the exhaust fan.

_____   **2.** A(n) _____ beam runs from the Southwest corner to the North wall of the building.

_____   **3.** The size of the _____ door is not given in the Door Schedule.

_____   **4.** _____ doors have marble thresholds.

_____   **5.** The teller area has a(n) _____ ceiling of $1/2''$ eggcrate on exposed tees.

_____   **6.** The roof plan is drawn to the scale of _____ $'' = 1'\text{-}0''$.

_____   **7.** Signs are to be affixed to doors B, C, E, and _____.

_____   **8.** Finished flooring in the storage vault is _____ tile.

_____   **9.** All _____ doors are tempered glass.

_____   **10.** Doors B, C, D, and E contain an $18'' \times 6''$ oak sight-proof _____.

_____   **11.** Parapet wall openings are capped with $7'' \times 18''$ steel plates _____ $''$ thick.

_____   **12.** The coat closet floor is _____.

_____   **13.** _____ $''$ diameter overflow pipes are provided on roof overhangs.

_____   **14.** All wood doors are specified to receive _____ hinges.

_____   **15.** The North wall of the teller area is finished with _____ wall cover.

_____   **16.** Finish 1 specifies two coats of _____ paint.

_____   **17.** Interior finish for the employee's lounge is the same as in the _____.

_____   **18.** Finish _____ is called for on counter shelves.

_____   **19.** All columns are _____ $''$ standard pipes.

_____   **20.** Storage vault walls are to receive Finish _____.

SHEET A-4
Completion

_____   **1.** The counter has a(n) _____ $''$ high toekick on the employee side.

_____   **2.** The built-up roofing contains _____ plies.

_____   **3.** _____ #4 rebars are run horizontally in the concrete foundation footings.

_____   **4.** Four $4''$ plastic pipes are required for _____ in all roof overhangs.

_____   **5.** The railing between the secretary's area and the teller area specifies a(n) _____ plate on the floor.

_____   **6.** The concrete curb is reinforced with two #_____ rebars top and bottom.

_____   **7.** Detail 6 shows the roof overhang on the _____ wall.

_____   8. Concrete blocks in masonry walls are to be reinforced on _____ courses.

_____   9. Parapet walls are _____ ″ solid brick.

_____   10. Ceiling height in both restrooms is _____ .

_____   11. Detail 7 is taken from a cutting plane shown in Section _____ .

_____   12. The exterior brick walls are anchored to the concrete block walls with _____ clips.

_____   13. _____ 1 plywood is used to finish the front walls of the counter in the teller area.

_____   14. Detail 7 is drawn to the scale of 1 ″ = _____ .

_____   15. The vault door can be seen behind the counter in Section _____ .

_____   16. Section _____ shows the restroom partition extending to the top of the steel joists.

_____   17. A minimum of _____ ″ of crushed stone is required below the concrete slab.

_____   18. Doubled _____ form the lintel over the North lobby window.

_____   19. The roof of the storage vault is a concrete slab _____ ″ thick.

_____   20. The wood shelf unit in the counter receives Finish _____ .

SHEET A-5
True-False

T   F   1. The West Exterior Elevation is drawn to the scale of $\frac{1}{4}$ ″ = 1 ′-0 ″.

T   F   2. The auto teller is not included in this contract.

T   F   3. Stone aggregate panels are placed completely around the building.

T   F   4. Exterior walls are brick on all sides of the building.

T   F   5. The exterior doors have a bronzed, anodized aluminum frame.

T   F   6. All plate-glass window walls are $\frac{1}{8}$ ″ polished glass.

T   F   7. A stepped foundation is required for the South Elevation.

T   F   8. The concrete foundation footing is 1 ′-0 ″ thick.

T   F   9. Two 12 ″ × 18 ″ openings are provided in the parapet wall.

T   F   10. The night depository is located on the South wall of the building.

Refer to Branch Bank Plans.

Multiple Choice

_____ 1. The Site Plan, Sheet A-1, shows that the _____.
  A. building is located 40'-0" from the North lot line
  B. face of the building is parallel to a true North-South line
  C. North and South lot lines are parallel
  D. all corner angles of the lot are 90°

_____ 2. Regarding elevations on the Site Plan, Sheet A-1, the _____.
  A. drive on the East and North sides of the building is at the same elevation for its entire length
  B. elevation of the finish floor is 101'-0"
  C. parking area South of the building slopes from East to West and North to South
  D. sidewalks vary in elevation as much as 2'-0"

_____ 3. Regarding foundation footings, _____.
  A. all footings are shown extending 8" beyond each side of foundation walls
  B. rebars in footings are ¼" in diameter
  C. the overall dimension of footings from North to South, including the auto teller pit, is 61'-2"
  D. the footings continue through the auto teller pit without changing elevation or size of reinforcement

_____ 4. Regarding the foundation and the auto teller pit, _____.
  A. the inside dimensions of the auto teller pit are 7'-0" × 8'-4"
  B. concrete block columns and pilasters support steel columns
  C. the cutting plane for the section view of the auto teller pit is taken looking East
  D. foundation walls are either 8", 12", or 16" thick

_____ 5. Drainage piping shown on the Site Plan, Sheet A-1, includes _____.
  A. connections to three downspouts in the walls passing under the floor slab to the discharge pipe
  B. a sump pump discharge connecting to the septic tank
  C. a soil pipe from the building to a 900-gallon septic tank
  D. 4" plastic pipe under the slab

_____ 6. Regarding walls and partitions shown on Sheet A-2, _____.
  A. all exterior masonry walls have the same thickness
  B. all masonry walls have brick facing
  C. the frame partitions for the closing office and the lounge have a nominal thickness of 6"
  D. the masonry partitions for the storage vault have lath and plaster over 1" × 2" furring on both sides

_____ 7. The Floor Plan, Sheet A-2, shows that the _____.
  A. workroom and janitor's closet exterior walls are stripped with 1" × 2" furring for the application of rocklath and plaster
  B. soffit extending around the outside of the building is 4'-8" wide
  C. soffit is finished with cement plaster and divided by expansion beads
  D. concrete curb is 2'-0" wide at the auto teller window

8. Regarding cutting planes and designations, _____.
   A. no cutting plane is taken through the septic tank
   B. all cutting planes are taken in a North to South direction
   C. all cutting planes extend either through the length or the width of the building
   D. all cutting planes are taken on the Floor Plan

9. Details 1, 2, and 3 on Sheet A-2 show that the _____.
   A. cove soffit and vertical wall finish above the teller counter are to be made with gypsum board for drywall
   B. restroom partitions are built with 2″ × 4″ studs and 2″ × 6″ plates
   C. fluorescent light fixtures are suspended from the ceiling
   D. ventilating fans are shown in the ceilings of the restrooms

10. Regarding the open web joists shown on Sheet A-3, _____.
    A. all joists designated 16 J 4 have square ends to support the facing panels of the roof projection
    B. the joists extending beyond the face of the North wall are supported by short W 8 × 17 beams and one W 14 × 34 beam
    C. the 7′-9″ dimension on the projection at the West side of the building is from the ends of the joists to the face of the lobby window wall
    D. all joists designated 20 J 6 are the same length

11. The Roof Plan and Details 1 and 2, Sheet A-3, show that the _____.
    A. two angles supporting the curb for the exhaust fan rest on the open web joists
    B. framework for the heat pump opening is made of steel angles and steel plates
    C. lintels over the closing office windows are steel angles
    D. wall surrounding the heat pump roof is made of concrete block with brick facing

12. The Room Finish Schedule, Sheet A-3, specifies _____.
    A. drywall on all walls in the janitor's closet
    B. gypsum board wall finish in the lobby but no paint finish
    C. acoustical tile ceiling with a plaster border in the lounge
    D. ceramic tile on floors and walls in restrooms

13. Regarding information on the Door Schedule, _____.
    A. the two doors to the lounge are identical
    B. doors D and G are alike except for the door construction and the lock
    C. all doors except the entrance doors and vault door are solid flush doors
    D. the doors to the closing office and manager's office have transoms above

14. Regarding the section views on Sheet A-4, the cutting plane for Section _____.
    A. 1 passes through the teller area
    B. 2 passes through the secretary's area
    C. 3 passes through the closing office
    D. 4 passes through the lobby and manager's office

15. The section views, Sheet A-4, show a floor to ceiling height of _____.
    A. 9′-7″ in the closing office
    B. 9′-7″ in the workroom
    C. 9′-10″ in the vault
    D. 8′-0″ in the teller area

—————— 16. Information on concrete work and masonry on Sheet A-4 includes _____.
   A. dimensions totaling 16'-8" from the grade to the top of the masonry
   B. a curb 10" × 2'-0" resting partially on the foundation wall
   C. 4" slabs for the floor and the ceiling in the vault
   D. dimensions for the footing and concrete columns supporting interior steel columns

—————— 17. The section views on Sheet A-4 show that _____.
   A. the ceiling in the lobby is hung flush against the open web joists
   B. the soffit and stone facing extend the same dimension away from the face of the building on three sides
   C. the same insulation is used to line the foundation between furring strips on masonry walls and over the ceiling
   D. joists are supported on concrete U blocks with steel rebars and concrete filling at exterior masonry walls

—————— 18. Regarding Details 6 and 7 and Joint Detail, Sheet A-4, _____.
   A. the metal window frame extends to the bottom of the W 14 beam
   B. Detail 6 is a section through the projection of the roof looking North
   C. lightweight concrete with welded wire mesh is placed over Corruform to make the roof slab
   D. the soffit is fastened to the bottom of the open web joists

—————— 19. The elevation views on Sheet A-5 show that _____.
   A. the bottom of the footing is 4'-0" below the finished floor line
   B. the finished grade and the top of the driveway pavement are at the same elevation
   C. the stone aggregate panels are only visible from the North, South, and West
   D. two 12" × 8" openings are provided for the roof area enclosing the heat pump

—————— 20. Regarding windows shown on Sheet A-5, _____.
   A. all of the windows in the lobby facing West and South are the same size
   B. all window frames except the auto teller's window frame extend to the floor level
   C. the lower portion of the closing office windows are hopper sash
   D. all windows are ¼" polished plate-glass

—————— 21. The tile field for the septic tank _____.
   A. is located on the West side of the building
   B. is located on the South side of the building
   C. runs parallel to the highway
   D. no septic tank and tile field are shown

—————— 22. Regarding Door H, _____.
   A. plastic laminate is used as a finish
   B. casings are not required
   C. a marble threshold is specified
   D. stainless steel butts are specified

—————— 23. Regarding the manager's office, _____.
   A. carpet is to be installed under the contract
   B. wallpaper will be hung by the owner
   C. baseboards are to be finished oak
   D. an acoustical tile ceiling is specified

24. The electrical panels are located on the _____ wall in the janitor's closet.
    A. North
    B. South
    C. East
    D. West

25. The _____ cannot be seen from the manager's office.
    A. main entrance
    B. side entrance
    C. teller's area
    D. restrooms

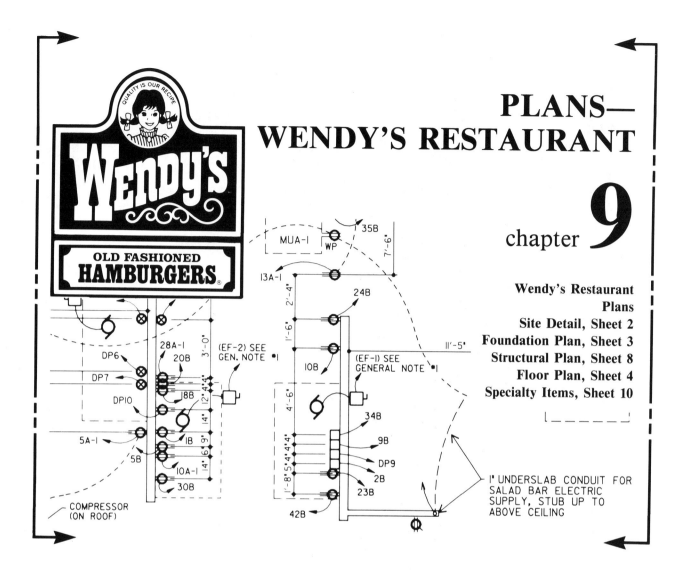

PLANS—
WENDY'S RESTAURANT

WENDY'S RESTAURANTS

Fast food restaurants have become firmly established throughout the United States over the past 30 years. Easily identified by their distinctive signs, these restaurants attract local patrons as well as the traveling public. Offering quality food products quickly and at moderate prices, fast food restaurants are located in cities, suburbs, and along major highways. See Figure 9-1.

Fast food restaurants are a vital part of a community's economic life because they provide jobs for local citizens. From the work generated in the building of a new restaurant to the serving of food, these restaurants employ millions of people. Building tradesworkers, material and equipment suppliers, food and beverage purveyors, utility companies, employees, and numerous other groups of people benefit from the economic opportunities. Additionally, government at all levels receives taxes generated by the establishment and operation of these facilities.

Wendy's Restaurants, with corporate headquarters in Ohio, has quickly become one of the more popular fast food restaurants. Using only the highest quality products and offering the staple attraction of such restaurants, the hamburger (in 256 different ways), customer loyalty has been developed. In addition, through clean, well-planned buildings designed for efficient service and containing pleasant areas for dining, Wendy's Restaurants has assured customer loyalty.

PLANS

The scope of work detailed in the set of plans is

Figure 9-1. Fast food restaurants are an integral part of the American way of life.

for a new restaurant, which is building type A-3 assembly (restaurant). The construction type is 5B (wood frame, unprotected). All posting requirements shall be met per OBBC and local requirements as follows:

Use Group......Assembly (A)
Fire Grading.........2 Hour
Live Loads...........100 PSF
(PSF = pounds per square foot)

Gross square footage of the restaurant is 3,018 sq. ft. Net square footage is as follows:

Dining Room......1,386 sq. ft.
Kitchen.............771 sq. ft.
Cooler-Freezer ......336 sq. ft.
Restrooms ....156 sq. ft.
Office..............62 sq. ft.

The restaurant has a seating capacity of 98 people. Design loads are as follows:

Floor ......100 PSF
Roof ....30 PSF
Wind ....15 PSF

All exitways shall comply with OBBC and all requirements for the handicapped, per OBBC and local requirements, shall be met. Fire dampers shall be installed per NFPA 96, OBBC, and local requirements. Ventilators shall comply with OBBC and local requirements. Architectural symbols used for this set of plans are standard symbols. See Figure 9-2.

The complete set of plans contains 15 sheets plus specifications. (Specifications are included as text in chapter 10.) The Site Plan, Sheet 1, is not included in this study. Site plans are developed after purchase of local property. They are drawn to meet all local requirements for zoning, easements, setbacks, landscape, appearance, sign placement, etc. See Figure 9-3.

SITE DETAILS, SHEET 2

The Site Details give information for construction outside the building. Curb and pavement markers are shown. The Trash Enclosure Plan with sections, details, and an elevation view give all dimensions and materials required for construction. Exterior signs and pole light details are shown. Plans for the ramp, recommended radius, and the paver details complete the drawings on this sheet. Note that the scale used for drawing the views on this sheet varies with different plans, details, elevations, and sections shown.

Three general notes are given on Sheet 2. Note 1 states that all signs shall be erected in accordance with all local codes and soil conditions. Note 2 indicates wind load designs of 15 PSF and calls for verification of local wind and soil conditions. Note 3 instructs the general contractor to furnish all pavement markers. These must be solid yellow.

Curb Details

Detail drawings are given for concrete and asphalt curbs. Determination of which drawing is to be used for a particular restaurant location is made in accordance with local requirements. The curb selected will then be noted on the Site Plan, Sheet 1. See Figure 9-4.

ARCHITECTURAL SYMBOLS	
	BRICK
	CONCRETE BLOCK
	CONCRETE
	GRAVEL
	INSULATION
	FRAMING LUMBER
	FINISH LUMBER
	STEEL
	STUDS
	DRYWALL

Figure 9-2. Standard architectural symbols are used.

INDEX OF DRAWINGS	
SHT	DESCRIPTION
I	SITE PLAN
2	SITE DETAILS
3	FOUNDATION PLAN
4	FLOOR PLAN
5	EXTERIOR ELEVATIONS
6	INTERIOR ELEVATIONS
7A	WALL SECTIONS
7B	WALL SECTIONS
8	STRUCTURAL PLAN
9	EQUIPMENT PLAN
IO	SPECIALTY ITEMS
II	HVAC PLAN
I2	ELECTRIC PLAN
I3	LIGHTING & REFLECTED CEILING PLAN
I4	ELECTRIC DISTRIBUTION
I5	PLUMBING PLAN
SI-5	SPECIFICATIONS

Figure 9-3. The complete set of plans contains 15 sheets plus specifications. The Site Plan, Sheet 1, is not included in this study.

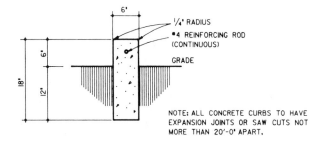

CONCRETE CURB DETAIL

SCALE: 1"=1'-0'

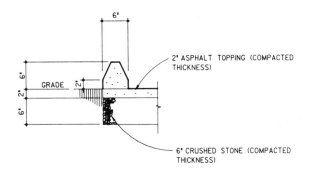

ASPHALT CURB DETAIL

SCALE: 1"=1'-0'

Figure 9-4. Details are required for curbs.

Concrete Curb Detail. The concrete curb is 6″ wide and 18″ high with 12″ of the curb below grade. A continuous #4 rebar is run horizontally through the curb and is generally centered in the 6″ portion of the curb above grade. Outside corners of exposed curb are rounded to ¼″ radius. All concrete curbs must have expansion joints or saw cuts not more than 20′-0″ apart. The concrete curb detail is drawn to the scale of 1″ = 1′-0″.

Asphalt Curb Detail. The asphalt curb detail is 6″ wide and 6″ high. It is placed on a 2″ asphalt topping (compacted thickness) over 6″ of crushed stone (compacted thickness). The profile view of the asphalt curb shows vertical walls extending 2″ from grade before sloping to meet the top surface of the curb. The asphalt curb detail is drawn to the scale of 1″ = 1′-0″.

Pavement Marker Details

Pavement markers are utilized to provide information to patrons and give directional information. Two pavement markers are shown. The upper plan gives dimensions for the PICK UP WINDOW and the lower plan shows dimensions for the EXIT ON-LY marker. Pavement marker details are drawn to the scale of ½″ = 1′-0″.

The PICK UP WINDOW pavement marker is triangular in shape with a 6′-0″ base and 30° sides. It is preceded by an 8″ × 4′-8″ rectangular bar placed 8″ in front of the triangle. Letters that are 8″ high are located in front of the rectangular bar. The EXIT ONLY pavement marker is similar to the PICK UP WINDOW marker and uses the same basic dimensions. Again, letters are 8″ high.

Trash Enclosure Plan

The plan, elevation, sections, and details for the trash enclosure occupy a large portion of Sheet 2. It is to be furnished and installed by the general contractor as specified in the note. The plan view is of primary importance as four sections (A/2, B/2, C/2, and H/2) and one elevation (Elevation 1) are taken from this view. One additional section (E/2) and five details (F/2, G/2, H/2, J/2, and K/2) are taken from these sections and elevation. The Trash Enclosure Plan is drawn to the scale of ¼″ = 1′-0″. See Figure 9-5.

The Trash Enclosure Plan has a 12′-0″ × 26′-0″ concrete slab as a base. It is 6″ thick and is reinforced with 6 × 6 wire mesh. The slab is sealed against grease absorption and slopes ¼″ per foot from back to front. Expansion joints are typical at each of the seven post footings. Corner posts are 6″ × 6″ and are set in 6″ from slab corners except at the front where they are set back 8′-0″. Wooden fences and gates are attached to the posts.

The trash storage area is separated from the grease barrel storage area by a wooden fence. Each area is accessible by a gate. The single gate for the grease barrel storage area is 3′-6″ wide. The double gate for the trash storage area is 10′-0″ wide.

Cutting planes for Sections A/2, B/2, C/2, and H/2 are denoted by circles containing these letters and numbers and cutting plane lines with triangular direction-of-sight arrows. The symbol denoting Elevation 1 is shown as the numeral 1 above a circle inscribed in a square. The numeral 2 inside the circle indicates that this elevation in located on Sheet 2. Direction-of-sight for Elevation 1, Sheet 2, is shown by the darkened upper corner of the square.

Section A/2. This section is taken from the Trash Enclosure Plan and shows details of the 12″ diameter concrete footings. These footings, which are 3′-0″ high, support the center posts. The tops of the round footings are flush with the top of the 6″ concrete slab. Both are 6″ above grade. Note the portion of the thickened concrete slab that is shown on the left side of the footing. Section B/2 shows that the slab is thickened to 12″.

A 6″ × 6″ treated cedar post is attached to the post base with four ⁵/₈″ diameter bolts. The 18″ high post base is shown as an isometric drawing in Detail F/2. Sides of the post base are bent ¼″ thick × 3″ wide plates. These are welded to a ¼″

× 6″ × 6″ plate. The plate is located 9″ from the bottom of the unit. The post base is pre-drilled for the ⁵/₈″ diameter bolts. Section A/2 is drawn to the scale of ³/₄″ = 1′-0″. Detail F/2 has no scale.

Section B/2. This section is taken from the Trash Enclosure Plan. It shows details of the thickened slab and the fence. The slab is thickened from 6″ to 12″ at its perimeter. The thickened portion extends 8″ horizontally before sloping up to the bottom of the slab. Wire mesh in the slab is indicated by the horizontal dashed line. A break line on the right side of the drawing indicates that the slab continues. The slab height is 6″ above grade.

The boards for the wooden fence are 1″ × 8″ rough-sawn cedar which is stained. These vertical boards are staggered on each side of 4″ × 4″ top-and-bottom cedar rails. The staggered boards are overlapped 1″ to prevent direct sight through the fence, which is 6′-6″ high above the concrete slab. Note that the bottom of the fence is 3″ above the concrete slab. The top rail is 4″ below the fence height and the bottom rail is 9″ above the concrete slab.

The cutting plane in Section B/2 refers to Section E/2. This section shows a portion of the fence as if viewed from above. The 8″ vertical cedar boards are denoted by the symbol for finish framing material. A 1″ overlap of boards is shown. Sections B/2 and E/2 are drawn to the scale of ³/₄″ = 1′-0″.

Section C/2. This section shows details of the concrete footings located at each corner of the slab and provides information on the steel tubing to which gate hinges are attached. The concrete footings at the corners are 12″ × 18″ × 36″. They extend 6″ above the concrete slab. Corner posts of 6″ × 6″ treated cedar are set into post bases as shown in Detail F/2. Additionally, a 3″ square steel tubing 9′-3″ long is set in each of the corner footings. Three hinges with removable pins are shop welded to the 3″ steel tubing. The note, "HOLD THIS DIMENSION," is critical to proper hanging of the gate which is aligned with the posts at the top. Section C/2 is drawn to the scale of ³/₄″ = 1′-0″.

Elevation 1. This elevation view provides basic information for constructing the gate. Specific width dimensions of the gate are shown in the plan view.

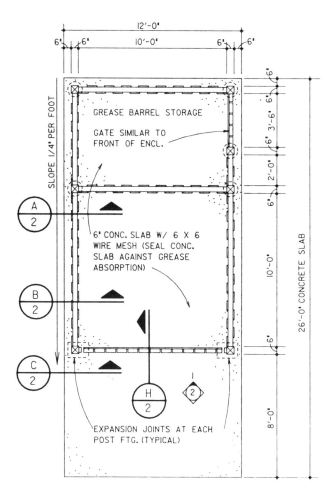

Figure 9-5. The trash enclosure allows placement of trash out of view.

Height dimensions are shown in Section C/2. The gate is basically 1″ square tubing shop welded with cross bracing. Plates are positioned behind all weld points. Rough-sawn 1″ × 8″ cedar boards 6′-4″ long are attached to the 1″ square tubing frame. A space of ½″ is specified between boards.

Detail G/2 shows the ⅜″ × 2″ × 2′-0″ steel gate arm that pivots on a ½″ diameter × 2½″ long square head bolt inserted through a 1⅜″ long sleeve. A ¼″ washer serves as a spacer to hold the gate arm off the gate boards.

Detail J/2 gives dimensions of the two open-top catches to receive the gate arm. These are made of ¼″ × 1″ wide steel plate and are bent as shown. A ½″ diameter sleeve maintains spacing of the open catch lip. The open catches are attached to the gate with ⅜″ diameter lag bolts.

Detail K/2 gives dimensions of the closed catch. It is similar in material and size to the open-top catches. Elevation 1 is drawn to the scale of ⅜″ = 1′-0″ and Details G/2, J/2, and K/2 are drawn to the scale of 3″ = 1′-0″.

Sign Details

These details provide information for the street sign(s) and the directional signs. The number of signs required is not specified on Sheet 2. This number is determined by the lot selected and their specific locations are detailed in the Site Plan, Sheet 1 (not included). See Figure 9-6.

Street Sign Detail. A wide variety of street signs are available for use. The particular sign(s) selected depends upon the location of the restaurant, the type of streets and roads in the area, and local ordinances. The details show the size of concrete foundations required for a two-pole sign with a 10″ standard steel pipe 23′-0″ long. The foundations, which are 3′-6″ × 3′-6″ × 6′-0″, are placed by the sign erector. The 10″ steel pipe is sunk to within 3″ of the bottom of the footing. Note that the footing extends ½″ above grade. The sign erector furnishes and sets the steel poles. The Street Sign Detail is drawn to the scale of ½″ = 1′-0″.

| READERBOARD | FEATUREBOARD | STAND-ALONE | ENTER, EXIT, OR PICK UP WINDOW |

STREET SIGNS   **DIRECTIONAL SIGN**

Figure 9-6. Street signs may include a readerboard, a featureboard, or may stand alone. Directional signs indicate traffic flow.

Directional Sign Detail. Directional signs are used to show traffic flow for entering and exiting the property and driving to the pick up window. The concrete foundation shown in the detail is 1'-0" × 1'-0" × 2'-6" deep. Again, the steel pipe is buried to within 3" of the bottom of the foundation and the top of the foundation is 1/2" above grade. The 2 1/2" standard steel pipe, which is 4'-6" long, is furnished and installed by the sign erector. The foundation is also placed by the sign erector. The Directional Sign Detail is drawn to the scale of 1" = 1'-0".

Exterior Pole Lights

The location and number of exterior pole lights is given on the Site Plan, Sheet 1 (not included). The detail shows that the general contractor is responsible for pouring the 18" diameter × 7'-0" tall concrete pier. The pier extends 2'-0" above grade and the top 1" is finished with 1" non-shrink grout with a smooth finish and 45° corners. The general contractor installs the anchor bolts which are supplied by the electrical contractor.

The steel pole, including the bottom plates and anchor bolts, is furnished by the electrical contractor who installs the pole. Mercury vapor floodlights and their required mountings are furnished and installed by the electrical contractor. The detail for Exterior Pole Lights is drawn to the scale of 1/2" = 1'-0".

Recommended Radius

This plan shows parking space size to be 10'-0" wide and 20'-0" long. The minimum radius is 18'-0". Location for the radius centerpoint is given. Note the 45° angle cut 3'-6" from the corner. The plan is drawn to the scale of 1/4" = 1'-0".

Handicap-Delivery Ramp

Plan dimensions are given for a ramp that may be used by handicapped individuals or for delivery of goods. The run of the 4'-0" wide ramp is 4'-0". A 1'-0" minimum taper is specified on each side of the ramp. Location and construction details must meet local requirements, and field verification is specified. The Handicap-Delivery Ramp is drawn to the scale of 1/2" = 1'-0".

Paver Detail

This detail shows a 2" to 12" coarse granular base that varies with the site. A 1 1/2" bedding course is placed over the base. Pavers with sand filled joints are placed on the bedding course. Pavers are 3 1/8" thick. There is no scale for the Paver Detail.

FOUNDATION PLAN, SHEET 3

The Foundation Plan gives complete horizontal dimensions for the foundation. Overall dimensions of the building are 38'-2 3/4" × 90'-5". All footings are 19" × 8" with two #4 rebars run continuously, unless otherwise noted. Footing depths must be verified to comply with local code requirements. All brick coursing begins 8" below the top of the 4" floor slab. Reinforcement for the floor slab consists of 6 × 6—W1.4 × W1.4 WWF placed on concrete blocks. The floor slab elevation is 100.00'. Footings are designed for 3,000 PSF soil-bearing pressure. Local soil-bearing capacity must be verified before footings are placed.

Plumbing runs are not shown on the foundation plan. Refer to Plumbing Plan, Sheet 15. The location for conduit runs are shown on the Electrical Plan, Sheet 12. Concrete pad locations are shown in Detail C/3. Three #4 rebars, 24" long, are placed through all door openings as indicated. The concrete slab is then poured through the openings. A control joint is centered on the wall at all door openings.

Foundation walls are either 8" or 10" concrete blocks as shown in the various section views referred to on the Foundation Plan, Sheet 3. Four cutting planes refer to Sections A, B, C, and D shown on Sheet 7A. Four additional cutting planes refer to Sections E, F, G, and H shown on Sheet 7B. The Foundation Plan, Sheet 3, is drawn to the scale of 1/4" = 1'-0".

Section A, Sheet 7A

This section is taken from a cutting plane through a wall of the Public Area, Room 101, as designated in the Room Finish Schedule, Sheet 4. Cutting plane A/7A is shown on the Foundation Plan, Sheet 3, and the Floor Plan, Sheet 4.

Section A, Sheet 7A, shows a foundation footing 1'-4" wide with two #4 rebars run continuously and an 8" concrete block foundation wall. A 4" concrete block is faced with three courses of brick above the

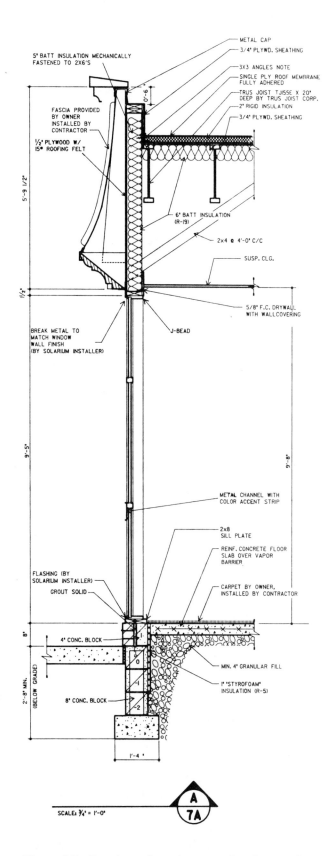

5' BATT INSULATION MECHANICALLY
FASTENED TO 2X6'S

METAL CAP
3/4" PLYWD. SHEATHING

3X3 ANGLES NOTE

SINGLE PLY ROOF MEMBRANE
FULLY ADHERED

FASCIA PROVIDED
BY OWNER
INSTALLED BY
CONTRACTOR

TRUS JOIST TJI55E X 20"
DEEP BY TRUS JOIST CORP.

2" RIGID INSULATION

3/4" PLYWD. SHEATHING

1/2' PLYWOOD W/
15# ROOFING FELT

6' BATT INSULATION
(R-19)

2x4 @ 4'-0" C/C

SUSP. CLG.

5/8" F.C. DRYWALL
WITH WALLCOVERING

BREAK METAL TO
MATCH WINDOW
WALL FINISH
(BY SOLARIUM INSTALLER)

J-BEAD

METAL CHANNEL WITH
COLOR ACCENT STRIP

2x8
SILL PLATE

REINF. CONCRETE FLOOR
SLAB OVER VAPOR
BARRIER

CARPET BY OWNER,
INSTALLED BY CONTRACTOR

FLASHING (BY
SOLARIUM INSTALLER)

GROUT SOLID

4' CONC. BLOCK

MIN. 4" GRANULAR FILL

1" "STYROFOAM"
INSULATION (R-5)

8" CONC. BLOCK

SCALE: 3/4" = 1'-0"

A
7A

Figure 9-7. Exterior wall sections are taken from cutting planes shown on the Foundation Plan and Floor Plan.

uppermost 8″ concrete block in the foundation wall. Anchor bolts are placed for attaching the 2″ × 8″ sill plate. After the foundation footings are poured and the foundation wall is laid, 1″ Styrofoam insulation (R-5) is placed inside the foundation walls to the bottom of the second 8″ block. Granular fill is then backfilled in the trench and spread to a minimum depth of 4″ to serve as a base for the concrete floor slab.

The 9′-5″ window wall resting on the sill plate is flashed by the solarium installer. The wall section above the window wall is framed and filled with 6″ batt insulation (R-19). Steel supporting the roof structure is shown and roofing materials and flashing are noted. The fascia above the window wall is provided by the owner and installed by the contractor. This fascia extends 5′-9¹⁄₂″.

Reinforcement is shown in the concrete floor slab, which is placed over a vapor barrier. Note that the owner provides the carpet, which is installed by the contractor. See Figure 9-7. This section, and similar sections, will be referenced by various trades as it shows information required by concrete workers, carpenters, glaziers, cement finishers, carpet installers, drywallers, steel erectors, and roofing workers. Section A, Sheet 7A, is drawn to the scale of ³⁄₄″ = 1′-0″.

Section B, Sheet 7A

This section is taken from cutting planes on the Foundation Plan, Sheet 3, and the Floor Plan, Sheet 4. The section shows the solarium area of Room 101. The use of a solarium brings natural light into the restaurant and expands floor space for patrons. The Left and Right Side Elevations, Sheet 5, also show the solarium. Note that the solarium is the same height as the window walls shown in Sections A and C, Sheet 7A. It extends 5′-7⁷⁄₈″ past the exterior wall and is provided by the owner and installed by the solarium installer. See Figure 9-8.

Details above the solarium are similar to details shown in Sections A and C, Sheet 7A. The fascia is the same. Space is provided above the suspended ceiling and below the roof joists to run ductwork to this portion of the building.

A 6³⁄₄″ × 36″ × 36′-8″ Glulam (glued-and-laminated) beam supports the structure above the solarium. This is also shown in Section G, Sheet 7B. The Foundation Plan, Sheet 3, shows the footings required for the beam support. Section B, Sheet 7A, is drawn to the scale of ³⁄₄″ = 1′-0″.

Section C, Sheet 7A

This section is taken from cutting planes through the exterior wall at the customer entrance door. It is shown on the Foundation Plan, Sheet 3, and the Floor Plan, Sheet 4. Notice that the concrete floor slab is thickened to provide additional load capacity at this entrance. The Foundation Plan, Sheet 3, shows the 8″ thickened slab extending 5′-11½″ from the outside of the foundation wall and running 9′-8¾″ along the foundation wall. Notes specifying details above the ceiling are similar to those given for Sections A and B, Sheet 7A.

The door is only shown to scale in this section. Its location and swing are shown on the Floor Plan, Sheet 4, and additional information is given in the Door And Hardware Schedule, Sheet 4. Section C, Sheet 7A, is drawn to the scale of ¾″ = 1′-0″.

Section D, Sheet 7A

The cutting plane for this section is shown on the Foundation Plan, Sheet 3, and the Floor Plan, Sheet 4. The cutting plane is taken through the counter portion of the Serving Area, Room 106. Sheet 9 lists all equipment on the Equipment Schedule and shows its location on the Equipment Plan.

Features of primary importance shown in this section are the raised concrete pad shown in plan view at C/3 and in a detailed elevation in E/3 and the dropped soffit area over the counter. Details are shown for framing the soffit and applying ⅝″ Firecode drywall to be covered with vinyl wallcover. The light in the soffit is an F-1 fixture. Nineteen

Figure 9-8. Solariums expand space and provide natural light.

of these recessed ceiling lights are specified on the Lighting And Reflected Ceiling Plan, Sheet 13.

The beam supporting the roof joists is made of three 1¾″ × 16″ members. Batt insulation 6″ thick (R-19) is shown and roofing information is repeated. Section D, Sheet 7A, is drawn to the scale of ¾″ = 1′-0″.

Section E, Sheet 7B

The cutting plane for this section is taken through the exterior wall at the pick-up window. This cutting plane is shown on the Foundation Plan, Sheet 3, and the Floor Plan, Sheet 4. The dimensions for vertical location of the pick-up window are of primary interest in this section. Window size given is 6′-0″ × 4′-8″ with a note to "SEE SPECS." Division 8, Doors, Windows and Glass, gives additional information. This window unit is to be a sliding glass door as manufactured by the Tubelite Corporation. It contains ⅝″ insulated glass, medium bronze color, and acrylic finish. The window is also shown on the Left Side Elevation, Sheet 5. A 4″ stone sill on the exterior and a white marble sill on the interior are shown.

Three 2 × 6s with ½″ plywood spacers form the window header and a 3½″ × 5½″ × 5/16″ steel angle serves as a lintel for the face brick. Note the use of the double soldier courses above the window and the single soldier course at the top of the wall. These are also shown in the Left Side Elevation, Sheet 5.

The inside of this wall is ⅝″ Firecode drywall covered with a laminated wall covering, which is detailed in the Specifications. The quarry tile floor and base are shown. Insulation for the wall is 6″ batt (R-19). The suspended ceiling is 9′-0″ above the finished floor. Section E, Sheet 7B, is drawn to the scale of ¾″ = 1′-0″.

Section F, Sheet 7B

The cutting plane for this section is shown on the Foundation Plan, Sheet 3, and the Floor Plan, Sheet 4. It is taken through the partition between the Serving Area, Room 106, and the serving line which is in the Public Area, Room 101.

A 2′-0″ × 2′-0″ × 13′-0″ concrete footing with three #5 rebars run continuously near the bottom of the footing and three #5 rebars run continuously at a higher level in the footing are indicated in the section view. The concrete floor slab is thickened to 8″ above the footing. The sill plate for the partition is secured with 3/4″ anchor bolts at 3′-4″ OC. Two hold downs are anchored into the concrete footing and bolted to the wall studs at each end of the partition. Hold downs may be used for transferring tension loads between floors, tying purlins to masonry, etc. They provide strong ties for securing wood walls to concrete or masonry. A large variety of hold downs are available for different applications. See Figure 9-9.

HOLD DOWNS

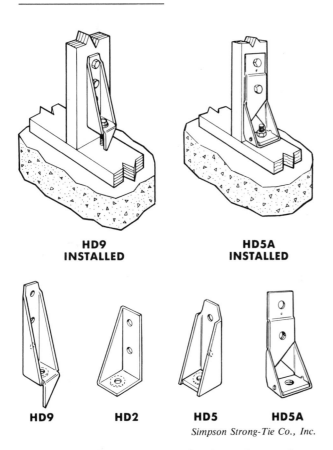

HD9 INSTALLED   HD5A INSTALLED

HD9   HD2   HD5   HD5A

Simpson Strong-Tie Co., Inc.

Figure 9-9. Hold downs are used to tie wooden members to concrete, masonry, or wood.

The partition in this section view is framed with 2 × 6s on 16″ centers. On the employee side of the partition, 5/8″ plywood is nailed with 10d nails at 3″ along panel sides to provide support for shelves that will be hung. The plywood is finished with a laminated wall covering. Note that the suspended ceiling heights are not the same on both sides of the partition. Section F, Sheet 7B, is drawn to the scale of 3/4″ = 1′-0″.

Section G, Sheet 7B

The cutting plane for this section view is shown on the Foundation Plan, Sheet 3, and the Floor Plan, Sheet 4. The primary purpose of this section view is to show the increased foundation footing and doubled wall required to carry the 6 3/4″ × 36″ × 36′-8″ Glulam beam which spans the distance between the two footings on opposite sides of the building.

The concrete foundation footing is 5′-0″ square and 1′-4″ high. It is reinforced with six #5 rebars each way. Concrete blocks for the doubled foundation wall are 10″ blocks set to give 2′-2 1/2″ wall thickness. Styrofoam insulation 1″ thick (R-5) is applied to the inside of the outer foundation wall.

Hold down anchors with two 3/4″ diameter through bolts and one 3/4″ diameter anchor bolt are embedded into the outer foundation wall and attached to the outer framed wall. Studs for this outer wall are 2 × 6s on 16″ centers with 1/2″ plywood sheathing attached with 10d nails spaced 4″ apart at panel ends and 12″ apart at intermediate supports. Face brick is laid and secured to the wall with corrugated masonry wall ties at 16″ OC vertically and horizontally. The wall ties are staggered. The double soldier course and single soldier course are shown.

The inside portion of the wall is secured to the foundation wall in the same manner as the outside wall. This is a brick wall and additional insulation is not specified. A prefabricated, prefinished, metal cap finishes off the top. This is supplied and installed by the sign supplier. Section G, Sheet 7B, is drawn to the scale of 3/4″ = 1′-0″.

Section H, Sheet 7B

This section is taken through the main wall along the rear of the building separating the Storage Area, Room 110, and the Cooler-Freezer, Room 107, from the remainder of the building. The Right Side, Left Side, and Rear Elevations, Sheet 5, show the storage module which is provided by the owner and installed by the general contractor. The primary purpose of this section view is to show the special treatment required for the concrete slab beneath the module and the wall detail.

The concrete floor slab is turned down (recessed) $5^{1}/_{2}$" to form an 8" wide bottom. One #4 rebar is run continuously through the turn down. The cooler-freezer slab is sloped $^{1}/_{2}$" from the edge of the building.

The header over the opening is three 2 × 10s with 1" plywood spacers. A $3^{1}/_{2}$" × 6" × $^{5}/_{16}$" steel angle is utilized to support and carry loads. The 2" × 6" stud wall at 16" OC is insulated with 6" batt insulation (R-19). The end of the truss joist is shown and roofing information is repeated. A metal cap is placed over the 2" × 10" top plate. Face brick is secured to the wall with corrugated metal wall ties fastened to the $^{1}/_{2}$" plywood sheathing, which is attached to wall studs with 18d nails on 6" centers at the panel edges. The cant strip for the transition of the rear building wall to the cooler-freezer roof is shown. Scuppers and downspouts are painted to match the ice box. Section H, Sheet 7B, is drawn to the scale of $^{3}/_{4}$" = 1'-0".

Safe Anchor, Detail A, Sheet 3

No cutting plane is shown to reference this detail. However, the note with the detail, "SEE SHEET 9, ITEM 70" indicates that the safe is a part of the Office Desk Assembly, Item 70. Item 69, Safe and File Cabinets, refers back to the Safe Anchor, Detail A, Sheet 3. A study of the plans shows that the office, Room 109, contains a symbol denoting reference to Interior Elevation 26, Sheet 6. This elevation view shows the safe as part of Item 70, Office Desk Assembly.

The primary purpose of Safe Anchor, Detail A, Sheet 3, is to show the tapered 12" × 12" cutout in the safe floor and the $^{7}/_{8}$" lag bolt, which is furnished with the safe, used to secure the unit. The Safe Anchor, Detail A, Sheet 3, is drawn to the scale of $1^{1}/_{2}$" = 1'-0".

Brass Post Anchor, Detail B, Sheet 3

This detail is referenced with the note, "SEE DETAIL B/3" on the Floor Plan, Sheet 4. The brass posts and wood railings are used to regulate patron traffic flow to the serving area. The detail shows that a 3'-0" long steel liner tube is embedded into the concrete floor slab, which is pocketed to receive the liner tube. The brass post is placed over the liner tube and secured to the floor by the floor flange. The railing is 3'-0" above the floor. Brass Post An-

chor, Detail B, Sheet 3, is drawn to the scale of $^{3}/_{4}$" = 1'-0".

Raised Concrete Pad, Plan C, Sheet 3

There is no specific reference in the set of plans for this particular plan view. However, a study of the Foundation Plan, Sheet 3, the Floor Plan, Sheet 4, Interior Elevations, Sheet 6, and the Equipment Plan, Sheet 9, locates this plan in the serving area, Room 106. The primary purpose of this plan is to show the raised concrete pads with the quarry tile base on which various counters and pieces of cooking equipment are placed. Note that quarry tile laid on the raised pads is placed diagonally. Also note that the pad height varies from 4" to 6" above the finished floor. Notes differentiate pad height and dimensions specify pad lengths and widths. When pouring the raised pads, allowance must be made for tile thickness. All measurements are to and from finished surfaces and all curbs must be level and square. The Raised Concrete Pad, Plan C, Sheet 3, is drawn to the scale of $^{1}/_{4}$" = 1'-0".

Detail E, Sheet 3. This detail is referenced by the cutting plane shown in the Raised Concrete Pad, Plan C, Sheet 3. The main item shown in this detail is the $^{5}/_{8}$" moisture-resistant plywood that extends 12" up the wall from the floor line. Two 4'-0" sections of $^{5}/_{8}$" drywall are placed above the moisture-resistant plywood. This detail is typical of all walls where drywall is used. Detail E, Sheet 3, is drawn to the scale of $^{3}/_{4}$" = 1'-0".

Brick Recess On Piers, Detail D, Sheet 3

Pier foundation footings are utilized to provide structural strength to carry the Glulam beam shown in Wall Section G, Sheet 7B, and referenced on the Foundation Plan, Sheet 3, and the Floor Plan, Sheet 4. The reference to the plan view for the Brick Recess On Piers, Detail D, Sheet 3, is given on the Floor Plan, Sheet 4. A note on the Left Side Elevation, Sheet 5, also references this detail by stating "RECESS BRICK 2" IN INDENTED AREA AS SHOWN, SEE DETAIL D/3." The plan detail shows that over the 4'-0" width, the bricks are indented 2" for a distance of 2'-8" centered on the space. The Brick Recess On Piers, Detail D, Sheet 3, is drawn to the scale of $^{3}/_{4}$" = 1'-0".

STRUCTURAL PLAN, SHEET 8

This plan shows placement of steel to support the roof and provide for wide expanses of open space in the building. The design load is based upon 30 PSI live load and 15 PSI dead load for a total load of 45 PSI.

Load Detail, C/8, gives information for loads exceeding 250 pounds on each side of the bottom flange of joists at 5'-0" OC provided the load is included in normal design loads. This detail also specifies that the contractor is responsible for nailing filler blocks (blocking panels) to the truss joist webs. The List of Accessories, Sheet 8, calls for 52 24" OC blocking panels and ten 36" OC blocking panels. R1, R2, and R3 truss joists are specified for the roof. See Figure 9-10.

R1 truss joists are to bear on the back wall and the center wall. The center wall, as shown in the Foundation Plan, Sheet 3, is 8" concrete block for 4'-0". Section F, Sheet 7B, then shows a 2" × 6" stud-bearing wall on 16" centers. This same portion of wall is shown on the Structural Plan, Sheet 8. Two bearing studs on each side of Door F (refer to the Floor Plan, Sheet 4) support a header made of three 2 × 10s. Over the serving area, three 1¾" × 16" × 15'-0" Micro=Lam® beams are nailed together to span the opening and support the truss joists. The Micro=Lam® beams are nailed together with a minimum of two 18d nails per foot, fully penetrating at least two pieces of lumber unless otherwise noted. The Micro=Lam® beam is supported by three bearing studs at each end. The top of the beam is placed 11'-7¹³/₁₆" AFF (above the finished floor) with equal bearing at both ends. Section D, Sheet 7A, shows the Micro=Lam® beam in end view and a longitudinal TJI 55E truss joist bearing on it. The height of the beam from the finished floor is repeated and ¼" plywood spacers are specified.

R1 truss joists are specified in the Material List And Engineering Specs, Sheet 8. These joists are 20" deep and 36'-0" long. Eighteen R1 truss joists are required. The total lineal feet of R1 truss joists is 648 lineal feet. The designation "R1" in large letters is located in the center of the back portion of the building, indicating location of R1 truss joists. The adjacent note, "20" TJI 55E, 18 REQ.," repeats information given in the Material List And Engineering Specs, Sheet 8, to clearly show specific joist placement.

TRUSS JOISTS

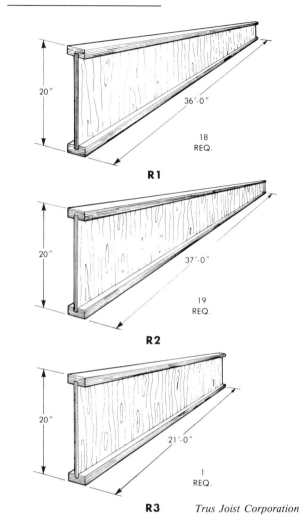

Figure 9-10. Trus Joist Corporation's TJI 55E truss joists are specified in Wendy's Restaurant Plans.

R1 joist bearing detail for the back wall is shown in Section H, Sheet 7B. Note the typical use of web stiffeners. The List Of Accessories, Sheet 8, specifies a quantity of one hundred fifty-two 20" web stiffeners. R1 joist bearing detail for the center wall is shown in Detail F, Sheet 7B. Again, web stiffeners are noted.

R2 truss joists are used in the front portion of the building as specified by the designation "R2" which is shown on the Structural Plan, Sheet 8. The note, "20" TJI 55E, 19 REQ." assures proper placement. R2 truss joists are 37'-0" in length and 19 are required for a total of 703 lineal feet.

R2 truss joists at the front of the building bear on the 6¾" × 36" × 36'-8" Glulam beam, which spans the width of the building. Section G, Sheet 7B, shows the end views of the joists bearing on the Glulam beam. Section B, Sheet 7A, shows a longitudinal section of an R2 truss joist (specified by the note, "20″ TJI 55E @ 24″ WITH 3-10D TOE NAILS") and a line indicated as "BOTTOM OF BEAM." The distance between the bottom of the joist and bottom of the beam scales out to 3′-0″, the height of the Glulam beam. The center wall supports the other end of the R2 joists as shown in Section D, Sheet 7A, and Section F, Sheet 7B.

One R3 truss joist is required in the Material List And Engineering Specs, Sheet 8. This joist is 20″ deep and 21′-0″ long. It is placed parallel to R1 and R2 joists along the lower side of the building. This joist rests on the center wall and the small exterior return wall for the pick-up window area.

All roof joists slope 13″ from the front of the building to the back of the building. Header, Detail B, Sheet 8, shows how joist hangers are used for 2× headers at rough openings in the roof. The rough openings designated as "R.O." on the Structural Plan, Sheet 8, shows two layers of ⁵/₈″ Firecode drywall to finish out the openings. Mechanical curbs extend the roof openings above roof height. Specific location and size dimensions for each rough opening is given. The HVAC Plan, Sheet 11, specifies the equipment to be installed on the roof over each rough opening. For example, exhaust fans are to be installed over the 28¹/₂″ × 28¹/₂″ rough openings and the main HVAC unit (RT-2) is to be installed on the roof over the dining area. Note that this unit's weight (2,240 lbs.) is spread over five joists. Ice machine compressor rails are shown tied to the roof steel.

The Right, Left, and Front Elevations, Sheet 5, specify an opaque (not transparent) mansard roof panel to be provided by the owner and installed by the general contractor. This fascia can also be seen in Sections A, B, and C, Sheet 7A. Note that the diagonal 2 × 4s @ 4′-0″ OC are called out by two notes on the Structural Plan, Sheet 8. This plan is drawn to the scale of ¹/₄″ = 1′-0″.

FLOOR PLAN, SHEET 4

Sheet 4 contains the Floor Plan, Room Finish Schedule, Door And Hardware Schedule, Door Elevations, Door Detail A, Corner Detail B, and General Notes. This sheet is used as a base sheet for studying particular details, which are referenced and shown on other sheets.

The Floor Plan, Sheet 4, contains overall dimensions of the building (38′-2³/₄″ × 90′-5″), location dimensions of partitions (the partition separating Room 106 and Room 108 is 24′-7″ from the rear wall), and size dimensions (the wall between Rooms 106 and 108 is 19′-4⁵/₈″ long). Cutting plane references (A/7A) refer to wall section views on Sheets 7A and 7B, and other references (6/14) refer to interior elevations on Sheet 6. Room numbers (100) are given in a rectangular box and doors (A) are identified by a letter in a circle. See Figure 9-11.

Specific notes such as "SEATING COUNTER BY OWNER" provide additional information. All objects above 5′-0″ are shown with dashed lines.

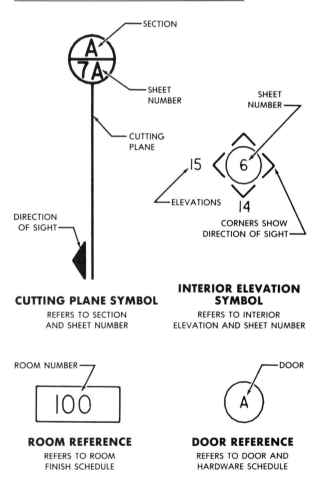

Figure 9-11. Reference symbols on the floor plan refer to specific views and schedules.

For example, the furred-down ceiling above the front counter in Room 106 is shown with dashed lines as the bottom is 8'-0" above the floor.

The Room Finish Schedule, Sheet 4, designates a specific number for each space shown on the plans. Floor, base, wall, ceiling, trim, and door finishes are given. Nine specific notes are referenced in the Room Finish Schedule and specific instructions are given. The Door And Hardware Schedule, Sheet 4, designates a specific letter for each door shown on the plans. Door location and swing are given on the plans and the schedule provides additional information on door size, type, frame, hinges, latch-catches, and accessories. Nine specific notes are also referenced in the Door And Hardware Schedule. Door Elevations, Sheet 4, contains letters identifying door types and notes and dimensions clarifying details.

General Notes, Sheet 4, are as follows:
1. All partitions not dimensioned are 3½" wood studs. (Metal studs may be used, all dimensions must be adjusted.)
2. Provide blocking as required in frame walls.
3. Rigid roof insulation is fiberboard—not foam.
4. Exterior dimensions are from out to out of masonry or plywood sheathing.
5. Interior dimensions are from face to face of framing or from face of masonry to face of framing.

The order of study for the floor plan is to relate the Exterior Elevations, Sheet 5, to the Floor Plan, Sheet 4, and then look at each room on the plan in the order designated in the Room Schedule and relate schedules, interior elevations, equipment, HVAC, electrical, reflected ceiling, and plumbing information as they apply to the particular room. This method presents a solid overview of the plans and allows the printreader to relate the work of various trades into the finished product. Additional study of specific plans is, of course, required for the actual construction.

Front Elevation, Sheet 5

The overall length dimension for this elevation is 38'-2¾" as shown on the Floor Plan, Sheet 4. The solarium and the opaque mansard roof panels, which are the main features of this elevation, are framed by the brick corners of the supporting structure for the Glulam beam. The solarium is to be installed by its manufacturer. The sign manufacturer

will fabricate a 6" red strip which will be installed by the general contractor.

Face brick is the exterior finish material with a double soldier course 7'-8" above the finish floor area and a single soldier course at the top of the wall. Height dimensions, which apply to this view, are obtained from the Left Side Elevation, Sheet 5. The overall height from the finished floor is 15'-8".

The awning and wrought iron railing on the Front Elevation are shown on the Left Side Elevation. Dashed lines show the foundation footings and walls. Refer to Wall Section B, Sheet 7A, and Wall Section G, Sheet 7B, for specific foundation dimensions. The Front Elevation, Sheet 5, is drawn to the scale of ¼" = 1'-0". See Figure 9-12.

Right Side Elevation, Sheet 5

The overall length dimension for this elevation is 90'-5" as shown on the Floor Plan, Sheet 4. The total height of the back half of the building is 15'-4" above the finished floor. This is 4" lower than the total height at the front of the building.

The end view of the solarium shown in the Front Elevation, Sheet 5, is shown and the note concerning the 6" red strip is repeated. Notice that this strip continues across the tempered glass area in this elevation and the Left Side Elevation, Sheet 5. Division 8 of the Specifications states that the storefront system (tempered glass) shall be by the solarium manufacturers using the same material and finish. The standard vertical glass is to be ⅝" double sealed insulated glass with ⅛" tempered bronze tinted on the outboard light and ⅛" tempered clear glass on the inboard light. This glass is also utilized for the storefront on the Left Side Elevation.

The note, "FACEBRICK—SEE SPECS" refers to Division 4, Masonry Specifications, where complete information is given for all masonry work. The particular face brick to be used is not given; however, directions for mortar mix, weather, conditions, method of laying, tying, cleaning, and painting are stated. Note the continuation of the single and double soldier courses, which appear on all sides of the building.

Five K-4 light fixtures are centered in the double soldier course. Location dimensions show horizontal spacing of these fixtures. The Lighting And Reflected Ceiling Plan, Sheet 13, specifies a mounting height of 8'-4" above the finished floor. Nine K-4 fixtures, as detailed in the Lighting Fixture Schedule,

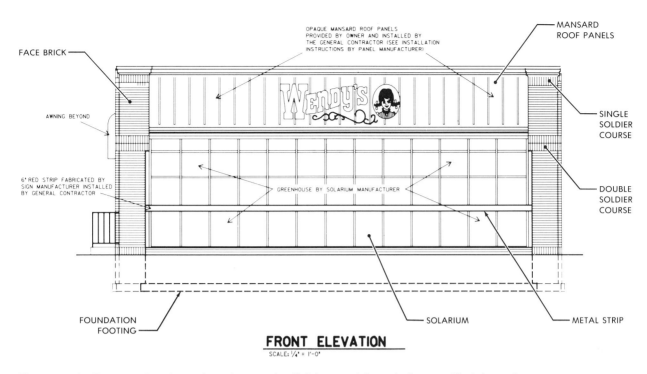

FRONT ELEVATION
SCALE: 1/4" = 1'-0"

Figure 9-12. Exterior elevations show the exterior finish materials and give specific information.

Sheet 13, are required. These are furnished with 100-watts/lamp, incandescent bulbs with white glass globes and standard fixture color and finish.

The dashed lines connecting five K-4 fixtures on this side of the building show that they are on the same circuit. The solid line terminated by an arrowhead and including the note "2A" indicates a home run for Circuit 2 to Panel A. See Figure 9-13. The schedule for Electric Panels, Sheet 14, shows that Panel A is a 225A, 120/208V, 3ϕ panel. Circuit 2 is specified for "Right Side Building Lights." This is

a 20A, 1ϕ circuit controlled by a single-pole CB. Conductors are run in 3/4" conduit.

The remaining light fixture shown on the Right Side Elevation, Sheet 5, is a K-3 fixture. This fixture throws light to the rear of the property and is also shown on the Rear Elevation, Sheet 5. Note that this fixture is mounted on top of the wall. Two K-3 fixtures are required for the building. These HP sodium fixtures contain 100-watt bulbs for floodlight use and are photocell operated. Circuit 6, Panel A, is a 20A, 1ϕ circuit. Conductors are run in 3/4" conduit and protected by a 20A, single-pole CB.

Additional items shown on the Right Side Elevation, Sheet 5, include the entrance vestibule door, sidewalk, outline of storage module, and foundation footings and walls. The Right Side Elevation, Sheet 5, is drawn to the scale of 1/4" = 1'-0".

Rear Elevation, Sheet 5

The overall length of this view is 38'-2 3/4". This is obtained by adding 4'-6", 30'-8", 2'-8 3/4", and 4" as shown on the Floor Plan, Sheet 4. The height of the rear wall is 15'-4". The main feature of this view is the note, "STORAGE MODULE TO BE PROVIDED BY OWNER AND INSTALLED BY

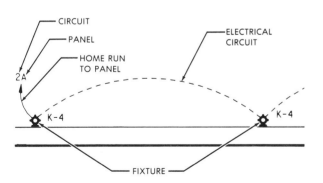

Figure 9-13. Dashed lines tie fixtures together in an electrical circuit. Solid lines show home runs to panels.

THE GENERAL CONTRACTOR.'' Division 6 of the Specifications states,

> Placement of pre-fabricated, walk-in freezer shall be part of this contract. Unit will be supplied by owners and will be shipped direct to store location with all uncrating and erection done by Contractor. Unit will be shipped with hardware and instructions. Installation of refrigeration to be done by Refrigeration Contractor and electrical hook-up by Electrical Contractor.

The door supplied with the Storage Module is shown. It has a viewer centered in the upper portion. A concrete ramp is specified. Electrical and plumbing work for the Storage Module are detailed in the discussion of Rooms 107 and 110. Other items on the Rear Elevation, Sheet 5, include the awning, fixed glass of the pick-up window, and the wrought iron railing shown in the Left Side Elevation, Sheet 5. Two K-3 light fixtures are mounted on top of the wall.

Two 16″ wide × 6″ deep × 9″ high scuppers with 4″ × 4″ downspouts are located on the rear wall with downspouts running over the Storage Module roof and down to grade. Additional information is given in Division 7 of the Specifications. The Rear Elevation, Sheet 5, is drawn to the scale of 1/4″ = 1′-0″.

Left Side Elevation, Sheet 5

The overall length for this view is 90′-5″ as shown on the Floor Plan, Sheet 4. Overall height at the front of the building is 15′-8″ above the finished floor level and overall height at the rear of the building is 15′-4″. Major features of this elevation are the tempered glass (storefront) with Exit Door K, the wrought iron railing, sidewalk, pick-up window with awning above, and exterior light fixtures.

The wrought iron railing is complete with newel posts, corners, flanged hose shoe and fittings. The design is 1/2″ square bars, alternately straight and twisted, on 6″ centers. The top rail and newel post are of standard design. Samples must be submitted to the owner for approval before installation. Division 8 of the Specifications states,

> Drive-thru window to be sliding glass door as manufactured by Tubelite Corporation, with 5/8″ insulated glass, medium bronze color and acrylic finish.

This is a 6′-0″ × 4′-8″ window as shown in Wall Section E, Sheet 7B.

A one-piece canvas dome awning is located above the pick-up window. The awning is 10′-0″ long, 4′-0″ high, and extends 3′-8 3/4″ from the back exterior side wall. The bottom of the awning is 8′-0″ above finished grade.

A junction box for two K-1 light fixtures is located above the pick up window. These are 60-watts/lamp, fluorescent fixtures, 4′ long connected end-to-end beneath the awning. Tube guards are provided. Conductors for K-1 light fixtures are run in 3/4″ conduit and are on Circuit 4, Panel A.

One K-2 light fixture is mounted on top of the wall above the pick-up window. This fixture is on the same circuit (6A) as the K-3 floodlights. The K-2 light fixture provides 50 watts/lamp and is photocell operated.

Four K-4 light fixtures are mounted on the exterior wall at the same height as the K-4 fixtures on the Right Side Elevation, Sheet 5. Dimensions are given for horizontal spacing of these fixtures. K-4 fixtures are on Circuit 4A, which is run in 3/4″ conduit. These incandescent lamps provide 100 watts each and are protected with white glass globes.

Additional features of this elevation are the foundation footings and walls, the note indicating the prefinished metal cap, and the note calling for recessed brick near the front corner. The Left Side Elevation, Sheet 5, is drawn to the scale of 1/4″ = 1′-0″.

Vestibule, Room 100, Sheet 4

The vestibule provides an entryway for customers. Two entry doors are utilized to help maintain an even temperature in the building. No interior elevations are shown for the vestibule. The size of the vestibule is not specifically given, although overall size (including walls) is 5′-8 3/4″ × 9′-0″.

Room Finish Schedule, Room 100, Sheet 4. The vestibule floor is finished with decorative tile set in a common bond pattern parallel to the front of the building. Wall finish is not specifically noted in the schedule although baseboard is to be decorative tile. Ceiling height for the vestibule is 9′-0″. The ceiling is acoustical tile.

Door And Hardware Schedule, Room 100, Sheet 4. Two doors are shown on the Floor Plan, Sheet 4, for the vestibule. The A door, which is 3′-0″ × 7′-0″, has an aluminum frame and tempered glass.

It is a keyed lock, self-closing door with push-pull bars, a panic lock, and door stop. A threshold is provided with the door. The A door is pivot-hinged.

The B door is also a $3'-0'' \times 7'-0''$ aluminum-framed, tempered-glass door. It is similar to the A door except that it is not keyed and does not have panic hardware and a threshold.

HVAC Plan, Sheet 11. This plan shows one $10''$ diameter duct from HVAC unit RT-2 supplying the diffuser in the vestibule. The C inside the hexagon refers to the Air Device Schedule, Sheet 11. C diffusers have an $8''$ neck and supply 100–200 cubic feet of air per minute. The 100 inside the hexagon gives CFM (cubic feet per minute) of this particular diffuser, which is a lay-in type used for supply. The diffuser and round neck are off-white.

Lighting and Reflected Ceiling Plan, Sheet 13. The supply air diffuser is shown in the reflected ceiling by two intersecting diagonal lines inside a square and the letters "SA." Return air is shown on this plan by one diagonal line inside a square. See Figure 9-14.

Incandescent light fixture F-1 is shown. These recessed, gold fixtures provide 75 watts per lamp. Supply conductors are two #12s with ground in $3/4''$ conduit. The F-1 light fixture in the vestibule

is on Circuit 5A, which is a 20A circuit protected by a single-pole CB. This circuit also supplies some of the dining room lights. Note: Recessed light fixtures must be thermally protected or insulated-covered type to protect the insulation of the fixture wiring.

Public Area, Room 101, Sheet 4

The Public Area is the largest single area in the building. It provides seating for 98 customers who are served by a 12-person crew. Basically, this area is $41'-10'' \times 33'-6^{1}/_{2}''$ including vestibule, salad bar, and serving areas.

A soffit is dropped to $7'-10^{1}/_{2}''$ above the finished floor to partially separate the solarium dining area from the remaining dining area. Coordinated wall, floor, and ceiling finishes are complimented by functional and attractive furniture placed for maximum use. Accessories and plants compliment and add to the decor. The Room Finish Schedule, Sheet 4, and the Door And Hardware Schedule, Sheet 4, detail finishes. Six interior elevations show details of the public area. These are Elevations 1, 2, 3, 4, 5, and 6 of Sheet 6. All interior elevations are drawn to the scale of $1/4'' = 1'-0''$. The Equipment Plan, Sheet 9, HVAC Plan, Sheet 11, Electric Plan, Sheet 12, Lighting and Reflected Ceiling Plan, Sheet 13, and Plumbing Plan, Sheet 15, give specific information for various tradesworkers.

Room Finish Schedule, Sheet 4. The floor of the public area is finished with carpet from a point beginning near door B and following a line around the seating counter to Door C. The note "CARPET" is specified and the line shows the break between carpet and decorative tile that covers the remainder of the floor in Room 101. Decorative tile is installed in a common bond pattern parallel to the front of the building. Decorative tile and oak are used for wall baseboards in Room 101.

Division 9 of the Specifications gives information pertaining to laminated wallcoverings and wallpaper (vinyl fabric) which is noted as either wallcover A, B, or C on the prints. Vinyl fabric and brick are used to finish walls in the public area.

The suspended ceiling in the public area is $9'-8''$ high. This dimension is found in the Room Finish Schedule, Sheet 4, and on Sections A and B, Sheet 7A. The acoustical ceiling is composed of lay-in

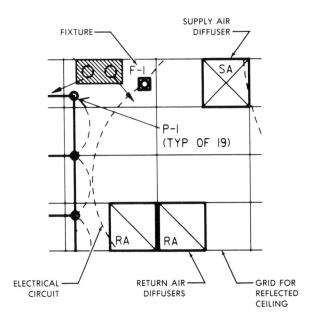

Figure 9-14. Two intersecting diagonal lines represent supply air. One diagonal line represents return air.

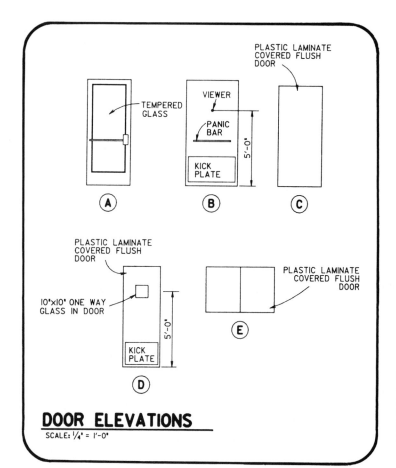

DOOR ELEVATIONS
SCALE: ¼" = 1'-0"

LOCATION	LEAF SIZE	ELEVATION
(A)	$3^0 \ 7^0$	A
(B)	$3^0 \ 7^0$	A
(C)	$3^0 \ 7^0$	A
(D)	$3^0 \ 6^8$	C
(E)	$3^0 \ 6^8$	C
(F)	$3^0 \ 6^8$	D
(G)	$3^0 \ 6^8$	C
(H)	$3^6 \ 6^8$	B
(J)	$2\text{-}2^4 \ 3^0$	E
(K)	$3^0 \ 7^0$	A

Figure 9-15. Door elevations give common information for doors shown on the plans.

panels with a matching grid. All trim in the public area is stained and doors are aluminum.

Door And Hardware Schedule, Sheet 4. Doors C and K are exit doors for the public area. Both of these doors are aluminum frame with tempered glass. Each is a 3'-0" × 7'-0" door with pivot hinges. Both doors are self-closing with push-pull hardware and door stops. Door C also has a panic bar, threshold, and a keyed lock. These doors are shown at A in the Door Elevations, Sheet 4. Other doors in the building are also shown in this elevation. See Figure 9-15.

Interior Elevations, Sheet 6. Elevation 1 is taken looking toward the right wall of the public area. On the far left side is a telephone on the wall covered with wallcover A below and wallcover B above. These two wallcovers are separated by a strip of wallcover C.

The salad bar with sneeze guard suspended above, counter with stools, "Z" booth-divider wall and brick pier are shown. The Equipment Plan, Sheet 9, shows the "Z" booth-divider as No. 113. Note that lighting fixtures are suspended 75″ above the finished floor. These are positioned above the tables and counter as shown on the Lighting And Reflected Ceiling Plan, Sheet 13.

Elevation 3, Sheet 6, is taken looking toward the left wall of the public area. The base cabinet and condiment shelf located past the end of the serving line is shown. Wallcover B is specified in this elevation.

Elevation 4, Sheet 6, is taken looking toward the serving area. The base cabinet and condiment shelf is shown on the left side with wallcovers A, B, and C separated by oak trim. Decorative tile cove base is shown. The counter-divider wall panel with six fixed stools is prominent. These are items No. 111 and 114 on the Equipment Plan, Sheet 9. Note the wood base on the counter.

The open portion of the serving area and part of its countertop are behind the counter and stools. An opening to the hallway is shown on the right side of the elevation and the lighting grid is also visible.

Elevation 5, Sheet 6, gives detailed information for the standard condiment counter base, which is a two-piece assembly. A piece of 5/8″ CDX plywood provides shelf support and is covered with laminated wallcovering. Wallcovers B and C and the decorative tile base add color to this area. Item No. 106 is two booster chairs.

Elevation 6, Sheet 6, is also taken looking toward the serving area; however, it is between the counter with stools and serving area. The condiment counter and shelf are shown on the left side. Wallcovers A, B, and C with oak trim and decorative tile cove base finish the wall. The serving counter is 3′-4″ above the finished floor level and has a 4″ drop laminate counter edge. The opening to the hallway and telephone are again shown.

Equipment Plan, Sheet 9. This plan shows all equipment and describes it in the accompanying Equipment Schedule. Room 101 has a substantial amount of equipment and furniture. Twelve 30″ × 30″ self-edged pedestal tables are located in the center of the public area. These are noted as item No. 109. Eight of these tables are equipped with four No. 105 chairs and four of the tables having three No. 105 chairs utilize the "Z" booth-divider for additional seating.

Twenty-two 20″ × 24″ self-edged pedestal tables are located around the perimeter of the public area. These are noted as item No. 108. Two No. 105 chairs are positioned at each of these tables. Two stacking high chairs, No. 107, are located near door C. Item No. 96 refers to the carpet and two carpet seams are shown running parallel to the front wall of the building. A carpet-tile transition strip, No. 94, separates the carpet from the decorative tile.

The counter-divider wall panel, No. 111, is installed by the general contractor. Six fixed stools, No. 114, are sleeved over steel posts set into cores in the floor slab.

HVAC Plan, Sheet 11. Room 101 is heated and cooled by an 11 ton HVAC unit mounted on the roof. This unit is designated RT-2. The HVAC Equipment Schedule, Sheet 11, shows a 208V, 3φ unit with a 3 HP blower motor.

The HVAC system is designed to meet outside temperatures of 93 °F in the summer and 0 °F in the winter. All ductwork is run above the suspended ceiling. Supply ducts and diffusers must be insulated. The HVAC plan, Sheet 11, shows the location of the RT-2 unit with a 24″ × 14″ main duct toward the rear of the building and a transition piece reducing to an 18″ × 14″ main duct toward the front of the building. Round ducts branching off the main duct supply lay-in ceiling-mounted diffusers and surface-mounted registers. Four diffusers are supplied by 12″ diameter ducts. These diffusers designated A/400 have a 12″ diameter and supply 400 cubic feet of air per minute. Diffuser color is off-white.

Three B diffusers are located in the ceiling toward the rear of Room 101. Two of these supply 300 CFM and one supplies 350 CFM. Three D registers supplying the atrium area are surface-mounted. Ductwork to these registers is 12″ in diameter. A round-to-rectangular transition is required from the 12″ diameter duct to the 30″ × 4″ register. See Figure 9-16.

Two returns with 16″ ducts to the unit return air for Room 101. Returns and supplies are also located

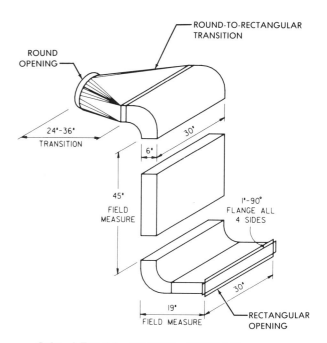

SOLARIUM DUCT DETAIL
NO SCALE

Figure 9-16. Transitions are required where duct shape or size changes.

and designated on the Lighting And Reflected Ceiling Plan, Sheet 13.

Electric Plan, Sheet 12. Information shown for Room 101 on this plan includes the location of three 20A, 120V, 1φ duplex receptacles placed 14″ above the finished floor. The dashed lines connecting the receptacles indicate circuit wiring from above. A 1″ conduit under the floor slab is stubbed up above the ceiling to carry conductors supplying the salad bar. Conduit in the slab is terminated at a J-box (junction box) in the floor beneath the salad bar. The J-box is 16′-7″ from the left wall and 11′-11″ from the wall between Room 101 and Room 106. The J-box in the ceiling, which is 21′-3″ from the left wall and 11′-5″ from the wall between Room 101 and Room 106, supplies sneeze guard lights and ceiling lights over the salad bar. This is run on Circuit 19 of Panel A. Circuit 19 is supplied with #12 conductors and protected by a 20A, single-pole CB.

Weatherproof duplex receptacles are shown on the roof. The letters WP placed near the symbol for the receptacle indicate that a weatherproof receptacle is specified. Circuit wiring is shown to all three rooftop units. The circuit marked 7A-1 is a 20A, 120V general purpose circuit. These receptacles are required by the National Electrical Code® to provide power for personnel servicing the HVAC equipment.

The disconnecting means for unit RT-2 is a three-pole rated switch. This is required by the NEC® to protect personnel from electrical shock while servicing the unit.

The telephone, located to the right of the entrance, is designated by a solid-color triangle. It is mounted 54″ above the finished floor. General notes on the Electric Plan, Sheet 12, gives specific mounting instructions for the telephone backboard and size and placement of 2″ conduit for the stub up.

Lighting And Reflected Ceiling Plan, Sheet 13. This plan shows the layout for the ceiling grid and all lighting fixtures. The grid lighting is the dominant lighting feature of the dining area. Two grids are shown with heavy object lines representing the wooden gridwork and solid circles at intersections and corners of the grid representing the 15 watts per lamp, decorative, incandescent bulbs. Fixture symbol P-1 designates fixtures for the grid lights. The larger grid unit, suspended over the major dining area, contains 54 P-1 fixtures and the smaller grid

unit, located above the brass railing at the rear of the dining area, contains 19 P-1 fixtures.

Always check local codes for the maximum number of lighting fixtures permitted on a general purpose branch circuit. Many local codes require a lighting outlet for a fixture to be computed at 1.5A per outlet. For example, this computation allows 13 outlets to be connected on a 20A circuit (20A CB/1.5A = 13.3).

Notice that 54 P-1 light fixtures, rated at 15 watts each, are specified on Circuit 9A. As the total volt-amps of this circuit does not exceed 80% of the 20A, 120V branch circuit, it would be accepted by some local authorities. The formula $I = VA/V$, where I = amps; VA = volt amps (or watts); and V = volts, is used in the computation to verify less than 80% loading of the branch circuit:

$$15W \times 54 = 810VA$$

$$I = \frac{VA}{V}$$

$$I = \frac{810VA}{120V}$$

$$I = 6.75A$$

A 20A branch circuit used at continuous duty is rated at 16A (20A × 80% = 16A). The 6.75A is well below the permitted load of the circuit.

The grid lighting is made of 2 × 6s with ¼″ oak veneer plywood covering the sides and oak veneer tape on the edges. P-1 fixtures are attached to the oak grid with a ¼″ hollow pipe providing space for the assembly routed to the wire molding raceway, which is positioned on the top edge of the grid. The oak grid is suspended from the ceiling by ceiling rods screwed to ⅜″ threaded rods, which are secured with recessed nuts. Drilled holes are plugged for appearance. See Figure 9-17.

Four E-1 fixtures are shown along each window wall of the dining area. Three E-1 fixtures are located between the two grid lights. E-1 fixtures are either 40 or 60 watts per lamps, depending upon the scheme (refer to the Lighting Fixture Schedule, Sheet 13). These fixtures are chain-hung.

Thirteen F-1 fixtures are recessed in the ceiling of Room 101. Each of these fixtures has one 75-watt incandescent bulb. F-1 fixtures are located above the telephone, along the entrance, serving, and condiment areas, and in the general dining area. F-1 light fixtures are supplied by two #12 conductors

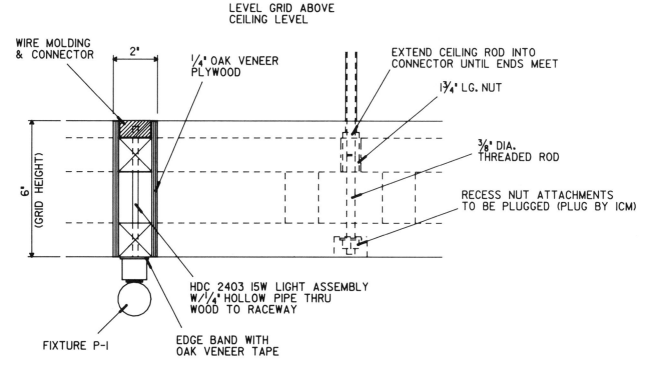

Figure 9-17. P-1 light fixtures are attached to the suspended oak grid.

with a #12 equipment grounding conductor pulled in ³/₄ ″ conduit protected by a 20A, single-pole CB.

Thirteen P-2 fixtures are wall mounted on the Glulam beam to provide lighting in the atrium area. P-2 fixtures are 40 watts per lamp, incandescent fixtures.

Emergency lights provide light for exiting the building should a power outage occur. These are shown on the plans by diagonal lines drawn through emergency light fixtures which are designated EM-1. Two EM-1 fixtures are recessed in the ceiling of Room 101. Lamps for these fixtures are furnished with the fixtures. Where general lighting circuits and emergency lighting circuits enter fixture enclosures or other enclosures, separation must be provided between the circuits per the NEC®.

Exit lights are positioned to clearly mark all exits. Two exit lights designated EX-1 are shown. Each is located at an exit door. These ceiling-mounted fixtures are furnished with lamps. Battery packs are permitted to be connected to the single-pole switch that controls a general lighting circuit in the same room as the battery pack. Emergency and exit lighting circuits cannot be routed in the same conduit system supplying illumination for required lighting per the NEC®.

Plumbing Plan, Sheet 15. Plumbing required for Room 101 is related to the salad bar. Two supply lines and one waste pipe are placed and roughed in before the concrete floor slab is poured. Supply lines are ¹/₂ ″, type K, soft copper tubing. Abbreviations CW and HW denote cold water and hot water supply lines. Sanitary waste piping is 3 ″ in diameter and of material required to meet local codes.

The salad bar is designated K-8. This designation is used to locate plumbing shown on the Sanitary Isometric and the Water Supply Isometric. The Salad Bar Drain Detail shows the 3 ″ sanitary waste piping with a trap beneath the concrete floor slab. A 12 ″ section of 2¹/₂ ″ pipe receives the cold pan drain line from the salad bar. Hot and cold water lines are also shown. See Figure 9-18.

Waitress Station, Room 102, Sheet 4

This small room provides a convenient work area for waiters and waitresses. It is conveniently located between the Public Area, Room 101, and the Serving Area, Room 106. Public view into this area is restricted by a 5′-0 ″ wide partition behind the condiment shelf and a 5′-0¹/₁₆ ″ partition set at a 45° angle.

The Floor Plan, Sheet 4, shows a pair of J doors for the base cabinet and one F door leading to the Serving Area, Room 106. Additionally, the symbol referencing interior elevations shows the direction of sight for interior elevations 7, 8, 9, and 10 found on Interior Elevations, Sheet 6.

Room Finish Schedule, Sheet 4. Notes 3 and 7 of this schedule refer to the floor finish for Room 102. Decorative floor tile is placed in a common bond pattern parallel to the front wall of the building. Plastic laminate covers the trash can area below the trash counter. The concrete floor slab is sealed with concrete floor sealer before finish flooring is applied. Decorative tile base is specified.

Walls in Room 102 are finished with vinyl fabric, and the suspended, acoustical ceiling is 9'-8" above the finished floor. Stain is applied to all wood trim in Room 102 and plastic laminate covers the doors.

Door And Hardware Schedule, Sheet 4. The F door, which is 3'-0" wide and 6'-8" high, is also shown in Elevation 10, Sheet 6. This plastic laminate covered, flush door is detailed in Door Elevation D, Sheet 4, which shows 10" × 10", one-way glass in the door. The glass is centered 5'-0" from the bottom of the door. A stainless steel kickplate on the bottom allows easy opening for workers carrying loads. Butt hinges, a privacy latch, a self-closing mechanism, and a door stop complete the hardware for the door.

J doors are provided by the kitchen equipment supplier. These two flush doors measure 2'-4" × 3'-0" and are covered with plastic laminate. Butt hinges and door stops are provided.

Interior Elevations, Sheet 6. The Floor Plan, Sheet 4, shows direction of sight for four interior elevations. These elevations provide additional detail for Room 102. They are drawn to the scale of 1/4" = 1'-0".

Elevation 7, Sheet 6, shows the 5'-0" wide wall. Decorative tile base is shown with wallcovers A, B, and C. Oak trim, spaced 1'-0" apart, out-to-out, is 3'-0" above the finished floor. The area between the oak trim is covered with wallcover C.

Elevation 8, Sheet 6, is taken looking toward the front of the building. A 3'-1 5/16" wall extends from the left exterior wall. A 5'-0 1/16" partition is set at a 45° angle off this wall. Base and wall cabinets are shown in section view and wallcover A is specified.

Elevation 9, Sheet 6, shows the front of the base and wall cabinets. Standard oak cabinets are placed on a 4" high, raised concrete pad. (Refer to the Raised Concrete Pad, Plan C, Sheet 3.) A quarry tile base is placed on the pad. Shelf support is provided by 5/8" CDX plywood under the plastic laminated wall. Wallcover A and decorative tile cove base complete the trim.

Elevation 10, Sheet 6, shows Door F and a sectional view of the base and wall cabinets. Again, one-way glass is noted for Door F.

Equipment Plan, Sheet 9. Equipment shown is keyed to the Equipment Schedule, Sheet 9, by encircled numbers. Item No. 91 refers to the base cabinet and No. 71 refers to the wall cabinet. Two waste containers, No. 61, are shown by dashed lines. The fire extinguisher, No. 87, is conveniently located. Two additional fire extinguishers are specified for other locations. The stainless steel kickplate for Door F is specified as No. 82 on the plan.

Electric Plan, Sheet 12. A 20A, 120V, 1ϕ duplex receptacle is shown on the right wall of Room 102. The box is 14" above the finished floor. No receptacles are shown between base and wall cabinets because this is not a preparation area and electricity is not required for work performed here.

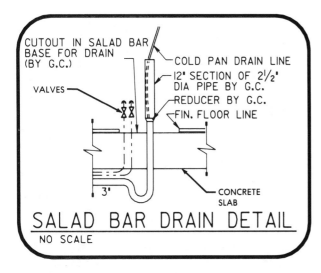

Figure 9-18. The salad bar supply and waste piping is run beneath the concrete floor slab.

Lighting And Reflected Ceiling Plan, Sheet 13. One C-3 fixture is shown in Room 102. This recessed, ceiling-mounted fixture measures 2′ wide × 2′ long × 4½″ deep. Two #12 conductors and one #12 ground are run in ¾″conduit to the fixture. Two 40-watt fluorescent lamps provide illumination.

Dashed circuit lines indicate that conductors for fixture C-3 in this area are routed through a box containing conductors for emergency and general lighting. This is permitted by the NEC® when proper separation of the two circuits is provided. This type of installation is used to provide emergency power when normal power is lost.

Hall, Room 103, Sheet 4

The hall leads from the entrance and dining area to the restrooms. Three interior elevations, No. 37, 38, and 39 are shown on Interior Elevations, Sheet 6. The hall, which is 3′-10⅞″ wide, is terminated toward the rear of the building by Door D leading to the Men's Room. Ceiling height in Room 103 is 8′-4″. A header, 8′-0″ above the finished floor, frames the entry to the hall.

Room Finish Schedule, Sheet 4. The floor in the hall is finished with decorative tile installed in a common bond pattern parallel to the front wall of the building. Decorative tile cove base is used on all walls. Vinyl fabric covers the walls and all wood trim is stained. The ceiling is suspended, acoustical tile.

Interior Elevations, Sheet 6. Elevation 37 shows the left wall of Room 103. Elevation 38 shows the rear wall and Elevation 39 shows the right wall. Wallcovers A, B, and C and oak trim are used to finish these walls.

HVAC Plan, Sheet 11. A ceiling-mounted supply diffuser is fed by an 8″ duct from HVAC unit RT-1. The diffuser is off-white and has a round neck. Metalaire model #71-5-00-0000-08, or equal, may be installed.

Electric Plan, Sheet 12. A 20A, 120V, 1ϕ duplex receptacle is shown on the left wall. The box is 14″ above the finished floor. The receptacle is wired on Circuit 1 of Panel A-1. A 20A CB provides overcurrent protection for this circuit.

The NEC® permits no more than 13 general-purpose outlets to be connected to a 20A circuit and no more than 10 to be connected to a 15A circuit. Verification of the permissible number of outlets is provided by the following procedure:

$$I = \frac{VA}{V}$$

$$I = \frac{180VA}{120V}$$

$$I = 1.5A \text{ per outlet}$$

$$I = \frac{20A\ CB}{1.5A} = 13 \text{ outlets per circuit}$$

$$I = \frac{15A\ CB}{1.5A} = 10 \text{ outlets per circuit}$$

Lighting and Reflected Ceiling Plan, Sheet 13. Two F-1 lighting fixtures are recessed into the ceiling of the hall. Each fixture has one 75-watt incandescent lamp. All fixtures are supplied by the electrical contractor who must verify the color scheme before placing an order.

The branch circuit rating and number of fixtures permitted is computed by the wattage of each incandescent lamp installed and by the ballast volt-amp rating of each fluorescent fixture. Note that the volt-amp rating of the ballast is used for the fluorescent lighting fixture and *not* the wattage rating of each lamp.

Restrooms, Rooms 104 and 105, Sheet 4

The Men's Room is L-shaped, measuring 10′-11¼″ wide by 6′-2″ deep with the entrance being 3′-10⅞″ wide × 4′-8½″ deep. The Women's Room measures 6′-8⅞″ × 9′-5″. Finish and equipment are similar in both restrooms with the exception of the urinal and urinal partition in the Men's Room. Standard plan symbols show the urinal, water closets, and lavatories.

Room Finish Schedule, Sheet 4. Floors in restrooms are decorative tile installed in a common bond pattern parallel to the front wall of the building. A decorative tile cove base is specified. All walls are ceramic tile. Any wood trim is stained. The ceilings consist of a drywall ceiling at 9′-0″ above the finished floor with suspended, acoustical ceilings at 8′-0″ above the finished floor. Doors are covered with plastic laminate.

Door And Hardware Schedule, Sheet 4. D and E doors are identical except for their swing. These are shown as type C doors in the Door Elevations, Sheet 4. The flush doors are 3'-0" × 6'-8". Each is undercut 1½". Aluminum-framed doors are covered with plastic laminate. The rough opening for these doors must be 1¼" wider and 1" taller than the door leaf. A room sign is applied to the outside of each door. Butt hinges, self-closing mechanisms, and door stops complete the door hardware required.

Interior Elevations, Sheet 6. Elevations 29, 30, 31, and 32 detail the walls in Room 104. Elevations 33, 34, 35, and 36 detail the walls in Room 105. Equipment on each wall is called out with a note or an equipment item number. All plumbing fixtures are detailed in the Specifications, Division 11. Ceramic tile with dark tile trim is shown on all walls in both restrooms.

Elevation 29 shows a side view of the lavatory in the Men's Rooms with a soap dispenser (No. 47) and an 18" × 36" mirror above. An electric hand dryer (No. 88) is to the right of the lavatory. Elevation 30, from left to right, shows Door D, the urinal partition, urinal, toilet partition, water closet, grab bar, and toilet paper holder. The grab bar is 2'-9" above the finished floor. Elevation 31 shows the left entrance wall and toilet partition. Elevation 32 shows the toilet partition and front view of the lavatory, soap dispenser, and mirror.

Elevation 33, from left to right, shows the toilet partition and Door E. Elevation 34 shows the electric hand dryer (No. 88) and side view of the lavatory with the soap dispenser (No. 47) and 18" × 36" mirror above. Elevation 35 shows the front view of the lavatory, soap dispenser, and mirror. A mounting height of 3'-8" above the finished floor is specified for the mirror. The toilet partition, lavatory, grab bar, and toilet paper holder complete this view. Elevation 36 shows the toilet partition with the base of the water closet visible at the floor.

Equipment Plan, Sheet 9. Two pieces of equipment are specified for each restroom. Item No. 47 on the Equipment Plan, Sheet 9, indicates soap dispensers to be furnished by the owner and installed by the contractor. Item No. 88 indicates electric hand dryers, which are part of the smallwares package. Electric hand dryers are installed by the general contractor.

HVAC Plan, Sheet 11. An 8" × 8" off-white grill, with a square to round transition, is connected to a 6" duct above the ceiling in each restroom. These ducts run to Exhaust Fan 5, which is equipped with a ¹/₁₅ HP, 115V, 1φ direct drive motor.

Electric Plan, Sheet 12. Electric hand dryers in both restrooms are shown. These are also shown on Interior Elevations, Sheet 6. Item No. 88 denotes the electric hand dryers. A 1.5kW heat lamp in the ceiling of each restroom is on Circuit 10 of Panel A-1. A 20A CB provides overcurrent protection. Exhaust Fan 5 is on Circuit 3 of Panel A. A 20A CB provides overcurrent protection.

Lighting And Reflected Ceiling Plan, Sheet 13. Two C-3 lighting fixtures in the Men's Room and one C-3 lighting fixture in the Women's Room provide illumination. A 1.5kW heat lamp in each ceiling is wired on Circuit 10 of Panel A-1. A 20A CB provides overcurrent protection for the heat lamps.

Plumbing Plan, Sheet 15. Plumbing fixtures are designated by letter and number on the plan and isometric views. All restroom plumbing fixtures are provided by the plumbing contractor. See Figure 9-19. The water closets (A-1) are supplied by ½" cold water pipes. They are set on 4" direct waste outlets and are vented through a 2" vent pipe to a 3" vent through the roof. The Specifications give the model number and additional information for water closet A-1. Water closet A-2 is provided for handicapped use.

The lavatories are designated B-1. These are wall-hung units with 1¼" direct waste outlets and a 1¼" vent. The mounting heights for supply and drain are as directed by the plumbing contractor. Lavatories are supplied by ½" lines. A thermostatic mixing valve, which delivers 110°F water, is set in line between the 52-gallon electric water heater and the lavatories.

The urinal (C-1) is supplied by a ¾" cold water line and is connected to a 2" waste. It is vented through a 1½" vent.

Serving Area, Room 106, Sheet 4

Room 106 is an activity-filled area with the final preparation, serving, and accounting of food ordered for customers eating in the dining area. The

WATER SUPPLY ISOMETRIC

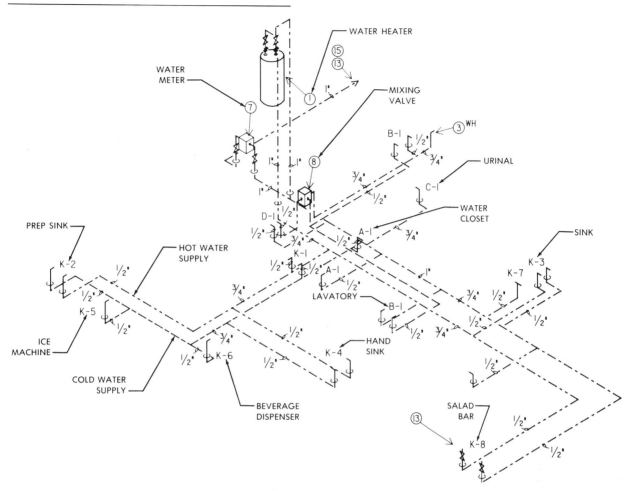

Figure 9-19. Water supply is shown with dashed lines in the Water Supply Isometric.

main portion of this L-shaped room is 27'-4⁵⁄₈" long and 9'-10" deep. Interior Elevations 11, 12, and 13 show wall details of the main area and Interior Elevations 14 and 15 show details of the pickup window area.

Dashed lines on the plan show locations for HOODS 1, 2, and 3 and the soffit area above the front counter assembly. Ceiling height in Room 106 is 9'-0" above the finished floor, which is quarry tile with a quarry tile base.

Interior Elevations, Sheet 6. Elevation 11 shows profile views of the rear counter assembly (No. 6), menu board, and front counter assembly (No. 1). The wall is finished with A, B, and C wallcoverings. Oak trim separates wallcover C from wallcover B (above) and wallcover A (below).

Elevation 12 shows a profile view, at the right-hand side, of the drive-thru cook counter assembly (No. 22) and exhaust hood with fan (No. 23), designated HOOD #3. Wallcover B is applied to the soffit area above the front counter assembly (No. 1). The ice bin (No. 2), carbonator (No. 3), cash register (No. 4), and coin changer (No. 5) complete the left side of Elevation 12. The center portion of the elevation shows the inside cook counter assembly (No. 13) with an exhaust hood with fan (No. 14) designated as HOOD #1 above. The wall in this area is ⁵⁄₈" CDX plywood under almond-colored wallcovering. The plywood provides shelf support for the multi-purpose holding unit (No. 16) which contains a bun warmer (No. 15), toaster (No. 18), toaster shelf (No. 19), storage shelf (No. 17), and hot dog bun griddle (No. 38). Door F, with viewer, leads to the Waitress Station, Room 102.

Elevation 13 is taken looking at the rear wall of Room 106. This wall is finished with almond-colored laminated wallcovering. The most visible feature shown on this elevation is the menu sign. See Figure 9-20. Detail A, Sheet 10, shows an elevation and section view of the menu sign. It requires a 43¼″ × 8′-2½″ rough opening for wall installation. The top of the sign is placed 8′-3″ above the finished floor. It is furnished by the owner and installed by the sign erector.

An exhaust hood with fan (No. 29), designated HOOD #2, is located above the custom fry center assembly (No. 28). The reach-in freezer (No. 30) and the dump and dry storage bin (No. 32) flank the custom fry center assembly (No. 28). A Frosty machine (No. 40) and rear counter assembly (No. 6) complete Elevation 13.

Elevation 14 shows the serving area for pick up window service. Equipment in this elevation is essentially the same as the equipment shown in Elevation 12 with the addition of the condiment holder (No. 21). The pick up window is shown on the right-hand side of the elevation.

Elevation 15 details the rear wall of the pick up window serving area. It contains a drink counter assembly (No. 25) with cash register (No. 4), an ice machine (No. 2) with carbonator (No. 3) above, and the Frosty machine (No. 40) shown in Elevation 14.

The wall is finished with almond-colored laminated wallcovering. A chime, to alert restaurant personnel that a customer has pulled up to the drive-thru menu sign, is located 7′-0″ above the finished floor. The speaker station, 5′-0″ above the finished floor, allows restaurant personnel to take drive-thru orders.

Equipment Plan, Sheet 9. All equipment for Room 106 called out on the Interior Elevations, Sheet 6, is also designated on the Equipment Plan, Sheet 9. Additionally, pieces of equipment that cannot be shown in elevation are shown on the plan view. This equipment includes the beverage machines noted, coffee machine and warmer (No. 7), ice tea dispenser (No. 8), and the hot chocolate machine (No. 9). A hand sink (No. 10) is shown with a soap dispenser (No. 47) and towel dispenser (No. 48) above. At the pick-up window serving area, items not shown on the Interior Elevations, Sheet 6, include the coffee machine and warmer (No. 7) and the ice tea dispenser (No. 8).

The Equipment Schedule, Sheet 9, lists each piece of equipment in numerical order and gives the quantity and a brief description, with remarks, of the equipment. General Notes 1 through 8 relate to the Equipment Schedule.

HVAC Plan, Sheet 11. Three exhaust fans, EF-1, 2, and 3, are located in Room 106. Each of these is equipped with a 6′-0″ × 3′-6″ exhaust hood with a 10″ × 20″ supply opening and an 8″ × 20″ exhaust opening ducted into a 14″ × 14″ duct feeding through 26″ × 26″ roof openings.

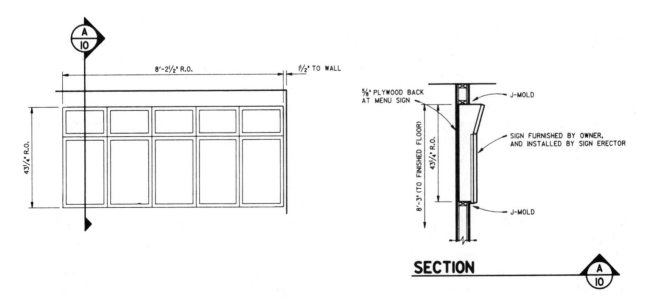

Figure 9-20. The menu sign is mounted on the wall in the Serving Area, Room 106.

HVAC units MUA-1 and RT-1 provide heating and cooling. Supply air is provided to Room 106 by two 12″ diameter A diffusers with 650 CFM capacity. Return air is handled by three 22″ × 22″ F grills.

Electric Plan, Sheet 12. Circuits and home runs are shown for all equipment in Room 106. For example, the note 35A-1 indicates that Circuit 35 supplies the Frosty machine in the indoor serving area. This circuit is fed from Panel A-1, which contains a 225A main on a 120/208V, 3ϕ service. On this set of plans, the symbol of an X in a circle indicates a 3ϕ circuit. Circuit 35 has a 30A, 3ϕ breaker.

Electrical circuits supplying the grills in Room 106 are fed directly from the Distribution Panel. These circuits are designated DP8 and DP9. Each of these is 3ϕ with 90A fuses for overcurrent protection. All circuits in Room 106 are designated by their circuit number and panel.

Additional electrical information is given in the form of notes. For example, reference must be made to Wendy's Wiring and Site Preparation Guide for installation of IBM point-of-sale cash register store loops.

Lighting And Reflected Ceiling Plan, Sheet 13. A variety of lighting fixtures are utilized in Room 106. Three F-1 fixtures are recessed into the soffit above the front counter assembly. These fixtures contain one 75-watt incandescent lamp. Three H-1 fixtures are shown over the rear counter assembly. The 2′ × 4′ recessed ceiling fixtures contain four 40-watt fluorescent lamps. The center H-1 fixture is drawn with 45° diagonal lines to indicate that it is on the night light circuit. Two B-1 fixtures contain four 40-watt fluorescent lamps and one B-2 fixture contains two 40-watt fluorescent lamps. The B-2 fixture is also on the night light circuit. EM-1 light fixtures provide emergency floodlighting. These are also indicated by 45° diagonal lines. A hanging fixture in each hood completes the lighting for Room 106.

Plumbing Plan, Sheet 15. Schedule 40 PVC beverage conduit, 6″ in diameter, is placed before the concrete slab is poured. It must slope down ⅛″ per foot toward the drink dispenser and is stubbed 6″ above the finished floor. It is sealed watertight at openings and must be free of foreign matter before drink lines are pulled. Dimensions are given on the plan for locating sanitary and water supply stubs. The isometrics specify pipe sizes and show vents.

Cooler-Freezer, Room 107, And Storage, Room 110, Sheet 4

The cooler-freezer and storage room is furnished as a module by the owner and installed by the general contractor. Consequently, only limited information concerning this unit is given in the plans. The module is 12′-0″ deep × 29′-0″ wide. It is divided into two rooms, Room 107 which is the cooler-freezer portion, and Room 110 which is the storage area. The exterior door for the module is Door H. This door is provided with the module. The module is entered from the opening in the rear wall of Room 108. A note on the Floor Plan, Sheet 4, specifies caulking and sealing around the opening.

The Foundation Plan, Sheet 3, shows the unexcavated area for the recessed slab, which is detailed in Section H, Sheet 7B. The Left Side and Rear Elevations, Sheet 5, give additional information.

Equipment Plan, Sheet 9. Item No. 62 is noted as the Walk-in Cooler-Freezer-Dry Storage Module. The freezer area contains one wire shelf unit (No. 64), which is 18″ deep × 60″ wide, and three freezer *palletiers* (No. 67). A palletier is a metal storage shelf with holes to allow circulation of air around items placed on the unit. The freezer area is separated from the cooler area which contains seven wire shelf units (No. 63) and one cooler palletier (No. 66). Sizes are given for each of these units. The dry storage area contains seven additional wire shelf units with sizes shown.

Electric Plan, Sheet 12. Circuit 15 to Panel A-1 contains a weatherproof disconnect for the bun freezer. The disconnect symbol is shown in the legend. WP indicates weatherproof. The three-phase load is protected by a 20A, three-pole circuit breaker that provides simultaneous tripping should a short circuit or ground fault occur. Two additional weatherproof disconnects are shown for electric motors for the cooler-freezer unit. The electrical contractor must provide two junction boxes with conduit at 108″ for hookup of the roof-mounted cooler-freezer unit. Circuits 37A and 38A provide power for the two roof-mounted units.

The storage module contains pre-installed conduit through which the electrical contractor will pull wire for the door buzzer. Pre-installed conduit is shown by a series of one long and two dashed lines.

Preparation Area, Room 108, Sheet 4

This area is 17'-5½" wide and 24'-7" deep. It is entered from the Serving Area, Room 106, and shares a 5½" thick common wall with the restrooms. The Office, Room 109, is located at the rear of Room 108 immediately behind the Employee Break Room, Room 111, and the Water Heater Closet, Room 112. The Walk-in Cooler-Freezer-Dry Storage Module is entered from Room 108. Floor-to-ceiling height in this room is 9'-0". Room finish is similar to the finish specified for Room 106, with minor changes.

Interior Elevations, Sheet 6. Five interior elevations are utilized to show details in the Preparation Area. These are numbered 16, 17, 18, 19, and 20. Interior Elevation 18 is an equipment elevation only. It shows equipment placed in the center floor area of Room 108.

Elevation 16, Sheet 6, shows the return wall for Room 111 extending 2'-0" into Room 108 and a 3'-6" extension, at reduced thickness, of the common wall between Room 108 and the restrooms. Plywood sheathing on this wall provides support for shelf units. Laminated wallcovering is applied as the wall finish.

Two pieces of stainless steel corner molding is applied to protect wall corners. Three wire wall shelving units (No. 50) 18" deep are hung above three 12" deep shelving units (No. 49). A quarry tile base with "J" molding is applied to the wall. Equipment located along the wall includes the coffee machine and warmer (No. 7) and the three-compartment sink (No. 46). Elevation 16 also shows an end view of the range (No. 34) with a stainless steel wall panel (No. 80) on the right side wall and HOOD #4 (No. 37) above.

Elevation 17 is taken looking toward the front of the building. The quarry tile base is extended along this wall where cooking equipment is located. The stainless steel wall panel (No. 80) is higher than the cooking equipment for sanitation and safety. HOOD #4 handles the exhaust air requirements for the electric modular range top with stand (No. 34),

baked potato oven with stand and timer (No. 33) and chicken pressure fryer assembly (No. 35). The chicken breading table assembly (No. 36), to the right of the cooking equipment, contains a built-in refrigeration unit. A hand sink (No. 44), soap dispenser (No. 47), and towel dispenser (No. 48) provide facilities for maintaining employee cleanliness.

Elevation 18 shows equipment in the center of Room 108. Walls are not shown. See Figure 9-21. Break lines on each end of the elevation define the area shown. A patty machine stand (No. 55) with a hamburger patty machine (No. 54) is located to the left of two bun racks (No. 59) beneath a 10'-0" worktable (No. 53).

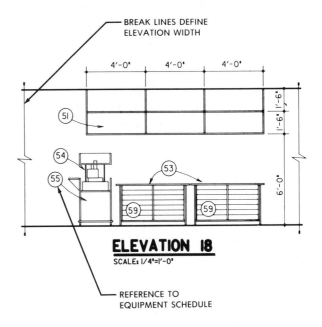

Figure 9-21. Break lines on each end of the interior elevation view define the width of an elevation taken in the center of a room with the wall behind not shown.

Three wire wall shelving units (No. 51) 18" deep × 3'-0" high × 4'-0" long are butted end-to-end and suspended from the ceiling by the general contractor. The bottom of these units is 6'-0" above the finished floor.

Elevation 19 is taken looking toward the left wall of the building. The return wall, shown on the left side of the elevation, extends 4'-9" to provide a separation from the pick-up window area. Stainless steel corner molding (No. 81) protects this corner. The Corner Molding, Detail A-9, shows this as a

$2'' \times 2'' \times 48''$ piece with five $1/4''$ diameter holes on $8''$ centers on one leg and six $1/4''$ diameter holes on $8''$ centers on the other leg. Spacing requirements for these holes begin on opposite legs to provide off-sets. The bottom $4''$ is flared to cover the floor tile. The corner molding is 16-gauge stainless steel. Stainless steel truss head machine screws ($\#8 \times 3/4''$) are used to fasten the molding to wall corners.

Equipment shown in Elevation 19 includes the syrup tank rack (No. 58), ice cube machine and bin (No. 41), and single-compartment sink (No. 45). The sink is used in the preparation of vegetables. Wire wall shelving units $12''$ deep (No. 49) and $18''$ deep (No. 50) are placed above the sink. Mounting heights above the finished floor are given for these wire wall shelving units.

Elevation 20 shows the rear wall of Room 108. The opening to the storage module is caulked and sealed tight since no door is specified. A portion of the break area can be seen on the right side of this elevation view.

Equipment Plan, Sheet 9. The equipment shown in Room 108 is referenced to the Equipment Schedule, Sheet 9, and the Interior Elevations, Sheet 6. The depth and length of wire wall shelving units are designated. For example, 12/60 denotes a shelving unit that is $12''$ deep and $60''$ long. A waste container (No. 61), not shown in the elevation view, is shown here in plan view along the right wall. Equipment on the front wall, not seen in elevation view, is the fire extinguisher (No. 87). The left wall shows the location for the Besco management board (No. 68). An additional fire extinguisher is placed on the rear wall near the opening to the storage module.

HVAC Plan, Sheet 11. The preparation room, Room 108, and the serving area, Room 106, contain cooking equipment that builds up heat and smoke during operation. Provisions are made to bring in outside air to replace exhausted air. Exhaust fans are installed over the cooking equipment to remove the heated, smoke-filled air. They are designed to provide proper air balance. Units RT-1 and MUA-1 are balanced with exhaust fans, which remove excess air, to provide heating, cooling, and ventilation for this area.

Exhaust fans under hoods must be connected to shunt-trip devices controlled by heat sensors that disconnect the circuit in the event of a fire. This prevents the fire from being fed into the system.

Electric Plan, Sheet 12. Unit RT-1 is wired to the distribution panel and noted on the plan as Circuit DP4. A 200A switch with 200A fuses is used to provide overcurrent protection to the branch circuit conductors supplying power to the unit. Circuit conductors are three $\#1/0$ THW copper with one $\#6$ ground. The 200A FRN fuses will hold five times their rating for 10 seconds. This holding power of 1,000A (200A $\times$ 5 = 1,000A) prevents nuisance tripping due to high head pressure resulting from high *ambient* (surrounding) temperature.

Circuits are traced through the Plan, Equipment & Connections Schedule, Equipment Schedule, and Panel Schedules to determine conductor size, overcurrent protection device type (CB or fuse), conduit size, and method of termination. The Equipment & Connections Schedule lists two methods of termination. T-1 is hard-wired (permanently connected). P & C refers to plug- and cord-connected equipment.

Circuit DP7 supplies the chicken pressure fryer assembly (No. 35). This unit is located along the front wall of Room 108. The Equipment & Connections Schedule, Sheet 12, shows a 12kW load on a 208V, 3ϕ circuit. A cord and plug is used as a disconnecting means. The connections are provided by a receptacle mounted $14''$ above the finished floor. The cord and plug is furnished by the electrical contractor who also provides the matching outlet.

The branch feeder circuit consists of three $\#6$ copper conductors with a $\#10$ equipment grounding conductor. These conductors are routed in $1''$ conduit from the distribution panel. To determine that conductors specified are sized properly to carry the circuit load, multiply the kW by 125% and divide by the voltage (208V x $\sqrt{3}$) to obtain the amperage rating. Note: When calculating 3ϕ problems, use the following values to eliminate one step from the mathematical computation:

for 208 volts $\times$ 1.732, use 360 volts
for 230 volts $\times$ 1.732, use 398 volts
for 240 volts $\times$ 1.732, use 416 volts
for 440 volts $\times$ 1.732, use 762 volts
for 460 volts $\times$ 1.732, use 797 volts
for 480 volts $\times$ 1.732, use 831 volts

For example:

$$I = \frac{VA}{V}$$

$$I = \frac{12,000VA \times 125\%}{208V \times \sqrt{3}} = 41.6A$$

$$I = 42A$$

A #6 copper conductor will supply power to a load of 42A. A 50A overcurrent protection device is selected based upon the ampacity of #6 copper conductors. Overcurrent protection is provided by 50A LPN fuses installed in a 60A disconnect. LPN fuses do not have time-delay characteristics. They are designed to hold five times their rating for $^1/_4$ to 2 seconds. This type of fuse cannot be used with loads having high inrush current. The inrush current of motors is usually 4 to 6 times the running current. Resistant heating loads (as specified here) have only 10% of the full-load current ratings of the heating elements.

All circuits should be traced in the preceding manner to determine that they comply with the minimum requirements of the NEC® and local codes. Always consult the authority having jurisdiction whenever discrepancies arise.

Lighting And Reflected Ceiling Plan, Sheet 13. The 2′ × 4′ grid system for the lighting and reflected ceiling is shown. Night lights, emergency lights, fluorescent lights, and exit lights are included. Additional lighting, which is part of the hood, is supplied by circuit 14A. The Equipment & Connections Schedule, Sheet 12, describes this circuit. The 1.6kW load is supplied by a 120V, 1φ circuit. The hood is hard-wired and the lights are controlled by a single-pole wall switch mounted 4′-6″ above the finished floor level. Two #12 conductors with one #12 equipment grounding conductor are routed in $^3/_4$″ conduit from Panel A to a junction box for the electrical connection to the hood lights. The branch circuit conductors are protected by a single-pole overcurrent protection device.

Plumbing Plan, Sheet 15. Floor drain FD-1 is located 2′-8$^1/_8$″ from the rear wall and 2′-0$^3/_{16}$″ from the partition at the opening to the Walk-in Cooler-Freezer-Dry Storage Module. This 3″ diameter sanitary waste piping is connected to the 4″ sanitary waste piping, which extends to the main sewer line on the property.

Floor drain FD-2 and the triple compartment sink, K-1, are connected to 3″ diameter sanitary waste piping running directly to the grease interceptor. This unit, with a minimum capacity of 200 gallons, provides collection and temporary storage of grease, which is removed before entry into the main sewer system. See Figure 9-22.

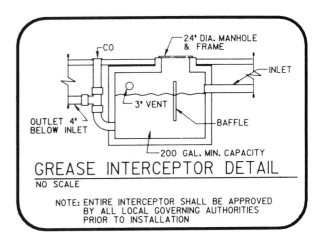

Figure 9-22. The grease interceptor allows accumulated grease to be removed before entering the main sewer system.

The prep sink, K-2, floor drain, FD-3, and hand sink, K-4, drain into the 3″ diameter sanitary waste piping, which is connected to the 4″ diameter sanitary waste piping leading directly to the main sewer line. Several cleanouts are shown on the sanitary waste piping by a small square or rectangle and the letters CO.

Hot and cold water lines and their respective diameters are shown for each piece of equipment requiring plumbing. The hot water line is represented on the plan by a solid line and the letters HW. The cold water line is represented on the plan by a solid line and the letters CW. All water lines in the water supply isometric are shown with dashed lines. The dashes alternate in length.

Office, Room 109, Sheet 4

The office measures 8′-6″ wide and 7′-3$^7/_8$″ deep. This room provides space for planning, purchasing, record-keeping, and other activities of management. The electrical panels are located on the rear wall and Interior Elevations 25, 26, 27, and 28 are utilized to show each wall.

Room Finish Schedule, Sheet 4. The floor in the office is finished with quarry tile with a quarry tile base. Walls are wood paneling. The ceiling is suspended, acoustical tile hung 8'-0" above the finished floor level.

Door And Hardware Schedule, Sheet 4. The office has one door, which is shown as a G door on the plan. This door is 3'-0" wide and 6'-8" high. It is undercut 1½" at the bottom to provide air circulation for the office. Note 4 in the schedule calls for the rough opening to be 1¼" wider and 1" taller than the door leaf, which is finished with plastic laminate. Butt hinges, dormitory lockset and a door stop complete the hardware for door G. The Door Elevations, Sheet 4, show door G as a C-type door.

Interior Elevations, Sheet 6. Elevation 25 shows a blank wall with the note FRP. Division 9 of the Specifications details this as a fire-rated Class A (flame spread) panel. These are available from either Kemlite Corporation or Marlite Products. The Kemlite Corporation panel is 4'-0" × 9'-0" and has a flame spread rating of 20. Marlite Products show two sizes, 4'-0" × 8'-0" and 4'-0" × 10'-0", with a flame spread rating of 25.

Elevation 26 is taken looking toward the front wall of the office. The office desk assembly (No. 70) is provided by the owner and installed by the general contractor. This unit contains two 2-drawer files and a safe (No. 69). (Refer to the Safe Anchor, Detail A-3 for anchoring the safe to the 4" concrete slab.)

Two 36" high wall cabinets are mounted above the office desk assembly. They are securely supported by ⅝" CDX plywood under the wall paneling.

Elevation 27 shows a profile view of the office desk assembly with wall cabinets above and the electrical panels. Door G is surrounded by wood paneling. The quarry tile base molding is shown on either side of the door.

Elevation 28 shows the electrical panels and ⅝" CDX plywood under wall paneling. Electrical panels are detailed on the Electric Distribution Plans, Sheet 14.

Equipment Plan, Sheet 9. The office desk assembly (No. 70) and wall cabinets (No. 71), which are shown

in Interior Elevations 26 and 27, are shown in plan view here. Additionally, the electrical panel is shown along the rear wall of the office. An office side chair (No. 72) completes the equipment for Room 109.

HVAC Plan, Sheet 11. A diffuser with 8" neck supplies heating and cooling for the office. This unit is off-white in color. It has a round neck to connect to the 8" duct from HVAC unit RT-1.

Electric Plan, Sheet 12. Room 109 contains the distribution panelboard with panels A, A-1, and B and the emergency disconnect, which is tapped ahead of the main. The service equipment, which consists of a distribution panelboard with an 800A main, is fed by a lateral from a pad-mounted transformer located outside of the building. The lateral is routed from the pad-mounted transformer to a CT (current transformer) enclosure mounted on the exterior wall of the building. See the Transformer Pad Details, Sheet 12, for additional information concerning the power company's equipment. Service-entrance conductors are routed from the CT enclosure and connected to the terminals of the 800A main and distribution panelboard. See Figure 9-23.

The service-entrance conductors are two sets of #500 MCM THW copper conductors, parallel per phase, routed in two 4" conduits. A #500 MCM THW copper conductor has an ampacity of 380A. See Table 310-16 of the NEC®. Two of these conductors, parallel per phase, have an ampacity of 760A. The NEC® allows the next larger standard size overcurrent protection device to be used up to 800A. The next standard size above 760A is 800A and is selected for use according to the total ampacity of the conductors per phase.

Electric Distribution, Sheet 14. The Distribution Panel Buss Detail, Sheet 14, shows the main service-entrance conductors terminated at the lugs of the main. The emergency disconnect, EM, is tapped ahead of the main and is located in a separate vertical section isolated from the main disconnect. The emergency system provides power for emergency lights, exit lights, and lighting in the event of an emergency shutdown in the kitchen.

The distribution panel contains control devices with control circuits shown in the HVAC Control Wiring Detail, Sheet 14. All thermostat wiring is #18

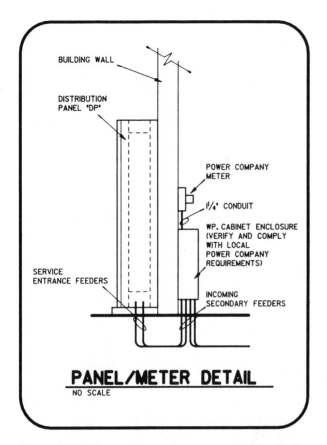

BUILDING WALL

DISTRIBUTION
PANEL "DP"

POWER COMPANY
METER

1¼" CONDUIT

WP. CABINET ENCLOSURE
(VERIFY AND COMPLY
WITH LOCAL
POWER COMPANY
REQUIREMENTS)

SERVICE
ENTRANCE FEEDERS

INCOMING
SECONDARY FEEDERS

PANEL/METER DETAIL
NO SCALE

Figure 9-23. The service equipment consists of a distribution panelboard supplied by underground service-entrance conductors from a CT enclosure located on the exterior of the building.

in size. The Control Panel Equipment Layout, Sheet 14, shows line connections for fan controls. For example, the control conductors for EF-1 terminate at L4, L5, and L6.

Lighting And Reflected Ceiling Plan, Sheet 13. One B-1 light fixture provides illumination for Room 109. This fixture with 40-watt, cool white, fluorescent bulbs in a recessed lighting fixture contains four 4' bulbs. Feeding this type of fixture is two #12 copper conductors with one #12 copper equipment grounding conductor. The conductors are routed in ¾" conduit and protected by a 20A CB.

Employee Break Room, Room 111, And Water Heater Closet, Room 112, Sheet 4

The Employee Break Room is located along the rear wall of the Preparation Area, Room 108. This area measures 2'-0" × 9'-2¼". Ceiling height and finish, and floor and wall finish are the same as for the preparation area.

Directly across from the Employee Break Room is the Water Heater Closet, which measures 3'-5⅞" wide and 3'-6" deep. A doubled header, at 8'-0" above the finished floor level, is indicated by parallel, dashed lines. Wall and floor finish is the same as for the preparation area.

Interior Elevations, Sheet 6. Four elevations are referenced on the Floor Plan, Sheet 4. These are Interior Elevations 21, 22, 23, and 24.

Elevation 21 is taken looking toward the office. The header for the closet, the doorway to the office, and profile view of the wall cabinet (No. 71) on the rear wall are shown. A broom holder (No. 83) and hose rack (No. 84) are located on this wall common to the office. The hot water heater (No. 86) is placed above two 12" deep wall shelves.

Elevation 22 is taken looking toward the front of the building. The hot water heater (No. 86) with one 18" deep wall shelf and two 12" deep wall shelves below are again shown. Wire wall shelving units (No. 49 & No. 50) are shown above the 5'-0" worktable in the preparation area. A vertical break line on the right-hand side of this interior elevation indicates that while the view could continue, it is terminated here.

Elevation 23 is taken looking toward the left side of the building. Stainless steel corner molding (No. 81) is shown on the corners of the kitchen wall and break area partition. A portion of the hot water heater (No. 86) with shelves below is also shown.

Elevation 24 shows features on the rear wall of the building. These include the wall cabinets (No. 71), time clock (No. 75), and timecard rack (No. 76). A 20" deep counter (No. 73), for employee use, is shown 42" above the finished floor level.

Equipment Plan, Sheet 9. The equipment noted in the interior elevation views is shown in plan view with two additional pieces of equipment. These are the Besco management board (No. 68) and six wooden stools (No. 74) for employees' use when sitting at the counter.

Electric Plan, Sheet 12. Circuit DP12 is shown for the hot water heater. This is a 12kW, 208V, 3ϕ unit requiring three #8 conductors and one #10 ground pulled in ³/₄ ″ conduit. A T-1 electrical connection specifies that the hot water heater is hard-wired. See Figure 9-24. Water heaters must have their kW rating increased by 125% to prevent nuisance tripping of the overcurrent protection device when the heating elements are activated to demand additional hot water.

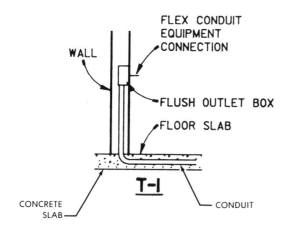

Figure 9-24. T-1 electrical connections are hard-wired.

Lighting And Reflected Ceiling Plan, Sheet 13. Single-pole wall switches are mounted 4′-6″ above the finished floor on the end partition in the break room. Circuit 17A controls service, office, and restroom lights with a 20A CB. Circuit 19A controls preparation area lights with a 20A CB. The lighting and reflected ceiling for this area is the same as for the preparation area.

SPECIALITY ITEMS, SHEET 10

Special systems required to complete the installation are an Ansul System, communication system, and menu signs. The Ansul System is a fire suppressant system installed in the hoods above cooking equipment. Equipment shown on the Floor Plan - Ansul System, Sheet 10, is identified by number and described in the Equipment Schedule, Sheet 10. The Isometric also shows the necessary connections for the system. See Figure 9-25.

The Ansul R-102 restaurant fire suppression system is designed to provide fire protection for kitchen ventilating structures such as hoods, plenums, ducts, and filters, and cooking appliances such as deep-fat fryers, griddles, range tops, upright natural or chain-type broilers and electric, lava rock, mesquite or gas radiant char broilers.

The basic system consists of an Ansul Automan Regulated Release Assembly, which includes a regulated release mechanism and a liquid agent storage tank housed within a single enclosure. Nozzles, detectors, and distribution piping are supplied in quantities needed for each fire suppression system arrangement.

The system provides automatic or manual actuation either at the Ansul Automan Regulated Release Mechanism, or through a remote manual pull station. The gas or electrical supply to all protected appliances will be immediately shut off upon actuation of the system.

The R-102 system suppresses fire by spraying the plenum area, the filters, cooking surfaces, and the exhaust duct system with a predetermined flow rate of Ansulex Liquid Fire Suppressant. When the liquid agent is discharged onto a cooking appliance fire, it cools the grease surface and reacts with the hot grease (*saponification*), forming a layer of soap-like foam on the surface of the fat. This layer acts as insulation between the hot grease and the atmosphere, thus helping to prevent the escape of combustible vapors.

Exhaust fans in the ventilating system should be left on. The forced draft of these fans assists the movement of the liquid agent through the ventilating system, which aids the fire suppression process. These fans also provide a cooling effect in the plenum and duct after the fire suppression system has been discharged.

The communication system provides a means of taking and placing orders. Customers, who are utilizing the convenience of the pick up window, place their orders directly from their cars to the employee working the pick up window. This employee then gives the order to personnel who fill the order. The microphone on the gooseneck and an additional speaker allow the same type of service to be provided for patrons wishing to eat in the dining area. Two equipment schedules give a complete list of the equipment needed for the communication system.

Plan and elevation views show necessary information for locating and installing the outside menu sign. The inside menu sign, which is located on the wall behind the rear counter assembly, is recessed into a 43¼″ × 8′-2½″ rough opening.

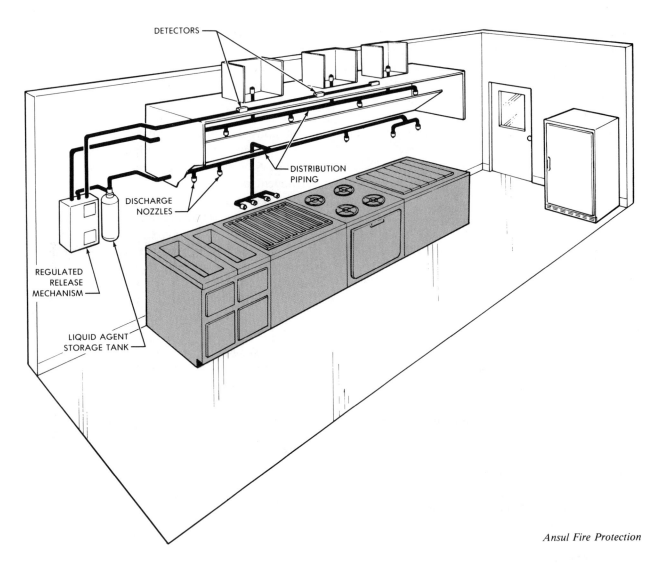

DETECTORS

DISTRIBUTION
PIPING

DISCHARGE
NOZZLES

REGULATED
RELEASE
MECHANISM

LIQUID AGENT
STORAGE TANK

Ansul Fire Protection

Figure 9-25. The Ansul Fire Suppression System provides fire protection for restaurant cooking equipment. Appliance energy sources are automatically shut off when a fire occurs.

Name   Date

Identification
Architectural Symbols

_____ **1.** Concrete

Ⓐ

Ⓑ

_____ **2.** Finish lumber

_____ **3.** Drywall

Ⓒ

Ⓓ

_____ **4.** Brick

_____ **5.** Earth

Ⓔ

Ⓕ

_____ **6.** Gravel

_____ **7.** Framing lumber

_____ **8.** Steel

Ⓖ

Ⓗ

_____ **9.** Concrete Block

_____ **10.** Insulation

Ⓘ

Ⓙ

True-False

T   F   **1.** Details are generally drawn to a larger scale than floor plans.

T   F   **2.** The radius of a circle contains 45°.

T   F   **3.** Pavers are solid brick capable of withstanding heavy loads.

T   F   **4.** Anchor bolts are used to secure drywall to wood or metal studs.

T   F   **5.** Exterior doors may be solid-core or hollow-core.

T   F   **6.** A 20A CB may be used to protect a 30A lighting circuit.

T   F   **7.** The net square footage of a room is found by multiplying the inside dimensions of length by the width.

T   F   **8.** Section views are identified by their equipment number and sheet on which the view is shown.

T   F   **9.** Door and hardware schedules specify door leaf sizes.

T   F   **10.** A restaurant is an A-3 assembly.

Identification

Plumbing Symbols

_____	1.	Vent thru roof	(A) — SAN —
_____	2.	Piping drop	(B) — 110 —
_____	3.	Wall hydrant	(C) — HW —
_____	4.	Sanitary waste piping	(D) — CW —
_____	5.	Hot water line	(E) - - - - - -
_____	6.	Cold water line	(F) ———O
_____	7.	Valve	(G) ———⊃
_____	8.	Tempered water line (110)	(H) —▷◁—
_____	9.	Piping rise	(I) —⊣ WH
_____	10.	Vent piping	(J) VTR

Completion

_____ 1. _____ receptacles are identified by symbol and the letters WP.

_____ 2. Dashes of alternating lengths on a plumbing isometric indicate _____.

_____ 3. _____ lines on a floor plan indicate equipment or material over 5'-0" above the floor.

_____ 4. Dimension lines are terminated by _____ lines.

_____ 5. Dimension lines may have arrowheads, _____, or dots on each end.

_____ 6. A scale of ¼" = 1'-0" indicates that the drawing is _____th actual size.

_____ 7. _____ collect rainwater from a roof and divert it to the ground through downspouts.

_____ 8. A(n) _____ glass will not slide or swing open.

_____ 9. Foundation footings on exterior elevations are shown with _____ lines.

_____ 10. Solariums are rooms with _____ walls.

_____ 11. Batt insulation 6" thick has an R value of _____.

_____ 12. The standard height for base cabinets is _____".

_____ 13. Installation of electrical equipment must conform to all local codes and the _____.

_____ 14. _____ is a thin layer of wood that is applied to a thicker core material.

_____ 15. Concrete slabs are _____ below piers to provide additional load-bearing capacity.

_____ 16. The minimum width for exterior doors is _____".

_____ 17. A(n) _____ course of brick is placed on end with the side exposed.

_____ 18. The symbol used to denote phase in electrical installations is _____.

_____ 19. _____ joints between concrete floor slabs and foundation walls provide for movement.

_____ 20. A #5 rebar is _____" in diameter.

Identification
Electrical Symbols

_____ 1. Weatherproof duplex receptacle

_____ 2. Telephone outlet

_____ 3. Disconnect switch

_____ 4. Buzzer

_____ 5. ON-OFF switch

_____ 6. Single-pole wall switch

_____ 7. Electric motor

_____ 8. Pushbutton

_____ 9. Hanging light fixture

_____ 10. Duplex receptacle

Math
Use $I = VA/V$ to solve 1–3.

1. $I = 20A$; $V = 120V$. Find VA.

2. $I = 15A$; $VA = 1,800VA$. Find V.

3. $VA = 7,200VA$; $V = 240V$. Find I.

4. The roof of a building requires 33 TJI 55E joists cut to 35′-9″ each. How many lineal feet of joists are required?

5. Rough-sawn cedar 1 × 6 boards are used to build an enclosure. At $485.00/M lineal feet, how much will 412 lineal feet cost?

6. A plan is drawn to the scale of ¼″ = 1′-0″. A line drawn 3 ½″ long on the plan represents what length on the actual building?

7. Two #12 THW copper conductors and one #12 equipment grounding conductor are pulled in a 46′-9″ run of ¾″ conduit available in 10′ lengths. How many total pieces of conduit are required?

8. A reflected ceiling plan for a room measuring 18′-0″ × 32′-0″ contains eight 2′ × 4′ recessed ceiling fixtures. How many pieces of 2′ × 4′ acoustical ceiling tile are required for the ceiling?

9. A 4″ concrete slab measures 18′-0″ × 24′-0″. How many yards of concrete are required?

10. At $48.00 per yard, delivered, what is the concrete cost for the slab in #9? Note: The next largest full yard of concrete is ordered.

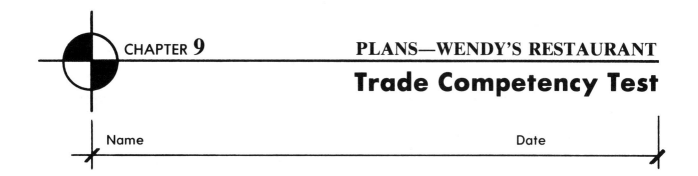
Refer to Wendy's Plans.

SITE DETAILS, SHEET 2

Completion

_____ **1.** The concrete slab for the trash enclosure is _____ ″ thick.

_____ **2.** Section A-2 specifies a(n) _____ ″ diameter concrete footing 3′-0″ high.

_____ **3.** Section _____ is a top view showing 1″ overlap of boards for the trash enclosure walls.

_____ **4.** The concrete slab for the trash enclosure slopes _____ ″ per foot.

_____ **5.** Detail J-2 is referenced in Elevation _____.

_____ **6.** Rough-sawn cedar boards for the trash enclosure sides are 1″ × 8″ × _____.

_____ **7.** Detail F-2 gives dimensions for the _____.

_____ **8.** The concrete piers for exterior pole lights extend _____ above finished grade level.

_____ **9.** Concrete foundations for directional signs are placed by the _____.

_____ **10.** Asphalt curbs extend _____ ″ above the asphalt topping.

SITE DETAILS, SHEET 2

True-False

T   F   **1.** The general contractor is to paint all pavement markers solid yellow.

T   F   **2.** Concrete curbs are reinforced with #4 rebars run continuously.

T   F   **3.** Bottom plates and anchor bolts are included with exterior pole lights.

T   F   **4.** The triangular pavement marker for the pick up window is larger than the triangular pavement marker showing the exit.

T   F   **5.** Detail F-2 is referenced in Section B-2.

T   F   **6.** Parking spaces are 10′-0″ wide, excluding the marker.

T   F   **7.** The sign erector must place 10″ standard steel pipe in 20′-0″ lengths for the street sign.

T   F   **8.** The gate arm for the trash enclosure is $3/8''$ × $2''$ × $2'-0''$ steel.

T   F   **9.** Four sections and two elevations are referenced on the plan view of the trash enclosure.

T   F   **10.** Exterior pole lights are designed for single or dual lights, depending upon the mounting bracket used.

FOUNDATION PLAN, SHEET 3
True-False

T   F   **1.** All raised concrete pads are elevated $4''$ for equipment placement.

T   F   **2.** Three #4 rebars, $24''$ long, are placed through exterior door openings.

T   F   **3.** Unless otherwise noted, $1/2''$ anchor bolts at $6'-0''$ are typical for all foundation walls.

T   F   **4.** Locations of all raised concrete pads are shown in Detail C-3.

T   F   **5.** Piping runs for plumbing are shown as dashed lines on the foundation plan.

T   F   **6.** Footing depths below grade must be verified with the local code.

T   F   **7.** Quarry tile for raised concrete pads is laid at a $45°$ angle to the walls.

T   F   **8.** Foundation walls at the front of the restaurant are $8''$ concrete block.

T   F   **9.** All footings are designed for 3,000 PSF soil-bearing pressure.

T   F   **10.** The thickness of the concrete floor slab is $4''$.

FOUNDATION PLAN, SHEET 3
Completion

_____   **1.** Brick coursing begins _____ $''$ below the top of the floor slab elevation.

_____   **2.** HD5 hold downs are required at _____ locations at the front of the building.

_____   **3.** The width of the widest raised concrete pad is _____.

_____   **4.** Control joints are centered on the _____ at exterior openings.

_____   **5.** The floor slab elevation is _____ $'$.

_____   **6.** Sawed joints must be cut within _____ hours of the slab pour.

_____   **7.** A(n) _____ $''$ high piece of $5/8''$ moisture-resistant plywood is placed at the base of $5/8''$ drywall.

_____   **8.** Reinforcement for the concrete floor slab is _____—W1.4 × W1.4 WWF.

_____   **9.** The Cooler-Freezer slab is sloped away from the the building a minimum of _____ $''$.

_____   **10.** The overall length of the building, including the Cooler-Freezer, is _____.

FLOOR PLAN, SHEET 4

Completion

_____ 1. All partitions not dimensioned are _____ ″ thick wood studs.

_____ 2. The floor in Room 101 is covered with _____.

_____ 3. Detail _____ provides additional information concerning brass posts and wood rails.

_____ 4. Overall dimensions of the Women's Restroom are 6′-8⅞″ × _____.

_____ 5. The hot water heater is located in Room _____.

_____ 6. Four A doors are shown at door locations _____ and K.

_____ 7. This restaurant is designed for an occupancy load of _____ people.

_____ 8. The drywall ceiling height in Room 104 is _____ above finished floor level.

_____ 9. Interior walls and partitions are covered with _____ ″ plywood sheathing, as noted, to provide shelf support.

_____ 10. _____ exhaust hoods are shown in Room 106.

_____ 11. All wood bases in Room 101 are to be _____.

_____ 12. The floor plan is drawn to the scale of _____ ″ = 1′-0″.

_____ 13. A(n) _____ wide rough opening is required for the sliding pick-up window.

_____ 14. Room 106 is entered through Door _____ from Room 102.

_____ 15. Room 108 has a(n) _____ ceiling 9′-0″ above the finish floor.

_____ 16. All electrical panels for the restaurant are located in Room _____.

_____ 17. The leafs of A doors are 3′-0″ wide × _____ high.

_____ 18. The illuminated sign in Room 106 is provided by the _____.

_____ 19. A dormitory lockset is required for the door to Room _____.

_____ 20. An exterior fascia runs along both sides of Room _____.

_____ 21. The width of the wall between Room 101 and Room 106 is _____ ″.

_____ 22. A(n) _____ is placed 8′-0″ above the finished floor at the front of the hall.

_____ 23. The wall separating Room 106 from the Women's Restroom and the Preparation Area is _____ long.

_____ 24. The overall length of the building excluding the Cooler-Freezer is _____.

_____ 25. _____ is applied to seal the opening between the Cooler-Freezer Area and Room 108.

FLOOR PLAN, SHEET 4
Identification

_____	**1.**	Room number
_____	**2.**	Door location
_____	**3.**	Direction of sight
_____	**4.**	Termination of dimension line
_____	**5.**	Sheet and interior elevation
_____	**6.**	Object above 5'-0"
_____	**7.**	Object below 5'-0"
_____	**8.**	Section and sheet
_____	**9.**	Detail and sheet
_____	**10.**	Framing member

(A) ——————+

(B) ◀

(C) [107]

(D) (6) 2

(E) (D / 7A)

(F) (D)

(G) - - - - - -

(H) —————

(I) ⊠

(J) (B / 4)

FLOOR PLAN, SHEET 4
True-False

T F **1.** The Waitress Station is designated as Room 102.

T F **2.** Interior dimensions are given from face-to-face of framing and from face of masonry to face of framing.

T F **3.** Three interior elevations are referenced for Room 105.

T F **4.** The Employee Break Room has a quarry tile floor.

T F **5.** All C doors are undercut 1½".

T F **6.** Customers enter and exit through A doors.

T F **7.** Water closets in restrooms are backed up to a common wall.

T F **8.** Exterior masonry walls, with interior finish, are 10⅞" thick.

T F **9.** The opening at the front wall of Room 106 is 2'-6" wide.

T F **10.** Both restrooms have quarry tile floors.

T F **11.** Exterior dimensions are from out-to-out of masonry or plywood sheathing.

T F **12.** The Cooler-Freezer measures 12'-0" × 30'-8".

T F **13.** The seating counter is supplied and installed by carpenters.

T F **14.** Three doors are specified as having security hinges.

T F **15.** Center-to-center distances between wood rails for customer traffic is 2'-2".

T F **16.** Return window walls for vestibules are 5'-8¾" long.

T   F   **17.** Hood 2 is 6'-0" long.

T   F   **18.** Blocking in frame walls is to be no more than 4'-0" apart.

T   F   **19.** Eight sections are referenced on the floor plan.

T   F   **20.** The rough opening for plastic laminate covered flush doors with adjustable metal frames is 3¾" wider than the door leaf.

EXTERIOR ELEVATIONS, SHEET 5
Completion

_____   **1.** A double _____ course of brick is shown on all elevations.

_____   **2.** Additional information regarding exterior light fixtures is found on Sheet _____.

_____   **3.** The _____ door is shown in the Left Side Elevation.

_____   **4.** The awning over the pick up window is seen in _____ elevations.

_____   **5.** Opaque mansard roof _____ are installed above window walls.

_____   **6.** The distance from the finish floor level to the top of the rear exterior wall is _____.

_____   **7.** _____ lines on the exterior elevations show foundation footings and walls.

_____   **8.** The awning over the pick up window is 4'-0" high and _____ long.

_____   **9.** The _____" red strip across the solarium is fabricated by the sign manufacturer.

_____   **10.** A junction box is shown for Fixture _____.

EXTERIOR ELEVATIONS, SHEET 5
True-False

T   F   **1.** Wrought iron railings are placed outside of the entrance and exit doors.

T   F   **2.** All exterior elevations are drawn to the same scale.

T   F   **3.** The glass in the Pick up Window Area which permits viewing of customers driving to pick up their orders is sliding glass.

T   F   **4.** Two scuppers with downspouts are shown on the Front Elevation.

T   F   **5.** Face brick is shown for all exterior brickwork.

T   F   **6.** Opposite sides of the building are illuminated with the same number of wall-mounted light fixtures.

T   F   **7.** The Wendy's logo is prominently displayed on the Front Elevation of the restaurant.

T   F   **8.** The storage module is provided by the general contractor.

T   F   **9.** Brick is recessed 2" in four indented areas on each side of the restaurant.

T   F   **10.** Tempered glass is specified for all window walls.

FLOOR PLAN, SHEET 4
INTERIOR ELEVATIONS, SHEET 6
EQUIPMENT PLAN, SHEET 9

Identification

_____ 1. Electric hand dryer

_____ 2. Fire extinguisher

_____ 3. Stainless steel corner molding

_____ 4. Water closet

_____ 5. Urinal

_____ 6. High chair

_____ 7. Hot chocolate machine

_____ 8. Booster chairs

_____ 9. Railing system

_____ 10. Carpet-tile transition strip

FLOOR PLAN, SHEET 4
INTERIOR ELEVATIONS, SHEET 6
EQUIPMENT PLAN, SHEET 9

Multiple Choice

_____ 1. Regarding Elevation 15, _____.
    A. this elevation is taken looking toward the front of the building
    B. a hot dog bun griddle is shown to the right
    C. equipment shown is located in Room 109
    D. a cash register is shown to the left

_____ 2. Regarding Elevation 4, _____.
    A. the hallway leads to the office
    B. details of the wall behind the front counter are not shown
    C. the reference for this elevation is in Room 101
    D. all details shown are also seen in Elevation 3

_____ 3. Regarding Elevation 12, _____.
    A. a type D door is shown to the right
    B. equipment shown is located in Room 108
    C. one cook counter assembly is shown
    D. the area open to the dining room is also shown in Elevation 14

_____ 4. Regarding Elevation 31, _____.
    A. the left wall of Room 105 is shown
    B. the opposite wall of this restroom is shown in Elevation 32
    C. the water closet shown is also seen in Elevation 35
    D. Elevations 29 and 30 are also for this restroom

_____   **5.** Regarding Elevation 21, _____.
      A. two 16″ deep wall shelves are shown
      B. a hot water heater is mounted on a solid shelf
      C. a broom holder is shown to the right of the hose rack
      D. this elevation is taken looking toward the left side of the building

_____   **6.** Regarding Item No. 51, _____.
      A. 49 are required
      B. these units are supplied by the electrical contractor
      C. placement is in Room 106
      D. wire wall shelving units are 18″ deep

_____   **7.** Regarding Item No. 113, _____.
      A. each unit has four seats
      B. four are required
      C. placement is in Room 108
      D. installation is by the general contractor

_____   **8.** Regarding the patty machine stand, _____.
      A. placement is in Room 106
      B. two are required
      C. this is part of the hamburger patty machine
      D. the general contractor provides the unit

_____   **9.** Regarding the Front Counter Assembly, _____.
      A. location is in Room 101
      B. two are required
      C. the cash register is included
      D. the general contractor provides labor for unloading at the building site

_____   **10.** Regarding customer stools, _____.
      A. six are required
      B. installation is by the owner
      C. these units are part of Item 109
      D. location is in Room 108

WALL SECTIONS, SHEETS 7A AND 7B

True-False

T   F   **1.** The typical 1′-4″ × 8″ concrete footings are reinforced with two #4 rebars run continuously.

T   F   **2.** Insulation above the ceiling in Room 100 is 6″ batt.

T   F   **3.** The soffit detail over the front counter assembly is shown in Section F, Sheet 7B.

T   F   **4.** Pier footings are reinforced with eight #5 rebars each way.

T   F   **5.** The double soldier course is 7′-8″ above the finished floor level.

T   F   **6.** Detail E-3 is referenced on Section A, Sheet 7A.

T   F   **7.** The roof membrane is two-ply rubber.

T   F   **8.** The bottom of the foundation footing must be a minimum of 2′-8″ below grade.

T	F	9. All sidewalks adjacent to exterior walls must have a minimum slope of ¼″ per foot.
T	F	10. Weep holes in exterior masonry are spaced at 4′-0″ OC.
T	F	11. Exterior sheathing is ⅝″ plywood.
T	F	12. The local frost line is to be verified before digging foundation trenches.
T	F	13. A cant strip is placed at the rear wall and the cooler-freezer roof to help assure water runoff.
T	F	14. Masonry wall ties are staggered at 16″ OC vertically and horizontally.
T	F	15. Anchor bolts in stud walls are typically ½″ × 12″ placed on 6′-0″ centers.

STRUCTURAL PLAN, SHEET 8
Completion

_____ 1. All roof joists slope _____″ from the front to the back of the building.

_____ 2. R1 joists have a cut length of _____.

_____ 3. The top of the Glulam beam is _____ above the finished floor level.

_____ 4. Exhaust Fan 5 is located _____ from the rear wall of the building.

_____ 5. Detail _____ shows the load detail for roof joists.

_____ 6. The Structural Plan is drawn to the scale of _____.

_____ 7. The Micro = Lam® beam above the front counter assembly must bear a minimum of _____″ on each end.

_____ 8. _____ lineal feet of R-2 joists are required.

_____ 9. Generally, roof joists are spaced on _____″ centers.

_____ 10. The R-3 joist is _____ in length.

_____ 11. _____ 20″ TJ1 55E joists are required in the front portion of the building.

_____ 12. The rough opening for Exhaust Fan 2 is _____″ square.

_____ 13. _____ layer(s) of ⅝″ Firecode-rated drywall is specified for roof openings.

_____ 14. Front-to-back locations for rough openings are taken from the _____ wall.

_____ 15. Diagonals bracing the exterior fascia are spaced on _____ centers.

_____ 16. _____ shows a typical roof opening detail.

_____ 17. The Micro = Lam® beam over the front counter assembly is supported by _____ bearing studs on each end.

_____ 18. The weight of RT-2 is spread over _____ joists.

_____ 19. Load Detail _____ is used for loads exceeding 250 pounds per joist.

_____ 20. _____ 20″ web stiffeners are required.

SPECIALTY ITEMS, SHEET 10
Completion

_____ **1.** The Ansul System is a hood _____ extinguishing system.

_____ **2.** The microswitch controlling the Ansul System is a double-throw, _____-pole assembly.

_____ **3.** Pull stations for the Ansul System are located at the _____ door.

_____ **4.** The door chime for the intercom main station is located _____″ above the the finished floor level.

_____ **5.** Hood # _____ contains one speaker for the communication system.

_____ **6.** The electrical contractor installs _____″ conduit for the communication system.

_____ **7.** When speaking to drive-thru customers, the communication system at the pick-up window is activated by a pedestal-mounted, heavy-duty _____ switch.

_____ **8.** The front counter equipment for the communication system contains one _____ microphone.

_____ **9.** The concrete base for the exterior menu sign is 18″ square and _____″ deep.

_____ **10.** The top of the interior menu sign is _____ above the finished floor level.

HVAC PLAN, SHEET 11
True-False

T F **1.** Cross-hatched plenums are located between joists.

T F **2.** Ductwork may run above or below the suspended ceiling as required.

T F **3.** Unit RT-2 is furnished with manual outside air dampers.

T F **4.** Wiring for Unit MUA-1 is completed by the electrical contractor.

T F **5.** Unit EF-3 is supplied by a 120V, 1ϕ circuit.

T F **6.** All supply air ducts and diffusers are to be insulated.

T F **7.** Three C diffusers are required.

T F **8.** The HVAC system is designed to meet an outside temperature of 98°F in the summer.

T F **9.** F grills are off-white in color.

T F **10.** The HVAC contractor is to use the Floor Plan, Sheet 4, for locating all equipment, curbs, and rails.

HVAC PLAN, SHEET 11
Completion

_____ **1.** Registers provide _____ air.

_____ **2.** The thermostat for RT-2 is located in the _____ room.

_____ 3. Disconnects for all HVAC equipment is provided by the _____ contractor.

_____ 4. Supply and return air duct drops from all roof units are isolated from unit vibration with _____ duct connectors.

_____ 5. A(n) _____ piece reduces the 24″ × 14″ duct of RT-2 to 18″ × 14″.

_____ 6. The kW ratings of electric heat units are listed 240V, 3φ and must be derated _____% when 208V, 3φ is used.

_____ 7. E grills are _____ mounted.

_____ 8. B diffusers are connected to RT-2 with _____″ diameter ducts.

_____ 9. All ductwork for exhaust hoods is to be fabricated per NFPA _____ and local codes.

_____ 10. D registers have a 30″ × 4″ _____ size.

ELECTRIC PLAN, SHEET 12
True-False

T   F   **1.** The double fryer is located on circuit DP10.

T   F   **2.** EF-1 is wired with three #12 conductors and one #12 equipment grounding conductor in ¾″ conduit.

T   F   **3.** T-2 electrical connections provide power for cord- and plug-connected equipment.

T   F   **4.** Ice machines are cord- and plug-connected.

T   F   **5.** Power to the hot water heater is controlled by a disconnect switch.

T   F   **6.** The location of the transformer pad may vary depending upon local conditions.

T   F   **7.** Electricians may correct circuits to the least amount of conduit run.

T   F   **8.** Fire disconnect switches are mounted at 3′-0″ above the finished floor level.

T   F   **9.** Outlet mounting height for the Frosty machine is 12″ above the finished floor level.

T   F   **10.** MUA-1 is controlled by a weatherproof disconnect located on the roof.

T   F   **11.** Eight telephone outlets are shown on the Electric Plan, Sheet 12.

T   F   **12.** A WP disconnect is utilized to shut-off power to the bun freezer.

T   F   **13.** Circuit 1A-1 serves duplex receptacles in the dining room.

T   F   **14.** The power company's meter is located on the rear wall of the building.

T   F   **15.** All control wiring for HVAC units is installed by the electrical contractor.

T   F   **16.** Primary service conductors are routed through 4″ conduit.

T   F   **17.** The cash register for the pick-up window has an isolated ground.

T   F   **18.** Momentary contact switches for the Ansul System are 120V.

T   F   **19.** The condiment warmer is hard-wired.

T   F   **20.** The circuit for the hot water tank contains a #8 equipment grounding conductor.

LIGHTING & REFLECTED CEILING PLAN, SHEET 13
Completion

_____   **1.** _____ lighting fixtures are shown on the plan by rectangles.

_____   **2.** A(n) _____ box is located above the ceiling for wiring of sneeze guard lights and ceiling lights over the salad bar.

_____   **3.** K-1 fixtures are _____-mounted.

_____   **4.** Two _____ fixtures are mounted on top of the rear wall to provide flood-lighting to the rear of the building.

_____   **5.** _____ P-1 fixtures are required for grid lighting in the dining room.

_____   **6.** The mounting height of K-4 fixtures is _____ above the finished floor level.

_____   **7.** Lighting for the entrance vestibule is provided by a(n) _____ fixture.

_____   **8.** The drive-thru sign at the rear of the property is wired on Circuit _____.

_____   **9.** _____ emergency lights are strategically located throughout the building.

_____   **10.** _____ for exit lights are furnished with the fixtures.

ELECTRIC DISTRIBUTION, SHEET 14
True-False

T   F   **1.** The distribution panel is located in Room 109.

T   F   **2.** The electrical contractor shall verify with the HVAC contractor which HVAC option is to be used for this building.

T   F   **3.** The scale for the Control Panel Equipment Layout is $1/4'' = 1'-0''$.

T   F   **4.** Exhaust hoods are controlled by 20A, three-pole breakers.

T   F   **5.** Right side building lights draw a .6kW load.

T   F   **6.** The main disconnect for emergency systems is connected ahead of other building main switches.

T   F   **7.** The distribution panel measures 90″ high × 84″ wide × 20″ deep.

T   F   **8.** All bussing shall be copper only.

T   F   **9.** Control wiring for MUA-1 is included in the HVAC contract.

T   F   **10.** Control wiring for RT-1 and RT-2 is included in the HVAC contract.

T   F   **11.** All circuit breakers shall be bolt-on only.

T   F   **12.** The total connected load of the water heater is 14kW.

T   F   **13.** The front counter drink system is controlled by a 20A breaker on Circuit A.

T   F   **14.** KTN fuses are specified for Panel B.

T   F   **15.** Panels A, A-1, and B shall be circuited as shown.

T   F   **16.** Cable-entrance cutouts for the distribution panel are located on the back of the panel.

T   F   **17.** The total connected load for the building is 235.30kW.

T   F   **18.** Dining room grid lights are on a 15A circuit.

T   F   **19.** Barriers shall separate all electric panels and control cabinets.

T   F   **20.** Rooftop receptacles are wired on four circuits.

PLUMBING PLAN, SHEET 15
Completion

_____   **1.** The salad bar is supplied by _____ " hot and cold water supply piping.

_____   **2.** _____ FD-1 floor drains are shown on the plan.

_____   **3.** _____ for beverage dispensers, coffee, tea, and hot chocolate machines are provided as directed by the equipment supplier.

_____   **4.** _____ lines in the Sanitary Isometric represent sanitary waste piping.

_____   **5.** _____ lines in the Sanitary Isometric represent vent piping.

_____   **6.** Sanitary piping for the salad bar is _____ " in diameter.

_____   **7.** The drain for the triple compartment sink is _____ ".

_____   **8.** A(n) _____ " drainage vent is provided for the water closets.

_____   **9.** The mounting height for the water supply to the triple compartment sink is _____ ".

_____   **10.** _____ cleanouts are shown on the Sanitary Isometric.

PLUMBING PLAN, SHEET 15
True-False

T   F   **1.** All piping is to be under the concrete slab unless otherwise noted.

T   F   **2.** Gas piping is to be omitted on electrically heated buildings.

T   F   **3.** The Grease Interceptor Detail is drawn to the scale of $1/4'' = 1'-0''$.

T   F   **4.** A 3" interceptor vent may be omitted if not required by local code.

T   F   **5.** A $1\frac{1}{2}''$ gas line run down inside the wall connects to the gas meter.

T   F   **6.** A $1\frac{1}{2}''$ water supply pipe is connected to the utility company's main service.

T   F   **7.** The plumbing contractor shall provide valves at each connection to all equipment.

T   F   **8.** Two hub drains are required for the sanitary system.

T   F   **9.** A $3/4''$ cold water and $1/2''$ hot water supply provide water for the urinal.

T   F   **10.** Water closets and lavatories are furnished by the plumbing contractor.

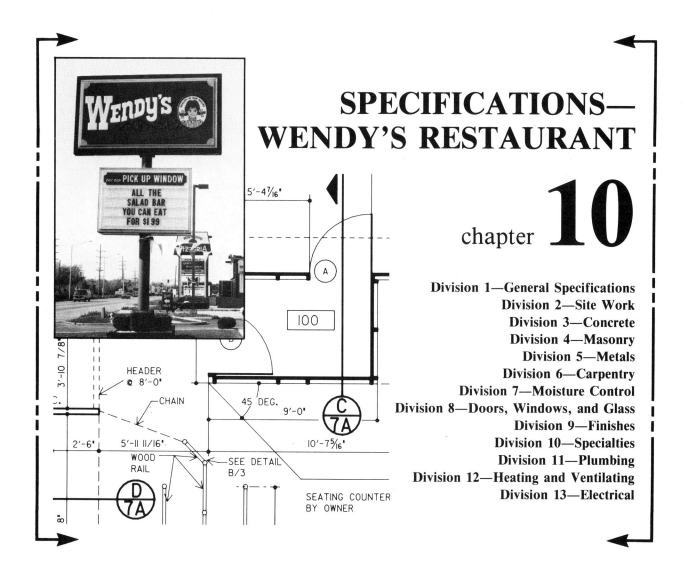

SPECIFICATIONS—WENDY'S RESTAURANT

chapter 10

SPECIFICATIONS

Specifications are written instructions for constructing a building. They may be printed on the plan sheets or bound in book form. Specifications define relationships and assign responsibilities of the owner, architect, contractor, and subcontractors. They also describe technical construction requirements for completing the job. The specifications are prepared after the plans are drawn and give *specific* information regarding the type, size, and location of material used to construct the project. Should a difference occur between the plans and the specifications, the specifications should be followed because they represent the specific intent of the architect.

The specifications may be changed by the owner during construction by issuing a *change order*, authorizing the contractor to make changes in location, layout, size, and type of material. The architect and contractor may also seek to make changes. Changes should be routed through the architect who verifies compliance with all local, state, and national requirements and completes the documents to assure completion and payment of the change order.

Specifications for Wendy's Restaurant follow the standardized format developed by the Construction Specifications Institute (CSI). In this format, 16 CSI divisions are arranged in trade work groups (carpentry, electricity, and so forth) in the same sequence as they occur on the job. The number of divisions for a particular job varies, depending upon the individual job requirements. For example, the specifications for Wendy's Restaurants contain 13 divisions.

INDEX TO SPECIFICATIONS

DIVISION 1—GENERAL SPECIFICATIONS

Specifications for Stipulated Sum Construction Agreement or for Cost of Work Plus Fee Construction Agreement

DIVISION 2—SITE WORK

Excavation, Backfilling, Grading
Asphalt Paving
Concrete Paving
Striping and Parking Blocks
Curbs
Landscaping
Plant Guarantee and Replacement
Utilities

DIVISION 3—CONCRETE

Footings
Slabs and Footings
Sidewalks and Ramps
Paving

DIVISION 4—MASONRY

Face Brick
Mortar for Face Brick
Concrete Block

DIVISION 5—METALS

Wrought Iron Railing (Outside)
Brass Railing (With wood handrail)

DIVISION 6—CARPENTRY

Rough Carpentry
Structural Lumber
Nailing Schedule
Truss Joists
"Z" Booths—Counter Wall and Seating
Finish Carpentry
Walk-in Cooler-Freezer

DIVISION 7—MOISTURE CONTROL

Caulking
Roofing and Sheetmetal
Single Membrane Roofing
Building Insulation

DIVISION 8—DOORS, WINDOWS, AND GLASS

Aluminum Entrance Doors & Storefront
Solarium Enclosure
Prefinished Doors
Windows
Mirrors

DIVISION 9—FINISHES

Gypsum Drywall
Suspended Ceiling System
Wall and Floor Finishes
Carpet
Wallpaper
Painting
Paint Schedule

DIVISION 10—SPECIALTIES

Toilet Partitions
Toilet Accessories
Room Identification Sign
Decorator Fascia Panels
General Signage
Communication System
Hood Fire Suppression System & Portable Fire
   Extinguishers
Exterior Trash Enclosure
Kitchen Equipment

DIVISION 11—PLUMBING

DIVISION 12—HEATING & VENTILATING

DIVISION 13—ELECTRICAL

DIVISION 1

GENERAL SPECIFICATIONS

FOR STIPULATED SUM CONSTRUCTION AGREEMENT OR
FOR USE WITH COST OF WORK PLUS FEE
CONSTRUCTION AGREEMENT

ARTICLE I.

DEFINITIONS

For the purposes of this contract, the following terms shall have the meanings hereinafter set forth:

A. The term *Wendy's* means Wendy's International, Inc., an Ohio corporation, whose principal address is 4288 West Dublin-Granville Road, Box 256, Dublin, Ohio 43017. Wendy's is also referred to herein as *owner*.

B. The term *contractor* means the person, firm, or corporation, identified as such in the agreement, responsible for the execution of the work contracted for by Wendy's.

C. The term *subcontractor* means, without limitation, any firm, corporation, or person working directly or indirectly for the contractor, whether or not pursuant to a formal subcontract, that furnishes or performs a portion of the work, labor, or material, according to the drawings and/or specifications. The term *principal subcontractor* means any subcontractor having one or more subcontractors requiring it to furnish work, labor, or material in an aggregate amount in excess of $500.

D. The term *agreement* means the construction agreement by and between Wendy's and the contractor.

E. The term *contract* means the agreement signed by Wendy's and the contractor, these specifications and all other documents listed as contract documents in Article I of the agreement.

F. The term *contract amount* means the contract amount as shown in Article IV of the agreement as revised by approved contract change orders.

G. The term *work* includes all labor necessary to produce the construction required by the contract, all materials and equipment incorporated or to be incorporated in such construction, and other items and facilities of every kind necessary to produce the construction required by the contract.

H. The term *change order* is a written order to the contractor signed by Wendy's, issued after execution of the contract, authorizing a change in the work or an adjustment in the contract amount or contract time.

I. The term *contract time* is the period of time alloted in Article III of the agreement for the completion of the work as revised by approved contract change orders. The term *guaranteed maximum cost* shall be the sum specified in Article V of the agreement.

ARTICLE II.
GENERAL REQUIREMENTS

A. The contractor warrants and represents that it has carefully examined all of the plans and specifications and all of the real property upon which the work is to be conducted, and has satisfied itself as to the conditions existing and the difficulties likely to be encountered in the construction of the work. The contractor agrees that any conditions that exist or that may hereafter exist, or any conditions or difficulties that may be encountered in the execution of the work, which should have reasonably been discovered upon such examination, will not constitute a cause for the reformation or recision of this contract, or a modification in the contract amount, or a termination hereof.

B. Contractor shall obtain and pay for all permits, licenses, certificates, tap charges, construction easements, inspections, and other approvals required both temporary and permanent to commence and complete the work. No additional cost to Wendy's shall be made because of this requirement except that contractor shall not be required to reimburse Wendy's for any permits, licenses, certificates, tap charges, construction easements, assessments, and other approvals obtained by Wendy's prior to the execution of the agreement.

C. In the event of non-acceptance of work by any regulating authority, the contractor shall perform the additional work required to bring the work into a condition of acceptance, and such additional work shall be done by the contractor without any further cost to Wendy's.

D. The contractor shall protect the work and all adjacent property from loss or damage resulting from its operations, and in the event of such loss or damage, shall make such replacements or repairs as required by Wendy's without additional cost to Wendy's.

E. Contractor shall furnish to Wendy's all permits and certificates permitting occupancy by Wendy's without restriction before any final payment shall be due to contractor.

ARTICLE III.
INTENT OF CONTRACT DOCUMENTS

A. The agreement and each of the contract documents are complementary, and they shall be interpreted so that what is called for by one shall be as binding as if called for by all. Should the contractor observe any conflicts within the contract documents, the contractor shall bring them to Wendy's attention for decision and revision at once. The contractor shall secure written instructions from Wendy's before proceeding with any work affected by conflicts, omissions, or discrepancies in the contract documents.

B. A duplication of work is not intended by the contract documents and any duplications specified shall not become a basis for extra cost to Wendy's.

ARTICLE IV.
SUBCONTRACTORS

A. The contractor may, at its discretion, elect to have certain portions of the work required to be performed by it hereunder, performed by others under subcontract, provided, however that no such work may be performed under subcontract unless prior written approval by Wendy's is obtained in each instance.

B. All contracts in connection with the work entered into by the contractor with subcontractors shall be subject to and governed by the terms and conditions of the contract. Upon any default by contractor, and upon receipt of written request from Wendy's, each subcontractor shall perform directly for Wendy's in accordance with the terms of its subcontract all of the work which it is required to perform pursuant to its subcontract.

C. No provisions of the contract nor of any contract between the contractor and subcontractors shall be construed as an agreement between Wendy's and the subcontractor, and neither the contract nor any contract between the contractor and the subcontractors shall give any said subcontractor rights against Wendy's unless Wendy's shall, upon default by the contractor, request the subcontract, in which event Wendy's shall be solely liable for payment of that portion of the amount due the subcontractor under subcontract for work performed after receipt of the request by Wendy's that the subcontractor proceed to complete the work.

The contractor shall be as fully responsible to Wendy's for the acts and omissions of a subcontractor, of the persons employed by a subcontractor, or of firms and/or subcontractors engaged by a subcontractor, as it is for the acts and omissions of its own employees.

ARTICLE V.
DELAYS AND EXTENSIONS OF TIME

A. If the contractor is unreasonably delayed at any time in the progress of the work by any act or neglect of Wendy's, or by any employee of Wendy's, or by any separate contractor employed by Wendy's, or by any changes ordered in the work, or by labor disputes, fire, or acts of God, or by any cause which Wendy's shall decide justifies the delay, then the contract time shall be extended by change order for such time as Wendy's may determine.

B. All claims for extension of time shall be made in writing to Wendy's no more than fourteen (14) days after the occurrence of the delay; otherwise they shall be waived. In the case of a continuing cause of delay, only one claim is necessary provided that Wendy's is notified in writing of the continuing delay with fourteen (14) days after the commencement of the continuing delay.

C. Extension of contract time by Wendy's, if any, shall be the contractor's sole remedy for delay.

ARTICLE VI.
WARRANTIES

A. The contractor warrants to Wendy's that all materials and equipment furnished under this contract shall be new unless otherwise specified, and that all work shall be free from defects in both material and workmanship.

B. All guarantees and warranties of equipment or materials furnished to the contractor or any subcontractor by any manufacturer or supplier shall be deemed to run to the benefit of Wendy's. Prior to final acceptance of the work, the contractor shall deliver to Wendy's copies of all guarantees and warranties on equipment and materials furnished by all manufacturers and suppliers to the contractor and all its subcontractors, with duly executed instruments properly assigning the guarantees and warranties to Wendy's. No retainage shall be paid until these copies and instruments are received by Wendy's.

ARTICLE VII.
ASSIGNMENTS

This contract or any rights thereunder shall not be assigned by the contractor without the prior written consent of Wendy's.

ARTICLE VIII.
COMPLIANCE WITH LAWS

Contractor shall be responsible for complying with all laws, ordinances, rules, and regulations affecting the work to be done by the contractor. Contractor will furnish to Wendy's such evidence as Wendy's may request from time to time to show compliance with all laws, ordinances, rules and regulations, but failure of Wendy's to request evidence of compliance with any laws, ordinances, rules and regulations shall not excuse contractor from complying with them.

ARTICLE IX.
PAYMENT AND PERFORMANCE BONDS

Prior to commencement of the work, the contractor shall furnish to Wendy's a payment bond and a performance bond in form and substance and with sureties acceptable to Wendy's. Both bonds shall be in the contract amount of in the amount of the Guaranteed Maximum Cost unless some other amount is specified in writing by Wendy's. The cost of obtaining said bonds shall be borne by the contractor.

ARTICLE X.
CLEANING

The contractor shall at all times keep the premises free from accumulation of waste materials or rubbish caused by its employees, subcontractors, or their work. At the completion of the work, the subcontractor shall remove from the building and the site all rubbish, tools, and surplus materials, and shall leave the work room clean unless otherwise specified. If in the opinion of Wendy's the contractor fails to keep the premises clean, Wendy's may remove waste materials and rubbish and charge the expense of such removal to the contractor.

ARTICLE XI.
INDEMNIFICATION

Contractor shall indemnify and hold harmless Wendy's, its agents, and employees from and against all claims, damages, losses, and expenses, including attorneys' fees, arising out of or resulting from the performance of the work, provided that any such claim, damage, loss, or expense (1) is attributable to bodily injury, sickness, disease, or death or to injury or destruction of tangible property, including the loss of use resulting therefrom; and (2) is caused in whole or in part by any act or omission of the contractor, and subcontractor, anyone directly or indirectly employed by any of them, or anyone for whose acts any of them may be liable regardless of whether or not it is caused in part by a party indemnified hereunder, and shall further indemnify and hold harmless

Wendy's, its agents and employees, from all expense of defending against all claims for damages, losses, and expenses which are claimed by any person, firm, or corporation to be caused in whole or in part by an act or omission of the contractor, any subcontractor, anyone directly or indirectly employed by any of them, or anyone for whose acts any of them may be liable, regardless of whether or not it is caused or claimed to be caused in part by a party indemnified hereunder. In any and all claims against Wendy's, or any of its agents or employees, by any employee of the contractor, any subcontractor, anyone directly or indirectly employed by any of them, or anyone for whose acts any of them may be liable, the foregoing indemnification obligation shall not be limited in any way by any limitation on the amount or type of damages, compensation, or benefits payable by or for the contractor or any subcontractor under any worker's compensation acts, disability benefit, or other employee benefit acts.

ARTICLE XII.
WORKER'S COMPENSATION AND INSURANCE

Contractor shall, at own expense, comply with all the provisions of the Worker's Compensation laws of the state in which the Wendy's Image Retail Facility is to be located. Before commencing work, contractor shall deliver to Wendy's a certificate showing compliance with the laws of such state.

Before commencing work, contractor shall deliver to Wendy's an insurance policy in form and company satisfactory to Wendy's, with limits of not less than $1,000,000 for injury to or death of persons and $200,000 for damage to property. Wendy's shall be named as a co-insured on such policy.

DIVISION 2
SITEWORK

EXCAVATION, BACKFILLING, GRADING

1. Remove all vegetation, refuse, or existing structures in confines of building construction and paving construction prior to commencement of work.
2. Excavate as required to provide sufficient working room for the laying of foundation walls. Excavate for all footings to be on undisturbed earth with a minimum depth as shown on drawings unless otherwise governed by local codes.
3. In the event that rock is encountered in the foundation excavation, and if this rock must be removed by dynamite or compressor, the owner will reimburse the subcontractor for the predetermined cost of these operations.
4. Backfilling of walls in interior areas where concrete slab will bear on grade shall be grits or bankrun gravel, well compacted, brought to a subgrade of 8″ below finish floor line.
5. Backfilling of exterior foundation walls shall be clean gravel, well compacted, brought to a subgrade of 8″ below finish sidewalk paving.
6. Backfilling over utilities running over paved areas shall be of grits.
7. Remainder of site shall be graded to assure drainage of surface water from building.
8. Remove excess soils from the site—if any.
9. Grades not otherwise indicated on the plans shall be uniform levels or slopes between points where elevations are given. Abrupt changes in slopes shall be well-rounded.

10. Soil tests shall be performed to insure soil will meet 3,000 PSF design strength. Contractor shall notify architect immediately if excavation on any part of the site reveals fill or ground water.

ASPHALT PAVING

All paving shall be installed in areas as indicated on site plan. Pavement design shall meet 10 year minimum design for local area as established by Asphalt Institute. The following guide should be used as minimum thickness required:

Soil Class	Minimum Pavement
Poor - CBR = 3.5 - Type, plastic when wet such as clay or fine silt, sandy loam	6″ coarse asphalt base binder (1½″ asphalt aggregate) plus 1½″ asphalt topping (max. ½″ aggregate)
Medium - CBR = 7.0 - Type, hard silty-sands, or sand gravels containing clay and fine silt	4″ coarse asphalt base (1½″ aggregate) plus 1½″ asphalt topping (max. ½″ aggregate)
Good - CBR = 12 - Type, clean sand and sand gravel free of clay, silt, or loam	3″ coarse asphalt base material (1½″ aggregate) plus 1½″ asphalt topping (max. ½″ aggregate)
	or
	6″ (compacted thickness stone base plus 2½″ asphalt topping) (max. ¾″ aggregate)

CONCRETE PAVING

See Concrete: Item 4 - Division 3

STRIPING AND PARKING BLOCKS

Concrete parking blocks and striping shall be installed as shown on drawings. All parking blocks shall be a minimum of 6′-0″ in length and a maximum of 5″ in height. Blocks shall be placed as shown on site plan.

CURBS

A. Concrete curbs—shall be full 6″ × 18″ formed curbs with expansion joints or saw cuts not more than 20′-0″ apart. All free-standing or integral curbs shall be reinforced with at least one #4 reinforcing rod continuous.
B. Asphalt curbs—shall be full 6″ machined formed curbs. Curbs shall be guaranteed for 90 days from the day of the store opening. Any defective curb shall be replaced by paving contractor at no expense to the owner.

LANDSCAPING

Provide all labor, materials, and equipment necessary to complete the seeding, sodding, landscape planting, earthwork, and edging as shown on the proposal. Landscape bidder shall submit a written proposal and landscape plan to the owner for approval. Proposal shall indicate size and number of planting and exact area to be sodded.

General contractor shall be responsible for installing topsoil to grade and for all rough grading. Area shall be free of debris and well drained before planting begins. No payments in excess of allowance shall be made unless approved by owner or general contractor in writing. Total proposal shall include all work including taxes where applicable.

PLANT GUARANTEE & REPLACEMENT

All plants and sod areas shall be guaranteed for one full growing season to extend from May 1st to September 30th. Any plants not in satisfactory vigor shall be replaced at no expense to the owner.

UTILITIES

1. The general contractor shall furnish all materials, labor, tools, transportation, incidentals, and appurtenances to complete in every detail and leave in working order all utilities called for herein and/or shown on the Construction Documents. This includes but is not limited to: Storm sewer, sanitary sewer, water service, gas service, electric service, roof drainage, etc.
2. All utilities including electric service to signs will be considered site work to within five feet of the building perimeter.
3. Required grease trap regardless of location shall be considered as part of the building cost and so reflected in all bidding.
4. The general contractor shall verify all taps and furnish any city drawings required prior to construction.

DIVISION 3
CONCRETE

All labor, materials, and equipment necessary to complete all concrete work including excavation, trenching, form work, reinforcing, cement finish, and precast concrete.
1. Footings:
Refer to drawings for sizes, depth, and reinforcement. Earth trench forms will be permitted for footings if conditions are favorable. Sides of trenches shall be clean, even, vertical and true, bottoms shall be level, clean, and without fill.

Reinforcing shall be unpainted and uncoated, free from rust or scale, and shall be cleaned and straightened before being shaped and placed in position. Accurately position reinforcement and secure against displacement. Where there is delay in pouring, reinspect reinforcement and clean off any dried cement, mortar, or rust.

All reinforcement shall be of size and spacing as called for on the drawings or as per local codes.

2. Slabs and Footings:

　　3,000 PSI concrete slabs to be reinforced with 6 × 6—W1.4 × W1.4 welded wire fabric installed in a manner that places that in the center of the slab. (Lap edges 6″)

　　Provide continuous 6 mil 'Visqueen' vapor barrier on leveled 4″ gravel base under all building slabs. Lap edges 6″ and seal (turn up at walls).

　　All concrete floors shall be poured level, except where floor drains occur, in which case they shall be sloped or warped to drain. Total slope is not to exceed ¾″ below floor level.

　　The contractor shall build into concrete work the following materials, which are furnished by other trades, and shall bed and secure same as required.

　　A. All plumbing and syrup lines, electric conduit, concrete inserts, hangers, anchors, floor clips, sleeves for all piping, etc., as and when required for all other trades.

　　B. Anchor bolts, plates, etc., for all equipment.

　　C. Concrete contractor shall install and pour in safe when equipment is delivered.

3. Side Walks and Ramps:

　　2,500 PSI air entrained concrete, 4″ thick, broom finish score with ¾″ deep contraction joints into approximately 4′-0″ squares or as shown.

4. Paving:

　　3,000 PSI concrete, 4″ thick reinforced with #10 - 6 × 6 wire or as shown on plan. Expansion joint spacing not to exceed 20′ apart and to be ³⁄₁₆″ cut with power saw. No wood expansion joints of any type to be accepted. All concrete to be vibrated and finished with float or belt finish.

DIVISION 4

MASONRY

　　All labor, materials, and equipment necessary to complete all brick and block work, including structural steel, wall ties, masonry reinforcing, etc.

1. General:

　　All work shall be laid true to dimensions, plumb, square, and in bond, or properly anchored. All courses shall be level with joints of uniform width. No joints shall exceed specified size and, if necessary, clipped courses shall be provided to level off.

　　Perform all masonry work in accordance with best trade practices. Brace "green" walls and protect mortar from "washing-out" at end of day's work using planks, weighted canvas, or similar means to cover wall. Cooperate with other trades in jointly executed work and built-in items. Patch openings as required for passage of mechanical and electrical trades. "Uncored" units must be used at all exposed and or semi-exposed conditions of brick rowlock caps, sills, etc. Window sills to be gray limestone. Size and location shown on construction documents.

2. Mortar, ASTM C-270, Type M or S

　　Cold weather admixture shall be "Trimix" as manufactured by L. Sonneborn Sons.

A. Temperature below 35 degrees F., and constant, use admixture (Trimix) for mortars at a ratio of three fourths (¾) quart to a bag of cement mortar.

B. Temperature 32 degrees F. to 25 degrees F., and constant, use admixture at ratio of one (1) quart to a bag of cement mortar.

C. Temperature dropping at 40 degrees F., add three fourths (¾) quart of admixture to a bag of mortar.

D. Temperature dropping at 35 degrees F., add one (1) quart of admixture to bag of mortar.

E. Temperature dropping at 30 degrees F., stop masonry work.

3. All concrete block and brick walls and partitions etc., as shown, noted, or indicated by hatching on the drawings, to be of masonry materials as hereinafter specified.

<u>Mortar for Face Brick</u> - shall be one part cement, one part lime, and five parts sand. The same brand of cement shall be used throughout the work.

Concrete Block shall conform to the following specifications.

    A. Concrete masonry units, hollow load bearing, ASTM C-90.

    B. Concrete masonry units, solid, ASTM C-145.

    C. Concrete brick, ASTM C-55.

    D. Use special blocks for all corners, piers, jambs, etc.

    E. Concrete block units to be of thickness indicated on drawings.

All brick shall be laid in a full mortar bed with a full end joint. All back-up block shall be parged with a uniform coat of mortar and the face brick laid immediately in a manner to prevent penetration of water. Face brick shall have tooled joints brought up to level approximately 16″ at a time.

All walls shall rise together, equally in height, at all periods of construction. Walls shall be tied and reinforced with corrugated wall reinforcement a minimum of one (1) tie every 16″ OC both to wood frame walls horizontally and vertically.

All lintels shall be of size and shape as shown or noted on the drawings and shall be structually sound for the spans and loads involved.

Build into masonry all materials furnished by other trades, such as angles, anchor bolts, flashing, steel lintels and framing, vents, sleeves, door frames, miscellaneous steel work with anchors, etc.

Clean and point all brick work and concrete block work at end of each working day. Clean all exposed brick work with water and fiber brushes at the completion of work as an entirety. No cleaning acids shall be used on any type of masonry.

DIVISION 5
METALS

Provide all labor, material, and equipment necessary to complete the miscellaneous structural and decorative metal work indicated on the drawings. All materials to meet ASTM A-36.

Provide all structural steel members as indicated on the drawings. All work shall be in accordance with the standards of the industry and all local governing codes. Fabrication shall be furnished to those trades prior to the execution of their work by the subcontractor for proper incorporation into their work.

1. Shop Drawings. Submit four (4) sets of shop drawings to the architect for approval and checking as required.

Provide proper anchor bolts as indicated.

All structural metal items to receive one coat of rust inhibitive shop primer.

Wrought Iron Railing (Outside)

Provide black wrought iron railings as indicated on the drawings. Railings shall be complete with newel posts, corners, flanged hose shoe, and fittings. Rail design shall be ½″ square bars in a design of alternate straight and twisted bars, 6″ OC. Top rail and newel post to be of standard design. Samples shall be submitted to owner for approval.

<u>Brass Railing</u> (With wood handrail)

Provide 2″ outside diameter (O.D.) oak handrail and brass post for the serpentine area as manufactured by Ship'n Out, Inc., Pawling, New York. Railings shall be complete with brass tubing, single line 2″ O.D. 5″ flange standard height 36″ brass railing post, steel tubeliners, 4″ wall flange, brass chain and ht. 36″ brass railing post, steel tubeliners, 4″ wall flange, brass chain and necessary fittings. Equal products must be approved by architect in writing. Available thru brass railing supplier and installed by general contractor.

DIVISION 6
CARPENTRY

<u>ROUGH CARPENTRY</u>

Furnish all labor, tools, equipment, and materials to complete all work under this heading as indicated on the drawings and described in the specifications.

Provide and maintain temporary enclosures, fences, and barricades as required by governing local ordinances. Provide temporary door and window enclosures as required.

All interior framing to be either $3^{5}/_{8}$″ metal studs or $5^{1}/_{2}$″ metal studs, or 2 × 4 studs 16″ OC, or 2 × 6 studs 16″ OC, double at openings, and triple at corners as shown on plan. Headers up to 36″, two 2 × 6's set on edge. All other openings to be as detailed on drawings. Provide bracing, as required, to support Glulam beam while it is being set and anchored.

<u>STRUCTURAL LUMBER</u>

1. All structural lumber shall be grade stamped per standard grading rules. Unless otherwise noted, all structural lumber shall be No. 1 Douglas Fir. Interior non-bearing stud walls shall be stud grade.
2. Plywood shall be DFPA grade stamped, type CDX 5 ply with exterior glue unless otherwise noted on plans.
3. Roof framing and sheathing shall be inspected prior to placing of roof.
4. Predrill all holes for 20d and larger nails and lag bolts.
5. Double top plates on all exterior and bearing partitions (not otherwise detailed). Plates shall lap 4′-0″ minimum at splices and have 6-16d nails minimum thru each side of splice.
6. Bolt holes for wood connections shall be $^{1}/_{32}$″ larger in diameter than normal bolt size.
7. Lag bolts shall have lead holes bored before driving. Hole diameters to be as follows:
   A. Shank portion - same diameter and length as shank.
   B. Thread portion - 0.6 to 0.75 diameter of thread and same length.
8. All bolt head and nuts bearing on wood shall have steel washers.

<u>NAILING SCHEDULE</u>

1. All nailing shall be common wire nails conforming to the latest edition of OBBC or UBC. Where automatic nailing is used, nails shall not penetrate plywood sheathing. Connections listed are minimum permissible. Details govern over schedule.
   A. Joist to sill or girder, toe nail...3-8d
   B. Bridging to joist or rafter, toe nail each end..........................2-8d

   C. Subfloor sheathing at all bearing
      1 × 6 or less, face nail...2-8d
      1 × 8 or wider, face nail.......................................3-8d
      2 × bind and face nail...2-16d
   D. Sole plate to joist or blocking, face nail........................16d @ 16″ OC
   E. Top plate to stud, end nail....................................2-16d
   F. Stud to sole plate, face nail...................................4-8d
   G. Double studs, face nail.......................................16d @ 24″ OC
   H. Double top plates, face nail..................................16d @ 16″ OC
   I. Top plates, laps and intersections, face nail....................2-16d
   J. Continuous header, two pieces (along each edge)................16d @ 16″ OC
   K. Ceiling joists or rafters to all bearings, toe nail...............3-8d
   L. Continuous header to stud, toe nail...........................4-8d
   M. Ceiling joists, laps over partitions, face nail..................3-16d
   N. Ceiling joist to parallel rafter, face nail.....................3-16d
   O. 1″ brace to each stud and plate, face nail.....................2-8d
   P. Built-up corner studs...16d @ 18″ OC
   Q. Joist or rafter to sides of studs
      up to and including 8″ depth.................................3-16d
      For each additional 4″ depth or less.........................1-16d
   R. Ceiling strips
      1″ × 4″ to underside of joists-each bearing-one
      slant and one straight.......................................2-8d
      2″ × 3″ to underside of joist-each bearing-one
      slant and one straight.......................................2-16d
      Use strong hold annulary grooved at gypsum board ceilings

TRUSS JOISTS

1. Joists to be used are supplied by Trus Joist Corporation.
2. Series used are TJI 55E in lengths and depths as indicated on drawings.
3. Shop drawings, nailing schedules, and connection details will be provided to contractor along with shipment of every order.
4. Trus Joist Corporation will also be supplying the Glulam beam and Micro = Lam® beam as indicated on Sheet 8 of the drawings.

"Z" BOOTHS—COUNTER WALL AND SEATING

General contractor shall provide and erect the prefabricated salad bar divider wall and "Z" booths. The divider wall and "Z" booth is available thru the approved millwork supplier and can be shipped directly to the store location. Contractor to receive, unload, uncrate, and erect the unit. Unit is shipped prefinished but does require general contractor to assemble. General contractor is to verify with approved millwork supplier what is not supplied with package.

ALUMINUM SOFFIT

Aluminum soffit shall be vented and non-vented, V-groove as manufactured by Alcoa Building Products, Inc. Color to be Sand Tone, catalog No. 12VN (vented) and No. 12VNT (non-vented). Twenty-five percent of soffit area shall be vented or approximately every four feet.

Install all rough hardware such as clips, straps, anchor bolts, etc. to provide a complete framing system as indicated on drawings.

FINISH CARPENTRY

Furnish all labor and materials to complete all work under this section as indicated on drawings and described in these specifications.

All hardware dimensions are to be net size and not nominal size. Material for interior finish shall be as follows:

A. Dining Room Trim - all trim shall be select Red Oak, no substitute.
B. Closet Shelves - 1 × 12 clear white pine stained.
C. Cleats - 1 × 4 white pine.
D. Laminated Wall Covering - as per specifications in Division 9. Wall & Floor Finishes - Laminated wall covering.
E. Countertops to be furnished by kitchen equipment supplier and installed by carpentry contractor.
F. For all finish materials not listed above, refer to the "Wendy's" Design Handbook.

WALK-IN COOLER-FREEZER

Placement of prefabricated, walk-in freezer shall be part of this contract. Unit will be supplied by owners and will be shipped direct to store location with all uncrating and erection done by contractor. Unit will be shipped complete with hardware and instructions. Installation of refrigeration to be done by refrigeration contractor and electrical hook-up by electrical contractor. See equipment plans sheet of the Construction Documents.

DIVISION 7
MOISTURE CONTROL

1. CAULKING

All surfaces to receive caulking to be dry and thoroughly cleaned of all loose particles of dirt and dust, oil, grease, or other foreign matter.

Caulk at exterior door frames, window frames, and elsewhere to insure a weatherproof job; using gun application.

MATERIALS

Polysulfide polymer base compound shall conform to American Standard Spec. A-116, 1960 Class A or B, and equal to that manufactured by Sonneborn or Pecora. (Exterior joints)

Butyl sealant shall be butyl rubber base compound equal to that manufactured by Sonneborn or Pecora. (All other caulking)

2. ROOFING AND SHEET METAL

Furnish and completely install the Duro-Last Roofing System per specifications and diagrams as outlined and furnished by Duro-Last Roofing, Inc. The Duro-Last Roofing System shall be installed exclusively by an approved Duro-Last applicator. Final inspection prior to warranty issuance shall be performed by an authorized Duro-Last Quality Control Field Inspector as per current specifications, installation, and inspection policies.

Any deviation from Duro-Last specifications and installation instructions shall void any warranty issuance unless the deviation is approved by a duly authorized Duro-Last representative in writing.

Shop drawings are required for ordering, manufacturing, and final inspection of the roofing system. All shop drawings shall include roof outline, size, all roof penetrations, insulation type and thickness, piece layout and parapet location. Orders and shop drawings shall be approved by Duro-Last Roofing and assigned a Duro-Last number.

MATERIAL REQUIREMENTS

All components of the Duro-Last Roofing System shall be products of Duro-Last Roofing, Inc. Substitutes must have prior acceptance by Duro-Last Roofing, Inc.

1. MEMBRANE

The membrane material shall be a high tenacity low shrink Celanese Fortrel Polyester Fabric coated with a thermoplastic alloy, conforming to the minimum physical properties as set forth by Duro-Last Roofing. One piece size shall not exceed 2,500 sq. ft. or 100' in length.

2. RELATED MATERIALS

B-1 Approved Fasteners
*Duro-Last Screws with special Dura-Coat coating. The length will vary to meet job conditions. A minimum size of $1/2''$ of the fastener point must protrude through the steel or wood roof deck. In reroofing over an existing roof and where additional approved insulation board is being attached, the screw shall be of the proper length to pass through all materials above the deck and protrude through the steel or wood deck a minimum of $1/2''$.

B-2 Distribution Plates
Duro-Last stress distribution plates formed from a minimum of 24 ga., G-90, C.Q. galvanized steel. A 0.252'' diameter hole is located in the center of the "plate." The metal screw is inserted through this hole and then properly secured into the deck. (Use for all metal and wood screws and toggle bolts for fastening insulation.)

B-3 Vents
M-105 Vents with Duro-Last Skirt attached: Install two-way vent for each 1,000 sq. ft. or fraction of roof area. One for each 75 sq. ft. if roof has been leaking badly. Minimum

of one vent on every Duro-Last Roof. Cut through old roofing and insulation to vapor barrier, if any, or to the roof deck, and remove. (This will allow entrapped moisture vapor and moisture from the building to escape.)

B-4   Sealant

Duro-Last SB-190 Urethane Silicone Sealant, evenly and continuously applied behind the material and above all termination or pressure bar, wall or parapet metal counterflashing, roof mounting or curb counterflashing, around top of Duro-Last stacks or at any location where a water seal may be improved. Use under all applications on drip edge, gravel stop, roof tie-ins, and drains. Use Duro-Last SB-240 or equivalent for night seals, under membrane around drains, filler for pitch pockets, and for added strength to hold flashing details in place. NOTE: All flashing shall still be mechanically fastened. (Do not use SB-240 or SB-190 to seal an imperfect weld.)

B-5   Stacks and Bands

Use factory formed Duro-Last stacks for all standard sized, circular roof penetrations, such as vent pipe, pipe supports (where possible), small exhaust vents, roof vents, etc. Properly apply Duro-Last silicone sealant at top portion of circular penetration where stack will be adhered and then strap top with stainless steel Panduit Bands as provided by Duro-Last Roofing or stainless steel adjustable band. Tighten to prevent water penetration. Trim top of stack and caulk with Duro-Last SB-190. Heat weld bottom of stack to Duro-Last roofing.

B-6   Drip Edge

Duro-Last special formulated weldable drip edge fastened every 8″ on center.

B-7   Water-Gravel Stop

Duro-Last special formulated weldable gravel stop with factory attached skirt, fastened to roof substrate every 8″ on center.

B-8   Termination Bar

Duro-Last special formulated reversible termination bar fastened every 6″ on center.

B-9   Sheet Metal

Formed metal shall be from 26 gauge galvanized. All metal counterflashing, coping, drip edges, gravel stops shall have a 3″ overlap for expansion and contraction.

B-10   Roof Scupper Linings

Cut Duro-Last roof scupper lining to fit roof scuppers, allowing adequate material for field welding to Duro-Last roof cover and base flashing. Apply Duro-Last adhesive to scupper. Install lining in scupper and make field welds to roof cover and base flashing. Apply Duro-Last SB-190 Sealant to all exterior edges of lining on exterior of wall, under and on top of the termination bar surrounding the edges.

B-11   Wood Members

All new lumber shall be #2 Southern Yellow Pine, Douglas Fir, or other approved species, and it shall be free from warping, excessive knots and grade marked. It shall be "Wolmanized" (CCA) pressure-treated and shall bear the trademark "Wolmanized" or an approved equal treatment.

MATERIAL STORAGE AND HANDLING

1. <u>DELIVERY</u>

All roofing and related materials shall be delivered to job site in original packaging and all shipping labels intact. If any shortages or damages are discovered upon delivery, do not accept them until the freight agent makes a damaged or short notation on your freight bill. In case of concealed loss or damage, it is necessary to notify your freight agent at once.

2. <u>STORAGE</u>

All roofing material shall be stored in original packaging to protect membrane from getting wet or being damaged and soiled. Adhesives and sealants shall be properly stored and protected as recommended by their manufacturers.

3. <u>HANDLING</u>

There should be adequate personnel and equipment to lift roofing material for placement on the roof to prevent damage to material. The material shall be deposited on the roof near the ends of joists or other roof load bearing members of the building frame and conveniently located for final placement.

SURFACE PREPARATION

The roof shall have an adequately prepared surface to receive the insulation, roofing, and flashing. Prior to onset of work the applicator shall inspect the entire area to be roofed, and any defects and improper conditions affecting the roof installation shall be corrected before application of the insulation of the Duro-Last Roofing System.

1. <u>WOOD DECKS</u>

Roof shall be clean, smooth, and suitable for acceptance of the Duro-Last system. Remove and replace all deteriorated wood nailers, roof curbs, and soured or badly deteriorated roof insulation. Any joints or cracks greater than $1/4''$ shall be repaired.

2. <u>INSULATION ATTACHMENT</u> (Mechanical)

The roof insulation boards shall be installed with factory approved fasteners and stress distribution plates as shown in installation drawing 5.02. The length will vary to meet the job conditions. A minimum of $5/8''$ of the fastener must protrude through the plywood deck.

MEMBRANE/ACCESSORY ATTACHMENT

1. WOOD DECK

Duro-Last screws and distribution plates; 12 " on center, 57 " laps. (Provide 1-90 wind up-lift). Buildings over 70' use 27 " lap, screws, and stress distribution plates 12 " on center.

2. FLASHINGS

All flashings or parapet walls shall be fastened 12 " on center along bottom on main deck with a minimum 6 " lap weldable to deck membrane covering Duro-Last approved fasteners. All parapet walls shall be covered minimum of 12 " high. If parapets or flashings are to be covered higher, the following shall be followed as per detailed drawing 6.03.

Flash and counterflash all items that pass through the roof. Provide "Pitch Pockets" as required to form a complete job.

Provide all necessary mounting clips, closures, fastenings, etc., required to complete the counterflashing, gravel stops, caps and copings, indicated on the drawings.

3. OVERNIGHT COVER

A temporary water seal shall be performed each night to avoid water penetrating underneath the installed membrane and causing damage to the building and the insulation being used.

Installation. With the membrane extended over exposed insulation (if used), set into a water resistant, non-bituminous sealant, generously applied over a dust, grease, and moisture free substrate. Fasten 12 " on center using termination bar.

4. PERIMETER LAPS

Any time a roof edge does not have a parapet wall or roof tie-in, (i.e.: drip edge, water-gravel stop, termination bar on edge, gutter, etc.) then the roof section must have a lap 27 " in from the edge and reversed. This helps reduce wind up-lift around perimeters and reversing the lap, allows contractor-applicator to place roof section away from the edge.

PROJECT/SITE CLEAN-UP

Upon completion, the roofing contractor shall remove all rubbish, waste materials, etc. from the roof, leaving the roof in a clean condition and further removing all such debris from the work site. A rigorous inspection for water tight field seams should be made after completion of job.

FIELD QUALITY CONTROL-QUALITY ASSURANCE

1. INSPECTIONS

Upon completion of each roofing job, contractor shall fill out inspection card and return to Duro-Last Roofing, Inc. Each room shall be inspected by an authorized Duro-Last Quality

Control Field Inspector to make sure application meets Duro-Last specifications, before issuance of warrant. Contractor shall accompany inspector on inspections and obtain signed warranty from customer and return to Duro-Last Roofing, Inc.

2. CONTRACTOR QUALIFICATION ASSURANCE

The roofing contractor shall be duly certified by Duro-Last Roofing, Inc. for complete application and installation of this roofing system. To maintain roof warranty, future repairs and alterations shall be made by personnel duly certified by Duro-Last Roofing, Inc. All applicators/contractors shall be trained on their first application of the Duro-Last Roofing System by an authorized Duro-Last Quality Control Field Inspector.

WARRANTY PROGRAM

WARRANTY

The owner shall be furnished and will sign for acceptance of a standard Duro-Last Roofing Manufaturer's 20 Year Limited Warranty. Any failure as a result of factory or field workmanship will be repaired and any defective material replaced up to the original contract price of the roof for the first ten years. Applicator/contractor assumes full responsibility for the first two years of warranty. The manufacturer will replace defective material only during this time. The cost of material will be prorated for the second ten years of this 20 year limited warranty. This warranty comes directly from the factory and is issued only after inspection by Factory Quality Specialist. (See Warranty Sec. 1.)

BUILDING INSULATION

Furnish all labor, materials, and equipment necessary to complete all work as indicated on the construction documents and described in the specifications.
   A. Vapor barrier under slabs-on-grade—6 mil ''Visqueen'' furnished and installed by concrete contractor. See Division 3.
   B. Exterior wall insulation—6″ thick fiberglass batts in the 2 × 6 stud walls of all cavity walls.
   C. Rigid roof insulation—furnished and installed by the roofing contractor. Insulation to be one layer, 2.1″, R-10, FES-CORE Thermal Roof insulation board by Johns-Manville. Permalite PK insulation board by Permalite, Inc. is an acceptable equal. Roof insulation shall be compatible with Duro-Last single-ply roof membrane material.
   D. Ceiling insulation—provide 6″ fiberglass batts attached to underside of roof decking.
   E. Perimeter insulation—1″ thick Styrofoam or equal on exterior foundation wall as shown on construction documents.

DIVISION 8
DOORS, WINDOWS, AND GLASS

1. ALUMINUM ENTRANCE DOORS AND STOREFRONT

Storefront system shall be by Solarium Manufacturer and of same material and finish. Equal products will be approved by architect if request is submitted in writing. Doors shall be Series 190 Narrow Stile door as manufactured by Kawneer or equal. All entrance doors shall be installed with offset pivots. Closers shall be heavy-duty surface mounted type No. 1605 as furnished by Norton or manufacturing by Yale. Locking hardware shall be dead bolt type and push-pull No. F-2 standard hardware as shown on drawings. Panic hardware shall be standard exit device, conventional design.

Personalized pull is available only with Kawneer Entrances. All keying shall be done to match rear and interior doors. (See wood doors below.) Finish shall be dark bronze No. 40 anodized finish.

2. SOLARIUM ENCLOSURE

A. Solarium glass enclosure shall be furnished by the owner and installed by a certified solarium installer. See approved glass suppliers list.
B. Construction documents are based on a solarium unit as provided by Solarium Systems, Inc. For all other brands four (4) sets of shop drawings shall be submitted to the architect for determination of compatibility and approval prior to the start of construction.
C. Shop drawings—Wendy's has approved shop drawings established by Solarium Systems, Inc. National Account. These drawings comply with the products and hardware requirements stated herein and are to be used as a guide by the local supervising architect, general contractor, and certified solarium installer to insure compliance with this specification. Copies of the approved shop drawings may be obtained by contacting Solarium Systems, Inc.
D. Color—Electrostatic Polyester Resin Powder Bronze Finish.
E. Shading—available as an option, contact solarium manufacturer for details.
F. Glass—
   1. Standard Vertical Glass
   Glass to be $5/8''$ double sealed insulated glass with $1/8''$ tempered bronze tinted on the outboard lite and $1/8''$ tempered clear glass on the inboard lite. The curved lite is the same tint but double strength insulated glass. Glazing caps shall be separated from the main bars by a thermal break.
   2. Standard Sloped Roof Glass
   $1/8''$ solar cool bronze reflective tempered outboard lite over $1/4''$ clear laminated lite.
G. Flashing—Refer to construction details for information on supply and installation of flashing pieces.
H. The contractor and the solarium installer shall guarantee all work installed under the contract to be free from defective workmanship and materials, usual wear expected, and should any such defects develop within a period of one year after acceptance of the building by the owner, the contractor shall repair and/or replace any defective items and all damage resulting from failure of the items, at no expense whatsoever to the owner.

3. PREFINISHED DOORS

Laminated doors—to be 1¾″ high pressure laminated solid core cross banded doors as manufactured by Marlite Products. All doors of this type to be furnished complete with adjustable prefinished aluminum frame.

Hardware to be Schlage—"D" Series:

Passage Latch	D-10-S Plymouth 605
Privacy Locks	D-40-S Plymouth 605
Keyed Locks	D-80-PD Plymouth 605
Dummy Knob	D-170 Plymouth 605
Dormitory Lock	D-73-PD Plymouth 605

Absolutely no substitutes accepted!

4. WINDOWS

Drive-thru window to be sliding glass door as manufactured by Tubelite Corporation, with ⅝″ insulated glass, medium bronze color and acrylic finish. See drawings for correct size and location.

5. MIRRORS

All mirrors shown on drawings to be ¼″ thick polished plate glass as manufactured by Pittsburgh Plate Glass Company, or Libbey Owens Ford Glass Company. Other brands must be approved by architect.

DIVISION 9

FINISHES

GYPSUM DRYWALL

Furnish all material and labor necessary to provide finished drywall surfaces in all areas scheduled to receive this finish on the drawings.

All drywall over furring and wood studs shall be ⅝″ Firecode gypsum. Materials shall be standard products manufactured by U.S. Gypsum, National Gypsum, or Gold Bond Gypsum Company.

SUSPENDED CEILING SYSTEM

Furnish all materials and labor to provide a complete system including tile, hangers, tees, and all moldings.

1. Acoustical ceiling material shall be as follows:

Tile—Armstrong, Cortega, minaboard No. 769A, 2 × 4 lay-in panels, white with matching grid.

Grid and Moldings—To be metal inverted tee, direct hung system with white color enamel finish as manufactured by Chicago Metallic Corp., or equal.

2. Washable ceilings shall be as follows:
   Tile—Vinyl-faced panels as manufactured by U.S. Gypsum. Panels shall be 24″ × 48″ × ½″, stipple almond lay-in type. All ceiling panels shall be held in place with a minimum of four TM type clips as furnished by manufacturers above. No substitutes accepted.
   Grid and Moldings—To be metal inverted tee, direct hung system with almond baked-on enamel finish as manufactured by Chicago Metallic Corp., Donn Corp., or equal.

WALL AND FLOOR FINISHES

Furnish all labor and materials to complete all work under this section as indicated on drawings.

1. Laminated Wall Covering (almond)—All areas designed as almond laminated plastic shall be surfaced with fiberglass reinforced polyester panels, ³/₃₂″ or .090″ thickness, as supplied by Marlite Products, Kemlite, or Contract Building Concepts.
2. Laminated Wall Covering (almond)—All areas designed as almond color laminated wall covering shall be surfaced with fiberglass reinforced polyester panels, ³/₃₂″ or .090″ thickness with matching "J" mold as furnished by Marlite Products, Kemlite, or Contract Building Concepts.
   NOTE: Fire-rated class A (flame spread) FRP panels available thru: Kemlite Corp., 4′ × 9′ almond, flame spread (20); Marlite Products, 4′ × 8′ and 4′ × 10′ only, flame spread (25).
3. Ceramic Wall Tile—All restroom wall area designated ceramic tile shall be 4¼″ × 4¼″ × ⁵/₁₆″ smooth glazed tile as manufactured by American Olean. Number 86 Espresso shall be used on perimeter trim and cove base for each wall, and No. 74 antique for wall space inside perimeter trim, or equal by Dal-Tile.
4. Restroom Floor Tile—Shall be unglazed ceramic mosaic tile, standard pattern No. P128-7030 as manufactured by American Olean. Colors are Driftwood, Beach Tan, and Reef Brown, or equal by Dal-Tile.
5. Quarry Tile—Shall be 6″ × 6″ × ½″ unglazed tile and cove base, round top trim units, Canyon Red Murray Tile Abrasive grain as manufactured by American Olean, or equal by Summitville Tile.
6. Decorator Floor Tile— Refer to Wendy's Design Handbook for type of tile and suppliers. Tile shall be set with thin-set mortar laid in running bond pattern parallel to front of building. Use bull nose cove base trim units. Grout shall be L & M Surco Acid R (or equal) color gray.

In general, workmanship shall be the best for the method of setting specified. Install tile in accordance with Tile Contractor's Association of America, Inc., specifications or the Tile Council of America, Inc. specifications.

CARPET

All carpet to be Axminster; special "Wendy's Pattern" as manufactured by Mohawk. All carpet and padding to be supplied by kitchen equipment supplier and installed by contractor.

Installation shall be in accordance with "Installation Instructions" as supplied with carpet. Critical items when installing Axminster style carpet include:

A. Floor should be clean and free of all foreign material.
B. Adhere padding to slab with Roberts No. 40-4001 cushion cement or equal.
C. Close all seams in padding with Roberts No. 50-111 pad tape or equal.
D. Follow instruction on pattern matching installation instructions.
E. Length seams and cross seams shall be hand sewn while carpet is tacked to cardboard cylinder. Stitches shall occur no farther apart than ½″.

F. After seam is sewn, reinforce seam by applying latex adhesive.

G. Tackless strip shall be Roberts architectural or equal. Strip must have three rows of pins to provide necessary anchorage.

H. Carpet-tile transition strip shall be a one-piece aluminum extrusion with solid vinyl saddle, $3'' \times {}^{11}/_{16}''$, clay red as manufactured by National Metal Shapes, Inc. and supplied by kitchen equipment supplier.

WALLPAPER

Refer to Wendy's Design Handbook for type of wallcovering.

All wallpaper shown on the drawings to be supplied by kitchen equipment suppliers and installed by contractor.

Wall shall be spackled and sanded as to receive paint. All areas shall be sized and allowed to dry thoroughly. Use only fresh vinyl paste. Wheat paste is not to be used under any circumstances.

Apply vinyl paste evenly giving special attention to edges. After pasting, fold, then roll, and allow to stand for at least five minutes. If blistering occurs, longer soaking will be required.

Apply and roll seams *lightly*. It is very critical the excess paste be washed from the wallcovering surface and woodwork. No overlapping will be permitted and all corners must be double cut to insure tight seams.

PAINTING

The intent of these specifications is to provide a satisfactory finish to all parts of the building, unless hereinafter noted otherwise. All surfaces shall be thoroughly covered. If the number of coats specified does not accomplish the intent, the contractor shall apply additional coats of material to give satisfactory coverage.

1. <u>EXTERIOR</u>

In general, the work shall include exposed angles above windows. Flashing to be included as exterior painting.

2. <u>INTERIOR</u>

All drywall work, millwork, etc., throughout the building shall be finished in accordance with the room finish schedule and the following specifications and paint schedule.

Before starting work, inspect all surfaces to be painted and report all defects therein to the owner in writing. The owner will cause all defects to be remedied. The commencing of work will indicate acceptance of surface.

The workmanship shall be of the very best. All materials shall be applied under adequate illumination, evenly spaced and smoothly flowed on without runs or sags. Only skilled mechanics shall be employed. Follow manufacturer's instructions for product use.

All surfaces to be clean and approved before painting. No painting during damp, rainy, or cold weather. Protect all work by others and clean-up, remove spots, and touch-ups as required.

All paints, varnish, stain, and enamel as manufactured by Benjamin Moore & Company; or equal, in colors and applied as per manufacturer's specifications.

PAINT SCHEDULE

The following schedule of Finishes is based on Benjamin Moore & Company and is used only to establish grades and types of material.

1. <u>EXTERIOR STEEL</u>

One coat Ironclad Rust Inhibitive Primer/Finish 163-60 (Bronzetone). Two coats Impervo High Gloss Enamel 133-60 (brown).

2. <u>EXTERIOR TRIM</u>

Two coats Ironclad Rust Inhibitive Primer/Finish 163-60 (Bronzetone).

3. <u>INTERIOR WOOD-STAIN</u>

A. All stained and varnished areas to match specified paneling.
B. One coat Benwood Urethane High Gloss Clear 428-00.
C. One coat Benwood Urethane Low Lustre Clear 435-00.

4. <u>EXTERIOR FENCES AND ENCLOSURES</u>

One coat Olympic Semi-Transparent Stain No. 707, or one coat Moorwood Semi-Transparent Exterior Stain No. 080-58.

<u>DIVISION 10</u>
SPECIALTIES

1. <u>TOILET PARTITIONS</u>

Toilet and urinal partitions shall be high pressure laminate partitions as manufactured by Marlite. Partitions shall be floor mounted and over-head braced. Doors and panels shall have a finished thickness of not less than $7/8$". Color to be No. 346 Natural Oak Design. See drawings for size and location of partition.

2. <u>TOILET ACCESSORIES</u>

Hand dryers shall be "World Dryer" Model No. A-5 as furnished by kitchen equipment supplier and installed by contractor.

Liquid soap dispenser shall be Bradley stainless steel Model No. 6541 or equal. Dispenser shall be furnished and installed by contractor.

Toilet tissue holder shall be Bradley stainless steel Model No. 540 double roll holder or equal. Holder shall be furnished and installed by contractor.

Handicapped grab bars shall be Bobrick Series No. B-610 stainless steel with exposed mounting. Finish shall be smooth and furnished complete with mounting kit. All items shown on drawings shall be furnished and installed by contractor.

3. ROOM IDENTIFICATION SIGN

All identification signs shall be furnished by kitchen equipment supplier and installed by contractor.

4. DECORATOR FASCIA PANELS

Exterior copper color fascia panel system; panels with standing seamed rib and roof crown moldings accented with copper stripe, shall be furnished by owner and installed by general contractor. See approved sign suppliers list.

5. GENERAL SIGNAGE

All free-standing signs and directional signs will incorporate the new cameo identity. Total signage including menu and speaker signs shall be furnished by owner and installed by licensed sign erector. See approved sign suppliers list.

6. COMMUNICATION SYSTEM

Total communication system as indicated on drawings, Sheet No. 10, shall be as manufactured by 3-M. System shall be furnished and installed by Owner. Contractor to furnish conduit, electrical connection, and coordinate installation with electrician.

7. HOOD FIRE SUPPRESSION SYSTEM & PORTABLE FIRE EXTINGUISHERS

Hood Fire Suppression System shall be as per specifications and drawings, (Sheet No. 10) as manufactured by Ansul. System shall be furnished and installed by general contractor unless otherwise instructed by owner. Verify with owner before construction. No substitutes accepted. Portable extinguisher shall be furnished by owner and shall be installed as directed by local fire control authority.

8. EXTERIOR TRASH ENCLOSURE

Trash enclosure shall be as per specifications and drawings, Sheet No. 2.

9. KITCHEN EQUIPMENT

Contractor to receive, unload all kitchen equipment, and install all items. Kitchen equipment service personnel will set up. Contractor to provide all hook-ups.

DIVISION 11
PLUMBING

1. Provide all labor, equipment, and materials necessary to execute the plumbing work indicated on the drawings, and as required by local codes and ordinances.
2. Pay all fees and arrange for execution of all taps, meters with required enclosures (if any), etc., inherent to the installation of new plumbing service.
3. Shall include all piping; domestic hot and cold water, sanitary and supply, and hook-up of all fixtures scheduled on the drawings; and insulation of designated piping runs. Shall also include all gas piping and equipment connections where required.
4. All items, such as fittings, etc., not mentioned but understood to be necessary to complete the plumbing system shall be included.
5. Soil, waste, and vent piping to be of material approved by local codes.
6. Provide cleanouts for soil and waste lines as shown on drawings, and of type approved by local codes.
7. All water supply piping below ground shall be type K soft copper tubing. (Avoid fittings below slab whenever possible) All water supply piping above ground shall be type L copper tubing.
8. Provide for draining water system, and cap all stubs until finish work is installed. Install drain valve at water meter with 3/4" hose thread and vacuum breaker.
9. Provide stops on water supplies to each fixture.
10. Gas piping for heating systems with gas-fired equipment shall be included in this contract. Gas piping shall be standard weight, black steel pipe, Schedule 40. Piping exposed to atmosphere or run below grade shall have polyethylene plastic coating. All gas piping, fittings, and installation shall be in accordance with requirements of utility company and all governing bodies.
11. Insulate all cold and hot water piping with Armstrong Company Armaflex "II" pipe insulation. Seal joints with Armstrong 520 adhesive.
    Important—Hold all cold and hot water piping to warm side of insulation to prohibit freezing.
12. Plumbing fixtures shall be furnished and installed where shown on the drawings. All fixture fittings and exposed fixture piping shall be brass chromium plated. All traps shall be cast brass. All fixtures shall be white. Fixtures shall be as manufactured by American Standard, Kohler, or Crane and equal in all respects to fixtures specified. Closet seats shall be Church, Olsonite, or Beneke.

A. Water closet (A-1)

   No. 2109.405 Elongated water-saver 'Cadet' vitreous china toilet.
   No. 169 McGuire flexible supply stop.
   No. 295 Elongated 'Church' open front white seat, not self-sustaining hinge.

Water Closet Where Required for Handicapped (A-2)

   No. 2108.408 Elongated water-saver 'Cadet' vitreous china toilet, 18" high.
   No. 169 McGuire flexible supply stop.
   No. 295 Elongated 'Church' open front white seat, not self-sustaining hinge.

B. Lavatory (B-1)

No. 0355.012 - 'Lucerne' vitreous china, 20″ × 18″.
4″ valve centers.
No. 8872 - McGuire - Adjustable cast brass 'P' trap with tubing drain to wall, 1¼″ inlet
and outlet, cleanout plug escutcheon.
No. 2103.886 - 'Heritage' faucet, valves, aerator, drain, with ½ GPM flow restrictor.
No. 167 - McGuire - Flexible tube riser, wheel handle stop, escutcheon.
Provide with wall hangers.

C. Urinal (C-1)

No. 6501.010 - 'Washbrook' vitreous china, washout, ¾″ top spud, wall hung.
No. 186YB - Sloan 'Royal' flush valve with integral stop.

D. Mop Basin (D-1)

No. MSB-2424 Flat molded stone basin.
No. 8344-111 'Heritage' faucet with vac. breaker.

E. Fixtures and Equipment (K-1 through K-8)

Fixtures and equipment by others. Rough-in and final connections of required waste, vent,
and water supply piping by plumbing contractor. All supply shall be valved.

13. Water meter is a positive displacement meter of the nutating disc type as required by local
utility company.
14. Electric storage water heater with glass lined tank as manufactured by A. O. Smith Model No.
DVE-52-12 or equal by Ruud or Lochinvan. Capacities shall be as noted on the drawings.
15. Wall hydrants shall be freezeless automatic draining type as manufactured by Woodford, Model
65, or equal by Josam or Wade.
16. Co-ordinate all work with electrical and heating contractor.
17. The contractor shall guarantee all work installed under the contract to be free from defective
workmanship and materials, usual wear expected, and should any such defects develop within
a period of one year after acceptance of the building by the owner, the contractor shall repair
and/or replace any defective items and all damage resulting from failure of these items, at
no expense whatsoever to the owner.
18. Backflow preventor to be installed when required by local code and is to be provided by and
installed by the plumbing contractor.

DIVISION 12
HEATING AND VENTILATION

1. Provide all labor, materials, and equipment necessary to complete the heating and ventilating
work indicated on the drawings and as required by local codes and ordinances.

2. Included in this section is all work to install kitchen exhaust hoods and room vents as shown on the drawings. All hoods and fans are to be Wendy's Standard Approved Suppliers. Roof mounted exhaust fans to be installed on prefabricated curb and furnished and installed by heating contractor.

3. Heating and cooling units as indicated on the drawings to be furnished and installed by heating contractor. Heating and ventilating units indicated on the drawings and hereinafter specified are designed to meet ASHRAE 90-65 based on Columbus, Ohio design conditions of 90° F summer and 0° F winter. (See Note 15.)

4. Diffusers, registers, louvers shall be as per model and size indicated on drawings. No substitutes shall be accepted unless approved by the owner or architect in writing. Diffusers and louvers not meeting specification as shown on drawings shall be replaced at the heating contractor's expense.

5. Final balancing of exhaust system shall be performed as outlined in instruction sheet furnished by exhaust hood manufacturer. Before final acceptance by owner, a manufacturer's representative of the exhaust hood manufacturer shall check entire system and submit a written report to the owner. Final balance of HVAC system shall be performed by mechanical contractor at the same time and in conjunction with the exhaust hood manufacturer. No final payment will be made until the above report has been received and both systems are in balance.

6. Where required by governing ordinances, provide fire dampers conforming to NFPA 90A. Supply ducts to have 1″ fiberglass insulation. Exhaust installation shall conform to NFPA 96.

7. Where required, provide Class "B" gas vent flues, complete with cap, collar, and flashing.

8. Install thermostat complete with all necessary wiring and controls, location as indicated on the drawings. Thermostat shall provide for automatic and manual fan operation.

9. Install and connect the complete system in strict accordance with all governing codes, ordinances, and the latest codes and manuals of the National Warm Air Heating and Air Conditioning Association.

10. A separate refrigeration contractor shall install cooler and freezer refrigeration system. Compressors, coils, controls, and valves shall be furnished by the refrigeration equipment supplier. This contract shall include providing refrigerant lines, necessary fittings, charging system with R-12 refrigerant, insulation, connection compressors, and coils.

   Refrigerant piping shall be Type "L" hard seamless copper tubing with ½″ thick closed cell foam plastic insulation on suction lines. Cooler piping—⅝″ suction lines, ⅜″ liquid line. Freezer piping—⅝″ suction line, ⅜″ liquid line.

11. Adjust all controls and equipment for proper operation. Lubricate and clean all equipment prior to acceptance of building owner.

12. Co-ordinate all work with electrical and plumbing contractors.

13. Furnish the owner with all operating manuals and maintenance instructions for equipment installed.

14. The contractor shall guarantee all work installed under the contract to be free from defective workmanship and materials, usual wear expected, and should any defects develop within a period of one year after acceptance of the building by the owner, the contractor shall repair and/or replace any defective items and all damage resulting from failure of these items, at no expense whatsoever to the owner.

15. For design conditions other than those shown in the HVAC Equipment Schedule of the construction drawings, see the selection charts below, in all cases the rooftop CFM's will be as listed but will utilize the duct system as shown on the plans. Only the duct drop sizes and roof openings as shown require modification.

STANDARD BUILDING

OPTION	WINTER SUMMER	TYPE	R. T. MARK	NOM. TON.	TRANE MODEL NO.	CFM	HI INPUT MBH*	HI OUTPUT MBH*	TOTAL CLG. MBH	MAX. FLA	O.A. CFM	DUCT DROPS S. A.	R.A.
A	0 °F	GAS	RT-1	11	BYC 130G3L	4,000	160	121.6	133	61.3	300	48 × 10	48 × 12
	94°–97°F		RT-2	11	BYC 130G3L	4,000	160	121.6	133	61.3	400	48 × 10	44 × 12
			MUA-1		GRNC 025	SAME AS STANDARD							
B	0 °F	GAS	RT-1	11	BYC 130G3L	4,000	160	121.6	133	61.3	300	54 × 10	48 × 12
	98°–102°F		RT-2	14	BYC 170G3L	5,000	160	121.6	168	68.5	400	48 × 10	54 × 12
			MUA-1		GRNC 025	SAME AS STANDARD							
C	–0 °F	GAS	RT-1	8.5	BYC 100G3H	3,000	250	187.5	103	42.9	300	40 × 10	40 × 12
	93 °F		RT-2	11	BYC 130G3L	4,000	160	121.6	133	61.3	400	48 × 10	48 × 12
			MUA-1		GRNC 025	SAME AS STANDARD							
D	10 °F	ELECT.	RT-1	11	BTC 130G3	4,000	19.5	14.6	133	41.0	300	48 × 10	48 × 12
	94°–97°F		RT-2	11	BTC 130G3	4,000	45KW	33.75	133	94.5	400	48 × 10	48 × 12
E	20 °F	ELECT.	RT-1	11	BTC 130G3	4,000	19.5KW	14.6	133	41.0	300	48 × 10	48 × 12
	98°–102°F		RT-2	14	BTC 170G3	5,000	45KW	33.75	168	94.5	400	54 × 10	54 × 12
F	+25 °F	ELECT.	RT-1	14	BTC 170G3	5,000	24KW	18KW	168	50.4	300	54 × 10	54 × 12
	+102 °F		RT-2	14	BTC 170G3	5,000	24KW	18KW	168	50.4	400	54 × 10	54 × 12
G	–10 °F	ELECT.	RT-1	8.5	BTC 100G3	3,000	44.1KW	33.0	103	94.5	300	40 × 10	40 × 12
	93 °F		RT-2	11	BTC 130G3	4,000	45KW	33.75	133	94.5	400	48 × 10	48 × 12

* Electric heating input shows KW rated at 240v capacity which is normal equipment ordering criteria, heating output is denoted for 208 volts, the typical operating conditions. Max. FLA is listed for 208 volt operation.

16. HVAC contractor is responsible to notify G. C. of required changes in roof openings for B. T. units due to change in equipment size dictated by appropriate option above.

17. HVAC contractor is responsible to notify G. C., electrical and plumbing contractors of changes in electrical and gas requirements due to changes in equipment capacities as dictated by appropriate option above.

DIVISION 13
ELECTRICAL

1. Provide a complete electrical system as indicated on the drawings and described herein.
2. Electrical work shall comply with the National Electric Code® as well as state and local governing codes.
3. Pay for permits and inspections and provide a certificate of inspection.
4. Provide required service and equipment grounding systems. The conduit system shall form a continuous path for ground and shall be safely grounded at the distribution panel. Provide grounding conductors where indicated or specified.
5. Materials shall be new with manufacturer's name printed thereon and Underwriter's Laboratory listed. The selection of materials and equipment to be provided under this contract shall be in strict accordance with the specifications and drawings. The contractor shall submit to the architect for approval 8 copies of equipment as follows: Main Switchboard and Disconnect Switches and Lighting Fixtures.
6. Identify disconnect switches with laminated phenolic nameplates with ¼" minimum height letters.
7. Provide power wiring and hook-up for each mechanical and kitchen equipment item. The contractor shall mount, provide wiring, and make final connections to equipment control panels (which include prewired starters, relays, etc.).
8. Provide devices, wiring, and hook-up for the emergency kitchen shutdown system as described and specified on drawings. Wiring shall be in conduit.
9. Disconnect switches shall be ITE heavy duty type in NEMA 1 enclosure. Equivalent Square D or Arrow-Hart is acceptable. Switches shall be quick-make, quick-break, externally operated and interlocked.

10. Switches shall be Hubbell 1221-I single pole or 1223-I three way. Duplex receptacles shall be Hubbell 5262-I. Sierra, Arrow-Hart, and Bryant shall be considered as equal. Ground fault interrupting receptacles shall be G.E. TGTR115F. Cover plates shall be as indicated on drawings.

11. Test electrical system for short circuits and megger test feeders and branch circuit wiring. Insure low inpedance ground system.

12. The electrical service to the site shall be verified by the contractor prior to bidding job. The contractor shall provide conduit, cable, concrete, connections, and other equipment required for an underground electrical system from the power company equipment to the new distribution panel "DP." It shall be the responsibility of the contractor to co-ordinate electrical service entrance work with the power company, securing contracts with power company for the installation of primary entrance, including charges by power company in bid; and performing work required by power company in accordance with power company rules and regulations to insure a complete electrical service.

    The contractor shall verify power company requirements and charges prior to bidding and include such in bid.

13. For service and panel feeder wiring, use Type THW or better cable. Use TW or better cable for interior branch circuit wiring except as noted. Design is based on copper conductors and all wiring shall be copper. Minimum #12 AWG. Wiring shall be in conduit. Splice wires #6 AWG and larger with approved solderless connectors such as Ilsco properly taped and insulated. Splice smaller wires with mechanical connectors such as "Scotchlock."

14. Provide rigid galvanized steel heavy wall conduit for service and panel feeder conduits. Fittings shall be steel, threaded, set-screw type with insulated throats. Furnish EMT conduit for interior wiring where physical damage is not a consideration. Minimum conduit size is ³/₄″ except for flexible runouts to fixtures, motors, etc., which may be ¹/₂″. Conduit shall be concealed wherever possible and shall be run parallel or perpendicular to building walls and ceilings. Conduit installed in or below slab shall be galvanized rigid conduit. No conduit larger than 1¹/₂″ diameter will be installed in slab.

15. Provide structural steel framework and hanging rods with braces and accessories where required to hold equipment in final position. Provide steel shapes and frames to support wall mounted equipment where normal wall strength may be inadequate. Electrical devices, motor starters, disconnect switches, etc., shall be supported independent of and isolated from equipment vibration.

16. Provide power to cash registers with the following grounding requirements.
    A. System power and ground must be made only at the main entrance panel. The ground conductor must be of insulated wire equal in size to the power conductor. (Conduit may not be used as the ground conductor.)
    B. The ground conductor must not be used as a return or neutral conductor for any equipment and must not be used as a ground for any equipment other than NCR 250 system equipment.
    C. A separate ground conductor is required for each receptacle into which a 250 system device is plugged.
    D. Receptacles for the registers must be 2 pole, 3 wire, 115 volts, 20 amperes. *The ground must be insulated from the mounting hardware.*
    E. For additional information, if required, contact Wendy's International, Inc., 4288 W. Dublin-Granville Rd., Dublin, Ohio.
    F. The NCR conduit must not be used for any other equipment.

17. Provide power to remote refrigeration equipment located on roof as shown on drawings.

18. Provide fixtures as listed on Lighting Fixture Schedule. Provide necessary mounting hardware for a complete installation. Provide lamps, ballasts, and special controls.

19. Furnish and install empty conduit, outlets, and backboard to accommodate telephone company wiring and equipment as shown on drawings. Work shall be installed in strict accordance with telephone company requirements.

20. The contractor shall guarantee work installed under the contract to be free from defective workmanship and materials, usual wear expected, and should any such defects develop within a period of one year after acceptance of the building by the owner, the contractor shall repair and/or replace any defective items and damage resulting from failure of these items, at no expense whatsoever to the owner.

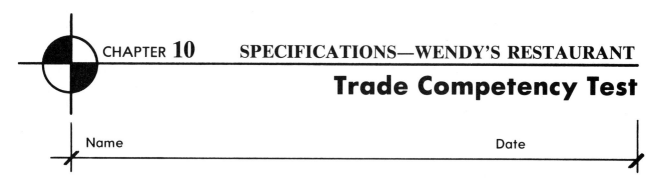

Trade Competency Test

Name   Date

Refer to Specifications for Wendy's Restaurant.

DIVISION 1—GENERAL SPECIFICATIONS
Definitions

1. Owner—

2. Contractor—

3. Subcontractor—

4. Agreement—

5. Work—

DIVISION 1—GENERAL SPECIFICATIONS
True-False

T   F   **1.** Under terms of the contract, the contractor will receive additional pay for all work necessary due to unforeseen difficulties.

T   F   **2.** The owner must secure and pay for all permits, licenses, tap charges, and inspections related to the job.

T   F   **3.** In the event of loss or damage to adjacent property during construction, the contractor is responsible.

T   F   **4.** No work may be performed under subcontract without prior written approval by Wendy's.

T   F   **5.** The contractor is fully responsible to Wendy's for all acts and omissions of all subcontractors.

T   F   **6.** The contractor's sole remedy for delay is an extension of the contract by Wendy's.

T   F   **7.** Wendy's requires that the contractor secure a payment bond and a performance bond prior to construction.

T   F   **8.** Waste material and rubbish on the job site are removed by the owner.

T   F   **9.** The contractor shall indemnify and hold harmless the owner from all claims due to injuries received on the job.

T   F   **10.** The contractor shall provide Worker's Compensation at the owner's expense.

DIVISION 2—SITE WORK

Completion

_____   **1.** All _____, refuse, and existing structures are removed prior to commencement of work.

_____   **2.** _____ excavations must be on undisturbed earth.

_____   **3.** Soil tests are taken to insure that site soil will meet _____ PSF design strength.

_____   **4.** _____ soil is defined as clean sand and sand gravel free of clay, silt, or loam.

_____   **5.** All parking blocks must be no more than _____″ high.

_____   **6.** Asphalt curbs are _____ formed.

_____   **7.** The _____ is responsible for all soil work.

_____   **8.** Plants and _____ are guaranteed for one full growing season.

_____   **9.** All _____ to within 5′-0″ of the building perimeter are considered site work.

_____   **10.** The general contractor must verify all _____ and furnish any city drawings required.

DIVISION 2—SITE WORK

True-False

T   F   **1.** Backfilling of foundation walls in interior areas shall be brought to a subgrade of 8″ below the finish floor line.

T   F   **2.** Crushed stone and sand shall be used as backfill over utilities.

T   F   **3.** All parking blocks shall be at least 6′-0″ in length.

T   F   **4.** Concrete curbs shall be reinforced with two #4 rebars running continuously.

T   F   **5.** Materials for landscaping are not part of the contract.

T   F   **6.** All bidders for landscape work shall submit a written proposal and landscape plan to the general contractor for approval.

T   F   **7.** All storm and sanitary sewer work is the responsibility of the general contractor.

T   F   **8.** Electric service to signs is considered as part of the site work.

T   F   **9.** The owner is responsible for verifying all utility taps.

T   F   **10.** Installation of the grease trap is not part of the contract.

DIVISION 3—CONCRETE AND DIVISION 4—MASONRY
Completion

_____   **1.** All _____ for footings shall be unpainted and uncoated.

_____   **2.** Concrete slabs are reinforced with 6 × 6—_____ WWF.

_____   **3.** WWF edges are lapped _____ before placing concrete.

_____   **4.** The total slope leading to floor drains shall not exceed _____″ below floor level.

_____   **5.** All concrete walks are 4″ thick with a(n) _____ finish.

_____   **6.** Concrete paving is to be reinforced with #_____—6 × 6 wire unless otherwise specified on the plans.

_____   **7.** All concrete must be _____ and finished with float or belt finish.

_____   **8.** All "green" brick walls must be _____ at the end of each day's work.

_____   **9.** All window sills are to be gray _____.

_____   **10.** An admixture of ¾ quart to a bag is to be mixed into mortar when the temperature drops below _____°F.

_____   **11.** All masonry work must cease when the temperature drops below _____°F.

_____   **12.** Mortar for face brick shall be one part cement, one part lime, and _____ part(s) sand.

_____   **13.** Hollow load-bearing concrete masonry units must conform to _____ specifications.

_____   **14.** All brick is to be laid with full mortar beds and full _____ joints.

_____   **15.** Back-up brick shall be _____ to prevent water penetration.

DIVISION 5—METALS AND DIVISION 6—CARPENTRY
True-False

T   F   **1.** Four sets of shop drawings showing all structural steel must be submitted to the architect for approval.

T   F   **2.** Wrought iron railings shall have ½″ square bars alternately straight and twisted.

T F **3.** Wrought iron railing samples must be submitted to the architect for approval.

T F **4.** Brass railings have a 2″ OD oak handrail.

T F **5.** All interior framing may be either metal studs or wood studs as shown on the plans.

T F **6.** Wooden 2 × 4 studs are placed 16″ OC.

T F **7.** Wooden studs shall be tripled at all openings and corners.

T F **8.** Unless otherwise noted on the plans, all structural lumber shall be No. 1 Douglas Fir.

T F **9.** CDX plywood with five plies and exterior glue is specified.

T F **10.** All holes for 16d and larger nails are to be pre-drilled.

DIVISION 5—METALS AND DIVISION 6—CARPENTRY
Completion

_____ **1.** _____ top plates shall be utilized on all exterior and bearing partitions unless otherwise detailed.

_____ **2.** Bolt holes for wood connections shall be _____″ larger in diameter than normal bolt size.

_____ **3.** Steel _____ shall be placed under all bolt heads and nuts bearing on wood.

_____ **4.** Nailing _____ govern over nailing schedules.

_____ **5.** Bridging to joists or rafters shall be toenailed at each end with two _____ nails.

_____ **6.** Double top plates shall be face nailed with 16d nails spaced _____″ OC.

_____ **7.** Continuous _____ shall be toenailed to studs with four 8d nails.

_____ **8.** Series _____ truss joists, as supplied by Trus Joist Corporation, are specified.

_____ **9.** _____% of the soffit area is to be vented.

_____ **10.** Dining room trim is to be _____.

_____ **11.** All closet shelves are to be _____ clear white pine boards.

_____ **12.** Countertops are to be installed by the _____ contractor.

_____ **13.** The cooler-freezer is supplied by the _____.

_____ **14.** The general contractor is responsible for the uncrating and _____ of the cooler-freezer.

_____ **15.** The cooler-freezer is to be shipped complete with _____ and instructions.

DIVISION 7—MOISTURE CONTROL
True-False

T F **1.** Caulking is to be applied to all exterior door frames and window frames to provide weatherproofing.

T F **2.** The roofing membrane shall not exceed 250 sq. ft. per piece.

T F **3.** Two-way vents shall be installed for each 1,000 sq. ft. or fraction of roof area.

T	F	**4.**	Drip edge sheet metal shall be fastened every 8″ OC.
T	F	**5.**	All metal counterflashing shall have a 3″ overlap for expansion and contraction.
T	F	**6.**	All roofing wood members shall be "Wolmanized."
T	F	**7.**	The roofing system is fully warranted for 20 years.
T	F	**8.**	All vapor barriers under concrete slabs shall be 6 mils thick.
T	F	**9.**	Fiberglass batts 4″ thick shall be placed in all exterior walls.
T	F	**10.**	Rigid roof insulation is to be one layer 2.1″ thick, R-10.

DIVISION 8—DOORS, WINDOWS, AND GLASS

Completion

_____ **1.** Doors shall be Series 190 as manufactured by _____ or equal.

_____ **2.** The solarium is to be furnished by the _____.

_____ **3.** All solarium framing is to have a(n) _____ finish.

_____ **4.** Vertical glass for the solarium must be _____″ double sealed and insulated.

_____ **5.** Sloped glass for the solarium shall be _____″ solar cool bronze reflective glass over ¼″ clear laminated glass.

_____ **6.** Solarium glass and installation are covered by warranty for _____ year(s).

_____ **7.** All laminated doors are to be _____″ thick.

_____ **8.** _____ locks shall be D-80-PD Plymouth 605.

_____ **9.** The drive-thru window is manufactured by _____ Corporation.

_____ **10.** All mirrors are to be _____″ polished plate glass.

DIVISION 9—FINISHES

Completion

_____ **1.** All _____ over furring and wood studs shall be ⅝″ Firecode gypsum.

_____ **2.** Washable ceiling tiles are _____ faced.

_____ **3.** Fire-rated Class _____ wall panels are specified.

_____ **4.** Restroom _____ tile is manufactured by American Olean.

_____ **5.** Cushion _____ is used to adhere the carpet pad to the floor slab.

_____ **6.** All walls to be papered must be _____, sanded, and sized before paste is applied.

_____ **7.** _____ paste is not to be used when papering walls.

_____ **8.** _____ coat(s) of primer and two coats of high gloss enamel paint are specified for exterior steel.

_____ **9.** Exterior trim is to receive two coats of _____ inhibitive primer before the finish is applied.

_____ **10.** All interior wood is _____ and varnished.

DIVISION 10—SPECIALTIES

True-False

T   F **1.** Toilet and urinal partitions are manufactured by American Standard.

T   F **2.** All partitions are floor-mounted and braced overhead.

T   F **3.** Handicapped grab bars are high-impact plastic.

T   F **4.** All room identification signs are supplied by the sign erector.

T   F **5.** The exterior fascia panel system is bronze in color.

T   F **6.** The communications system is manufactured by 3-M.

T   F **7.** No substitutes are acceptable for the hood fire suppression system specified.

T   F **8.** Portable fire extinguishers are sized by the local fire control authority.

T   F **9.** The plumber is to receive and unload all kitchen equipment.

T   F **10.** The contractor will provide hook-ups for kitchen equipment.

DIVISION 11—PLUMBING

Completion

_____ **1.** Soil, waste, and vent piping material must meet all local _____.

_____ **2.** Type K, soft _____ tubing is used for water supply piping below ground.

_____ **3.** All water supplies to fixtures must be equipped with _____.

_____ **4.** Schedule _____ black steel gas piping is to be used for all heating systems.

_____ **5.** All water supply piping must be placed to the _____ side of insulation.

_____ **6.** Traps for all plumbing fixtures are to be cast _____.

_____ **7.** The urinal is to be _____ hung.

_____ **8.** The water heater has a(n) _____ lined tank.

_____ **9.** _____ hydrants must be freezeless and automatic draining types.

_____ **10.** The backflow preventor, if required by local code, is to be provided and installed by the _____ contractor.

DIVISION 12—HEATING AND VENTILATION

True-False

T   F   **1.** The installation of kitchen exhaust hoods is covered by this section.

T   F   **2.** Heating and cooling units are designed to handle normal temperatures in Columbus, Ohio.

T   F   **3.** The final balance of the HVAC system shall be performed by the mechanical contractor.

T   F   **4.** All supply ducts must be wrapped with a minimum of 2″ insulation.

T   F   **5.** The thermostat is required to provide manual operation only.

T   F   **6.** The refrigeration contractor must charge all refrigerant lines.

T   F   **7.** Freezer piping shall be $3/8$″ suction line and $5/8$″ liquid line.

T   F   **8.** The heating contractor must coordinate work with the electrical and plumbing contractors.

T   F   **9.** The warranty period for HVAC work is one year.

T   F   **10.** The owner assumes no responsibility for expenses incurred in repairing the HVAC system while it is under warranty.

DIVISION 13—ELECTRICAL

Completion

_____ **1.** All electrical work shall comply with the _____, state, and local codes.

_____ **2.** The _____ system shall form a continuous path for ground.

_____ **3.** All electrical equipment must be _____ by Underwriter's Laboratory.

_____ **4.** All disconnect switches shall be mounted in _____ enclosures.

_____ **5.** All feeder and branch circuits must be _____ during the electrical system test.

_____ **6.** Type _____ or better cable is required for service and panel feeder wiring.

_____ **7.** Electrical design is based on _____ conductors.

_____ **8.** All wiring shall be run in _____.

_____ **9.** Wires #6 AWG and larger must be _____ with approved solderless connectors.

_____ **10.** No conduit larger than _____″ is to be installed in the floor slab.

_____ **11.** Disconnect switches shall be _____ from equipment vibration.

_____ **12.** The system ground conductor must be of _____ wire.

_____ **13.** The ground conductor must not be used as a return or _____ conductor for any equipment.

_____ **14.** The _____ for the cash registers must be isolated from the mounting hardware.

_____ **15.** _____ for NCR equipment must not be used for any other equipment.

APPENDIX

AREA—PLANE FIGURES

SQUARE OR RECTANGLE

Area = Length × Width

$A = L \times W$

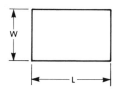

TRIANGLE

Area = $\frac{1}{2}$ *(Base × Altitude)*

$A = \frac{1}{2} (b \times a)$

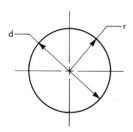

CIRCLE

Area = .7854 × Diameter²

$A = .7854 \times d^2$

Area = π × Radius²

$\pi \times r^2$

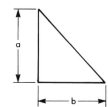

VOLUME—SOLID FIGURES

RIGHT RECTANGULAR PRISM

Volume = Length × Width × Height

$V = L \times W \times H$

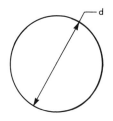

SPHERE

Volume = $\frac{1}{6}$ *× π × Diameter³*

$V = \frac{1}{6} \times \pi \times d^3$

CYLINDER

Volume = .7854 × Diameter² × Height

$V = .7854 \times d^2 \times H$

Volume = π × Radius² × Height

$V = \pi \times r^2 \times H$

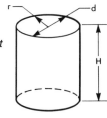

DECIMAL EQUIVALENTS

COMMON FRACTIONS	DECIMAL EQUIVA-LENTS	COMMON FRACTIONS	DECIMAL EQUIVA-LENTS	COMMON FRACTIONS	DECIMAL EQUIVA-LENTS	COMMON FRACTIONS	DECIMAL EQUIVA-LENTS
1/64	.015625	17/64	.265625	33/64	.515625	49/64	.765625
1/32	.03125	9/32	.28125	17/32	.53125	25/32	.78125
3/64	.046875	19/64	.296875	35/64	.546875	51/64	.796875
1/16	.0625	5/16	.3125	9/16	.5625	13/16	.8125
5/64	.078125	21/64	.328125	37/64	.578125	53/64	.828125
3/32	.09375	11/32	.34375	19/32	.59375	27/32	.84375
7/64	.109375	23/64	.359375	39/64	.609375	55/64	.859375
1/8	.125	3/8	.375	5/8	.625	7/8	.875
9/64	.140625	25/64	.390625	41/64	.640625	57/64	.890625
5/32	.15625	13/32	.40625	21/32	.65625	29/32	.90625
11/64	.171875	27/64	.421875	43/64	.671875	59/64	.921875
3/16	.1875	7/16	.4375	11/16	.6875	15/16	.9375
13/64	.203125	29/64	.453125	45/64	.703125	61/64	.953125
7/32	.21875	15/32	.46875	23/32	.71875	31/32	.96875
15/64	.234375	31/64	.484375	47/64	.734375	63/64	.984375
1/4	.25	1/2	.50	3/4	.75		

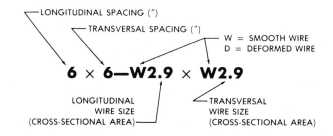

LONGITUDINAL SPACING (")

TRANSVERSAL SPACING (")

W = SMOOTH WIRE
D = DEFORMED WIRE

6 × 6—W2.9 × W2.9

LONGITUDINAL
WIRE SIZE
(CROSS-SECTIONAL AREA)

TRANSVERSAL
WIRE SIZE
(CROSS-SECTIONAL AREA)

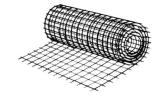

ROLL

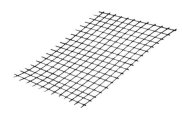

SHEET

COMMON STOCK SIZES FOR WELDED WIRE FABRIC

STYLE DESIGNATION		STEEL AREA SQ. IN. PER FT.		WEIGHT APPROX.
NEW DESIGNATION (BY W-NUMBER)	OLD DESIGNATION (BY STEEL WIRE GAUGE)	LONGIT.	TRANS.	LBS. PER 100 S.F.
ROLLS				
6x6—W1.4xW1.4	6x6—10x10	.028	.028	21
6x6—W2.0xW2.0	6x6—8x8	.040	.040	29
6x6—W2.9xW2.9	6x6—6x6	.058	.058	42
6x6—W4.0xW4.0	6x6—4x4	.080	.080	58
4x4—W1.4xW1.4	4x4—10x10	.042	.042	31
4x4—W2.0xW2.0	4x4—8x8	.060	.060	43
4x4—W2.9xW2.9	4x4—6x6	.087	.087	62
4x4—W4.0xW4.0	4x4—4x4	.120	.120	85
SHEETS				
6x6—W2.9xW2.9	6x6—6x6	.058	.058	42
6x6—W4.0xW4.0	6x6—4x4	.080	.080	58
6x6—W5.5xW5.5	6x6—2x2	.110	.110	80
4x4—W4.0xW4.0	4x4—4x4	.120	.120	85

Wire Reinforcement Institute

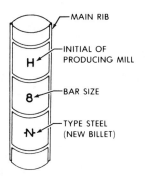

MAIN RIB

INITIAL OF PRODUCING MILL

BAR SIZE

TYPE STEEL (NEW BILLET)

**LINE SYSTEM
GRADE MARKS**

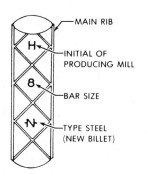

MAIN RIB

INITIAL OF PRODUCING MILL

BAR SIZE

TYPE STEEL (NEW BILLET)

**NUMBER SYSTEM
GRADE MARKS**

STANDARD REBAR SIZES

BAR SIZE DESIGNATION	WEIGHT PER FOOT		DIAMETER		CROSS-SECTIONAL AREA SQUARED	
	LB	KG	IN.	CM	IN.	CM
#3	0.376	0.171	0.375	0.953	0.11	0.71
#4	0.668	0.303	0.500	1.270	0.20	1.29
#5	1.043	0.473	0.625	1.588	0.31	2.00
#6	1.502	0.681	0.750	1.905	0.44	2.84
#7	2.044	0.927	0.875	2.223	0.60	3.87
#8	2.670	1.211	1.000	2.540	0.79	5.10
#9	3.400	1.542	1.128	2.865	1.00	6.45
#10	4.303	1.952	1.270	3.226	1.27	8.19
#11	5.313	2.410	1.410	3.581	1.56	10.07
#14	7.650	3.470	1.693	4.300	2.25	14.52
#18	13.600	6.169	2.257	5.733	4.00	25.81

WIRE SIZE COMPARISON				
W & D SIZE NUMBER SMOOTH	DEFORMED	AREA (SQ. IN.)	NOMINAL DIAMETER (IN.)	AMERICAN STEEL & WIRE GAUGE NUMBER
W31	D31	0.310	0.628	
W30	D30	.300	.618	
W28	D28	.280	.597	
W26	D26	.260	.575	
W24	D24	.240	.553	
W22	D22	.220	.529	
W20	D20	.200	.504	
		.189	.490	7/0
W18	D18	.180	.478	
		.167	.4615	6/0
W16	D16	.160	.451	
		.146	.4305	5/0
W14	D14	.140	.422	
		.122	.394	4/0
W12	D12	.120	.390	
W11	D11	.110	.374	
W10.5		.105	.366	
		.103	.3625	3/0
W10	D10	.100	.356	
W9.5		.095	.348	
W9	D9	.090	.338	
		.086	.331	2/0
W8.5		.085	.329	
W8	D8	.080	.319	
W7.5		.075	.309	
		.074	.3065	1/0
W7	D7	.070	.298	
W6.5		.065	.288	
		.063	.283	1
W6	D6	.060	.276	
W5.5		.055	.264	
		.054	.2625	2
W5	D5	.050	.252	
		.047	.244	3
W4.5		.045	.240	
W4	D4	.040	.225	4
W3.5		.035	.211	
		.034	.207	5
W3		.030	.195	
W2.9		.029	.192	6
W2.5		.025	.177	7
		.021	.162	8
W2		.020	.159	
		.017	.148	9
W1.4		.014	.135	10

Wire Reinforcement Institute

CONCRETE SLABS SQ. FT. PER CU. YD.	
SLAB THICKNESS	SQUARE FEET
1″	324
2″	162
3″	108
4″	81
5″	65
6″	54
7″	46
8″	40
9″	36
10″	32
11″	29.5
12″	27

CONCRETE FOOTINGS VOLUME PER LINEAL FOOT		
WIDTH	DEPTH	VOLUME PER LINEAL FOOT
1′-0″		.50
1′-2″	6″	.59
1′-4″		.67
1′-6″		.75
1′-0″		.67
1′-2″	8″	.78
1′-4″		.89
1′-6″		1.00
1′-0″		.83
1′-2″		.97
1′-4″		1.11
1′-6″	10″	1.25
1′-8″		1.39
1′-10″		1.53
2′-0″		1.67
1′-2″		1.17
1′-4″		1.33
1′-6″	12″	1.50
1′-8″		1.67
1′-10″		1.83
2′-0″		2.00

VERTICAL COURSING TABLE FOR MODULAR BRICK[1]

No. of Courses	Nominal Height (h) of Unit[2]				
	2″	2⅔″	3⅕″	4″	5⅓″
1	0′- 2″	0′- 2¹¹⁄₁₆″	0′- 3³⁄₁₆″	0′-4″	0′- 5⁵⁄₁₆″
2	0′- 4″	0′- 5⁵⁄₁₆″	0′- 6⅜″	0′-8″	0′-10¹¹⁄₁₆″
3	0′- 6″	0′- 8″	0′- 9⅝″	1′-0″	1′- 4″
4	0′- 8″	0′-10¹¹⁄₁₆″	1′- 0¹³⁄₁₆″	1′-4″	1′- 9⁵⁄₁₆″
5	0′-10″	1′- 1⁵⁄₁₆″	1′- 4″	1′-8″	2′- 2¹¹⁄₁₆″
6	1′- 0″	1′- 4″	1′- 7³⁄₁₆″	2′-0″	2′- 8″
7	1′- 2″	1′- 6¹¹⁄₁₆″	1′-10⅜″	2′-4″	3′- 1⁵⁄₁₆″
8	1′- 4″	1′- 9⁵⁄₁₆″	2′- 1⅝″	2′-8″	3′- 6¹¹⁄₁₆″
9	1′- 6″	2′- 0″	2′- 4¹³⁄₁₆″	3′-0″	4′- 0″
10	1′- 8″	2′- 2¹¹⁄₁₆″	2′- 8″	3′-4″	4′- 5⁵⁄₁₆″
11	1′-10″	2′- 5⁵⁄₁₆″	2′-11³⁄₁₆″	3′-8″	4′-10¹¹⁄₁₆″
12	2′- 0″	2′- 8″	3′- 2⅜″	4′-0″	5′- 4″
13	2′- 2″	2′-10¹¹⁄₁₆″	3′- 5⅝″	4′-4″	5′- 9⁵⁄₁₆″
14	2′- 4″	3′- 1⁵⁄₁₆″	3′- 8¹³⁄₁₆″	4′-8″	6′- 2¹¹⁄₁₆″
15	2′- 6″	3′- 4″	4′- 0″	5′-0″	6′- 8″
16	2′- 8″	3′- 6¹¹⁄₁₆″	4′- 3³⁄₁₆″	5′-4″	7′- 1⁵⁄₁₆″
17	2′-10″	3′- 9⁵⁄₁₆″	4′- 6⅜″	5′-8″	7′- 6¹¹⁄₁₆″
18	3′- 0″	4′- 0″	4′- 9⅝″	6′-0″	8′- 0″
19	3′- 2″	4′- 2¹¹⁄₁₆″	5′- 0¹³⁄₁₆″	6′-4″	8′- 5⁵⁄₁₆″
20	3′- 4″	4′- 5⁵⁄₁₆″	5′- 4″	6′-8″	8′-10¹¹⁄₁₆″
21	3′- 6″	4′- 8″	5′- 7³⁄₁₆″	7′-0″	9′- 4″
22	3′- 8″	4′-10¹¹⁄₁₆″	5′-10⅜″	7′-4″	9′- 9⁵⁄₁₆″
23	3′-10″	5′- 1⁵⁄₁₆″	6′- 1⅝″	7′-8″	10′- 2¹¹⁄₁₆″
24	4′- 0″	5′- 4″	6′ 4¹³⁄₁₆″	8′-0″	10′- 8″
25	4′- 2″	5′- 6¹¹⁄₁₆″	6′- 8″	8′-4″	11′- 1⁵⁄₁₆″
26	4′- 4″	5′- 9⁵⁄₁₆″	6′-11³⁄₁₆″	8′-8″	11′- 6¹¹⁄₁₆″
27	4′- 6″	6′- 0″	7′- 2⅜″	9′-0″	12′- 0″
28	4′- 8″	6′- 2¹¹⁄₁₆″	7′- 5⅝″	9′-4″	12′- 5⁵⁄₁₆″
29	4′-10″	6′- 5⁵⁄₁₆″	7′- 8¹³⁄₁₆″	9′-8″	12′-10¹¹⁄₁₆″
30	5′- 0″	6′- 8″	8′- 0″	10′-0″	13′- 4″
31	5′- 2″	6′-10¹¹⁄₁₆″	8′- 3³⁄₁₆″	10′-4″	13′- 9⁵⁄₁₆″
32	5′- 4″	7′- 1⁵⁄₁₆″	8′- 6⅜″	10′-8″	14′ 2¹¹⁄₁₆″
33	5′- 6″	7′- 4″	8′- 9⅝″	11′-0″	14′- 8″
34	5′- 8″	7′- 6¹¹⁄₁₆″	9′- 0¹³⁄₁₆″	11′-4″	15′- 1⁵⁄₁₆″
35	5′-10″	7′- 9⁵⁄₁₆″	9′- 4″	11′-8″	15′- 6¹¹⁄₁₆″
36	6′- 0″	8′- 0″	9′- 7³⁄₁₆″	12′-0″	16′- 0″
37	6′- 2″	8′- 2¹¹⁄₁₆″	9′-10⅜″	12′-4″	16′- 5⁵⁄₁₆″
38	6′- 4″	8′- 5⁵⁄₁₆″	10′- 1⅝″	12′-8″	16′-10¹¹⁄₁₆″
39	6′- 6″	8′- 8″	10′- 4¹³⁄₁₆″	13′-0″	17′- 4″
40	6′- 8″	8′-10¹¹⁄₁₆″	10′- 8″	13′-4″	17′- 9⁵⁄₁₆″
41	6′-10″	9′- 1⁵⁄₁₆″	10′-11³⁄₁₆″	13′-8″	18′- 2¹¹⁄₁₆″
42	7′- 0″	9′- 4″	11′- 2⅜″	14′-0″	18′- 8″
43	7′- 2″	9′- 6¹¹⁄₁₆″	11′- 5⅝″	14′-4″	19′- 1⁵⁄₁₆″
44	7′- 4″	9′- 9⁵⁄₁₆″	11′- 8¹³⁄₁₆″	14′-8″	19′- 6¹¹⁄₁₆″
45	7′- 6″	10′- 0″	12′- 0″	15′-0″	20′- 0″
46	7′- 8″	10′- 2¹¹⁄₁₆″	12′- 3³⁄₁₆″	15′-4″	20′- 5⁵⁄₁₆″
47	7′-10″	10′- 5⁵⁄₁₆″	12′- 6⅜″	15′-8″	20′-10¹¹⁄₁₆″
48	8′- 0″	10′- 8″	12′- 9⅝″	16′-0″	21′- 4″
49	8′- 2″	10′-10¹¹⁄₁₆″	13′- 0¹³⁄₁₆″	16′-4″	21′- 9⁵⁄₁₆″
50	8′- 4″	11′- 1⁵⁄₁₆″	13′- 4″	16′-8″	22′- 2¹¹⁄₁₆″
100	16′- 8″	22′- 2¹¹⁄₁₆″	26′- 8″	33′-4″	44′- 5⁵⁄₁₆″

[1] Brick positioned in wall as stretchers.

Brick Institute of America

[2] For convenience in using table, nominal ⅓″, ⅔″ and ⅕″ heights of units have been changed to nearest ¹⁄₁₆″. Vertical dimensions are from bottom of mortar joint to bottom of mortar joint.

VERTICAL COURSING TABLE FOR NON-MODULAR BRICK[1]

No. of Courses	2¼-in. High Units		2⅝-in. High Units		2¾-in. High Units	
	⅜" Joint	½" Joint	⅜" Joint	½" Joint	⅜" Joint	½" Joint
1	0'- 2⅝"	0'- 2¾"	0'-3"	0'- 3⅛"	0'- 3⅛"	0'- 3¼"
2	0'- 5¼"	0'- 5½"	0'-6"	0'- 6¼"	0'- 6¼"	0'- 6½"
3	0'- 7⅞"	0'- 8¼"	0'-9"	0'- 9⅜"	0'- 9⅜"	0'- 9¾"
4	0'-10½"	0'-11"	1'-0"	1'- 0½"	1'- 0½"	1'- 1"
5	1'- 1⅛"	1'- 1¾"	1'-3"	1'- 3⅝"	1'- 3⅝"	1'- 4¼"
6	1'- 3¾"	1'- 4½"	1'-6"	1'- 6¾"	1'- 6¾"	1'- 7½"
7	1'- 6⅜"	1'- 7¼"	1'-9"	1'- 9⅞"	1'- 9⅞"	1'-10¾"
8	1'- 9"	1'-10"	2'-0"	2'- 1"	2'- 1"	2'- 2"
9	1'-11⅝"	2'- 0¾"	2'-3"	2'- 4⅛"	2'- 4⅛"	2'- 5¼"
10	2'- 2¼"	2'- 3½"	2'-6"	2'- 7¼"	2'- 7¼"	2'- 8½"
11	2'- 4⅞"	2'- 6¼"	2'-9"	2'-10⅜"	2'-10⅜"	2'-11¾"
12	2'- 7½"	2'- 9"	3'-0"	3'- 1½"	3'- 1½"	3'- 3"
13	2'-10⅛"	2'-11¾"	3'-3"	3'- 4⅝"	3'- 4⅝"	3'- 6¼"
14	3'- 0¾"	3'- 2½"	3'-6"	3'- 7¾"	3'- 7¾"	3'- 9½"
15	3'- 3⅜"	3'- 5¼"	3'-9"	3'-10⅞"	3'-10⅞"	4'- 0¾"
16	3'- 6"	3'- 8"	4'-0"	4'- 2"	4'- 2"	4'- 4"
17	3'- 8⅝"	3'-10¾"	4'-3"	4'- 5⅛"	4'- 5⅛"	4'- 7¼"
18	3'-11¼"	4'- 1½"	4'-6"	4'- 8¼"	4'- 8¼"	4'-10½"
19	4'- 1⅞"	4'- 4¼"	4'-9"	4'-11⅜"	4'-11⅜"	5'- 1¾"
20	4'- 4½"	4'- 7"	5'-0"	5'- 2½"	5'- 2½"	5- 5"
21	4'- 7⅛"	4'- 9¾"	5'-3"	5'- 5⅝"	5'- 5⅝"	5'- 8¼"
22	4'- 9¾"	5'- 0½"	5'-6"	5'- 8¾"	5'- 8¾"	5'-11½"
23	5'- 0⅜"	5'- 3¼"	5'-9"	5'-11⅞"	5'-11⅞"	6'- 2¾"
24	5'- 3"	5'- 6"	6'-0"	6'- 3"	6'- 3"	6'- 6"
25	5'- 5⅝"	5'- 8¾"	6'-3"	6'- 6⅛"	6'- 6⅛"	6'- 9¼"
26	5'- 8¼"	5'-11½"	6'-6"	6'- 9¼"	6'- 9¼"	7'- 0½"
27	5'-10⅞"	6'- 2¼"	6'-9"	7'- 0⅜"	7'- 0⅜"	7'- 3¾"
28	6'- 1½"	6'- 5"	7'-0"	7'- 3½"	7'- 3½"	7'- 7"
29	6'- 4⅛"	6'- 7¾"	7'-3"	7'- 6⅝"	7'- 6⅝"	7'-10¼"
30	6'- 6¾"	6'-10½"	7'-6"	7'- 9¾"	7'- 9¾"	8'- 1½"
31	6'- 9⅜"	7'- 1¼"	7'-9"	8'- 0⅞"	8'- 0⅞"	8'- 4¾"
32	7'- 0"	7'- 4"	8'-0"	8'- 4"	8'- 4"	8'- 8"
33	7'- 2⅝"	7'- 6¾"	8'-3"	8'- 7⅛"	8'- 7⅛"	8'-11¼"
34	7'- 5¼"	7'- 9½"	8'-6"	8'-10¼"	8'-10¼"	9'- 2½"
35	7'- 7⅞"	8'- 0¼"	8'-9"	9'- 1⅜"	9'- 1⅜"	9'- 5¾"
36	7'-10½"	8'- 3"	9'-0"	9'- 4½"	9'- 4½"	9'- 9"
37	8'- 1⅛"	8'- 5¾"	9'-3"	9'- 7⅝"	9'- 7⅝"	10- 0¼"
38	8'- 3¾"	8'- 8½"	9'-6"	9'-10¾"	9'-10¾"	10'- 3½"
39	8'- 6⅜"	8'-11¼"	9'-9"	10'- 1⅞"	10'- 1⅞"	10'- 6¾"
40	8'- 9"	9'- 2"	10'-0"	10'- 5"	10'- 5"	10'-10"
41	8'-11⅝"	9'- 4¾"	10'-3"	10'- 8⅛"	10'- 8⅛"	11'- 1¼"
42	9'- 2¼"	9'- 7½"	10'-6"	10'-11¼"	10'-11¼"	11'- 4½"
43	9'- 4⅞"	9'-10¼"	10'-9"	11'- 2⅜"	11'- 2⅜"	11'- 7¾"
44	9'- 7½"	10'- 1"	11'-0"	11'- 5½"	11'- 5½"	11'-11"
45	9'-10⅛"	10'- 3¾"	11'-3"	11'- 8⅝"	11'- 8⅝"	12'- 2¼"
46	10'- 0¾"	10'- 6½"	11'-6"	11'-11¾"	11'-11¾"	12'- 5½"
47	10'- 3⅜"	10'- 9¼"	11'-9"	12'- 2⅞"	12'- 2⅞"	12'- 8¾"
48	10'- 6"	11'- 0"	12'-0"	12'- 6"	12'- 6"	13'- 0"
49	10'- 8⅝"	11'- 2¾"	12'-3"	12'- 9⅛"	12'- 9⅛"	13'- 3¼"
50	10'-11¼"	11'- 5½"	12'-6"	13'- 0¼"	13'- 0¼"	13'- 6½"
100	21'-10½"	22'-11"	25'-0"	26'- 0½"	26'- 0½"	27'- 1"

Brick Institute of America

[1] Brick positioned in wall as stretchers. Vertical dimensions are from bottom of mortar joint to bottom of mortar joint.

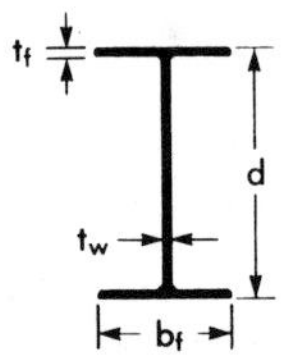
t_f
d
t_w
b_f

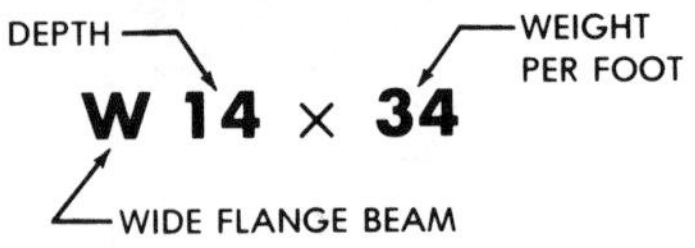
DEPTH
WEIGHT PER FOOT
W 14 × 34
WIDE FLANGE BEAM

W SHAPES-DIMENSIONS FOR DETAILING

DESIGNATION	DEPTH d (IN.)	FLANGE		WEB THICKNESS t_w (IN.)
		WIDTH b_f (IN.)	THICKNESS t_f (IN.)	
W18 x 119	19	11 1/4	1 1/16	5/8
x 106	18 3/4	11 1/4	15/16	9/16
x 97	18 5/8	11 1/8	7/8	9/16
x 86	18 3/8	11 1/8	3/4	1/2
x 76	18 1/4	11	11/16	7/16
W18 x 71	18 1/2	7 5/8	13/16	1/2
x 65	18 3/8	7 5/8	3/4	7/16
x 60	18 1/4	7 1/2	11/16	7/16
x 55	18 1/8	7 1/2	5/8	3/8
x 50	18	7 1/2	9/16	3/8
W18 x 46	18	6	5/8	3/8
x 40	17 7/8	6	1/2	5/16
x 35	17 3/4	6	7/16	5/16
W16 x 100	17	10 3/8	1	9/16
x 89	16 3/4	10 3/8	7/8	1/2
x 77	16 1/2	10 1/4	3/4	7/16
x 67	16 3/8	10 1/4	11/16	3/8
W16 x 57	16 3/8	7 1/8	11/16	7/16
x 50	16 1/4	7 1/8	5/8	3/8
x 45	16 1/8	7	9/16	3/8
x 40	16	7	1/2	5/16
x 36	15 7/8	7	7/16	5/16
W16 x 31	15 7/8	5 1/2	7/16	1/4
x 26	15 3/4	5 1/2	3/8	1/4
W14 x 730	22 3/8	17 7/8	4 15/16	3 1/16
x 665	21 5/8	17 5/8	4 1/2	2 13/16
x 605	20 7/8	17 3/8	4 3/16	2 5/8
x 550	20 1/4	17 1/4	3 13/16	2 3/8
x 500	19 5/8	17	3 1/2	2 3/16
x 455	19	16 7/8	3 3/16	2
W14 x 426	18 5/8	16 3/4	3 1/16	1 7/8
x 398	18 1/4	16 5/8	2 7/8	1 3/4
x 370	17 7/8	16 1/2	2 11/16	1 5/8
x 342	17 1/2	16 3/8	2 1/2	1 9/16
x 311	17 1/8	16 1/4	2 1/4	1 7/16
x 283	16 3/4	16 1/8	2 1/16	1 5/16
x 257	16 3/8	16	1 7/8	1 3/16
x 233	16	15 7/8	1 3/4	1 1/16
x 211	15 3/4	15 3/4	1 9/16	1
x 193	15 1/2	15 3/4	1 7/16	7/8
x 176	15 1/4	15 5/8	1 5/16	13/16
x 159	15	15 5/8	1 3/16	3/4
x 145	14 3/4	15 1/2	1 1/16	11/16
W14 x 132	14 5/8	14 3/4	1	5/8
x 120	14 1/2	14 5/8	15/16	9/16
x 109	14 3/8	14 5/8	7/8	1/2
x 99	14 1/8	14 5/8	3/4	1/2
x 90	14	14 1/2	11/16	7/16
W14 x 82	14 1/4	10 1/8	7/8	1/2
x 74	14 1/8	10 1/8	13/16	7/16
x 68	14	10	3/4	7/16
x 61	13 7/8	10	5/8	3/8
W14 x 53	13 7/8	8	11/16	3/8
x 48	13 3/4	8	5/8	5/16
x 43	13 5/8	8	1/2	5/16
W14 x 38	14 1/8	6 3/4	1/2	5/16
x 34	14	6 3/4	7/16	5/16
x 30	13 7/8	6 3/4	3/8	1/4
W14 x 26	13 7/8	5	7/16	1/4
x 22	13 3/4	5	5/16	1/4

DESIGNATION	DEPTH d (IN.)	FLANGE		WEB THICKNESS t_w (IN.)
		WIDTH b_f (IN.)	THICKNESS t_f (IN.)	
W12 x 336	16 7/8	13 3/8	2 15/16	1 3/4
x 305	16 3/8	13 1/4	2 11/16	1 5/8
x 279	15 7/8	13 1/8	2 1/2	1 1/2
x 252	15 3/8	13	2 1/4	1 3/8
x 230	15	12 7/8	2 1/16	1 5/16
x 210	14 3/4	12 3/4	1 7/8	1 3/16
W12 x 190	14 3/8	12 5/8	1 3/4	1 1/16
x 170	14	12 5/8	1 9/16	15/16
x 152	13 3/4	12 1/2	1 3/8	7/8
x 136	13 3/8	12 3/8	1 1/4	13/16
x 120	13 1/8	12 3/8	1 1/8	11/16
x 106	12 7/8	12 1/4	1	5/8
x 96	12 3/4	12 1/8	7/8	9/16
x 87	12 1/2	12 1/8	13/16	1/2
x 79	12 3/8	12 1/8	3/4	1/2
x 72	12 1/4	12	11/16	7/16
x 65	12 1/8	12	5/8	3/8
W12 x 58	12 1/4	10	5/8	3/8
x 53	12	10	9/16	3/8
W12 x 50	12 1/4	8 1/8	3/8	5/8
x 45	12	8	5/16	9/16
x 40	12	8	5/16	1/2
W12 x 35	12 1/2	6 1/2	5/16	1/2
x 30	12 3/8	6 1/2	1/4	7/16
x 26	12 1/4	6 1/2	1/4	3/8
W12 x 22	12 1/4	4	1/4	7/16
x 19	12 1/8	4	1/4	3/8
x 16	12	4	1/4	1/4
x 14	11 7/8	4	3/16	1/4
W10 x 112	11 3/8	10 3/8	1 1/4	3/4
x 100	11 1/8	10 3/8	1 1/8	11/16
x 88	10 7/8	10 1/4	1	5/8
x 77	10 5/8	10 1/4	7/8	1/2
x 68	10 3/8	10 1/8	3/4	1/2
x 60	10 1/4	10 1/8	11/16	7/16
x 54	10 1/8	10	5/8	3/8
x 49	10	10	9/16	5/16
W10 x 45	10 1/8	8	5/8	3/8
x 39	9 7/8	8	1/2	5/16
x 33	9 3/4	8	7/16	5/16
W10 x 30	10 1/2	5 3/4	1/2	5/16
x 26	10 3/8	5 3/4	7/16	1/4
x 22	10 1/8	5 3/4	3/8	1/4
W10 x 19	10 1/4	4	3/8	1/4
x 17	10 1/8	4	5/16	1/4
x 15	10	4	1/4	1/4
x 12	9 7/8	4	3/16	3/16
W8 x 67	9	8 1/4	15/16	9/16
x 58	8 3/4	8 1/4	13/16	1/2
x 48	8 1/2	8 1/8	11/16	3/8
x 40	8 1/4	8 1/8	9/16	3/8
x 35	8 1/8	8	1/2	5/16
x 31	8	8	7/16	5/16
W8 x 28	8	6 1/2	7/16	5/16
x 24	7 7/8	6 1/2	3/8	1/4
W8 x 21	8 1/4	5 1/4	3/8	1/4
x 18	8 1/8	5 1/4	5/16	1/4
W8 x 15	8 1/8	4	5/16	1/4
x 13	8	4	1/4	1/4
x 10	7 7/8	4	3/16	3/16

THICKNESS — LONGEST LEG — SHORTEST LEG

SHORTEST LEG — LEG THICKNESS — ANGLE — $\angle$ **6** × **4** × **5/16″** — LONGEST LEG

ANGLES (UNEQUAL LEGS)—DIMENSIONS FOR DETAILING

SIZE AND THICKNESS (IN.)	SIZE AND THICKNESS (IN.)	SIZE AND THICKNESS (IN.)	SIZE AND THICKNESS (IN.)	SIZE AND THICKNESS (IN.)	SIZE AND THICKNESS (IN.)
L 9 x 4 x 1	L 7 x 4 x 7/8	L 5 x 3 1/2 x 3/4	L 4 x 3 x 5/8	L 3 x 2 1/2 x 1/2	L 2 1/2 x 1 1/2 x 5/16
7/8	3/4	5/8	1/2	7/16	1/4
3/4	5/8	1/2	7/16	3/8	3/16
5/8	9/16	7/16	3/8	5/16	L 2 x 1 1/2 x 1/4
9/16	1/2	3/8	5/16	1/4	3/16
1/2	7/16	5/16	1/4	3/16	1/8
L 8 x 6 x 1	3/8	1/4	L 3 1/2 x 3 x 1/2	L 3 x 2 x 1/2	L 2 x 1 1/4 x 1/4
7/8	L 6 x 4 x 7/8	L 5 x 3 x 1/2	7/16	7/16	3/16
3/4	3/4	7/16	3/8	3/8	1/8
5/8	5/8	3/8	5/16	5/16	L 1 3/4 x 1 1/4 x 1/4
9/16	9/16	5/16	1/4	1/4	3/16
1/2	1/2	1/4	L 3 1/2 x 2 1/2 x 1/2	3/16	1/8
7/16	7/16	L 4 x 3 1/2 x 5/8	7/16	L 2 1/2 x 2 x 3/8	
L 8 x 4 x 1	3/8	1/2	3/8	5/16	
7/8	5/16	7/16	5/16	1/4	
3/4	1/4	3/8	1/4	3/16	
5/8	L 6 x 3 1/2 x 1/2	5/16			
9/16	3/8	1/4			
1/2	5/16				
7/16	1/4				

DEPTH — WEIGHT PER FOOT — $\textsf{C}$ **12** × **20.7** — AMERICAN STANDARD CHANNEL

THICKNESS — EQUAL LENGTH LEG — EQUAL LENGTH LEG — LEG LENGTHS — LEG THICKNESS — $\angle$ **4** × **4** × **5/16″** — ANGLE

AMERICAN STANDARD CHANNELS

DESIGNATION	DEPTH d (IN.)	FLANGE		WEB THICKNESS t_w (IN.)
		WIDTH b_f (IN.)	AVERAGE THICKNESS t_f (IN.)	
C 15 x 50	15	3 3/4	5/8	11/16
x 40	15	3 1/2	5/8	1/2
x 33.9	15	3 3/8	5/8	3/8
C 12 x 30	12	3 1/8	1/2	1/2
x 25	12	3	1/2	3/8
x 20.7	12	3	1/2	5/16
C 10 x 30	10	3	7/16	11/16
x 25	10	2 7/8	7/16	1/2
x 20	10	2 3/4	7/16	3/8
x 15.3	10	2 5/8	7/16	1/4
C 9 x 20	9	2 5/8	7/16	7/16
x 15	9	2 1/2	7/16	5/16
x 13.4	9	2 3/8	7/16	1/4
C 8 x 18.75	8	2 1/2	3/8	1/2
x 13.75	8	2 3/8	3/8	5/16
x 11.5	8	2 1/4	3/8	1/4
C 7 x 14.75	7	2 1/4	3/8	7/16
x 12.25	7	2 1/4	3/8	5/16
x 9.8	7	2 1/8	3/8	3/16
C 6 x 13	6	2 1/8	5/16	7/16
x 10.5	6	2	5/16	5/16
x 8.2	6	1 7/8	5/16	3/16
C 5 x 9	5	1 7/8	5/16	5/16
x 6.7	5	1 3/4	5/16	3/16
C 4 x 7.25	4	1 3/4	5/16	5/16
x 5.4	4	1 5/8	5/16	3/16
C 3 x 6	3	1 5/8	1/4	3/8
x 5	3	1 1/2	1/4	1/4
x 4.1	3	1 3/8	1/4	3/16

ANGLES (EQUAL LEGS)—DIMENSIONS FOR DETAILING

SIZE AND THICKNESS (IN.)	SIZE AND THICKNESS (IN.)
L 8 x 8 x 1 1/8	L 3 1/2 x 3 1/2 x 1/2
1	7/16
7/8	3/8
3/4	5/16
5/8	1/4
9/16	L 3 x 3 x 1/2
1/2	7/16
L 6 x 6 x 1	3/8
7/8	5/16
3/4	1/4
5/8	3/16
9/16	L 2 1/2 x 2 1/2 x 1/2
1/2	3/8
7/16	5/16
3/8	1/4
5/16	3/16
L 5 x 5 x 7/8	L 2 x 2 x 3/8
3/4	5/16
5/8	1/4
1/2	3/16
7/16	1/8
3/8	L 1 3/4 x 1 3/4 x 1/4
5/16	3/16
L 4 x 4 x 3/4	1/8
5/8	L 1 1/2 x 1 1/2 x 1/4
1/2	3/16
7/16	5/32
3/8	1/8
5/16	L 1 1/4 x 1 1/4 x 1/4
1/4	3/16
	1/8
	L 1 x 1 x 1/4
	3/16
	1/8

TYPICAL APA REGISTERED TRADEMARKS

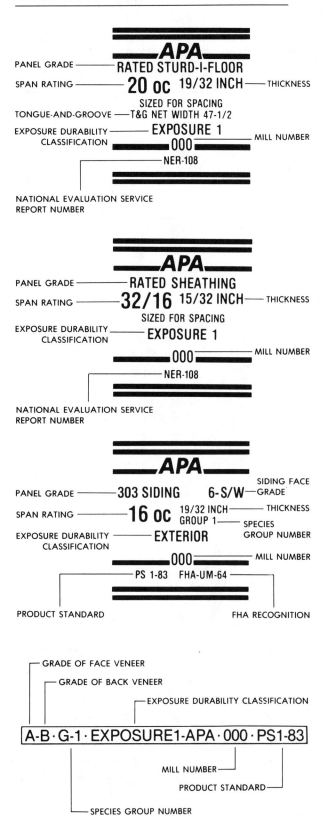

PANEL GRADE — **APA** RATED STURD-I-FLOOR

SPAN RATING — **20 oc** 19/32 INCH — THICKNESS

SIZED FOR SPACING

TONGUE-AND-GROOVE — T&G NET WIDTH 47-1/2

EXPOSURE DURABILITY CLASSIFICATION — EXPOSURE 1

000 — MILL NUMBER

NER-108

NATIONAL EVALUATION SERVICE REPORT NUMBER

PANEL GRADE — **APA** RATED SHEATHING

SPAN RATING — **32/16** 15/32 INCH — THICKNESS

SIZED FOR SPACING

EXPOSURE DURABILITY CLASSIFICATION — EXPOSURE 1

000 — MILL NUMBER

NER-108

NATIONAL EVALUATION SERVICE REPORT NUMBER

APA

PANEL GRADE — 303 SIDING 6-S/W — SIDING FACE GRADE

SPAN RATING — **16 oc** 19/32 INCH — THICKNESS

GROUP 1 — SPECIES GROUP NUMBER

EXPOSURE DURABILITY CLASSIFICATION — EXTERIOR

000 — MILL NUMBER

PS 1-83 FHA-UM-64

PRODUCT STANDARD   FHA RECOGNITION

GRADE OF FACE VENEER

GRADE OF BACK VENEER

EXPOSURE DURABILITY CLASSIFICATION

A-B · G-1 · EXPOSURE1-APA · 000 · PS1-83

MILL NUMBER

PRODUCT STANDARD

SPECIES GROUP NUMBER

APA PERFORMANCE-RATED PANELS

APA RATED SHEATHING

TYPICAL TRADEMARK

APA RATED SHEATHING
32/16 15/32 INCH
SIZED FOR SPACING
EXPOSURE 1
000
NER-108

Specially designed for subflooring and wall and roof sheathing. Also good for broad range of other construction and industrial applications. Can be manufactured as conventional veneered plywood, as a composite, or as a nonveneered panel. For special engineered applications, veneered panels conforming to PS 1 may be required. EXPOSURE DURABILITY CLASSIFICATIONS: Exterior, Exposure 1, Exposure 2. COMMON THICKNESSES: $5/16$, $3/8$, $7/16$, $15/32$, $1/2$, $19/32$, $5/8$, $23/32$, $3/4$.

APA STRUCTURAL I RATED SHEATHING[3]

TYPICAL TRADEMARK

APA RATED SHEATHING
STRUCTURAL I
48/24 23/32 INCH
SIZED FOR SPACING
EXTERIOR
000
PS 1-83 C-C   NER-108

Unsanded all-veneer plywood grades for use where shear and cross-panel strength properties are of maximum importance, such as panelized roofs and diaphragms. EXPOSURE DURABILITY CLASSIFICATIONS: Exterior, Exposure 1. COMMON THICKNESSES: $5/16$, $3/8$, $15/32$, $1/2$, $19/32$, $5/8$, $23/32$, $3/4$.

APA RATED STURD-I-FLOOR

TYPICAL TRADEMARK

APA RATED STURD-I-FLOOR
20 oc 19/32 INCH
SIZED FOR SPACING
EXPOSURE 1
000
NER-108

Specially designed as combination subfloor-underlayment. Provides smooth surface for application of carpet and possesses high concentrated and impact load resistance. Can be manufactured as conventional veneered plywood, as a composite, or as a nonveneered panel. Available square edge or tongue-and-groove. EXPOSURE DURABILITY CLASSIFICATIONS: Exterior, Exposure 1, Exposure 2. COMMON THICKNESSES: $19/32$, $5/8$, $23/32$, $3/4$.

APA RATED STURD-I-FLOOR 48 oc (2-4-1)

TYPICAL TRADEMARK

APA RATED STURD-I-FLOOR
48 oc 1-1/8 INCH 2-4-1
SIZED FOR SPACING
EXPOSURE 1
T&G 000
UNDERLAYMENT
PS 1-83 NER-108

For combination subfloor-underlayment on 32- and 48-inch spans and for heavy timber roof construction. Manufactured only as conventional veneered plywood. Available square edge or tongue-and-groove. EXPOSURE DURABILITY CLASSIFICATIONS: Exposure 1. THICKNESS: $1\frac{1}{8}$.

APA PANEL CORNER BRACING

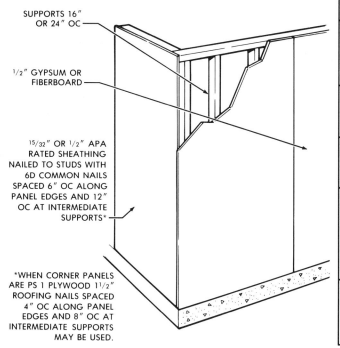

SUPPORTS 16″ OR 24″ OC

½″ GYPSUM OR FIBERBOARD

¹⁵/₃₂″ OR ½″ APA RATED SHEATHING NAILED TO STUDS WITH 6D COMMON NAILS SPACED 6″ OC ALONG PANEL EDGES AND 12″ OC AT INTERMEDIATE SUPPORTS*

*WHEN CORNER PANELS ARE PS 1 PLYWOOD 1½″ ROOFING NAILS SPACED 4″ OC ALONG PANEL EDGES AND 8″ OC AT INTERMEDIATE SUPPORTS MAY BE USED.

VENEER GRADES	
N	Smooth surface "natural finish" veneer. Select, all heartwood or all sapwood. Free of open defects. Allows not more than 6 repairs, wood only, per 4 × 8 panel, made parallel to grain and well matched for grain and color.
A	Smooth, paintable. Not more than 18 neatly made repairs, boat, sled, or router type, and parallel to grain, permitted. May be used for natural finish in less demanding applications.
B	Solid surface. Shims, circular repair plugs and tight knots to 1 inch across grain permitted. Some minor splits permitted.
C Plugged	Improved C veneer with splits limited to ⅛-inch width and knotholes and borer holes limited to ¼ × ½ inch. Admits some broken grain. Synthetic repairs permitted.
C	Tight knots to 1½ inch. Knotholes to 1 inch across grain and some to 1½ inch if total width of knots and knotholes is within specified limits. Synthetic or wood repairs. Discoloration and sanding defects that do not impair strength permitted. Limited splits allowed. Stitching permitted.
D	Knots and knotholes to 2½ inch width across grain and ½ inch larger within specified limits. Limited splits are permitted. Stitching permitted. Limited to Exposure 1 or Interior panels.

BRICK VENEER OVER APA PANEL SHEATHING

APA RATED SHEATHING

1″ AIR SPACE

BRICK VENEER OR MASONRY

"WEEP HOLES" IN BOTTOM COURSE EVERY 4′

HOLD PANEL EDGE ½″ ABOVE BASE FLASHING

EXTEND FLASHING UP BEHIND SHEATHING AT LEAST 6″

BUILDING PAPER MAY BE REQUIRED WITH BRICK VENEER*

*CHECK LOCAL BUILDING CODE FOR REQUIREMENTS

STUCCO OVER APA PANEL SHEATHING

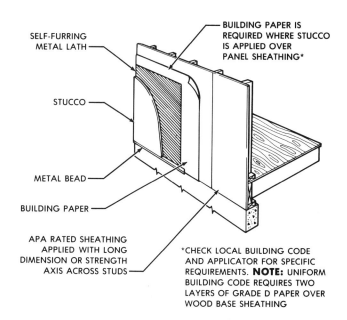

SELF-FURRING METAL LATH

STUCCO

METAL BEAD

BUILDING PAPER

APA RATED SHEATHING APPLIED WITH LONG DIMENSION OR STRENGTH AXIS ACROSS STUDS

BUILDING PAPER IS REQUIRED WHERE STUCCO IS APPLIED OVER PANEL SHEATHING*

*CHECK LOCAL BUILDING CODE AND APPLICATOR FOR SPECIFIC REQUIREMENTS. **NOTE:** UNIFORM BUILDING CODE REQUIRES TWO LAYERS OF GRADE D PAPER OVER WOOD BASE SHEATHING

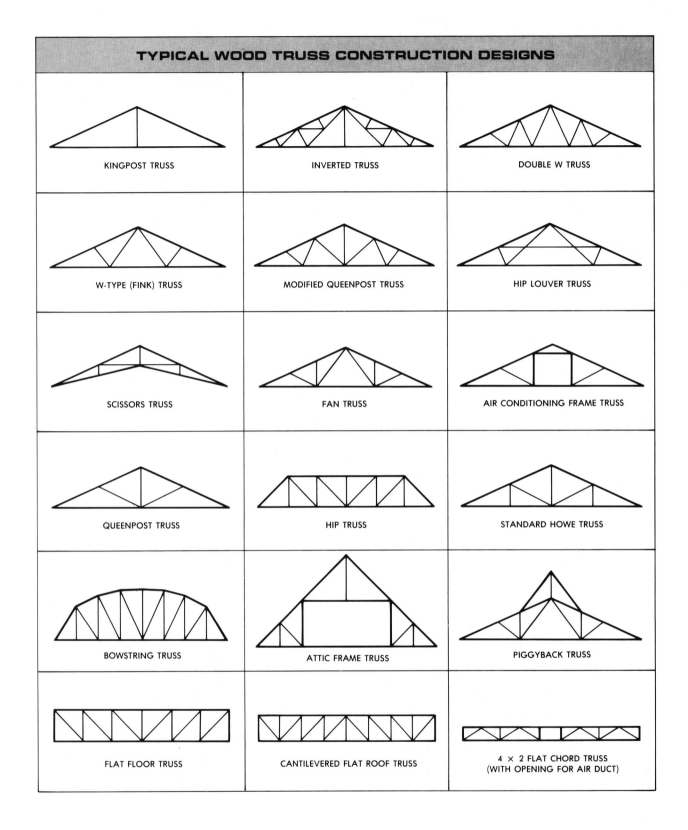

TYPICAL WOOD TRUSS CONSTRUCTION DESIGNS

KINGPOST TRUSS

INVERTED TRUSS

DOUBLE W TRUSS

W-TYPE (FINK) TRUSS

MODIFIED QUEENPOST TRUSS

HIP LOUVER TRUSS

SCISSORS TRUSS

FAN TRUSS

AIR CONDITIONING FRAME TRUSS

QUEENPOST TRUSS

HIP TRUSS

STANDARD HOWE TRUSS

BOWSTRING TRUSS

ATTIC FRAME TRUSS

PIGGYBACK TRUSS

FLAT FLOOR TRUSS

CANTILEVERED FLAT ROOF TRUSS

4 × 2 FLAT CHORD TRUSS
(WITH OPENING FOR AIR DUCT)

TRUSSED WOOD RAFTERS

TYPE	CONSTRUCTION	USE
LAMINATED CHORDS WITH PLYWOOD WEB	Chords—2″ × 3″ laminated wood Webs—³/₈″ plywood	20′–60′ spans
WOOD CHORDS AND WEBS WITH STEEL PLATES	Chords—wood Webs—wood with steel plate connectors	40′–60′ spans
WOOD CHORDS WITH STEEL WEBS	Chords—2 × 6 wood Webs—1″-1¹/₂″ diameter tubing	40′–80′ spans
DOUBLE WOOD CHORDS WITH STEEL WEBS	Chords—Double 2 × 6 wood Webs—2″ diameter steel	60′–100′ spans

STANDARD LUMBER SIZES

TYPE	THICKNESS		WIDTH	
	NOMINAL SIZE	ACTUAL SIZE	NOMINAL SIZE	ACTUAL SIZE
COMMON BOARDS	1″	³/₄″	2″ 4″ 6″ 8″ 10″ 12″	1¹/₂″ 3¹/₂″ 5¹/₂″ 7¹/₄″ 9¹/₄″ 11¹/₄″
DIMENSION	2″	1¹/₂″	2″ 4″ 6″ 8″ 10″ 12″	1¹/₂″ 3¹/₂″ 5¹/₂″ 7¹/₄″ 9¹/₄″ 11¹/₄″
TIMBERS	4″ 6″ 8″	3¹/₂″ 5¹/₂″ 7¹/₂″	4″ 6″ 8″ 10″	3¹/₂″ 5¹/₂″ 7¹/₂″ 9¹/₂″
	6″	5¹/₂″	6″ 8″ 10″	5¹/₂″ 7¹/₂″ 9¹/₂″
	8″	7¹/₂″	8″ 10″	7¹/₂″ 9¹/₂″

FLOOR JOIST SPAN TABLE

40# Live Load
10# Dead Load

Design Criteria:
Strength—10 lbs. per sq. ft. dead load plus 40 lbs. per sq. ft. live load.
Deflection—Limited to span in inches divided by 360 for live load only.

L/360

Species or Group	Grade*	2 × 6			2 × 8			2 × 10			2 × 12		
		12″ O.C.	16″ O.C.	24″ O.C.	12″ O.C.	16″ O.C.	24″ O.C.	12″ O.C.	16″ O.C.	24″ O.C.	12″ O.C.	16″ O.C.	24″ O.C.
DOUGLAS FIR-LARCH	2	10-11	9-11	8-6	14-4	13-1	11-3	18-4	16-9	14-5	22-4	20-4	17-6
	3	9-3	8-0	6-6	12-2	10-7	8-8	15-7	13-6	11-0	18-11	16-5	13-5
DOUGLAS FIR SOUTH	2	10-0	9-1	7-11	13-2	12-0	10-6	16-9	15-3	13-4	20-5	18-7	16-3
	3	9-0	7-9	6-4	11-9	10-3	8-4	15-1	13-1	10-8	18-4	15-11	13-0
HEM-FIR	2	10-3	9-4	7-7	13-6	12-3	10-0	17-3	15-8	12-10	20-11	19-1	15-7
	3	8-3	7-2	5-10	10-10	9-5	7-8	13-10	12-0	9-10	16-10	14-7	11-11
MOUNTAIN HEMLOCK- HEM-FIR	2	9-5	8-7	7-6	12-5	11-4	9-11	15-11	14-6	12-8	19-4	17-7	15-4
	3	8-3	7-2	5-10	10-10	9-5	7-8	13-10	12-0	9-10	16-10	14-7	11-11
WESTERN HEMLOCK	2	10-3	9-4	7-11	13-6	12-3	10-6	17-3	15-8	13-4	20-11	19-1	16-3
	3	8-8	7-6	6-1	11-5	9-11	8-1	14-7	12-8	10-4	17-9	15-5	12-7
ENGLEMANN SPRUCE LODGEPOLE PINE (Englemann Spruce- Alpine Fir)	2	9-5	8-7	6-11	12-5	11-2	9-1	15-11	14-3	11-7	19-4	17-3	14-2
	3	7-5	6-5	5-3	9-9	8-6	6-11	12-6	10-10	8-10	15-3	13-2	10-9
LODGEPOLE PINE	2	9-8	8-10	7-3	12-10	11-8	9-7	16-4	14-11	12-3	19-10	18-1	14-11
	3	7-10	6-10	5-7	10-5	9-1	7-5	13-4	11-7	9-5	16-3	14-1	11-6
PONDEROSA PINE- LODGEPOLE PINE	2	9-5	8-7	7-0	12-5	11-4	9-3	15-11	14-5	11-9	19-4	17-7	14-4
	3	7-7	6-6	5-4	10-0	8-8	7-1	12-9	11-1	9-1	15-7	13-6	11-0
WESTERN CEDARS	2	9-2	8-4	7-3	12-0	11-0	9-7	15-4	14-0	12-3	18-9	17-0	14-11
	3	7-10	6-10	7-6	10-5	9-1	7-5	13-4	11-6	9-5	16-3	14-0	11-6
WHITE WOODS (Western Woods)	2	9-2	8-4	6-10	12-0	11-0	9-0	15-5	14-0	11-6	18-9	17-0	14-0
	3	7-5	6-5	5-3	9-9	8-6	6-11	12-6	10-10	8-10	15-3	13-2	10-9

*Spans were computed for commonly marketed grades. Spans for other grades can be computed utilizing the WWPA Span Computer.

Western Wood Products Association

WOOD SCREW HEADS

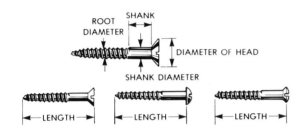

FLAT   **ROUND**   **OVAL**

HEAD RECESSES

SLOTTED   **PHILLIPS**

WOOD SCREW SIZES

NAIL SIZES

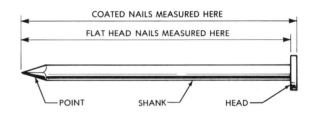

WIRE SIZE	APPROXIMATE DIAMETER	LENGTH
0	1/16″	1/4″–3/8″
1	5/64″	1/4″–1/2″
2	5/64″	1/4″–3/4″
3	3/32″	1/4″–1″
4	7/64″	1/4″–1 1/2″
5	1/8″	3/8″–1 1/2″
6	9/64″	3/8″–2 1/2″
7	5/32″	3/8″–2 1/2″
8	5/32″	3/8″–3″
9	11/64″	1/2″–3″
10	3/16″	1/2″–3 1/2″
11	13/64″	5/8″–3 1/2″
12	7/32″	5/8″–4″
14	1/4″	3/4″–5″
16	17/64″	1″–5″
18	19/64″	1 1/4″–5″
20	21/64″	1 1/2″–5″
24	3/8″	3″–5″

LENGTH (IN IN.)	PENNY	GAUGE	DIAM. OF HEAD (IN IN.)	NO. OF NAILS PER LB.
1	2	15	11/64	847
1 1/4	3	14	13/64	543
1 1/2	4	12 1/2	1/4	296
1 3/4	5	12 1/2	1/4	254
2	6	11 1/2	17/64	167
2 1/4	7	11 1/2	17/64	150
2 1/2	8	10 1/4	9/32	101
2 3/4	9	10 1/4	9/32	92.1
3	10	9	5/16	66
3 1/4	12	9	5/16	66.1
3 1/2	16	8	11/32	47.4
4	20	6	13/32	29.7
4 1/2	30	5	7/16	22.7
5	40	4	15/32	17.3
5 1/2	50	3	1/2	13.5
6	60	2	17/32	10.7

NAIL HEADS

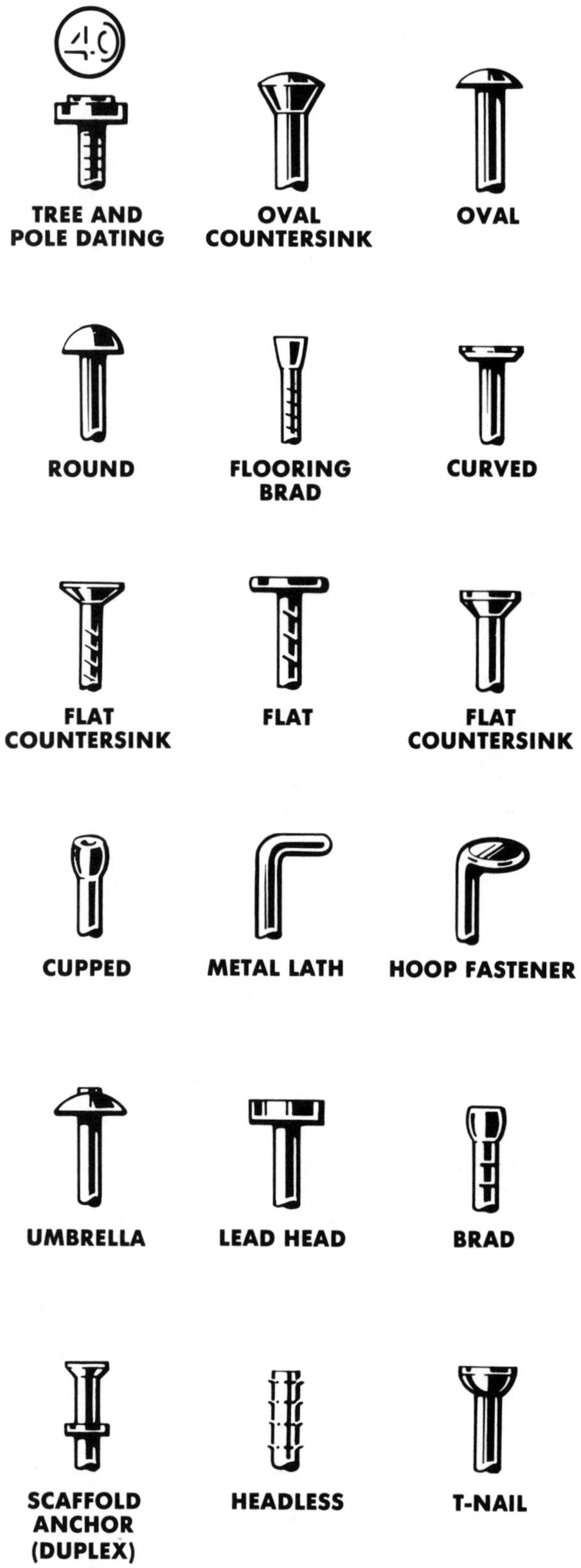

TREE AND POLE DATING

OVAL COUNTERSINK

OVAL

ROUND

FLOORING BRAD

CURVED

FLAT COUNTERSINK

FLAT

FLAT COUNTERSINK

CUPPED

METAL LATH

HOOP FASTENER

UMBRELLA

LEAD HEAD

BRAD

SCAFFOLD ANCHOR (DUPLEX)

HEADLESS

T-NAIL

NAIL SHANKS

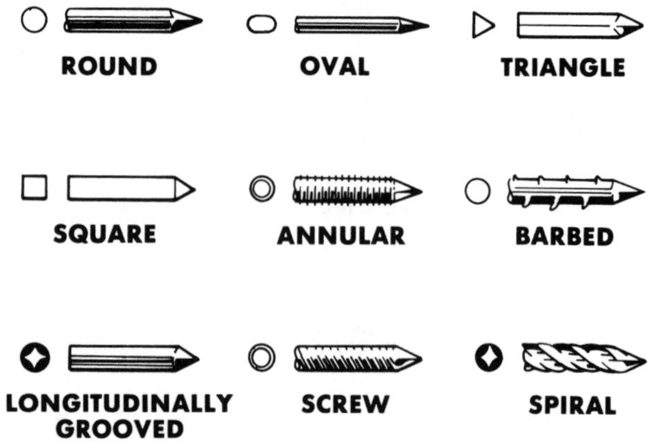

ROUND

OVAL

TRIANGLE

SQUARE

ANNULAR

BARBED

LONGITUDINALLY GROOVED

SCREW

SPIRAL

NAIL POINTS

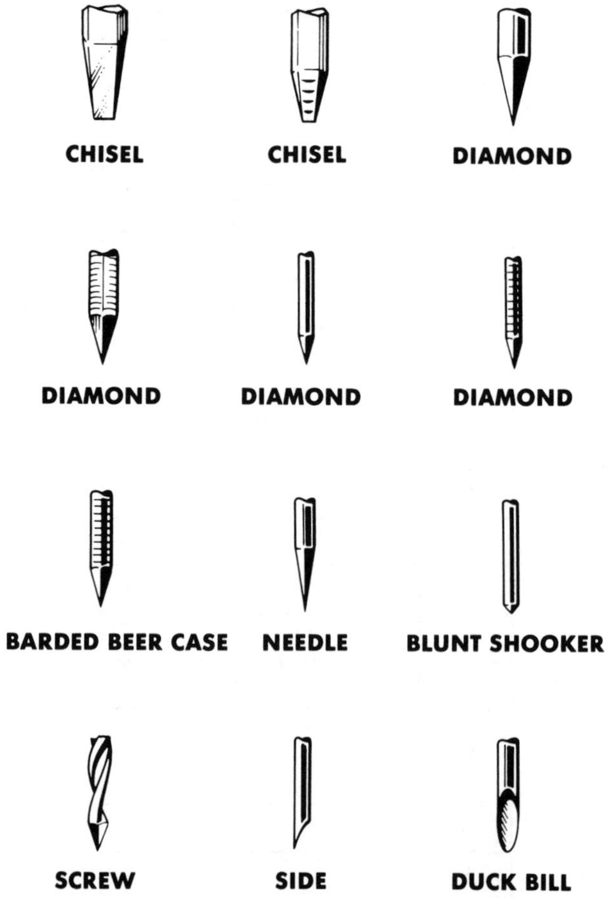

CHISEL

CHISEL

DIAMOND

DIAMOND

DIAMOND

DIAMOND

BARDED BEER CASE

NEEDLE

BLUNT SHOOKER

SCREW

SIDE

DUCK BILL

GLOSSARY

A

A frame. A building with a gable roof extending to the foundation.

Accordion door. Door made of wood slats or fabric arranged to fold back and forth in the plane of the door frame.

Acoustical tile. Ceiling tile with small holes which serve as sound traps to reduce the reflection of sound.

Acrylic. 1. In plastic, a thermoplastic used in molded plastic parts. 2. In painting, a bonding resin in latex paint.

Actual size. The true size of lumber in contrast to nominal size. The actual size of a 2 × 4 is 1½″ × 3½″.

Additive. Chemical added to concrete to alter its properties. Accelerators, retardants, and air entraining agents are examples of additives.

Aggregate. Gravel, broken stone, or other hard inert material used in concrete.

Agricultural tile. Clay drain tile usually laid with open joints to permit water to enter.

Air duct. Pipe, usually rectangular or round and made of sheet metal, used to conduct hot or cold air in heating or cooling systems.

Air entrainment. In concrete, a process by means of a chemical admixture causing the formation of tiny air bubbles uniformly throughout the mixture. Air entrainment improves the workability of the fresh mix and the frost and de-icing salt resistance of the final structure.

Alkyd. A synthetic resin used as the base for surface coatings.

Allowable span. Distance allowed between supporting points for various sizes of girders, joists, and roof rafters.

Aluminize. To coat with aluminum.

Amp. Measurement of electrical current. Designated I in formulas. Abbreviated as A.

Anchor bolt. Metal bolt used to secure a wood sill to a masonry or concrete foundation wall.

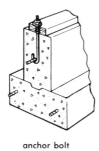

anchor bolt

Angle. The number of degrees between two intersecting lines of a flat plane.

Angle iron. Piece of structural steel formed with a cross-sectional shape of a right angle.

Annular ring nail. Nails with fine rings on the shanks having strong holding power.

Anodize. To protect metal with an aluminum oxide film produced by an electrolytic process.

ANSI. American National Standards Institute.

Apron. 1. In concrete, the flat concrete slab in front of a garage. It occasionally has a slight pitch for drainage purposes. 2. In carpentry, an inside trim member on a window.

Architect. Person qualified and licensed to design and oversee construction of a building.

Ashlar masonry. Masonry composed of sawed, squared, or dressed stone in rectangular or square shapes.

ASME. American Society of Mechanical Engineers.

Asphalt. A waterproof petroleum product, obtained from crude oil, used as the base of many products for roof, wall, and floor covering.

Asphalt shingle. Shingle made of felt saturated with asphalt and a surface covered with mineral granules. Used as a finish roofing material.

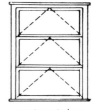

awning window

Attic. Space between the ceiling and roof of a building.

Awning window. A type of window in which each sash opens outward with hinges placed at the top of the sash.

AWS. American Welding Society.

Axonometric. Pictorial drawing in which the axes vary depending upon the type. Three types are isometric (most common), dimetric, and trimetric.

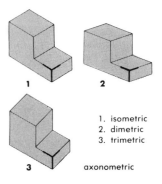

1. isometric
2. dimetric
3. trimetric

axonometric

B

Backfill. Coarse earth, or other material, used to build up the ground level around foundation walls or in low areas.

Backsplash. The rear vertical piece of a countertop that is placed along a wall.

Balcony. An above-grade deck projecting from the wall of a building.

Balloon framing. Framing method in which studs extend from the sill plate to the roof. Second floor joists, which are spiked into the studs, receive their main support from a ribbon notched into and nailed to the studs.

Baluster. Upright support for a rail.

Balustrade. A row of balusters topped by a rail.

Baseboard. Molding placed at the base of a wall and fitted to the floor. Also called *base molding.*

Base cabinet. Kitchen cabinet placed against a wall and resting on the floor. Standard size of base cabinets is 24″ deep and 36″ high.

Base shoe. Molding placed against a baseboard at the floor.

Batt insulation. Blanket insulation in widths to fit between studs. Common widths fit between studs on 16″ or 24″ centers.

Batten. A narrow strip of wood used to cover the joint between two vertical pieces of siding.

Batterboard. A construction of stakes and horizontal boards from which lines are hung to define the building lines.

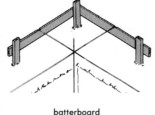

batterboard

Beam. A general term for a major horizontal supporting member.

Bearing. The actual amount of surface on which a supporting member rests.

Bearing partition. Interior wall that supports a vertical load and its own weight.

Bearing plate. A steel plate used to support ends of heavy structural members.

Bench mark. In surveying, a mark on some object firmly fixed in the ground from which distances and elevations are measured. It is usually a mark established by the local government as a local point of reference.

Bending stress. External and internal forces acting on a horizontal member tending to cause it to deflect.

Bevel. An angled cut from surface to surface of a board.

Beveled siding. Siding that is tapered from one edge of the board to the other.

Bid. Offer to perform work for a specified price.

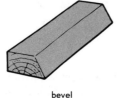

bevel

Bi-fold doors. Doors arranged so that a pair of folding doors are hung on each side of an opening.

Board-and-batten siding. Siding consisting of wide boards with narrow boards (battens) nailed over the board joints.

Board foot. Unit of measure for lumber based on the volume of a piece 12″ square and 1″ thick. A board foot contains 144 cubic inches.

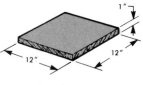

board foot

Bond beam. A reinforced concrete beam at the top of a wall or over an opening designed to strengthen a masonry wall.

Bond pattern. Patterns formed by exposing faces of masonry units.

Bond, structural. Tying wythes of masonry units together by lapping units one over another or connecting them with metal ties.

Branch circuit. In electrical work, the circuit conductors between the final overcurrent protection device and outlet.

Bridging. Bracing between joists or studs to add stiffness to the floors and walls. See *Cross bridging* and *Solid bridging.*

Brown coat. The second coat of a three-coat plaster job. The first coat is the *scratch coat* and the third coat is the *finish coat.*

Buck. Frame placed inside a concrete form to provide an opening for a door or window.

Building brick. Brick made from common clay without a special surface treatment. Also called *common brick.*

Building code. Set of regulations that establish the required standards for the materials and methods of construction in a city, county, or state. Building codes are enforceable by law.

Building lines. Lines laid out to establish the faces of exterior walls.

Building permit. Legally required authorization for construction work.

Butt. A hinge for a door.

Butt joint. Joint in which one piece butts squarely against another.

C

Cabinetmaker. Person who works in a cabinet shop and is skilled in the layout, construction, and installation of wood cabinets.

CAD (computer-aided drafting). Graphic representation of designs using special computer equipment.

Cantilever. Projecting beams or slabs supported at one end.

Cantilevered joists. Joists projecting from the wall in order to support a floor or balcony that extends past the wall below.

Cant strip. Angular board installed at the intersection of a roof deck and wall to avoid a sharp right angle where the roofing is to be installed.

Cased opening. Finished interior opening without a door.

Casement window. A window in which each sash opens outward on hinges placed at the side of the sash.

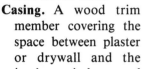

casement window

Casing. A wood trim member covering the space between plaster or drywall and the jamb at windows or doors.

Casing bead. Metal bead used at the edge of plaster or openings to provide a stop.

Casing nail. A type of finishing nail.

Caulk. Nonhardening paste used to fill cracks and crevices.

Cedar shingles. Shingles cut from western red cedar logs and used as a finish roofing and siding material.

Ceiling grid. Light metal framework supporting the tiles for a suspended ceiling.

Ceiling tile. Rectangular or square fibrous pieces used to finish off ceilings.

Cement. A binding agent capable of uniting dissimilar materials into a composite whole. The binding part in a concrete mix.

Central heating. System in which heat comes from a single source and is distributed by ducts or pipes to all parts of a building.

Central processing unit (CPU). The control center of a CAD system. The CPU receives information from an input device, manages the information, and produces an output image.

Ceramic tile. Thin flat piece of fired clay attached to walls or floors.

Chamfer. A cut from the surface of a board to an adjacent edge.

Channel. A rolled piece of structural steel with a straight web and 90° flanges on the same side.

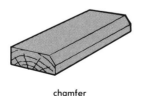

chamfer

Chord. Main horizontal member of a truss or open web joist.

Circuit. A complete electrical path. Dashed lines on plans show circuit wiring. Solid lines with arrowheads indicate home runs.

Circular stairs. Type of winding stairway in which all the steps radiate from a common center.

Cleanout. 1. In concrete work, an opening at the foot of a chimney or fireplace to remove ashes and debris. 2. In plumbing, a plugged opening in drainage piping.

Closed stringer. A stair stringer constructed by routing out grooves for the ends of treads and risers. The tread and riser ends are concealed in the finished stair.

CMU (concrete masonry unit). Building material such as cinder block or concrete block. See *Concrete block.*

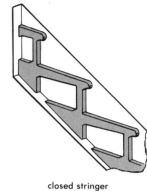

closed stringer

Collar tie. Horizontal member connecting two opposite rafters. Usually placed at every second or third pair of rafters.

Column. A vertical supporting member.

Common bond. Pattern of bricks in a stretcher position with every sixth course being a header course.

Common brick. See *Building brick.*

Common nail. Flat-head nail used most often in rough work.

Common rafter. Roof member that extends from the top wall plate to the ridge of a gable roof.

Compass direction. Direction based on the compass points North, South, East, or West.

Component. A part of a house assembled before delivery to the building site. Examples of components are a wall, floor, roof section, or truss.

Compression. Stress in a structural member caused by loading, which tends to compress it either parallel or at right angles to its axis.

Compressor. 1. In HVAC, one of the main parts of an air conditioning system in the cooling cycle to condense the gas to a liquid coolant. 2. A piece of equipment that compresses air and delivers it to a pneumatic tool.

Concrete. A mixture of cement, sand, and gravel with water in varying amounts according to the use of the finished product.

Concrete blocks. Precast blocks, solid or hollow, used in the construction of walls. Also known as CMU's.

Concrete mix. The proportion of cement, sand, and gravel in a mixture of concrete.

Concrete pour. Term used in the trade to mean placing concrete.

Concrete wash. Thinned concrete applied with a brush.

Conductor. 1. In electrical work, any material that conducts electricity. Copper is an excellent conductor. **2.** In plumbing, a pipe that carries water to the ground or storm sewer. Also known as a *leader* or *downspout*.

Conduit. Metal tubing used to carry electrical conductors.

Contact cement. Adhesive that adheres instantly on contact. Used to apply plastic laminate when making countertops.

Contour lines. Lines on a plot plan drawn to pass through points having the same elevation. Dashed lines represent the natural grade; solid lines represent the finish grade.

Convenience outlet. An electrical outlet in the wall or floor that can be used for lamps and appliances.

Convention. A simplified way of representing a building component on prints.

Coping. The cap or top course on a masonry wall.

Corbel. The shelf or ledge formed by projecting successive courses of masonry out from the face of the wall.

Cord- and plug-connected. Wiring method in which equipment is connected with a cord and plug to a receptacle.

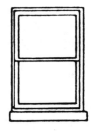

Corner bead. A protective metal piece fastened to corners of walls that are to be plastered or finished with drywall compound.

cord- and plug-connected

Cornice. A horizontal projection that crowns or finishes the eaves of a building.

Course. 1. In masonry, one horizontal layer of brick, stone, or other masonry material. **2.** In roofing, a horizontal row of shingles.

Cove mold. Concave molding used on inside corners.

Crawl space. The space between the ground and bottom of the joists in a house which does not have a basement.

Crimp. To fold the edges in a pinching action. A crimping tool is used to fasten certain metal studs to floor and ceiling channels.

Cross bridging. Bridging made of pieces of wood or metal placed diagonally between joists. See *Bridging*.

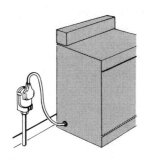

cross bridging

Cul-de-sac. A street with only one outlet. A turn-around.

Culvert. Large pipe used as a drain under a road.

Curing. Chemical process by which concrete dries, hardens, and attains its load-bearing strength. Also called *hydration*.

Cutting plane. Line (identified by letters) that cuts through a part of a structure on a drawing. It refers to a separate plan, section view, or detail drawing given for that area.

D

Damper. Movable metal plate in a fireplace throat used to regulate the draft.

Damp-proofing. Vapor barriers placed over walls and roofs before applying exterior finish.

Datum point. Point of reference, established by ordinance, from which levels and distances are measured.

Dead bolt. Locking device consisting of a solid metal bar that can be thrown or retracted with a knob or key.

Dead load. Weight of the permanent structure of a building, including all materials that make up the unit.

Decking. Steel plates or formed metal sheets used to support a concrete roof deck. Also, 2″ (nominal) wood members used for exterior flooring.

Degree. In plane measurement, 1/360th of a circle.

Detail. Enlarged drawing showing a particular feature of construction.

Diazzo. A process for making blue, black, or sepia-colored line prints.

Diffuser. Air register transferring forced air from a duct to a room.

Dimmer switch. Electrical control device that permits gradual dimming of lights.

Diverter. Raised strip of sheet metal fixed to the surface of a roof to divert rainwater to a desired location.

Door hand. Direction in which a door swings.

Double-hung window. A window with upper and lower sashes that slide up and down in the grooves of the window frame.

Dowel. A vertical reinforcing and positioning steel bar embedded in a footing and extending in to a column.

double-hung window

Downspout. Vertical pipe used to carry rainwater from the gutter to the ground or sewer. Same as *leader.*

Drain tile. Rough, unglazed tile pipe laid with open joints around the footing to conduct water to a point from which it is diverted away from the building. Plastic drain pipe is commonly used.

Drip. Wood or metal piece used to throw off rainwater.

Drywall. A system of interior wall finish using sheets of gypsum board with taped joints.

Duct. 1. In HVAC, a large round or rectangular pipe used for carrying air. 2. In electrical work, a rectangular-shaped trough that serves as a wireway.

E

Easement. Legal right-of-way provision on another person's property.

Eggcrate ceiling. Ceiling made of intersecting metal strips on edge and arranged in a square pattern. Light from fixtures above the ceiling is directed downward and diffused.

Elevation. 1. In drafting, the orthographic view of any of the vertical sides of a structure or the vertical view of interior walls. 2. In measurement, the height of a point above sea level or some datum point.

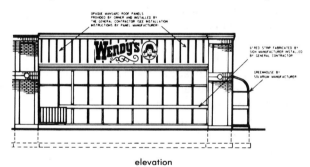

elevation

Expansion bead. Metal strip used between adjoining materials.

Expansion shield. A masonry bolt and anchor that works on the principle of a shell to expand and grip the inside of a hole.

Exterior finish. Materials such as roof shingles, wall siding, or window and exterior door frames used to finish the outside of a building.

Extrude. To shape heated plastics or metal by forcing it through dies.

F

Face brick. Brick made of select clays to produce a desired color.

Face nail. To drive a nail perpendicular to the surface of the wood.

Fascia. The flat outside horizontal member of a cornice placed in a vertical position.

Fiberboard. Building material of wood or other vegetable fibers that are compressed and bonded into sheet form.

Field tile. A type of porous tile that is placed around the outside of a foundation wall of a building to absorb excess water and prevent seepage through the foundation.

Fill insulation. Granulated mineral wool or pellets made from substances such as glass, slag, rock, and expanded mica.

Finish floor elevation. Height of the finished first floor in relation to the bench mark established on the construction site.

Finish flooring. Material used for the exposed, finished surface of a floor such as hardwood flooring, tile, or rugs.

Finish grade. Various levels of the lot surface after final grading work has been completed.

Finish hardware. Hardware that is visible, such as hinges, locks, catches, door stops, door closers, coat hooks, etc.

Fire block. Horizontal piece placed between studs to slow down flames.

Firebrick. Brick made from pure clays that have special heat resistance.

Fire cut. Angled cut made at the end of a joist or wood beam that is inserted into a masonry wall.

Fixed-sash window. Window with sashes that do not open. Often used in combination with double-hung, awning, or hopper windows.

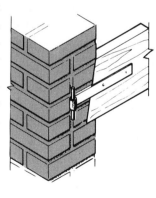

fire cut

Flanges. 1. The two parallel faces of a structural steel beam separated by the web. 2. In plumbing, a collar used for connecting sections of pipe.

Flashing. Sheet metal used in roof and wall construction to make them waterproof.

Flight. Series of steps between landings or the floors of a building.

Flexible metal conduit. Electrical conduit consisting of a spiral-wound steel strip.

Floor joist. Common joist supporting the rough floor material.

Floor plan. Drawing(s) in a set of prints that give a plan view of each floor of the building.

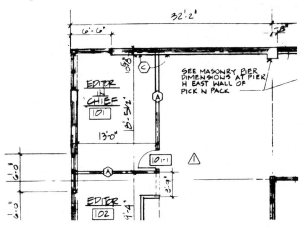

floor plan

Flume. An inclined channel to conduct water.

Flush door. Door with a flat surface on both sides.

Form. In concrete work, braced structure built to the shape of the structural member for which concrete is placed.

Form tie. Metal device to tie the two sides of foundation wall forms together and, at the same time, space them the proper distance apart.

Formwork. Construction of concrete forms.

Foundation. The part of a building resting on and extending into the ground that provides support for structural loads above.

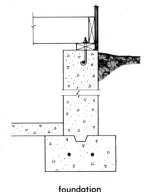

Foundation footing. The part of a foundation resting on bearing soil and supporting the foundation wall. The base for a column.

foundation

Foundation plan. Drawing(s) in a set of prints giving a plan view and section views of the foundation of a building.

Furring. Strips fastened to a wall, floor, or ceiling for the purpose of attaching covering material.

G

Gable roof. Type of roof that slopes in two directions from the ridge. Most common type of roof used in residential construction.

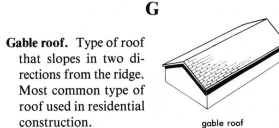

gable roof

Galvanizing. Zinc coating applied by electroplating or hot dipping to protect base metal from atmospheric corrosion.

Gambrel roof. Type of roof with a double slope in two directions from the ridge.

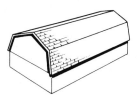

gambrel roof

Gauge. 1. In metal work, a uniform standard for wire diameters and for thickness of metal sheets. **2.** In concrete work, the proportion of the various materials in mortar or plaster mix.

General contractor. Licensed individual or firm in charge of a construction project.

GFCI (ground-fault circuit interrupter). A device used to detect leakage of current and trip the circuit open at 5 milliamps or less.

Glass block. A hollow, translucent, non-load-bearing masonry unit.

Glazing. Installing glass in a window sash or door and applying putty.

Grade. The level of the ground around a building. See *Finish grade* and *Rough grade*.

Grade beam. Horizontal load-bearing foundation member that usually rests on footings or caissons spaced at intervals.

Granular fill. Sand or fine gravel used as a base for concrete slabs.

Gravel. Crushed rock. Particles range in size from ¼″ to 1½″ in diameter.

Gravel stop. A strip of metal that is formed with a vertical lip. It is used at the edge of a built-up roof.

Green concrete. Trade term for freshly placed concrete.

Grid. Lines drawn in squares on paper used to help make drawings to modular measure. A ¼″ grid is a common size.

Ground. 1. In plastering, a piece of wood fastened to the rough framework that serves as a stop and thickness gauge for plaster. **2.** In electrical work, a conducting connection between equipment or circuit and the earth or other approved device.

Grout. Thin mortar that pours readily. Used in masonry to fill joints and cavities.

Gutter. A horizontal rain trough at the edge of a roof.

Gypsum board. Air-entrained core of gypsum between two layers of fibrous absorbent paper.

Gypsum lath. Essentially the same as gypsum board except for size and thickness.

H

Hardboard. Reconstituted board made by exploding wood chips into a fibrous state, then pressing them in heated hydraulic presses to form a dense rigid board.

Hardware. The physical components of a CAD system. Common hardware items are the keyboard, graphics tablet, display monitor, and plotter.

Hard wired. Wiring method in which conductors are routed and connected permanently to equipment.

Head. The top of a window or door frame.

Head jamb. The top horizontal member of a window or door frame.

Header. Joist(s) placed at the ends of an opening in the floor used to support side members. The top rough framing member(s) over a window or door opening.

Header course. Course of bricks arranged so that the ends of the brick laid horizontally make a continuous row.

Headroom. The clear, vertical dimension between the sloped line passing over the nosing of stair treads and the ceiling or stairs above.

Heat pump. Combined heating-cooling system that extracts heat from the outdoor air and transfers it indoors in winter. In summer, it reverses the cycle absorbing heat indoors and disposing of it to the outside.

hip roof

Hip roof. Roof that slopes in four directions from the ridge.

Hold down. Metal anchoring device for securing framing members to concrete or masonry.

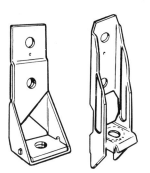

hold down

Hollow-core door. Flush door made of strips of wood glued together on edge to form the core and covered with veneer plies. For interior use only.

Hopper window. A type of window in which the upper sash opens inward with hinges at the bottom of the sash.

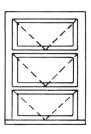

hopper window

Hose bibb. Water faucet or valve connection for a garden hose.

HP (horsepower). Unit of power equal to 746 watts.

HVAC. Heating, ventilating, and air conditioning.

Hydration. Chemical reaction that occurs when water is combined with cement, sand, and gravel in a concrete mix. Hydration causes concrete to harden. See *Curing.*

I

Input device. Hardware that enters information into a CAD system. Common input devices include keyboard, stylus, and mouse.

Insulating glass. Two sheets of glass separated by an air space and sealed around the edges with either a glass or metal closure.

Isometric. Type of pictorial drawing in which horizontal lines of the object are drawn at a 30° angle from the horizontal. The isometric axis is drawn on a 120° angle.

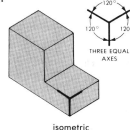

isometric

J

Jamb. Main member of a window or door frame, forming the sides and top.

Joist. Framing member that directly supports the floor.

Joist hanger. Metal stirrup for supporting the end of a joist that is flush with and nailed against another joist.

Joist tie. Wood or metal piece notched into the tops of joists where they butt together over a wall or girder.

K

Kerf. Width of cut produced by a saw blade.

Keyway. Groove in one *lift* of concrete that is filled with concrete of next lift. Commonly found in a foundation footing when foundation wall is concrete.

L

Lally column. Metal pipe filled with concrete and used to support beams or girders.

Laminated glass. Glass made with several layers of thin glass with tough plastic sheets between layers.

Landing. A platform to change the direction of the stairway or to break the run.

Latchset. Unkeyed door hardware with beveled bolts.

Lateral. In electrical work, underground conductors that connect the power company's transformer to the service equipment.

Lath. Metal mesh or gypsum board that is fastened to structural members to provide a base for plaster.

Leader. Vertical pipe used to carry water from a roof gutter to the ground or to the sewer. Same as *downspout*.

Leech line. Tile line from septic tank for dispersing water into the earth.

Let-in brace. Diagonal brace notched into the studs of a wood-framed wall.

Level. 1. Horizontal. **2.** A builder's instrument, which revolves only in a horizontal plane, used to transfer points in laying out foundations. **3.** Tool used to level building parts during construction. **4.** To adjust into a horizontal position.

Lift. In concrete work, the dimension from the top of one placement of concrete in a form to the top of the next placement. For example, concrete may be placed in 8″ lifts.

Light. A pane of glass.

Light construction. The building of residential and small- to medium-sized commercial buildings.

Lintel. A support for masonry over an opening. Usually made of steel angles or other structural shapes individually or in combination.

Live load. All loads that are not part of the structure. For example, people, furnishings, snow, and wind.

Load-bearing wall. Wall that bears its own weight and other loads.

Lockset. Keyed door hardware with rectangular, beveled, or rectangular and beveled bolts.

Longitudinal. Lengthwise.

Lookout. Horizontal wood structural member projecting beyond the face of the building.

Loose-fill insulation. Insulation poured directly from a bag or blown into place with a pressurized hose.

Lot. Piece of land with established boundaries.

Louver. 1. A slatted opening used for ventilating attics and other roof spaces. **2.** A slatted opening in a door.

M

Main. 1. In electrical work, the primary overcurrent protection device that protects the busbars in a panelboard. **2.** In plumbing, the major supply pipe for gases or liquids.

Mansard roof. Roof with a double slope in four directions.

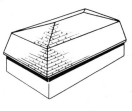

mansard roof

Masonry. Construction using molded or shaped construction material such as concrete blocks, bricks, stones, and tiles.

Masonry control joint. Vertical joint built into a masonry wall to allow slight movement. The joint is filled with a flexible material.

Masonry veneer. Exterior finish cover of brick or stone, usually applied over a wood stud wall.

Membrane. A thin pliable sheet of plastic material used for waterproofing.

Mil. One thousandth of an inch (.001″).

Minute. As related to plane measurement, 1/60th of a degree.

Mixture. Proportions of ingredients in concrete. Also called *mix*.

Modular measure. A system of measurement designed so that parts fit together on a grid of a standard module of 4″.

Module. 1. A unit of measure established at 4″. **2.** A complete part of a building (such as a bathroom or a kitchen) assembled in a shop.

Mold. Strips of wood or metal used for interior or exterior finish. Also called *molding*.

Monolithic. In one piece. For example, concrete placed in one pour.

Mortar. A mixture of cement, sand, and water used for joining brick or other masonry units. Lime may also be used for the mixture.

Mosaic tile. Ceramic tile in small square or rectangular shapes.

Muntin. The smallest member or bar dividing the glass light in a window sash.

N

Nailer. A block of wood used to fill a space and provide a means to nail material in place.

Natural grade. The various levels of the lot surface before any finish grading occurs.

Nominal size. Descriptive size, not actual measured size. For example, 2″ × 4″ is the nominal size of a piece of wood actually measuring 1½″ × 3½″.

Non-load-bearing wall. Wall that supports its weight only.

Nonmetallic sheathed cable. Type of cable used for residential structures and small commercial buildings. The cable contains two to four conductors with a nonmetallic jacket protecting the conductors.

Nosing. The extension of a stair tread beyond the face of the riser.

O

Oblique. A type of axonometric drawing with one surface shown as a true (normal) view and having receding lines of 30°–45°. Obliques may be cabinet or cavalier drawings.

oblique

Open stringer. A stair stringer cut so that the profile of treads and risers is visible from the side.

Open web steel joist. Floor and roof supporting member made with steel angle top and bottom chords and bars bent back and forth between them.

Orientation. 1. In building, the position of a building on a lot and the direction which the different walls face. **2.** In printreading, the method of relating one part of a print to another.

Orthographic. Method of projecting planes at right angles.

Out-to-out. In measurement, an overall dimension.

Overcurrent protection device. Either fuse or circuit breaker (CB) used to protect circuit conductors from overload.

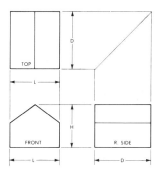

orthographic

P

Package door. A factory-assembled door complete with frame, lock, and butts.

Panelboard. Metal enclosure which houses *overcurrent protection devices.*

Panel door. A door made of solid strips or boards arranged to hold thin panels.

Parapet. A low, solid brick wall at the edge of a roof.

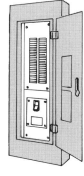

panelboard

Parging. In masonry, the application of mortar to the back of facing material or the face of backing material for waterproofing and bonding purposes.

Parquet flooring. Type of manufactured wood flooring in which adjacent pieces are laid at right angles.

Partition. An interior wall separating rooms.

Pass-through. An opening in a wall, usually between a kitchen and the dining area.

Paver. A dense variety of brick made of special clays and baked longer than usual. Also known as *paving brick.* They have a high resistance to heavy loads.

Penny. Measure of nail length, abbreviated by the letter d. For example, an 8d nail is 2½ ″ long.

Perlite. Volcanic siliceous rock that has been crushed and heated to a high temperature, causing it to expand and its combined water to vaporize. The resulting product takes the form of glassy particles. It is used as a lightweight aggregate, especially for concrete and plaster.

Perspective. Type of pictorial drawing in which receding lines converge.

The Garlinghouse Company

perspective

Pictorial drawing. A drawing that shows three surfaces of an object. See *axonometric, oblique,* and *perspective.*

Pier. A supporting section of wall between two openings.

Pilaster. Rectangular masonry column attached to a wall.

Pitch. The slope of a roof expressed as a ratio of rise to span. For example, a 8 in 12 roof rises 8 ″ vertically per 1 ′-0 ″ of horizontal measurement.

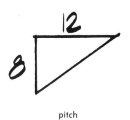

pitch

Plan view. A view looking down. **1.** In orthographic projection, a top view. **2.** In architecture, a floor plan, roof plan, or plan view of a cabinet, etc.

Plancier. Board that forms the underside of an eave or cornice.

Plaster. Pasty composition that hardens upon drying. Used for coating wall and ceiling surfaces.

Plastic laminate. Product made of three or four layers of plastic material bonded together under high heat and pressure. Used to surface countertops, wall surfaces, shelving, cabinets, etc.

Plate. In frame construction, the top horizontal structural member of a frame wall or partition.

Platform. Flat, level surface at the top or bottom of a flight of stairs.

Platform framing. System of wood-frame construction in which studs are one story high. A platform is built on plates over the studs and acts as a base for the next floor. Also called *western framing*.

Plot plan. Plan view showing information about a lot and the location of the building on the lot.

Plumb. 1. To be vertical. 2. To adjust into a vertical position.

Plywood. Product made of *veneer* sheets glued at right angles to one another and pressed together under high heat and pressure.

Pocket. Recessed area in a foundation wall in which a beam rests.

Pocket door. Door that slides into a partition.

Point of beginning. The point on the lot from which horizontal and vertical measurements are made.

Pointing. Troweling mortar into joints after the masonry units are laid.

Polyethylene membrane. Sheet of plastic used for waterproofing.

Portland cement. Hydraulic cement consisting of silica, lime, and alumina mixed in proper proportions and burned in a kiln. The klinkers, or vitrified product, when ground fine, form an extremely strong cement.

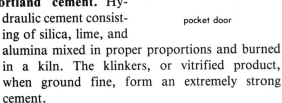

pocket door

Powder-actuated fastener. Metal pin or stud driven with an explosive cartridge. Used to fasten wood or other materials to concrete, brick, or steel.

Precast concrete. Concrete structural member that has been cast and cured in a casting yard or factory and then delivered to the job site.

Primer. A first coat of paint used to fill pores of wood or coat metal.

Property lines. Recorded, legal boundaries of a piece of property.

Q

Quarry tile. Unglazed tile made from natural clays and shales.

R

Rabbet. Groove cut in the surface or on the edge of a board to receive another member.

Rafter. A sloping roof member that supports the roof sheathing.

Rail. Horizontal member of a door or a window sash.

Random. A manner of laying stones without regular patterns or courses.

Range. Squared stone laid in horizontal courses of even height.

Rebar. Steel bar used for reinforcing concrete structural members.

Receptacle. Electrical contact device installed at the outlet for the connection of a single attachment plug.

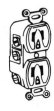

receptacle

Register. A grill through which heated or cooled air flows into or out of a room.

Resilient tile. Type of floor tile that yields when pressure is applied, then returns to its original position.

Retaining wall. Masonry or wood wall constructed to hold back earth.

Ribbon. In balloon framing, a narrow strip of board that fits into cuts in the edge of studding to help support joists.

Ridge. Top horizontal member of a roof framed with rafters.

Rigid insulation board. Wood or vegetable fiber pressed together to make a board or panel. Usually impregnated with bituminous waterproofing.

Ripping. Narrow board cut lengthwise from a wider board.

Rise. 1. Vertical measurement from the support to the ridge of the roof. For example, a rafter may have a 3″ *rise* per foot of run. 2. Vertical measurement from the top of a tread to the top of the next higher tread.

Riser. 1. In plumbing, a vertical water supply line. 2. In carpentry, the vertical part of a stair step. 3. In HVAC, a vertical heating supply duct.

Roof beam. The part of the roof structure of a post-and-beam building to which roof decking is nailed.

Roof jack. Sheet metal device surrounding a pipe through the roof to make the opening waterproof. Used for plumbing vent stacks.

Roof truss. A prefabricated structural roof unit made of top and bottom chords tied together with web members. The top chord serves as a roof rafter and the bottom chord serves as a ceiling joist.

Rough grade. Various levels of the lot before grading has been completed.

Rough hardware. Hardware items used in the rough structure such as nails, screws, fastenings, anchors, hangers, metal bridging, etc.

Rout. To cut a slot or groove with a router.

Rowlock. A method of laying brick on edge so that the vertical ends appear in the face of the wall.

Rubble. Wall made of rough stones, irregular in size and shape, laid without pattern.

Run. 1. Horizontal measurement of a rafter. For example, a rafter may have a 3″ rise per foot of *run.* **2.** In plumbing, the horizontal measurement of a section of inclined pipe.

R-value. In insulation, resistance to heat flow. The higher the R-value, the better the insulating qualities of the material.

S

Sash. The frame in which the window lights (glass) are set.

Scaffold. Elevated platform to support workers, material, and tools while working on a building.

Scale. 1. In general, to measure. **2.** In architecture, to make a drawing proportionately smaller than the building or building part. **3.** In drafting, the instrument used to make drawings to scale.

Scratch coat. The first coat of a three-coat plaster job. The rough plaster is left with a crisscross, scratched surface to provide a good bond for the next coat (*brown coat*).

Screed. 1. Grade level forms set at desired elevation so that concrete may be leveled by drawing a straightedge over their surface. **2.** A straightedge.

Screen block. Decorative concrete masonry units.

Scupper. Outlet in the wall at the roof to permit water to drain off.

Sealant. Liquid substance used to seal cracks and porous surfaces. It solidifies to make a waterproof bead.

Second. In plane measurement, equals ¹/₆₀th of a minute.

Section view. A view made by passing a cutting plane through the building or building part.

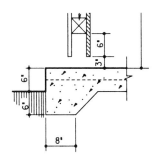

section view

Septic tank. A tank in which sewage is deposited so that bacterial action may cause disintegration of organic matter.

Service equipment. In electrical work, the main enclosure containing *overcurrent protection devices* controlling all electrical loads in the building.

Setback. Required distance a building must be placed from a given boundary as established by ordinance.

Settling basin. Reservoir for groundwater to permit silt to settle before the water goes through the sump pump to be expelled.

Shakes. Hand-split wooden roof or wallcoverings.

Sheathing. First layer of exterior wallcovering applied over the framing. Types of sheathing include fiberboard, gypsum board, plywood, etc.

Shed roof. Roof that slopes in only one direction.

Sheet glass. Window glass manufactured in a continuous sheet and cut into required sizes.

Sheet goods. Resilient floor covering, such as linoleum or vinyl, supplied in continuous rolls of wide width.

shed roof

Sheetrock. Trade name for gypsum wallboard.

Shim. Any tapered piece of wood used to fill space.

Shingles. Machine-cut roof or wallcoverings. Mineral-based roofing material in single units or strips usually with three tabs.

Shiplap. Lumber that has been rabbetted along each edge to provide a close lapping joint when two pieces are fitted together.

Sill. 1. In frame construction, the bottom rough structural member that rests on the foundation. **2.** In general construction, the bottom exterior wood member of a window or door frame. **3.** In masonry, the lowest member below window or door in a masonry wall.

Sill cock. Valve connection or water faucet placed about sill height on the outside of a building.

Site. The location of a building.

Slab. A horizontal flat area of concrete.

Slab-on-grade. Ground-supported concrete foundation system consisting of foundation walls and concrete slab.

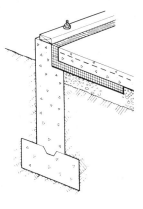

slab-on-grade

Sleeper. Wood strip laid over a concrete slab or rough flooring to which finish flooring is applied.

Smoke shelf. Horizontal area at base of chimney part of a fireplace in back of the throat.

Snap bracket. In formwork, a wedge used with a *snap tie* in a single waler form system.

Snap tie. Patented tie system with cones acting as spreaders. Grooved snapbacks provided for snapping off the ends of the ties extending from the hardened concrete wall.

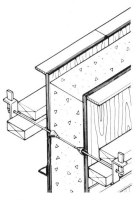

snap tie

Soffit. A lower horizontal surface such as the underface of eaves, cornice, or beam.

Software. The operating system of a CAD system. Software is commonly found as magnetic disks or tapes.

Soil stack. Vertical pipe carrying waste including that from water closets. Extends through the roof to ventilate the system.

Solar energy. Energy derived from the sun's rays.

Solar screen. Arrangement of wood strips to provide degree of shade.

Solarium. Glass-enclosed area of a building.

Soldier course. In masonry, a course of brick set vertically on end.

Sole. In frame construction, the horizontal member of a frame wall or partition that rests on the floor.

Solid bridging. Bridging made of solid blocks of wood placed between joists. See *Bridging.*

solid bridging

Solid-core door. Flush door made of solid wood blocks glued together to make a core, then covered with plies of veneer. Can be used as interior or exterior door.

Span. Total clear distance between supports.

Specifications. Written document included with a set of prints clarifying and supplying additional data.

Square. 1. In layout, a 90° angle. **2.** In roofing, the amount of roofing that will cover 100 sq. ft. when laid.

Stair flight. Section of stairs going from one floor or landing to another.

Stair landing. Platform between one flight of stairs and another.

Stair pitch. The slope of a set of stairs.

Stair ratio. Ratio between the unit rise and unit tread of a set of stairs expressed as a formula ($T + R = 17"$ to $18"$).

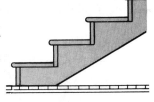

stair pitch

Staircase. Entire assembly of stairs, landings, railings, and balusters.

Stairwell. Opening in the floor provided for stairs.

Standpipe. Discharge pipe connected to the sewer or drainage system.

Stepped foundation. Foundation with a change in elevation to provide for a change in grade or special building condition.

Stile. Side vertical part of a door or window sash.

Stool. Shelf-like piece that crosses the bottom of a window.

Stop. In plumbing, a valve at a plumbing fixture.

Strap anchor. Fasteners made of narrow strips of steel used to secure rough framing members to each other and to masonry walls.

Stretcher. Masonry unit laid with its length horizontal and parallel to the face of the wall.

Stretcher bond. Masonry bond consisting entirely of stretchers.

Stringer. The member on each side of a stair that supports the treads and risers.

Strike plate. Metal piece mortised into a door jamb. It receives the latch bolt when the door is in a closed position.

Stucco. A cementitious exterior coating.

Stud. Vertical structural uprights that form the walls and partitions in a frame building.

Styrofoam. Chemical substance used for insulation. Provided as insulation board or applied by blowing it into enclosed spaces.

Sump pump. Pump used to remove water from a pit in the basement floor.

Survey. A plan or map of a lot prepared by a licensed surveyor showing lot dimensions, angles at corners, elevations, and other data.

Swale. The slopes on a lot to ensure water drainage away from the building.

T

Tack weld. Short welding bead deposited at intervals. Used to hold supplementary angles and beams in position and to hold steel decking to steel beams.

Take-off. Estimate of the amount of material required for a job.

Temperature bar. In concrete onstruction, a metal bar used to counteract stress caused by temperature changes.

Tempered glass. Glass with increased mechanical and thermal properties.

Tension. A stress in a structural member that tends to stretch the member or pull it apart.

Terra cotta. Ceramic material molded into masonry units before it is baked.

Thermopane. Insulating glass.

Thermoplastic. Characteristic of becoming soft when heated and hard when cooled.

Threshold. Piece of material over which a door swings.

Throat. The part of the fireplace at the damper where the fireplace walls converge.

Tier. A row. See *Wythe.*

Tilt-slab construction. Method of construction where concrete walls are constructed in flat panels and tilted up into position.

Toekick. Recessed space at the bottom of the front sides of base cabinets and vanities.

Toenail. To nail diagonally to hold a framing member that butts against another.

Toggle bolt. A hollow wall fastener.

Tongue-and-groove. Lumber or wood sheeting in which one edge is cut with a projecting tongue and the other edge is cut with a recessed groove.

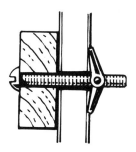

toggle bolt

Topsoil. Uppermost layer of soil that is capable of supporting vegetation.

Transit. Surveyor's instrument used by builders to establish points and elevations. Operates on both horizontal and vertical planes.

Translucent. Permits passage of light but diffuses it so that objects cannot be clearly distinguished.

Transverse section. View made by a cutting plane cut across the object on its shorter dimension.

Tread. The horizontal board in a stairway.

Trimmer. Beam or stud into which a header is joined for an opening.

Truss. Structural assembly with primary and secondary members arranged to form a triangle.

Trussed rafter. Roof truss that supports the roof and ceiling construction.

U

Underlayment. Floor covering of plywood or fiberboard used to provide a level surface for carpet or other resilient flooring.

Underslung joist. Open web steel joist supported by its top flanges.

Unit rise. 1. For roofs, the number of inches a common rafter will rise vertically for each foot of run. 2. For stairs, the riser height calculated by dividing the total rise by the number of risers in a stairway.

Unit run. 1. For roofs, the unit of total run based on 12″ (17″ for hip roofs). 2. For stairs, the width of the tread calculated by dividing the total run by the number of treads in the stairway.

Utilities. Electric, gas, water, and sewerage services provided to the public.

V

V-joint boards. Boards cut on the edges so that when assembled a V-shaped groove is exposed.

Valley. Angle formed by two inclined sides of a roof. A valley rafter is the rafter supporting the valley.

VA tile. Vinyl asbestos tile used as a floor covering.

Vanity. Base cabinet with a sink used as a lavatory. Standard size of vanities is 20″ deep and 30″ high.

Vapor barrier. Watertight material used to prevent passage of moisture or water vapor into walls or slabs.

Veneer. 1. In masonry, a facing of brick, stone, or other units placed over a frame superstructure. 2. In carpentry, a thin layer of wood.

Vent stack. Vertical pipe connected to the plumbing vent pipes and soil waste stacks to remove gases and relieve pressure in the system.

Vinyl. Type of plastic material used for floor and wall covering, exterior siding, gutters and downspouts, and for weatherproofing.

Vitrified clay tile. Tile used primarily for underground drainage.

Volt. Pressure that forces the flow of electrons in an electrical circuit. Designated *E* in formulas. Abbreviated as *V*.

Volt-amp. *Volts* × *amps* × *power factor* in an electrical circuit. Designated *VA*.

W

W beam. A structural steel member with a cross-sectional shape resembling the letter *H*. Formerly called *wide flange beam*.

Wainscot. Treatment of the lower part of an interior wall with special finish.

Waler. Horizontal piece placed on the outsides of form walls to strengthen and stiffen the walls. The form ties are also fastened to the walers.

Wall cabinet. Upper cabinets attached to a wall. Standard size of wall cabinets is 12″ deep and either 30″ or 42″ high.

W beam

Watt. Measurement of electrical power. Designated *P*. Beginning with 1984 NEC®, termed *VA* for calculations. See *Volt-amp*.

Web. In steel construction, the connecting part of a beam between flanges.

Wedge tie. Patented tie consisting of a strap and wedge. Used with plank-forming systems.

Weep hole. Small holes in masonry and masonry veneer walls provided to release water accumulation to the exterior.

Welded wire fabric. A mesh made of heavy wire in a rectangular or square pattern welded at intersections of the wire.

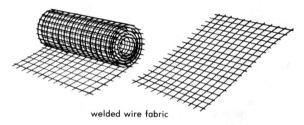

welded wire fabric

Wide flange beam. See *W beam*.

Working drawings. Set of plans that contain all dimensions and structural information needed to complete a construction project. Also called *prints*.

Wythe. Continuous vertical section of masonry that is one unit in thickness.

INDEX

A

A frame, 183–184, *185*
Abbreviations, on plans, 27, *28, 29*
Air registers, 108, 110
Aluminum, 83
Aluminum members, 191
American Institute of Architects, 124
American National Standards
  Institute, 27
American Society of Mechanical
  Engineers, 27
American Society for Testing and
  Materials, 83
American Welding Society, 27
Anchor bolts, 179, *179*
Angles, steel, 82–83, *83*
ANSI. *See* American National
  Standards Institute
Architectural symbols, 250, *251*
ASME. *See* American Society of
  Mechanical Engineers
Asphalt shingles, 197
ASTM. *See* American Society for
  Testing and Materials
Awning windows, 30, *31*
AWS. *See* American Welding Society
Axonometric, 2–6, *3, 4*

B

Balloon framing, 181–183, *184*
Basements, 194
Batt insulation, 86, *86*
Batterboards, 186, *186*
Beams
  box, 181, *182*
  channel, 162, *162, 163*
  floor, 183
  Glulam, 256
  grade, 19, 197
  Micro = Lam®, 260
  roof, 183
  W, 162, *162*, 163, *163*, 192, *192*, 193
Bearing partition, 179
Bench marks, 20, 226, 227
Blocking, 163–164, *164*, 165
Blueprint process, 1–2
Blueprints. *See* Prints
BOCA Basic Building Code, 165
Box beam, 181, *182*
Bracing
  corner, 179, *180*
  diagonal, 179
Branch Bank, 225–237
  concrete work for, 230
  details, 235–236
  doors, 231
  elevation views, 230–231
  exterior finish, 229

exterior walls, 229
floor plan, 228–230
foundation plan, 231–232
interior partitions, 229–230
plot plan, 226, *227*
roof, 230
schedules, 236
section views, 234–236, *237*
steel structure of, 232–234
windows, 231
Brick, 75–79, *76, 77, 78, 79,* 185
  building, 76, 77, *77,* 161
  common, 76, 77, *77,* 161
  face, 75–77, *76, 77,* 161
  fire-, 76, 77, *76*
  jumbo, 24, 75
  laying, 77, 78, *79*
  manufacture of, 76–77
  modular, 77, *77, 78*
  Norman, 77, *77*
  Roman, 77, *77*
  rowlock courses, 231
  SCR, 77, *77,* 189, 190
  standard, 77, *77*
Brick bonds, 78, *79*
  common, 78, *79*
  English, 78, *79*
  Flemish, 78, *79*
  stack, 78, *79*
Brick veneer, 79, 111
  laying, 114
Brick veneer walls, 190, *191*
Brickwork, positions for, 78, *78*
Bridging, 113, 163, *163,* 193, *195*
Brown coat, 88
Building
  brick, 76, 77, *77,* 161
  codes, 20
  lines, 208, 226
Building Materials Directory, 124
Built-up roofing, 197
Bullnose blocks, 81

C

Cabinet drawings, 6–7, *8*
Cabinets, kitchen, 109, *109*
CAD. *See* Computer-aided drafting
CAD-generated drawings, *43*
Carpentry
  finish, 209, 210–211
  rough, 209–210
Carport, 111, 112
Casement windows, 30, *31*
Cavalier drawings, 7, *8*
Cavity walls, 190, *191*
Ceilings, 193
  eggcrate, 236
Cement masonry construction, 185–188
Central processing unit, 47, *47*
Ceramic tile, 81–82, 212
Channel beam, 162, *162, 163*

Chimneys, openings for, 179
Clay facing tile, 81
Commercial Building, 159–168
  concrete work for, 160–161
  doors, 167
  exterior walls, 161–162
  heating, 167, *168*
  rough structure, 161
  windows, 167
Common
  bond, 78, *79*
  brick, 76, 77, *77,* 161
Compression
  across grain, 72, *75*
  parallel to grain, 72, *75*
Computer-aided drafting, 40–48
  hardware, 41, *44*
  input devices, 41, 42, 44–47, *45, 46*
  output devices, 48, *48*
  software, 41, *44*
Concrete, 73–74, *76*
  green, 185
  monolithic, 73
  ready mix, 185
Concrete block, 78, 80–81, *81*
  decorative, 81
  types of, 80–81, *80*
  for exterior walls, 196
Concrete
  construction, monolithic, 184
  floors, reinforcement for, 83
  formwork, 74
  masonry units, 208, *208*
  mixture, 73–74
  piers, 196, *198*
  work, 160–161, 208–209, 230
Construction Specifications
  Institute, 125, *126,* 127
Contour lines, 20, *207*
Coping, wall, 81
Corbel, 189, *189*
Corner
  blocks, 81, *81*
  bracing, 179, *180*
CPU. *See* Central processing unit
Crawl space, 194, 195
Cross bridging, 113, *113*
CSI. *See* Construction Specifications
  Institute
Cursor, 42
Cutting plane
  horizontal, 21
  vertical, 24

D

Damp-proofing, 232
Datum points, 20, 226, 227
Dead load, 193
Degrees, 226
Details, 25, *26*
Diagonal bracing, 179